To Lilian and Richard,
with very warm regards
of 25 years of conviviality and friendship,
Martin [signature]
x

'A Grand City' – 'Life, Movement and Work':
Bristol in the eighteenth and nineteenth centuries

'A Grand City' – 'Life, Movement and Work': Bristol in the eighteenth and nineteenth centuries

————

Essays in Honour of Gerard Leighton, F.S.A.

————

Edited by

M. J. Crossley Evans

The Bristol and Gloucestershire Archaeological Society
2010

ISBN 978-0-900-197-74-1

Printed by
4word Ltd, Bristol

Contents

H. G. M. Leighton, M.A., F.S.A.

AN APPRECIATION

It is appropriate that the Society celebrates the year 2010 for two distinct but inter-connected reasons. Firstly, this marks the centenary of the association between our Society and the family of one of its most distinguished members and secondly, it concludes 40 years of tireless service by Gerard Leighton as our treasurer and almost 60 years of membership.

In Roman historiography it was often held that no true assessment of a man could be made without seeing him in the context of his ancestry. To understand the interests and enthusiasms of our former treasurer it is first necessary for us to look at those of his family.

His father, Wilfrid Leighton, J.P., F.S.A., (1886–1967),[1] a native of Bishopwearmouth, became a member of the Society in 1910, and served as chairman of Council (1933–1936), as honorary treasurer (1928–1937)[2], chairman of its Records Section and its Archaeological Trust, and as president between 1947 and 1948.[3] He also represented the Society on the committee of management of Leigh Woods. His tireless efforts in preserving the heritage of Bristol and Gloucestershire can be seen in his work as chairman of the Council for the Preservation of Ancient Bristol, and as the chairman of the Theatre Royal Preservation Appeal Committee, which culminated in the successful purchase, preservation and restoration of the Theatre Royal, Bristol in 1942–1943,[4] and his efforts in 1949 to raise the money necessary to transfer Arlington Row, Bibury, from the Society to the National Trust. He represented Gloucestershire on the newly organised Regional Council of the C.B.A. from 1943 onwards, and his distinguished services to archaeology and history were recognised by his election as an F.S.A.

Wilfrid Leighton's friendships in the Society were many and varied. They included the Revd. Canon M. A. Rauceby Thorold Cole (1874–1948), rector of Christ Church with St. Ewen, Bristol, and Arthur Cecil Powell (1868–1949)[5], the distinguished historian of both the glass and pottery industry, and Freemasonry in Bristol. From his father Gerard Leighton learned many facts about the Society during the inter-war period, the membership, and the excursions. They included his father's recollections of an elderly cleric belabouring another with his umbrella during a heated disagreement on the patronal attribution of a church they were visiting! An

---

[1] He died 12 April 1967.

[2] The dates are derived from R. Austin, *T. B. & G. A. S.*, *General Index to volumes 55–60, (1930–1939), with a separate index to[…] Lists of Officers of the Society*[…], (Gloucester, 1942), pp. 4–5.

[3] For his presidential address, 'Endowed Charity in Bristol and Gloucestershire', *T. B. & G. A. S.*, LXVII, (1946–7–8), pp. 1–20.

[4] *The Architects' Journal*, 27 May 1943, p. 345. The theatre re-opened in May 1943 as the first State theatre in the country.

[5] *Corona Gladiorum: Transactions of the Bristol Masonic Society*, (2004–2005), pp. 5–7.

Fig. 1. Mr. Gerard Leighton, [Copyright Sarah Buttenshaw].

entertaining conversationalist and raconteur, Gerard Leighton's fund of stories ranging from Winchester, and Oxford common rooms, to personalities in the commercial
worlds of Bristol and London, are worthy of a volume in their own right and would
rank with the literary table talk compiled in the eighteenth and nineteenth centuries.

A chartered accountant by profession, Wilfrid Leighton was secretary to the Bristol
Municipal Charities for many years, representing them on the Portbury Sea Wall
Commission from 1922 until his retirement. He served as clerk to the governors of the
Endowed Schools, Queen Elizabeth Hospital, Bristol Grammar School, and the Red
Maids, and took an active interest in the management of the trustees' almshouses,
(Foster's, and Bengough's, and Trinity Hospital).[6] It is consequently no surprise that
his first publication in our *Transactions* was a detailed history of one of their number.[7]
Thereafter his contributions to the *Transactions* were numerous and include: 'The
grant of Arms to Queen Elizabeth's Hospital, Bristol';[8] 'The Brass of Nicholas
Thorne';[9] 'Blackfriars, now Quaker's Friars, Bristol';[10] 'The manor and parish of
Burnett, Somerset';[11] and 'King Street, Bristol'.[12] From his father Gerard Leighton
developed both his knowledge of and his interest in heraldry, country houses, and
monumental brasses. A keen shot and motorist, Wilfrid Leighton's extensive social
connections within the city were consolidated by his membership of the Bristol
Savages, where he numbered among his friends men such as the Revd. Canon John
M. D. Stancomb (1890–1955), the vicar of St. Nicholas, Bristol Bridge, and former
precentor of the cathedral,[13] and most of the leading architects, artists and musicians
in the city.[14] He was of sufficient importance for a cartoon of him to be published in
the Bristol press attached to a poem by 'Woofler' who, 'disdaining the subtleties of
rhyme' wrote:

> On Bristol Charities and Schools
> A very fount of knowledge he.
> He Charts. Accounts., and shoots and mo tes
> And dotes on Archaeology.[15]

---

[6] He was clerk to the governors between 1915 and 1946, C. P. Hill, *The History of Bristol
Grammar School*, (Bristol, 1950), p. 219; *Bristol Municipal Charities Yearbook, 1935–36*, (Bristol, 1935),
pp. 11, 16. He was an A.C.A.

[7] W. Leighton, 'Trinity Hospital, Bristol', *T. B. & G. A. S.*, XXXVI, Part II, (1913), pp.
251–287.

[8] *Ibid.*, LI, pp. 109–121;

[9] *Ibid.*, LIV, pp. 58–61.

[10] *Ibid.*, LV, pp. 151–190.

[11] *Ibid.*, LIX, pp. 243–285.

[12] *Ibid.*, LXV, pp.157–160.

[13] He had been one of Canon Cole's curates at Christ Church with St. Ewen, Broad Street
in the early 1920s.

[14] For a history of the Bristol Savages see: J. Hudson, *The Savage Spirit: One Hundred Years of
Bristol Savages*, (Bristol, 2004).

[15] *Bristol Times and Mirror*, Wednesday, 21, March 1928. The bound volume, entitled 'Bristol
Personalities Extracted from the "Bristol Times and Mirror" during the years 1922–1932' is to
be found in the Local Studies section of the Central Library, College Green, class mark B
21637, and the cartoon of Wilfrid Leighton is on f. 155.

Fig. 2. Wilfrid Leighton as seen in the Bristol press.

Wilfrid Leighton's important and significant contributions outside the city of Bristol were recognised by his appointment as High Sheriff of the county of Somerset.[16]

Wilfrid Leighton was married on 17 November 1931 to Miss Margaret Mather (1900–1993)[17] of Nether Staveley, Westmorland. She was the daughter of Harold Mather, J.P. (1862–1941),[18] a wealthy landowner who was originally from Bolton, (where his family were cotton mill owners). His main residence until the early 1920s was St. Anne's on Sea, Lancashire,[19] but in *c.* 1925 he left St. Anne's and settled permanently in Nether Staveley[20] where he took a leading part in life in the village, and was a major benefactor to the community.[21] Harold Mather purchased woodland, extensive farmland and bobbin mills, the latter to assist in his cotton spinning interests in Lancashire. He settled at Sidegarth, which commands fine views of the village of Staveley and the mouth of the Kentmere valley, and it was here that Gerard Leighton spent many of his holidays as a schoolboy. His grandfather was a member of the Cumberland and Westmorland Archaeological and Antiquarian Society, an association valued and continued by his grandson, and he had a fine appreciation of gardens, employing a leading Edwardian landscape gardener to transform his grounds at Sidegarth.[22] Gerard Leighton retains commercial interests in Staveley. He is a member of the Staveley and District History Society, and recently supported the initiative to move the monument of a local worthy, James Tyson J.P. (1836–1911), from the derelict Wesleyan chapel to the parish church.

Henry Gerard Mather Leighton was born on 15 August 1932. After education at Winchester College,[23] and Corpus Christi College, Oxford, where he read History, graduating with a B.A. in 1953 and an M.A. in 1957, he followed in his

---

[16] *T. B. & G. A. S.*, LXXXVI, (1967), pp. 211–212, obituary notice by Mrs. Elsie M. Clifford, F.S.A.; LXXXVII, (1968), p. 224, Report of Council for the Year 1967.

[17] She was born at St. Anne's on Sea, Lancashire, on 7 March 1900, and died 20 August 1993. I am grateful to Mrs. Gerard Leighton for this information.

[18] Harold Mather died on 7 November 1941, aged 79, and was buried in the churchyard at St. Ann, Ings, Westmorland, where there is a monument to his memory and to his wife, Margaret Ada, who died on 12 August 1930, aged 62. I am most grateful to Mr. O. B. Peachey for helping me to locate and transcribe the stone during Easter 2009. There is also a stained glass window set into the north wall of the parish church of St. James, Staveley, illustrating the parable of The Good Samaritan, which was erected to the memory of Mrs. Mather. Harold Mather was a director of the New End Spinning Co., Eagley, near Bolton.

[19] J. Lyon, 'Early Year Memories [...] early days at Sidegarth', *The Journal of the Staveley and District History Society*, Winter 2008–9, Issue 14, pp. 6–9.

[20] They were near neighbours of the parents of the poet (and Bristol graduate), Charles Hubert Sisson, C.H., (1914–2003) who had retired to live in the Kentmere valley.

[21] J. Scott, *A Lakeland Valley Through Time: A History of Staveley, Kentmere and Ings*, (Kendal, 1995), pp.16, 72, 104, 105. Harold Mather was a J.P. for Westmorland, chairman of the Village Institute opened in 1936, for which he gave the land, and a trustee of the War Memorial recreation ground.

[22] For a picture of the house and an account of life there in the 1920s and 1930s see: J. Lyon, *loc. cit.*, pp. 6–9.

[23] C. F. Badcock and J. R. La T. Corrie, *Winchester College Register*, (1992). He was in Kingsgate House "K" or "Beloe's" as it is known among Wykehamists, from Common Time (Spring Term) 1946 to Common Time 1950. I am indebted to my cousin, Dr. T. G. B. Howe, *quondam* pre-clinical dean in Medicine and senior lecturer in Bacteriology at the University of Bristol, for this information.

father's footsteps and was articled to Ernest Harbottle, qualifying as a chartered accountant in 1957.[24] He was a partner of Grace, Darbyshire and Todd, Bristol, between 1959 and 1968, and served as a director of the Tyndall Group Ltd. and Subsidiaries, including the Tyndall and Company Bank in Princess Victoria Street, Clifton (1962–1986)[25] and of Gateway Securities Ltd. (1965–1977). He was appointed a director of the Jordan Group Ltd. in 1968, became chairman in 1985, and is a director of a major publishing company.[26]

His successful and demanding commercial career has not prevented Gerard Leighton from following his father in other fields of endeavour. In 1961 at the age of 29 he was elected a Fellow of the Society of Antiquaries of London, and he has been actively involved with its affairs for nearly half a century, serving on its Finance Committee, and as a member of its William and Jane Morris Fund Committee.

He became a member of the Bristol and Gloucestershire Archaeological Society at the age of 19 in 1951. When the treasurer, the Honorable W. R. S. Bathurst, died in office in 1970, Gerard Leighton stepped into the breach and served as treasurer *pro tem* until he was elected at the next Annual General Meeting. His publications in our *Transactions* include: 'The Overseas Meetings of the Society', 118, pp. 263–274, and he has represented the Society on the committee of management of Leigh Woods, The Council for the Preservation of Ancient Bristol and on the Theatre Royal Trust. He has regularly supported field meetings, both at home and overseas, and was elected president of the Society for the year 2004–2005, in recognition of his long and distinguished service.[27]

He served as chairman of the Bristol Diocesan Advisory Committee for the Care of Churches (1974–1994), which deals with the ecclesiastical exemption of parish churches from the planning regulations; as chairman of the Somerset Record Society (1977–2009); as honorary treasurer of the Friends of Somerset Churches; as a chairman of Christ Church Lands Trust (Bristol), and St. Ewen's Lands; as a member of the committee of All Saints' Lands, Bristol; as a member of the council of the Bristol Record Society, and he has served on the Bristol Cathedral Fabric Fund (from 1990), and as the chairman of the Friends of Lydiard Tregoze, the former home of the St. John family, viscounts Bolingbroke. He was the chairman of the Wells Cathedral Fabric Committee (1987–2007), and is a trustee of the Wells Cathedral Preservation Trust. Gerard Leighton became a member of the Somerset Archaeological and Natural History Society in 1958 during his father's presidency, and became president of the Society exactly fifty years later.[28]

---

[24] C. F. Badcock and J. R. La T. Corrie, *op cit.* A. W. Peake prize and West of England prize, Institute of Chartered Accountants, 1956; A.C.A., 1957; F.C.A., 1967.

[25] Tyndall was sold to Globe, and The West of England Trust Ltd. was formed after these transactions were completed. Gerard Leighton is a director of the company. I am grateful to Mrs. Judith Young of Jordans and Mr. Ian Harbottle for this information.

[26] *Who's Who in Bristol & Avon*, (Bristol, 1991–2), p. 160; and private information.

[27] For his presidential address: 'Country Houses Acquired with Bristol Wealth', see *T. B. & G. A. S.*, 123, (2005), pp. 9–16.

[28] *SANHS News, The Newsletter of the Somerset Archaeological & Natural History Society*, No. 78, Autumn 2008, p. 2.

In his many interests he has been fortunate to receive the tireless support and encouragement of his wife, (formerly Miss Amanda Juliet Buttenshaw, by whom he has two children, a son and a daughter).

Gerard Leighton's trenchant and uncompromising views, clearly enunciated and forcefully expressed, on a wide range of publishing and conservation matters in general; on the publication of archaeological reports; the conduct of liturgy in the Church of England; and the impracticality and lack of financial experience and acumen of most of the clericy and many academics are well known. His financial prudence and good sense have enabled many organisations to weather the vagaries of the financial markets and to emerge financially strengthened in order to undertake the tasks for which they were intended. For example, through successful fund raising and the careful husbanding of resources it was possible for him to establish the St. Andrew's Conservation Trust from the surplus funds from the restoration of Wells cathedral. These are employed to assist with small restoration projects such as the conservation of hatchments and monuments in churches in Somerset and the South West.

This collection of essays reflects some of Gerard Leighton's wide range of interests: Bristol cathedral; funerary hatchments and Royal coats of arms; the churches of Bristol, and Christ Church, Broad Street, and St. Ewen in particular; the 'historic built environment'; the work of Thomas Paty (in Clifton Hill House and Christ Church);[29] the Tyndall family; music; and the eighteenth century in general.

Christ Church with St. Ewen, Broad Street, was known irreverently by wags as 'the Bristol and Gloucestershire Archaeological Society at prayer'![30] The Society, guided by our past honorary general secretary, Dr. Elizabeth Ralph, was instrumental in ensuring that the church remained open as a place of worship between the 1950s and the 1980s when the diocesan authorities were firstly in favour of its demolition, and later made repeated attempts to have the church declared redundant. Its survival and current position as the headquarters of the Prayer Book Society for the diocese of Bristol owes much to their efforts and to those of Gerard Leighton in his capacity as the chairman of the Diocesan Advisory Committee. Gerard Leighton, wrote the current visitors' guide to the church. These factors explain the decision to include essays on the church and the associated, but now demolished, church of St. Ewen in this volume. The restoration of the four Tyndall hatchments and the Royal coat of arms in Christ Church has been partly funded on Gerard Leighton's recommendation by the St. Andrew's Conservation Trust.

It also a happy coincidence that that the centenary of the connection of the Leighton family with the Bristol and Gloucestershire Archaeological Society falls within the centennial year of the University of Bristol.[31] This has facilitated publica-

---

[29] M. J. Crossley Evans and H. G. M. Leighton, review of Gordon Priest's, 'The Paty Family: Makers of Eighteenth-Century Bristol', *T. B. & G. A. S.*, 123, (2005), pp. 190–193.

[30] Dr. Ralph's sister, Jeannette, attended the church as well as successive membership secretaries of the Society, (Mr. Vivian Mildren and Mrs. Joyce Morris); Bristol secretaries, (Mr. Robert Knapp and the editor of this volume), and members of Council, (Mr. John Stevens *et al.*).

[31] Henry Edward Buttenshaw Leighton, Gerard Leighton's son, who was at Winchester between 1997 and 2002, is a graduate in Mathematics from the University. *Old Wykehamist Address Roll*, (2007).

tion of a number of papers within this volume elucidating the history of important Georgian buildings in its care: Clifton Hill House, Goldney House, Richmond House and the Royal Fort.

From its place on the shelves of the members of this Society, the Publications Committee hopes that this volume will serve as a permanent record of Gerard Leighton's many achievements, and to his huge contribution, over half a century, to furthering the realisation of our shared aims and objectives.

EDITOR'S NOTE

'Of making many books, there is no end'.
Ecclesiastes, XII, v. 12.

My thanks are many and varied, but must principally go to my editorial assistant, Mr. David Smith, our former honorary general secretary, upon whom I have relied heavily and whose scholarly attention to detail and consistency have been invaluable to me, as well as to my academic readers. I am indebted to many people for their technical assistance: particularly to Dr. Wilson and Mrs. Winnie Wong, and to Messrs. Simon A. Allatt, Owen B. Peachey and Joseph S. Selit-Renny, and to Miss Helen L. Poole.

Thanks are due to Mrs. Sheena Stoddard, keeper of Fine Art at Bristol Museum and Art Gallery, and the staff of the Local Studies Library, in the Central Library, College Green; to Mrs. Anne Bradley, and the staff of the Bristol Record Office; to my colleagues Mr. Michael T. Richardson, special collections librarian, University of Bristol, and Ms. Hannah Lowery, archivist of the University of Bristol, for their unfailing courtesy and patience, to Dr. Myra F. K. Stokes, *quondam* Senior Lecturer in English, University of Bristol, and to Mr. Jamie Carstairs, of Special Collections for his photographic work. I am indebted to Mrs. Mary V. Campbell for being able to draw upon her detailed knowledge of Clifton and the Society.

I would also like to thank Mr. John Roost and the staff of '4Word' for their professionalism, and the Publications Committee of the Bristol and Gloucestershire Archaeological Society for their support during the last two years. I thank my authors for their helpfulness, and good humour in the face of tight deadlines and I accept full responsibility for any errors or omissions.

Notes on Contributors

STEPHEN BANFIELD is Stanley Hugh Badock Professor of Music at the University of Bristol and founded CHOMBEC, its Centre for the History of Music in Britain, the Empire and the Commonwealth, in 2006. Author or contributing editor of seven books on English and American music, he is currently preparing two histories of music in the British world beyond the metropolis, in the West of England and in the Empire.

JOSEPH H. BETTEY was formerly Reader in Local History at the University of Bristol, and is author of numerous books and articles on various aspects of the history of Bristol and the West Country. He was President of the British Association of Local History, and of the Bristol and Gloucestershire Archaeological Society, and served as General Editor of the Bristol Record Society. He is Chairman of the Fabric Advisory Committee of Bristol cathedral and is particularly interested in the ecclesiastical history of Bristol and in the agricultural history of the neighbouring counties.

SHEILA B. BRENNAN was born in Liverpool on 2 August 1922, graduated in English from St. Margaret's Hall, Oxford, in 1944, trained as a school mistress and taught at Dame Alleyne's School for Girls at Dulwich. She subsequently lectured in Education at the University of Bristol (1952–1955); Fourah Bay College, Sierra Leone (1955–1959); Newton Park, Bath (1959–1964), and the University of Malawi (1964–1969), before returning to the University of Bristol, where she was Special Lecturer in Education, Warden of Clifton Hill House (1969–1984) and Manor Hall (1974–1984), and Advisor to Overseas Students. She was interested in literature and spent many years researching the history of Clifton Hill House. Before she was able to complete her research on Paul Fisher she died on 12 February 2005. Her ashes are buried in the gardens of Manor Hall. [Ed.]

ANNIE M. BURNSIDE was born in November 1944, brought up in Paris and read English at the Sorbonne where she was awarded a Diplôme d'Etudes Supérieures (D.E.S.) in 1967 for her work on 'Horace Walpole and Clara Reeve as pioneers of the Gothic Novel', and the Certificat d'Aptitude Professionnelle à l'Enseignement du Second Degré (C.A.P.E.S.) in English Language and Literature. She obtained her M.A. in Classical French Literature from the University of Bristol in 1972, became language assistant in the Department of French in 1980, and Warden of Clifton Hill House in 1988. In 1980, she founded the Ecole Française de Bristol and the Alliance Française de Bristol in 1983. She was Présidente de l'Union des Français du Sud-Ouest de Grande Bretagne from 1982 to 2004. She is 'Officier dans l'Ordre des Palmes Académiques', and 'Officier dans l'Ordre National du Mérite'. She has been French Honorary Consul for Bristol and the South West of England since 2003. In 2004 she was appointed one of the two Deputy Marshals of the University. She has a special interest in art, architecture and literature.

MARTIN J. CROSSLEY EVANS was born in Wirral, and read Archaeology and Geology at the University of Bristol, where his personal tutor for two years was Dr. A. J. Parker. He trained as a school master, and taught at Shrewsbury and Gresham's School, Holt, before taking a doctorate in Ecclesiastical History at Bristol. His interest in Bristol's history owes much to the encouragement of Mr. G. C. Boon, Dr. A. B. Cottle and Miss Elizabeth Ralph. A past President of the Bristol Masonic Society, and one of the church wardens of St. Ewen, he is currently Senior Warden, and Historic Collections' Officer of the University of Bristol, and has been Warden of Manor Hall since 1984. He is one of the two Deputy Marshals of the University, a magistrate, and was a made an M.B.E. in 2001 for 'services to higher education'.

WILLIAM L. H. EVANS, author of a history of Abbot's Leigh, and whose work on Hannah More's family, and on other eighteenth century subjects has been printed in our *Transactions*, worked as a lawyer with local and other public authorities, including the former Avon County Council from 1974 to 1986. In 1989 he was appointed Secretary and Solicitor to Bristol Polytechnic, and then to the University of the West of England, Bristol, until he retired in 1997. His amateur interest in local history has led to him becoming Honorary Treasurer of Avon Local History and Archaeology, the Bristol Record Society and, since 2009, of our Society. His curiosity about Lord Botetourt springs from the University of the West of England's main campus forming a part of what was formerly Botetourt's Stoke Park estate.

ROBERT A. GILBERT is a writer and retired antiquarian bookseller, born and educated in Bristol. He read Philosophy and Psychology at the University of Bristol, and was recently admitted to the degree of Doctor of Philosophy by the University of London, for his thesis 'The Great Chain of Unreason', a study of the publication of esoteric literature in Victorian England. He is a past President of the Bristol Masonic Society, the former editor of the premier journal of Masonic research, *Ars Quatuor Coronatorum*, and has written extensively on the history of western esotericism. He currently edits *The Christian Parapsychologist* for the Churches' Fellowship for Psychical and Spiritual Studies.

COLIN GODMAN is a retired writer and broadcaster living in Bristol. Early experience in field archaeology led to St. Catharine's, College, Cambridge and the study of Archaeology, and Anthropology with Fine Arts and Architecture. Despite the inspiration of Sir Leonard Woolley, the encouragement of Miss Elizabeth Ralph, Professor Philip Rahtz and Messrs L. V. Grinsell and G. C. Boon and the teaching of Professor Glyn Daniel he was distracted by more ephemeral delights. Professional work in the theatre led to a career with the British Broadcasting Corporation as a television producer. Archaeology was never quite abandoned and he has published his work on a sub-Roman cemetery on Kings Weston Down near Bristol and a desktop assessment of the mediaeval manor of Ashton Phillips in Long Ashton in North Somerset.

JAMES HOBSON is a research student in the department of music at Bristol University. His particular area of interest is the Bristol-born composer, Robert Lucas Pearsall (1795–1856), and the revival of the madrigal and other renaissance music in nineteenth century Britain. He is also the administrator of CHOMBEC, the Centre for the History of Music in Britain, the Empire and the Commonwealth, whose home is at the Victoria Rooms, Bristol.

LORNA F. HUGHES read English at Lady Margaret Hall, Oxford, and went on to teach English and English Literature until her retirement. She held posts at two former Clifton schools: La Retraite High School and Clark's Grammar School. She is a member of the Bristol and Clifton Dickens Society, with a particular interest in the religious life of the nineteenth century. This has led to her research on the connection of Dr. Pusey with Bristol, a subject which was of great interest to our former Honorary General Secretary, Miss Elizabeth Ralph.

ROGER H. LEECH was born in Cheshire 13 days after D-Day, and is a graduate of the Universities of Cambridge and of Bristol, where his Ph.D. dissertation in 1978 under the supervision of Dr. A. J. Parker was on 'Romano-British Rural Settlement in South Somerset and North Dorset'. He was the first Director of the Cumbria and Lancashire Archaeological Unit in the University of Lancaster (1979–1984), moving then to the Royal Commission on the Historical Monuments of England (now merged with English Heritage), firstly as head of the former Ordnance Survey Archaeology Division and then as head of Archaeology. He has been the President of both the Society for Post-Medieval Archaeology and the Bristol and Gloucestershire Archaeological Society, and is now visiting Professor of Archaeology at the University of Southampton. His work on Bristol includes the first two volumes of an intended series on the topography of the city published by the Bristol Record Society; a study of Bristol town houses to be published by English Heritage in association with the City of Bristol is approaching completion.

DEIRDRE LE FAYE is an independent scholar, who has researched the life and times of Jane Austen for more than thirty years. She has published a new edition of *Jane Austen's Letters* (O.U.P., 1995, 1997), and also the definitive factual biography, *Jane Austen, a Family Record* (2nd ed. C.U.P., 2004), as well as numerous articles and other books concerning Jane Austen and her works.

MICHAEL J. H. LIVERSIDGE, is Emeritus Dean of Arts in the University of Bristol where he taught History of Art between 1970 and 2008, specialising in British painting and landscaping in the eighteenth and nineteenth centuries, co-directed the Master of Arts in Garden History, and was Head of Department. He served on the Board of Management of the Area Museums Council for the South West; was a member of (1980–2004) and Chairman of the Council of the Bristol and Gloucestershire Archaeological Society (1986–1989); Honorary Secretary of the Friends of Bristol Art Gallery; and President of the Bristol Decorative and Fine Arts Society. He is Governor of the British Institute of Florence, and of Dauntsey's School. He has been a Resident Fellow at the Yale Center for British Art, and has co-organised and co-edited catalogues for major exhibitions, including *Canaletto and England* (1993), and *Imagining Rome: British Artists and Rome in the Nineteenth Century* (1996). He is the author of *The Bristol High Cross* (1978), and *William Hogarth's Bristol Altar-Piece* (1980).

A. J. 'TOBY' PARKER taught archaeology in the Departments of Classics and Archaeology, University of Bristol, from 1973 to 2002. Among the courses he introduced during those years was one entitled 'Bristol', in which he tried to integrate site visits and field-work with the study of plans, records and artefacts. Since his retirement he has intensified his interest in historic Bristol by founding 'Bristol Harmony', a West Gallery quire which places a special focus on the music of Bristol and the West of England, *c.* 1700–1850. A notable feature of the vernacular music of that period is the fragility of the resource, by which much is preserved only in unique copies, whether printed or manuscript: its documentation and performance are thus important, even urgent. He is a Fellow of the Society of Antiquaries of London.

LIONEL R. REEVES, is a Bristolian who, after 15 years in commerce, was appointed a library assistant at Bristol Technical College. He subsequently trained as a school teacher at Newton Park, obtaining his degree from the University of Bristol, and taught in local primary schools until retirement. He is currently head guide at Bristol cathedral. Through participation in amateur dramatics he was introduced to the Bristol and Clifton Dickens Society, elected to the committee, and served as Honorary Secretary for 18 years, during which time he organized two international Dickens Fellowship conferences at Clifton Hill House.

DAVID J. H. SMITH learned his trade as a professional archivist at the Bodleian Library in 1964–1965. Between 1980 and 2000 he was City, County, and Diocesan Archivist of Gloucestershire. From 1986 until 2006 he was Honorary General Secretary of this Society. He is a Fellow of the Society of Antiquaries of London and an Honorary Fellow of the University of Gloucestershire. Since his retirement he has continued to work as archivist for the Berkeley family as well as holding several voluntary positions. He runs workshops on archives skills and gives lectures on historical subjects mainly relating to Gloucestershire.

PEGGY K. STEMBRIDGE became interested in the Goldney family when she was a tutor in a hall of residence, in a house once owned by Thomas Goldney III, adjacent to his main house and garden in Clifton. Wide-ranging research led to new information about the history and significance of the family, particularly in the seventeenth and eighteenth centuries. Some of the results have been included in a thesis for the University of Bristol in 1982 and in a range of books and articles. Serendipity also led to tracing a collection of family papers and to Sir Henry Goldney's generous gift of them to the University of Bristol.

JOHN R. STEVENS was born and bred in Dorset and educated at Dorchester Grammar School and Downing College, Cambridge, where he read Law. He began his professional career in Bournemouth, qualifying as a solicitor and moving to Bristol in 1984. He now practises in government service and his main historical interest is in the political history of the eighteenth and nineteenth centuries: he is currently researching Bristol at the time of the Reform Act of 1832. He sits on the Council of the Bristol and Gloucestershire Archaeological Society and on the P.C.C. of Christ Church with St. Ewen.

JOHN TOMAN spent thirty years in education as a teacher, lecturer and schools inspector. He read English at the University of Nottingham and completed a B.Phil. in Language and Education at the University of Birmingham. He taught in secondary schools, was a lecturer at Jordanhill College of Education in Glasgow, and County Inspector for English in Lincolnshire. During the last eighteen years, he has made an intensive study of Kilvert's background and Kilvert's Diary. His *Kilvert's Diary and Landscape*, (Lutterworth Press, 2009) is the second part of a revaluation of the diarist that began with his *Kilvert: The Homeless Heart*, (Logaston Press, 2001).

KATHARINE WOODGATE-JONES after training in the conservation of paintings, worked for the Area Museums' Council for the South West based in Bristol. In 1976 she took up a position as Senior Conservator with the Canadian Conservation Institute which was followed by a contract with the New Zealand government as National Conservator based in Auckland City Art Gallery. She returned to the U.K. in 1983 and is now in private practice.

Abstracts

Bristol Cathedral during the early eighteenth century,
by Joseph H. Bettey, F.S.A.
The eighteenth century church has been much criticized for somnolence, pluralism, non-residence and failure to display sufficient energy in proclaiming the gospel. The records of Bristol cathedral for this period reveal the presence of all these failings. Nonetheless, the unique survival of a detailed account of expenditure on the cathedral during the period 1699–1745, the so-called *Book of Particulars*, provides a different view and forms the basis of this article. It shows that whatever else was amiss, the cathedral continued to be well-maintained, the services were regularly provided and were accompanied by music and singing. It reveals the regular expenditure on craftsmen and builders, the decoration of the interior, the costs of the organ, the charitable contributions of the Chapter and other details which would be quite unknown without this source of information. Other surviving records of the period are used to present as full an account as possible of the building, its precinct, the cathedral clergy and community.

**Pitt the Elder and the financial discomfiture of Norborne Berkeley,
Lord Botetourt**, by William L. H. Evans, M.A., (Oxon).
Norborne Berkeley (1717–1770) had his seat at Stoke Park in the parish of Stoke Gifford. In 1741 he was returned as one of the M.P.s for Gloucestershire, in the Tory interest. On the accession of George III Berkeley obtained a post in the royal court. In 1764 he successfully revived a claim to a peerage in abeyance, the entitlement to which his father had researched but not pursued, and entered the House of Lords as Lord Botetourt. He invested heavily in William Champion's zinc manufactory at Warmley, and fronted the Warmley Company's application for a charter of incorporation. When Pitt the Elder failed to execute the charter, Champion fraudulently withdrew his capital from the company, which collapsed. This paper explores how that came about, and suggests that Botetourt was not as blameworthy as he was made out by his detractors, who included Edmund Burke, then not yet M.P. for Bristol. This article involved a detailed study of Lord Botetourt's accounts.

Richmond House and the manor of Clifton, by Roger H. Leech, F.S.A.
Richmond House is one of the less well-known historic houses owned by the University of Bristol. Recent research is beginning to reveal much more of the history and architectural development of this house, providing new insights into the history and location of the manor house and later the two manors of Clifton. Looking at Richmond House in more detail, as an early suburban villa or garden house, provides a further understanding of the architectural development of Clifton in the seventeenth and eighteenth centuries.

Paul Fisher, linen-draper and merchant, of Clifton Hill House,

by Annie M. Burnside, M.A., and the late Sheila B. Brennan, M.A.(Oxon), (1922–2005).

This study assesses the part that Paul Fisher, a respected merchant, and linen draper, played in the commercial development of eighteenth century Bristol. The sources of his immense wealth were many and included the slave trade in which he was involved for more than 30 years. A philanthropist, he played an important role in the early years of the Bristol Infirmary, and was a trustee of Redland chapel. Paul Fisher's enduring legacy is Clifton Hill House. The design by the London architect, Isaac Ware, marks a turning point in the architecture of the Palladian style of villa.

Thomas Goldney II and Thomas Goldney III: The Creation of the Goldney estate, by P. K. Stembridge, B.A., M.Litt.

Goldney house and garden in Clifton, Bristol, were largely the creation in the eighteenth century of two Bristol Quaker merchants: Thomas Goldney II (1664–1731) and his son Thomas Goldney III (1696–1768). The father leased a gentleman's house and a two-acre garden on Clifton Hill in 1694 and extended the house in the 1720s, probably using profits from a famous privateering expedition. From 1733, the son enlarged the estate to some 13 acres, chiefly using income from his business interests in the iron trade and banking. Thomas Goldney III re-designed the garden with unusual and unique features; even before it was finished, the grotto in particular was well known beyond Goldney's own circle. In the twentieth century the house and the garden features have been listed as II or II* and the grotto is Grade I.

Christ Church, City, its fabric and re-building during the eighteenth century, by M. J. Crossley Evans, F.S.A.

Christ Church occupied one of the most prominent positions in the mediaeval city of Bristol, at the junction of Corn Street, Broad Street, High Street and Wine Street. The mediaeval structure, which is believed to have contained elements dating from the eleventh century onwards and at least one integral priest's house, had large sums of money spent on its fabric in the eighteenth century. None the less, by 1786 it was judged to be in such a perilous situation that it was decided to demolish and rebuild the church. The reasons behind these decisions and the claim that the design of the new church was by William Paty, are explored.

Music at the Bristol chapel of the Countess of Huntingdon's Connexion, by A. J. 'Toby' Parker, F.S.A.

Hymn singing was an important part of worship for the Calvinistic Methodists led by Selina, countess of Huntingdon (1707–1791). A tune-book compiled *c.* 1788 by Benjamin Belcher, clerk of the Bristol congregation, survives in a unique copy in Bristol Reference Library. Study of Belcher's tunes, and comparison with other tune-books of the Bristol and Bath chapels, show some originality and independence of taste on his part, while emphasizing how much 'the Old Methodist way of singing' came to diverge from mainstream English psalmody in the later eighteenth century. The music of the Bristol chapel was simpler, on the whole, than that at Bath—perhaps in keeping with the waterfront location and restricted site of the eighteenth century chapel, now completely vanished.

The cemetery under the tower: Christ Church, Bristol; and the destruction of St. Ewen's Church, by Colin Godman, M.A., (Cantab), and M. J. Crossley Evans, F.S.A

The discovery of a sealed vault, beneath the tower of Christ Church with St. Ewen, Broad Street, Bristol, in 1958, containing a large number of bones and coffin fragments, presented a problem of interpretation. The surviving eighteenth century parish church replaced the mediaeval Holy Trinity, or Christ Church, demolished in 1786. Were the remains those of the dead of the earlier church, or had they been carried from the nearby St. Ewen's church when it was demolished in 1824? A 'cemetery under the tower' had been referred to by the eminent antiquarian Canon Rauceby Cole, rector of Christ Church with St. Ewen from 1903 to 1938. Canon Cole's notebooks and archive were found to contain a number of clues. The study of the photographs taken in 1958 when combined with research amongst the respective parish records, vestry accounts, and town clerk's records allows an identification of the material.

The Church of St. Thomas the Martyr: Demolition and Re-building 1786–1793, by Joseph H. Bettey, F.S.A.

The church of St. Thomas the Martyr was founded at the end of the twelfth century. Although it was on a restricted site, the church was re-built on the grandest scale during the later Middle Ages and was expensively furnished. The survival of copious documentary evidence reveals the continuing expenditure by the church wardens, and the large sums spent on new furnishings during the eighteenth century. In spite of the lavish expenditure, however, it was decided during the 1780s that the structure was in such a bad condition that it had to be demolished and re-built. This essay considers the possible reasons for this decision and traces the re-building of the new church in an elegant classical design.

Blotting out Bristol. Humphry Repton's Royal Fort 'Red Book', by Michael J. H. Liversidge, F.S.A.

Humphry Repton's manuscript 'Red Books' for the gardens and landscapes he created, together with the books he published on the theory, practice and aesthetics of landscaping and garden design, describe in detail the development of his ideas over a period of some thirty years when he was one of the principal protagonists in the debates around what constituted the picturesque and was a formative influence on a nascent 'natural' vision in English landscape art at the start of the nineteenth century. The pleasure grounds and park he designed and improved for Thomas Tyndall around The Royal Fort overlooking Bristol between 1799 and 1801 are an unusual example of his landscaping for a suburban villa, contrived to preserve the amenity of a gentleman's country seat and insulate it from the populous city encroaching on its environs. The Royal Fort 'Red Book', published here for the first time, reveals Repton's clever use of a landscape artist's pictorial manipulation of scale and perspective effects to manage the views from, as well as those of, the house and its grounds, together with the social and cultural values he expressly sets out to inscribe on a landscape that constructs a 'natural' hierarchy of possession and position separating the polite from the populace in Georgian England.

Jane Austen and Bristol, by Deirdre Le Faye

It is well-known that Jane Austen visited Bath and later lived there for some years in the early nineteenth century, during which time she probably became acquainted with Bristol as well. This paper considers her possible reasons for visiting Bristol, and the influence that city had upon her two novels *Northanger Abbey* (1818) and *Emma* (1815).

The Catholic Question in Bristol public life 1820–1829, by John R. Stevens, M.A., (Cantab).

This essay is a narrative of the impact on Bristol public life of the Catholic crisis of the 1820s. The emphasis is placed on the years 1828–1829 when the question of Catholic Emancipation became of the first importance, nationally and locally. The crisis is followed through the speeches, sermons, writings and activities of Bristol's M.P.s, bishops, clergy and civic leaders. Attention is also paid to public opinion as reflected in the press and in popular demonstrations. A brief concluding section considers the nature and consequences of the Catholic question.

Parochial burials in Bristol in the eighteenth and nineteenth centuries, exemplified by Christ Church, City, by M. J. Crossley Evans, F.S.A.

Although there was an increase in the number of burial places in Bristol following the Reformation, the provision did not keep up with the increasing demand for space. By the early eighteenth century the city's churchyards were overcrowded and insanitary, but the first major new cemetery was not opened until 1836. This paper looks at the problems this created for the small central parish of Christ Church, and places them in the context of those faced by parishes elsewhere in the city.

The Restoration of the Funerary Hatchments and the Royal Coat of Arms in Christ Church with St. Ewen, Bristol, by K. Woodgate-Jones, F.I.I.C.

Christ Church, Bristol, was fortunate to have survived the air raid on the night of the 24 November 1940. The destruction of the shops in Wine Street adjoining the south wall of the church, caused damage to the interior. Amongst the fittings affected were the two funerary hatchments closest to the source of the fire. In 2008 a long overdue assessment revealed that in addition to fire damage, these and a number of the other hatchments had been subject to damage from water, possibly during the year following the death of the person they commemorate when they were hung outside the front of the house of the deceased. It was also discovered that the Royal coat of arms in the vestry needed conservation. This study places the hatchments and the Royal arms into their contemporary context in Bristol and discusses the methods and materials used to repair, to clean and to conserve them.

Bristol and the Foundation of its Madrigal Society, by James Hobson, B.A., P.G.Dip.(Law).

The Bristol Madrigal Society was founded in 1837 by a group of enthusiastic amateur musicians who had been inspired by the visit of the eminent lecturer, Edward Taylor, in January that year. In the early nineteenth century, Bristol's musical life was spasmodic. War and economic depression affected the overcrowded city, and entertainment suffered accordingly. However, the 1830s saw a revival of musical culture, and by 1837 Bristol was ripe for new ventures. This paper puts into historical, musical and social context the years leading up to the foundation of the Bristol Madrigal Society, and considers the men who formed the society of which Bristol became so proud.

Dr. Pusey: Visitor to Bristol, by Lorna F. Hughes, B.A., (Oxon).
This paper attempts to explore something of the spiritual and personal sides of the life of the Revd. E. B. Pusey D.D. through his association with Bristol. A considerable body of information is fortunately available, from letters, news articles and studies of the period; the chief focus here being the years from 1831 to 1851. The intention has been to place some of the fascinating details of local interest within the historical context of the Oxford Movement and Tractarian doctrine at national level.

'A Grand City': Kilvert and Bristol, by John Toman, B.A., B.Phil.
Kilvert was drawn to admire Bristol by various factors in his background, education and personality. The entries he wrote in his diary about his regular visits to it are a guide to its significance for him. Of utmost importance was its dominance in the region as a trading centre and he had a particular affinity with the Quakerism that had figured so strongly both in his own family and in Bristol's commercial history. He had a tradesman grandfather and was brought up to admire people who had raised themselves by their own efforts and contributed to the amelioration of society. Bristol also satisfied Kilvert's love of poetry and romance and his passion for the past. His stance towards the city exemplifies the ambivalence of his personality.

Captain Francis George Irwin: his private press and his Rosicrucian rivals, by Robert Andrew Gilbert, B.A., Ph.D.
In the later nineteenth century, Bristol was home to a variety of peculiar esoteric and quasi-masonic institutions, many of them under the *aegis* of the adjutant of a Bristol Battalion of Volunteers—Captain F. G. Irwin. By profession a soldier, Irwin was an occultist by inclination and from 1867 until his death in 1893, he drew in fellow enthusiasts to the Rosicrucian and other Orders that he had variously joined, directed or invented. He sought also to instruct his acolytes with the aid of short papers that he wrote and badly printed himself, but they were too few in number, and too lacking in dedication, to keep Irwin's esoteric creations alive. Nor did Bristolians follow other esoteric paths and a near total lack of support led to the collapse of the 'Bath Occult Reprints', a publishing venture of Robert Fryar, Irwin's only local contemporary in the field of esoteric dreams.

They came, they stayed and they went: musicians and Bristol in the nineteenth century, by Stephen Banfield, M.A., D.Phil., F.R.C.O.
Working with a collection of around 75 genteel (as opposed to proletarian) musicians born between *c.* 1760 and 1880 for whom biographical facts have been easily retrieved, this essay looks at the demographic career patterns into which Bristol's musicians fitted. A striking contrast between mobility and stasis emerges. The city acted as a gateway or staging post between the west country and London, but with its cathedral establishment and, after 1862, Clifton College, it also possessed an

infrastructure that could generate long musical careers *in situ*. Movement to and from other provincial regions within Britain proves rare but emigration is frequent and fruitful, whether or not this has anything to do with Bristol's status as a port.

Lovers of Dickens: The formative years of the Bristol and Clifton Dickens Society, by Lionel R. Reeves, B.Ed.

The Bristol and Clifton Dickens Society was founded in 1902 to encourage Bristolians 'To form a bond of union among lovers of Dickens'. Two years later this statement was amplified by adding: 'with the avowed object of spreading his love of humanity [...] and to give practical effect to his teachings by following the example he set'. As such the Society has a small niche in the sociology of the city and may have influenced the formation of the international Dickens Fellowship. In the absence of original documentation in the Society's archive, 'Lovers of Dickens' sets out to collate from newspaper reports and other sources the circumstances in which the Bristol and Clifton Dickens Society was born and to show how it developed during the first decade of its existence.

The Society's Archives: Gloucestershire Archives D7996, by David J. H. Smith, M.A., F.S.A.,

Until relatively recent times the Society's records were preserved haphazardly both in Bristol and Gloucester, as well as in the homes of current and former officers. During his years as Honorary General Secretary, David Smith tried to rationalise their custody and storage and to produce a list which would reflect the way the Society has operated and consequently has recorded its activities. The results are summarised in this article which also charts the main changes in the Society's organisation since its foundation.

I

Bristol Cathedral during the early eighteenth century

JOSEPH H. BETTEY, F.S.A.

IT IS appropriate to include an essay on Bristol cathedral in this collection produced to honour Gerard Leighton and pay tribute to the many voluntary activities in which he has been involved. For many years he has been a valued member of the Fabric Advisory Committee of Bristol cathedral, and has contributed a great deal of expertise and advice, based on his long chairmanship of Wells Cathedral Fabric Advisory Committee. In addition, he was for 20 years chairman of the Bristol Diocesan Advisory Committee, using his detailed knowledge of the churches of the diocese to provide advice on developments in architecture and furnishings and on the appropriate care and maintenance of church buildings.

Bristol cathedral, together with the diocese and bishopric of Bristol, was founded by order of Henry VIII in 1542, when Bristol was first designated as a city. The site and buildings of the former Augustinian abbey, which had been suppressed in 1539, were vested in a Dean and Chapter, with the abbey church as the cathedral and the former abbot's lodging as the residence of the bishop. During the final decades of the abbey's existence work had slowly been going on to replace and enlarge the nave of the abbey church. Great quantities of building stone had been brought to the site, and work had started on new walls outside the twelfth century nave. With the suppression of the abbey all work had stopped, and during the upheaval caused by the end of the abbey and the creation of the new cathedral establishment, the existing nave was demolished. Soon afterwards the stone which had been assembled for the new nave was removed. The new cathedral church therefore consisted only of the chancel, Lady Chapel, side chapels, crossing and transepts of the former abbey church. This cramped inconvenient arrangement was to last until the mid-nineteenth century. Likewise, the new diocese was very difficult to administer since it consisted of the 18 parishes within Bristol, 14 parishes in south Gloucestershire, and the parish of Abbots Leigh across the river Avon in Somerset, together with the county of Dorset. Moreover, some 40 Dorset parishes remained as 'peculiars' of the Dean and Chapter of Salisbury Cathedral and were effectively outside the jurisdiction of the bishop of Bristol. This administratively-impossible situation, ignoring the fact that the nearest part of Dorset is more than 40 miles from Bristol, was to last until the mid-nineteenth century.[1]

Without a nave, accommodation for congregations within the cathedral was limited. The situation was made worse by the solid stone screen or *pulpitum* which

---

[1] For a complete account of the abbey and cathedral see the Revd. J. Rogan, (ed.), *Bristol Cathedral: History and Architecture*, (2000). Details of the dissolution of the abbey are contained in J. H. Bettey, *The Suppression of the Religious Houses in Bristol*, Bristol Historical Association, 74, (1990).

divided the chancel from the transepts and by the large monuments which further constricted the space within the cathedral. The high altar and choir stalls were moved east into the former Lady Chapel, but most of the congregation had to be confined to the area west of the massive screen where a pulpit was erected for the sermons which were regarded as such an important part of the services. Later records have several examples of complaints about overcrowding and the difficulty of obtaining a seat. The area to the south and west of the cathedral was crowded with houses belonging to various members of the cathedral, and by the dwellings erected on the site of the former nave during the later sixteenth century. The schoolroom for the cathedral school was situated on the west side of Lower College Green.

The cathedral was endowed with the income from widespread and numerous lands, properties in Gloucestershire, Wiltshire and Somerset, and houses, shops, inns and industrial premises in Bristol. The endowment provided an adequate though far from lavish income for the Dean and Chapter and for the various members of the cathedral. The income of the bishop was less than that enjoyed by any other episcopal see. Consequently few bishops remained long in Bristol before seeking a more lucrative bishopric elsewhere. The average length of stay of a bishop in Bristol during the eighteenth century was little more than four years, and this is distorted by one bishop (Dr. Thomas Newton) who, unusually, stayed for 21 years.

Henry VIII's Foundation Charter of 4 June 1542 evidently expected the cathedral community to resemble closely the Augustinian abbey which it replaced, and envisaged a group of men, both priests and laymen, living a communal life and maintaining a constant round of prayer and praise to God. The establishment consisted of a bishop, dean, six canons, six minor canons, one deacon, six lay-clerks or choirmen, one master of choristers, two schoolmasters, four almsmen, a sexton or sacrist, a porter or verger, a butler and two cooks. This ideal of a religious community was soon abandoned when during the mid-sixteenth century it became lawful for priests to marry and as many of the canons became pluralists, holding other benefices and coming to Bristol only to fulfil their allotted periods of residence.[2]

In contrast to the Augustinian abbey for which few documentary sources survive, Bristol cathedral has a remarkably fine collection of records. These include charters, statutes, Chapter minutes and annual accounts or *Computa* for most years from 1550 onwards. There are also administrative records, surveys, correspondence and numerous documents relating to the building itself and to the administration of the estates.[3] The following paper describes the life of the cathedral during the first decades of the eighteenth century and is largely based on a unique survival. This is known as the *Book of Particulars* and consists of the detailed account in English, showing annual receipts and expenditure and from which the summary accounts or *Computa* were compiled in Latin. Only one Book of Particulars survives, covering the years 1691–1745. [4] This gives a much more detailed insight into all aspects of the life of the cathedral than

---

[2] Bristol Record Office (B.R.O.), DC/A/7/1/1, Charter of Foundation, 4 June 1542; DC/A/7/1/3–5, Cathedral Statutes 1544.

[3] For a complete list of the cathedral records which are now in the Bristol Record Office see I. M. Kirby, *The Records of the Diocese of Bristol*, (1970). For a detailed description of the records with extracts see J. H. Bettey, *Records of Bristol Cathedral*, Bristol Record Society, (hereafter B.R.S.), 59, (2007).

[4] B.R.O., DC/A/9/2/1, *Book of Particulars* 1699–1745.

exists for any other period until the late nineteenth century. It reveals the way in which the building was used, maintained and decorated, and the various people involved in administering the estates. The contents of this remarkably detailed source will be described later.

The *Computa* for 1699 show the typical annual income and expenditure of the whole establishment. The total rental income for the year was £807 8s 7d. From this the dean received £100 per annum and each of the six canons received £20. Like the lands of most large estates of the time, the Dean and Chapter properties were leased, generally for three lives, at a nominal rent but with a substantial fine levied at each renewal. Thus the ordinary income of the dean and canons was occasionally increased when a major lease was renewed and a large fine was paid. The dean received a fourth part of the additional income and the six canons each received an eighth share. An example of this uncertain, but no doubt welcome, good fortune occurred in 1724 when £2,000 was received for a renewal of the lease of the rectorial tithes of Halberton, Devon, £300 was paid by Sir Abraham Elton for a new lease of the manor of Blacksworth which included the right to operate the lucrative Rownham ferry across the Avon to Long Ashton, and a further £700 was obtained for the renewal of sundry smaller leases. Another example occurred in 1746 when a lease of the area to the east of the cathedral, known as the 'Masonrie and Covent Garden' granted to the Bristol lawyer, Jarrit Smith, brought £750 of additional income to be shared by members of the Chapter.[5]

Each year the four minor canons were paid £6, the schoolmaster received £20, the six singing-men or lay-clerks were each paid £12, and the four boy choristers £4. The organist was paid £20 per annum and each of the four almsmen was paid £6 13s 4d. Sundry other small payments for specific duties such as treasurer, sub-sacrist, auditor, chapter clerk, verger and keeper of the clock and keeper of the organ were also made. These payments, together with statutory obligation to donate alms for the relief of the poor and repair of roads, as well as £151 18s 0d spent on the maintenance of the cathedral church brought the total expenditure for the year to £769 15s 2d, leaving a surplus of £37 13s 5d in the treasury.[6]

The original intention of constant attendance by all the canons or prebendaries and a communal life similar to that of a monastery had long since broken down and been abandoned. The dean and each of the canons were generally resident for less than two months each year, according to a rota agreed at Chapter meetings. By the eighteenth century, even the short periods of statutory residence were not always scrupulously observed by the canons. Dr. Thomas Newton (bishop 1761–1782) in his autobiography published in 1782, wrote that he had been in Bristol during successive summers 'for months together, without seeing the face of Dean, or Prebendary, or anything better than a Minor Canon'.[7] Almost all of the canons had other benefices or positions at Oxford or Cambridge, and came to Bristol only for their periods of residence, generally letting their canonical houses to laymen. For example, Robert Boothe, who was dean from 1708 until 1730, held several other ecclesiastical offices including the rectory of Richmond, in Yorkshire; his successor, Samuel Creswicke

---

[5] B.R.O., DC/A/9/1/8–9, *Computa* 1682–1754.
[6] *Ibid.*
[7] The Rt. Revd. T. Newton, *Works*, (1782), pp. 94–97.

(dean 1730–1739), was also chaplain to George II, rector of St. James, Bristol, and of Marden, Wiltshire. Nathaniel Lye (canon 1691–1723) was also archdeacon of Gloucester, and rector of Dursley, Gloucestershire; James Harcourt (canon 1711–1739) was rector of All Saints', Bristol, and of Tellisford and South Petherton, Somerset. Charles Livesay (canon 1693–1739) was rector of St. Stephen, Bristol and of Rushden, Northampton, as well as enjoying the lucrative living of Sutton Bonnington, Nottingham, which was in the patronage of the Dean and Chapter of Bristol. John Baron (canon 1713–1721), can have spent little time in Bristol since as well as holding several other benefices he was also Master of Balliol College, Oxford. The minor canons were similarly pluralist, many of them holding positions as incumbents, curates and lecturers in Bristol churches in addition to their duties in the cathedral.[8]

The regular cathedral services were conducted by the minor canons, assisted by the lay-clerks and choristers, although most of the lay-clerks also served as organists or choir-masters in other Bristol churches, and could give only a strictly limited amount of time to their cathedral duties. The minor canons derived some additional income from conducting weddings and funerals in the cathedral. The cathedral register shows that it was popular for marriages, mostly of persons who had no connection with it. There were few baptisms, but for those who could afford it, burial in the cathedral or cloisters was evidently regarded as highly desirable. The number of eighteenth century memorial tablets on the floor of the cathedral is an indication of this popularity, and archaeological work during repairs to the floor regularly reveal large numbers of eighteenth century graves, many of them quite shallow. Up to 1762 the fee for such burials was £10 for the choir and £5 for the transepts or cloisters.[9]

A DESCRIPTION OF THE CATHEDRAL IN 1727
BY BROWNE WILLIS

A careful description of the cathedral buildings in 1727 was made by the antiquary, Browne Willis, as part of a survey of ten English cathedrals. In his account of Bristol cathedral he gave details of the statutes and organisation prescribed by Henry VIII, listing all the officials named in the Charter of Foundation. He then proceeded to a survey of the buildings, starting with the bishop's palace which was the former abbot's lodging on the south side of the cathedral. This he described as large but not very convenient, although in good repair and with a small chapel containing a good deal of painted glass in the windows. The deanery was at the west end of the cathedral, adjacent to the Norman gateway which gave access to the abbey precinct. Browne Willis thought that the deanery was 'a better house than the episcopal palace'. He also commented on the canons' houses within the precinct, some of them having been erected on the site of the nave of the abbey. The cloisters, or what remained of them, he thought were mean and covered 'with a sloped Roof like a Shed'. He was, however, greatly impressed by the Norman Chapter House and its elegant entrance,

---

[8] Details of the additional preferments held by many of the cathedral clergy during this period are listed in J. Foster, *Alumni Oxonienses*, (Oxford, 1887–1892) and J. & J. A. Venn, *Alumni Cantabrigienses*, (Cambridge, 1922–1927).

[9] B.R.O., DC/A/8/2, Chapter minutes 1751–1801, entries for 1762 and 1776.

and he noted that the library and archives were kept there and that four large sash windows had been inserted in place of the original circular window.

Finally, Browne Willis gave a description of the cathedral church. Lacking a nave, it was inevitably small, cramped and crowded, and he described it as 'one of the meanest Cathedrals in the Kingdom'. This dismissal was tempered by his praise for the condition of the building and the excellence of its fittings. His description continued:

> It is so well adorn'd, that it wants for no Cost or Art to render
> it beautiful, and is daily improving, and may be said to be kept
> in as good Repair as any Church whatsoever.
> The Organ is large and good, the Choir Stalls very regular, the
> Altar which is ascended to by black and white Marble Steps, and
> laid with Pavement of the same, is embellish'd with costly
> Painting and Gilding; and the East Window being large, and
> glaz'd with painted Glass, looks very magnificent and indeed,
> the whole Structure is kept so decent, that the example of this
> Chapter, is worthy to be recommended to the Imitation of our
> richest and most antient Cathedrals.[10]

THE BOOK OF PARTICULARS 1699–1745

As already mentioned, these detailed accounts of receipts and expenditure on the cathedral from which the Latin summaries in the annual *Computa* were compiled, are the fullest and most informative of all the financial accounts relating to the cathedral, and it is regrettable that only one volume has survived. Inevitably, there is much repetition of regular items of income and expenditure year after year, but these accounts provide details of many aspects of cathedral life which would otherwise be completely unknown. Above all, they confirm the verdict of Browne Willis that in spite of long periods of non-residence by the dean and canons, the cathedral was well maintained, and the regular daily services with musical accompaniment continued to be conducted by the minor canons with the assistance of the lay-clerks and boy-choristers.

Each year the accounts include a note of the arrangements made for the periods of residence of each member of the Chapter, together with the cost of letters sent to and received from the canons. There were frequent expenses for the administration of the estates from which the bulk of the cathedral income was derived, costs of collecting rents and of occasional visits to particular estates by the dean or one of the canons. For example, in 1717 £13 17s 9d was spent on 'Charges of Visiting the Severall Estates belonging to the Dean and Chapter of Bristol in the Counties of Devon and Somerset by Dr. Harcourt, Sub-Dean and Mr. Waterman, Treasurer'. In 1719 £16 3s 11d was spent on 'a Progress into Gloucestershire, Buckinghamshire and Wiltshire' in order to visit and inspect the estates. Each year a formal audit of the accounts was held in the Chapter House and there were substantial payments for the 'Audit Dinner'. In 1716 'Ann Shall the Cook' was paid £1 8s 0d for providing the Audit Dinner, and a further 18s 9d was spent on wine. Later in the eighteenth century these dinners became much

---

[10] B. Willis, *A Survey of the Cathedral of Bristol*, (1727).

more elaborate and expensive, and were held in local taverns. [11] The Chapter took its responsibilities towards its estates and tenants seriously, and each year there were payments to the poor in specific estates chosen in turn. In addition, occasional financial assistance was given to incumbents and curates, or for work done on parish churches or schools. In 1718, for example, £4 18s od was given towards the repair of the vicarage house at Puxton and £1 1s 6d towards 'Beautifying the Chancel at Churchill'. Occasionally the cost of apprenticing poor children from the estates was met by the Chapter. In 1723 £10 os od was spent on 'Placeing out of Katherine Barrett a poor Child of Banwell parish', and in 1724 the costs of an apprenticeship for Anne Badman, a poor child from Churchill came to £8 8s od'.

Expenses for the choir and the organ naturally figure largely in the accounts. As well as their stipends, the choirmen were given Christmas bonuses and occasional dinners, and there were frequent payments to the organist for copying out the words and music of new anthems. Thomas Bell was paid £5 5s od 'for writing anthems' in 1716, and almost every year there were costs for music and anthems, either purchased or copied. A new organ had been built and installed above the choir screen or *pulpitum* in 1682–1683 by the distinguished organ-builder, Renatus Harris. This magnificent organ with its finely-carved case consisted of a great organ with three manuals and 12 stops, an echo organ with seven stops and a choir organ. In 1719 Renatus Harris came to live in Bristol, occupying a house near the cathedral, and from then until his death in 1724 he was paid an annual salary of £6 os od. In 1719 he undertook a major overhaul of the organ and was paid £140 for:

> The Trumpett Stopp and the Eccho Trumpett and the addition
> of the C fol and the Key in the Organ of the Cathedrall Church
> and for all other work and repaires by him done on the same
> Organ, and in full for all other Moneys due to him.

Contributions were evidently sought towards the costs of this work, and gifts were recorded from the bishop of London £20, Edward Colston Esq. £50, Richard Moustin £5 and John Romsey the town clerk £5. [12] Nathaniel Priest, who was organist and choirmaster from 1723 until his death in 1734, was an accomplished musician who organized concerts in the cathedral, as well as musical events elsewhere in Bristol. Evidently he drew choristers from some distance, since in 1726 an advert from Nathaniel Priest appeared in the Bristol newspapers announcing that one of the choirboys, James Parry aged 14–15 years and from Carmarthen, had run away. [13] Priest's most notable concert in the cathedral took place on 22 November 1727 (St. Cecilia's Day) when more than 30 musicians and singers performed Handel's *Te Deum Jubilate*, the first time it had been heard outside London. [14]

There are frequent references to unspecified expenditure on the choirboys, and it is evident from later records that this was partly due to apprenticeships provided for

---

[11] For examples see J. H. Bettey, *Records of Bristol Cathedral*, B.R.S., 59, (2007), pp. 161–166.
[12] B.R.O., DC/A/9/2/1, entries for 1719.
[13] *Felix Farley's Bristol Journal*, 25 February 1726.
[14] The concert was advertised in *Felix Farley's Bristol Journal*, 18 November 1727.

the boys when they left the choir, and for suits of clothes given to them at the same time.[15] It is a clear indication of the importance attached to music and singing in the cathedral services that such large sums were regularly spent on it. Likewise there were recurring costs for the maintenance of the bells, for ropes, oil and payments to the ringers. Benjamin Long was paid £3 3s 0d in 1712 'for new hanging the Great Bell', and a bell was re-hung in the tower in 1716 costing £2 5s 0d. There were also regular costs for the care of the clock, and in 1714 £7 17s 9d was paid to 'Mr Whitemore for putting up the Quarters, mending the Clock and altering the Striking Hammer'. Drains and gutters or 'gouts' were regularly cleaned, and wire guards were fixed to the outside of windows, as in 1724 when £4 5s 0d was paid 'for Lattice Wire for the painted window in the south aisle'.

There are few detailed references to the Cathedral School, although the Dean and Chapter were closely involved in its management, the maintenance of the schoolroom and in the appointment of the headmaster and under-master. At the beginning of the eighteenth century the school occupied a building on the west side of Lower College Green, near the schoolmaster's house, but this was superseded in about 1720 by a new schoolroom on the south side of the Green, adjacent to Canons Marsh. The Chapter minutes for 1718 record the grant of a lease of the old schoolroom and other buildings in Lower College Green to Thomas Maddocks, carpenter, for 40 years at an annual rent of £10, in consideration that Maddocks was to build a new schoolroom.[16] The *Book of Particulars* records several payments of small sums during 1719–20 to workmen building the new schoolroom. There are also notes of regular payments each year of £1 0s 0d to 'the Boys at the Grammar School' or 'paid by order of the Dean and Chapter to the School-boyes', presumably to provide an annual treat.

The obligation to maintain four pensioners or almsmen was carefully observed throughout the eighteenth century. They were appointed by the Crown, and according to the Statutes drawn up by order of Henry VIII in 1544 they were to be former royal servants, soldiers or sailors 'oppressed with want and poverty, broken down or maimed in the wars, weakened by age, or any other ways disabled, and reduced to want or misery'. They were to take part in the daily services, clean the church, toll the bells, light the candles and undertake similar duties. As well as their regular pension of £6 13s 4d, some of the almsmen were paid additional sums for such tasks as lighting the fire in the Chapter House, winding the clock, acting as sexton or assistant organist, or pumping the bellows for the organ. The Statutes also laid down that every year each pensioner was to be provided with a new coat for him to wear in the cathedral, each coat decorated with an elaborately-embroidered device made of silk in the form of a Tudor rose. This requirement continued to be observed and each year there were entries for the new coats and for 'four roses' each costing between 3s 0d and 5s 0d to make.

Other annually recurring expenses included washing the altar linen, scouring the wax from the candlesticks and from the brass eagle lectern, cleaning the marble floor of the chancel and 'Christmas Boxes' for the various tradesmen employed about the cathedral. Candles were expensive and occur frequently in the accounts. Wax candles

[15] B.R.O., DC/A/11/1/1, Letters and Receipts concerning choristers and lay-clerks 1705–1837.
[16] B.R.O., DC/A/8/1, Chapter minutes 3 April 1718.

were purchased in London, whereas the much cheaper tallow candles could be obtained in Bristol. For example, during the winter of 1723–1724 £10 7s 10d was spent on wax candles and a further 6s 6d 'for carriage of them from London'. By contrast only £1 19s 0d was spent on tallow candles.

The obligation which the Statutes imposed on the Dean and Chapter for charitable giving continued to be observed. Each year a contribution of £20 was made to the poor and another £20 for the maintenance of roads and bridges, as well as the relief which was given to the poor on the cathedral estates. Twenty widows in Bristol were each given £1 at Christmas and other sums were given to the poor and to travellers during the year. Preachers were paid for additional sermons at Christmas, Easter, 5 November, the commemoration of the execution of Charles I on 30 January and the Restoration of Charles II (Oak Apple Day) on 29 May. In 1705 a 'half hower Glasse' was purchased for 7d to remind preachers of the passage of time. The Gunpowder Plot was also remembered with an annual bonfire on 5 November, presumably held on College Green. Occasional royal visits to Bristol involved the Dean and Chapter in the expense of paying men to carry the cathedral arms and provide an escort in the welcoming procession. For example, when Queen Anne came to Bristol in 1703 two men were paid 4s 0d 'for carrying Armes when the Queen came,' and a further 2s 0d was spent 'for cleansing the Armes and powder'. In 1728 £1 10s 0d was spent in 'Expenses when Princess Amelia came to Bristol'. Each year at Christmas and Easter the cathedral was decorated with holly and other greenery. For example, in 1703 Hugh Jones was paid 5s 0d 'for dressing the Church twice', and in 1712 Arthur Redwood was paid 5s 0d 'for dressing the Church twice with Greenes'.

Evidence that the cathedral was well maintained comes from the regular and substantial payments which were made to masons, plumbers, joiners, glaziers, tilers and smiths for work on various parts of the building and on the Chapter House, cloisters and other structures within the precinct. The *Book of Particulars* show that the interior walls of the cathedral were plastered and whitewashed or 'white limbed'. Hugh Jones was paid £2 0s 0d in 1701 'for white limbing the church'. All the surfaces were treated in this way, as is evident from the expenditure of 8s 0d in 1703 'for Canvass to naile about the Organ when the Church was White limb'd'. In 1723 a major re-painting and cleaning of the interior of the cathedral was undertaken as is evident from the following entries in the Book of Particulars:

Extraordinary Expenses in Beautifying the Cathedral Begun June 17 & finished Augt. 3rd 1723

		£	s	d
June 18	For Mops and Brushes	00	06	00
July 5	For Cleansing the Marble	00	10	00
6	For a Pail and a Mop	00	03	00
18	For Mops and Brushes	00	10	00
25	To Sherwood the Buttmaker [Barrel-maker] his Note	00	15	00
	Given to his Man	00	01	00
Augt 1	To Horwood the House Painter his Note	13	08	00
	Given to his man at Severall times	00	07	06

Oct. 21	To Mr Degroot for Cleansing & repairing the Painting at the Altar & in the body of the Church	05	16	00
Nov. 16	To Michael Sidwell Freestone Mason his note	11	00	00
	Given to his man at Severall times	00	05	06
	To John Cole Plaisterer his Note	51	04	00
	Given to his Workmen at Severall times	01	06	00
19	To Andrew Ruddock Sailmaker his Note	01	11	06
	To the men who laid the Sails in the Church	00	01	00
Dec .10	To John Thomas the Smith his Note	01	10	05
	To G: Stringer Upholster his note	01	10	00
Jan. 13	To Jones the Glazier his Note	12	05	00
	Given to the Pensioners for their work & Attendance	03	03	00
27	To Madox the Carpenter his Note	07	05	00
	Given to his Man	00	05	06
	John Newman the Plummer	02	09	06
	For Brushes	<u>00</u>	<u>03</u>	<u>08</u>

As well as regular expenditure on the fabric of the cathedral, much care was evidently taken over the maintenance of College Green. There were frequent charges for cutting the grass, planting and caring for trees, for repairing the fences around the Green and for 'pitching and paving' the paths which ran across it. In 1712, for example, the sum of £12 os od was paid to 'Lynford the Pitcher on College Green' for what must have been very extensive work. Paul Powell was paid £3 9s od for trees in 1700, and trees purchased for the Green in 1724 cost £2 8s 6d; in 1735 £3 os od was paid to 'Robine the Gardiner for looking after the Green'. One curious entry which occurs each year is the sum of £1 1s od which was paid to 'Mr Morgan's Keeper'. This was no doubt William Morgan of Tredegar, whose family had leased the manor of Peterstone, near Cardiff from the Dean and Chapter from 1661. William Morgan died in 1740, but the payment continued to be made to 'Lady Rachel Morgan's Keeper'. The reason for this annual entry is that the manorial custom of Peterstone required the lessee to present a deer to the Dean and Chapter every year, and the payment was made to the keeper as a reward for bringing the gift to Bristol.

CHAPTER MINUTES

In contrast to the detailed information which can be derived from the Book of Particulars, the Chapter minutes or Act Books, for the early eighteenth century are much less rewarding. They record the arrangements for residences each year, the appointment of minor canons, lay-clerks, the schoolmaster and other members of the cathedral community, but are mostly concerned with the management of cathedral property, the granting or renewal of leases, and the distribution of the occasional large fines. The Dean and Chapter were required formally to elect each new bishop, but this merely involved acceptance of the person named in 'the King's Writ of *congé d'elire*'. These elections are carefully recorded in the minutes, and because of the rapid changes of bishop in Bristol, they happened frequently. There is a long gap in the minutes between 1684 and 1714, so there is no reference to the major damage caused to the cathedral by the great storm of the night of 26–27 November 1703 which caused so much devastation throughout the West Country. It is known from other sources that the rose window in the west wall of the cathedral dividing the crossing from the former nave, was blown out in the storm, together with a large window on the north side, and that the cloister roof was badly damaged.[17] The rose window had been installed by Dr. Robert Wright (bishop 1623–1633) during a major refurbishment of the cathedral in 1630, for which he had collected £510 6s od from numerous benefactors. The only evidence of the damage caused by the storm in the cathedral records is found in payments listed in the Book of Particulars. These include clearing rubble from the cloisters, and large payments to Thomas Sumpsion, freemason, Thomas Reynolds, rough mason, William Jones, glazier, and William Humbelstone, tiler.

A major addition to the cathedral furnishings which was acquired in 1712 is not mentioned at all in the records. This was the splendid pair of silver candlesticks given to the cathedral by the Bristol town clerk, John Romsey. He had made a large profit by investing in the privateering voyage of Captain Woodes Rogers to the rich Spanish colonies in the Pacific. Two ships, the *Duke* and *Dutchess* left Bristol in 1708 and returned in 1711, having seized various prizes and providing a large return for the investors. As a thank-offering Romsey gave the two beautifully-designed silver candlesticks for use in the cathedral. They were made by a London maker, Gabriel Sleath, and bear the arms of Romsey and of the cathedral. They cost £114.[18]

DEAN HENRY BEEKE'S NOTES

The missing section of the Chapter minutes between 1684 and 1714 can be partly filled from the detailed notes made by Dean Henry Beeke, who came to the cathedral in 1814 and remained until his death in 1837. Dr. Henry Beeke was a distinguished scholar and writer on economic affairs. Before coming to Bristol he had been Regius Professor of Modern History at Oxford, and was widely respected as a writer and authority on political economy and taxation. At Bristol he took a great interest in the history of the Augustinian abbey and the cathedral and left copious notes on various aspects of the building, the cathedral statutes, the various dignitaries associated with it and on the estates from which the Chapter income was derived. Among his notes are some extracts from the lost Chapter minutes relating to a controversy over the houses built on the site of the former nave. Soon after the demolition of the nave in the mid-sixteenth century, houses had been erected on the site and were occupied by members of the cathedral community or were leased to various tenants who had no connection with the cathedral. The impropriety of using the consecrated site of the nave for secular dwellings seems not to have provoked any criticism until the late seventeenth century. According to Dean Beeke's notes based on the now-vanished

---

[17] The Revd. S. Seyer, *Memoirs Historical and Topographical of Bristol*, II, (1823), pp. 552–555; J. Latimer, *The Annals of Bristol in the Eighteenth Century* (Bristol, 1893), p. 57.

[18] D. Jones, *Captain Woodes Rogers' Voyage round the World 1708–11*, Bristol Historical Association, 79, (1992), pp. 23–24.

Chapter minutes, when one of the leases became due for renewal in 1693 two of the canons, Richard Towgood and Charles Livesay, objected on the grounds that the houses and their residents 'do greatly annoy the Church and very much endanger the foundations of the tower and west part of the church'. Their objection was over-ruled, but when another lease became due for renewal in 1712 the two canons objected again and insisted that the reasons for their dissent should be entered in the minutes. Henry Beeke's notes provide details of their objections which were that the former nave was consecrated, that 'houses of office' and chimneys had been built against the walls of the cathedral, impairing the fabric, and some of the houses were occupied by people of unsuitable character. The two canons further stated that if a new lease was granted they would refuse to accept any share of the profit and would apply the money in ways which would 'atone for any guilt which may fall on us in this matter, though not consenting to it'. They went on to hope that the nave might be restored to 'its primitive religious use and design', and that pious benefactors might be found who would complete the fabric of the cathedral. Again, their protest was in vain, and re-building was not to take place for another century and a half. Not until the early nineteenth century was the granting of leases ended. The last lease finally expired in 1835, and demolition of the houses could begin. By that time, according to Henry Beeke, who as dean was responsible for the site, the houses had become 'notoriously a Receptacle for Prostitutes'.[19]

THE MASONRIE AND TRINITY STREET

The increasing population of Bristol during the eighteenth century led to the development of much of the land around the cathedral. During the second half of the century streets were laid out and houses built around the lower slopes of Brandon Hill on land which had previously been open. Earlier development took place on the land to the east of the cathedral around the parish church of St. Augustine the Less. This area was known as the 'Masonrie and Covent Garden' and was leased to the Bristol lawyer, Jarrit Smith, whose large house occupied part of the site. Jarrit Smith was the legal representative and land agent for many prominent Bristol families, including Sir John Smyth of Ashton Court, whose sister, Florence, Jarrit Smith married and whose estate he eventually acquired. He also acted as land agent, auditor and legal adviser to the Dean and Chapter of Bristol Cathedral. He served as M.P. for Bristol during the years 1756–1768. His lease of the 'Masonrie' was renewed in 1733 on payment of a fine of £73 14s 0d, and Jarrit Smith began the construction of houses on the site, laying out a street immediately east of the cathedral which was to be known as Trinity Street. By 1746 when the lease was again renewed the value of the area had greatly increased and the fine was £750. [20]

[19] B.R.O., DC/A/7/9/1, Notes on the Cathedral Records by Dean Henry Beeke.
[20] B.R.O., DC/E/1/5, Register of Leases 1720–40; DC/E/40/64, Leases and Surrenders of Properties in Trinity Street 1746–1816.

THE BISHOP'S PALACE

The relatively poor endowment of the Bristol bishopric meant that few bishops stayed long or spent much time in Bristol. As a result the bishop's residence was neglected and successive bishops were unwilling to spend money on it. The remark of Browne Willis in 1727 that the bishop's house, although large, was inconvenient and not as good as the Deanery has already been quoted. Even Dr. Thomas Secker (bishop 1735–1737) who was a particularly energetic bishop and who was unusually active in the diocese, stayed only two years at Bristol before moving on to Oxford and eventually to Canterbury and did little to improve the residence.[21] His successor, Dr. Thomas Gooch (1737), lasted such a short time that he never came to Bristol at all. The next bishop was Dr. Joseph Butler, the most notable of all the bishops of Bristol, whose episcopate lasted for 12 years (1738–1750), and who completely refurbished the bishop's palace. In 1736 Butler had published his book *The Analogy of Religion, Natural and Revealed, to the Condition and Course of Nature*, which was to become the leading Anglican theological work of the eighteenth century. He was a diligent bishop, highly respected and popular in Bristol, who spent long periods in the city. He combined the bishopric with the lucrative position of dean of St. Paul's Cathedral in London, and as a wealthy bachelor with modest tastes he was able to spend large sums on his residence and its garden. He virtually re-built the house, spending some £5,000 of his own money on it, undertaking a full restoration of the small episcopal chapel, and creating what William Barrett in 1789 described as 'a handsome and commodious dwelling'. His work on the chapel included covering the walls with a cedar wainscot, using wood said to have been donated by Bristol merchants. He also installed a new altar complete with a cross, a feature which was criticised strongly by Protestant Bristolians as a dangerously Popish article. Sadly, most of his work was destroyed by the rioters in 1831 although the chapel survived. Bishop Butler also created a peaceful garden around his house. [22] In 1743 he acquired land to the east of the bishop's palace from the Dean and Chapter in return for land in Canons' Marsh, and was thus able to create a garden with secluded walks and arbours, where he was accustomed to spend long periods in contemplation. [23]

CONCLUSION

The picture which emerges from a study of the cathedral records of the early eighteenth century, is of pluralist and largely non-resident senior clergy, whose attitudes and concept of their duties would be quite at variance with the views of their successors during the next century. Nonetheless, the regular round of services was maintained by the minor canons, although they also had additional preferments in

[21] For details of Bishop Secker's activities in the diocese see J. H. Bettey and E. Ralph, 'Bishop Secker's Diocese Book', in P. McGrath, (ed.), *A Bristol Miscellany*, B.R.S., 37, (1985), pp. 21–78.
[22] W. Barrett, *The History & Antiquities of the City of Bristol*, (Bristol, 1789), pp. 284–286.
[23] B.R.O., EP/E/2/1, Deed of Exchange 1743. See also J. H. Bettey, *Records of Bristol Cathedral*, B.R.S., 59, (2007), pp. 145–149.

local parish churches. The festivals of the Church's year were observed with sermons on special occasions. The cathedral was decorated with holly and other greenery at Christmas and Easter, music and singing continued to be a major feature of the services, and, judging by the complaints about overcrowding, attendances remained high. Above all, there is ample evidence in the records that the cathedral estates continued to be carefully administered and that the building itself was well maintained and cared for, even though the completely white-washed interior is difficult for the modern observer to visualize.

II

Pitt the Elder and the financial discomfiture of Norborne Berkeley, Lord Botetourt

BY WILLIAM L. H. EVANS, M.A., (OXON)

NORBORNE BERKELEY, LORD BOTETOURT

NORBORNE BERKELEY (1717–1770) was the only son of John Symes Berkeley, head of a branch based at Stoke Gifford in South Gloucestershire, of the Berkeley family, whose main seat is at Berkeley castle. After attending Westminster School and undergoing private tuition, Berkeley went on a Grand Tour, during which his father died and he inherited the Stoke Gifford estate. In 1740 Berkeley's sister married Lord Charles Noel Somerset, younger brother of the third duke of Beaufort. In 1741, standing as a county Tory with the support of the Jacobite Beauforts, Berkeley was elected a Member of Parliament for Gloucestershire. Kept out of public office by the Hanoverians' proscription of the Tories, Berkeley busied himself with constituency and landowner duties, local charitable works (a ward at the main hospital in Gloucester is named after him), and the improvement of his house at Stoke and its grounds, in which he was assisted by the gentleman-designer Thomas Wright. Berkeley was active in the militia, of which he became a colonel in 1758. That year, to some disapproval, because he was the guardian of his infant nephew, the fourth duke of Beaufort, Berkeley went on the expedition to attack St. Malo and Cherbourg. Politically Berkeley was a Hanoverian Tory, not a Jacobite like his father and his in-laws: after the 1745 rebellion he signed the Association pledging allegiance to the king, and he generally supported the government. He showed independence and principle, however, over issues such as Jewish naturalisation, the cider excise, the Stamp Act and the Townshend duties imposed on the American colonies.

On the accession in 1760 of George III, who had been tutored by the Tory, John Stuart, marquis of Bute, Berkeley was allotted a place at court as a groom of the bedchamber. A suggestion that he be appointed Secretary-at-War was blocked. In 1764 Berkeley renewed a claim to the abeyant Botetourt peerage, which his father had investigated but not pursued, and entered the House of Lords as Lord Botetourt. He invested heavily in William Champion's zinc manufactory at Warmley in South Gloucestershire, and lost his investment when the enterprise collapsed. This paper explores the background to that, and suggests that Botetourt was not as blameworthy as he was made out by his detractors, who included Edmund Burke, who was then not yet M.P. for Bristol. In 1768 Botetourt, who in 1766 had moved the fateful resolution in the House of Lords insisting that the English parliament had the power and the right to legislate for Britain's colonies 'in all cases whatsoever', was appointed governor of Virginia where, notwithstanding the movement towards independence, his polite and courtly manner did much to maintain order and good relationships in the colony. Impulsive and hot-tempered, but generous to a fault, Botetourt died of a fever in October 1770, genuinely mourned in Virginia. What course the American Revolution would have taken had he survived, we can only speculate.

A MARKET FOR BRASS

In the first half of the eighteenth century the market for manufactured brass in the Bristol area was lucrative: brass went into many sorts of articles, from basic pots and pans and tools to the new steam engines and the machinery they powered. Bristol brass contributed to the production of Guinea wares, objects which Bristol slavers would take on the first leg of the Atlantic trade, to barter for enslaved Africans to take to the sugar plantations in the Caribbean. The Bristol area was well-placed for making brass: calamine (zinc carbonate) and blende (zinc sulphate) ores were mined on Mendip, less than 30km away; copper was shipped to Bristol from Cornwall; and coal was dug in Bristol itself and immediately to the east in Kingswood and Warmley.

Until the 1760s the local market for brass was supplied mainly by two businesses: the Brass, Brass Battery Wire and Copper Company of Bristol (the Bristol Company), and the Warmley Company. They competed, but neither was powerful enough to destroy the other. The Bristol Company, a joint stock limited liability company, had been formed about 1700 by five Quakers led by Abraham Darby. By 1708 Darby had left the partnership in order to pursue his own interests in iron, and later moved to Coalbrookdale in Shropshire. By 1720 the Bristol Company was being led by Nehemiah Champion II, who had patented a process for making copper, was smelting copper at Crew's Hole and was making brass at Baptist Mills in Bristol. By 1760 it was also manufacturing articles from brass, using water mills to drive hammers, at various places along the rivers Avon and Chew. Sampson Lloyd and Thomas Goldney III were partners.[1]

The Bristol Company employed William Champion, Nehemiah's youngest son. He patented a process for smelting calamine to produce zinc. In 1738 he formed his own business off Bristol's Old Market, and after much friction with his employers, perhaps because some of them thought he ought to work only for the Bristol Company, not on his own account as well, he formed a separate firm in 1746 with three of the Bristol company partners.[2] After his Bristol premises were closed down because of nuisance to the neighbourhood, he transferred his operations to Warmley. From then on Champion's firm was known as the Warmley Company, though in law it was a partnership. William Champion was an awkward customer. Joseph

---

[1] For the Goldney family and the three Thomas Goldneys (I, 1629–1694; II, 1664–1731; III, 1696–1768), see P. K. Stembridge, *Goldney: a house and family*, (Bristol, 1969, 4th ed., 1982): and *id.*, *Thomas Goldney, man of property*, (Bristol, 1991).

[2] Attorney General's report, 16 September 1767, Gloucestershire Archives (hereafter G.A.), D2700 QP13/2. I am grateful to His Grace the duke of Beaufort for access to and permission to use his family's records at G. A. and at Badminton Muniments (hereafter Bad. Mun.).

Hornblower, who built the steam engine for Champion's Warmley works, said of him: 'As to Mr Champion, I think there are few mortals queerer'.[3]

The metal smelters needed fuel. The scarcer charcoal became as the timber it was burned from was cut down, the more the demand for coal increased. The main owners of coal mines and coal mining rights in the Kingswood area were Charles Whittuck of Hanham Hall to the south-east of Kingswood; Charles Bragg of Cleve Hill to the north-east of Bristol; and Norborne Berkeley of Stoke Park, who held mining rights in the coalfield that included collieries in the parish of Stapleton, then more extensive than it is today. Berkeley did not employ people directly to mine his coal: he had a coal manager, who negotiated leases of the mining rights to small partnerships and individuals. They paid a royalty on what they produced, or sold the coal to Berkeley, whose manager sold it on. Berkeley's wealth in that regard was reputed to be notable: in 1743 a French government spy reported home, albeit with exaggeration and inaccuracy, that:

> C'est le nombre prodigieux de gens qui travaillent aux mines de charbon dans ses terres aux environs de Bristol qui rend M Norborne Berkeley [...] un des plus considérables de la noblesse du royaume.[4]

A more accurate idea of the value of Norborne Berkeley's coal holdings can be obtained from the accounts his mother kept of her guardianship of his personal estate during the remainder of his minority.[5] Over the two years 1736 and 1737 his total income was £4,738, of which £3,095 came from 'the coal works at Stapleton'.

A BUSINESS PLAN

In 1761, when Norborne Berkeley was a year into the second phase of his re-fashioning of Stoke Park House, William Champion devised a new business strategy for the Warmley Company. He had several objectives, some of them inter-related. First, he aimed to produce more brass. For that he needed more copper. To produce more copper he proposed to build 80 new furnaces at Kingswood. Those new furnaces would need reliable supplies of fuel, and in huge quantities. At the same time Champion planned to attack the market share of his main competitor, the Bristol Brass Company. He proposed to do that by signing up the main Kingswood coal owners as his partners, and then getting them to promise, first to sell coal only to the Warmley Company (which would be in their interests once they became partners with him), and secondly not to sell coal to the Bristol Company.[6] That would force the Bristol Company to look elsewhere for its coal which, having to be hauled from further away, would be more expensive to produce and dearer to sell. Champion

---

[3] J. Day, *Bristol Brass*, (Newton Abbot, 1973), p. 85, citing R. Jenkins, 'The zinc industry in England', in *Transactions of the Newcomen Society*, (1946), p. 42.

[4] Archives du ministère des affaires étrangères: *Mémoires et documents, Angleterre* (Paris) 82, ff. 4–23: 'It is the stupendous number of people who work in the coalmines in his lands around Bristol that makes Mr. Norborne Berkeley one of the most important members of the nobility of the kingdom'.

[5] Bad. Mun., Fm S/F 4/4.

[6] C. Whittuck to Bragg, 19 June 1761, G.A., D421/B1; D2700 QP13/1.

reckoned that this would damage the Bristol Company's Crew's Hole works in particular, which would, in turn, severely damage the Bristol Company's business as a whole.

To fund all of this Champion proposed that the Warmley Company raise £100,000 by issuing 800 tickets or partnership shares of £125 each. To get Berkeley on board, Champion did not approach him directly. Instead, Champion persuaded Whittuck and Bragg to join him, and then got Bragg to sell the scheme to Berkeley. Bragg did so with an enthusiasm he was later to acknowledge as an 'infatuation'. Berkeley promised to invest £5,000 in the Warmley Company, though his initial investment was in fact only £1,500.[7] In June 1761 Norborne Berkeley and the other two coal owners met the Bristol Company's owners and, no doubt scripted by the absent Champion, demanded much higher prices for coal delivered to the Bristol Company's works at Crew's Hole and Baptist Mills.[8] As might have been expected, the Bristol Company refused the demands. So in one manoeuvre Champion achieved two of his objectives: a reduction in supplies of local coal to the Bristol Company; and three big local coal owners who no longer had a major local customer for their coal. They could be expected instead to want to sell it to the Warmley Company, but for lack of an alternative market they would be able to do so only at a discount of 20% from the prices they would have received from the Bristol Company. Having secured the prospect of improved and probably cheaper and more reliable supplies of coal, in July 1761 Champion started to build his new copper furnaces.[9]

Once the lessees of the mining rights got wind of what Champion was planning, and particularly once it was evident that the Warmley Company intended to build a large number of new furnaces, they boosted their production of coal to meet the expected rise in demand. Many of them invested heavily in new plant and equipment, the cost of which could be met in most cases only by selling more coal. The result was that they over-produced. Because the Warmley Company did not yet have the furnaces to cope with all the coal produced, the surplus coal found its way to the Bristol Company,[10] so the impact of the cartel on his competitor was not as severe as Champion had intended.

A PROBLEM OF CAPITAL

At this stage Berkeley did not draw dividends, but allowed them to accumulate in the firm, thus in effect increasing his partnership share to that extent. He did not add lump sums to his initial investment in the Warmley Company. Perhaps he realised that the sale of surplus coal to the Bristol Company was undermining the Warmley Company's strategy, but a more likely reason is that until 1764 Berkeley had other calls on his income. He was improving Stoke Park; he was undertaking the second phase of the re-fashioning of Stoke Park House; he had become Lord Lieutenant of Gloucestershire, colonel of the militia and an honorary freeman of Bristol; and in 1764 he had successfully claimed the Botetourt peerage.

---

[7] Share account, G.A., D2700 QP13/2.
[8] C. Whittuck to Bragg, G.A., D421/B1.
[9] 7 and 21 July 1761., *ibid.*
[10] C. Whittuck to Bragg, 6 October 1764, *ibid.*

There may also have been another reason for Botetourt not sinking more cash into the Warmley Company: it was not as profitable as expected. By 1764 only 17 new furnaces had been built at Kingswood.[11] The main reason for that was that Champion had raised little more than a quarter of the sum he needed: Sampson Lloyd (but with a reduced share), Charles and Samuel Whittuck and Thomas Goldney III were still partners in the company, but Botetourt, Bragg, and Michael Newton, another local landowner, had not put in all the cash they had promised. They had been joined by James Matthews, another landowner, and also by Charles Arthur, Botetourt's coal manager, and Silas Blandford, Botetourt's estate manager at Stoke Park. Between them they had raised only some £29,250. Champion had borrowed, in the Company's name, another £131,400. As a result, more than half the Company's operating profits went on the payment of interest, leaving only some £2,500 net profit to be split amongst the subscribers.[12]

By the beginning of 1765 Champion had decided that the Company needed more capital. He first put pressure on those partners who had not yet done so to subscribe the balance of what they had promised. To overcome any reluctance to invest further in an enterprise whose profits had not come up to expectations Champion first reminded them of their personal liability for the debts of the partnership, now standing at over £131,000. Having thus frightened them he then offered a way out: if the Company was to raise a further £158,000 capital by way of subscriptions, that could be used to pay off the existing loans. To induce outsiders to subscribe capital he proposed that a plan be adopted to make shares in the company transferable, and therefore marketable: people might invest more readily if they saw some prospect of being able to get out, whether at a profit or to cut losses, by selling their shares.[13]

The only legal way of making shares in the enterprise transferable was to turn the business into a joint stock company. That would also have the advantage that proprietors' losses would be limited to the money they had subscribed or lent to the company, so that their private fortunes would be safe from creditors should the company become insolvent, whereas in a partnership each member was liable to his last farthing. By section 18 of the *South Sea Bubble Act* of 1720, however, it was unlawful to carry on a joint stock company except with the authority of either an act of parliament or a royal charter, and by section 19 of the Act infringement of section 18 was a criminal offence.[14] So Champion set about applying for a charter. In the meantime, he tried to increase the Warmley Company's production of copper by buying ore from Cornwall, and he made the company diversify into making its own brass products, including articles for the Guinea trade and pins, in the manufacture of which many Gloucester people worked. On 31 March 1765 Bragg wrote to Berkeley enclosing a copy of Champion's proposals.[15]

Either because as a man of honour Botetourt considered himself bound to subscribe to the Warmley Company up to the sum that he had promised in 1761, or because he now saw a reasonable prospect of making a satisfactory return on his

[11] *Ibid.*
[12] Account, 25 March 1767, G.A., D2700 QP13/2.
[13] Statement, 25 March 1765, G.A., D421/B1.
[14] *6 Geo.1 c.18.*
[15] G.A., D421/B1.

investment, Botetourt invested a further £3,000 on 1 February 1766, another £300 later the same month, and a further £450 on 1 March 1766, in order to bring his total investment up to his promised £5,000.[16]

PITT THE ELDER

Towards the end of July 1766 there was a change of government: George III offered leadership of the administration to William Pitt. Pitt's conditions for acceptance were that the duke of Grafton, in the House of Lords, should be in charge of the treasury; Seymour Conway should be leader in the Commons; and Pitt himself, ennobled as the earl of Chatham, should hold the office of Lord Privy Seal and direct operations from the House of Lords. He did so only for three months. In October 1766 Chatham fell ill, and went to Bath. He returned, but having made only two speeches in the House of Lords, on 11 November and 12 December 1766,[17] he again returned to Bath early in January 1767. On 11 January he set out for London, but an attack of gout forced him back to Bath and into bed. Both Horace Walpole[18] and Rockingham[19] suspected that Chatham's indisposition was pretended or political, because he did not want to face up to difficult decisions to be made about government relations with the East India Company. Beckford, whom Chatham had detailed to lead in the Commons on India matters, asked for Chatham's advice, but received no reply.[20] From this point on events were dominated by government ministers apparently unwilling or unable to act without Chatham's approval or guidance, and Chatham evidently unable and perhaps unwilling to communicate with them on any official business whatever.

A CASE FOR A CHARTER

Meanwhile, Champion had prepared the Warmley Company's case for a charter of incorporation. This involved two principal documents: the petition itself and a statement of the Company's affairs. Early in 1767 he lodged the petition, with Botetourt named as governor of the company and Champion as deputy governor and treasurer, and proposing an authorised share capital of £400,000.[21] Botetourt prepared to pave the way with Chatham: he moved from London to Stoke House so as to be ready to visit Chatham at Bath at short notice.[22] But on 12 January 1767 Grenville, who led one of the Whig opposition groups, told Botetourt that his brother-in-law Chatham was

---

[16] Share account, G.A., D2700 QP13/2.

[17] J. Black, *Pitt the Elder*, (Cambridge, 1992), p. 270.

[18] H. Walpole, *Memoirs of the Reign of King George the Third*, (re-ed.), G. F. Russell Barker (London, 1894), (hereafter Walpole, *Memoirs*), ii, p. 293.

[19] Rockingham to Newcastle, 24 January 1767, B.L., Add. MSS. 32979, f. 311.

[20] J. Brooke, *The Chatham Administration*, (1956), pp. 99, 100.

[21] Draft charter, G.A., D2700 QP13/2.

[22] On 13 January he chaired at Bristol's Merchant Tailors' Hall a contested election to a post of physician at the Bristol infirmary: G. Munro Smith, *A History of the Bristol Royal Infirmary*, (Bristol, 1917), p. 426.

'confined to his bed with a strong fit of the gout in his hands and feet', and suggested that Botetourt delay meeting him.[23]

In his statement of the Warmley Company's affairs to accompany the petition Champion seriously misrepresented the financial state of the firm.[24] He valued its fixed assets at about £105,000 and its manufactured stocks, including large quantities of brass articles, some of them explicitly branded for the Guinea trade, at £94,000. Stocks of ores and coal were put at £8,000. Debts due to the Company he valued at £93,000, a large figure, with no indication whether he regarded them as recoverable or bad. Thus Champion put the Company's total worth at some £300,000, which he misrepresented as financed by £100,000 from contributions by members, and borrowings of £200,000. In fact the members' contributions at that stage were little more than £50,000, and the borrowings a little above £130,000: Champion was claiming that the Warmley Company was worth over double its actual value and had nearly double its actual capital. In the petition for incorporation itself Champion stated that the company had capital of £200,000 and wanted to raise a further £200,000 by issuing shares.[25] A couple of months later, in March 1767, on a paid-up capital of only £50,000 the company returned an operating profit of £7,182, which after interest of £4,682 left a net profit of barely £2,500.[26]

Because most M.P.s were themselves property owners or represented boroughs in the pocket of property owners, they had an interest in keeping the poor rates as low as possible. So petitioners for a charter of incorporation routinely emphasised how much employment the company generated for poor people. Champion argued that his company's works gave employment, directly or indirectly, to 2,000 poor men, women and children.[27] Champion also contended that with a capital of £400,000 the company would be able to expand its production so as to avoid altogether any need to import brass wares into Britain from abroad, thus appealing to both the pockets and the patriotism of those who would decide whether the Crown should grant the petition. Meanwhile in March 1767 Botetourt lent the Company a further £1,000 on the strength of a promissory note.[28]

It is surprising that no objections were lodged at that stage to the Warmley Company's petition. On 18 April 1767 the Attorney General, William de Grey, certified that there was no objection to the proposal in point of law, and on 24 April the Privy Council issued a warrant for preparation of the Warmley Company's charter of incorporation, with a proposed new capital of £400,000. The warrant issued from the Privy Council to the office of Chatham, the Lord Privy Seal, whose responsibility it was to affix the royal seal to the charter. On 4 May 1767 Shelburne, then Secretary of State for the southern department, told Botetourt that a warrant had gone to the Attorney General and that the charter should issue in a couple of weeks.[29] Botetourt lent the Company another £500.

---

[23] Grenville to Botetourt, 12 January 1767, G.A., D2700 QP13/2.
[24] Statement, G.A., D421/B1.
[25] Attorney General's report, 16 September 1767, G.A., D2700 QP13/2.
[26] Account, 25 March 1767, *ibid.*
[27] B.L., Add. MSS. 22675, f. 70.
[28] Bad. Mun., Fm L 6/3/43.
[29] Shelburne to Botetourt, 4 May 1767, G.A., D2700 QP 13/3.

PITT'S INACTION

By May 1767 the government's difficulties with the East India Company had been resolved,[30] and it turned to deal with issues arising out of riots in America against the Stamp Act. Chatham, supposed to be acting as Prime Minister, remained resolutely incommunicado. On 27 May 1767 Grafton wrote pleading for a quarter of an hour with him for advice, but Chatham refused.[31] Two days later Grafton repeated his request and Chatham again refused. On 30 May the king himself wrote and asked Chatham to give Grafton five minutes. Grafton saw Chatham on 31 May and 4 June, and found his 'nerves and spirits [...] affected to a dreadful degree,' and described the interviews as 'truly painful.' Chatham simply assured Grafton of his support, telling him not to worry, because if he disagreed with anything Grafton did, Chatham would smooth it over later. On 13 June 1767 Chatham told the king he was 'utterly incapable of the smallest effort of thought'.[32] A week later he indignantly contradicted a rumour that his heath had improved.[33] Chatham described himself as 'under a health so broke as renders at present application of mind totally impossible.'[34] On 3 July 1767 Sir Gilbert Elliot had a conversation with Grafton:

> I saw the duke of Grafton this morning, and learnt in conversation with him that he had not seen Lord Chatham, nor heard from him since the 4th of June, that in his opinion there was no hope of his ever being a man again, that Lord President and himself had represented in writing to the king, how necessary it was in the present state of affairs, and in the present situation of Administration, that Lord Chatham should either appear and assist in filling up the vacancies that must immediately happen, or otherwise quit all thoughts of being Minister, as it was impossible to continue any longer in this state of suspense. [...] The king transmitted this very paper to his Lordship but the answer it appeared he wished Mr Conway's place might be supplied, and the system still go on as it had done all the session. This his Grace seemed to think impossible; he had expected that Ld Chatham would himself have given facility to the king to make an effectual arrangement, by declining on account of his health to act any longer as Minister, as he had for six months not been able to attend so much as one cabinet.

In July 1767 an acquaintance wrote: 'Pitt disabled by dejection of spirit almost approaching to insane melancholy—scarce anyone sees him but Lady Chatham—criminal to ask how he does—servants turned off for inquiring'.[35]

For reasons not clear, the Attorney General delayed issuing the bill, a legal document which would have told the Lord Privy Seal to issue the charter. In that time ten petitions against the grant of the charter were lodged with Shelburne, Secretary of

---

[30] Brooke, *Chatham Administration*, pp. 133–134.

[31] *Ibid.*, 149; H. Grafton, (ed.), W. R. Anson, *Autobiography and political correspondence*, (Edinburgh, 1898), p. 133.

[32] J. W. Fortescue, *The Correspondence of King George the Third from 1760 to 1863*, (1928), (hereafter *Correspondence of George III*), I, p. 531.

[33] *Ibid.*, I, p. 536.

[34] *Ibid.*, I, p. 538.

[35] Lyttelton to Harris, July 1767, J. Harris, *Correspondence and Diary of James Harris, first Earl of Malmesbury*, J. H. Harris, (ed.), (1844).

State for the southern department. The petitions came from the Society of the Mines Royal and the Society of the Mineral and Battery Works, both of London; the Company of Copper Miners in England; John Lockwood & Co. of London; Thomas Patten & Co., brass and copper manufacturers of Warrington in Lancashire in north-west England; the guild of pin makers in the city of Leeds in Yorkshire; Gloucester corporation; several pin makers in Gloucester; the Pinmakers Guild of London; Charles Roe & Copper Company of Macclesfield in Cheshire; John Freeman and the Copper Company of Bristol; and the Bristol Brass, Brass Battery, Wire and Copper Company.[36] They attacked the award of a charter on the grounds that because of limits on the supply of ores it would not be possible to expand the Warmley company's trade to the extent Champion claimed; that such a big increase in capital would enable the Warmley Company to dominate the market; and that its effect would be to destroy the pin-making industry in Gloucester, putting 1,200 men, women and children out of work. Between 23 May and 14 July Shelburne forwarded these objections to the Attorney General, and told him to re-open consideration of the petition. The Attorney General heard counsel for the petitioners between 17 and 28 July, and reserved his decision. On 16 September 1767 he issued a written adjudication, confirming that there was no objection in law to the grant of the proposed charter.

In November 1767 George III appointed Botetourt a Lord of the Bedchamber, on a salary of £1,000 a year.[37] Botetourt lent the Company another £500.[38] In December 1767 Shelburne wrote to Chatham for advice on a proposal to carve his office of Secretary for the southern department into two so as to create a separate Secretary of State for the colonies. Chatham refused to advise.[39] The same month, no doubt encouraged by the prospect of the charter being granted, Botetourt lent a further £6,000 to the Warmley Company, bringing his total investment to £13,000: £5,000 in partnership capital and £8,000 in loans. The warrant for the charter, however, now lay in Chatham's office, unactioned. Around Christmas 1767 Botetourt decided to take matters into his own hands. He asked Lady Chatham, who was now handling all Chatham's communications, to ask her husband to take action. Not wanting to upset Chatham, she asked her brother to convey her reply to Botetourt.[40] Grenville did so, and wrote back to her:

> I related to him […] that you were convinced Lord Chatham would not consent to put the seal to the Warmly company's grant, without first hearing the parties who opposed it; that the state of his health made it impossible for him to appoint that hearing at present; and, under these circumstances, you could not venture to trouble him with any thing upon the subject; therefore, lord Botetourt must be left to take whatever measures he may think best for his own satisfaction.

[36] *Cal. Pap. Dom. Home Office*, 1767–1769, p. 705; the full list is in Attorney General's report, 16 September 1767, G.A., D2700 QP13/2.

[37] Huntingdon to Botetourt, 5 November 1767, Bad. Mun., Fm S/G 4/19.

[38] Bad. Mun., Fm L 6/3/43.

[39] Lady Chatham to Shelburne, 14 December 1767, Lansdowne MSS.

[40] Grenville to Lady Chatham 16 January 1768; W. S. Taylor and J. H. Pringle, (ed.), *Correspondence of William Pitt, Earl of Chatham*, (1838–1840), (hereafter *Chatham Correspondence*), pp. 306–307.

Grenville said Botetourt received the message 'with tranquillity,' but said that if that was the case then he would ask the king to put the privy seal in commission (that is, to appoint a group of other privy counsellors to act instead of the Lord Privy Seal) 'in the most respectable manner possible to Lord Chatham.'

The same day Botetourt lent a further £4,000 to the Warmley Company.[41] Of that, he appears to have borrowed £50 from his butler, William Marshman,[42] which suggests that Botetourt had run out of cash of his own. Botetourt had now put £5,000 of his own money into the Company and lent it another £12,000, much of which was itself borrowed money. Botetourt then saw the king, and told him what he intended to do; the king said he could not give an answer on the spot.[43] Botetourt wrote to Grafton, in Chatham's absence the administration's senior minister in the House of Lords:

> Your Grace's fair and noble manners, entitle you to notice, that I mean tomorrow to move the House, that a day be appointed and lords summoned, in order to take under consideration a matter of justice, and to declare that I shall then complain of the Earl of Chatham for delay in his office.[44]

Grafton, who regarded the terms of the notice as impolite, asked Botetourt to delay until the king had made a decision, and Botetourt complied with that request. Grafton must have communicated with Grenville, because Grenville wrote to Lady Chatham explaining what putting the seal in commission would involve, but added that Grafton was not willing to arrange that without Chatham's consent, and urged her to speak to Chatham. Lady Chatham replied the same day that Chatham's state of health made a hearing of the objectors impossible, nor could he fix any time for it, and that he thought he should give up the privy seal.[45] Grafton then wrote to Chatham, feigning ignorance of Grenville's letter, suggesting putting the seal into commission temporarily, and citing some precedents.

> I would suggest to your Lordship an expedient, as natural as it has been usual, to remove the difficulty which the peculiar character of the noble lord who presses his grant seems to make necessary. For, on one hand, no persuasion has weight with him, and if threats were added, he is of a temper more likely to add it to his complaint, than to drop from hence his resolution; on the other, I dread alike the bankruptcy of the company he is engaged in; and when, if it should happen, as certainly as falsely, the ill natured clamour of the world will lay their ruin to the grant's having been delayed and not heard before the privy seal. [46]

Camden, also professing ignorance of Grenville's letter, wrote in similar terms to Chatham:

> It is impossible to describe how much we have been embarrassed by Lord Botetourt's unreasonable proceeding. [...] It is in vain to tell him that he is suing

---

[41] Share account, G.A., D2700 QP13/2; promissory note, Bad. Mun., Fm L 6/3/43.
[42] *Ibid.*
[43] Grenville to Lady Chatham, 20 January 1768, *Chatham Correspondence*, p. 307.
[44] Botetourt to Grafton, 19 January 1768, G.A., D2700 QP13/2.
[45] Lady Chatham to Grenville, 20 January 1768, *Chatham Correspondence*, pp. 310–311.
[46] Grafton to Chatham, 21 January 1768, *ibid.*, p. 312.

for a favour; that the delay hitherto has been trifling; that the House of Lords have no right to interfere; that if his company are in doubtful circumstances, the very mention will make them bankrupt. His answer to this and every thing else is, that he and his friends in that undertaking are upon the brink of ruin, and that neither private nor public considerations shall make him change his resolution.[47]

On 23 January 1768 Lady Chatham wrote to Grafton that 'The gout not fixing, Lord Chatham is so extremely ill and weak [...] he desires only to say, with regard to the privy seal, that as he can have nothing so much at heart as the King's pleasure and what is judged to be most for his Majesty's service, he is all obedience with respect to the commission'.[48] Meanwhile the king wrote to Chatham politely but clearly: 'I wish you would take such steps as have not been unusual, to conclude this unpleasant business'. Chatham replied that he had already told Grafton of his acquiescence in the expedient proposed.[49] Even then, Chatham continued to quibble, questioning the applicability of the precedents for putting the seal into commission. Not until 18 February did Lady Chatham write to Camden acquiescing in the legal opinion that the precedents were sound.[50] Not until 20 March did a commission of privy counsellors, one of whom was Botetourt's distant kinsman Lord Berkeley of Stratton, attend Chatham and the seal was taken out of Chatham's hands.[51]

On 25 March 1768 the partners in the Warmley Company gave Botetourt a bond for £12,748, equivalent to Botetourt's loans to the Company of £12,000 plus interest accrued. Again, as Botetourt was himself a giver of the bond jointly with the other participants, it is difficult to see what legal benefit the bond would have been. But before any further steps could be taken to issue the charter, William Champion fraudulently withdrew his capital from the company, without telling his fellow contributors. It was not until well into April 1768 that they found out, and expelled him. Champion issued a printed defence of his actions, in which he claimed to have been persuaded, against his judgment, by Bragg and the others to expand the Warmley business and to increase the capital of the company. He claimed that his partners had peremptorily thrown him out of the company for no reason. He omitted any mention of his having secretly withdrawn his own capital.

COLLAPSE OF THE WARMLEY COMPANY

The Warmley Company was left hopelessly undercapitalised. In July 1768 Charles Bragg, who independently of the Warmley Company owed several hundred pounds to Botetourt, proposed a scheme for 'a new partnership on a moderate capital' to run the Warmley side of the operation, and invited Botetourt to subscribe £5,000.[52] Polite

---

[47] Camden to Chatham, 22 January 1768, *Chatham Correspondence*, pp. 314–315.

[48] Lady Chatham to Grafton, 23 January 1768, *ibid.*, 316; Grafton to the king, 23 January 1768, *Correspondence of George III*, II, p. 582.

[49] The king to Chatham; Chatham to the king, *Chatham Correspondence*, pp. 318, 319; *Correspondence of George III*, II, pp. 583, 584, 585.

[50] Lady Chatham to Camden, 18 February 1768, *Chatham Correspondence*, pp. 322–323.

[51] Camden to Chatham, 20 March 1768, *ibid.*, p. 323.

[52] Bragg to Botetourt, 23 July 1768, G.A., D421/B1.

as ever, Botetourt declined: he said he was paying interest on the £12,000 he had already lent the Warmley Company, and was not prepared to invest any more: 'Fresh money I have none'. He had lost all the £5,000 capital he had invested in the company and the £12,000 he had lent it. All his other cash had been spent on Stoke Park and its house and his other financial commitments. He owed several thousand pounds to various creditors. If he was in fact paying interest on the £12,000, then he must have borrowed all of it, not just the £50 he had borrowed from his butler. Horace Walpole described him as ruined,[53] 'like patience on a monument, smiling at grief', and people gossiped that 'schemes about mines' had brought it about.[54]

Chatham was not so ill that he was unable to conduct a vigorous correspondence with Sir William Draper, a Bristol man, who in 1762 had commanded the forces which captured Manilla, and who sought approval to the inscription he proposed to have cut on a triumphal pillar in his garden in honour of Chatham.[55] Lady Chatham gave the impression that the initiative for her husband's resignation came from Chatham himself: 'The very weak and broken state' of her husband's health 'reduced him to the necessity of asking the King for permission to resign', she wrote.[56]

A CASE OF MISREPRESENTATION

Botetourt's financial loss was brought about by a combination and a succession of contributory events. At the outset, William Champion's scheme was too ambitious. As Bragg later confessed in what almost amounted to an apology, it was Bragg's 'infatuation' with Champion's scheme that led him to persuade Berkeley, as he then was, to invest.[57] Champion overstated the worth of the company to its members, and to the Privy Council. He misrepresented the size of the company's business. Having a business with £180,000 capital, he caused the petition to be for a company more than twice as big. That understandably alarmed the Bristol Company, who formed a lobby against the charter. Once it appeared that the objections had not been upheld, Botetourt lent the Company comparatively large sums, unaware that Chatham, whatever his reason or motive, was not going to seal the grant. Chatham's failure to apply the seal, which Botetourt accurately and justifiably described as a dereliction of public duty, led to Champion fraudulently withdrawing his capital, and the company collapsed.

According to Horace Walpole Botetourt tried to get the company incorporated, not in order to improve its prospects of raising capital, but to protect his private estates from his creditors.[58] A similar allegation was later made in the *Letters of Junius*, and was repeated by Edmund Burke. As with Botetourt's involvement over the Northampton

---

[53] H. Walpole to Mann, 13 August 1768. W. S. Lewis, W. H. Smith and G. L. Lam, (eds.), *Horace Walpole's Correspondence with Sir Horace Mann*, (New Haven, Conn., 1954).

[54] J. A. Home, (ed.), *The Letters and Journal of Lady Mary Coke*, (Edinburgh, 1889–1896), II, p. 323; E. Stuart Wortley, (ed.), *A Prime Minister and his Son*, (1925), p. 235.

[55] Now on Clifton Down, near Christ Church. See J. Dreaper, *Bristol's forgotten victor: Lieutenant-General Sir William Draper, K.B., (1721–1787)*, Bristol Historical Association, 94, (Bristol, 1998).

[56] Lady Chatham to Anne Pitt, 21 October 1768, B.L., Add. MSS 69289, no. 66.

[57] Bragg to Botetourt, G.A., D2700 QP13/2.

[58] Walpole, *Memoirs*, III, p. 108.

dowry,[59] Walpole had got hold of only half the story: whilst the partners must have been attracted by the limited liability that a joint stock company would give, their main object was to facilitate the raising of more capital, and incorporation was the only way they were going to achieve that. So long as Botetourt's creditors did not press for immediate repayment of any money owed them, he was not insolvent. He was never made bankrupt, and he still had his income from his estates and his £1,000 a year as a Lord of the Bedchamber. Because Botetourt was a former protégé of Lord Bute and a supporter of the government, it was only to be expected that Burke and the anonymous Junius should exploit Botetourt's discomfiture as part of the normal currency of political invective.

If that excuses politicians, it does not exonerate professional historians who, mostly without reference to original sources, have uncritically repeated the Burke diatribe. In his edition of Walpole's *Memoirs* Denis le Marchant claimed that 'Lord Bottetort's proposal was absolutely monstrous, being nothing less than a gross fraud on his creditors'.[60] In his edition of Grafton's correspondence William Anson claimed that 'Lord Botetourt appears to have contemplated a fraud on his creditors by incorporating a Company on such terms as would save his private estates from the creditors of the Company'.[61] John Brooke, following Walpole, narrated that 'Botetourt had engaged in a copper works that had failed; he had applied for a charter of incorporation to prevent his estates being liable for the debts'.[62] Joan Day described Botetourt, having turned down Bragg's rescue proposal, as 'shortly to flee to America to escape his debts'.[63] Frank O'Gorman, citing Burke's correspondence and the anonymous *Letters of Junius*, described Botetourt as 'destitute and sinister'.[64] Others have suggested that Chatham blocked the grant of the charter because he perceived the scheme as an attempt to defraud the Company's creditors. In fact, although incorporation would have facilitated transfer of risk from lenders to the business to the wider range of investors who might have bought shares in the company, the primary purpose of the charter was to raise more capital, not to evade debt; Chatham's dereliction of his public duty in not sealing and issuing the charter was not motivated by any such perception, but was a consequence of his general incapacity, coupled with his irrational and obstinate unwillingness to relinquish office.

In the event the Warmley Company's premises and stock were sold, unpaid capital was called in, debts were collected and the firm's creditors were eventually paid off. Botetourt, Bragg, Silas Blandford and all the others lost the money they had subscribed or lent to the firm, but that was all. Botetourt was not bankrupted, he did not seek to evade his creditors, his estate was never in danger, and no one was defrauded. With an income of several thousand pounds a year even before he went to Virginia, Botetourt could hardly be described as destitute. Nor was his financial discomfiture the prime reason for his appointment as governor of Virginia: but that is another story.

---

[59] W. Evans, 'Paradise on a Limited Budget: how Norborne Berkeley funded his improvements at Stoke Park', *T. B & G. A. S.*, 126, (2008), pp. 157–166.
[60] Walpole, *Memoirs*, III, p. 108, footnote.
[61] H. Grafton,(ed.) W. R. Anson, *op. cit.*, p. 184.
[62] Brooke, *Chatham Administration*, p. 368.
[63] Day, *op. cit.*, p. 93.
[64] F. O'Gorman, *The Rise of Party in England: the Rockingham Whigs 1760–82*, (1975), p. 233.

III

Richmond House and the Manor of Clifton

ROGER H. LEECH, F.S.A.

INTRODUCTION

RICHMOND HOUSE is one of the less well-known historic houses owned by the University of Bristol. (Fig. 1) Most people who are knowledgeable about the historic architecture of Bristol would find it difficult to identify its location and significance. Yet this is a house deserving far more attention than it has hitherto received.[1] Generations of students at Manor Hall who have lived in Richmond House, one of Manor Hall's annexes, may not always have been aware that this is one of Clifton's oldest houses, built on the site of the Manor House of Clifton as a suburban villa for one of Bristol's wealthiest citizens at the very beginning of the eighteenth century. Recent research is beginning to reveal much more of the history and architectural development of this house.

This paper will first examine the history and location of the manor house of Clifton, and will then look at Richmond House in more detail, as an early suburban villa.

THE MANORS OF CLIFTON

By the fifteenth century there were two separate manors of Clifton. The smaller of these, sometimes referred to as the manor of Clifton St. Lawrence, belonged first to the hospital of St. Lawrence on the east side of Bristol and was then given in 1463 to the College at Westbury-on-Trym, a religious foundation dissolved by Henry VIII at the Dissolution of the Monasteries; a survey of 1625 now in the Bristol Record Office gives many valuable insights into the lands of this manor.[2] The larger manor appears with clarity in the historical records only at a later date, as the manor acquired by the Society of Merchant Venturers' *c.* 1686. The lands of both manors were widely scattered across the parish of Clifton, but looking at part of the map of the larger manor (Fig. 2), made for the Society of Merchant Venturers in 1746 by Jacob de Wilstar, may give some clues as to why this was so, and why there were two separate manors.[3]

[1] This first paragraph repeats what Dr. M. J. Crossley Evans and I wrote in *Nonesuch* in the Autumn of 2002: M. J. Crossley Evans, and R. H. Leech, 'Richmond House', *Nonesuch*, 13, no.1, (2002), pp. 41–43.

[2] B.R.O., AC/M/15, a survey, view and value of the manor of Clifton belonging to Rafe Sadleir of Stondon, Herts., Esq., 1625, transcribed in L. J. U. Way, 'The 1625 Survey of the Smaller Manor of Clifton', *T. B. & G. A. S.*, XXXVI, (1913), pp. 220–250.

[3] B.R.O., SMV/6/5/4/3.

Fig. 1. Richmond House, from Lower Clifton Hill, erected 1701–1703, a pencil sketch by Harold John Stops, R.W.A. (1925–2002), [The Stops Gallery, Manor Hall, University of Bristol].

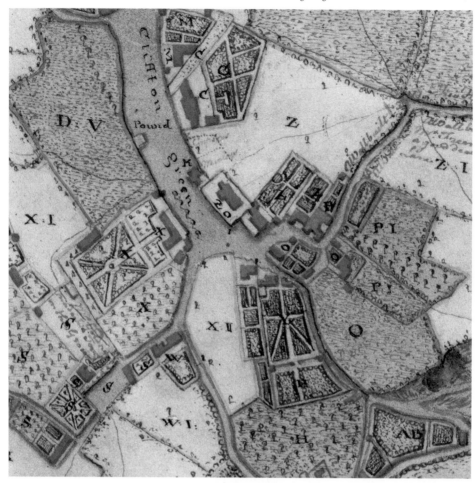

Fig. 2. Extract from the map of the manor of Clifton made for the Society of Merchant Venturers in 1746 by Jacob de Wilstar, [B.R.O., SMV/6/5/4/3].

The separate index to de Wilstar's map reveals the existence of two manors. 'Mr Hodge's freehold' included 'The Mansion House with a new messuage thereunto adjoining, together with offices, gardens, courts and a close called Church Close' marked 'Z', also 'the church and churchyard of Clifton' marked 'ZO' and the 'The Three Acre Paddock' marked 'Z.I' (Fig. 2). These lands half encircled two other holdings, those of Mr. Freeman and Mrs. Phippen. It can be argued from their being adjacent to one another and from their manorial associations that these two holdings resulted from the division of the manor house and barton or manorial centre of the larger manor of Clifton.

'Mr. Freeman's holding' was marked on the map of 1746 (Fig. 2) as P, 'a messuage with offices, garden, court and orchard, and P.I, the 'Home Close [...] divided into two parcels with a coach house and stable adjoining'. Earlier leases for this property show that in 1666 this was the toft of a messuage lately burnt and the garden plot adjoining. From 1694 onwards this property was the subject of a series of leases to members of the Freeman family. A lease of 1788 to Richard Bowsher gent. noted that

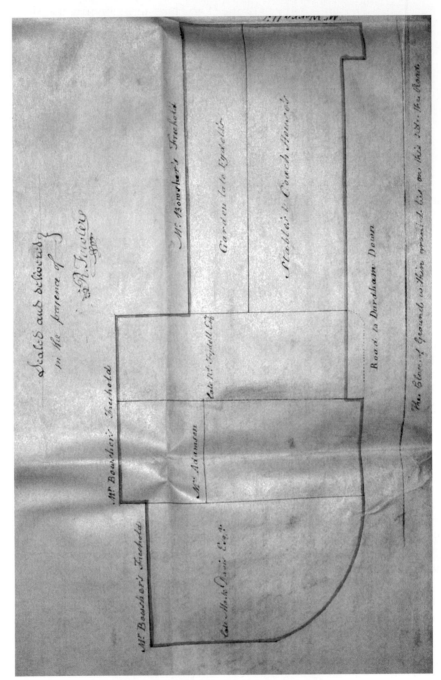

Fig. 3. Plan from lease of 1788 to Richard Bowsher gent. showing the location of the three tenements on the west side of Clifton Place; these are now the Muset Restaurant, the Lansdown Public House and the house, set back (see Fig. 4) and now divided, between these, [B.R.O., SMV/6/2/2/3].

the messuage demised in 1666 had been 'pulled down' and that three tenements with coach houses and stables had since been built in its place. A plan shows the location of the three tenements, on the west side of Clifton Place; these are now the Muset Restaurant, the Lansdown Public House and the house, set back and now divided, between these (Fig. 3). There was a stipulation in leases from 1678 onwards that the lord of the manor would retain the right to keep the manorial court in the said messuage twice in each year, and to have on these occasions the use of the kitchen for 'the dressing of provisions'. It can be concluded that this had been the site of the manor house for the manor purchased by the Society of Merchant Venturers.[4]

Possibly the messuage demised in 1666 was not entirely pulled down, but in part re-incorporated in the house that is now partly re-used as the Muset Restaurant. This formed part of what in 1909 was then still known as 'the Manor House Hotel'.[5] This incorporates part of a substantial two-room wide house of five bays; at least one of the windows in this house facing Clifton Road is of a form constructed in the seventeenth century, with brick quoins to an opening formed in coursed rubble (Figs. 4 and 5).[6]

Adjacent to the manor of the Merchant Venturers' was another property (Figs. 1, 7, and 8), later to be known as Richmond House, also part of their manorial lands, formerly burnt and of sufficient distinction to have been called 'the old castle'. This was in 1746 'Mrs. Phippen's holding', 'two messuages, garden, orchard, courts, stables and one close of pasture adjoining' marked as 'O' on de Wilstar's map (Fig. 2). Mrs. Phippen's holding was in 1701 the 'scite or ruines of the late greate house or capitall messuage ... heretofore burnt downe by fire ... since in the holding of Mary Hodges spinster ... and called the old Castle And the barton & paddock or close of meadow adjoyning called the Home Close', leased by the Society of Merchant Venturers to Whitchurch Phippen, mercer.[7]

It can be suggested that these two holdings, both belonging to the Society of Merchant Venturers, were formerly one, constituting the manor house or manorial centre of the larger manor of Clifton. From the above it will be seen that the manor houses and home closes of the two manors, the smaller and the larger manor, were topographically contiguous. I suggest that the most probable reason for this is that the two manorial centres were also formerly one, divided before the Dissolution, possibly when the smaller manor was first granted to the College of Westbury-on-Trym. The grant to the College was most probably made for devotional reasons. The grantor may at the same time have retained part of the manor for reasons unknown, this becoming the larger manor. This same process can be paralleled in the centre of Bristol where nos. 18 and 19 Small Street formed one property belonging to the

[4] B.R.O., SMV/6/2/2/3.

[5] B.R.O., Building Plans, Volume 56, fol. 4c.

[6] The technique of providing brick quoins to window and door openings was well known by the mid-seventeenth century to masons across southern England working in areas with building stone unsuited to construction in ashlar. Examples of surviving seventeenth century buildings with brick dressings to windows and/or doorways are particularly concentrated in East Anglia, but are found also in Barbados. For further discussion see R. H. Leech 'Alleynedale Hall, Barbados—A Plantation House of the Seventeenth Century', *Journal of the Barbados Museum and Historical Society*, 48, (2002), pp. 123–141.

[7] B.R.O., SMV/6/2/2/3.

Fig. 4. Behind the Muset Restaurant is part of a substantial two-room wide house of five bays; at least one of the windows in this house facing Clifton Road is of a form constructed in the seventeenth century, with brick quoins to an opening formed in coursed rubble, (see Fig. 5), [Copyright, author].

merchant Richard Erle until the early 1500s, which was then divided following his death to be used for two separate purposes.[8]

By 1738, when leased to Jane Phippen widow, the Richmond House property included two principal dwellings, the Old Castle, now 'converted into a tenement [...] and now of William Lewis dancing master as tenant to Jane Phippen, together with the barton and pasture called the Home Close, *c*. 3 acres including the part lately taken into the highway 'for the making the same way more commodious' and the 'part of the close lying next to the highway is lately enclosed with a stone wall'.[9] The making of the highway as more commodious may be relevant to the origin of the property as part of the manorial centre of Clifton. The tortuous course of the present day road around the front of Richmond House and then northwards as Clifton Road,

---

[8] R. H. Leech, *The Topography of Medieval and Early Modern Bristol, part 1: Property Holdings in the Early Walled Town and Marsh Suburb North of the Avon*, B.R.S., XLVIII, (1997), p. 158.
[9] B.R.O., SMV/6/5/2.

Fig. 5. Window with brick quoins opening to Clifton Road, the ground floor of the Manor Hotel, now partly the Muset Restaurant and much altered since the plan of 1909, [Copyright, author].

Lauridge Lane, in the 1625 survey, may represent the former entry into the barton or enclosure around the mediaeval manor house which consisted of both the Old Castle and the Freeman family's holding on the opposite side of the road (Figs. 2 and 6).

In summary, the manor of Clifton appears to have been divided in mediaeval times, one part becoming the smaller manor owned before the Dissolution by Westbury College and the other part becoming the larger manor which was purchased by the Society of Merchant Venturers *c.* 1686. Prior to this division the manor house and the barton extended from the churchyard eastwards to include what is now Richmond House. Following the division the manor house and barton of the larger manor constituted both Richmond House and the properties on the opposite side of Clifton Place. This was itself divided and let as two separate properties by the Society of Merchant Venturers from the early eighteenth century. Before turning to the physical remains of these properties, it will be necessary to say something of the second residences which members of Bristol's urban elite were acquiring from at least the fifteenth century onwards, known in the fifteenth century as lodges, by the seventeenth century as garden houses, and by the eighteenth century as summer houses.

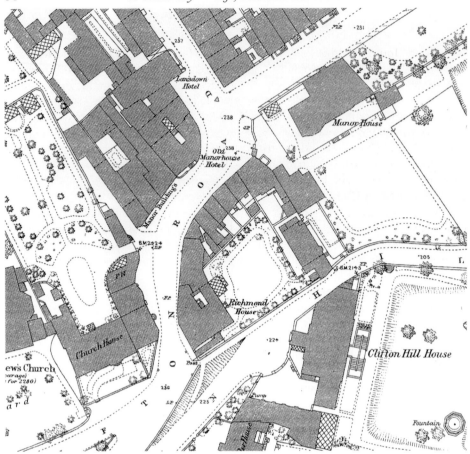

Fig. 6. Extract from the Ordnance Survey plan of 1884, showing the area depicted on Fig. 2.

GARDEN HOUSES AND SUBURBAN VILLAS

From at least the fifteenth century the wealthiest citizens of Bristol were acquiring second residences, built for the most part in suburban gardens or on the slopes overlooking the increasingly congested and densely occupied city. Many such houses were built on the slopes of St. Michael's Hill, now within the precinct of the University.[10] More such houses were being built by the late seventeenth and early eighteenth centuries on the slopes of Clifton, a little further away from the city but overlooking the Avon and the shipping upon which the wealth of so many citizens rested. Some of these houses will now be examined in detail.

[10] R. H. Leech, *'The Topography of Medieval and Early Modern Bristol, Part 2: The St. Michael's Hill Precinct of the University of Bristol'*, B.R.S., 52, (2000), p. 158; R. H. Leech, 'The garden house: merchant culture and identity in the early modern city', in S. Lawrence, (ed.), *Archaeologies of the British, Explorations of identity in Great Britain and its colonies 1600–1945,* One World Archaeology Series, 46, (2003), pp. 76–86.

RICHMOND HOUSE

Richmond House was built on the site of the 'late Great House or Capital Messuage' burned by Prince Rupert's soldiers in 1645, and known by the later seventeenth century as 'the Old Castle'. The research being undertaken by Dr. Martin Crossley Evans and myself into the history of Richmond House[11] arose from the notion that this new house was built out of the ruins of the old, the evidence for this being the exposed stone hood moulds over apparently partly blocked window openings on the rear elevation. The removal of rendering from two of the elevations has now shown that this was not so, and that the house that we see today is the creation of Whitchurch Phippen the Elder, a linen draper and mercer of the parish of All Saints', who lived at No. 9 High Street until his death in 1710.[12]

Phippen's suburban dwelling was built very much in the tradition of the larger garden houses to be found on the slopes of St. Michael's Hill by *c.* 1700. It occupied a prominent position on the crest of the hill, affording distant views, and readily seen from afar. It was exceptionally well lit, with tall narrow mullioned and transomed windows probably on all four elevations, some of these only recently exposed by the removal of render (Figs. 7 and 8).

Externally, stone hood moulds and moulded timber lintels over the windows echoed seventeenth century practice. The absence of gables and the five-bay symmetrical design with paired windows to each side of a central bay was repeated in the building of houses in St. James's Square in the same decade.[13] Internally, the positioning of windows rather than cupboards in the spaces between chimney stacks and side walls echoed a seventeenth century preference, as did the centrally placed entrance and stairs' hall. The introduction of a 'double pile' or two room deep plan foreshadowed what would become standard practice for larger houses in eighteenth century Bristol.[14] The paucity of kitchen and other service accommodation, together with the space given over to a splendid baroque stair which still survives (Fig. 9), marked the house out as one given over to entertainment and less than regular use. That this was an occasional residence is indicated also by the entries in the rates and land tax assessments for the parish of All Saints', which record Whitchurch Phippen as living at no. 9 High Street until his death in 1710.[15]

Richmond House subsequently passed to Phippen's widow, Maria, and his son Whitchurch Phippen the Younger (*c.* 1685–1739). It was the fate of many garden houses to become permanent residences. At some time in the late 1720s, or early 1730s, the son moved with his family from Richmond House to a new property, which he had built on part of the land that he leased from the Society of Merchant Venturers, which later became known as Manor House. We can only speculate on

[11] See note 1.
[12] Render which was deemed 'unsafe' was removed by the Bursar's Office of the University. This has assisted the re-appraisal of the historic form of the house in advance of restoration; for Phippen's leases see ref. 7, for his property at No. 9 High Street in the parish of All Saints', see B.R.O., F/PR/AS, All Saints' rates, correlated with entry in R. H. Leech, *Topography*, 1, p. 74.
[13] W. Ison, *The Georgian Buildings of Bristol*, (1952), Fig. 24b.
[14] For other examples of the seventeenth century see Stoke Bishop House of 1669 (now the Trinity Theological College) and No. 6 King Street.
[15] See note 1.

Fig. 7. Richmond House, north elevation, window openings of the seventeenth century with freestone hood moulds over mullioned and transomed frames with leaded lights, [Copyright, author].

why Whitchurch Phippen the Younger made this decision, but a likely reason was the increasing number of merchants' houses on the slopes of Lower Clifton Hill, which obscured the view of Brandon Hill, the spire of St. Mary Redcliffe, and the distant hills of Somerset, from the windows of Richmond House.

Other houses close to Richmond House were also possibly built as garden houses or occasional residences. Goldney House was possibly first purchased and then rebuilt as the second residence for Thomas Goldney II and his family who then lived at No. 22 High Street in the city centre parish of St. Nicholas;[16] possibly it fulfilled a similar function for his father Thomas Goldney I living at Castle Green;[17] his widow, Mary, subsequently moved to live with her son Thomas Goldney II at the Clifton house. Here it needs to be highlighted that Goldney House was built as a rather smaller house than has been generally assumed. Professor Mowl has assumed that the early eighteenth century house was of five bays in width, suggesting that 'its garden front has survived Alfred Waterhouse's nineteenth century additions [1864–1865], the east wing intact, the west sensitively refaced'.[18] Analysis of Waterhouse's drawing, and

---

[16] For the Goldney residence at No. 22 High Street, see B.R.O., F/PR/St N, St Nicholas rates, correlated with the entry in R. H. Leech, *Topography* 1, p. 77.

[17] P. K. Stembridge, *The Goldney Family, a Bristol Merchant Dynasty*, B.R.S., XLIX, (1998), pp. 86 and 111–114.

[18] T. Mowl, *To Build the Second City: Architects and Craftsmen of Georgian Bristol*, (Bristol, 1991), p. 14.

Fig. 8. Richmond House, East elevation, window openings of the seventeenth century with freestone hood moulds over blocked openings, [Copyright, author].

Fig. 9. Richmond House, the stairs, [Copyright, author].

comparing the 1828 map with that of 1884 show that only the eastern half formed the house built by Thomas Goldney. (Figs. 10–12). This was the distant house shown on a watercolour of the Clifton hillside painted in *c.* 1790,[19] and on Booth's painting of Granby Hill in 1822.[20] (Fig. 13) To the south and west of Goldney House were further garden houses. To the south of Goldney House is another garden house, now the

---

[19] Bristol City Museum and Art Gallery, M.4178.
[20] Bristol City Museum and Art Gallery, K.101.

west part of Clifton Wood House, and probably of *c.* 1700 (Fig. 14). To the west is Emmaus House, built in the early 1700s as a development of two garden houses by the merchant James Hollidge, probably the two gabled houses shown on a painting of the early eighteenth century.[21] (Fig. 15). Another garden house was possibly that demolished by the merchant Paul Fisher for the construction of Clifton Hill House. The earlier house, in use when Fisher lived in High Street, was possibly that shown in the distance on the Buck's prospect of Bristol from the south-east. (Fig. 16).

Research into the function of the garden house has shown that they served principally as places to which to retreat from the noise and bustle of the city. They were places for entertaining, for visiting on a Sunday, and offered space for a garden and cultivation which could not be found in the centre of the city. The merchant George Lane leased a lodge or garden house adjacent to what later became Tyndall's Park; his possessions in the parlour of this house in 1613 indicate that it served as a dining room and included a lute and Venetian glasses.[22] When James Hollidge leased one of his garden houses to John Matthews, a gardener in 1710, he stipulated that the fruit trees and standers were to be properly pruned and not removed at the end of the lease.[23] From the records of the Goldney family we might deduce also that they were places more amenable for events such as the birth of a child. From 1696 onwards all seven Goldney children recorded by Thomas Goldney II were born at Clifton, and not in the city centre parish of All Saints'.[24] The garden house may also have functioned as a place for meeting neighbours and friends. On summer evenings and at weekends the Goldneys and Phippens might well have trod the same path from town house in High Street to garden house on Clifton Hill.

RICHMOND HOUSE AND THE MANOR OF CLIFTON

If Richmond House was not the manor house of Clifton where then might we look for the remains of the manor house? A first thought might be to look at the house long known as the Manor House in York Place. (Fig. 17). This it has already been suggested was not the Manor House but was the 'new erected messuage lately built by Whitchurch Phippen and now of Jane Phippen' first mentioned in the lease of 1738. The Manor House, which gives its name to Manor Hall, is quite possibly of this date. Chimneypieces on the first floor can, for instance, be compared with those being installed in other houses of the middle decades of the eighteenth century. (Fig. 18). The compact plan of this house and its relationship to its garden again echoes the arrangements of earlier garden houses. Was this an up to date replacement for Richmond House? It was certainly not the Manor House.

We might also look for the manor house across the road from Richmond House, on the opposite side of Clifton Place. The complex of buildings now occupied partly by the Muset Restaurant and the Lansdowne Public House has already been noted as possibly including fragments of the earlier manor house, not withstanding that it was

---

[21] Bristol City Museum and Art Gallery, K.4646.
[22] R. H. Leech, *Topography*, 2, pp. 42–43.
[23] B.R.O., 1281 (3).
[24] P. K. Stembridge, *op. cit.*, pp. 86–88.

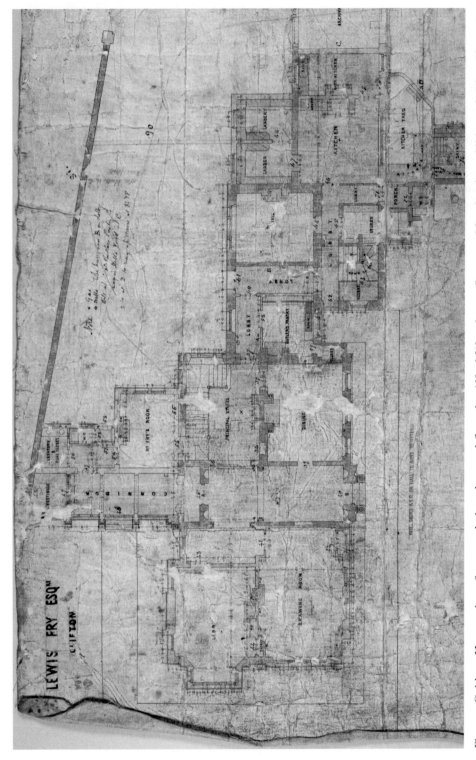

Fig. 10. Goldney House, plan of proposed altered ground floor, by Alfred Waterhouse, January 1864, showing additions of 1864–1865 to the original house, [Bristol University Library, Special Collections].

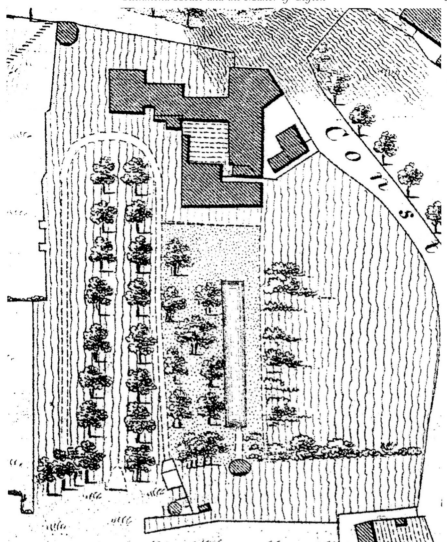

Fig. 11. Goldney House, outline of plan in 1828 as shown on the map of Bristol by Ashmead and Plumley, [B.R.O., SMV/6/4/14/15].

described in 1788 as having been pulled down; certainly the remains should be there below ground, awaiting discovery by a future generation of archaeologists.

That I hope will be one useful outcome of this contribution to this volume: to have flagged the archaeological importance of this little corner of Clifton, with the remains of a manor first divided in mediaeval times, and one half of it then further divided by the beginning of the eighteenth century. A second useful outcome may be to raise awareness of the difficulties surrounding the question facing the University of Bristol, English Heritage and the planning authority: how might Richmond House be best restored? To what extent should the early eighteenth century elevation of paired mullioned and transomed windows below hood moulds be respected or restored?

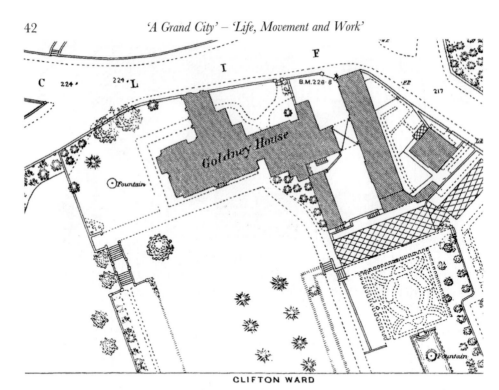

Fig. 12. Goldney House, outline of plan as extended *c.* 1864–1865, as shown on the Ordnance Survey plan of 1884.

Fig. 13. View of Goldney House and St. Andrew's church, Clifton, detail from the watercolour painting of Granby Hill, Clifton, from the west (1822), by Lieutenant Colonel William Booth (1748–1826), [Bristol City Museum and Art Gallery, K101].

Fig. 14. Clifton Wood House viewed from the west: the part closest to the camera is a garden house of *c.* 1700, [Copyright, author].

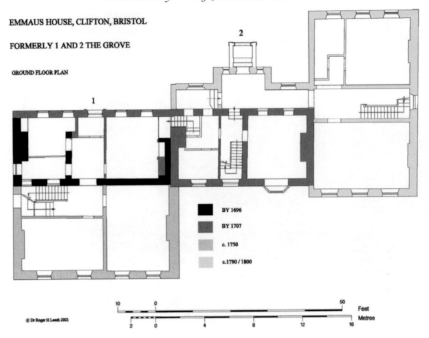

EMMAUS HOUSE, CLIFTON, BRISTOL

FORMERLY 1 AND 2 THE GROVE

GROUND FLOOR PLAN

BY 1696

BY 1707

c. 1750

c.1790 / 1800

10   0   50
                                                        Feet
© Dr Roger H Leech 2002   Metres
 2   0   4   8   12   16

Fig. 15. Emmaus House, Clifton Hill, possibly built around two garden houses of the later seventeenth and early eighteenth centuries, plan of the ground floor, [Copyright, author].

Fig. 16. Another garden house was possibly that demolished by the merchant Paul Fisher for the construction of Clifton Hill House. The earlier house, in use when Fisher lived in High Street, was possibly that of three gables to the right of the number '4' shown in the distance on the Bucks' prospect of Bristol from the south-east (1734). Richmond House was possibly the house of five windows in width shown immediately above, [Author's collection].

Fig. 17. The Manor House, York Place, from a sketch by Anton Bantock M.B.E., [The Stops Gallery, Manor Hall, University of Bristol].

Fig. 18. The Manor House, York Place, chimneypiece on the first floor, [Copyright, author].

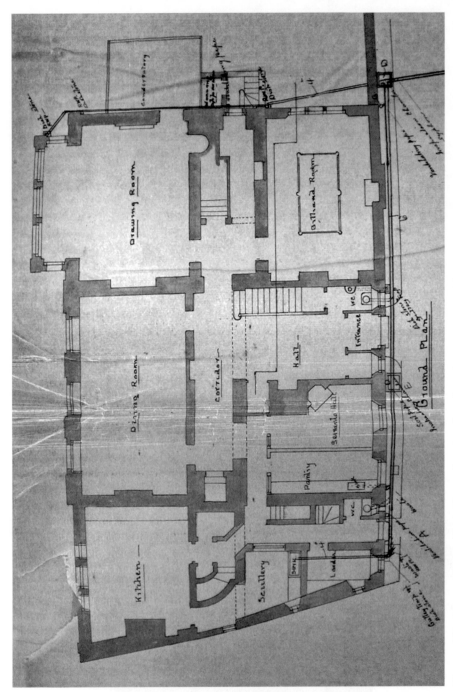

Fig. 19. The Manor House, York Place, plan showing alterations as proposed in 1891–1892; the compact plan of this house and its relationship to its garden again echo the arrangements of earlier garden houses, [B.R.O., Building Plans, Volume 27, fol. 31b].

IV

Paul Fisher, linen-draper and merchant, of Clifton Hill House

ANNIE M. BURNSIDE, M.A.
AND SHEILA B. BRENNAN, M.A. (OXON).[1]

PAUL FISHER was one of most the prominent merchants who contributed to Bristol's commercial life of the eighteenth century. Something of him is known from the factual records of his career, and from the revealing minutiae of his will. From this evidence he emerges as an energetic, industrious, and above all conscientious man who enjoyed a reputation as a philanthropist.

Fisher was born in the small town of Somerton, Somerset, in 1692,[2] the son of John Fisher, an apothecary, surgeon and sometime church warden.[3] Fisher probably went to school in Somerton, to the school which had been endowed in 1675 to teach the boys of the town and the parish.[4] He had a good educational grounding. The range of his interests, his correspondence and his extensive library illustrate this, quite apart from his shrewdness, which brought him both a fortune and the respect of his contemporaries.

Seventeenth century Somerton had been a busy cloth-town, with many markets and fair-days. By the end of the century trade was beginning to decline; it was a good time to send a son to the city of Bristol. In 1708, Fisher was sent to Bristol to be apprenticed to Robert Smith, mercer, and Sarah, his wife. Unusually, Fisher's family agreed to provide 'his apparel of all sorts',[5] and his master and mistress were 'discharged there from, any custom of Bristol to the contrary thereof in any wise notwithstanding'.[6] Nothing is known of him between 1708 and the end of his

---

[1] This article on Paul Fisher is a revision of the research carried out by Miss Sheila Barbara Brennan (1922–2005), formerly warden of Clifton Hill House and Manor Hall, and special lecturer in Education at the University of Bristol, for a lecture delivered to the Bristol section of the Bristol and Gloucestershire Archaeological Society in February 1992, entitled 'The life of Paul Fisher, an eighteenth century Bristol merchant', and subsequently delivered as one of the University of Bristol's series of Convocation Lectures given in July 1992 in the Junior Common Room at Clifton Hill House. A synopsis of this article is to be found in A. Burnside, *A Palladian Villa in Bristol: Clifton Hill House and the People who lived there*, (Bristol, 2009), pp. 5–23.

[2] The registers of Somerton only date back to 1697; the date of Fisher's birth is derived from his age at death as recorded on the monument in St. Andrew's, Clifton.

[3] D. Jones, *A History of Clifton*, (1992), pp. 40–41 claims that he was the son of a Paul Fisher who was also a merchant resident in Clifton. He designates them as Paul Fisher Senior, and Junior. John Fisher was married to Elizabeth, who died in 1727.

[4] *Victoria County History of Somerset*, III, pp. 136, 153.

[5] B.R.O., 09467 (1), Paul Fisher, apprenticeship to Robert Smith, 23 September 1708.

[6] *Ibid.*

apprenticeship in 1715 when he was referred to as 'Mercer and Linnen-draper'.[7] In November of that year, he was admitted to the liberties of the city as a burgess some months after his friend and future nephew-in-law, Christopher Willoughby.[8] Christopher was a grandson of Alderman John Willoughby of Kenn, in the parish of Yatton; he had been apprenticed to Peter Day, a prosperous Bristol merchant, at the same time as Fisher was apprenticed to Robert Smith. Another descendant of Alderman John Willoughby was Mary Puxton.[9] She and her sister Sarah had inherited considerable property from their father, Thomas, a wealthy soap-boiler.[10]

Fisher was hardworking and shrewd and his business prospered. In 1717 Fisher married Mary Puxton. By then he was referred to as a linen-draper, but it is clear from the marriage-settlement that Mary's grandmother and uncle[11] were determined to watch closely over her interests. The articles state simply that Mary is 'worth in money and goods the value of £1,600',[12] whereas Fisher 'is not at present seized or Possessed of any real estate' with which to make a competent settlement on Mary.[13] The Puxtons would therefore continue to control £1,000 of her inheritance, paying the interest to Mary for her own separate use. The settlement specifies that Paul was not to 'intermeddle'[14] with these monies. In addition, it was specified that if Paul predeceased Mary, she was to take back her goods and chattels including her gold jewellery and silver plate. If she died first, these were to be delivered within a month to whomever she had designated as her beneficiary in her will. Her goods included 'a gold locket, one Charles the first's head in gold painted on Christall, and a silver porringer marked with M.P., three silver castors marked with a Cypher T.P. and two silver salts marked with T.P.'[15] In return Paul agreed to leave £1,500 to Mary from his estate should she survive him.

Upon this foundation Fisher continued to establish his career. The 1720s were marked by great expansion in Bristol, in trade, in building, and in population. Paul and Mary lived in the High Street in the parish of St. Nicholas. Their elder daughter, Mary, was born *c.* 1720 and their second child was christened Elizabeth at St. Nicholas on 9 September 1722.[16] Mary Fisher's sister Sarah had married John Baker in 1718,[17] and Christopher Willoughby married an heiress, Mary Birkin.[18]

---

[7] B.R.O., 04359/6, 'Burgess Books'.

[8] The Revd. A. B. Beaven, *Bristol Lists: Municipal and Miscellaneous*, (Bristol, 1899), pp. 235, 407. Christopher Willoughby was appointed chamberlain of the city on 16 May 1739, and died in his house at 43 Prince Street, on 4 June 1773. He served as master of the Society of Merchant Venturers between 1747 and 1748, and as treasurer between 1747 and 1773. He was warden of St. Stephen's Ringers in 1733.

[9] Mary Puxton was the grand-daughter of Mary Puxton, *née* Willoughby.

[10] B.R.O., 09860/8, will dated 22 July 1708, proved 7 September 1708.

[11] Michael Puxton was a member of the Common Council of the city between 1721 and 1732, served as sheriff between 1725 and 1726 and died about November 1732, The Revd. A. B. Beaven, *op. cit.*, p. 306.

[12] B.R.O., 09471/14 (a, b, c), Marriage Articles of Paul Fisher and Mary Puxton, 1717.

[13] *Ibid.*

[14] *Ibid.*

[15] *Ibid.*

[16] *Ibid.*, St. Nicholas Parish Registers, P/St.N./R/1 (j).

[17] B.R.O., 09471/15 (b), marriage bond dated 11 August 1718.

[18] B.R.O., 09463/7 (a), marriage settlement 2 February 1726/7.

Fisher's name appears in the wharfage books in the late 1720s. At first his ventures into shipping were tentative, with only a few hogsheads of goods exported each year, but there was an increasing quantity of imports, mainly of linen, but with occasional small amounts of sugar and rum. The wharfage entries between 1727 and 1733 show a constant expansion in his commercial interests especially in imports: cotton, linen, sugar, rice, redwood, logwood, wine, deerskins, calfskins and lime juice. In partnership with John King, Fisher was also importing tobacco from Virginia. They paid the 10% duty on £50,000 worth of leaf between 1728 and 1731. In 1729, Fisher is named as 'Master of the Mercers and Linnen-drapers Companie', and he had become part owner of a ship called the *Post-Boy*. Fisher appears as an agent for his partner Thomas Jennys in the shipment of rice from Carolina in 1731, and is also mentioned as a privateer, or licensed pirate, holding letters of marque from his government to prey on enemy shipping during the war of Austrian Succession (1739–1748).[19] His vessels included the 300 ton *Eagle*, the *Jamaica*, 290 tons, and the *North Cape*, 306 tons, but the *Jamaica* was lost at sea in the West Indies in 1746 together with 500 hogsheads of sugar, and the *North Cape* was captured by the French after a four hour battle off Antigua.[20] His imports in 1731 on his own behalf included cambrick and Holland linen, probably from the Austrian Netherlands, and in partnership with Mr. Bruton, one ton and 60 gallons of Flemish brandy.[21] He was also actively involved in the slave trade as early as 1729–1730. The period between 1730 and 1745 saw a large expansion in the Bristol slave trade. 'Bristol was [then] the premier British port trading to Africa. However, the level of its involvement in the trade varied substantially during the period'.[22] His partners, Thomas Jennys[23] and Slade Baker, were known slaving agents. In 1731, the *Post-Boy* returned with a telltale cargo of redwood from West Africa and cowries, which had been surplus to requirements when slaves were bought, and they were returned for lack of sale. In 1733, Fisher is named with Jennys and Co. for the sale, on 7 August, of slaves transported on the *Post-Boy*. In 1735, Fisher is also recorded as part owner of the *Scipio*, from which Jennys and Baker sold 204 adults and 58 children in South Carolina in June of the same year. Many of the voyages were from what is now Angola to Jamaica or the Carolinas. He also had an interest in a plantation in Grenada.[24] His involvement in the Africa trade lasted for more than 30 years. In 1750 he became one of the Company of Merchants trading to Africa, which succeeded to the Royal Africa Company's forts and trading posts, when the latter was dissolved and the former established by Act of Parliament. He is listed among the 237 individual members of the Company as a resident of Bristol in June 1759.[25]

[19] Thomas Jennys, merchant of Yeoville; W. E. Minchinton, 'The Trade of Bristol in the *Eighteenth Century*', B.R.S., XX, (1957), p. 20.

[20] D. Jones, *op. cit.*, (1992), pp. 40–41.

[21] W. E. Minchinton, *op. cit.*, pp. 30–31.

[22] D. Richardson, '*Bristol, Africa and the Eighteenth-Century Slave Trade to America: The Years of Ascendancy 1730–1745*', B.R.S., XXXIX, (1987), pp. xiii and xiv.

[23] Thomas Jennys was a co-owner with Fisher and Robert Smith, among others, of the *Post-Boy* and the *Scipio*. Both vessels were used to trade in slaves in return for various imports from the Carolinas.

[24] M. J. Dresser, *Slavery Obscured: The Social History of the Slave Trade in Bristol*, (Bristol, 2007), p. 109.

[25] D. Jones, *op. cit.*, p. 88. George Daubeny is also listed. He was probably the father and namesake of one of Fisher's trustees named in his will.

Fisher's business was not only imperilled by storms, piracy, privateers, fluctuating demand and the bankruptcy of trading partners, it also posed temptations to thieves, and we find that at a Gaol Delivery held at the Bristol Newgate on 27 August 1750 one Thomas Hickes was condemned to 'be hanged by the neck until he shall be dead' for 'feloniously stealing the Goods of Messrs Fisher, Baker and Griffin to the value of 5£ in their Warehouse in this City'.[26]

The scale of Fisher's commercial interests is partly revealed by the second codicil of his will dated 16 September 1761. In this he mentions 'a large field of profitable business under the direction and management of Mr. John Kelsall of Warrington in the county of Lancashire, as my agent', which his executors were to carry on until Christopher Willoughby the Younger reached the age of 24. They were given a capital sum of £15,000 to be 'constantly employed therein'. Tantalisingly we are not told the nature of this trade.[27]

At home Fisher had gone into partnership with Slade Baker[28] and William Griffin and engaged in the linen-trade with Ireland.[29] By 1739 he was the dominant partner, putting up $7/_{12}$ths of the £18,000 capital. The agreement was made in 'consideration of the mutual trust and confidence they had in each other',[30] and the trade was to be carried on in Fisher's warehouse in High Street, or where he thought fit. Accounts were to be carefully kept, and each partner would draw a proportionate salary. Fisher's was to be £42 a month, and in addition to this sum he was to have £200 yearly for his 'Extraordinary Expenses in Entertaining Customers and Dieting and Lodging of Servants'.[31] The partnership continued until Fisher's death in 1762.

In the 1730s, Fisher began to look away from the 'smoak and stir' of Bristol to the heights of Clifton, where several successful merchants had already leased land or built houses, Whitchurch Phippen[32], Robert Smith and Daniel Goizin[33] among them. As early as 1721 Robert Smith, the wealthy mercer and linen draper to whom Fisher was

[26] G. Lamoine, *Bristol Gaol Delivery Fiats 1741–1799*, B.R.S., XL, (1989), p. 8.

[27] The National Archives, PROB 11/884.

[28] It has been suggested that he was related to Mary Fisher's brother-in-law, John Baker. Slade Baker was governor of the Incorporation of the Poor in 1764–1765 and died 26 October 1784, The Revd. A. B. Beaven, *op. cit.*, p. 319.

[29] Slade Baker and William Griffin, who were linen drapers and Fisher's co-partners, were also involved in the slave trade. Slade Baker and his son, Jeremy, became trustees of Redland Chapel, together with Paul Fisher, in 1757.

[30] B.R.O., 09476 (2), Agreement of 1739 between Paul Fisher, Slade Baker and William Griffin; K. Morgan, *Bristol and the Atlantic trade in the eighteenth century*, (Cambridge, 1993), p. 162.

[31] B.R.O., 09476 (2).

[32] Whitchurch Phippen the Elder, linen draper of the parish of All Saints' built Richmond House, Lower Clifton Hill in 1701–1703 on the ruins of part of the mediaeval manor house destroyed during the Civil War. His son and namesake, who died in 1738, was church warden in 1725–1726 and subsequently erected a new residence called Manor House a short distance from his home, *c.* 1732 in anticipation of the erection of Clifton Hill House, which would rob him of his views of Somerset and Brandon Hill. Notes by Dr. M. J. Crossley Evans upon the re-opening of Manor House 21 April 1999; A. J. Green-Armytage, *Concerning Clifton: A Historical Narrative from Saxon Times until the Present Day*, (Clifton, 1922), p. 76.

[33] Merchant and friend of Paul Fisher, and part-owner of the ship *Katherine* 1730–1733. He served with Paul Fisher as one of the first nine visitors upon the foundation of the Bristol Infirmary in 1737.

apprenticed, had commissioned the architect George Tully to build Clifton Wood House for him. Robert Smith's estate of twenty acres covered the slopes below Thomas Goldney's house and included a vineyard and orchards.

The church wardens' accounts of Clifton show that Fisher was paying rates for property in Clifton from 1734 onwards.[34] In 1735, Fisher acquired a pew in St. Andrew's church, Clifton.[35] He paid 'the sum of five shillings apiece of lawful British money[36] to [....]Walter Fisher, Peter Hardwicke[37] and William Jefferis'[38] At the same time he bought the leases of various lands in Clifton.[39] He paid £743.10.00 for these in 'good British money'.[40] However, he did not begin to build his house for some years.

Although his thriving business took some of his attention, Fisher was able to devote time and energy to charity. He had taken his turn as the treasurer of the Incorporation of the Poor between 1725 and 1726 and later on served as governor between 1742 and 1743.[41] In 1737 the Bristol Infirmary was founded, after 'some well-disposed persons held a meeting in which they resolved to endeavour at the establishment of a public charity'.[42] Seventy-eight persons signed, all promising between two and six guineas. Fisher gave his full support to this new venture. As the son and brother of apothecaries this is likely to have been to have been of keen

[34] B.R.O., P/StA/V/I/I, in 1734 he paid £0.3.9 for premises, late Philpotts, and in 1735 there is an entry for Mr. James Hardwick, late Mr. Edward Jones, now Mr. Fisher's.

[35] This might indicate that Fisher and his family already lived in Clifton at that time. The land that Paul Fisher eventually bought had been in the tenure of Daniel Goizin since 1731.

[36] B.R.O., 09467 (6b). Indenture of 20 May 1737. Walter Fisher was the son of Rachel Fisher whose brother Edward Jones merchant, deceased, had held the land upon which Clifton Hill House was built, after Daniel Goizin and Thomas Gaynes. Walter Fisher is termed 'of the City of London, Blackwell Hall, Factor', and his partners 'Peter Hardwicke Doctor of Physics and William Jefferies Esq. both of the City of Bristol'. Mr. Donald Jones in his history (*op. cit.*, p. 41) states that in the Vestry Book for 1734 there is an entry granting Fisher the right to erect a seat in the gallery of the church dated 22 February 1734.

[37] Peter Hardwicke, physician of the Infirmary 1737–1747, died 1 September 1747, The Revd A. B. Beaven, *op. cit.*, p. 355; G. Munro Smith, *A History of the Bristol Royal Infirmary*, (Bristol, 1917), pp. 11, 16, 18, 420, 421, 483.

[38] William Jefferis, member of the Common Council 1722–1752; alderman 1742–1752; (Redcliffe 1742–1746, St. Nicholas 1746–1752); sheriff 1724–1725; mayor 1738–1739; governor of the Incorporation of the Poor 1743–1745; treasurer of the Incorporation of the Poor 1727–1728; warden of the Merchant Venturers 1737–1738; treasurer, Merchant Venturers 1730–1732; died April or May 1752; The Revd. A. B. Beaven, *op. cit.*, p. 298.

[39] B.R.O., SMV/6/1/8/8, lease from the S.M.V. of Dean's Close and Honey Penn Hill Field. Paul Fisher paid £150 for a lease of Dean's Close (5 acres) and Honey Penn Hill Field for three lives, his own, and his daughters Mary and Elizabeth, at a yearly rent of 20 shillings. On 29 September 1750 Paul Fisher surrendered the lease and paid £25, 'the said Elizabeth Fisher is since dead'. The new lease was granted for three lives, Paul Fisher, Mary his daughter and Slade Baker, linen draper. On 13 June 1754 Paul Fisher again surrendered his lease as the 'said Mary Fisher is since dead'. The new lease was granted for three lives, Paul Fisher, Slade Baker and Jeremy, son of Slade Baker, aged 12 years.

[40] The de Wilstar survey of the manor of Clifton in 1746 shows that he then owned only one acre of freehold land, but rented a further 17 acres from the Merchant Venturers, D. Jones, *op. cit.*, p. 32.

[41] The Revd. A.B. Beaven, *op. cit.*, p. 346.

[42] G. Munro Smith, *op. cit.*, p. 6.

interest to him, and as most apothecaries at the time also practised the art of surgery
we can be sure that he was well-informed on the subject. He was involved at every
stage of the project, he was seventh on the list of subscribers, he was among the first
trustees who met at Mrs. Barry's coffee-house in February 1736/7 to approve the new
premises, and was one of the committee appointed to prepare the house to receive its
first patients. The committee also recommended a matron, approved an apothecary,
and gave a vote of thanks to Mr. Elbridge, the principal benefactor and enthusiast.

The committee agreed that the Infirmary should open on 13 December 1737. Every
subscriber was summoned to meet at the Infirmary 'at 10 of the clock in the Morning,
and to Dine at the Nag's Head Tavern in Wine Street'.[43] More importantly, they
appointed a committee of nine to serve as 'house visitors'. Fisher was re-appointed in
January and became one of another group appointed to serve in the same capacity
for three months a little later on. He rapidly became indispensable: sometimes serving as the chairman, sometimes running the Brewing Committee, holding the keys to
the poor box, and so on. In 1752, the city council complained that Infirmary patients,
after being cured, or discharged as incurable, remained in the city and were continually charged with acts of vagrancy and then, having applied to be admitted to St.
Peter's Hospital, they subsequently became a charge on the city. Fisher was one of
those deputed to reply to the council's allegations.

The visitors took their duties very seriously, and Fisher was assiduous in the execution of his responsibilities. Some of the nine visited the hospital nearly every day, and
made a report. On some days there was 'noe complaint'.[44] The visitors were meticu-
lous; and on Fisher's first visit he was one of the four who examined the beer 'and
found it not good enough for the price'.[45] The visitors ordered chimneys to be mend-
ed, surgery boxes with panakins, a powdering tub and £10 for the matron;
they recorded a 'Complaint against Robt. Clare for giving abusive language to the
Nurse',[46] and sent for a kilderkin of ale. Fisher was present on fifteen of the first
seventeen visits.

It is clear that he enjoyed this kind of work, and his services to the parish church in
Clifton were equally painstaking. He served as a church warden in 1750–1751, and as
a vestryman during most of his years in Clifton.[47] His name appears in the records as
a man to rely on, whether it was to give orders about repairing the tower of the
church, or 'to Amend and Repair the Churchway leading from Jacob's Well to the
said Church'[48], or merely to sign the accounts and approve the 'payment at 4d each
for 34 hodge hoggs for the hole yeere'.[49] On 1 October 1761 the church warden and
Fisher reported on the repairs to the church that they had undertaken as directed at
the Easter Vestry. Fisher appears to have overseen the work, which amounted to

[43] *Ibid.*, p. 24.
[44] *Ibid.*, p. 27.
[45] *Ibid.*
[46] *Ibid.*
[47] A. J. Green-Armytage, *op. cit.*, p. 76.
[48] J. Latimer, *The Annals of Bristol in the Eighteenth Century*, (Bristol, 1893), p. 313.
[49] *Ibid.*

Fig. 1. Clifton Hill House. Plate 40 from *A Complete Body of Architecture*.

£109.4.0, and presented the tradesmen's accounts, which included a payment of £22.6.0 to 'Mr. Thomas Patty freemason'.[50]

He decided to build a house in the parish which, while reflecting his solid prosperity, was not pretentious. His land on Clifton Hill was at the end of the ridge, stretching down towards Clifton Wood and the river. He did not choose a local builder, but turned to the London architect, Isaac Ware, who designed a Palladian semi-rural villa for him. (Fig. 3). The plans appear in Ware's *A Complete Body of Architecture* (1756), (Plate 40).[51] (Fig. 1). C. F. W. Dening, the first historian of the architecture of eighteenth century Bristol, states: 'The building relies for its effect entirely upon its excellent proportions, and it is an admirable example of the dignity that may be obtained by absolutely simple methods'.[52] In his book on Georgian Bristol, *To Build the Second City*, Professor Timothy Mowl describes the house as an 'immaculately restrained and utterly correct Palladian villa'.[53]

As the original plan shows, the house stood high on its rustic podium; originally this ground floor projected at each side, but later additional rooms were extended on the 'piano nobile', and the main block now appears less commanding. On the garden

[50] B.R.O., P/StA/V/I/I. Paty was subsequently responsible for erecting a south aisle and porch to the parish church in 1768, at a cost of £419.14.4, to which Thomas Goldney III and his sister Ann both contributed £26.5.0 each, Paty received the balance of his account on 22 January 1770; B.R.O., P/StA/V/I/2.
[51] W. Ison, *The Georgian Buildings of Bristol*, (1952), p. 177. Ison's work and A. Gomme, M. Jenner and B. Little, *Bristol: An Architectural History*, (1979), pp. 151–154, contain excellent accounts of the house.
[52] C. F. W. Dening, *The Eighteenth-Century Architecture of Bristol*, (Bristol, 1923), pp. 165–166.
[53] T. Mowl, *To Build the Second City: Architects and Craftsmen of Georgian Bristol*, (Bristol, 1991), p. 14.

Fig. 2. The two cartouches on Clifton Hill House, [Copyright Mrs. A. M. Burnside].

front the perron and double staircase are reminiscent of Chiswick; Ware was a pupil and a protégé of Lord Burlington. The tympanum of the pediment on the garden side bears Fisher's armorial shield. On the other side are the date, 1747, and the monograms of Paul and Mary Fisher. (Fig. 2). The construction took four years (1746–1750).

There are still some rough accounts for the house building.[54] Thomas Paty, the mason and carver, was paid over £2,000 'to realise the chilly serenity of Isaac Ware's designs'[55] between 1746 and 1752. Samuel Glascodine was the house-carpenter. Joseph Thomas, the tyler and plasterer did break out from Ware's Palladian severity; his beautiful ceilings, although framed in geometrical panels, have a natural liveliness with Rococo swirls and curves, C- and acanthus scrolls, shell motifs and floral garlands. Thomas received £400 for his plaster work at Clifton Hill House.

It is probable that Fisher erected a cold bath within his grounds sometime after 1746. The bath, of mid-eighteenth century date, is of fine ashlar Bath stone lining and pennant paving, and was attached to an anteroom, associated with the thirteenth century conduit of St. Augustine's abbey. The cold bath was erected on the land and orchard that he rented below Clifton Hill House from the Society of Merchant Venturers. It is situated in what is now 47 Jacobs Well Road/Gorse Lane.[56] Originally it was open to the air, and must have born striking similarities to the bath erected in Bristol by the Venetian merchant, Bartholomew de Dominiceti, in the 1760s and described as being 'of polished stone and shaded with apple and pear blossom'. The bath room is seven feet by 14 feet and would have contained a maximum of five feet of water and is similar to that situated in John Pinney's house in Great George Street, constructed in 1791.[57] The cold bath was let in 1786, together with the surrounding cold bath orchard, to James Cross of Clifton Hill House, distiller.[58] It was subsequently detached from the Clifton Hill House estate following his death in 1791 and the lease was sold to a speculative builder, who erected Bellevue and establish its pleasure grounds.[59]

The interest that Fisher took in the minutiae of house-keeping matters during his residence in Clifton is shown by the following passage in the second codicil to his will which was inserted to ensure that his family always had the benefit of fresh meat and milk: 'I further will and direct that that my Grounds at Clifton shall be kept in the hands of my Executors for the benefit of Cows and other Cattle to be used for the Family in my said House in Clifton according to my directions in respect thereto and as my self hath used the same'.[60]

---

[54] B.R.O., 09467 (12a).

[55] T. Mowl, *op. cit.*, p. 62.

[56] *Bristol and Avon Archaeology*, 18, (2001), p. 113.

[57] J. G. P. Erskine, 'The Excavation and Preservation of a Georgian Cold Bath at Gorse Lane, Clifton, Bristol', *Bristol and Avon Archaeology*, 20, (2005), pp. 7–16.

[58] B.R.O., SMV/6/1/8/8, lease 25 May 1786, containing a map.

[59] Sale particulars of Clifton Hill House in the *Bristol Gazette*, announcing the auction on 3 June 1830 following the death of a subsequent owner, Robert Bush, mention that the house had acquired 'a bathing-room and water closet' on the ground floor and a further water closet on the first floor. The bathing room may have been added to the property following the detachment of the cold bath and cold bath orchard following the death of Mr. Cross.

[60] T.N.A., PROB 11/884.

By the time he moved in to Clifton Hill House Fisher was in his late fifties. His daughter, Elizabeth, had been suitably married in 1743 to Edward Gwatkin[61], a wealthy Bristol soap-boiler, but she died before September 1750. The marriage agreement made extensive provision for possible heirs but a little note scrawled on the back says, 'Mrs. Gwatkin is since dead and left no children'.[62] Edward Gwatkin remained on good terms with his father-in-law and was one of the executors of his will. Paul Fisher's elder daughter, Mary, was dead before June 1754 and is not known to have married. His wife died in January 1755 and Fisher placed a tablet to her memory on the north aisle of St. Andrew's church, Clifton:[63]

> In a Vault near this Place is deposited the Body of MARY the Wife of PAUL FISHER, of this Parish, there to rest till it shall be raised in Incorruption, and to be re-united to her immortal Soul in everlasting Life, thro' the Mercy of God, and Merits of Jesus Christ. Oh Grave, where is thy Victory? She died the 8th January 1755. Also the body of Paul Fisher, who departed this life the 4th of December 1762, aged 70.

Paul Fisher's elder brother, James Fisher, apothecary of Somerton, died in 1728 leaving his daughter Rebecca as Fisher's ward.[64] Her considerable fortune was left in trust to him and to Graffin Prankard, another merchant who also came originally from Somerton. In 1745 Rebecca married Paul Fisher's contemporary and long standing-friend, Christopher Willoughby, by then a prosperous Merchant Venturer, chamberlain of the city, and a widower.[65] A son and heir, Christopher, was born to the couple between 1746 and 1748, followed by a younger son, Benjamin, who was later drowned in 1758. *Felix Farley's Bristol Journal* recorded the tragedy in the following laconic manner: 'Thursday a Son of Mr. Willoughby, Chamberlain of the City, had the Misfortune to fall into the Bason in Mr. Fisher's garden at Clifton, and was drown'd before he was discover'd'. This was probably the open air cold bath situated in Paul Fisher's orchard below the house, and may explain why it was subsequently roofed over.

Following the death of two of the original trustees of the Redland chapel, Fisher was called upon by John Cossins (1681/2–1759) of Redland Court to give his services as a trustee for the maintenance and the smooth running of the chapel. Slade Baker,

---

[61] The Revd. A. B. Beaven, *op. cit.*, p. 354. Elizabeth Fisher married Edward Gwatkin at St. Nicholas's on 7 April 1743. He died 30 October 1764. For his will see B.R.O., 00414e, proved 23 November 1764. He was warden of St. Stephen's Ringers in 1745 and 1746. After the death of Fisher's daughter Edward Gwatkin married Miss Ann Lovell, *Felix Farley's Bristol Journal*, 13 October 1753.

[62] B.R.O., 09467 (10). Articles, Marriage of Elizabeth Fisher and Edward Gwatkin, 7 April 1743.

[63] This was destroyed when the church was gutted during the air raid on Sunday, 24 November 1940. The shell of the church was demolished in the 1950s. *Felix Farley's Bristol Journal*, 11 January 1755, gives the date of her death as the 9th; *The Bristol Weekly Intelligencer*, 11 January 1755, gives the 7th; Thomas Goldney III (1695–1768) in his register book gives the 8th; P. K. Stembridge, *The Goldney Family: A Bristol Merchant Dynasty*, B.R.S., XLIX, (1998), p. 157.

[64] Somerset Record Office, DD/BR U/19 N/39, will dated 3 September 1728, proved 25 September 1728.

[65] B.R.O., 09465/5/g, for their marriage settlement.

his friend and business associate, and his son Jeremy, or 'Jeremiah', as Fisher terms him in his will,[66] then a minor, and who was later nominated by Fisher as one of the trustees of his will, were also among the new trustees appointed in August 1757.[67] Fisher was assiduous in the execution of his duties, and attended most general meetings of the trustees until his death in 1762. Fisher's involvement in the affairs of Redland chapel was due to the fact that Slade Baker's wife, Elizabeth, *née* Innys, was the niece of John Cossin's wife, Martha (1689–1762), and her son Jeremy Baker, became the eventual heir of the Redland Court estate.[68]

During his last years Fisher continued to busy himself with the affairs of the Infirmary and the Church. He was one of the commissioners for a new church, St. George, at Kingswood in 1751, and he wrote to Isaac Ware to ask him to pull together Samuel Glascodine's inept plans for the roof and the tower.[69]

His own trade prospered, although in common with most Bristol merchants he endured anxiety during the Seven Years' War, and in December 1759 his partner William Bull, ship owner, was made bankrupt, leaving Fisher and Slade Baker, linen draper, as his chief creditors.[70]

Paul Fisher died at his residence on 4 December 1762, aged 70 years,[71] possibly attended by his friend and executor, John Deverell, surgeon.[72] Fisher drew up his will in 1761. It is both very exact and all-embracing. He makes detailed arrangements for his funeral, including the cost of the clothes of the six poor men who are to be his

[66] Jeremy Baker, member of the Common Council 1771–1798; sheriff 1771–1772; declined the offices of mayor, 1789 and alderman 1792, died 29 April 1798, The Revd. A. B. Beaven, *op. cit.*, p. 276. Jeremy Baker inherited Redland Court and his monument in Redland chapel states that he died 2 May 1798, aged 58, The Revd. H. J. Wilkins, *Redland Chapel and Redland*, (Bristol, 1924), pp. 67, 83, 85. Fisher appointed two other trustees: John Griffin, son of his other partner, William Griffin, and Jeremy Baker's brother-in-law George Daubeny, who was a member of the Common Council between 1769 and 1806; alderman 1787–1806, (St. James); sheriff 1769–1770; mayor 1786–1787; M.P. 1781–1784; master of the Merchant Venturers 1784–1785; governor of the Incorporation of the Poor 1788–1790; president of the Dolphin Society 1775, died 26 May 1806, The Revd. A. B. Beaven, *op. cit.*, p.285.

[67] The Revd. H. J. Wilkins, *op. cit.* p. 35. See also note 27.

[68] According to the deed of consecration of Redland chapel (1790), Elizabeth was the only daughter of Jeremy Innys, (1682/3–1764) of Redland Court, master of the Society of Merchant Venturers 1725–1726 and church warden of St. John the Baptist in 1716. The Revd. A. B. Beaven, *op. cit.*, p. 363; The Revd. H. J. Wilkins, *op. cit.*, pp. 41, 54, 85. H. C. M. Hirst, *History of the Church of St. John the Baptist, Bristol*, (Bristol, 1921), p. 30 contains many inaccuracies about the Innys family, some were subsequently quoted by Dr. Wilkins. Jeremy Baker came into possession of the estate in 1778 and was forced to mortgage it for £3,000. He died heavily in debt. The estate was subsequently sold by order of the Master in Chancery in 1799. J. Charlton, and D. M. Milton, *Redland 791 to 1800*, (Bristol, 1951), pp. 50, 52–57.

[69] B.R.O., The Commissioners' Minutes 04225 (1); 04225 (a-c); A. Gomme, M. Jenner and B. Little, *op. cit.*, p. 149.

[70] W. E. Minchinton, *op. cit.*, pp. 185, 189.

[71] *Felix Farley's Bristol Journal*, 11 December 1762, 5 March 1763.

[72] Fisher appointed four executors, Christopher Willoughby and John Deverell, who proved the will and his former son-in law, Edward Gwatkin and his friend, Michael Atkins, who renounced their executorships. Deverell was one of the trustees of the marriage settlement between Elizabeth Fisher and Edward Gwatkin.

bearers. It was to consist of: 'A compleat suit of broad cloth at not less than 9/- a yard, a Hat Stockings Shoes each a shirt of Irish Linnen not less than fifteen pence a Yard and a Cravat of Muslin at not less than three shillings a yard'.[73]

He asked to be laid 'in the Vault which was made by me at the East End of the Church in Clifton Church Yard and therein laid by my dear wife'.[74] After the funeral '100 twelve-penny loaves are to be distributed to the poor of the parish generally, and £5 each to such Housekeepers not receiving alms of the parish: and the health and numbers of such poor familys I will may be enquired into and considered'.[75] All this was to cost no more than £200. He also ordered that a good fat ox to the value of £10 should be purchased and distributed to the poor of Clifton 'a few days before the Christmas day next after my decease in the like manner I used to do'.

Fisher made many small bequests to friends and servants for mourning and mourning rings. Servants who did not have specific sums bequeathed to them were to have a year's wages in lieu. His family in Somerton and Cork in Ireland were remembered and twenty poor families of the town of Somerton, not receiving alms, were to have £100 divided among them; the trustees were to ensure that the recipients came from the most pious and numerous families in the town, but were also to constantly attend church and to be regular communicants. He left £50 to the poor of the parish of St. Nicholas, Bristol Bridge, under the same conditions,[76] and the new parish church of Kingswood was endowed with a sum of £300 to ensure that there were prayers, additional sermons, and a monthly administration of the sacrament.[77]

He left £2,000, for the Society for the Propagation of the Gospel in Foreign Parts; £500 of this was to establish English Protestant schools in Ireland, £500 for the propagation of the Gospel in America and £1,000 was to be 'applied towards the establishment of an Episcopal see in America, according to the Principles and Usage of the present established Church in England'.[78]

He left £200 to 'that Useful and necessary charity, the Magdalen House' in London established for the treatment and the assistance of reformed prostitutes: he left £200 to the Bristol Infirmary; £500 to the mayor of Bristol in trust for 'a Foundling Hospital' and another £500 for a 'Lying-in-Hospital for Poor Married Women'.[79]

---

[73] T.N.A., PROB 11/884, Paul Fisher's Will, 16 September 1761, codicils 1 December 1761 and 24 November 1762, proved 22 February 1763.

[74] Ibid.

[75] Ibid.

[76] The charitable gift does not appear in the pages of T. J. Manchee, *The Bristol Charities, Being the Report of the Commissioners for Inquiring Concerning Charities in England and Wales*, II, (Bristol 1831), relating to those charities attached to the parish of St. Nicholas, and so must have been intended as a 'one off' distribution and not as monies to be invested.

[77] B.R.O., 09860 (16a), is a receipt from the mayor and commonalty of Bristol for £300 from the will of Paul Fisher, paid to them by Christopher Willoughby and John Deverell, of Mangotsfield, dated 22 July 1769.

[78] T.N.A., Paul Fisher's Will, PROB 11/884. The interest was to be added to the principal and the see was to be founded within 25 years of his death.

[79] Neither of the latter two endowments appears to have been used for the purposes for which they were bequeathed. Fisher stated that if the Foundling Hospital was not built within 20 years of his death the monies were to go to the Foundling Hospital in London. If the Lying-in-Hospital was not erected the money was destined for the Magdalen Hospital in London.

The new parish of Kingswood was endowed with £500 to establish a school 'wherein poor children shall be taught to read at such hours as they can be best spared from Labour or otherwise, and instructed in the Cathechism',[80] and another £1,000 was bequeathed for the purpose of providing marriage portions for poor single young women 'of honest and reputable characters in the city of Bristol', in sums not exceeding £5, to be paid on the day of marriage after procuring a certificate from the minister. Fisher hoped that 'this would encourage marriage among the lower class of people'.[81]

His extensive library was left to the city of Bristol. The range of subjects of his books was wide: history, theology, and many collections of sermons, travel, biography and works of general reference, including Palladio's books on architecture. He left his own books of devotion, his watch and personal ornaments to the younger Christopher Willoughby.

He made careful arrangements for Clifton Hill House. By this time, 1761, he had two housekeepers, to whom he left annuities and the organisation of his funeral.

> It is my Will and I do hereby direct and order my executors that good housekeeping shall be observed and kept up in my present Dwelling House at Clifton and the Garden supported and taken care of after my decease in the same manner they were kept by me while living for the Space of one whole year after my decease.[82]

The bulk of his estate was left to his niece Rebecca and her husband Christopher Willoughby, in trust for their son. Fisher obviously hoped that the 15–year old boy would marry and settle down in Clifton Hill House, although he made provision for the eventuality that Christopher Willoughby the Younger might die without issue before the age of 24 years by appointing three men of the younger generation as additional trustees of his estate together with his executors; Slade Baker's son and son-in-law, George Daubeny, and John Griffin, the son of his other partner, William Griffin. In his will Paul Fisher had stated that it was his 'will desire and intention that my Dwelling house at Clifton shall be at no time void'. In spite of this, neither Christopher moved to Clifton Hill House.[83] The association of Clifton Hill House

---

[80] T.N.A., Paul Fisher's Will, PROB 11/884.

[81] *Ibid.*

[82] *Ibid.*

[83] B.R.O., SMV/6/1/8/8. On 20 April 1763 the Society of Merchant Venturers gave a 99 year lease with one life to John Deverell of land that 'was in the tenure of Daniel Goizin and now Christopher Willoughby, £75 being paid by John Deverell on behalf of Christopher Willoughby the younger, aged 15 years or thereabouts'. On the 1 December 1773 there was an assignment of the lease from Christopher Willoughby to John Vaughan. Deverell was the unsuccessful candidate for the physician's post at the Infirmary in 1741, G. Munro Smith, *op. cit.*, p. 420. Deverell may have resided in Clifton Hill House as a tenant following Fisher's death. He had for some years resided at Hill Close and complained that his view of the country was being ruined by speculative building, but in 1758 he applied for 40–year building leases from the S.M.V., D. Jones, *op. cit.*, pp. 39, 66. The Clifton church wardens' accounts show that he was a vestryman and overseer of the poor in 1763. In 1798 he left the yearly interest of £50 to the poor of the parish to be distributed in bread.

with the tragedy of the drowning of their younger son must have been too painful for Rebecca and Christopher, and they stayed in their house of 43 Prince Street, where Christopher the elder died in 1773.[84]

The younger Christopher (1746/8–1808) disposed of his interest in Clifton Hill House and the estate shortly after his father's death.[85] By 1776 the house was the home of Edward Elton, who was born in 1746, served as warden of the Society of Merchant Venturers in 1770–1771 and died 20 September 1811. His grandfather Jacob Elton (1684–1765) was a younger brother of Sir Abraham Elton 2nd Bart., (1679–1742) of Clevedon Court. Edward's house in Clifton was described as a 'messuage together with fixed grates, venetian blinds', three coach houses, three stables and a garden.[86] Edward's wife died in 1780 leaving him with six children under the age of eight and this may have induced him to move to a more manageable house in Clifton. In the 1780s he neglected his own business interests, which included shipping, coal, sugar, olive oil, copper, banking, the Bristol Crown Fire Office, and his office in George Street, to attend to his wife's extensive business interests, which frequently took him away from Bristol.[87] By 1786 Clifton Hill House was the residence of James Cross, a wealthy distiller, formerly of 7 Temple Cross,[88] who served as church warden of the

[84] B.R.O., 09463 (10), will 18 May 1773, proved 8 November 1773. *Felix Farley's Journal*, 23 June 1773.

[85] B.R.O., SMV/6/1/8/8, lease from Christopher Willoughby of Baldon in the county of Oxford Esquire to John Vaughan for the sum of £3,000; in 1776 John Vaughan let the same to Edward Elton for £3,500 and he in turn let a close called Honey Penn Hill of 7 acres, and one other close 'commonly called or known by the name of the Dean [where the Artillery Ground is now situated] of 5 acres be it more or less' and 'one other little close', White Stile Hill, together with his freehold messuage for £4,200 to James Cross in 1781. This mention of a freehold messuage and the sum involved almost certainly indicates that the property was Clifton Hill House. John Vaughan was master of the Merchant Venturers in 1787–1788, president of the Colston Society in 1787. He died on the 10 September 1795. He appears as living at 1 Clifton Hill in *Sketchley's Bristol Directory 1775*, (Kingsmead Reprints, Bath, 1971), p. 99.

[86] The sale particulars of the house in the *Bristol Gazette*, announcing the auction on 3 June 1830 mention 'a double coach house, six-stall stable, gig house, and harness room'.

[87] M. Elton, *Annals of The Elton Family: Bristol Merchants and Somerset Landowners*, (Stroud, 1994), pp. 78, 92, 100, 105, 236. The Revd. A. B. Beaven, *op. cit.*, pp. 344, 402. Edward Elton subsequently served as church warden of Clifton in 1784–1785; A. J. Green-Armytage, *op. cit.*, p. 77.

[88] *Sketchley's Bristol Directory 1775*, p. 22; in 1793–1794 Cross, Harris and Co. distillers were listed at Temple-backs. B.R.O., SMV/6/1/8/8, lease from the S.M.V. of Dean's Close and Honey Penn Hill Field to James Cross, dated 25 May 1786 with plan. Cross was president of the Grateful Society in 1776 and died 27 June 1791, The Revd. A. B. Beaven, *op. cit.*, p. 337. Mr. Cross appears as resident in Clifton Hill House in *A Plan of Clifton and Hotwells*, (11 August 1787), by M. B. Hall. Cross also leased for three lives a 3–acre 'tenement, gardens, extending from the Garden Turrets unto Jacob's Well', formerly leased to Paul Fisher which was subsequently assigned by Cross's representatives to an attorney and speculative builder, Harry Elderton, who began building Bellevue Terrace on the site, but left the 19 houses unfinished due to the financial crisis in 1793–1794, and his subsequent bankruptcy in 1796, D. Jones, *op. cit.*, p. 75.

parish church in 1790–1791 [89] and the Bristol Directories show a Mrs. Sarah Cross resident there from 1793 until 1821–1822.[90]

Christopher the younger subsequently bought the estate of Marsh Baldon near Abingdon in Oxfordshire.[91] He became a famous agriculturalist. For his work he was granted not only a baronetcy in 1794, but also a D.C.L. from the University of Oxford. He was greatly praised by Arthur Young in his *General View of the Agriculture of Oxfordshire* (1813) for his innovative and successful farming practices. Rebecca, his mother, spent her last years living with him and she is recorded on a monument in Marsh Baldon church as having died in 1799, aged 99. [92]

Paul Fisher was one of the most prominent merchants who contributed to Bristol commercial life of eighteenth century Bristol. Regrettably, like many of his famous contemporaries, he took part in the slave trade, which helped to establish his extensive wealth. However, he was also a philanthropist and keen churchman concerned with the welfare of the poor and of the community. This is clearly demonstrated by his many bequests. He has come down to us as someone of great energy, a man to be relied on, thorough, conscientious and warm-hearted.

His lasting legacy is Clifton Hill House, one of the most important Palladian villas in the South West of England. By the provisions for the house in his will, Fisher was expressing the hope that his house and gardens would be lived in and well looked after following his death.

In many ways, his wishes have been met. In 1909, the House was opened as a 'Women's Hostel' for the newly established University of Bristol, accommodating 15 young ladies. Clifton Hill House is now a popular mixed hall of residence, housing a vibrant community of 225 students. One of the drawing rooms of Fisher's original house is named after him, and a copy of the portrait by Andrea Soldi,[93] of his

[89] A. J. Green-Armytage, *op. cit.*, p. 77. A monument to his memory carved by William Paty is to be found near the south doorway of Westbury-on-Trym parish church. He died 27 June 1791, aged 51 years. The monument also records the death of his widow, Sarah, on 8 April 1821, aged 82. Their daughter, Charlotte (1775–1850), married John Sayce of Cote Lodge, Westbury, who died on 21 July 1834, aged 63.

[90] *Mathews's Bristol Directories* for 1825 and 1829 and the Clifton Lighting and Watching Rate Books (eg. B.R.O., F/CLR/2, f. 58, (1825–1826)), show that Robert Bush the Elder was resident there from 1821–1822, until his death on 4 March 1829, aged 67. He was a widower and a wealthy Bristol merchant. In 1793–1794 he was principal of the firm of Robert Bush and Co., pewterers and brass and copper smiths of 20 High Street and Thomas Street, and later of 30 College Green. Bush was master of the Society of Merchant Venturers in 1823–1824; president of the Dolphin Society 1825; and president of the Gloucestershire Society 1809; The Revd. A. B. Beaven, *op. cit.*, p. 280; the MS. diaries of James Bush (1804/5–1866), No. 1, ff. 1, 37, in possession of Dr. M. J. Crossley Evans. Bush was admitted into the S.M.V. in 1803, P. McGrath, *The Merchant Venturers of Bristol*, (Bristol, 1975), p. 547. There is a monument to his memory in the church of St. Thomas, City.

[91] *Victoria County History of Oxfordshire*, V, pp. 32, 35, 40–41, 46.

[92] Some doubt may be placed on her age. If she was born *c.* 1700, then both her sons were born when she was aged between 46 and 50. James Fisher's will (1728) notes that his daughter, Rebecca, was then still a minor, and consequently she must have been born after 1707.

[93] Andrea Soldi, born in Florence in 1703, died in London in 1771. He began his career by painting British Turkey merchants in the Levant, and it was on their recommendation that he came to England to make his fortune in 1736. By the mid-1740s he was so successful that he was: 'willing to be thought a count or marquis rather than an excellent painter'. The copy of the portrait was commissioned in 1992 from the Bristol artist Marek Gregor, by the present warden, *The University of Bristol Convocation Yearbook*, (1992), p. 16.

Fig. 3. Isaac Ware by Andrea Soldi, [after the copy by Marek Gregor in Clifton House].

architect, Isaac Ware holding the plans of Wrotham Park built in 1754 for Admiral John Byng, hangs on one of the walls, helping to draw the attention of the younger generation to the enduring and visible results of Fisher's business acumen and his refined and elevated tastes in art and architecture. (Fig. 3).

ACKNOWLEDGEMENT
In writing this article I am greatly indebted to Dr. M. J. Crossley Evans for his help, advice and encouragement, as well as for his suggestions and scholarly additions.

V

Thomas Goldney II and Thomas Goldney III: The Creation of the Goldney Estate

P. K. STEMBRIDGE, B.A., M.LITT

GOLDNEY AND the garden in Clifton, Bristol, represent over 300 years of development and change from the late seventeenth to the present early twenty first century. The most significant period is the eighteenth century when the estate was owned by two generations of the Goldney family, father and son, both called Thomas. It is convenient to label Thomas the elder (1664–1731) Thomas II, as his father was also Thomas.[1] He was a second generation member of the Society of Friends, more commonly known as Quakers, as his parents, Thomas I and Mary, had been among the first converts in Bristol in the 1650s. He was a grocer and tradesman, a freeman able to trade from Bristol.[2] Although he suffered some persecution and fines levied on Quakers in the late seventeenth century, he was fairly prosperous. He lived in a house in High Street, near Bristol Bridge, with his wife Martha, and three surviving children and was recorded in a survey in 1696 as a £600 householder.[3] His income came from the grocery trade, from fishing off Newfoundland, shares in small trading vessels, and some house rents. These sources are shown in a surviving account book: Waste Book no. 1; in this Thomas Goldney II entered daily notes relating to his financial affairs before they were 'posted' into the appropriate ledgers.[4]

Two years before the survey, in 1694, he leased one of the few gentlemen's houses outside the busy city, in the healthier and more fashionable area on Clifton hill. Possibly built after the destruction of houses in Clifton during the civil war, the property had belonged to and been occupied by an Irish peer, Lord Folliott, who had given it in 1692 as part of his daughter's marriage settlement. The house was in need of some repairs, for which Goldney was allowed £13 of the £150 consideration for the 99–year lease. There was already a landscaped garden with 'statues, figures & flower pots'.[5] Professor Leech suggests that Goldney, like some other city merchants who

---

[1] The major printed works on the Goldney family are: P. K. Stembridge, *Goldney: A House and a Family*, (Revised ed., Bristol, 1991); P. K. Stembridge, *Thomas Goldney: Man of Property*, (Bristol, 1991); P. K. Stembridge, *Thomas Goldney's Garden: The creation of an eighteenth century garden*, (Bristol, 1996); and P. K. Stembridge, 'The Goldney Family: A Bristol Merchant Dynasty', B.R.S., XLIX, (1998). [Ed.]

[2] B.R.O., 04359/3(b), Burgess Book 1662–1689, f. 489.

[3] E. Ralph and M. Williams, (eds.), 'Inhabitants of Bristol in 1696', B.R.S., XXV, (1968).

[4] University of Bristol Library Special Collections (U.B.L.S.C.), Waste Book no.1 1708–1713, DM 1466/9.

[5] The University of Bristol has a large collection of estate deeds relating to Goldney property; these are now in U.B.L.S.C., DM 1911/3. Unless otherwise stated, all references to deeds are to items in this collection.

had a second property, wanted it as a summer house. His family were certainly in residence when a son, Thomas III, was born 'at my house in Clifton' in July 1696, and the father recorded the births there of six more children in the next 11 years.[6]

In 1705, perhaps using part of a legacy from his father-in-law, Thomas Speed, Goldney bought the house 'wherein said T. Goldney now dwells together with orchard & garden thereto belonging & appurtenances [...] for ever' for £100, so that the estate was secured as the main home for his growing family and household servants. In 1722, however, he was cautiously checking the legality of his title to the property,[7] before he set about building and enlarging the house by adding a considerable wing suited to a gentleman's family. He employed local craftsmen and used some local materials, including Hotwell marble, but also newly fashionable mahogany imported *via* the West Indies and Dutch tiles that he had probably bought on a trip to Holland in 1725.[8]

Goldney's will, first drawn early in 1724, suggests he had removed to one of the houses he owned in Castle Green while the new building was going on.[9] As well as time, the building, decorating and furnishing of the new house required considerable funds and the source of these is of significant interest, for both social and economic historians. Some 15 years earlier, Thomas Goldney II had made investments in two important enterprises. In Bristol a project was being planned in 1708 to fit out two small ships, the *Duke* and the *Dutchess*, funded at considerable outlay by a group of Bristol merchants, including Goldney, ostensibly for a 'trading adventure to the South Seas'. Thomas Goldney's account book recorded payments he made towards the fitting out and supplies for the ships.[10] Captain Woodes Rogers, who was in charge of the expedition, had letters of marque which gave permission to attack the Queen's or the country's enemies, who were at this time the Spanish. Privateering was not ruled out and the chief object was, if possible, to capture one of the large Spanish treasure ships that sailed annually between Manila in the Philippines and Acapulco on the coast of Mexico.

The voyage proved to be remarkable in many ways and merits the description 'Fabulous Voyage' given by the two modern American authors of their book about the adventure.[11] Woodes Rogers and another captain, Edward Cooke, both published accounts of the voyage soon after their return. Other authors of modern books and articles give accounts of the voyage, and also consider surviving documents dealing with its results and finances.[12] After a series of fights in the Atlantic and raids on the west coast of South America, the adventurers did indeed encounter and capture one of the great treasure ships and its contents. Then the final accomplishment was to sail

[6] U.B.L.S.C., Memorandum by Thomas Goldney II, DM 1398/E/22, 1745–1764.

[7] U.B.L.S.C., Letter from lawyer 1722, DM 1911/3/1. Bundle 3.

[8] U.B.L.S.C., 'Journal of a Tour in Europe'. Goldney's account of his travels includes a description and cost of tiles. DM 1466/11.

[9] The National Archives, PROB 11/648/304, (f. 180).

[10] U.B.L.S.C., 'Waste Book no. 1' 1708–1713, DM 1466/9.

[11] F. MacLiesh and M. L. Krieger, *Fabulous Voyage*, (1963).

[12] B. M. H. Rogers, 'Woodes Rogers's Privateering Voyage of 1708–11', *The Mariner's Mirror*, XIX, (1933); B. Little, *Crusoe's Captain: Being the Life of Woodes Rogers, Seaman, Trader, Colonial Governor*, (1960); D. Jones, *Captain Woodes Rogers' Voyage round the World 1708–11*, Bristol Historical Association, 79, (1992).

on round the world, an historic feat in itself. After three years of great physical perils followed by difficult negotiations with the East India Company, the ships eventually reached London in 1711. It took more time and argument to sort out the profits. It has been calculated that Thomas Goldney received something over £6,800 for an outlay of £3,726 for 36 shares. It had been a risky investment; Woodes Rogers himself acknowledged this when he wrote thanking his sponsors 'who had the courage to adventure your Estates on an undertaking which to men less discerning seemed impracticable'.[13]

There were some other interesting consequences of the voyage. A marooned sailor, Alexander Selkirk, rescued from several years of isolation on the island of Juan Fernandez, became the model for Defoe's hero in *Robinson Crusoe*. The South Sea Company was founded, and was able to make use of the valuable collection of Spanish charts of unfamiliar seas that had been brought back.[14] The optimism about the trading possibilities, which Woodes Rogers himself suggested 'may bring vast riches to Great Britain', probably contributed to the South Sea Bubble a few years later.

Some of Goldney's new capital was immediately useful for another venture. Before the house building, Goldney had already invested a large portion of the profits in a very different concern. In 1708 a fellow Quaker, Abraham Darby, had moved from Bristol to Coalbrookdale on the river Severn in Shropshire to set up a new enterprise, smelting iron with coke instead of charcoal to cast hollow iron goods. From Goldney's account book, it is clear that he had been making small and irregular contributions to Darby for the iron works. Eventually, in April 1713 Goldney replaced other backers, becoming the chief sponsor, when he lent £1,700 against Darby's security of $^8/_{16ths}$ of the works.[15]

After Abraham Darby's early death in 1717, instead of continuing the loan as before, Goldney bought six shares for £1,200; two further shares were security for the remaining £500. He also installed his elder son Thomas, nearly 21 and coming to the end of his apprenticeship in Bristol, as cashier at the works. The following year he rewarded his son with two shares, making him a partner; later he bought another share so that the Goldneys had a controlling interest, $^9/_{16ths}$ of the new Dale Company formed in 1718.[16] From 1717, Thomas Goldney II became in effect the managing partner, running the business from Bristol, organising the sale of goods sent down the river by trow to the Bristol docks, and managing the finances.

His son, Thomas III, (1696–1768) worked at Coalbrookdale with an excellent practical manager there, Richard Ford, for the next five years or so. He was closely involved with all aspects of the iron trade from acquiring raw materials to selling the finished products, to dealing with customers by collecting orders and payment. This was experience he was to put to good effect for the rest of his working life. The close connection between the Goldney family and Coalbrookdale was to last very satisfactorily for both sides for another 60 years.

[13] Captain Woodes Rogers, *A Cruising Voyage round the World*, (1712).

[14] D. Jones, *op. cit.*, p. 14.

[15] Wiltshire and Swindon Record Office (W.S.R.O.), 473/156. This small set of papers among a large collection of Goldney family documents had escaped the notice of earlier writers on this period referring to Abraham Darby and Coalbrookdale.

[16] W.S.R.O., 473/156.

When Thomas Goldney II died in June 1731, his shares, which he estimated had increased at least five times in value,[17] were distributed to his daughters, with two going to his younger son Gabriel. Thomas III added his father's role and work to that he had been doing for the firm for more than a dozen years. This now included managing their shares on behalf of his sisters. Although one historian[18] has written that he was 'by no means such an outstanding man as his father had been' this is a considerable underestimate of the younger man's abilities. He may well have been different in character, not a risk taker, but he had years of practical and varied experience of the iron trade, and of its finance, and was a very capable business man. He became the managing partner, respected and consulted by the managers and Darby partners at Coalbrookdale on various aspects and developments of the trade for the next 37 years.

Born in the old house in 1696, now 35, a bachelor, Thomas III inherited the newly extended fashionable house, with most of its contents: furniture, silver, paintings, books,—and the gardens. As a merchant, he concentrated on managing the Coalbrookdale company, mainly from Bristol. For this, he had a salary of £50 a year, and dividend income from his shares. With rents from the family's houses in Castle Green and from invested capital, he was comfortably off for a single man with no family.

Surviving deeds and a few notebooks[19] show what soon became his abiding leisure interest—adding land to the estate, and developing what was already considered a gentleman's garden, described by a visitor in 1735 as 'very fine [...] with Walks, Greens, [evergreens] Water-works, Summer Houses &c'.[20] Since there were no estate agents, land deals were generally made by private negotiation and lawyers. Goldney drew up some documents himself and perhaps did some of his own surveying, with the help of his gardener sent out with a measuring wheel to check distances.[21]

As well as the fortunate survival of the collection of deeds relating to Goldney property, there is the valuable map drawn in 1746 by Jacob de Wilstar for a Survey of the Manor of Clifton commissioned by the Society of Merchant Venturers. The Survey lists the owners of properties and some of the acreage. Although this shows ownership at a specific date in the middle of the period under consideration, it is possible to identify on it most parts of the Goldney estate. (Fig. 1). The Goldney house and rectangular garden acquired by Thomas Goldney II can be seen in the centre of this portion of the map.

Thomas Goldney's first purchase, completed in 1733, was the adjacent house on the east, now Clifton Hill Cottage, with its 1½ acre paddock and 3–acre close of meadow across the road leading down to Jacob's Well. Much legal work was involved, and the purchase price of £500 was probably made up from income from Goldney's salary

[17] Will of Thomas Goldney II, see note 9.

[18] A. Raistrick, *Dynasty of Ironfounders*, (2nd impression, 1970), p. 65, where the death of Thomas Goldney II is incorrectly given as 1738. The book first came out in 1953, and Dr. Arthur Raistrick had not seen the relevant documents in the Goldney collection, and possibly not the family pedigree, as relationships of the various Gabriels and Thomases are confused in his account.

[19] U.B.L.S.C., Goldney collection, DM1398, DM1466.

[20] Friends' House, London, Diary of John Kelsall 1734-1737, (V) Ms. Vol. S 193.

[21] U.B.L.S.C., A measuring wheel is listed in the Inventory of Furniture & Effects, 1768.

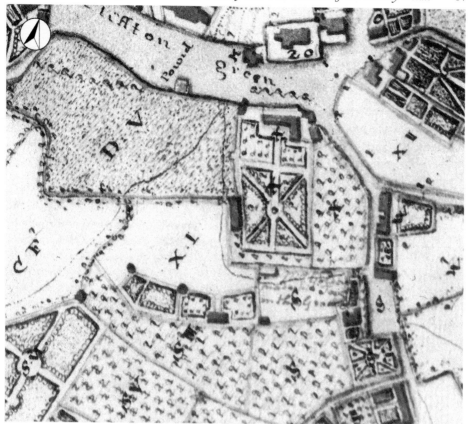

Fig. 1. Section of the map of Clifton 1746 by de Wilstar, [courtesy of the Society of Merchant Venturers, now in the B.R.O.].

X indicates 'Mr Goldney's Freehold: the Mansion house with Courts, Stables, Gardens & Orchards' [3½ acres]

DV Hill Close **XI** the fort garden; to the south are the individual plots, all acquired by Goldney by 1753. The single line to the south and west of Goldney's original garden indicates the intrusive footpath.

S indicates the property owned by Robert Smith in 1746, including the 'Great Messuage, coach house, stables, gardens and orchard', all acquired by Goldney.

and dividends from Coalbrookdale, house rents in Bristol and investment money. Ten years later some of the outlay was recouped by selling the meadow across the road to the Revd. Thomas Taylor, land which has now become part of the University of Bristol's hall of residence, Clifton Hill House. The paddock became part of Goldney's kitchen garden, chiefly for an orchard and for growing wall fruit.

Having extended his eastern boundary, Goldney looked to the south and west of his main garden, to the land owned or leased by his neighbour Robert Smith. Smith was a linen-draper and merchant who some years earlier had acquired a good deal of property and land in Clifton Wood. Between the southern boundary of Goldney's garden and the northern boundary of the larger estate of his merchant neighbour, and separated by some 'void' or unused ground and a footpath, were some small garden plots, rather like allotments, belonging to other Bristol tradesmen. These are not individually identified in the Survey.

It seems that at the time of Goldney's interest in expansion to the south these occupants were not interested in giving up their property. Instead, in July 1737, Robert Smith granted Goldney a plot, about 110 feet by 40–48 feet, to the south-west of Goldney's garden, with permission to make 'a subterraneous passage' to the new plot. The deed mentions that it was for the 'grotto garden', and this is the earliest indication of Goldney's ambitious scheme to construct a grotto at the southern end of his garden with a tunnel leading to a small garden.

The following year, in October and November 1738, he was again negotiating with Smith, for land beyond his western boundary. The first of these agreements, in Goldney's handwriting, signed and sealed by both men and witnessed, concerned a close of some five or six acres, called Hill Close, which adjoined Goldney's garden on the west. It was 'bounded to the north by Clifton Hill or Common' and to the west by 'a lane leading from the said Hill towards Hotwell Road'. Robert Smith had leased the close from the Society of Merchant Venturers in 1715, and was now assigning the remainder of the 99–year term to Goldney for £300. This meadow was not intended to become part of the garden, but was to help maintain the privacy of the heart of his garden. Used occasionally for grazing horses and for the hay crop, it was overlooked by 'the Octogon', [sic] a two-storey summer house in the north-west corner of the garden. With this purchase Goldney extended and protected the western boundary of his garden,[22] but he had to tolerate the continued use of the footpath now passing through his property, which he was not able to close and which was a source of annoyance to him for some years. Later, he sent his gardener out to measure the distances using the footpath or going round by the road, to prove that the latter way was some yards shorter.[23]

The second agreement, also put into effect at the end of January 1739, was for the conveyance from Smith to Goldney of a further piece of land of about 2½ acres to the south of Hill Close together with an enclosed garden, one of the previously mentioned plots, planted as a vineyard. Goldney made a note that this land was for 'the Fort garden'; the 'fortification', perhaps showing Vanbrugh's influence, came to be known as the Bastion and may have been developed from the 'new wall' Goldney had built at the northern boundary of the plot he had bought earlier. The new plot was freehold, but Goldney seems only to have paid five shillings and agreed to pay £11.10.0. rent in quarterly instalments.

In spite of not yet having obtained all the land he needed for his garden plans, Goldney continued fairly rapidly with his grotto-building, so that the main shell was finished and roofed over by 1739. The date and his initials are recorded in a pattern of shells round the western roof light in the grotto. At some time before 1745, Goldney had made a small encroachment on his neighbour's land when he 'sunk a Trench & Digg'd out a Cave, at the Backside of his Grotto';[24] Robert Smith, however, now in 1745 agreed to grant it 'free from all Claim' without any further payment beyond the already agreed rent. This seems generous of Smith but an entry in Goldney's Day

[22] On part of this land the University of Bristol's student hall of residence, Goldney Hall, was built and opened in 1969.

[23] U.B.L.S.C., Memorandum book kept by Thomas Goldney III, DM1398 Box E/22.

[24] This encroachment is shown as a small rectangle at the southern edge of Goldney 's main garden on de Wilstar's map, (Fig. 1).

Book[25] shows that he had lent Smith £120 the previous year. Robert Smith also had more urgent matters on his mind at this time than the possession of a small piece of void land, as he had financial difficulties which would lead to bankruptcy within two years.

In the spring and summer of 1747, the remaining three plots immediately to the south of Goldney's garden were changing hands. Goldney missed one opportunity, but he was successful in acquiring from Smith a large and important piece, about ³/₄ of an acre to the south-east. It adjoined the southern boundary of his kitchen garden and part of his main garden. He was later to extend his terrace and to build the tower for his 'fire engine'—a Newcomen pumping engine—on this ground. At the same time Goldney made a preliminary agreement for the plot tenanted by William Jones adjacent to the vineyard he had bought some 10 years before. Six months later, in January 1748, Jones gave up his life interest and sold his plot, with its summer house built over an underground kitchen, to Goldney for £200.

By September 1747, all the rest of Robert Smith's land and property was in the hands of trustees for sale to pay off his remaining debts. Some of it was heavily mortgaged, including the handsome Clifton Wood House, built in the 1720s, with its extensive grounds, coach house and stables, walled garden and 2½ acre orchard. Thomas Goldney contracted to buy the house and estate in February 1748, but it was the end of September before the deal was settled. Goldney paid £2,200 and took over responsibility for the payment of an annual ground rent to a previous owner. This was Goldney's most expensive purchase and, unlike earlier ones for which he had been able to pay out of income or ready capital, this time he had to borrow. He withdrew some money from his London bank account and borrowed £2,000 from a fellow Bristol merchant, Isaac Elton.[26] For the first year Goldney paid interest at 5%, the legal rate, but this was later reduced to 4% until the whole capital and final half year's interest were repaid in April 1754.[27]

This was the first of several purchases in the area of Clifton Wood which were not intended to form part of Goldney's own estate but were for investment, and so are not all relevant to this article. However, the Clifton Wood estate is of special interest, as some of the grounds remained linked with Goldney's estate for 100 years and the house and its garden for 250 years. Like Goldney house and garden, they also came to be owned in the mid-twentieth century by the University of Bristol and were part of a hall of residence.[28]

Thomas Goldney III was an astute business man and saw the possibilities for letting this house and garden to wealthy visitors to the Hotwells. According to a Bath and Bristol guide for 1755, the spa was 'much frequented by the Gentry for its Waters' and for the social season. One of the aristocratic visitors was Selina, countess of Huntingdon, and for a few years she became Goldney's regular tenant at Clifton Wood, so that he actually referred to the house as 'Lady Huntingdon's'. She was

[25] W.S.R.O., 473/295. In this large ledger Goldney entered daily business transactions, which were later transferred or 'posted' to other appropriate ledgers.

[26] Isaac Elton (1711–1776). M. Elton, *Annals of the Elton Family: Bristol Merchants and Somerset Landowners*, (Stroud, 1994), pp. 76–81 and ff.

[27] W.S.R.O., 473/295.

[28] Clifton Hill House.

certainly in residence in April 1753 when an incident was reported in *Felix Farley's Bristol Journal*: a horse had been stolen from her stable and ridden off towards Gloucester, but the horse 'insisted on stopping at the Bell where it was well-known,' so the rider was suspected and the horse recovered.

Finally, in 1753 Goldney was able to buy the last plot on the southern boundary that he needed to complete the landscaping of his garden. He had missed the opportunity six years earlier and he had to pay £550, twice what the previous buyer had paid. At the time he was receiving good dividends on his Coalbrookdale shares, and considerable profits from a new mining adventure he had embarked on in Flintshire.[29] Throughout the previous 15 years, work had continued on construction and decoration of the garden's centrepiece, the grotto, but this latest purchase led to a new burst of activity in the gardens. Goldney could at last plant trees along his southern boundary, and build the great terrace, which he recorded took two years 'for making it only in the rough'.[30]

The Rotunda, possibly an original summer house above the eastern end of the bastion walk, became a feature at the western end of the terrace; Goldney noted that he finished it 'with the Colonade round it' in 1757. Long since removed, this can now only be seen in a drawing by S. H. Grimm of 1788, though the plinths for the columns remain in the surrounding wall. The Bastion with its long walk, also shown in the drawing, had been in place by 1748. It could have been developed from the 'new wall' by the Fort garden built in the late 1730s; it provided a good lookout from which to watch for ships and trows on the river, the latter vessels bringing iron goods from Coalbrookdale in to the Bristol docks.

The main grotto entrance from the north was completed in 1757 'all save the Freestone Window Frames'; Goldney recorded payments for work on these and for further shell work by 'Mr. Warwell'.[31] There were some major changes carried out in the main garden, although at the time Goldney was much occupied with important expansions connected with the works at Coalbrookdale. The considerable work to create the long rectangular canal was done in 1758–1759. Obviously intended to be on an axis with the Orangery, the two were in place when the duchess of Northumberland visited in the early 1760s, but there seems to be no reference to the moving of the original greenhouse from the western boundary, nor to the building of an elegant new structure. Fortunately, the duchess was so impressed by all she saw that she wrote a long account in her journal.[32]

The date of the arrival of the lion and lioness in their cave in the grotto is a similar mystery; it was ready for them by 1745 but they were not included there in any of the surviving early accounts by visitors, though they are one of the unique features in a grotto. The floor tiles which are also unique in a grotto[33] had been chosen by Goldney

[29] W.S.R.O., 473/295; U.B.L.S.C., Memorandum book, DM 1398/E/22, 1745–1764.

[30] U.B.L.S.C., Memorandum book, DM 1398/E/22, 1745–1764.

[31] W.S.R.O., 473/295.

[32] Duke of Northumberland MS 121/177, Alnwick Castle, Notebook of the duchess of Northumberland (1716 -1776).

[33] Information from the late Professor R. J. G. Savage (1927–1998), emeritus professor of Vertebrate Palaeontology at the University of Bristol, who visited every grotto he could discover in the country. See R. J. G. Savage, 'Goldney Garden Grotto, Clifton, Bristol', reprint, undated, but *c.* 1987, from *Garden History*, 17, No. 1, pp. 1–40.

from tile works near Coalbrookdale. The Bristol craftsman Thomas Paty was paid for fitting and laying them in the early 1760s and the duchess of Northumberland commented on them.

Although Thomas Goldney was in his late sixties he was still adding to and improving the garden features. He noted that he had built a tower in 1764 to house 'my Fire-engine'.[34] This was a small Newcomen engine to raise water from the well to supply the cascade in the grotto. Most of the working parts were supplied in instalments from Coalbrookdale[35] to be erected by local workmen. Various adjustments had to be made and replacements were sent to get it in to working order, probably achieved a year or two before Goldney's death in December 1768.

From his study window on the first floor, looking south, he had been able to survey the progress of most of his achievements in the heart of his garden. Over a period of 35 years he had created a gentleman's garden on a moderate scale, decorated with several statues, water works, and unique features, and kept it well planted and cared for by loyal and hardworking gardeners, all much appreciated by visitors.

In the absence of any other contemporary map than de Wilstar's, George Cully Ashmead's map of 1828 is a useful record showing Goldney's garden with features surviving into the nineteenth century. (Fig. 2) The Octagon was soon to be removed for road widening in the 1830s, the house itself to be altered and enlarged in the late 1850s; housing and road development (Randall Road) took land on the south from the Clifton Wood estate. More such development followed on the west in the twentieth century, leaving only the nucleus to be bought by the University of Bristol in 1956. In 1969, the blocks of a new university hall of residence were built on the remaining part of Hill Close and the 'fort garden', and named Goldney Hall, perpetuating the name of the family who had owned the estate for over 150 years.

CONCLUSION

Some of the achievement and legacy of these two enterprising Bristol merchants can be seen in material survivals: the house and particularly the garden, with its unique features, the principal concern of this article. In Bristol there is also the Quaker Meeting House in Quakers Friars, now a restaurant, after many years as a Registry Office. Thomas III was a member of the committee responsible for the construction of this building, begun in 1747, and the family contributed to the building fund.

Apart from the visible legacy, these two men made considerable contributions to trading history, not only in Bristol but also nationally. In economic history, the sources of finance for industrial development are important. Money the Goldneys earned from the various enterprises was often re-invested in continuing development. Both father and son were involved in the growth of the iron industry throughout the first three quarters of the eighteenth century. During all his working life, Thomas III was closely involved with developments at all the iron works connected with Coalbrookdale, and particularly in the expansion in the 1750s and 1760s. With his share in the founding of the second bank in Bristol in 1752 Thomas III contributed to

[34] U.B.L.S.C., Memorandum book, DM 1398/E22.
[35] W.S.R.O., 473/295.

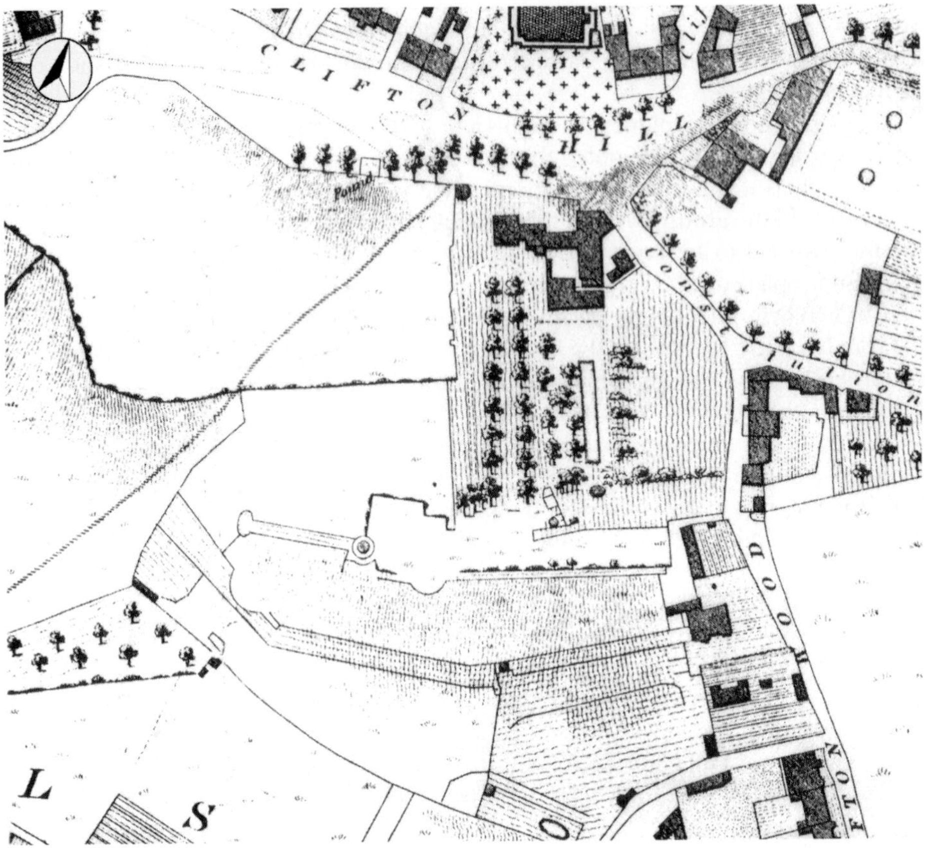

Fig. 2. Section of map of Clifton 1828 by George Cully Ashmead, [Local Studies Library, Bristol Reference Library].

This shows the enlarged house of the 1720s, with the later Orangery and the long Canal to the south. A tree-lined walk leads south to the entrance to the grotto below the great terrace. At the western end of this is the Rotunda, with the Bastion beyond. The tower is not clearly shown; it should be a little to the south-east of the grotto entrance, on the northern side of the terrace. The octagon is clearly shown to the north-east of the house.

To the S. E. near the road is Clifton Wood House, with its stable block to the north.

the development of provincial banking.[36] Without the finance and expertise of these two Goldneys, Abraham Darby's Coalbrookdale would not have been rescued and developed to be considered as the 'Birthplace of the Industrial Revolution' and to become the heart of the Ironbridge Gorge Museum, denoted a World Heritage site in the late twentieth century.

[36] The portrait of Thomas Goldney III which originally hung in the mahogany parlour in Goldney house has recently been acquired (after 40 years in the U.S.A.) by the Bristol Museum and Art Gallery and is intended for display, in the planned Museum of Bristol, to represent eighteenth century merchants. It would be gratifying if the portrait of Thomas Goldney II could be recovered to accompany it.

VI

Christ Church, City, its fabric and Re-building during the eighteenth century

M. J. CROSSLEY EVANS, F.S.A.

During the second half of the eighteenth century four of Bristol's mediaeval churches were demolished and rebuilt: St. Nicholas, Bristol Bridge, (1762–1768); St. Michael and All Angels on the Mount Without, (1775–1777); Christ Church with St. Ewen, Broad Street, (1786–1790) and St. Thomas the Apostle (1790–1793).[1] This essay looks at Christ Church and seeks to place the reasons for the decisions in their historical context.[2] It also looks at the claims of various architectural historians since the 1950s who have sought to attribute the design of the new building solely to William Paty (c. 1755–1800).

THE FABRIC c. 1720–1782

James Millerd illustrated the church and the church clock in his plan of 1673. (Fig. 1). The most complete illustration of the eighteenth century church is to be found in William Barrett's *The History and Antiquities of the City of Bristol*, (Bristol, 1789). This drawing was made *post*-1751–1753, when the stone flaming classical urns were added to the parapet.[3] Certain liberties were taken in the illustration and the church is shown with the high cross in the foreground which had been dismantled and removed 20 years before. (Fig. 2).

The church was believed to date from late Saxon times and a stone purporting to carry the date 1003 or 1004 was stated to have been found in 1765 during work on the spire. Barrett recorded that the church:

> Was no very beautiful structure [...] It was a low building of the model of a quar-
> ter cathedral, the tower being very near the center [*sic*]; from the ground to the bat-
> tlements of the tower about 70 feet high, on the center of which a spire of freestone
> rose about the same height [...] The tower handsome, [...] and had four pinnacles
> of solid freestone about 12 feet high, with copper vanes on them. In the tower was

---

[1] P. Brown, 'Architectural and Interior Changes in Bristol Churches', J. H. Bettey, (ed.), *Historic Churches and Church Life in Bristol*, (Bristol, 2001), pp. 109–133.

[2] St. Leonard was pulled down to lay open Clare Street. It was closed in 1766, and demolition began in 1771. St. Werburgh was taken down in part, and rebuilt in 1760–1762. One of the reasons was to widen Small Street.

[3] It is possible that it may date prior to 1763 when the Gothic parapet was removed by Thomas Paty and replaced with a plain one of dressed ashlar, however considering the liberties taken in the copper plate it is not possible to be certain.

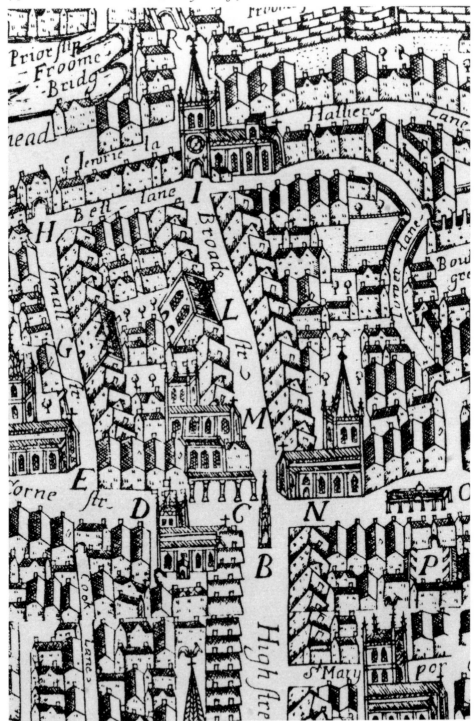

Fig. 1. Millerd's Plan of Bristol 1673 showing the junction of High Street, Corn Street, Broad Street and Wine Street, the High Cross, St. Ewen (M), and Christ Church (N).

Fig. 2. Christ Church, Broad Street. This engraving is taken from the south and shows the shops in Broad Street and Wine Street, *c.* 1760–1780. The four small arched windows on the far right of the church, under the tower, are believed to have been part of a mediaeval priest's house. The entrance into the church from Wine Street can be clearly seen. The picture is a composite, the high cross having been taken down before the flaming urns were erected on the parapet, [William Barrett, *The History and Antiquities of the City of Bristol*, (Bristol, 1789)].

a peal of ten bells, which chimed at the hour of one, six and eleven, with two dial plates to the clock at the west end of the south aile, one facing Corn-Street and the other High-Street. [...] The middle aile in length from the high altar to the west door was 94 feet, from the ground to the cieling [*sic*] of the same aile, 41 feet high, the length of the chancel 18 feet. The north and south ailes each 59 feet long. The body of the church was supported on the north and south side with four arches and five pillars. The width of the church from the north to the south door 54 feet.[4]

The south door was approached by steps from Wine Street.[5] The description of the church possessing four internal arches and five pillars may suggest the existence of priest's houses to the north and south of the chancel and although the former cannot be seen in the surviving drawings of the church, the presence of a priest's house on the south side is suggested in Barrett's drawing by the presence of four small windows under the tower. The churches of All Saints' and St. Mary le Port both contained one, or more, priest's houses.

The vestry on 13 November 1721 expressed the concern they felt about the state of one of the pillars in the southern part of the church and the damage that had been done to it:

> From a room in the dwelling house of Mr. Georg(e) Adams, goldsmith in Wine Street,[6] which room being over part of the said church and being used as a kitchen and as wee suppose considerable quantities of water being thrown down in the said kitchen sinks thro the floor to the pillar of the said church and is the cause of the damage done to the said pillar and may occasion much farther dammage to the pillar aforesaid and even to the tower itself if not timely prevented.[7]

This indicates that at least one priest's house was formerly an integral part of the church, and that following the Reformation it was let out for secular purposes. The church wardens subsequently viewed George Adams's house and we may assume that they took steps to rectify the problems with the water, although the damage had caused permanent problems to the structure, as we shall see later.

The church records also indicate that at least part of a crypt under the church formed a shop which provided the vestry with a useful source of revenue.[8] In 1748 we know that this was being used by a watchmaker.[9] We do not know the point of access to this crypt, or if it had any natural light, but access was likely to have been through Mr. Joseph Smith's shop in Broad Street, which was situated under the portico of the church. Although of a small area we are told that the shop was one of the main meeting places for the clergy in the city.[10] The Braikenridge Collection in the City

[4] W. Barrett, *The History and Antiquities of the City of Bristol*, (Bristol, 1789), pp. 464–466.

[5] B.R.O., P/XCh/HM/5, p. 29, 26 December 1760.

[6] R. H. Leech, 'The Topography of Medieval and Early Modern Bristol: Part 1: Property Holdings in the early Walled Town and Marsh Suburb North of the Avon', B.R.S., XLVIII, (1997), p. 172.

[7] B.R.O., P/XCh/ ChW/4(ix), p. 5.

[8] *Ibid.*, p. 32; '1738, three shillings and two pence for disbursements for the shop under Christ Church being what [*sic*] paid for smiths worke'.

[9] *Ibid.*, p. 48.

[10] Bristol City Library, Reference Section, Braikenridge Collection, XV, pp. 35, 36.

Fig. 3. Christ Church, Broad Street, *c.* 1785. A water colour drawing by Miss Bird (1822). This is a copy of a drawing which was then in possession of William Tyson, bookseller of Clare Street. The original was given to him by Thomas Howell, professor and seller of music of 12 Clare Street, whose father, Robert Howell, a silversmith, cutler and jeweller, had served his apprenticeship with Joseph Smith, the watchmaker, whose shop was situated under the portico of the church. Robert Howell commissioned the original painting before the demolition of the old church, [Bristol City Museum and Art Gallery, Braikenridge Collection Mb 9].

Museum and Art Gallery contains a copy of a drawing made in *c.* 1785 for the father of Thomas Howell, professor of Music in Clare Street, who had served his apprenticeship there.[11] (Fig. 3). The plan in Dr. R. H. Leech's, *The Topography of Medieval and Early Modern Bristol: Part 1: Property Holdings in the early Walled Town and Marsh Suburb North of the Avon*, Bristol Record Society, XLVIII, (1997),[12] gives no indication of the presence of this cellar. It does, however, show the premises known as Nos. 1–8 Wine Street hard against the church's south wall.

Between 1727 and 1729, the parish spent significant sums of money on repairing the church tower; the steeple; re-roofing the building; adding two treble bells, which were cast by Mr. Rudhall of Gloucester; taking down and replacing the dragon weather vane; repairing and beautifying the outside of the church's clock, dial plates and clock house; setting up chimes, and beautifying the church and chancel.[13]

Notwithstanding these improvements it was decided a decade and a half later to undertake further work to the church and in 1745 William Halfpenny (*c.* 1695–1755), the architect of Redland chapel, was asked to draw up plans for re-seating and beautifying the church. On 4 June 1746 it was agreed to undertake the repairs and improvements according to Halfpenny's plans, and to approach the chancellor of the diocese to obtain the necessary authority. Before this could be undertaken the church found itself having to provide an additional churchyard, and the costs of this were sufficiently heavy for the work on the main building to be delayed. In 1750 a faculty was granted for raising the church floor and repairing the church, and Barrett tells us that the work, which finally commenced in 1751, turned out to be very extensive:

> A new strong arch was turned under the belfry by the pulpit with inverted arch under ground. [*sic*]. The old tower-stairs were at the same time converted into solid wall and filled up, to strengthen and support the tower, which was much cracked and a new stair-case was made in the churchyard. Also a strong arch was built under the old one at the east end of the south aile.[14]

This was to repair the damaged pillar noted in 1721. This work, together with the re-gilding and repair of the Renatus Harris organ, took two years and ten months to complete, and the church was not reopened for worship until 18 November 1753. The work was under the supervision of Thomas Paty (1713–1789), who was termed 'architect to the vestry'. He undertook the removal of at least four monuments in the church, two of which we know were subsequently replaced (Brent's and Pye's);[15] flaming urns were added to the Wine Street parapet, and a new altar piece containing the Ten Commandments, the Creed and the Lord's Prayer was added,[16] but still the

---

[11] Bristol City Museum and Art Gallery, A88, George Weare Braikenridge, manuscript catalogue to the topographical collection of Bristol. The copy made by Miss Bird in 1822 was an exact copy of the one held by William Tyson, bookseller of Clare Street.

[12] R. H. Leech, *op.cit.*, p. xxii.

[13] B.R.O., P/XCh/HM/5, pp. 35, 37, 39.

[14] W. Barrett, *op.cit.*, p. 466.

[15] It took two men one day to remove Mr. Rossco's monument, and half a day each to remove Mr. Brent's, Mr. Pye's and Mr. Skinner's.

[16] They may have been re-used in the new church erected between 1786 and 1790 and disposed of by the Revd. E. P. Cole in the 'restoration' of 1881–1883.

work remained incomplete.[17] In March 1755 the vestry noted that the work had 'been unavoidably neglected', and a committee was set up to relieve John Willis of some of his duties to do with the re-building. It was decided that if the money in hand was insufficient then the leases on some of the church lands would be sold for three lives determinable on years in order 'to finish so tedious an undertaking and thereby enable the s[ai]d Mr Willis to extricate himself from the last five years trouble he has had by passing his sundry accts as soon as possible'. In July of the same year it was noted that the 'great arch in ye church is painted a handsome marble, the dials a good stone col[ou]r, the boys to be properly beautify'd, the church door to be painted' and a handsome covering added to the font. In 1756 the bells were repaired and a new branch, or candelabra, made for the middle aisle at a cost of £62[18] and one each was made for the side aisles by William Westborough at a cost of £60 in 1757–1758, which were attached by ornamental irons to the centre of the ceilings. The chancel branch was erected in 1759–1760.[19]

At a meeting of the vestry on 8 July 1761 concern was expressed at the state of the top of the church spire which was found to lean very heavily to one side. The church wardens were asked to employ the West Indian, James Bridges 'the architect', who was then engaged on the restoration and partial re-building of St. Werburgh, Corn Street, the re-building of Bristol Bridge and the erection of Royal Fort House, and Thomas Paty, to survey the spire.[20] Owing to the extensive work being undertaken on the Christ Church upper graveyard James Bridges's report, made ten days later, was not considered by the vestry for over twelve months until 6 October 1762. Bridges reported that he found it:

> Absolutely necessary two fifth[s] of the said spire should be taken down as soon as possible and when rebuilt the ashlar to be yeoled with lead only, also to take down the four leaning pinacles at the four corners and not to rebuild them again and in the place of the decay'd Gothic parapet or breast rail to erect a plain battlement.

One of the church wardens was asked to obtain estimates of the cost of the work.[21] Bridges's bill for making an estimate of the alterations needed to the tower and spire was one guinea. The vestry celebrated their decision to restore the tower with a supper of bread, wine, lobsters, ale and porter.[22] The meeting held nine days later considered three estimates:

James Bridges £188
Thomas Paty £230, and if begun in March 1763 £200
James Paty   £262

It is not known why the vestry declined the estimate of James Bridges, but it may have been due to the fact that he had recently accepted the commission to re-build

---

[17] B.R.O., P/XCh/Ch W/4 (ix), pp. 50, 51, 52, 54a, 55, 56, 58, 61, 62, 63, 66–70.
[18] These were much admired, *Mathews's Bristol Directory, 1793–4*, p. 70 refers to 'a most beautiful set of brass chandeliers'.
[19] B.R.O., P/XCh/HM/5, pp. 89–91, 95, 97, 105, 107, 109, 113.
[20] *Ibid.*, pp. 121, 8 July 1761.
[21] *Ibid.*, pp. 129, 131; P/XCh/ChW/4 (v).
[22] B.R.O., P/XCh/ChW/4 (ix), p. 96.

St. Nicholas, Bristol Bridge and had heavy work commitments. In the end the vestry, decided that the necessary work should begin after their meeting in March 1763.[23] An agreement was drawn up between the vestry and Thomas Paty,[24] 'freestone mason'. In return for £220 he would:

> Take down two fifths of the spire belonging to this parish church and rebuild the same (the dragon and ladder on the inside only excepted) [...] also to take down the Gothic parrapett and four pinnacles at the corners and erect an open battlement as described in a plan now produced.

He was also to: 'lower and finish the open pedestal wherein the market bell [is] hung and repair the Gothick parrapett next Wine Street'. Good freestone was specified for the work, and Thomas Paty was given the old material for his use. The work was to be done between 1 March and 1 October 1763.[25]

The wardens experienced problems with the church pavement, no doubt caused by the honeycombs of vaults under all, or part, of the church. These may well have also adversely affected the structure of the whole building. The church wardens' vouchers contain a bill for the employment of a stone mason and a labourer for two days for 'taking up a stone, opening a vault in the church & covering down ditto with timber as like to fall in at the communion table'.[26] In addition to the hazards caused by uneven pavements constantly being raised and re-laid to allow for burials under them, there was likely to have been the inescapable stench of human corruption which would have pervaded the building and was complained of by the habitual worshippers in many other ecclesiastical buildings of the period, such as Bath abbey.[27]

THE ADVOWSONS, THEIR UNION AND THE RECTORS OF CHRIST CHURCH AND ST. EWEN 1785–1788

The corporation had cast acquisitive eyes upon the church of St. Ewen throughout the seventeenth and eighteenth centuries because they hoped to employ the space for their own uses. They had held the patronage of the living since the 1630s, but as their nominees, once presented and inducted to the living by the bishop or his agent, held the freehold they could not be easily dislodged from their parish. The rector since 1762 had been the Revd. Rumney Penrose Junior,[28] whose stipend was £31.10.0 p.a.[29]

---

[23] B.R.O., P/XCh/HM/5, p. 133.

[24] *Ibid.*, p. 96, the contract was signed on 12 November 1762.

[25] *Ibid.*, pp. 135, 137; The dragon was repaired and re-gilded; *ibid.*, pp. 143, 145, 12 November 1762, P/XCh/Ch/4 (ix), p. 99. Thomas Paty was paid £100 on 7 October 1763 and allowed interest of 5% on the remainder, which was paid on 20 January 1764, P/XCh/HM/5, pp. 149, 150.

[26] *Ibid.*, p. 93, 15 August 1761; P/XCh/Ch/4 (v).

[27] *New Prose Bath Guide for the Year 1778*. The stench was aggravated by poor ventilation.

[28] W. Barrett, *op. cit.*, pp. 419, 478, 481. J. Foster, *Alumni Oxonienses 1715–1886*, III, (Oxford, 1888), p. 1096. Rumney Penrose Senior, son of Thomas of Clifton, gentleman, matriculated Merton College, 17 October 1717, aged 16, B.A., 1721, M.A., 1724, he was successively rector of St. Werburgh 1729–1743 and of St. Michael and All Angels on the Mount Without from 1743 until his death on 19 July 1749. He was buried at Bedminster. He was also vicar of

In 1784 we are told that the mayor and aldermen treated with the rector in an attempt to gain his assent to the union of his living and the parish with that of Christ Church and to take down the church and to enlarge the Council House, 'but the incumbent seems to have refused his assent'.[30] His health had obviously broken down by the autumn of 1784 and the parish was served by curates during his final illness.[31] The timing of his death in the autumn of 1786[32] could not have been more opportune for the corporation.[33]

The Revd. Daniel Debat (*c.* 1724–1785),[34] the rector of Christ Church, had been in dispute with the feoffees of the Christ Church lands when he discovered that he was not being paid what he was entitled to receive as his stipend. He was forced to take the feoffees to court and filed a bill in the court of Chancery in October 1776. The court found in his favour in June 1782 and ruled that he should receive £80 p.a., back-dated, but the delay, financial worries, and anxiety, impaired his health. Barrett tells us that 'it is certain he visibly declined in his health' and that he 'had several fits of ill-ness, and a paralytic stroke, of which he for sometime recovered'.[35] The recovery was short-lived and he died suddenly in April 1785 at his residence at 57 Queen Square.[36] His death left the living, which was in the gift of the corporation, vacant.[37] The living by this time was without a parsonage house and both the next two incumbents were non-residents.[38] The Poet Laureate, Robert Southey (1774–1843), who was born in the

Westbury-on-Trym and the first minister of Redland chapel, The Revd. H. J. Wilkins, *Redland Chapel and Redland*, (Bristol, 1924), pp. 31, 81, 79. Rumney Penrose Junior matriculated at Wadham College, Oxford 26 May 1749, aged 16; B.C.L. St John's 1756 and was a fellow of his college.

[29] W. Barrett, *op. cit.*, p. 478; states that he was allowed £19 by the vestry, received 6s 8d p.a. for a gift sermon and received contributions from his parishioners.

[30] J. Latimer, *The Annals of Bristol in the Eighteenth Century*, (Bristol, 1893), p. 470. B.R.O., The Proceedings of the Common Council 1783–1790, pp. 47–48, 10 July 1784.

[31] B.R.O., P/StE/V/2, f. 97, 101.

[32] B.R.O., The Proceedings of the Common Council 1783–1790, pp. 129, 130.

[33] Bristol City Reference Library, Braikenridge Collection, XV, p. 533, states that he was buried at Bedminster leaving two daughters, Elizabeth, who died unmarried and another who married Mr. Seymour, woollen draper of Messrs. Llewelyn, Seymour and Llewellyn, High Street. Their son George Penrose Seymour was a barrister who inherited the estate of Mr. Edward Turner of Wraxall, Hannah More's beaux. Miss Elizabeth Penrose was paid £6. 12s. 5d by Dr. Ireland in consideration of her father's claims for payment of Queen Anne's Bounty and the Easter offerings of St. Ewen at the time of his death, *ibid.*, p. 56.

[34] J. and J. A. Venn, *Alumni Cantabrigienses*, Part I, II, (Cambridge, 1922), p. 27; pensioner of the Queens' College, Cambridge, 29 January 1741–2, of Middlesex, matriculated 1742, B.A. 1745–6, M.A. 1749, ordained deacon Lincoln 5 June 1748, priest 18 December 1748, will P.C.C. 1785, as of Bristol, clerk.

[35] W. Barrett, *op. cit.*, pp. 467–469.

[36] B.R.O., P/XCh/R/1 (d), he was buried in/under the chancel on 10 April 1785; The Proceedings of the Common Council 1783–1790, pp. 77–78, his death was reported on 28 April 1785.

[37] The corporation obtained the patronage of the living in the reign of Elizabeth I.

[38] Dr. Ireland resided firstly in Brislington (1796), and then at Bourton on the Water, Gloucestershire, and performed his duties by employing stipendiary curates. The Revd. Robert Watson resided in Bedminster; C. R. Hudleston, 'Non-resident clergy of Bristol and Gloucester', *T. B. & G. A S.*, XCVI, (1978), p. 3.

Fig. 4. The entrance to the new Christ Church with St. Ewen, Broad Street, and part of the Old Council House (1823). A watercolour drawing by Hugh O'Neill (1784–1824). This shows the window in the tower which provided the light for the St. Ewen's Vestry Room. In 1835 the Chepstow and Newport Steam Packet Office was removed and the fronts of the three shops in Broad Street belonging to the parish and situated between the church and the White Hart Inn were taken down and set back to a level with the front of the church to allow the widening of Broad Street. See Braikenridge MS., XV, f. 13, situated in the Bristol City Reference Library, College Green, Local Studies' Library, [Bristol City Museum and Art Gallery, Braikenridge Collection M2333].

Fig. 5. Christ Church with St. Ewen from Corn Street (1824). A watercolour by Edward Cashin, showing the site cleared for the new Council House, [Bristol City Museum and Art Gallery, Braikenridge Collection M2341].

parish and baptised in the church, writing in March 1806, says of Mr. Debat that he was 'a humdrum somnificator, who, God rest his soul for it! made my poor mother stay at home Sunday evenings, because she could not keep awake after dinner to hear him'.[39]

The Revd. Dr. Thomas Ireland (1743–1816),[40] and the Revd. Robert Watson (1758–1842)[41] petitioned the common council for the living of Christ Church. Both were subsequently interviewed by members of the council and the former, who was the mayor's chaplain and no doubt felt to be more amenable, appointed to the living in May 1785.[42] Southey's views of him were not, on the whole, favourable, and perhaps also not wholly accurate. Referring to Dr. Ireland he says: 'A worldly-minded man succeeded, and effected, by dint of begging and impudence, a union between the two parishes of Christ Church and St. Ewins[sic], for no other conceivable reason than that he might be rector of both'.[43] This paints a rather different picture than the one depicted on his memorial tablet on the wall of the south aisle: 'as a clergyman he was conscientiously and zealously attached to the doctrine of the discipline of the Church of England. In situations of provincial importance and trust, as a Deputy Lieutenant and a magistrate for the counties of Somerset and Gloucester his conduct was distinguished by equal integrity and talent'.[44]

Following the death of Penrose the corporation employed a curate to serve the parish, but appointed no successor to the living of St. Ewwn. It was later noted that a Mr. Cook was in possession of the living, but as he had not taken out a licence from the bishop he was given an ex-gratia payment of £40 which appears to have disposed of any claims that he might have had to the living.[45] Subsequently on 11 November 1786 the corporation passed a resolution agreeing to unite the living of Christ Church with St. Ewen, if the bishop would agree.[46] On 12 March 1787 the bishop directed the union of the parishes and ordered that in future the vestry of St. Ewen should pay a

[39] The Revd. C. C. Southey, (ed.), *The Life and Correspondence of Robert Southey*, III, (1850), p. 33.

[40] J. A. Venn, *Alumni Cantabrigienses*, Part II, III, (Cambridge, 1947), p. 730 ; son of Thomas Ireland of Hereford, gentleman, matriculated, Brasenose College, Oxford, 11 March 1761, aged 17, B.A., 1764, The Queens' College, Cambridge, M.A. 1767, B. and D.D. 1779, prebendary of Bristol and Wells cathedrals, patron and rector of Bourton on the Water, Gloucestershire.

[41] J. Foster, *Alumni Oxonienses 1715–1886*, IV, (Oxford, 1888), p. 1511, son of George Watson of Yeovil, esquire, Trinity College, Oxford, matriculated 29 November 1779, aged 21, subsequently vicar of Temple, Bristol, and rector of Christ Church with St. Ewen in succession to Dr. Ireland from 1816 until his death on 11 August 1842. For an account of his funeral, the service conducted by the Revds. Henry Rogers and S. E. Day and the burial in the crypt see: Bristol Central Library, Reference Section, Braikenridge Collection XV, p. 97.

[42] B.R.O., The Proceedings of the Common Council 1783–1790, p. 82. Apparently he lost the living by one vote, Bristol Central Library, Reference Section, Braikenridge Collection XV, p. 97.

[43] The Revd. C. C. Southey, (ed.), *op. cit.*, III, (1850), pp. 33–34.

[44] Southey goes on to say: 'However, he was a great man; and it was the custom once a year to catechise the children, and give them, if they answered well, a good plum-cake a-piece in the last day of the examination', The Revd. C. C. Southey, (ed.), *op. cit.*, p. 34.

[45] B.R.O., P/XCh/1/4, p. 17.

[46] B.R.O., The Proceedings of the Common Council 1783–1790, p. 86, 11 November 1786; P/XCh/1/4, p. 16.

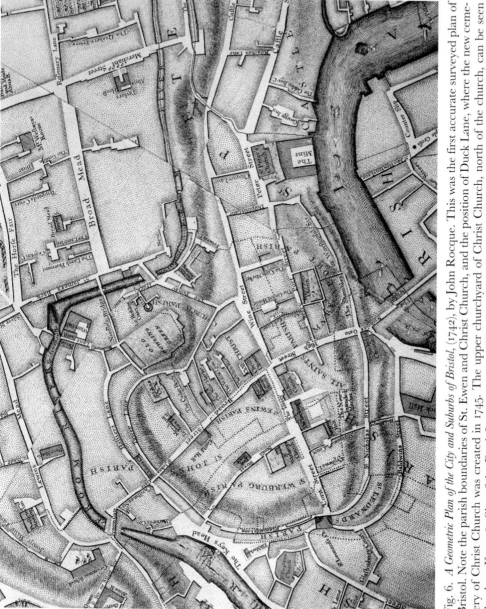

Fig. 6. *A Geometric Plan of the City and Suburbs of Bristol*, (1742), by John Rocque. This was the first accurate surveyed plan of Bristol. Note the parish boundaries of St. Ewen and Christ Church, and the position of Duck Lane, where the new cemetery of Christ Church was created in 1745. The upper churchyard of Christ Church, north of the church, can be seen clearly. Key: ○ Site of the Duck Lane cemetary, [The Special Collections of the University of Bristol].

fifth of the cost of the repairs to Christ Church. Although the parishioners of St. Ewen were opposed to the union their objections were of no account, particularly when weighed against the memorial in favour of the union signed by 145 of the 150 house-holders in the parish of Christ Church.[47] It is likely that the church of St. Ewen was used by the parishioners of Christ Church during the period 1786–1790 whilst their own church was being rebuilt.

The corporation decided to include the demolition of St. Ewen and the union of the benefice with Christ Church in the terms of a private Act of Parliament which was read and agreed in draft form by the council on 28 February 1788.[48] The bill received the Royal Assent on 11 June 1788.[49] We do not know what promises or inducements the corporation could have offered Dr. Ireland to still any moral scruples that he might have had about their decision to acquire the site of St. Ewen's church, which had become their Naboth's vineyard, but by not presenting him to the vacant living prior to the Act they ensured that he had no legal say in the matter, nor do we know what induced the vestry of St. Ewen on 24 March 1788 to vote that Dr. Ireland's stipend as rector should be increased from £31.10.0 to £50 per annum.[50] It is inter-esting to note that notwithstanding the resolution of the vestry in 1788 he was still receiving £31.10.0 in 1796 and that it was not until 1800 that he was paid the increased stipend which was voted to him twelve years earlier.[51]

THE DECISION TO DEMOLISH THE CHRIST CHURCH AND REBUILD THE STRUCTURE 1783–1785

On 5 June 1783 the vestry, having noticed that there were problems with the struc-ture of Christ Church ordered the church wardens to employ:

> The usual workmen to put two iron bars across the middle aisle for the support of the roof of the church, to whitelime the church, to repair the pavement, to fasten some of the ornaments on the outside of the church which are lose.

Three weeks later the workmen appeared before the vestry and reported that 'many of the beams and the rafters were quite rotten and that many parts of the church were in a very dangerous state'. On 19 July Thomas Paty, William Daniel, Richard Hill and George Grist presented a damning report on the state of the building:

> No repairs can be made which would add sufficient strength and permanency to the building without the whole being taken down and rebuilt (the tower and chancel excepted). As the present walls, pillars and arches are so much out of an

[47] B.R.O., P/XCh/1/4, pp. 15–17.
[48] B.R.O., The Proceedings of the Common Council 1783–1790, p. 201. If Dr. Ireland had been presented to the living in 1786 he would have held it by means of personal union with Christ Church before the bishop agreed to the consolidation of the benefices and the Act of Parliament was obtained.
[49] B.R.O., P/XCh/PM/14.
[50] B.R.O., P/StE/V/2, f. 126.
[51] Ibid., ff. 186, 206, 215.

upright that any attempt to make the fabrick strong and durable would be attended by great expense and would be insufficient when done'.

The meeting accepted the report and the vestry decided to treat with their tenants who held estates adjoining the church, for the surrender of their leases.[52] In August it was decided to dismantle the organ. As time progressed the huge costs of the proposed work became apparent. Thomas Paty was present at the vestry meeting on 10 September 1783, when 'its being proposed to have the state of the church surveyed by some architect in conjunction with him, he much approved thereof', and Paty and John Palmer (1738–1817), architect and builder of Bath, were asked to survey the church.[53] A plan was to be made of the church, the streets adjoining, and the shops which it was felt would need to be taken down, together with notes giving the terms of the leases and what the tenants would accept for the surrender of their leases.

John Palmer wrote to the vestry on 30 September 1783:

> The south, west and north walls, together with the inside pillars are in a very ruinous state, and much out of an upright. And that the whole of the church from the tower westward ought to be taken down and rebuilt […] an attempt to repair the said building would amount almost to an impossibility, as the main timbers, wall plates &c., appear to be greatly decay'd in those parts that bears on the walls.

It must have been with heavy heart that the vestry accepted the advice of John Palmer and began to calculate the cost of the work, put at £1,500 and upwards for the surrender of the leases of the properties adjoining the church, and Thomas Paty's estimate for taking down and re-building the church, which was put at £2,000.[54] Having grasped the enormity of the task before them, the church wardens and vestry, with the aid of a solicitor, prepared a memorial which they submitted to the common council on 10 December 1783.[55] This pointed out that if certain buildings in Wine Street and Broad Street adjoining the church were taken down and the ground 'whereon they stood were thrown out for the use of the public the passages into Wine Street and Broad Street wo[ul]d be considerably widened and improved'. The narrowness of the streets at the heart of the city had already caused problems with access, ingress and egress, and this had led to the removal of the High Cross to College Green in 1733.[56] In parts Wine Street was only seventeen feet wide and the opportunity to widen the street and ease congestion was welcome to the corporation.

---

[52] B.R.O., P/XCh/ChW/6, Declaration of Trust (1787–1788) as to monies advanced on the security of rates and assessments by Joseph Lansdown for re-building the church; see P/XCh/F/14–18; and P/XCh/D/72–76, which deals with the re-building of the parts of Wine Street closest to the church, 1789–1792.

[53] John Palmer was noted for his designs for churches in Bath, including St. James (now demolished); St. Swithin, Walcot; and All Saints' chapel. He designed Lansdown Crescent, and as the city architect of Bath from 1792 onwards he was largely responsible for the Pump Room and the Theatre Royal. He was noted for his 'sober good taste and excellent craftsmanship'. W. Ison, *The Georgian Building of Bath from 1700 to 1830*, (Kingsmead Reprints, Bath, 1969), pp. 43–44.

[54] B.R.O., P/XCh/HM/6, unfoliated.

[55] *Ibid.*, 20 and 27 November 1783.

[56] B.R.O., The Proceedings of the Common Council 1783–1790, p. 26; J. Latimer, *op. cit.*, p. 186; M. J. H. Liversidge, *The Bristol High Cross*, Bristol Historical Association, 42, (Bristol, 1978), p. 2.

The common council referred the matter to a sub-committee, but made no reply to the memorialists. The vestry continued to receive no answer to their petition, and the situation becoming critical they waited on the mayor on 7 June 1784. On 9 July they were informed of the corporation's requirements and asked to attend a meeting with the mayor and aldermen later in the day. Following a hasty conference the vestry noted that the cost of re-building the church's tower and steeple, which 'would not otherwise be necessary' would amount to £2,000, that the purchase of the leases of the vestry's properties was likely to amount to a further £1,250 and they would have to fund the cost of obtaining a private Act of Parliament, consequently they asked the corporation for a grant of £3,250.[57]

The vestry were so anxious about the costs involved that they asked Thomas Paty to view the church once more and report if the re-building of the walls on the west and south sides of the church would make the buildings safe.[58] Thomas Paty reported to the vestry on 23 September that 'the building of walls on the inside thereof would not render the same safe, but that the church might be secured by lying in the walls with iron bars and repairing the most defective parts'. The vestry still had not received an answer to their memorial to the corporation dated the previous November or to their resolutions of 9 July. In desperation they resolved that unless they heard from the corporation within a month of their meeting they 'shall be disposed to give effectual assistance towards the re-building'. Paty was requested to begin the emergency repairs to the church that he had reluctantly suggested, and probably believed would ultimately prove ineffectual.[59]

At its meeting on 4 December the vestry noted that the scheme, which was under the consideration of the sub-committee of the common council, had included the proposal to re-build the church without pulling down the tower. The aggregated cost, minus various matters which could be set against the cost left a short fall of £3,445.

The sub-committee recommended on 8 December 1784 to the common council that an offer of £1,500 be made to the vestry if they:

> Will carry up the wall of the said church on the south side the[reo]f and the ffronts of the houses in Wine Street in the possession of Mary Thorn, baker and company and Mary Rossiter on a line to be drawn from the eastward corner of the Council House to the eastward end of the said Rossiters house according to a dotted line laid down on Mr. Patys plan marked with the letter A herewith annexed, and give to the public in Wine Street, all the ground which shall be cut off by such line and on which a part of the said church and sundry shops and the said houses are at present standing.[60]

The vestry accepted the offer with alacrity. They decided to raise the shortfall of the monies that they needed by selling the leases of some of their properties, and to raise by means of a parochial rate and/or the sale of annuities, a further £1,000. The church wardens requested Mr. Paty 'to prepare immediately Plans and Estimates of the Expence of re-building the whole of the Church and Tower'.

[57] B.R.O., P/XCh/HM/6.
[58] *Ibid.*, 28 July 1784.
[59] B.R.O., P/XCh/HM/6.
[60] B.R.O., The Proceedings of the Common Council 1783–1790, pp. 61–62.

On 7 January 1785 Thomas Paty produced a plan for re-building the church, which is believed to be in his own handwriting and is amongst the parochial papers. The vestry whilst broadly supportive of the plan felt that:

> The seats should run in a contrary direction; that the pulpit should be placed against the north-east corner [rather than centrally]; that the middle Aisle should be more than six feet wide; that the organ loft should not run so far out into the body of the church & that there should be Galleries on each side of it.

Paty was instructed to complete his estimates and to value the ground which would be left over once the church was built.

Among the church wardens' vouchers we find a bill of William Paty's dated 1790 for work undertaken for the vestry of Christ Church in October 1784 by his father, who was by then dead.[61]

> To taking a plan of the several dimension[s]
> of the present church and drawing a plan and
> section of the same   £3.03.00
> To drawing one D[itt]o to be built on the old foundation
> together with the elevation against Wine Street   £2.02.00

In November Paty drew a further two plans at a cost of a guinea a piece, to help the members of the corporation with their deliberations, one of which showed the south-west corner rounded off.[62]

In December he was engaged in drawing a further plan for the use of the Society of Merchant Venturers at the cost of a guinea and he was called upon by the vestry to draw up a plan for their own use:

> To one D[itt]o with 2 isles supposing the tower
> and steeple to be taken down with rough sketch
> of church and tower   £2.02.00[63]

The church wardens, William Oldham and Richard Pearson, together with a small committee consisting of the noted blacksmith, Walter Swayne, Henry Pater, and Thomas Willis[64] were asked to prepare a memorial to solicit financial assistance from the Society of Merchant Venturers and the public. The Merchants at their meeting on 26 March 1785 granted £500 towards the re-building of the church.[65] The Merchant Tailors' Company also made a grant of £100 towards the cost of re-building.[66]

[61] B.R.O., P/XCh/HM/1 (c).

[62] C. F. W. Dening, *The Eighteenth-Century Architecture of Bristol*, (Bristol, 1923), p. 133.

[63] B.R.O., P/XCh/HM/1 (c).

[64] Thomas Willis asked to be excused from serving on the committee and was replaced by William Carr.

[65] B.R.O., SMV/2/1/1/11, The Society of Merchant Venturers, H.B., XI, p. 130, 26 March 1785; P. McGrath, *The Merchant Venturers of Bristol*, (Bristol, 1975), p. 207.

[66] J. Latimer, *op. cit.*, pp. 459–460.

Thomas Paty presented his estimates of the cost of building the new church to the vestry on 25 February 1785.

Rough masons work & ffrestone work for the church and tower digging & halling included	£1,750.03.06
Carpenters Work	£432.05.00
Tyling Plaistering and Painting	£162.10.00
Plumbers Work	£216.15.00
Glazing	£77.00.00
Smiths Work	£50.00.00
Crowd	£217.02.00
Gallerys	£80.00.00
Ringing Lofts and hanging Bells	£123.06.00
Altering and making good the pews	£100.00.00
Fencing the church in during the time of Building	£30.00.00
	£3,239.01.06

This estimate made no allowance for the cost of a new altar, or altar piece, and it is possible that it was envisaged re-using the painted boards with the Creed, the Ten Commandments and the Lord's Prayer from the existing altar piece. No account was made for the cost of the communion rail; the pulpit or for re-erecting the organ; nor was there an estimate of the cost of acquiring the leases of the shops and tenements adjoining the church in the possession of the vestry, or the estimated costs of obtaining a private Act of Parliament to enable the work to progress.[67]

At the meeting of the vestry held on 6 May 1785 it was resolved to present a draft bill to the House of Commons with a view to have it passed into law before the end of the Parliamentary Session. It appears that the procurement of the Act was delayed and that it had not been passed by 15 September 1785.[68] The Act, *25 George III cap. III*, shortly afterwards received the Royal Assent and passed into Law.

THE RE-BUILDING 1786–1790

Between March and August 1786 the Patys prepared further plans, details of which have survived among the church warden's vouchers.[69]

---

[67] B.R.O., P/XCh/HM/6.

[68] B.R.O., The Proceedings of the Common Council 1783–1790, p. 92.

[69] Transcribed in: C. F. W. Dening, *op. cit.*, p. 133.

[70] The trustees were: Dr. Ireland; John Townsend (1730–1800), 'an eminent surgeon of this city', attached to the Infirmary 1754–1781, of 52 Broad Street; Samuel Townsend (1736–1801) a drysalter, in partnership with Thomas Tyndall, brother of the preceding, both buried in Christ Church; Daniel Burgess (church warden in 1789), attorney at law, and notary public, Clerk of Arraigns of 50 Wine Street, (born 1756/7, died 10 April 1791, buried in Christ Church and commemorated by a memorial brass plate in the north aisle); George Thorne; Thomas

1786 March

To Drawing 2 Setts of plans for the Workmen to estimate from, [*sic*] in each were as follows:

The south, north, and west Elevations- The Section of the west-end, -The Section of the Tower and middle Isle, the plan of the Church -The plan of the different orders of the Tower with the sett off, and projections -a Drawing of the Capitals for the Columns in the inside with the whole of the Entablature to a large Scale. -The different mouldings of the ceiling to their full size. Making a rough model of ciel-ing [*sic*] and drawing the ornaments in the same.

April.

To Drawing two plans, describing the manner in which the pews were to be fixed in the new Church, with written Instructions for taking down the old pewing. Drawing up Instructions for the Mason's work, Carpenter's do. Plumber's do. Tyler's plasterers and Painter's, Glazier's, and Smithswork with Copies of the same, and attendance on the making the model of the Roof
Expence of the model and various attendances etc.   ..£33. 9. 0

July

To Making a design and drawing of another Tower...   ..£ 2. 2. 0

Aug.

To taking a Correct plan of the Ground and marking thereon the most elegible part for the intended Church...   .. £1. 1. 0

To Drawing a Section of the south side, with the Windows elevated, together with a Section of the houses on the south side, describing what part of the Ground would be lost in the different Floors, to give light to the Windows of the Church on that side, To Drawing a Section of the east end, and Elevation of an Alter-piece [*sic*], with various attendances, Writing different Instructions for the several Trades occasioned by the alterations.   .. £5. 5. 0

1788 Feb.

To making a finished Drawing of the Tower together with a design for a spire.
          ..£3 . 3. 0

Once the Act was passed the vestry ceased to be involved in the work and their place was taken by men named in the Act as trustees to oversee the demolition and re-building the church.[70] They would have determined the date when the church would close for services and when the demolition of the old structure would begin.

Culliford (1749–1800), linen draper of 21 Wine Street, who is buried in the crypt; Thomas Sheppard (buried in Christ Church, 27 December 1792), and Richard Jones, probably wine merchant of 26 Corn Street.

The delay allowed the fine organ built by Renatus Harris[71] between 1708 and 1709, and the eight bells cast by Abraham Rudhall of Gloucester in 1716,[72] to be dismantled and stored for safety. Other fixtures salvaged from the condemned church included the gilded dragon weather vane dating from 1727; the old parish chest dating from the fourteenth century; the benefaction boards, which contained the names of those parishioners who had left money for charitable purposes; the pews;[73] the mayoral sword rest, dating from the reign of Charles II, and the chandeliers.[74] The trustees were keen to re-use whatever they could in order to keep their expenses to a minimum. The clock with its two dial plates on the west end of the south aisle facing Corn Street and Wine Street and its two quarter jacks were dismantled[75] and subsequently disappeared,[76] the latter not returning to the church until the time of Canon M. A. R. T. Cole in 1913. The monument to the Revd. Richard Standfast (1603–1681), one of Charles I's chaplains, a prebendary of Bristol cathedral, who was ejected from the living of Christ Church during the Civil War, was saved, minus its white surround, marble hour glass and death's head.[77] The monument to the Revd. Charles Brent (1666/8–1729)[78] was moved to Wraxall,[79] but the mediaeval monu-

---

[71] For a good account of the work of Renatus Harris see: D. Gwynn, *The Renatus Harris Organ at St. Botolph Aldgate*, (Worksop, 2007).

[72] One of these carries the name of Charles Brent the rector. Two treble bells were cast by Abraham Rudhall in 1727 and added to the previous eight. They were probably re-cast in 1789.

[73] The church wardens' vouchers contains the following, dated 1791, 'To Edward Stocks a/c for taking down, lodging and re-fixing the seats £182'.

[74] B.R.O., P/XCh/1/16; P/XCh/ChW/4 (viii); Thomas Sheppard was paid (1790–1792) for cleaning and lacquering 1, 36 light chandelier; 3, 24 light chandeliers; and 6 double pulpit lights. These together with the lights at the organ, the church wardens' seats, the reading desk, the orchestra and the gallery, and the central ceiling rods to which the main chandeliers were attached must have ensured that the church was well illuminated. The vestry agreed on 2 September 1820 that they should be sold to the 'new church in Bathwick', St. Mary, Raby Place, (erected between 1814 and 1820), for one hundred guineas. Their decision was made in anticipation of the installation of gas lighting into the church. It is not certain that the sale went ahead.

[75] The Bristol City Museum and Art Gallery, Braikenridge MS Catalogue, II, states that when the clock was dismantled it was found to be ruinous. Mr. Oldham, a Wine Street haberdasher, purchased the clock and the quarter boys. They subsequently appeared in the procession to mark the coronation of George IV in 1821. It is claimed that the vestry put the money so raised towards the purchase of some communion plate for the new church, but no record of this fact has been found in Canon Cole's exhaustive printed account of the church's plate.

[76] Southey's father, a linen draper, was keen for it to be restored, and loved the quarter-boys, but he could not prevail upon his fellow parishioners to help find the necessary finances, 'the Wine Streeters had no taste for the arts, and no feeling for old friends and God knows what became of the poor fellows', The Revd. C. C. Southey, (ed.), *op. cit.*, III, (1850), p. 34.

[77] W. Barrett, *op. cit*, pp. 469–470.

[78] J. Foster, *Alumni Oxonienses*, Part I, I, (Oxford, 1891), p.174; he was of Balliol College, Oxford, matriculated 22 November 1682, aged 14; B.A. 1687; M.A., 1 March 1691/2; rector of St. Werburgh, Bristol, 1691, or according to Barrett 1694–1729; prebendary of St. David's cathedral 1707; canon residentiary 1715–1716; died Bristol 10 June 1729. There was formerly an inscription to him in St. Werburgh. He was the author of *The Nature and Guilt of Lying*, (1711), dedicated to Edward Colston.

[79] Notes by Canon M. A. R. T. Cole, in possession of the author.

mental brasses and the other more recent monuments were removed and not subsequently returned to the new structure.[80] An exception was the palimpsest brass to Thomas Farmer (1541–1624), mayor and alderman, who died in November 1624. The brass was engraved on both sides and according to Canon Cole was discovered among a quantity of rubbish in the coal hole of the old vestry in 1836 and was then re-placed by the vestry door.[81] It was in the church as late as 1955 and has subsequently disappeared.[82] The old altar piece was purchased by a Mr. Markham, who presented it to the church at Yatton, in Somerset.[83]

The trustees were engaged in dealing with the urgent need to demolish and rebuild the church's properties in Broad Street and Wine Street. The vestry clerk, Jeremiah Osborne, a solicitor, also borrowed money to enable the trustees to commence the work and among the church wardens' vouchers there is a bill showing that £1,000 was borrowed on mortgage from Francis Weaver. The principal and the interest, amounting to £72.13.6, was not finally repaid until 1 October 1792. Thomas Paty and Sons drew elevations of the properties to be re-erected, while the trustees negotiated the conveyances of shops and premises from their tenants which they subsequently re-mortgaged between 21 September 1785 and September 1788.[84] Much of this work was done very swiftly and the articles of agreement between the trustees and Thomas Lewis, apothecary dated 1 June 1786 specified that in return for £84 he would rebuild his messuage in Wine Street within six months. The front of the property was to be in a straight line with the adjoining properties and in agreement with the elevation drawn by Thomas Paty and Sons. The articles carry the endorsement that the contract had been satisfactorily completed, together with the date, 8 December 1786.[85]

The parish officers advertised on 20 May 1786 for contractors to submit quotations before the 30 June for the cost of the demolition of the old building and the erection of the new structure.[86] Barrett states that the demolition of the church took place in 1786.[87] We can be certain that the removal of the old structure was swiftly accomplished between July and September, because the crowd, or crypt, and the

---

[80] The Revd. J. Evans, *The History of Bristol, Civil and Ecclesiastical*, II, (Bristol, 1816), p. 140, 'its monuments have perished'. Bristol City Library, Reference Section, Braikenridge Collection, XV, pp. 134, 136, 137, notes that one of these was the monument to the well-respected Dr. Samuel Pye (1685–1759), erected in 1760. George Braikenridge toured the church with his friend the rector, the Revd. Robert Watson, in June 1821, but concluded that the monuments recorded by Barrett as being in the old church but not found in the new structure, had perished at the time of the demolition.

[81] Canon Cole extracted this information from the Braikenridge MS, in the Central Library, Vol. XV, on 2 December 1922. Thomas Farmer gave lands to the parish, the income to be used to supply the poor in bread or coals.

[82] The Revd. C. M. J. Turner, *Christ Church or Holy Trinity*, (Bristol, 1955), p. 23; S. G. Tovey, *Cursory Observations on the Churches of Bristol, by an Occasional Visitor*, (2nd ed., Bristol, 1843), p. 106.

[83] C. F. W. Dening, *op. cit.*, p. 132. Bristol City Library, Reference Collection, Braikenridge Collection, XV, p. 35; The Revd. J. Collinson, *The History and Antiquities of the County of Somerset*, III, (Bath, 1791), p. 619. The altar piece blocked most of the chancel window.

[84] B.R.O., P/XCh/ChW/4 (ix), nos. 138, 141, 142, 144; P/XCh/F/10, 15, 16, 17, 18.

[85] R. H. Leech, *op. cit.*, pp. 48–50, 170–174.

[86] W. Ison, *The Georgian Buildings of Bristol*, (Kingsmead Press, Bath, 1978), p. 25.

[87] W. Barrett, *op. cit.*, p. 466.

foundations of the new structure were sufficiently far advanced for the foundation stone of the new building to be laid on Monday, 30 October 1786.[88] The young Robert Southey was present in the middle of a crowd to celebrate the birth of the new church and placed money under the commemorative stone.[89] 'Several members of the corporation attended on the occasion, together with the Gentlemen of the Vestry, the principal inhabitants of the parish and a vast number of spectators, Mr. Alderman Baugh[90] laid the foundation stone in absence of the Mayor, [George Daubeny][91] who was indisposed [...] Dr. Ireland gave a short commendatory prayer and concluded the ceremony. The Vestry dined together at the White Lion Inn and were honour'd with the company of Mr. Sheriff Daniel[92] who generously and unsolicited gave Ten Guineas towards building the Church'. The foundation stone carries the names of the rector, Robert Southey[93] and William Carr, the church wardens, the vestrymen, and 'Thomas Paty & Sons, Architects'.[94]

Charles Viner of Bath acted as the contractor for the work. He built the church and the tower and was responsible for taking down the cemetery, clearing the vaults, disposing of the dead and re-building the cemetery. He charged £2,394.11.6½ and was paid in instalments for the work between 12 January 1787 and October 1792.[95] Relations between the trustees and Viner were strained and we find the vestry clerk, Jeremiah Osborne, being sent to Bath in an attempt to resolve a dispute which had arisen.[96] William Paty acted as a clerk of works and from about this time he authorises the bills of the tradesmen, which were submitted to him before he passed them in turn on to the trustees for settlement.

The land adjoining the church in Wine Street which was not required for building or road improvement was sold at auction on 2 March 1789 and excited considerable interest from speculators and investors at the height of the building boom. The four lots were of a whole length of 101 feet and very shallow in depth. A perpetual ground rent for the land of £2.2.0 'per running foot' was obtained for the whole.[97]

---

[88] *Felix Farley's Bristol Journal*, 4 November 1786.

[89] The Revd. C. C. Southey, (ed.), *op. cit.*, pp. 34–35.

[90] The Revd. A. B. Beaven, *Bristol Lists: Municipal and Miscellaneous*, (Bristol, 1899), p. 277; Isaac Baugh, common councilman 1748–1786; alderman 1768–1786 (Redcliffe 1768–1771, St. Ewen 1771–1781, St. James 1781–1786); sheriff 1748–1749 and 1751–1752; mayor 1765–1766; master of the Merchant Venturers 1759–1760; died 25 December 1786.

[91] The Revd. A. B. Beaven, *op. cit.*, p. 285. George Daubeny, common councilman 1769–1806; alderman 1787–1806; sheriff 1769–70; mayor 1786–1787; M.P. 1781–1784; governor of the Incorporation of the Poor 1788–1790; master of the Merchant Venturers 1784–1785, died 26 May 1806.

[92] Thomas Daniel died 6 April 1854, variously said to have been aged 91 and 93; common councilman 1785–1798; alderman 1798–1835; sheriff 1786–1787; mayor 1797–1798; J.P. 1841; master of the Merchant Venturers 1805–1806; the Revd. A. B. Beaven, *op. cit.*, pp. 68, 285; partner in the firm of Ames, Cave and Company, bankers; sugar merchant, son of Thomas Daniel of Barbados, C. H. Cave, *A History of Banking in Bristol from 1750 to 1899*, (privately printed, Bristol, 1899), p. 113.

[93] Father of the future Poet Laureate.

[94] The Revd. C. M. J. Turner, *op. cit.*, pp. 28–29.

[95] B.R.O., P/XCh/ChW/4 (viii).

[96] He was paid for his time and services and the hire of a horse, 21 October 1788.

[97] J. Latimer, *op. cit.*, p. 485.

The financial burden of the re-building of the church continued to be felt long after it had been re-opened for worship and the celebratory ball in the White Lion had been held.[98] The vestry had still not received £500 of the £1,500 promised by the corporation in 1801. In October 1801 they decided upon legal action against the corporation. It was not until 10 August 1803 that a repayment schedule was agreed which meant that the final instalment would not be received until Christmas 1805. The clerk was instructed to tell the corporation that the vestry required the payment of interest on each instalment of the money. The final entry relating to the re-building in the minutes of the vestry records that on 2 June 1806 the remaining monies due from the parish in the form of loans for the re-building would be discharged 'on or before 21 December next with interest'.[99]

The new church structure and its fixtures and fittings will not be discussed in detail here. Almost everything of any importance on the subject has already been treated by C. F. W. Dening in his masterly work, *The Eighteenth-Century Architecture of Bristol*, (Bristol, 1923).[100] Dening, a close friend of the rector, Canon M. A. R. T. Cole, had access to the church wardens' vouchers and the other surviving contemporary documents and he made full use of them. His work has been subsequently augmented by Walter Ison's, *The Georgian Buildings of Bristol*, (1952),[101] and *Bristol: an Architectural History*, by A. Gomme, M. Jenner, and B. Little (1979). The former claimed that Thomas Paty was responsible for re-building Christ Church, but attributes the design to his son William.[102] William Paty, with his brother John, had been working with their father since *c.* 1777. Gomme, Jenner and Little state: 'the building accounts show that it was designed by William'.[103]

This statement is based on a misconception, firstly because Thomas Paty was the architect to the vestry and had been for thirty years or more at the time the plans were drawn up; secondly the only plan of the projected new church known to survive is in his handwriting; thirdly Thomas Paty is mentioned, together with his Christian name, at one of the vestry meetings (26 June 1783) and fourthly, the reason why the bills which were generated by the firm from 1790 onwards carry William Paty's name is that Thomas died the previous year. The building is actually a joint effort, a point made by Dening, who attributed the survey of the old church and the plans of the new, to the Patys, plural. The other references to Paty in the vestry minutes all call him 'Mr. Paty'. In the convention of the period this would have signified the father. The sons during their father's life time would have had their Christian names inserted before the surname. William Paty is not mentioned by name in the minutes and the designation of the firm as 'Thomas Paty and Son' does not aid transparency.

---

[98] C. F. W. Dening, *op. cit.*, p. 132.

[99] B.R.O., P/XCh/HM/6, Vestry Minutes 1783–1824; 28 October 1801; 2 November 1802; 5 May and 10 August 1803. J. Latimer, *The Annals of Bristol in the Nineteenth Century*, (Bristol, 1887), pp. 8–9. The corporation claimed that Broad Street had not been widened as much as had been previously agreed and in places it was not 23 feet wide.

[100] C. F. W. Dening, *op. cit.*, pp. 132–138.

[101] W. Ison, *op. cit.*, pp. 72–76. The Revd. Maurice Turner was influenced in his attribution of the architecture to William Paty by reading Ison, (personal information).

[102] *Ibid.*, pp. 25, 72–73.

[103] A. Gomme, M. Jenner, and B. Little, *Bristol: an Architectural History*, (1979), p. 184.

Subsequent authorities have been content to remove any mention of Thomas Paty from involvement with the new church.

Professor Timothy Mowl in his book, *To Build the Second City: Architects and Craftsmen in Georgian Bristol*, (Bristol, 1991), speculates that Thomas Tyndall 'seems to have been its [the church's] inspiration. Christ Church in the city centre was his parish church and he was, by his wealth, a highly influential parishioner'.[104] There is no contemporary evidence of Tyndall having anything to do with the re-building of the church. Whilst parts of his business interests were situated in the parish, he was a non-resident and as such he was not eligible to hold parochial office. He was certainly not a parishioner from at least 1760, as his home, the Royal Fort House, was situated in the parish of St. Michael and All Angels on the Mount Without, and when he sold the house he went to live in Berkeley Square which was in the parish as St. Augustine the Less. Historically his family had a vault in the old church and his family continued to be buried there. Thomas Tyndall subsequently acquired a family vault in the new church, and this, together with the possible addition of a subscription to the cost of re-building seems to have been the extent of his involvement in the re-building of the new church. Professor Mowl also accepts William Paty as the sole architect.[105] The most recent architectural historians to deal with the building are Mr. Gordon Priest, *The Paty Family: Makers of Eighteenth-Century Bristol*, (Bristol, 2003)[106] and Dr. Andrew Foyle in his *Pevsner Architectural Guide to Bristol*, (2004).[107] Both have continued the practice of removing any mention of Thomas Paty as playing a part in the design of the church, a view which should be now revised.

The date of the completion of the new church is variously put at 1790 and 1791 and Dening also notes that the re-opening was marked by a grand ball in the White Lion, without giving any date.[108] The Braikenridge papers in the City Library state that the ball was for wives and daughters of parishioners.[109]

William Barrett writing in 1788–1789 stated that the new church 'will soon exhibit a beautiful structure in the center [*sic*] of the city, and afford good accommodation for the parishioners resorting to it. The new spire is beautiful, and the whole building much admired, and is a great ornament to the center of the city, as you go up High-street'.[110] Those alive at the time of the construction of the church were enthusiastic

---

[104] T. Mowl, *To Build the Second City: Architects and Craftsmen in Georgian Bristol*, (Bristol, 1991), p. 73.

[105] *Ibid.*, pp. 98–99.

[106] G. Priest, *The Paty Family: Makers of Eighteenth-Century Bristol*, (Bristol, 2003), pp. 106–112, reviewed by H. G. M. Leighton and M. J. Crossley Evans, *T. B. & G. A. S.*, 123, (2006), pp. 194–197.

[107] A. Foyle, *Pevsner Architectural Guide to Bristol*, (2004), p. 94.

[108] C. F. W. Dening, *op. cit.*, p. 132.

[109] Bristol City Library, Reference Section, Braikenridge Collection XV, p. 75. Mr. Burgess and Mr. Thorne are called the 'active promoters and chief planners'. Both lived in Wine Street, almost opposite the church. We are also told on p. 71 that almost all the Wine Street traders kept horses in those days which were stabled in Duck Lane and that on Sundays they rode across Durdham Down to the Ostrich, which was a famous inn formerly on the site of Down House, the home of Alderman Sir William Howell Davies M.P. It served subsequently as an annexe of Wills Hall, one of the University of Bristol's halls of residence, *ibid.*, p. 75, *The Bristol Times*, 31 August 1850.

[110] W. Barrett, *op. cit.*, p. 466.

about the building. The Revd. John Evans, writing in 1816 stated that: 'The present Christ church is certainly a neat, and is frequently denominated an elegant fabric. Its monuments are few but those few are in the best taste, either being tablets, or in the form of cenotaphs. In these simple forms monuments best harmonize with the surrounding objects, and may constitute elegant appendages to the principal structure'.[111] Views changed over time, and S. G. Tovey, an enthusiastic champion of the Gothic style, writing in 1843 was rather dismissive of the structure:

> Time, that beautifies ere it destroys, has not yet removed from this Church that appearance of freshness, which indicates the lateness of its erection, nor shed upon it that mellow tranquillity which marks the repose of years; even were it so [...] the peculiar character of its architecture would still fail in commanding that respect and hallowed reverence, with which we are accustomed to gaze upon temples belonging unto antiquity [...] The present [church] built in what is termed the light and graceful character of the Grecian style, though simple and chaste, is at the same time little and unimposing, and in itself would not be an object of sufficient interest to claim a notice.[112]

He was, however, forced to concede that the interior was 'tastefully decorated in accordance with the modern style in which it is designed. There is no mixture of styles to offend the eye, but every portion is finished with a harmonious effect of the whole'.[113] The 'Bristol Churchgoer', Joseph Leech, called it a 'handsome and convenient classical structure' and although he was a man of Gothic tastes, he went on to admit that 'the interior is imposing'.[114]

It is a great pity that the Revd. Edward Pattinson Cole (1844–1926), the rector between 1880 and 1896[115] and 1896 and 1903, did not feel the same sentiments before he embarked upon the disastrous restoration of the church, which was undertaken by a second or third-rate architect in a sub-Florentine manner between 1881 and 1883. This destroyed much of the 'elegant fabric' that he found, and caused his son to spend the period between the wars trying to reverse its baneful effects. This was managed with some success with the help of his friend, the architect, C. F. W. Dening, but their efforts form no part of this story.

[111] The Revd. J. Evans, *op. cit.*, II, (Bristol, 1816), pp. 139–140.

[112] S. G. Tovey, *op. cit.*, pp. 97–98.

[113] *Ibid.*, p. 103.

[114] J. Leech, *The Church Goer: Being a Series of Sunday Visits to the Various Churches of Bristol*, (2nd ed., Bristol, 1845), p. 167.

[115] Canon Cole senior's health was not robust. In 1896 illness caused him to resign the living in favour of an old friend, who subsequently died before he could be inducted into the living. The bishop of Gloucester and Bristol, Dr. Ellicott, encouraged Canon Cole to resume charge of his cure of souls.

VII

Music at the Bristol chapel of the Countess of Huntingdon's Connexion

A. J. PARKER, F.S.A

OF THE sources for English church music listed by Nicholas Temperley in *The Music of the English Parish Church*[1] and detailed (for the eighteenth and early nineteenth centuries) in *The Hymn Tune Index*,[2] only one is cited as surviving uniquely in Bristol Central Library. This is a small, 124–page music book, entitled: *SACRED MELODY, being A collection of Psalm and Hymn tunes, IN THREE PARTS. As made use of at the Right Hon, the Countess of Huntingdon's Chapel and other Places of Worship in BRISTOL, but particularly suited to the last edition of her Ladyship's hymns to their various measures, in Two parts.*[3] *Sacred Melody* was published at Bristol by the author, Benjamin Belcher, clerk of the chapel, apparently between 1786 and 1788. Some of the tunes bear local-sounding names, such as 'Broad Street' or 'Keynsham', and a few at least appear to be unique, i.e. 'Bristolian'. What sort of an institution was this chapel, and was its music distinctive compared with others of its kind?

Selina Hastings, countess of Huntingdon, was an early associate of George Whitefield and the Wesleys in the eighteenth century reinvigoration of the Church in England. Her aristocratic status meant that she was able to construct private chapels for religious meetings without impinging on the local Church benefices, and, although she followed Whitefield in adopting a Calvinist view of salvation, like the Wesleys and other revivalists of the period she remained within the Church for as long as she could. In 1781, however, property issues became too strong and she was forced to secede, thus forming a sect, i.e. the Connexion named after her.

The countess had a long association with Bristol. She heard John Wesley preach in the New Rooms in Broadmead in the early 1740s, and in the summer of 1749 Bristol was the setting of her meeting with Whitefield, and the Wesley brothers. In January 1751 the countess was very ill and her life was despaired of by both her family and friends. She received a visit from Whitefield, and once pronounced out of danger she followed the advice of her friends and travelled to Bristol. (Fig. 1). Subsequently in 1752 she leased Clifton Wood House from Thomas Goldney III, and was to spend much of the 1750s resident there, visiting Charles and Sally Wesley in Charles Street, and taking the waters of the Hotwells for the benefit of her health.[4] In November 1753 Whitefield's Tabernacle in Penn Street, Bristol was opened, largely funded by the

---

[1] N. Temperley, *The Music of the English Parish Church*, (Cambridge, 1979).

[2] http://hymntune.library.uiuc.edu/ (consulted 8 July 2008). This splendid resource, instituted by Professor Nicholas Temperley, is invaluable for studies such as the present. Also invaluable has been advice from Margo Chaney, a contributor to the *Index*, who has made a special study of the Bristol and Bath musicians reviewed here.

[3] Bristol Reference Library: SR81–783.3.

[4] F. Cook, *Selina Countess of Huntingdon*, (Edinburgh, 2001), pp. 27, 71, 82, 129, 138–139, 142–150, 170.

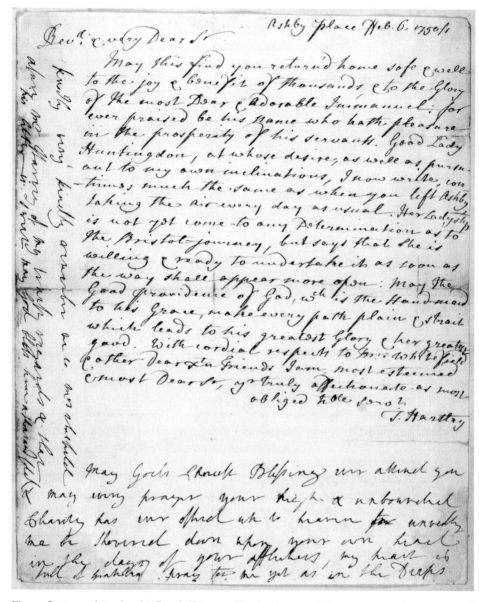

Fig. 1. Letter written by the Revd. Thomas Hartley (1709–1784), secretary to the countess of Huntingdon, addressed to George Whitefield, and dated from Ashby, 6 February 1750/1, with a postscript in the hand of the countess. The letter mentions her forthcoming journey to Bristol, [Collection of the Revd. Dr. John Stoughton, now in possession of M. J. Crossley Evans].

countess. The chapel continued to be filled to overflowing with worshippers and was enlarged in 1774.[5]

Twenty years after the foundation of the Penn Street Tabernacle, perhaps partly in response to the decision to change the conduct and style of worship there and to make it plainer and less in accordance with the rubric laid down in the *Book of Common Prayer*, the countess decided to found a chapel closer to her home and to the fashionable visitors to Clifton and Hotwells. She noticed and decided to lease the old Assembly Rooms in St. Augustine's Place. Obtaining the premises for £40 a year[6] the countess's chapel was opened in August 1775.[7] It is said to have been called Salem chapel, but this name does not appear in the tune-books of 1778 and 1786–1788, which seems unusual. Something of the atmosphere surrounding such ventures can be judged from what happened in Bath.[8] The countess, we are told, resolved to erect a house for herself and a chapel in Bath. She secured an appropriate piece of ground in the Vineyards and a place of worship was opened in October 1765. In a letter to a friend, Whitefield describes the opening:

> Could you have been present at the opening of the Chapel, you would have been much pleased. The building is extremely plain, and yet equally grand. A most beautiful original! All was conducted with great solemnity. Though a wet day, the place was very full, and assuredly the Great Shepherd and Bishop of souls consecrated and made it holy ground by His presence.

This, the fourth of Selina's chapels to be opened, survives, as the Building of Bath Museum—a stylish Gothic building by a leading architect.

The Bristol chapel was a charming but simpler building, seen in a drawing of 1824 in the Braikenridge collection in Bristol City Museum.[9] (Fig. 2). Now completely vanished, it occupied the upper floors of 3 St. Augustine's Place, on the west side of St. Augustine's Back, on the right bank of the Frome; it was thus only a few yards away from the intensive activity of the eighteenth century Quay. In the Middle Ages this had been the site of the Carmelite Friary church, and the east wall of the church may have formed the foundation of the front wall of the Georgian building.[10] After the Dissolution, the site had become part of the yards and outbuildings of 'The Great House', and during the seventeenth century was built up with housing and industrial buildings.[11] Millerd's map of 1673[12] shows that the former east wall of the monastic

[5] F. Cook, *op. cit.*, pp. 155, 343; the Revd. I. Jones, *Bristol Congregationalism: City and County*, (Bristol, 1947), pp. 23–27.

[6] F. Cook, *op. cit.*, pp. 343–344.

[7] G. F. Stone, *Bristol as it was, and as it is*, (Bristol, 1909), pp. 149–150; Bristol Urban Archaeological Database, Monument Record no. 418 M, (courtesy of Peter Insole).

[8] http://www.cofhconnexion.org.uk/ (consulted 8 July 2008).

[9] 'Lady Huntingdon's Chapel seen from the Drawbridge', 1824, by George W. Delamotte (BRSMG M 2531); see S. Stoddard, *Bristol before the Camera: The City in 1820–30*, (Bristol, 2001), p. 53, fig. 51.

[10] J. E. Pritchard, 'Bristol Archaeological Notes for 1904', *T. B. & G. A. S.*, XXIX, (1906), pp. 127–141.

[11] Alan Baxter & Associates, Desk Based Assessment (April 2006), in Bristol Sites & Monuments Record.

[12] Bristol City Museum; widely reproduced, e.g. as Plan B (beween pp. 135 & 136) in F. Neale, *William Worcestre: The Topography of Medieval Bristol*, B.R.S., 51, (2000).

Fig. 2. The Countess of Huntingdon's Chapel in Bristol, by George W. Delamotte (1824), [Bristol City Museum and Art Gallery].

complex served as the basis of a yard wall. When the Great House became Colston's School in 1708, the site was sold off, and a row of flat-pedimented houses, including an assembly room, was built along the St. Augustine's Place frontage: from about 1726, the assembly room was occupied by a theatre (used by Charles Williams's Company and Thomas Lewis and his company). It remained a place of entertainment until it was bought by Selina Hastings and opened as a place of public worship. The 1824 drawing and a late nineteenth century photograph[13] show that in the east wall was a big, four-light Gothic window with a double-light at each side on the first floor, facing out over the port, and three sash windows on the second floor above. The rooms indicated by sash windows over the passageway at the side may have belonged to the chapel; it is possible, but seems unlikely from the nineteenth century photographs, that the Gothic windows were inserted when the chapel took over the building. The side passageway climbed several steps and then ascended the rising hillside to a narrow paved court behind; the entrance to the chapel was by a short flight of steps some 25 ft from the street frontage, where a 6 ft wide doorway gave access to the interior.[14] A photograph of the 1890s taken from Lady Huntingdon's Court, at the top of the side passage, shows the sloping pavement and enables an estimate of the height of the windows (about 5 ft) above the floor level:[15] the cellar doors visible on the street frontage thus gave access only to storage beneath the chapel floor. (Fig. 3). There was one four-light window on each side of the chapel, about 50 ft from the east wall: otherwise it had no light, being hemmed in by other buildings on both sides and at the rear. From the 1890s photographs it is not clear whether the sash windows on the second storey lit a suite of rooms above, or were a clerestory for the main chapel, but the former seems more likely.[16] At the rear, the roof was hipped and the roof-line descended below the top of the sash window line, suggesting there was little space for a gallery at that end, although there was a gallery situated somewhere inside the chapel by the middle of the nineteenth century. Maybe the chapel was provided by the countess with the pulpit and possibly with a reading desk at the east end, in front of the big windows; however, so far no information about the internal arrangement of the building at this period has come to light.

A description of the interior at a later date has survived. This is from the period between October 1842 and the late 1870s when it was used by the Brethren as a place of worship under the ministry of the Revds. George Müller and Henry Craik. The author of this description, Edward Rendle Short,[17] subsequently clerk to the directors and head of the office staff at Fry's, attended the chapel when a young man. He wrote:

[13] Pritchard, *op. cit.*; R. Winstone, *Bristol As It Was, 1845–1900*, (1983), pl. 86; photo by C. H. Horton.

[14] Pritchard, *op. cit.*, plan, p. 135.

[15] Winstone, *op. cit.*, pl. 94; photo by E. Brightman & Son.

[16] R. Winstone, *Bristol: As It Was 1866–1860*, (Bristol, 1967), pl. 9, indicates a possibility that there was a structure of some sort inside the chapel which cut across the upper part of the central Gothic window and obscured the light into the chapel.

[17] His son was Professor Arthur Rendle Short (1880–1953), who held the chair of surgery at the University of Bristol between 1933 and 1946; see: W. Melville Capper and D. Johnson, *Arthur Rendle Short: Surgeon and Christian*, (1954), p. 14.

Fig. 3. The Countess of Huntingdon's Chapel: view from the north side, 1890s. Note that a second four-light window can be seen through the Gothic window on the facing wall, and that the roof-line dips downward towards the rear wall of the chapel (off the right of the photograph) so that the west part of the chapel (approx. 25 ft beyond the right-hand side of the window) was effectively of only one storey, [Reece Winstone collection].

Salem was an insanitary and uncomfortable place. There were high raised seats each side of the pulpit, over which was a sounding board. These seats were usually called by the frivolous "The Throne", and there were large dark boxes under the gallery at the other end which was known as "The Manger" [...] and in the middle with its closed pews with their narrow seats and upright backs with a beading which kept the sitter rather more than upright and just rubbed the shoulder bones; but neither the discomfort of the sitting nor the unpleasant smells could keep the people away.[18]

It was a relatively narrow building, some 80 ft x 50 ft, and it is not clear how it provided 500 seats, as it is said to have done in the later nineteenth century.[19] Nothing appears to be known of its equipment or furnishings, or how much it retained of its previous theatre fittings; from what one can guess, with a relatively low ceiling, it would have had a warm but not flattering acoustic. In 1831 the congregation of the Countess of Huntingdon's Connexion moved to a much more capacious building round the corner in Lodge Street;[20] the original chapel was demolished between 1904 and 1906, and Lodge Street chapel was closed for worship on 27 March 1910, converted to a printer's warehouse and finally pulled down in 1967.[21]

The music of the Church in the eighteenth century was extremely varied, but an important characteristic was that the main singing in both town and country services was not hymns, but psalms. Even the 'hymns' of Isaac Watts (the early eighteenth century Independent) are usually based on scriptural texts. The revival of the middle part of the century brought a change to this: especially at open-air meetings, Charles Wesley and other writers instituted hymns of their own composition, which often expressed very personal sentiments and emotions, and these hymns became an important part of Methodist and (eventually) other worship. In the Bristol tune-book, the words which are underlaid are, for the most part, taken from Selina's own collection of hymn texts,[22] and are often highly charged with personal feeling. Many of the newly written hymns were in unusual metres (compared with the straightforward 'ballad' measures of the metrical psalters) and so had to have new music provided for them. This music came from a variety of sources: from Moravian and German

---

[18] K. and A. Linton, 'I Will Build My Church': 150 years of local church work in Bristol, (Bristol, undated, but c. 1979), pp. 23, 43. See R. Winstone, Bristol: As It Was 1866–1860, (Bristol, 1967), pl. 9.

[19] O.S. 6-inch 1st edition, 1884. At this time the building was used by the Salvation Army, but no information has been found as to what furnishings (if any) were inside.

[20] The original chapel was the home of the controversial Dissenting minister and 'eccentric', Thomas Conolly Cowan (1776–1856), and his congregation, between 1837 and 1841–1842; see Mathews's Bristol Directory, (1838), pp. 33–34, (1840), pp. 36, 84, (1841), p. 32 ; M. J. Crossley Evans, 'The Life and Times of the Revd. Thomas Conolly Cowan (1776–1856), of Clifton, a "restless and enquiring spirit" or "a wolf in sheep's clothing"'? in J. H. Bettey, (ed.), Archives and Local History in Bristol & Gloucestershire, Essays in Honour of David Smith, (Bristol, 2007), p. 258.

[21] G. F. Stone, op. cit., pp. 149, 150; Arrowsmith's Dictionary of Bristol (2nd ed. 1906) p. 53; G. Pryce, A Popular History of Bristol, Antiquarian, Topographical and Descriptive (Bristol, 1861), p. 158; A. Gomme, M. Jenner, and B. Little, Bristol: an Architectural History (1979) p. 297; the Revd. I. Jones, Bristol Congregationalism: City and County, (Bristol, 1947), pp. 33–35. References and information kindly provided by Dr. M. J. Crossley Evans, who has improved this paper in many respects.

[22] A Select Collection of Hymns to be universally sung in all the Countess of Huntingdon's Chapels. Collected by her Ladyship (1780); B.R.O., ref. 9492/86.

Lutheran tunes, from opera and even popular songs, and from new compositions. Among musicians who contributed especially to this process was the chaplain of the Lock Hospital (for women suffering from venereal disease), the Revd. Martin Madan, who composed tunes himself and persuaded others to contribute as well. Most of the proprietors of chapels and meeting houses, especially in London, put together collections of words and music, as indeed both Whitefield and John Wesley had done in the 1740s; often enough these compilers drew on a wide range of sources and were vague (or even deceitful) as to the composer of a melody. Such a tune, which appears in the Bristol tune-book, is 'Portsmouth': this tune is first known from the 1765 edition of Thomas Knibb's *The Psalm Singers Help, being a Collection of Tunes in three Parts, that are now us'd in the several dissenting congregations in London*. Also known by the name 'Trumpet', it was at one time attributed to Handel, but without authority. Usually known nowadays as 'Portsmouth New', this tune came to be widely adopted by all kinds of congregations: it is in 6.6.6.6.8.8. metre, which was (unusually) used in the Old Version (1562) of the metrical psalms for Psalm 148, and used again in the New Version (1696) for Psalms 136 and 148, so it was by no means limited to hymns. However, in Belcher's Bristol tune-book, it is given over the words, 'Ye virgin souls, arise; with all the dead awake', a hymn first known in English publication from *The Spiritual Psalmodist's Companion* of 1772.

The three-part setting of 'Portsmouth' in the Bristol tune-book (Fig. 4) is not much like choral four-part settings such as that by Thomas Clark of Canterbury in *The Sunday School Union Tune Book* (1837).[23] In the Bristol book, the air is placed in the middle part; the top part, also in the treble clef, for much of the time lies a third or more above the air, but it also drops below the air, especially at the beginning and the end. The third part, obviously a bass, is much more plainly written, and could well be intended for an accompanying instrument. These features can be found in many other sources, and can be partly explained by their occurrence in some of Madan's tunes for the Lock Hospital: there, much as at the Magdalen Hospital[24], the unfortunate women inmates sang from the gallery, screened from the general congregation below, and were probably accompanied by the organ. In such cases the women and girls would have split the two upper parts between them, high men's voices would have taken the second part (the air) an octave lower, and low men's voices would have sung the bass. Unsatisfactory though this might seem to us, it was apparently a widespread procedure in the later eighteenth and the nineteenth centuries, and may well have been adopted even in rural parish churches where there were 'charity children' or Sunday school pupils to be schooled in singing the upper parts. This, the 'Old Methodist way of singing', allowed the whole congregation to take a part with the minimum of practice, but practice many chapels must have had, especially Selina's chapel at Bath, where Benjamin Milgrove (precentor *c.* 1766–1772) wrote four-part hymn settings with sections for 'Women alone', 'Men alone' and 'All together'[25]: as

---

[23] Published in a performing edition with historical notes by R. Woods, E. Macadam, and S. Girling Smith, *Praise & Glory. A selection of the Psalms of David set to the metrical psalm tunes used by West Gallery quires 1740–1860*, (Oxford, 2000), pp. 220–221.

[24] Temperley, *op. cit.*, p. 211.

[25] N. Temperley, and S. Drage, (eds.), *Eighteenth-Century Psalmody*, (Musica Britannica, 85, 2007), no. 41, pp. 74–75.

Fig. 4. 'Portsmouth' set for three voices to the Countess of Huntingdon's Hymn 82: from *Sacred Melody*, compiled by Benjamin Belcher, Bristol, [1786–1788], [Bristol Reference Library].

Temperley[26] puts it, 'He was writing here for congregation, choir and organ, allotting contrasting phrases to the women in the congregation, a custom that reflected widespread Methodist practice'. Such musical opportunities not only appealed to the more cultured worshippers found at Bath, but anecdotally are supposed to have drawn attendance away from churches to chapels, especially Methodist chapels, where 'hearty' singing was both encouraged and enjoyed.[27]

This more complicated music comes from Milgrove's Book III of *Hymns dedicated to the Countess of Huntingdon* (1781): neither this nor the second book (1771) were used by any of the three Bristol collections which survive from this general period. On the other hand, no fewer than six of the 16 tunes in Milgrove's first book, published 1768, are found in Belcher's tune-book of 1786–1788, but not in the other two collections. Perhaps Milgrove came to the Bristol chapel when it was set up, and left copies of his music there, to be used by Belcher a dozen years later.

The other Bristol collections, besides Belcher's, which belong to this period are two. The first, *Twenty Psalm Tunes in Three Parts[...] sung [...] at the Cathedral and most other places of worship in Bristol [...] Compos'd by the late Mr Coombes and other eminent masters* (Longman, Lukey & Co. for T. Naish, London, *c.* 1775), contains 16 tunes, each prescribed for a psalm (not hymn). George Combes was organist at Bristol cathedral between 1756 and 1759 and 1765 and 1769.[28] The second, *Musica Sacra, being a Choice Collection of Psalm and Hymn Tunes, and Chants [...] as they are used in [...] the Countess of Huntingdon's Chapels, in Bath, Bristol, &c.* (W. Gye, Bath, *c.* 1778)[29] contains no fewer than 115 tunes (29 more than Belcher's tune-book). Neither of these draws on Milgrove. *Musica Sacra* has eight tunes (or variations thereof) which are in *Twenty Psalm Tunes*, but Belcher has eleven. Of the tunes in *Twenty Psalm Tunes*, seven are attributed to Combes, and all of these are found in *Musica Sacra* or Belcher or both – an unexpected use of Anglican compositions – whereas six of the tunes in *Twenty Psalm Tunes* are attributed to 'Smith' or 'Wm. B', and none of these is taken up by the Selina chapels collections.[30]

[26] N. Temperley, 'More Psalms, Hymns and Anthems', *CHOMBEC News*, (No. 3, Summer 2007), pp. 4–5 [ISSN 1751–3308].

[27] Cf. W. Vincent, *Considerations on Parochial Music*, (1787), quoted by P. Gailiunas, 'The Hawks Family and the Progress of Church Music on Tyneside before the Oxford movement', *Archaeologia Aeliana*, 36, (2007), pp. 309–323, at p. 15.

[28] W. Shaw, *The Succession of Organists of the Chapel Royal and the Cathedrals of England and Wales from c. 1538*, (Oxford, 1991). Combes was associated with the performances of Handel's music which took place in Bristol during August 1758. It seems logical that the 'late Mr Combes' referred to in the title of the *c.* 1775 collection is George, and not (*pace* the Hymn Tune Index) an obscure William Combes; conversely, George Combes can scarcely have been the compiler of the collection, as the British Library catalogue implies.

[29] This is the estimated date of the copy used by the Hymn Tune Index, which is followed here; there is, in fact, what might be an earlier edition in the University of Bristol Library [Restricted Hta], but this has not been used in the present analysis.

[30] Mr. Smith, composer of Psalm 23 in *Twenty Psalm Tunes*, might be the associate of Handel who settled in Bath as Professor Stephen Banfield has suggested: the appropriately pastoral feel of the setting for two high voices and bass suits such an identification, even though it is conjecture. 'Wm. B.,' composer of five psalm settings in the same collection, could be William Bromfeild, who contributed tunes to Madan's Lock Hospital Collection and had compositions published in 1762 and 1769; alternatively, the composer could be William Boyce (1710–1778), whose *Cathedral Music* appeared between 1760 and 1778, and was certainly acquired and used in Bristol cathedral.

The relationship between the collections of *Musica Sacra* and Belcher is close, but not very close. Of Belcher's 86 tunes, 39 or 45% came from *Musica Sacra* or an unknown predecessor of them both; conversely, Belcher did **not** adopt 76, or 66%, of the tunes in *Musica Sacra*. The Bristol collections analysed here thus show a considerable degree of independence, even though their titles and close dates of publication would suggest one should expect to find a good deal of common material. This emphasizes the energy which went into writing, setting and selling music of all kinds in the second half of the eighteenth century. The clerks, if not the choirs and any instrumentalists, in Bristol chapels and churches of the 1770s and 1780s must have been changing their music books all the time. Of course, this reflects the activity, outside worship, of musical societies, glee clubs, and oratorio productions which flourished even in small country towns at this period.

The tunes from Milgrove which appear in Belcher's book bear, for about the half part, local names (e.g. 'Bath', 'Marshfield', or 'Chappel'). Those in *Twenty Psalm Tunes*, in the original merely labelled for a psalm, appear in *Musica Sacra* and Belcher sometimes with local names: thus Belcher renames Psalm 105 'Werburgs', and Psalm 23 'St. Johns'.[31] Curiously, Belcher includes Psalm 21 from *Twenty Psalm Tunes* under that name, but in London collections of *c.* 1778 and 1784 the tune is named 'Bristol': of course, Belcher already had one tune named 'Bristol' and could not use just the same title for this tune, but one would like to know how the tune came to the attention of London compilers under that name.[32] However, the origin of tune names is often quite mysterious: the Bristol Selina compilers (*Musica Sacra* and Belcher) are the only source for the tune-name-matches of 'Truro' and 'Wigstone', but neither name has any evident Bristol connotation. Conversely, there are three tunes known only from *Musica Sacra* and Belcher: these are 'Keevil' (in Wiltshire), 'Reading' (in Berkshire) and 'St. Michael' (which could be in Bristol!).

Of the chief sources for Belcher's tune-book, the earliest of note is *The Divine Musical Miscellany* (London, *c.* 1754), said to be 'for use with George Whitefield's *Hymns for Social Worship* [...] *Design'd for the use of the Tabernacle Congregation in London, 1753'*. These early Calvinist books were no doubt on the shelf in Selina's chapels at Bath and Bristol, and all or nearly all of the nine tunes from *The Divine Musical Miscellany* which are in Belcher's book were previously included in *Musica Sacra*. Sometimes such tunes were renamed by the Bristol compilers: such happened to 'Italian' (or 'Maryland') which Belcher renamed 'Clifton'—surely a local reference. Another major source for Belcher's tunes was the *Sacred Melody* of John Wesley, which was issued in various

---

[31] The church of St. John the Baptist was one of the churches in Bristol in which Whitefield preached with 'wonderful effect' in 1737 prior to going as a missionary to Georgia; I. Jones, *op. cit.*, p. 24. He also preached at St. Mary Redcliffe, St. Stephen, and probably at St. Philip and St. Jacob and St. Werburgh also. See: the Revd. A. D. Belden, *George Whitefield- the Awakener*, (undated but *c.* 1925), pp. 33–36.

[32] Of the eleven tunes which appear in *Twenty Psalm Tunes* and in Belcher's collection, five have the same or a similar arrangement in Belcher, four are different, and two are well-know tunes from which no conclusion can be drawn. The implication is that Belcher was prepared to adopt the 'duetting' style of setting most of the time, but at other times chose to rearrange the tune so as to provide a strong Air for the congregation to sing: the music of the Connexion chapel, under Belcher's clerkship, thus enjoyed an easy-going relationship with that of the cathedral.

editions 1765–1782: the 1765 edition was reissued in Bristol in 1770 and 1773, and this is reflected in at least six tunes from it being included in *Musica Sacra* and by Belcher. Madan's *Lock Hospital Collection* (1763–1769) yielded some ten tunes for Belcher's tune-book, again for the most part having already been included in *Musica Sacra*. Some of these, such as 'Helmsley' or 'Hotham', were (and still are) widespread favourites, but Madan's links with Selina emphasize the rather partial feel to the Bristol compilers' selections.

Most of the tunes in Belcher's book have some kind of dissenting or Methodist link, even those (a dozen or more) for which there is no obvious single source. Conversely, there is only a handful of tunes which came from a mainstream West Gallery source: such are the widely known 'Otford' (Belcher 'Ps. 8'), 'Burford' (Belcher 'Stroud'), and 'Wiltshire' (curiously named 'Bradau' by Belcher).[33] One reason must be that the Bristol compilers for Selina's Connexion were shy of fully-blown fuguing tunes (like 'Otford' and 'Wiltshire'), preferring duetting or homophonic settings more suitable for congregational use.

Lastly, did Benjamin Belcher himself compose any singable tunes? Eight of the tunes in his book are known only from that source—they are named 'Bristol', 'Broad Street' (Fig. 5), 'Keynsham', 'Llandilo', 'Morning', 'Nailsey' (Fig. 6), 'St. Philips', and 'St. Stephens':[34] all but two are Bristol place-names. 'Broad Street' (Fig. 5) sits uneasily in the three-part setting, though it is quite singable if the middle part (the Air) is taken by high men's and low women's voices: like several of these tunes, it is generally similar to other 'enthusiastic' tune of the period, and may not be original at all. The air bounces along well and one can imagine this tune being popular among the Bristol congregation.[35] 'Nailsey' (Fig. 6) by contrast conforms rather to the style of the more elegant compositions in *Twenty Psalm Tunes*, and could possibly be sung by two treble parts and a bass. From the fact that it is set to the first hymn in the congregation's book, one might suppose that this tune would be especially favoured at the Bristol chapel: it is a rather charming tune, and unusually varied in the way it develops from line to line. These two examples, whether or not they were composed by Benjamin Belcher, give us a taste of the variety and expressiveness of the singing at the Bristol chapel, for all their simplicity and sometimes awkward harmonies.

In conclusion, it looks as if Benjamin Belcher should be added to the roll of Bristolian composers, though the tunes which we suppose are his compositions are scarcely outstanding or worth widespread revival. There seems to have been a division between the music of the Countess of Huntingdon's Connexion and that of the Church, and the Connexion's tunes tended to be drawn from their own collections

---

[33] A distinctive setting of a Selina's Connexion hymn, 'Evening', in Belcher's collection (HTI 6053a). turns out to be a truncated version of 'Christmas Day', published in November 1748 in *The Gentleman's Magazine* and apparently of Anglican origin (HTI 1887a).

[34] This was another of the churches in Bristol in which Whitefield preached with 'wonderful effect' prior to going as a missionary to Georgia; I. Jones, *op. cit.*, p. 24.

[35] 'Broad Street' is set to Selina's Hymn 44, 'Jubilee'. In *Sacred Melody* there is another setting of this hymn, entitled 'Trumpet' (HTI 5285b): no earlier publication of this tune is cited by the Hymn Tune Index, but it is hardly likely that Belcher would write two tunes for the same hymn. 'Trumpet', unusually for *Sacred Melody*, is in only two parts: in later publications, it appears (unattributed) as 'Jubilee' or 'Jubilee New'. No doubt it originates from a mid-eighteenth century nonconformist collection.

Broad Street

Countess of Huntingdon Collection Hymn XLIV 'The Jubilee' v. 1   Benjamin Belcher (?) of Bristol *c.* 1786

Fig. 5. 'Broad Street', from Belcher's *Sacred Melody*. Transcribed by A. J. Parker (2008) from *SACRED MELODY, being A collection of Psalm and Hymn tunes, IN THREE PARTS. As made use of at the Right Hon, the Countess of Huntingdon's Chapel and other Place of Worship in BRISTOL, but particularly suited to the last edition of her Ladyship's hymns to their various measures, in Two Parts* (Benjamin Belcher, Bristol *c.* 1786–1788), pp. 106–107 [Bristol Reference Library SR81–783.3]. Hymn Tune Index 18059. Voice parts identified by ed.; words corrected and supplemented from *A Select Collection of Hymns, etc.* (London, 1780), [B.R.O, 9492/86].

rather than even those of John Wesley; however, in Bristol, there is a surprising overlap of tunes between the cathedral and chapel in the clerkship of Benjamin Belcher. There is no evidence, at least from Belcher's tune-book, that the Bristol chapel sang such complicated music as that at Bath, though there was clearly much interaction between the two congregations and one may suppose that Milgrove visited Bristol at some stage to help with the music there. Nor can one detect any whiff of sea-air, or of rum or tobacco, drifting up from the quayside below to lend an exotic flavour to the music of the devotees of the Countess of Huntingdon's Connexion in St. Augustine's Place.

Countess of Huntingdon's Collection no. 1 v. 1

Nailsey

Benjamin Belcher (?) of Bristol *c.* 1786

Fig. 6. 'Nailsey. PM. Hymn 1st, Page 1st.' in *Sacred Melody* (published by B. Belcher & T. Mills, Bristol [1786–1788]), p. 80. Bristol Reference Library SR 81–783.3. Hymn Tune Index 18063. Transcribed by A. J. Parker (2008): the parts are not labelled in the original. Original notes corrected in bars 28 & 30 as shown. Words from 'Hymn I. To the BLESSED SPIRIT. For Whitsunday' in the Countess of Huntingdon's Collection.

VIII

'The Cemetery Under the Tower': Christ Church, Bristol; and the destruction of St. Ewen's Church

COLIN GODMAN, M.A., (CANTAB), and
M. J. CROSSLEY EVANS, F.S.A.

> Where once, St. Ewen, pious soul
> Could every earthly wish controul;
> On that same spot, now mark me well,
> I Brushes make and Brushes sell.
> Here dwelt the saint in hut of clay,
> And here his manhood pass'd away.[1]

SOME FIFTY years ago a small group[2] assembled in the crypt of Christ Church in Broad Street, Bristol. Electricians working beneath the church had made a discovery which had unnerved them. Curious about a blocked ventilation grille a few feet above floor-level, and wondering if something lay beyond the west wall of the crypt , they had forced a small opening and found an unexpected void. They were shocked by what they saw.

My notebook suggests that our visit was made in the last week of February 1958. We had been invited to see what had startled the workmen, take photographs, make rough measurements and attempt an interpretation of their discovery and answer some questions. The men had pushed a short ladder though the opening and, using a lamp, had seen a great mound of bones, skulls and coffin-boards. The officers of the church, including the church warden and later patron of the living, Mr. (later the Revd.) C. Maurice J. Turner (1913–1997)[3] were puzzled, having assumed that they were standing beneath the west end of their church with nothing but the natural earth below Broad Street beyond the whitewashed end wall of their crypt.

When the old church of Christ Church, or Holy Trinity, was demolished and the site cleared in 1786 the Patys marked out a simple rectangle 70 feet long, 50 feet wide. The new church was to be four bays long and three wide with gold and white

---

[1] Bristol City Reference Library, Braikenridge Collection, XV, p. 553, advertisement for Samuel Tayler's Brush Manufactory, No. 51 Corn Street, opposite All Saints' church, *circa* 1820.

[2] This group consisted of myself (C.G.) and fellow pupils in the Vth form at Bristol Cathedral School: the late Michael Dyer, the son of the organist and choir master of Christ Church, Mr. Cecil Dyer, and Robert Andrew Gilbert.

[3] Church warden of Christ Church 1947–1962. An active mason, Worshipful Master of The Burnett Lodge 1976–1977 and chaplain 1983–1997. Provincial Grand Chaplain of the Mark degree.

Fig. 1. Photograph of one of the six massive masonry piers supporting the Corinthian columns in the church above. Built by Thomas and William Paty in 1786, as soon as the burials beneath the mediaeval Christ Church were cleared, the stonework was roughly plastered and white-washed. The 1958 photograph shows the north-east pier beneath the chancel, and old pan-elling stored against the east wall, [Photograph by Colin Godman].

shallow domes supported by six slender Corinthian columns. In the crypt below, these columns were to stand on stout square pillars of coursed rubble. (Fig. 1). Sturdy vault-ing was to support the floor above and the walls and springing of the arches in the crypt were to be roughly plastered and whitewashed.

   We wondered in 1958 if a vault might have continued westwards under Broad Street, beyond the limit of the Patys' foundations? After a moment's confusion we realized that the Patys' church has a western tower and spire that encloses a grand entrance porch with steps leading from street-level up to the body of the church. The base of the tower, roughly 25 feet square, is masked by shops to west and south that combine to give the impression of a wide façade. The vaulted space with the bones lies directly below the tower and so did not extend beyond the ground plan of the Patys' church. Our rough measurements taken in 1958 confirmed that the vault fits snugly into the square space created by the thick foundation walls of the tower. Before asking where the bones might have come from we might ask whether the photographs offer any dating evidence for the jumbled remains.

Fig. 2. Pen and ink drawing of central Bristol in 1600, as imagined by Bristol illustrator Frederick George Lewin R. W. A., (1922). The relationship of old Christ Church to St. Ewen's Church, facing each other across Broad Street is clear, [Collection of Colin Godman].

THE PHOTOGRAPHS

A 35mm Leica camera with standard lens and an electronic flashpack was employed, but the absence of light in the vault made framing and focussing a matter of luck rather than judgement. This writer, the photographer, was held on a rope with foot on the ladder while aiming the camera in total darkness.

It is apparent that the walls of the vault, or charnel, had been whitewashed and display two phases of construction. The first employed roughly squared ashlar blocks of local sandstone and millstone grit with random pieces of dressed freestone, perhaps re-used material from the demolished mediaeval church. The work is well-jointed and rises some seven courses from the imagined ground level on the north and south. A simple barrel vault springs out from these walls but the east and west faces rise vertically and, above the well-built foundation courses, employ flat pennant sandstone, and unworked rubble masonry.[4]

The photographs were taken looking towards the west wall and floor, and it seems that the human remains are scattered over the whole of the floor area and rise,

---

[4] This second stage, which included the arched vault that supports the floor of the porch above must have been completed by candlelight, (electricity was not introduced into the church until the end of the nineteenth century when it replaced gas).

having settled over the years, to a calculated height of five feet at the centre of the mound. The vault offered approximately 150 square feet of space. Apart from the broken ventilation grille that permitted a wriggling entry no other doorway or step was immediately apparent. There was some evidence in the top north west corner of the vault of repairs, as if the vault had been penetrated from above. Unfortunately this feature was not to appear in the photographs.

Directly below the ventilation grille was seen a circular stone-lined well, all but completely blocked with tumbled bone and coffin fragments.[5] It was not possible to judge the depth of this 'well' but later speculation let us to wonder if it served the duty of a lidded cistern to contain decayed bones and debris in the context of a parochial vault had that been the purpose of the Patys' use of the space. Faint marks on the western wall, seen in the photographs, may indicate traces of the shelving employed for coffins. If so any structures had been stripped out before the vault was called into use as a specific charnel to store remains introduced from elsewhere.

Close inspection of the photographs suggests an eighteenth century date for the later material. The 1700s saw the fashion for the 'triple coffin' for intramural burial. The dead, embalmed or not, dressed in shroud or clothes, were first placed in a sturdy coffin of oak or elm boards, well jointed and screwed together. The joints would have been sealed with pitch and a layer of bran or sawdust introduced beforehand to absorb any natural corruption. Next, a lead shell would be added, affording an airtight and watertight protection to the inner coffin. Plumbers would form and solder the lead work before the coffin-makers provided the third and final casing. Again, oak or elm would have been employed, boards glued and screwed tightly together around the lead shell. Richer clients would expect their cases to be covered with black velvet or fine scarlet cloth decorated with gold or silver studs and a finely engraved *depositum* (nameplate). Fragments of all three casings can be seen in the photographs.

The lead shells seem to have been damaged and torn, suggesting their rough removal from graves with hooks and chains, or their subsequent partial collapse when roughly stacked one upon another. Most of the coffins are smashed and rotten, suggesting long decay in earth burials before they were brought here in a state of advanced decomposition. Elsewhere, some bones and skulls seem to have been carried here from other charnels or vaults; dry and disarticulated but generally unbroken, they hint at careful exhumation followed by brisk and violent deposition in this vault. It seems they were dropped from above, in time sliding or collapsing into the position they assume now.

Two fairly complete lead shells have survived in the north-west and south-west corners of the vault. The former is almost complete, only the foot end has damage that reveals a slender tibia and fibula where they would be expected. (Fig. 7). A jumble of other bones has been placed on its lid; an old adult femur, a youngster's femur,

---

[5] A similar 'well' containing skulls was discovered at the time of the restoration of the crypt of St. Nicholas, Bristol Bridge, in 1893. Some of these bones were 'liberated', including numerous skulls, and were housed in the crypt where they were used to frighten the choir boys during practice in the 1950s. Subsequently they were moved to the City Museum for analysis. The bones were photographed in the crypt by the Revd. Stanley Tate Collins (1886–1964), second master of Bristol Grammar School, in the 1930s and some of the prints finally came into the possession of Dr. Arthur Basil Cottle. This information is conflated from verbal information provided by the Revd. C. M. J. Turner, Mrs. M. V. Campbell, and Mr. R. C. Metcalfe.

Fig. 3. Photograph taken in 1958 of the disturbed material covering the floor of the vault show-ing the west wall. It reveals the human remains exhumed from earth-burial, some with little more protection than a copper-pinned woollen shroud. Fragments of simple wooden coffin boards are jumbled together with the shells of the fashionable triple cases of the eighteenth cen-tury. In these the wrapped body had originally been placed in a lead shell, itself protected by a simple wooden coffin. Enclosing these were decorative wooden cases, often velvet uphol-stered with studs and ornamental embossed plates. These coffins would have been lifted from family vaults or brick-lined graves protecting their contents from damp or interference, [Photograph by Colin Godman].

parts of a pelvis and an odd iron coffin handle seem to have been tossed here. The latter coffin is massive, the lead shell has been propped on its head and also betrays rough handling. When its photograph was printed it betrayed a secret; someone had scratched a name with a nail, level with the occupant's left knee: 'Thos TYNDALL: 1766'. (Fig. 8). Research has now shown him to have been an attorney[6], the King's Proctor to George II and George III and a Fellow of the Royal Society.[7] He was also a first cousin to Thomas Tyndall (1722–1794) of Royal Fort House, and his father, Thomas Tyndall (1690–1735), merchant, was buried in the old Christ Church.[8]

[6] We are grateful to Ms. Theresa Thom, the Librarian of Gray's Inn and to Mr. Lim Ming Wang for confirming that the King's Proctor was an attorney and not a barrister.

[7] T. Thomson, *History of the Royal Society from its Institution to the End of the Eighteenth Century*, (1812), Appendix No. IV, p. *l*; elected 25 November 1762, never admitted, died 7 September 1766. Thomas Tindal [*sic*] was appointed to the office of King's Proctor on 31 July 1750. The post required him to represent the interests of the Crown in Marriage, Divorce and Admiralty proceedings.

[8] C. H. Cave, *A History of Banking in Bristol from 1750 to 1899*, (Privately printed, Bristol, 1899), pp. 248–249.

Fig. 4. 1958 photograph looking downward from the ventilation grille towards the vault floor. A stone-lined well or cistern is apparent, close against the inside or E. wall of the vault. Decayed coffin boards and torn fragments of lead shells have tumbled into the void, [Photograph by Colin Godman].

The parish registers show that Thomas died in London in 1766 and his coffin, probably originally triple lined, was transported to Bristol, and buried in a vault in the old church.[9] What was left of the coffin was roughly exhumed when the vaults of the old church were cleared. The family were Unitarians in the early eighteenth century and so far no record has been found of their return into the fold of the Established Church prior to the early nineteenth century. The grandfather of the King's Proctor resigned from the corporation during the reign of Queen Anne upon the enactment of the Occasional Conformity Act owing to his religious scruples.

No pattern emerges from the mound but the way that long bones seem to lie bundled together, side by side, suggests they may have been dumped from bags or baskets. (Fig. 9). Fifty years ago all we could propose was they seemed to represent a series of burials with the most recent being of eighteenth century date cleared either from a disused burial ground or the product of a radical alteration to a church that required the emptying of vaults and graves.

THE SOURCE OF THE REMAINS

Clearly Christ Church itself replaced an earlier mediaeval church: Christ Church or Holy Trinity. Could the remains be the burials disturbed by the Patys' workmen? In

[9] B.R.O., P/XCh/R/1 (d), 16 September 1766, 'Thomas Tyndale from London: Buried'.

Fig. 5. The skulls in the crypt of St. Nicholas raised from the church's bone hole in 1893 and photographed *in situ* in September 1934, [Collection of M. J. Crossley Evans].

1958 one of the church wardens, Mr. Turner, gently reminded us that the church's present name: Christ Church with St. Ewen, was a reminder of her old neighbour, swept away to clear its site for a new Council House. What had happened to the dead of St. Ewen's parish? Had they been removed from the vaults and the burial ground after the church was closed? Were there other parish burial grounds that had been closed and cleared for building? Were they the dead beneath Christ Church tower? My notes suggest that we drew a plan of the vault without, I regret, realizing how neatly it fitted into the space beneath the tower. Our modest report referred to three authorities. The first was William Barrett, *The History and Antiquities of the City of Bristol* (1789), described the old Holy Trinity. The church was:

> A low building [...] the middle aisle in length from the high altar to the west door was 94 feet [...]the length of the chancel was 18 feet[...] the north and south aisles

Fig. 6. The north-west corner of the vault showing triple coffins, [Photograph by Colin Godman].

were each 59 feet long. The width of the church from the north to the south was 54 feet (William of Worcester says, "the length of the Holy Trinity is 22 yards, its breadth 35 steps")

Barrett continued: 'In 1751 [...] a new strong arch was turned under the belfry by the pulpit with inverted arch underground'. On reading this we were interested but we were then unaware that the old church tower stood above the crossing, not at the west end. The 'belfry by the pulpit' reference should have alerted us. The tower was not to migrate west until the Patys' design.

Barrett's page reminded us that 1786 saw the demolition and intent to re-build Christ Church 'on the same ground, only allowing some space to widen the street there'. Unfortunately we were unaware of the release of land on the Wine Street side of the church and incorrectly assumed it was Broad Street that was affected. Consequently we wondered if setting back the west front of the church might have isolated a western extension of the mediaeval crypt or, perhaps, a seventeenth century vault under Broad Street.

J. F. Nicholls and John Taylor's *Bristol—Past and Present*, volume III, chapter XIV, (1881), offered a brief summary of the events of 1786: 'old Christ Church was taken down and the foundation of the present structure was laid November 4th' and later 'a faculty was obtained on March 10th in answer to a petition presented on 15th January 1786 for uniting St. Ewen's Parish with that of Christ Church. The last sermon was preached in St. Ewen's on 15th May 1791. The bells and material of the inside of the church were sold by auction 1st August 1791'.

Fig. 7. A small lead shell lying in the north-east corner of the vault. The 1958 photograph suggests that the foot-end of the coffin was torn open when it was moved here. Several bones have fallen or been placed on the shell: a tibia, a small femur, a pelvis and they are accompanied by an iron coffin handle, [Photograph by Colin Godman].

Our third authority was the eminent church warden, Maurice Turner, whose *Christ Church or Holy Trinity* (1955), offered a valuable introduction to the history of his parish. Amongst the records of 1746 Turner recorded a 'new churchyard in the parish at some distance from the church has lately been consecrated and the skull house was repaired'. In his forward, church warden Turner acknowledged his gratitude to 'Mrs. A. M. Cole who so graciously placed the notes and documents of the late Canon R. T. Cole M.A., F.S.A' at his disposal.

Having come to no particular conclusion in 1958 about the source of the bones all we could do was note the several opinions of the church warden, Mr. Cecil Dyer the organist and choir-master, and others, and agree that the dead of either Christ Church or St. Ewen's were the most likely candidates. By 1959 we had prepared a tidier plan and section for the authorities (Figs. 10a and b) and we hoped that wiser scholars after us would solve the puzzle at some time in the future.

Fig. 8. A large lead shell, standing on its head end, against the south-east corner of the vault. The lead at the head end seems to have been levered outwards perhaps damaged when being drawn upwards out of a brick-lined grave. Close examination of the 1958 photograph revealed an inscription, scratched into the metal: 'THOS. TYNDALL 1766'. This may be discerned, with a glass, just above the occupant's supposed left knee, [Photograph by Colin Godman].

RECENT RESEARCH

Almost fifty years later a black-bound exercise book, with pages numbered 1 to 131, carefully entitled 'Christ-Church with St. Ewen: Record of Monuments and Gravestones made by the Revd. R. T. Cole, Rector 1914–1922' provided some of the answers.[10]

The book was the work of former president of the Bristol and Gloucestershire Archaeological Society, an honorary canon of Bristol cathedral and rector of Christ Church with St. Ewen: the Revd. Marwood Anselm Rauceby Thorold Cole M.A.,

[10] In possession of Dr. M. J. Crossley Evans.

Fig. 9. A closer view of the pile of exhumed bones carelessly arranged at the top of the heap. Photograph taken in 1958 from a position below the ventilation grille. Easily identifiable are human leg bones (femurs and tibias), a female pelvis, and a jumble of ribs and arm bones (humerus and ulnas) and vertebrae. The random mixing of adult and immature materials with grave debris suggests a fairly brisk exhumation and hurried dumping in this place, [Photograph by Colin Godman].

F.S.A. (1874–1948), who served as the rector between 1903 and 1938. The rector's notebook contains detailed measurements of wall monuments, their inscriptions and notes recording their removal or re-erection in the church.

Of particular interest are the accounts of removals from St. Ewen in 1791. Canon Cole turned his attention to the inscriptions in the crypt; those on the ledger slabs covering brick-lined graves in the 'cemetery' under the church. He was able to match names on wall monuments above to names on the stones below. In 1958 we had noted the scattering of large pennant sandstone ledgers but in 1920 Canon Cole had made a careful, methodical survey of the graves noting every inscription no matter how incomplete. Canon Cole's plan and index offer the most complete evidence of the surviving gravestones.

Does the Canon's work explain the presence of the bones under the tower? He noted that the church records differentiate between 'cemetery' and 'graveyard'. The former clearly related to burials in the floor of the crypt, the latter to either of the two burial-grounds, that landlocked by buildings to the north of the church wall and that maintained by the vestry at Duck Lane discussed elsewhere in this volume by Dr. Crossley Evans. On p. 23 Canon Cole noted the wall monument to one of the city's bankers: 'In the cemetery of this church are deposited the remains of Thomas Tyndall Esq., late of this city, who died April 17th 1794 aged 72 years'. It also records 'those of

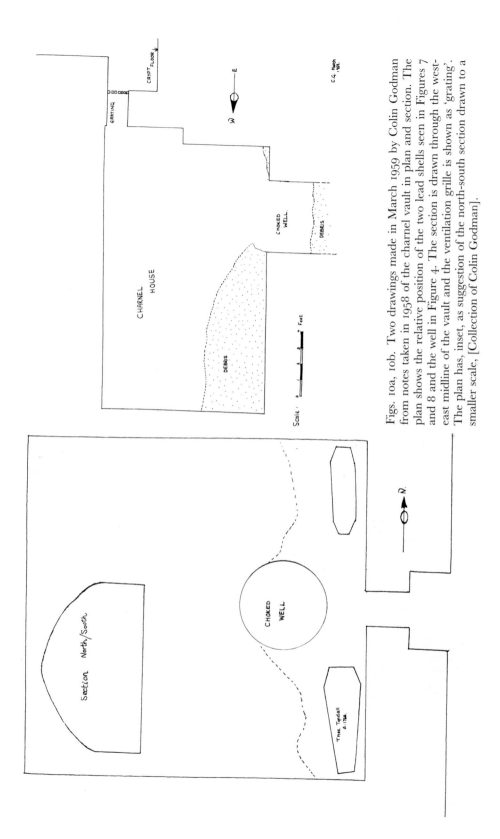

Figs. 10a, 10b. Two drawings made in March 1959 by Colin Godman from notes taken in 1958 of the charnel vault in plan and section. The plan shows the relative position of the two lead shells seen in Figures 7 and 8 and the well in Figure 4. The section is drawn through the west-east midline of the vault and the ventilation grille is shown as 'grating'. The plan has, inset, as suggestion of the north-south section drawn to a smaller scale, [Collection of Colin Godman].

Fig. 11. A reconstruction of St. Ewen's Church in the eighteenth century looking up Broad Street towards the High Cross by the artist A. C. Fare, R. W. A. Formerly in possession of the Revd. Canon Cole. This view is an idealisation: the south front of the church would not have been visible from this point owing to the buildings in Broad Street and along the church passageway. The south wall of the church is not shown with its doorway and the entrance to the tower should have been portrayed on the east side rather than the south side of the structure, [Collection of M. J. Crossley Evans].

Alicia, his wife, who died February 2nd 1764 aged 31 years'. As Mrs. Tyndall had died over twenty years before the new church re-opened she must have required translation from old Christ Church to new. Canon Cole noted that the monument was moved to the porch in 1882 and returned to the body of the church in 1927. He related it to the 'Tyndall Vault in the Crypt: No. 47'. Canon Cole had located this in his survey to the west end of the 'cemetery', quite close to the ventilation grille of the charnel beneath the tower.

On page 31 of the Cole notebook there is a discussion of the Holmes memorial: 'Near this Stone Lieth Interred Mr. Thomas Holmes late of the Parish of St. Nicholas in this City Merchant, who full of Days, and ripe for his expected Summons, departed this life in the Faith and Fear of Christ in sure and certain Hope of a Resurrection unto Glory on the 24th day of July in the year 1761, in the 73rd Year of his Age. 'Also beneath this Trophy of the Victories of Death lieth Interr'd ELIZABETH the Daughter of Thomas Holmes [...] And of Mrs. Mary Holmes relict of the said Thomas Holmes who died Septr. 27th 1789 Aged 85 Years'. Canon Cole wrote against it: 'interred in Crypt No. 5'. In faint pencil he added 'Elizabeth lies in cemetery under the tower'. It had long been the practice to grant the parson the privilege of burial beneath his chancel. The rector would also occasionally grant such a position to his favourites as it was in his gift. In 1920 Canon Cole placed the Holmes grave at the east end of the crypt beneath the transept, two plots away from the Reverend Dr. Ireland's family vault. Had Elizabeth been buried in the vault beneath the tower she would have been lying far away at the west end. How did Canon Cole know that the family had been divided?

A clue can be found in the rubbings the Canon had made of inscribed lead plates, similar to but not *deposita*, a few inches long and to be found attached to pp.101, 103 & 105 of the Cole notebook. They may be read as 'C. Brent', 'Mr. Skinner & Family', 'Mr. Banister's Family' and 'Miss Holmes'. These labels had been found in 'the cemetery under the Tower in Christ Church'. Canon Cole had typed out his transcriptions of each and added 'there are two more large lead plates in the strong room from the Coffins of Tyndall and Banister, both from Cemetery under Tower'. Canon Cole added a sketch of the 'Tyndall' label '11" by 10⅝"' In 1958 we noted a 'strong room' in the north-east corner of the crypt next to the furnace which was above Canon Cole's 'vault No. 5'.

The lead labels hint strongly at a more formal use of the 'cemetery under the tower'. In the eighteenth century a parish vault, or vestry vault, offered a fashionable space for the worthy dead to share rather than suffer being crammed one upon another in the narrow brick-lined family vaults marked by ledger stones elsewhere in the crypt. The labels were employed to guide the sexton when re-uniting new coffins with family members who had predeceased them. In that sense the sexton had the same duty to the dead that the pew-openers had to the living worshippers above.

'C. Brent' was evidently the marker for the Revd. Charles Brent, rector of both Christ Church (1682–1729) and St. Werburgh. His bones may have remained behind when the Brent memorial was moved to Wraxall church in Somerset when Christ Church was demolished in 1786. 'Miss Holmes' is surely identified as Elizabeth who died in 1772. Her mother must have been able to arrange for the coffins of her husband, who died in 1761, and her daughter to be stored between 1786 and the opening of the new cemetery. As Mary Holmes had died in 1789 one wonders why her executors did not re-unite all three members of the family in 'No. 5'?

The families identified by Canon Cole may be given more than a name and a date by recourse to the trade directories of the time. *Sketchley's Bristol Directory*, published for the broker and auctioneer in 1775, allows the reader to follow the merchants of Wine Street to their final rest, side by side in death just as they traded side by side in life. We find the dry salters Tyndall, Power & Townsend with their neighbour Daniel Burgess, the attorney. There were many linen drapers: William Baylis was one as were his competitors Peter Goodwin, James Hill, Culliford & Usher and Mary Stephens the hosier. Another attorney, Jacob Kirby, might well have served the same customers as his neighbour: Ann Raymond the upholder. Upholders provided all the fashionable fabrics of a funeral, as well as the palls, shrouds and gloves they supplied the cockades and elaborate swags and drapes that transformed the homes and workplace of the living into dark caverns of mourning for the dead. That upholders traded in the heart of a street of linen drapers and haberdashers is unsurprising and Ann Raymond would have felt at home with her customers in her grave under Christ Church.

In Broad Street, James Sketchley identifies Gravenor & Carr at their 'ribbon & stuff warehouse', James Skynner, the excise officer, John Townsend the surgeon, and another hosier: Ann Jackson. William White kept the White Hart alongside Job Williams the grocer and chandler, James Edwards the chemist, Ann Edwards and Arthur Palmer both tea-dealers, and Robert Langford a bank-clerk. It is easy to imagine these traders, disgusted by conditions in the overcrowded city burial grounds, being tempted to buy plots cut in the soft sandstone below their bright new church.

THE END OF ST. EWEN'S CHURCH

Canon Cole felt closely attached to the church and was intrigued by the plight of the dead of St. Ewen's parish. He was to choose drawings used by the B. & G. A. S. that showed St. Ewen's church in 1795 on the Christmas cards sent from his home at 7 Great George Street, one of Paty's townhouses, which the Coles were to leave to the citizens of Bristol and is now preserved as the popular museum: The Georgian House. He also commissioned the Bristol artist, Arthur C. Fare (1878–1958), R.W.A., in the 1920s to paint a re-construction of St. Ewen's church looking up Broad Street towards the High Cross,[11] and upon leaving Bristol in 1938 he called his new home St. Ewen's.[12] (Fig. 11).

Canon Cole, when consulting papers and sketches in the Braikenridge Collection on 2 December 1922, was pleased to find a mention of the 'discoveries made on the digging for the foundations of the New Council House 1824' and noted that there was 'nothing above ground on St. Ewen's site' as demolition had taken place in 1820.[13] Fourteen stone graves cut from entire pieces of Dundry stone, each to fit a

---

[11] J. Hudson, *The Savage Spirit*, (Bristol, 2004), pp. 153, 164. He was president of the Savages in 1927–1928, and was succeeded by another friend of Canon Cole, the architect C. F. W. Dening, R.W.A.

[12] Situated in Westover Road, Milford on Sea, Hampshire.

[13] In fact demolition, for the most part, appears to have taken place in 1823–1824.

body and covered with long flat stones, were sketched 'three feet below ground [...] bodies placed into these stone spaces, tightly packed with no coffins'.[14] They were found 'under the Examination Room and Large Hall of the Old Council House' in what had formerly served as the south aisle of St. Ewen's church. A capital fashioned in the Norman style, parts of fluted bases and stone coffins, one with a cross fashioned on the lid, were uncovered. Things that intrigued Braikenridge delighted Canon Cole and he listed the coins found: a shilling of Henry VIII, a sixpence of James I (c. 1603), a shilling of Charles I and a handful of copper coins and tokens. He was moved by a lock of female hair found in a coffin behind Mr. Davis's shop (the glover's) with a wrapped miniature oil painting of a bewigged man of the early 1700s.

Amongst the odd scraps collected by Canon Cole was the important note that 'the remains of 1,000 skeletons at least were dug up in the site of the old church of St. Ewen's and churchyard and there were nearly 500 skulls mostly in good preservation and many with the teeth quite perfect'.[15] It seems they were 'carefully collected and put into a large shaft dug for that purpose and securely covered down with stone and mortar'. Canon Cole added the important observation 'probably that in the cemetery under the tower in Christ Church: R.T.C.'. This offers the strongest suggestion that Canon Cole was aware of the remains under the tower and suspected their origin was, indeed, the clearance of St. Ewen in 1824.

Might the mound of remains photographed in 1958 have contained '1,000 skeletons at least'? In the 130 years since the material was roughly tipped into the vault it has subsided into a pile with a volume of about 350 cubic feet which could easily represent the remains of 500 individuals. No allowance has been made for the well or any other pit dug into the vault floor and covered by the deposit so perhaps more burials may be represented. Might the fragmentary account in the Braikenridge Collection be an eye-witness account or merely hearsay? What can we make of the 'large shaft dug for that purpose'? Had an opening been made into the vault from overhead, perhaps through the floor of the porch near the staircase leading up the tower? Alterations made since the Patys finished their porch would have masked any backfilled hole in the floor and there is nothing to detect now. Such a hole made into the vault below might have resembled 'a shaft' and 'stone and mortar' would certainly have been employed to close-up the hole and repair the vault.

The tipping of the St. Ewen's materials straight into the vault would certainly explain the tumbling mound that we saw in 1958 and would offer the most efficient if the least respectful means of disposal of the remains. Eager to clear the site in readiness for celebrations of mayoral foundation-stone laying surely the city corporation would have paid for the work? Might proof be found in the accounts of the two vestries involved? Was Canon Cole mistaken and were the remains, after all, the disturbed burials cleared from the old Christ Church? The latter possibility will be considered elsewhere in this volume.

[14] Bristol Reference Library, Braikenridge MS XV, f. 455.
[15] Notes in possession of Dr. Crossley Evans, extracted by Canon Cole from Bristol Reference Library, Braikenridge MS XV, f. 457.

BURIALS AT ST. EWEN 1700 TO 1791

Although St. Ewen was a small parish (Fig. 12) there were on average slightly more than three burials per annum between March 1700 and December 1775, making a total of 242 burials for this period. [See Table 1]. The registers make no record of the burials which took place from 1776 until the church closed in 1791 but there may have been a further 60 to 70 during this period. The last marriage took place on the 22 March 1790 and the last baptisms were on the 5 May 1790 and the 25 August 1791.[16]

We know that many of the burials for the period 1755 to 1767 were for people resident outside the parish, for example two of the three in 1755, three of the five in 1756, and all of the four in 1758. Of the 36 burials in this period 26 were of people non-resident in the parish. This situation was so serious that the vestry at its meeting on 17 July 1778 discussed: 'the future burying of the poor who claim a right of being buried in the churchyard'. They agreed: 'that whenever any application in future shall be made for the above purpose, the church warden for the time being, shall and may allow and pay unto such persons so applying the whole expense attending such burial in any other place that shall be [...] convenient for that purpose'.[17] This was to ensure that there was sufficient burial space in the church and the churchyard for the vestrymen and their families. Such drastic measures to encourage the families of the poor to bury their dead elsewhere explains, in part, their panic at the implication of the union of their parish with Christ Church, whose problems with their burying grounds were well-known. On 5 May 1788 the St. Ewen's vestry minutes recorded that the members:

> throw themselves under [the bishop's] protection and request his attention to their interests and particularly that a proper burying ground may be assured to the parish or that a sufficient sum may be paid them to enable them to purchase ground for that purpose—And this is the more material to the parish as the burying grounds of Christ Church are very small.[18]

In spite of the fact that the upper churchyard of Christ Church and the crypt of the new church were to be reduced further in area to allow part of the land to be commercially let in order to ease the cost of re-building, the bishop, Dr. Christopher Wilson,[19] did nothing in response to the petition of the vestry.

The town clerk, Samuel Worrall (1756–1821),[20] was more forthcoming and certified on the same day:

> In consideration of the parishioners of Saint Ewen's in making no opposition to the

---

[16] B.R.O., P/St E/R/1(b), unfoliated.

[17] B.R.O., P/St E/V/2, f. 80.

[18] *Ibid.*, f. 128.

[19] Bishop from 1783 until his death on 18 April 1792; E. Boswell, *The Ecclesiastical Division of the Diocese of Bristol*, (Sherborne, *c.* 1826), p. 6.

[20] Town clerk, 30 June 1787, resigned following the failure of the bank of which he was a partner 1819, the Revd. A. B. Beaven, *Bristol Lists: Municipal and Miscellaneous*, (Bristol, 1899), p. 235. Forever haunted by the 'Caraboo' hoax of 1817 when the Worralls entertained the young Devon vagrant, Mary Ann Baker, at Knole Park, Almondsbury, Gloucestershire, believing her to be a shipwrecked princess, J. Wells, *Princess Caraboo: Her True Story*, (1994).

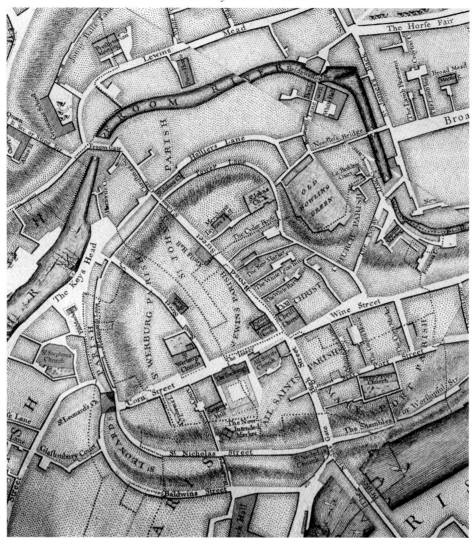

Fig. 12. The parishes of St. Ewen and Christ Church illustrated from Rocque's map of Bristol, 1750, [Special Collections, University of Bristol].

church bill now before Parliament, we do promise in case it shall appear that the parish church of Christ Church to which the parish of Saint Ewen's is now annexed shall not be large enough for the parishioners of Saint Ewen's to bury therein or they sho[ul]d have no right to bury therein by the Act of Union that we will recommend to the corporation to provide a piece of ground for the parish of Saint Ewen's for the purpose of a burying ground in lieu of that which is intended to be taken away by the Act now about to be passed.[21]

---

[21] B.R.O., P/St E/V/2, pasted onto the last page.

By this time the Common Council were fully aware of what they had proposed in the draft Act submitted to Parliament for 'enlarging the Council House and Guildhall and for taking down St. Ewen's and certain houses and buildings in the city' because it had been read in the council on 28 February 1788.[22] The Act was passed later in the year.

John Weeks, one of the church wardens of St. Ewen, formally gave the church to the mayor on 10 December 1791 and two days later the mayor formally took possession of the building on behalf of 'the mayor, burgesses and commonality', and informed the Common Council that they could now dispose of the church and appurtances according to the terms of the Act.[23] This was done without any provision being made for the future burials of the residents of the parish.

Allowing for the fact that the parish was more populous prior to 1700, and if the estimate of the number of skeletons removed in 1824 is accurate, namely about one thousand, and that just over 300 burials took place at St. Ewen's between 1700 and 1791, many of the remains cleared from the churchyard may have dated from the earlier centuries.

Table 1. Burials in St. Ewen's church and churchyard March 1700—December 1775 [24]

1700	8	1716	5	1732	7	1748	1	1764	4
1701	2	1717	2	1733	1	1749	2	1765	3
1702	1	1718	-	1734	5	1750	5	1766	2
1703	2	1719	2	1735	1	1751	2	1767	1
1704	4	1720	8	1736	2	1752	2	1768	2
1705	5	1721	6	1737	7	1753	6	1769	7
1706	5	1722	3	1738	4	1754	2	1770	2
1707	2	1723	3	1739	5	1755	3	1771	-
1708	3	1724	3	1740	5	1756	5	1772	2
1709	1	1725	2	1741	3	1757	3	1773	1
1710	4	1726	1	1742	1	1758	4	1774	2
1711	7	1727	2	1743	5	1759	5	1775	4
1712	2	1728	3	1744	3	1760	1		
1713	3	1729	1	1745	4	1761	2		
1714	7	1730	4	1746	4	1762	2		
1715	2	1731	4	1747	2	1763	1	Total	242

ST. EWEN'S CHURCH AND VAULT

We know that there was a crypt or vault underneath the chancel window of St. Ewen facing Broad Street. The proctors of St. Ewen paid a rent to the corporation for shop premises here in the first half of the seventeenth century. We also know that in 1700 the feoffees of St. Ewen's charity leased the parsonage adjoining the church together with a 'new deep cellar lately digged by the churchwardens' which also extended

---

[22] B.R.O., Proceedings of the Common Council 1783–1790, p. 201.
[23] B.R.O., Proceedings of the Common Council 1791–1796, p. 88.
[24] Taken from P/St E/R/1(b) unfoliated.

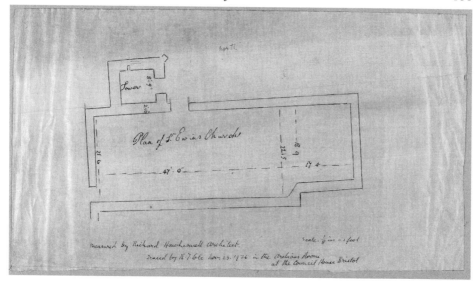

Fig. 13. Canon Cole's sketch of the plan of St. Ewen, made in 1926 from an unidentified original, [Collection of M. J. Crossley Evans].

under the chancel, to George Lewis bookseller.[25] In the following year a vault adjoining and also situated under the chancel was constructed to house the remains of John Creswick(e), gentleman.[26] By the end of the eighteenth century the Creswick vault was let by the feoffees as a vintner's store.

It is possible that the rest of the church was underpinned by a crypt, but there is no direct evidence of this. The record of burials between 1768 and 1775 lists the actual places of burial as follow:

Table 2. Places of interment at St. Ewen 1768 to 1775

Year	Total Burials	Church	Churchyard
1768	2	2	
1769	7	7	
1770	2		2
1771	-		
1772	2	1	1
1773	1		1
1774	2	1	1
1775	4	4	
	20	15*	5

*It is possible that all of these were burials under the floor of the nave of the church rather than in specific vaults.

[25] R. H. Leech, *The Topography of Mediaeval and Early Modern Bristol*, B.R.S., XLVIII, (1997), pp. 30–31.
[26] He came from one of the leading families in the city which provided three mayors in the seventeenth century, and a dean of Bristol cathedral in the eighteenth.

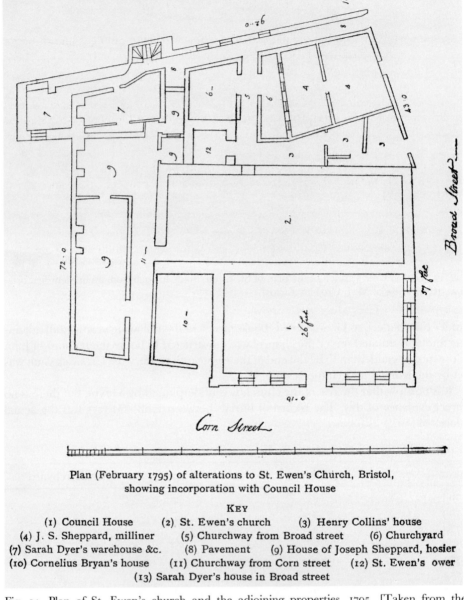

Plan (February 1795) of alterations to St. Ewen's Church, Bristol,
showing incorporation with Council House

KEY

(1) Council House   (2) St. Ewen's church   (3) Henry Collins' house
(4) J. S. Sheppard, milliner   (5) Churchway from Broad street   (6) Churchyard
(7) Sarah Dyer's warehouse &c.   (8) Pavement   (9) House of Joseph Sheppard, hosier
(10) Cornelius Bryan's house   (11) Churchway from Corn street   (12) St. Ewen's ower
(13) Sarah Dyer's house in Broad street

Fig. 14. Plan of St. Ewen's church and the adjoining properties, 1795, [Taken from the
T.B. & G.A.S. XLVIII, (1926), p. 235, and reproduced by kind permission of the Bristol and
Gloucestershire Archaeological Society].

THE SEXTONS OF ST. EWEN, 1762–1829

The sexton and the dead of the parish had a close connection. Little is known of the post of sexton at St. Ewen in the eighteenth century. The work was light and the salary a mere £4 per annum. The vestry minutes of 21 April 1762 note that Richard Thomas had neglected his duties as parish clerk and sexton, and 'after several repeated adm[on]itions' he was removed from the post of sexton. The minutes do not record the name of his successor,[27] but it was probably John Grabham who resigned from the post on 26 December 1769 and was replaced by Henry Crook 'during pleasure'.

There are records of monies received for two burials in 1783, one at 6/8d (a child), and another at 13/4d.[28] There were three burials in 1785 two at 13/4d and one at 11/7d.[29] Money was expended on cleaning the churchyard as late as 1785.[30] A Miss Davis was buried in November 1786 and the accounts note that the minister's fee for the burial was one guinea and that the cost of the use of the church was 13/4d. We know from Christ Church that this was the sum paid for the ground used for the burial. By this date Mr. Crook's widow, Hannah, was sexton.[31] In 1789–1790 her quarterly payments amounted to £11.19.2d.[32] As her salary was then £7 per annum she must have undertaken a considerable number of additional tasks on behalf of the vestry, like her counterpart at Christ Church.

On 3 January 1799 it was noted that Mrs. Crook had become Mrs. Smith.[33] She continued to be paid by the vestry of St. Ewen as their sextoness after the congregation moved to Christ Church.

Sextons of St. Ewen

Richard Thomas		–1762
John Grabham	1762	–1769
Henry Crook	1769– before	1784
Hannah Crook	before	1784–1829
(As Mrs. Smith	from	1789).

After the amalgamation of the parishes in December 1788, the vestry paid Mrs. Smith ten shillings annually each December from the forty shillings which they received from Alderman Harrington's and Alderman Kitchen's gifts.[34] When Hannah Smith finally died at a great age in January 1829 it was noted that she had been 'partly supported for a considerable time past by her [...] son in law', Thomas Crook, who received her half yearly salary. It appears that the actual work of sexton for the

---

[27] B.R.O., P/St E/V/2, f. 34, f. 56.
[28] These occur in 1784, but were in the accounts of Charles Prosser, who was church warden between the Easter vestries in 1782 and 1784.
[29] *Ibid.*, ff. 96, 104, 108.
[30] *Ibid.*, f. 108, 21 December 1785 'pd Charles Chapple for doing up the ch. yd. £1.11.8d'.
[31] *Ibid.*, ff. 122–123.
[32] *Ibid.*, f. 141. In 1786–1787 they were £12.12.10d, ff.122–123.
[33] *Ibid.*, f. 206.
[34] *Ibid.*, f. 129. This may have been the practice prior to this date.

parishioners of St. Ewen had been undertaken since at least 1817 by Mrs. Charlotte Jones, who was subsequently sexton of Christ Church. It is presumed that following the union of the parishes, Mrs. Crook would have been responsible for the burial of all the residents of the old parish of St. Ewen in the churchyards and the crypt of Christ Church. No doubt it was she, by then an elderly woman, who played an important role, either directly or through a deputy, in the disposal of the dead of St. Ewen after the church was demolished. In 1824 John Evans[35] records the digging for the foundations of the new Council House. Referring to the events of *c.* 1823 he says: 'Generally, the contents of the cemetery appear to have been rudely disturbed on the demolition of the church, when those who, laying claim to the ashes of relatives, had them re-interred in Christ Church'.

After 5 July 1829 the salary of the sextoness of St. Ewen was £8 p.a. 'including all extra charges', which was to be divided equally between Philip Jones, the parish clerk, and his wife, who was now the 'sextoness' of both Christ Church and St. Ewen. The vestry minutes of St. Ewen note: 'the allowance to the clerk and sextoness [*sic*] is gratuitous (except such part as they are entitled to by wills) and may be discounted at the pleasure of the vestry'.[36] The clerk and the 'sextoness' were also given five shillings each at the annual vestry dinner of St. Ewen.

THE DEMOLITION OF ST. EWEN[37]

The vestry was very concerned to learn that the corporation wanted to take down the church of St. Ewen and petitioned them on the subject in November 1786.[38] The approaching closure of the church meant that Thomas Pierce Junior, a former church warden laid claim to his former gift of the clock inside the church.[39] It is quite possible that in spite of the apparent supine attitude of the vestry to the plans of the corporation for its church at this stage, there was opposition. The parishioners of St. Ewen were firmly opposed to the union.[40] John Ellis[41] served as junior church warden between 1781 and 1783 and wished to stand again for election at the Easter vestry in 1787. There was an objection to his nomination on the grounds that he lived 'upon Kingsdown' with his family. The question was referred to Mr. Hobhouse[42] and it was noted that 'Mr. Ellis stands rated in the parish books and pays both landlord and tenant's taxes and also a proportional part towards the maintenance of the apprentices,

---

[35] J. Evans, *Chronological Outline of the History of Bristol and the Stranger's Guide*, (Bristol, 1824), p. 368.

[36] B.R.O., P/St E/V/3, ff. 130, 132.

[37] For an account of the church and its demolition, see, R. Jackson, 'Excavations at the Old Council House, Corn Street, Bristol, 2005', *Bristol and Avon Archaeology*, 22, (2007), pp. 49, 50.

[38] B.R.O., P/St E/V/2, f. 116, no copy of the petition is to be found amongst the vestry minutes.

[39] *Ibid.*, f. 119. A watchmaker and goldsmith of 8 Broad Street, he was church warden from 1778 to 1780, and from 1785 to 1787.

[40] B.R.O., P/XCh/1/4, p. 16.

[41] He was a peruke maker and hair dresser of 9 Broad Street. B.R.O., P/XCh/R/1 (d), unfoliated, buried in Christ Church in a vault in the church 28 February 1797.

[42] Probably the man mentioned in *Sketchley's Bristol Directory 1775* as a counsellor, at 7 Clifton Hill.

but he neither eats, drinks or sleeps in the said house' in Broad Street which was resided in by his partner. Mr. Hobhouse deemed him non-resident and therefore inel-igible to serve as church warden. The next in rotation eligible to serve in the office was Charles Prosser, a silk mercer at 7 Broad Street, who had served as junior church warden between 1770 and 1772, and between 1775 and 1777, and as senior church war-den between 1782 and 1784, but who, for reasons which are not explained was 'also deemed ineligible'.[43] The junior church warden between 1783 and 1785, William Bulgin (1758–1831),[44] was then duly elected and appears to have offered no opposition to the bill before Parliament or to the demolition of the parish church. Charles Prosser again served as church warden of St. Ewen between 1791 and 1793, by which time the church had ceased as a place of worship and he was unable to oppose the corporation's plans for the church.[45]

On the 24 April 1788 the vestry noted that the proposed Act of Parliament[46] was principally designed as a road widening measure with the demolition of the church and the removal of the churchyard as an adjunct. It was noted that the bill made no mention of any compensation for the materials of the demolished church and ground and the vestry determined to try to obtain compensation 'how trifling soever it may be' through petitioning their M.P., Matthew Brickdale (1734–1831). This achieved nothing and he was as helpless, as compromised, or as indifferent to the plight of the parishioners and the vestry as the bishop.[47] The vestry also noted that their annual income would suffer as a result of the passage of the Act because 'under part of the church (viz. the chancel) there is a vault or cellar now occupied by [John] Manwaring, for which he pays and the occupiers of the tenem[en]t held by him, have for a long time since paid a rent to the parish'. There was also the loss of the revenue from the vault of Mr. Creswick which had been constructed in 1701 and subsequently rented out as a store-room to one of their tenants, John Weeks, vintner of the Bush tavern[48] at 40 Corn Street, for five shillings per annum.[49]

[43] B.R.O., P/St E/V/2, f. 120. See Appendix 2.

[44] The Revd. A. B. Beaven, *op. cit.*, p. 328. B.R.O., P/XCh/R/4 (a), p. 42, of Royal Fort House, buried 5 October 1831, aged 73. He may well have been related to the Tyndall family. We find one William Tindall Bulgin of St. James's Place, buried at Christ Church on 11 June 1833, aged 38.

[45] He died *c.* 1797.

[46] *28 Geo. III (1788), cap. 67: An Act for widening and rendering commodious a certain Street called Broad Street within the city of Bristol; and for enlarging the Council House and the Guild Hall of the said city, and providing Public Offices thereto, and Repositories for the Books, Papers and Records of the said city.*

[47] The Revd. A. B. Beaven, *op. cit.*, p. 279, he was a member of the common council between 1767 and 1824, served as M.P. between 1768 and 1774 and 1780 and 1790 and died 8 September 1831, aged 97.

[48] The Birmingham diligence and a Bath coach went from the inn and Mr. Weeks let post chaises for hire. One of the leading inns in the city, it was the home of the masonic lodge, where Dr. William Howley, Queen Victoria's first archbishop of Canterbury was initiated, and the setting of part of Dickens's novel, *Pickwick Papers*.

[49] B.R.O., P/St E/V/2, ff. 127, 128, See f. 104, 6 July 1785 when John Weeks was recorded as paying £2.10.0d as rent for the vault. He served as junior church warden from 1790 to 1791 and as senior church warden from 1791 to 1792: f. 141 shows that John Manwaring paid £25 rent in June 1790. Monies were still being paid for the upkeep of Mr. Creswick's vault in 1792–1793 and Mr. Manwaring's rent was paid up to and including the 12 March 1793. P/St E/M/1, 1701 copy will of John Creswick, gentleman of Bristol, P/St E/D/29, 26 June 1793

Fig. 15. The remains of St. Ewen's tower adjoining the Old Council Chamber. This view is taken from the church passage way which opened out into Broad Street looking towards the obscured north wall of the church (1820). The doorway into the tower which faced east is obscured by the lean-to buildings erected against the north wall of the church following its closure. Watercolour by Hugh O'Neill (1784–1824), [Bristol City Museum and Art Gallery, Braikenridge Collection M2308].

It should be noted that the antipathy caused by the union of the two parishes and the demolition of St. Ewen lasted into the early 1880s. Not only did the vestry of St Ewen's continue to have their own sexton, and subsequently hire and pay their own choir members, who were independent of those of Christ Church with predictable musical results, but they elected their own church wardens, who acted as junior wardens to those of Christ Church, and maintained their own vestry room in the tower of the new church.

THE DEAD OF ST. EWEN'S PARISH

If we accept that the remains found under the tower of Christ Church, with a few exceptions, cannot represent the dead raised by Paty's workmen from the church and churchyard in 1786, then were they, as a church warden suggested in 1958 echoing the thoughts of Canon Cole in 1922, the dead of St. Ewen?

No entry in the burial registers of either parish supports the premise but the removal and re-burial of the dead would not warrant registration. Some parsons or clerks would add a brief note of clarification but it would not be done as a matter of course.

St. Ewen's church had been something of a Cinderella having to live so close to big sisters All Saints' and Christ Church.[50] The church in the eighteenth century consisted of a nave,[51] and a churchyard on its north side. (Figs. 13 and 14). The south aisle which had formed the chapel of St. John the Baptist was surrendered to the corporation of Bristol in 1551 for an annual rent of 6/8d. The corporation absorbed the chapel and the parish subsequently 'added to' the tower next to the north door in 1631.[52] (Fig. 15). The church was small but adequate for its congregation. *Mathews's Bristol Directory* for 1793–1794 called it 'the smallest Church in Bristol, having only

lease of house in Corn Street by the feoffees of St. Ewen's to John Weeks, vintner, to be a coffee room called *Jack's Coffee Room*. For Weeks as an actor and eccentric, see G. H. Gibbs, *Bristol Postscripts: being a selection of articles which have appeared in the Bristol Evening Post*, (Bristol, undated, c. 1950), pp. 89–98.

[50] The late Dr. Arthur Basil Cottle intended to write a detailed history of all the churches dedicated to St. Ewen or St. Owen in the British Isles, but he died before this project could be completed. His notes, photographs and maps have been recently deposited in the Special Collections of the University of Bristol where they join his other papers.

[51] In their introduction to *The Church Book of St. Ewen's, Bristol 1454–1584*, (1967), p. xiv, the editors Miss Betty Masters and Dr. Elizabeth Ralph described the fifteenth century church with two aisles. The volume was dedicated to Canon R.T. Cole. F. G. Lewin in his depiction of the church c. 1600 shows a north aisle, which is not known to have existed, F. G. Lewin, *Portfolio of Sketches of Bristol in the XVIIth and XVIIIth Centuries*, (Bristol c. 1922), unpaginated. Frederick George Lewin, (1861–1933), R.W.A., was a prolific self-taught artist, best known for his Bristol scenes.

[52] This is the official story, but the surviving illustration of the church tower as it existed in a truncated form in 1820 shows that the bottom storey of the tower was certainly of mediaeval date and contained a window of possibly fourteenth century date, see J. S. Prout, *Picturesque Antiquities of Bristol: Drawn from Nature and on Stone*, (Bristol, undated but c. 1835), unpaginated, contains as plate No. 26, a lithograph showing the 'Remains of the Old Tower of St. Ewen's', painted originally in 1820 by Hugh O'Neill, (see Fig. 15).

one aile 66 feet long'.[53] Its close proximity to the buildings which surrounded it, particularly to the west *via* the narrow passage way and the small opening called St. Ewen's Court, caused problems. We learn that a door made into the wall of John Kimber's 'coffe [*sic*] and tipling house' nearly opposite the church's west door, had led, in an earlier age, to 'divers dissolute, idle and disorderly persons sitting Tippling and Smoaking Tobacco in the said Coffee house at the time of saying Divine Service, and doing other Holy Offices in the same church, [who] do with Derision and Contempt look on such as are at their Devotions in the said Parish Church, and by their Tipling and Tobacco taking there do offend and interrupt such as are [...] at Church'.[54]

The Corporation tried to acquire and convert St. Ewen into a library in 1657. The necessary Act of Parliament was obtained but nothing was done until 1787. The Act suggested that it was hoped to join St. Ewen's parish with All Saints' in 1657. A fresh Act was obtained in 1788 but, again, action was delayed while after the closure of the church the council used the old nave and tower for document storage. By 1820 the council's financial situation had improved, the long war with France was concluded and it had become clear that a new Council House was not only needed but possible and the St. Ewen's site would permit the desired expansion. John Latimer in *The Annals of Bristol in the Nineteenth Century* (Bristol, 1887) chronicles the decisions taken. He suggested that the church building was taken down in 1791, and whilst the upper part of the tower was removed in 1795 it appears that the body of the church remained. The chamberlain ordered the tower to be sketched and measured, together with the plans showing their intended incorporation into the old Council House, the church yard and the Churchways to the church from Corn Street and Broad Street together with their adjoining properties.[55] (Fig. 14). No new building was started before Sir Robert Smirke presented his designs for the Council House in 1823. His designs were rejected for not permitting a desired widening of Corn Street and Broad Street so Smirke made modifications and the work began. The mayor, John Barrow,[56] laid the foundation stone in May 1824.

A search of the Braikenridge manuscripts in Bristol's Reference Library revealed an interesting eye-witness account of the removal of the dead of St. Ewen written in the 1840s:[57]

> It was a singular sight, at the same time that this same St. Ewen's churchyard was being cleared, to see people coming from all quarters and carrying away their long gone relatives, at dead of night, in mouldering coffins, like so many resurrectionists.

---

[53] *Mathews's Bristol Directory for 1793–4*, p. 71. It also mentions its two bells and tower 60 feet high with battlements on the top.

[54] MS notes by Canon Cole, extracted from the Braikenridge MS XVII, 'The Grand Jurie's address to the Mayor of Bristol, 1681'.

[55] N. Dermott Harding. 'The Archives of the Corporation of Bristol', *T. B. & G. A. S.*, XLVIII, (1926), pp. 234–235, Figures 2 and 3. B.R.O., 00228 (22). A sketch plan of the church was prepared in 1795 by Richard Hawkeswell, architect, and copied by Canon Cole on 23 November 1926.

[56] Great uncle of Charles Dickens.

[57] Bristol Reference Library, Braikenridge MS XV, f. 81.

Thus we know that some of those buried in the churchyard and church, who had family alive at the time of the clearance of the site, were to find a resting place in the new Christ Church. Others were, perhaps, to be moved to family plots and vaults elsewhere in the city. The large majority of human remains, however, would have had no one to lay claim to them.

A search was made for payments from the Council for clearing the graves from the church and churchyard but the Town Clerk's record in the B.R.O. lacked the convincing item. He did, however, charge large sums to the building of the New Council House and the money was handed to Edward Brigden, the clerk of works. For example £170.18.0 was paid in June 1824 for sundry expenses associated with the laying of the foundation stone. Other payments were more transparent: Brigden's salary, modest sums to the church wardens of Christ Church (19.4½d and £10.18.0)[58] and, for comparison, £3.15.0 was enough for the sheriff's sergeant (William Silvey) to pay forty men to carry books and papers to the Guildhall in September.

However the job was paid for it had happened by 21 February 1825 when Sarah Poston accepted £22 to give all the workmen a good dinner to celebrate 'completing the shell of the building'. From that date onward regular sums were paid to Joseph Phillips the mason, Charles Whiting the plumber, William Edkins the painter, John Crispin the carpenter and the ironmongers Underwood & Co. Smirke claimed £210 for the sculptor who supplied the statue over the entrance. The work proceeded briskly and by 1827 the Town Clerk's journal was noting payments for all the furnishings, stained glass, blinds, picture frames, gas lights, inkstands and the engraving of the new great council seal. Nothing has emerged since we began our search in 2007 to account for the moving of the St. Ewen's burials. Might the work have been considered too sensitive to record in detail? Might the £170 in cash have gone some way to transporting the remains into the tower cemetery? Perhaps vouchers or receipts will turn up in time but it seems doubtful as, in 1824 alone the Town Clerk wrote off £1,334.3.4 to cash without recording any detail.

THE BURIAL REGISTERS

Before 1813 the parish clerks or parsons of Christ Church merely entered a year, a day, a name and the parish of the deceased if other than Christ Church. The actual place of burial was rarely noted after the re-opening in 1791, but there are instances of 'lower churchyard' (Duck Lane), 'upper churchyard' (next to the church), 'in the church' or 'in the crowd'. These two last referred to the cemetery beneath the church and were often one and the same; brick-lined graves beneath the paved floor. Was there a link with the cemetery under the tower? The survival of a Tyndall shell there could hint at a more prestigious intent for the space.

A recurring family name amongst the Tyndalls was 'Thomas' of whom the most important was Thomas Tyndall for whom the splendid Royal Fort had been built. Canon Cole proudly recorded the Tyndall family wall monuments, including a modest celebration of Thomas who died in 1794 aged 72 and Alicia, his wife, who had died thirty years earlier in 1764 aged 31.

[58] These may, however, disguise payments for the removal of the bodies from St. Ewen.

The register confirms that the crowd was the chosen place of rest for the Tyndalls. In 1804 another Thomas (son of Thomas) died on 23 July and was buried a week later 'in the crowd' as was his wife Marianne, who had died on 15 November 1805 and was buried on 23 December. A year later their daughter Alicia joined them 'in the crowd' in 1806. Another generation of Tyndalls were to follow: Mary Sybelle Tyndall on 21 August 1822, of Royal Fort, St. Michael's aged 31[59], and her husband Thomas Tyndall in 1841.

Canon Cole had noted that one of the regular row of substantial ledger stones guarding the west end of the cemetery, number 47 on his plan, was inscribed 'Thomas Tyndall Esq: Burial Ground'. It might be supposed that he, in the burial register denominated as 'Thomas Tyndall Senr', had purchased a double-width vault suited to his family's status before his death in 1794. The other Thomas, whose burial in 1766 'from London' was favoured with an invitation to a place in the family grave in Bristol, was presumably moved to the 'cemetery under the tower' in the late 1780s. Five other members of the family are found in the register between 1747 and 1764 buying burial at Christ Church. We cannot know whether they were moved to the new vault.

Those coffins favoured with burial in the vault under the tower before the re-opening of the church seem to be either ancestors or close relatives of worshippers alive in 1790; Canon Cole's handful of lead labels affirms this. How were the coffins carried into the vault? Apart from the ventilation grille we had noticed no obvious entrance way in 1958. We revisited the crypt in 2005 and again in 2007.

'THE CEMETERY UNDER THE TOWER' REVISITED

In September 2005 we noted that the damaged ventilation grille had been blocked with bricks, cement and a sealed iron inspection cover. The grille had been in the centre of an arched opening in the west wall four feet wide (122 cm). From the crypt floor to the inside top of the arch is also four feet. The arch is built of well dressed ashlar blocks and it echoes the arches in all the crypt walls. A well-drawn plan of Christ Church made in 1887 by the architect Henry Williams of Clare Street in Bristol confirms that the arches lie directly below the surface features such as windows or doorways.[60] The Patys would have appreciated that the arch was strong and allowed a saving of stone.

The stonework around the old grille is set back 27" (69cm) from the face of the crypt wall. Small blocks of coursed, undressed pennant sandstone were used, bound with a lime mortar. Although similar to the mortar found elsewhere in Paty's work of the 1780s some repairs seemed to be of a nineteenth century date.

We noted that the ledger slabs recorded by Canon Cole continue without interruption along the west end of the crypt and seemed to rule out a stairway descending from the crypt floor to the 'cemetery under the tower'. In 2005 we wondered if the blocking of the vault and backfilling hid a redundant flight of steps which might have afforded space for another grave. Canon Cole observed, as we did, small packing pieces of freestone separating the grave slabs near the putative 'entrance'.

[59] B.R.O., P/XCh/R/4 (a), p. 23, Burials 1813–1854.
[60] B.R.O., P/XCh/PP/11/2.

Two years later, in September 2007, we were invited to reconsider the possibility of lost steps surviving that would have permitted access to the vault under the tower. It was no longer easy to see the crypt as Canon Cole once saw it but the six grave slabs indentified by him as those of Kirby,[61] Salway,[62] 'W.A.',[63] Robertson,[64] Tyndal [sic][65] and Townsend were still accessible. That of Charles Robertson of Balliol College, Oxford, marks a burial on 3 July 1793. It lies directly in front of the ventilation grille of the tower vault.

A non-invasive 12" (30cm) square sounding was cautiously made east of the free-stone packing blocks. Should a set of steps have been laid there to the vault evidence might have survived. It was clear that the massive sandstone grave slabs capped, as supposed, brick-lined graves. The brickwork of 'W.A.''s grave appeared in section and indicated that the graves were closed by small pennant slabs laid flat-side down on to the top of brick sides of the vault. Above this a layer of loose packed earth allowed ledgers of different thickness to be laid evenly. 'W. A.'s grave was not disturbed in any way but the gaps between the small capping stones allowed sight of a dry, sound grave. The grave had been dug to a depth of 92" (234cm). The brick work rose 80" (203cm) to the 3" (8cm) capping stones, allowing for some four or five coffins to be laid one upon another. The grave inspected contained only a single coffin, supported on two iron bars. Some 5" (13cm) of soil had been placed upon the capping stones and this, in turn, supported the heavy pennant sandstone ledger, in this case 4" (10cm) thick. The small test pit was backfilled after measurement and photography.

Another small sounding was made west of the Robertson grave slab against the arch containing the grille. The unstratified material offered few dating suggestions. The mix was of red natural earth and builders' rubbish, including modern window glass and window lead that suggested modern diamond panes. Clay pipe fragments of mid to late nineteenth century date suggested the sweeping of floor rubbish into the alcove under the arch in question.

No evidence was found of steps leading to the lower vault level and the dates of the first burials in the run of the graves all being of the years closely following the reopening of Christ Church in 1790 argue against a formal entrance to the tower vault from the crypt having ever existed. Re-examination of the stonework closing the arch suggested it was of an inferior quality to that closing the other arches in the crypt and perhaps carried out at a later date in the building schedule. It seems that 'the cemetery under the tower' was more likely to have offered accommodation to the respected dead of the parish, buried prior to the demolition of the church in 1786 but, when disturbed, given decent re-burial. When all the work was complete and no more remains

---

[61] Jacob Kirby, attorney of 58 Wine Street, buried 13 February 1793. B.R.O., P/XCh/R/1 (d), unfoliated.

[62] B.R.O., P/XCh/R/4 (a), p. 26, Burials 1813–1854, George Salway, Montague Street, St. James, buried 28 April 1824, aged 64. The family originally lived in the parish of St. Ewen and Sarah Salway's body was removed from the church of St. Ewen and buried at Christ Church on 11 April 1793, B.R.O., P/XCh/R/1 (d), unfoliated. See B.R.O., P/StE/V/2, f. 108, 'cash for burial 5 July 1785 Mrs. Selway (sic), 13/4d'.

[63] Unidentified.

[64] B.R.O., P/XCh/R/1 (d), unfoliated, Charles Robertson, buried 3 July 1793.

[65] Ibid., the vault was probably purchased to contain the remains of Alicia Tyndall, the grand daughter of Thomas Tyndall, who was buried on 28 December 1793.

required re-burial the vault was closed, the crypt floor levelled and used for the first brick-lined vaults recorded by Canon Cole. In 1824 it offered an easy solution to the problem of the two vestries in providing a home for the human remains which had to be removed from the church and churchyard of St. Ewen.[66]

Re-visiting the crypt allowed us to note that the entrance from the north seems to be the only one in use. A second entrance through a trapdoor in the floor of what was the choir-vestry had been closed. Our sketch plan of 1958 also noted a side vault above floor height in the north-west corner of the crypt wall in the space afforded by the arch below the Baptistry, which was erected in 1898.

Recently a study of the faculty granted on 25 June 1887 to re-build and enlarge the vestry room of Christ Church, to remove the gallery in the church and extend the seating in the church by removing the partition wall and the entrance lobby,[67] has provided some possible answers to our questions. The extension of the seating area meant that pews were placed under the organ gallery. The removal of the west gallery required the removal of the steps that led to it. The church wardens' vouchers for the erection of the church include an entry in November 1789 for 'penant steps to church yard',[68] but these were to improve access to the upper churchyard beyond the north wall of the church. The steps that led the parishioners from the porch up to the floor of their church, which were also of pennant stone, were to be removed and relaid to rise from a point closer to the west door. The floor of the porch would require relaying and this work would have obliterated any trace of an access trap made to the charnel beneath over the sixty years before. (Fig. 16). This work was undertaken between 1888 and 1894.[69] Most of the work applied for under the faculty was not completed until September 1892.[70] The faculty also made provision at a future date for a doorway on the north side of the church leading into the churchyard, to be converted into an apsidal recess to contain the font, and 'if necessary to provide it with an outer door'.[71]

---

[66] It is possible that the remains disturbed in the upper churchyard as a result of the erection of the choir vestry in 1887, which covered about a quarter of the upper churchyard, and the erection of a clergy vestry in 1908 may have found their way into this vault. There are no faculties dealing with the exhumation of human remains which would be normally required to enable this work to proceed, or for the disposal of any remains thus uncovered.

[67] B.R.O., P/XCh/ChW/9.

[68] B.R.O.. P/XCh/ChW/4 (viii).

[69] Notes by the Revd. Edward Pattinson Cole, in possession of Dr. M. J. Crossley Evans. B.R.O., P/XCh/1/16, notes by his son Canon M. A. R. T. Cole, state that the vestibule under the tower was altered in 1894. He states that 'a small flight of steps with a hand rail on each side led up to the floor of the church. A stone staircase on either side of the vestibule gave access to the gallery'.

[70] B.R.O., P/XCh/PM/22. *The Western Daily Press*, 23 September 1892.

[71] B.R.O., P/XCh/PP/11/2, an undated plan of Christ Church by the architect Henry Williams, c. 1887 in the possession of Dr. M. J. Crossley Evans shows both the north door and a door into the churchyard from the choir vestry. Subsequently a clergy vestry linked the baptistery and the choir vestry and denied access to the churchyard at any point other than *via* the entrance to the old vestry in the north-east corner of the church.

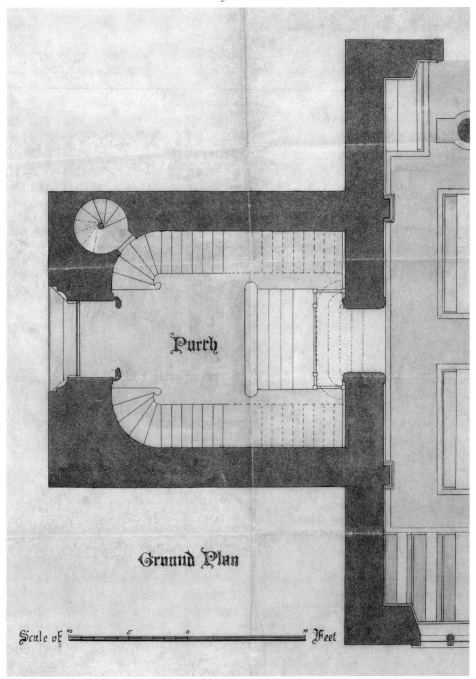

Porch

Ground Plan

Scale of   10   5   0   10 Feet

Fig. 16. The porch of Christ Church with St. Ewen, drawn by the architect Henry Williams, *c.* 1887. The plan has a note that 347 worshippers could be seated in the church as surveyed. The drawing shows the steps leading up to the nave and aisles and the twin stairs then used to reach the gallery, [Collection of M. J. Crossley Evans].

AFTERWORD

Four years after our visit to the vaults of Christ Church in 1958 screens were being put up around the forlorn remains of St. Augustine-the-Less on College Green in Bristol. The modest city church sitting in its old graveyard was facing demolition in 1962. It had suffered the misfortune of some very minor damage in the blitz of 1940–1941 which sealed its fate. Rebuilt in 1482 and 1840, I can recall its agreeable eighteenth century plaster work. Twenty years of neglect and decay and a potential danger, imagined rather than real, when combined with the aspiration of the owners of the Victorian Royal Hotel next door and the wish of the Diocesan Board of Finance to capitalise on the interest of the owners, led to the city council's decision to allow the demolition of the old church.[72]

The thunder of sledge hammers attracted our attention and we found that workmen had been ordered to smash any inscribed stones into small pieces. The graves had all been opened and their contents briskly bundled into plain wooden crates for dispatch to unmarked pits in the local council cemetery at Canford in Westbury-on-Trym. We saw no archaeological supervision or recording, just the grim determination to leave no word, no trace of the dead of St. Augustine-the-Less. We were moved to see amongst bones crushed into the mud by bulldozers, touching reminders of the past: a Bristol delftware saucer, with the stub of the last candle left alight against the darkness of a vault closed, (the mourners might have hoped two hundred years earlier for eternity), disappearing under the wheels of the contractor's lorry.

We were told that the council had instructed the workmen to carry out work as discreetly as possible, as secretly as possible and as quickly as possible. The clearances of graves in Christ Church in 1786 and at St. Ewen in 1823 seemed only too close. Some twenty years later, in the winter of 1983 and 1984, the site of the church was properly excavated. A note appeared at the time in the *T.B.&G.A.S.*, 104, pp. 211–214, and Eric Boore published his full report in *Bristol and Avon Archaeology*, No. 4, (1985), pp. 21–33. Ironically Boore's excavation included the painstaking recovery of the fragments of stone, their careful reassembly and thoughtful transcription. It is to be regretted that no such chronicler was at hand in 1786 and 1823 in Broad Street, Bristol.

APPENDIX

The despoliation of the church and the fate of the fixtures and fittings of St. Ewen 1792–1823/4

The list below shows that the despoliation of the church was a gentle, if progressive, process which took place over 30 years. We know that some of the fixtures of the church were sold at auction in August 1791.

---

[72] M. J. Crossley Evans, 'The Church of England and the City of Bristol: change, retreat and decay- reform, revival and renewal?' in J. H. Bettey and N. Knight (eds.), *Post-War Bristol 1945–1965: Twenty years that changed the city*, (Bristol, 2000), pp. 57, 81.

a) The bells

The vestry minutes for 1792–1793 note that one of the two church bells was sold at one shilling per pound in weight, at a total of 89lb at £4.9.0, which was purchased by the Methodists. The cash book of Portland Wesleyan chapel records that this was acquired during the construction of the chapel on 13 February 1792: 'Paid to Mr. John Weeks[73] for a bell £4.10.6'. It bears the inscription: 'Come away; make no delay' and the year 1698, and was hung in small belfry above the roof of the chapel and rung for five minutes half an hour before service and for five minutes immediately before the service began.[74] 'The large bell of St. Ewin's [sic] Church was taken down the 29 Jany 1795 and sent to Mr. Brown's at the Back Hall. The weight of it was 10.1.14, including the iron with the clapper of the bell is deposited at Mr. Davis's Bell hanger, Milk Street- the inscription on it was 'Peace and good neighbourhood. God save the King, 1698'.[75] Its removal relates to the demolition of the upper parts of the church tower for safety reasons in 1795. The whereabouts of this bell are not known. Both bells were cast by Abraham Rudhall I (1657–1735/6), the celebrated bell founder of Gloucester.[76] When Portland Chapel was closed and subsequently demolished in the 1960s the smaller bell was housed briefly in Victoria Methodist Chapel, Whiteladies' Road, before being transferred to a warehouse in Temple Meads Station. In 1996 it was acquired from the trustees of Portland Chapel by the parochial church council of Christ Church with St. Ewen, Broad Street, and hung inside Christ Church with monies donated for the purpose by the friends and colleagues of the late Dr. Arthur Basil Cottle F.S.A., (1917–1994), sometime reader in Mediaeval Studies at the University of Bristol, president of this Society, and one of the church wardens of St. Ewen between 1984 and 1994.

b) The font

The plain octagonal font from St. Ewen rests on an octagonal stem and is variously stated to date from the first and the second half of the seventeenth century. It appears to have remained in the church following its closure in 1791, and was not removed until c. 1820–1823.[77] It was subsequently housed in the crypt of Christ Church. In 1849 it is said to have been placed in the church, where 'it superseded' the portable fluted mahogany baptismal urn made for the new church.[78] This move was probably as much a reflection of the reaction to Georgian ecclesiastical fixtures and fittings at this time as it was in obedience to number LXXXI of the Canons of 1604, which required

---

[73] Church warden of St. Ewen.

[74] A. J. Lambert, *The Chapel on the Hill*, (Bristol, 1930), pp. 42–43, this also makes the statement that the bell was sold at auction with other materials in August 1791. The difference in price between that recorded by the vestry and the chapel may be accounted for by the cost of carriage.

[75] B.R.O., P/St.E/V/2, ff. 160, 175, 178.

[76] M. Bliss and F. Sharpe, *Church Bells of Gloucestershire*, (Gloucester, 1986), pp. 57–70.

[77] A. B. Cottle, *Christ Church, City of Bristol: A Guide for the Welcome Visitor*, (privately printed, 1992), p. 4, makes the curious and inaccurate statement that this font was where Robert Southey was baptised. This font is believed to have been destroyed at the time of the demolition of Christ Church in 1786.

[78] It stood between the verger's pew and the north door into the churchyard, which now opens out into the baptistry.

all fonts to be made of stone.[79] In 1898 it was cleaned and re-erected in the newly-built baptistry of Christ Church. The Georgian font, largely undamaged, was turned into a lectern. It was changed back to its original condition in the 1940s and is currently housed in the vestry of Christ Church.

c) **The church monuments**

The funerary monument commemorating one of the church wardens, George Lewis (died 1769), his mother, Martha (died 1750), and sister, Martha (died 1737/8), who were buried in a vault, was removed from St. Ewen in 1791, a fact recorded on their monument. [80] No doubt this was followed shortly afterwards by whatever was left of their remains.[81]

At the time of the church closure at least one other monument in the church was rescued. This recorded the life of Samuel Hardwicke, apothecary and church warden, (died 1765), Anne and Mary his wives, Henry (1740–1761), his son by his first wife, and a further five of his children who died young. It was re-erected in Chipping Sodbury church where it was seen and transcribed by Canon M. A. R. T. Cole in the church tower on 10 April 1915.[82]

d) **The vestry chest**

The church's muniment chest was not finally removed from St. Ewen until 1794–1795 when it was found that assistance was needed to open it. The vestry of St. Ewen was allocated their own room in the tower of Christ Church[83] where the chest was kept until 1801. Although this room now lacks natural light it was formerly lit by a circular window which was subsequently filled with the clock face on Broad Street. The chest was damaged and for the security of its documents the vestry paid 14 shillings on 6 July 1801 for making a new box to deposit their papers and deeds. This chest was still in the tower in the first decade of the twentieth century and was subsequently moved to the choir vestry of Christ Church.[84]

e) **The banner of the guild of merchant tailors**

The standards (c. 1740) of the Guild of Merchant Tailors which originally worshipped in the south aisle of St. Ewen were not transferred to Christ Church, and following the closure of the church in 1791 they passed into other hands.[85] In the early nineteenth

---

[79] See A. C. Fryer, 'Gloucester Fonts: Part XV', *T.B. & G.A.S.*, XLVII, (1925), pp. 184–185, he stated the font was made about the year 1630. Fryer contradicts and updates information to be found in A. Harvey, 'Church Furniture and Decoration of the Renaissance Period in Bristol', *T.B. & G.A.S.*, XXXII, (1909), p. 150.

[80] Probably related to the George Lewis, glover, undertaker and breeches maker of 16 Broad Street, mentioned in *Sketchley's Directory* for 1775.

[81] This monument was removed from the body of the church during the 'restoration' of 1882, and placed on the north side of the inner wall of the porch. In November 1927 it was re-erected in the church on the central projection of the south aisle.

[82] Notes by Canon Cole in possession of Dr. M. J. Crossley Evans.

[83] B.R.O., P/StE/V/2, f. 178.

[84] *Ibid.*, f. 219.

[85] A. B. Cottle, *op. cit.*, p. 5, claims that the one in Christ Church dates from 1763 and that it had hung there since the re-building.

century there were said to be twelve of them, but only two survive, the other being housed in the Folk Museum at Blaise Castle.[86] Canon Cole noted that the banner, which is seven feet eight and a half inches long, was lent to the church by the trustees of the Merchant Tailors' Charity in 1931.[87] Canon Cole hung the banner loose from the top of the old altar piece which had been recently re-erected as a chancel screen. It was ripped down and disposed of by vandals in 1990. Subsequently rescued from a dustbin in Broad Street, it was conserved by staff at the city's Museum and Art Gallery and framed. It now hangs over the north-east entrance to the vestry.

f) The cushions
As late as 1802 we find the vestry receiving three guineas from the rector of Christ Church, Dr. Ireland, in return for the old velvet cushions taken from St. Ewen. These were formerly placed in the pulpit and on the ledges of the clerk's and the reading desks.[88]

g) The benefaction board
The benefactions to St. Ewen's parish were recorded on a board, heavily varnished and blackened, which was transferred to Christ Church at some unknown date, possibly at the same time as the font, and stored with it in the crypt, where it remains, in the company of the benefaction boards from Christ Church which were removed in 1786, re-erected in 1790 under the organ gallery and removed once more in 1882. It measures five feet by eight and six-eighth inches tall by two feet seven inches wide, and was transcribed by Canon Cole as follows:

Benefactions
of St Ewens
Mr Robert Kitchen Aldm
Gave Twenty Shillings pr
Annm to the Poor for ever.
Mr George Harrington Aldm.
Gave Twenty Shillings pr.
Annm to the Poor for ever.
Mr Thomas Hobson for a
Sermon on the 6th July.
Six Shillings and Eight
Pence and Three Shillings
and Four Pence in Bread
For Ever.
1753 Mr. John Willis late
Clerk of this Parish gave
Forty Pounds towards
erecting the Altar.

[86] The Revd. C. M. J. Turner, *Christ Church or Holy Trinity, Bristol*, (Bristol, 1955), p. 38.
[87] Notes by Canon Cole in possession of Dr. M. J. Crossley Evans; a letter written to Canon Cole, dated 9 April 1931, by F. Percy Jenkins, clerk to the trustees, refers to a letter sent to Canon Cole, dated 7 October 1930, outlining the terms of the loan.
[88] B.R.O., P/StE/V/2, f. 226.

Saml Hardwick Gentn.
gave £ the Interest
viz. £ to the
Minister for a Sermon
on Mich. Day-£ 0.3.6 to
the Clerk and the Rest to
the Poor in Bread for Ever

h) The altar

The benefaction board refers to John Willis's gift in 1753 towards the erection of a new altar at St. Ewen.[89] Volume II of the bound catalogue of George Weare Braikenridge's[90] collection held at the City's Museum and Art Gallery mentions three stone panels from this altar which, in 1823, were fixed in his library at Broomwell House. He writes:

> I purchased these tablets 26 June 1823 of Wm Housley, mason No 4 Water Street who assured me he picked them out of Rubble removed from the spot on which the altar of St Ewin's Church stood. He took them out of the carts whilst loading with the rubble & they were then quite filled with mortar & yellow wash- He thinks they were originally a part of the old altarpiece of the above named Church- a fig-ure of the Virgin Mary crushing the Serpent came also from the same rubble and was a part of the same altar piece.

The three carved tablets were of remarkable character and in October 1823 their likenesses were captured by the artist Hugh O'Neill, who worked for Mr. Braikenridge. They represent: Abraham offering up his son Isaac; Adam, Eve, a rather battered serpent and the forbidden fruit; and Cain slaying Abel.[91]

i) The communion plate

The church plate remained unused following the closure of the church until at a meeting of the vestry on 7 July 1796:

> It was agreed to sell to the best Bidder the old & useless Plate belonging to the said Parish of St. Ewen- And the same weighing seventy nine ounces ten pennyweights was accordingly sold to Mr. Henry Brown Silversmith (he being the best Bidder) for the sum of twenty Guineas- which Plate consisted of the following Articles; one Flagon,[92] one patin, one Bread Plate,[93] one communion Cup[94] & Cover. Which

---

[89] T. J. Manchee, *The Bristol Charities Being The Report of the Commissioners for Inquiring Concerning Charities in England and Wales, so far as relates to The Charitable Institutions in Bristol*, I, (Bristol, 1831), p. 395, says 'no trace whatever is found in the parish books of this gift'.

[90] (1775–1856). For a detailed account of his life and collections see: S. Stoddard, *Mr Braikenridge's Brislington*, (Bristol, 1981).

[91] Bristol Museum and Art Gallery, Braikenridge Collection; Mb 14 the sacrifice of Isaac; Mb 15 Adam and Eve; Mb 16 the death of Abel.

[92] In an inventory of 1737.

[93] In an inventory of 1737.

[94] Probably the one purchased in 1571.

sum of twenty Guineas Mr. Charles Prosser Ch[urch]warden was instructed to lay out for the augmentation of the Parish Fund.[95]

j) The church way

The sign entitled 'The Church Way', was a carved oak board of eighteenth century date, which was formerly erected over the narrow passageway which ran from Broad Street to the north of the church and led to the churchyard and the north door.[96] The passageway formed part of the premises of No 3 Broad Street, in the occupation of Charles Frost, bookseller, and adjoined number 2, occupied by Mr. Sheppard, a milliner. It was removed at the time of the demolition of the church and numbers 1 and 2 Broad Street in 1823–1824. At this time it was either given to, or purchased by, the collector and retired dry salter, George Weare Braikenridge from Charles Frost.[97] It was re-erected over an ornamental wooden doorway in his garden at Broomwell House, Brislington, and captured in a pencil and sepia wash by T. L. S. Rowbotham, c. 1826–1827.[98] Its current whereabouts are unknown.

k) The corbel heads

When the church was demolished many of the finer pieces of carving from the church were fought over by Bristol's small group of enthusiastic collectors and connoisseurs. One of them was Thomas Garrard (1786–1859),[99] who was the city's chamberlain or treasurer between 1822 and 1856. He acquired at least seven extraordinarily fine corbel heads from the building. Unable to acquire them himself, Braikenridge gained permission for them to be painted by Hugh O'Neill, and their likenesses remain in his collection. The originals disappeared from view following Mr. Garrard's death and their current whereabouts are unknown.

l) St. Ewen's vestry and church wardens

When the small parish and the living of St. Leonard, Bristol, was joined to St Nicholas, Bristol Bridge, the vestry continued to exist and to elect church wardens, who acted as deputies to the church wardens of St. Nicholas. This custom continued until after the war. St. Nicholas was bombed in 1940 and the crypt was closed for worship in 1958.

The closure and subsequent demolition of St. Ewen did not bring its vestry or church wardens to an end. The vestry continued to meet in Christ Church in its own vestry room in the tower and to elect two wardens annually at its Easter vestry meeting. Subsequently, from about 1912 or 1913 when the window space was filled by the church clock, its meetings and muniments were moved to the choir vestry, where, following the abolition of select vestries, it has continued to meet and transact business as the re-constituted St. Ewen's Lands Trust.

[95] B.R.O., P/StE/V/2; see the Revd. R. T. Cole, *The Church Plate of The City of Bristol*, Part I, The Bristol and Gloucestershire Archaeological Society, (1932), pp. 27–29.

[96] Bristol Museum and Art Gallery, Braikenridge Collection M2306, an undated watercolour by Joseph Manning.

[97] Bristol City Reference Library, Braikenridge MS, XV, f. 456.

[98] S. Stoddard, *op. cit.*, p. 38, pl. 33.

[99] The Revd. A. B. Beaven, *op. cit.*, p. 349; Bristol Museum and Art Gallery, Braikenridge Collection M2309; M2310; M2311; M2312.

The church wardens of St. Ewen, who act as deputies to the wardens of Christ Church, are now elected at the annual parish meeting of Christ Church, but the trustees manage their own investments. When the bishop agreed to the union of the parishes in 1786 it was on the understanding that a fifth part of the cost of the upkeep of Christ Church would be met by the parishioners of St. Ewen. This proved a heavy burden. It was an on-going source of dispute and resentment by the vestry in the early nineteenth century and the division between the officers and parishioners of the two parishes was maintained. A writer in the 1840s said that all that remained of St. Ewen 'is a brace of church wardens, who were obliged to seek shelter in Christ Church when they no longer had a place or a pew of their own in which to hide their diminished heads'.[100] *The Bristol Churchgoer* writing on 26 February 1844 stated, incorrectly, that the church of St. Ewen had 'preserved none of the parochial honours and possessions beyond a pair of blue wands with a couple of church wardens made to match'.[101]

By the 1950s one of the two early nineteenth century gilt-tipped black church wardens' staves used by the wardens of St. Ewen in formal processions, and verging important visitors to the church on civic occasions and on visits by the archdeacon, and visiting preachers, had disappeared and the other one was badly damaged. They have recently been replaced by two wands of original design through the generosity of Mr. David Morton Selwyn, one of the two church wardens of St. Ewen and an English master at Bristol Grammar School.

APPENDIX 2

Church Wardens of St. Ewen from 1747 until the present[102]
The records indicate that the selection of church wardens in the eighteenth and the early nineteenth century was done by rota.

William Fry	1747–1749
George Lewis	1747–1748, 1750–1752, 1754–1756, 1760–1762[103]
Samuel Hardwick	1748–1750, 1752–1754, 1758–1760, 1763–1765[104]
John Mills	1749–1751, 1753–1755, 1759–1761, 1765–1767
Richard Winpenny	1751–1753, 1757–1759, 1762–1764[105]

[100] Bristol City Reference Library, Braikenridge MS, XV, f. 81.

[101] *Ibid.*, f. 43.

[102] The church wardens were elected by the rector and the vestry with the warden in his first year of office serving as the junior church warden and as senior for the second. I am most grateful to Mr. John Edward Heal, *quondam* clerk to the trustees of the St. Ewen's Lands Charity for extracting from the records the names of the church wardens *post*-1890. The names of the church wardens for 1747–1813 come from B.R.O., P/St E/V/2 and those for 1814–1889 come from B.R.O., P/St E/V/3.

[103] Died 1769, possibly a glover, undertaker, and breeches' maker, 16 Broad Street.

[104] Died 1765, apothecary. He left the church wardens £40 the interest of which was to provide a guinea for a sermon at Michaelmas, three shillings and six pence for the clerk, and the residue to provide bread for the poor on 29 September, 1 January and the Sunday following. The £40 was paid on 6 July 1765. B.R.O., P/StE/V/2, f. 46.

[105] Richard Winpenny was in partnership with Mr. John Freeman as a vintner. They opened the newly re-built Three Tuns Tavern in Corn Street in 1748. Their partnership was

James Wade	1755–1757, 1761–1763, 1767–1769
William Shipman	1756–1758, 1764–1766, 1768–1770
John Headington	1769–1771, 1774–1776, 1779–1781, 1786–1788[106]
Charles Prosser	1770–1772, 1775–1777, 1782–1784, 1791–1793, 1796–1797[107]
Captain Jasper Hawkins	1771–1773, 1776–1778[108]
Matthew Mease	1772–1773[109]
Charles Brown	1773–1774
Thomas Peirce or Pierce, Junior	1773–1775, 1778–1780, 1785–1787, 1789–1791[110]
Thomas Dunbar	1777–1778, 1784–1786[111]
John Weeks	1780–1782, 1787–1788, 1790–1792, 1797–1799[112]
John Ellis	1781–1783, 1787 elected but deemed ineligible[113]
William Bulgin	1783–1785, 1787–1788[114]
Joseph Sheppard	1788–1789, 1795–1796[115]
Samuel Williams	1788–1790, 1796–1798[116]

dissolved on 10 January 1756 when the former retired to Clifton. Winpenny retired *c.* 1766; Bristol City Reference Library, Braikenridge MS, XV, f. 631.

[106] Apothecary of 14 Broad Street.

[107] Silk mercer of 7 Broad Street. Died *c.* 1797.

[108] Retired master mariner and later vintner of the Three Tuns Tavern, 43 Corn Street, one of the embarkation points for the Bath coach. Captain Hawkins took over the premises from Richard Winpenny, and re-opened them on 10 January 1767. They were later incorporated into the Bush Tavern. Bristol City Reference Library, Braikenridge MS, XV, f. 631. A. C. Powell and J. Littleton, *Freemasonry in Bristol*, (Bristol, 1910), pp. 484–486, Captain Hawkins was an active mason, a member of The Sea Captains' Lodge from 1768 and Worshipful Master in 1784.

[109] Buried at Christ Church in the crowd, 13 December 1800.

[110] Watchmaker and goldsmith 8 Broad Street.

[111] Milliner and haberdasher, 59 Broad Street.

[112] Vintner of the Bush Tavern, 40 Corn Street; the Birmingham diligence and one of the Bath coaches went from this inn. 'Jack' Weeks also let post chaises. He was 'an ardent friend of Church and State', whose establishment was famous for the quality of its turtles, venison and limes, and the Christmas bill of fare. Many leading visitors to Bristol in the eighteenth century, such as Admiral Rodney in 1782, stayed there. It ceased to be a hotel and hostelry in 1846. Bristol City Reference Library, Braikenridge MS, XV, f. 565, 581–582, 588, 599ff, 623. He retired in the early nineteenth century. For Weeks as an actor and eccentric, see G. H. Gibbs, *Bristol Postscripts: being a selection of articles which have appeared in the Bristol Evening Post*, (Bristol, undated, *c.* 1950), pp. 89–98. Member of The Sea Captains' Lodge of freemasons from 1782, A. C. Powell and J. Littleton, *op. cit.*, pp. 486–488. He died 18 June 1819, aged 74. A monument bearing his bust is situated in the cloisters of Bristol cathedral. I am grateful to Mr. Gordon E. Jones for this information.

[113] Peruke maker and hair dresser, 9 Broad Street.

[114] Buried 5 October 1831, aged 73, of the Royal Fort. In 1793–1794 *Mathews's Bristol Directory* lists Bulgin and Sheppard, booksellers and stationers, Wine Street, and Bulgin and Rosser, printers of the *Bristol Mercury*, Broad Street.

[115] Joseph Sheppard, hosier, Corn Street. His property was one of those adjoining the passage which ran from Corn Street to the west door of St. Ewen's church. In 1793–1794 he was a stocking manufacturer in Corn Street.

[116] Apothecary in Broad Street in 1793–1794.

Richard Errington	1792–1794[117]
James Stuart Webb	1793–1795, 1799–1801, 1811–1812[118]
Joseph Francis Sheppard	1794–1796, 1804–1806, 1807–1808, 1811–1812, 1814–1816, 1821–1822, 1823–1824[119]
Michael Mogg	1798–1800
George Salway	1800–1802, 1805–1807[120]
Henry Rudhall or Rushall	1801–1803
John Ross	1802–1804
John Owen	1803–1805, 1808–1810[121]
William Holmes	1807–1809
Edward Powell	1807 elected, but declined office.
Charles Frost	1809–1811, 1816–1817, 1820–1822, 1824–1825, 1826–1828[122]
John Mereweather	1811–1813[123]
William Webb	1812–1813[124]
Richard Knight	1813–1814
William Davies	1813–1816, 1817–1819, 1822–1823[125]

[117] Grocer in Broad Street in 1793–1794.

[118] Glover and undertaker of Broad Street in 1793–1794.

[119] Haberdasher and milliner of 2 Broad Street in 1793–1794. Trustee from 1807, alive 1838, dead by 1845. His property in Broad Street was demolished to make way for the new Council House.

[120] *Mathews's Bristol Directory, 1793–1794*, p. 103, George Salway, hair dresser, Broad Street, Bristol. Buried at Christ Church, as of Montague Street, St. James, 28 April 1824, aged 64.

[121] Possibly the John Owen, who was a tailor at 21 Broad Street in 1793–1794.

[122] Account book manufacturer, bookseller and stationer; Lottery Office keeper, vendor of patent medicines, of 3 Broad Street. Claimed to have 20,000 books on sale, Bristol City Reference Library, Braikenridge MS, XV, f. 467.

[123] John Mereweather (1771–1845), was in business at the junction of Corn Street and Small Street, from at least 1820, as a fruiterer. He subsequently served as a church warden of St. Werburgh, Corn Street. His first wife, Ann Grimes (*c.* 1775–1809) was buried in the crypt of Christ Church on 18 August 1809 in the vault of her mother and step father, and his second wife, Anna Maria Davies (1778–1831), was buried in the same vault on 5 March 1831, aged 52. His first wife's step father, Henry Mathews, a fruiterer of 3 Broad Sreet was buried in the crypt at Christ Church on 29 December 1799. John Mereweather retired from business in 1839, and as a 'gentleman' settled at 2 Tottenham Place, Clifton, now part of Manor Hall, one of the University of Bristol's halls of residence. His only child by his second wife, the Revd. John Davies Mereweather (1816–1896), English chaplain at Venice 1855–1887, knight of the Order of the Crown of Italy, was baptised at Christ Church on 3 October 1816. He was an author and poet, and is believed to have inspired the works of Frederick Rolfe, Baron Corvo, the author of *Hadrian VII*, whose literary style, known as 'Corvine', has attracted many unlikely admirers such as the late Dr. A. B. Cottle. The Revd. Mr. Mereweather was cremated and his ashes buried in Stockholm. I am most grateful to Mr. Ole Pein of Stockholm for this information, exchanged in March, April, and August 2009.

[124] Possibly the William Webb, who by 1820 was in business as a linen draper at 1 Bridge Street.

[125] In 1820 glover, breeches maker, hosier and undertaker of 1 Bridge Street. By 1829 he had moved his business to 17 Corn Street and lived at 16 College Street.

Samuel Tayler   1816–1818, 1819–1821, 1822–1826[126]
James French   1818–1820, 1825–1829[127]
Charles Muskett   1828–1831[128]
William Cannicott   1829–1835[129]
Samuel Dight Senior   1831–1836[130]
George Edwards Senior   1835–1839[131]
Samuel Dight Junior   1836–1838, 1841–1842[132]
John Smith   1838–1841[133]
Christopher Tapprell   1839–1841[134]
George Davey Senior   1841–1845[135]
William Cannicott Junior   1842–1846, 1847–1854[136]
Charles England   1845–1849, 1854–1878[137]
William James Pickering   1849–1850[138]
Thomas Henry Weston   1850–1852[139]
Alfred Pickering   1853–1854[140]

[126] Trustee from 1838; brush, bellows, mop, patten and sieve maker. Until 1824 his business was situated at 51 Corn Street. These premises were torn down to facilitate the enlargement of the Council House. He then moved to 16 Broad Street and latterly to 27 Upper Arcade. Bristol City Reference Library, Braikenridge MS, XV, ff. 547, 549, 551, 553, 555. By 1820 his home address was 5 Wilson Terrace, Wilson Street, St. Paul's.

[127] Silversmith, watchmaker, jeweller and engraver. Premises facing the Exchange by 1820. By 1829 he was also a dealer in dollars, doubloons and Portugal coin and had shops in Corn Street and 49 High Street. Trustee from 1838, alive 18 August 1859.

[128] Resident at Park Gate House, St. Michael's Hill in 1830 and 1831. Gentleman.

[129] Hairdresser, perfumer and ornamental hair manufacturer of 2 Broad Street.

[130] Straw hat maker. In 1829 he was resident at 8 Broad Street, trustee from 1838. By 1841–1842 Samuel Dight and Co. had expanded the business to include drapery, and hosiery as well as straw hat manufacture and moved to 23 Bridge Street.

[131] Cordwainer, trustee from 1838. In 1838 called a boot and shoe maker, wholesale and retail, 11 Broad Street and 24 Small Street, lived at 36 Stokes Croft.

[132] Some of these dates may refer to the father rather than the son and *vice versa*.

[133] Hairdresser of 2 Broad Street, trustee from 1838.

[134] Tea dealer, trustee 1838–1841. In 1841 Tapprell and Co. were situated at 12 Broad Street. He later became bankrupt and left the parish.

[135] He left the parish in 1848. Trustee from 1838. Stationer, publisher, printer, account book manufacturer, binder, and book seller of 1 Broad Street and elected church warden on 23 April 1832 but declined to take the usual oaths due to 'religious scruples'. William Cannicott was elected in his place. He also had an exhibition room where he sold paintings on commission; Bristol City Reference Library, Braikenridge MS, XV, ff. 469, 471. In 1841 he resided at 3 Portland Square.

[136] Hairdresser and perfumer of 2 Broad Street.

[137] Hairdresser, peruke and scalp [*sic*] manufacturer of 10 Broad Street; trustee from 24 September 1864, retired in 1878 after 34 years of service to the church, died 1882.

[138] Left the parish, possibly the W. J. Pickering who is listed as the proprietor of an ale and porter store at 1 Frog Lane in 1852.

[139] In 1852 he was a bookseller, stationer and print seller, situated opposite the Exchange in Corn Street, and resident at Kensington Villa, Upper Montpelier.

[140] In 1849 he was a second hand book seller, binder, stationer, and account book manufacturer, and proprietor of a circulating Library at 27 Lower Arcade. He was resident at 3 Belmont, Clifton. By 1852 he had moved his business to 8 Broad Street. On 28 December 1854 it was stated that he was about to leave England.

Henry Knight	1855–1859[141]
James George Hobbs	1859–1866[142]
Alexander Halcombe	1866–1868[143]
John Dexter	1868–1895[144]
Lieutenant-Colonel David Macliver	1878–1884[145]
Fairfax Spofforth	1884–1928 [146]
John Tremayne Lane	1895–1921[147]
Richard Greenway Hort	1921–1946[148]
Lewis Tenison Mosse	1928–1936 [149]
Roland Greenway Hort	1936–1945[150]
Francis Everard Alford Long	1945–1959[151]
Philip William Hort	1946–1977[152]
George Edwin Portingale	1959–1978[153]

[141] In 1852 of 1 Broad Street, stated to have been formerly of Hardings. Frederick Harding was a well-known ladies' boot and shoe maker of 25 Lower Arcade.

[142] Attorney, 1 Baldwin Street, resided at Gothic Villa, Ashley Hill in 1852. By 1859 he is listed as a solicitor with Hobbs and Peters, at Bank of England Chambers, 12 Broad Street. By 1867 his private address was Hampton Lodge, Durdham Park. Trustee from 24 September 1864.

[143] In 1867 termed 'posting and job master, omnibus and funeral carriage proprietor', Broad Street.

[144] Appointed trustee on 12 April 1882. Died 16 July 1921 at 2 Berkeley Square, aged 85, stockbroker.

[145] Appointed trustee on 12 April 1882. Thanked by the vestry for his service as church warden and for 'the very liberal manner in which he has contributed to the recent alterations', vestry minutes, 15 April 1884. He left the parish. Partner in the *Western Daily Press*. An active freemason, a member of The Lodge of Agriculture, No. 1199, joined The St. Vincent Lodge No. 1404, May 1880, worshipful master 1885–1886, died January 1888 at Cannes, aged 45, *Bristol Times and Mirror*, 17 January 1888.

[146] Property lawyer for whom Mr. Edward Heal, a leading figure in the life of Christ Church, worked for two years, lectured in church history and took an active part in the defence at the time of the Welsh Disestablishment Bill, alderman, born 1857, died 1928, an active freemason, worshipful master of The Royal Clarence Lodge no. 68, 1896–1897. Although in 1898 he is said to be 'formerly' a church warden of St. Ewen and the people's warden of St. Mary, Tyndalls Park, he does not appear to have relinquished the former post. Member of the Bristol and Gloucestershire Archaeological Society from 1903 until his death. W. T. Pike, (ed.), *Bristol in 1898: Contemporary Biographies*, I, (Brighton, 1898), p. 71.

[147] Appointed treasurer of the city and county of Bristol 1881 and remained in office until his death at 3 Windsor Terrace, Clifton, on 14 April 1921, buried Clifton parish church. W. T. Pike, (ed.), *op. cit.*, p. 83. J. Lyes, *Bristol 1920–1926*, (Bristol, 2003), p. 10. His death was recorded at a meeting of the vestry on 6 June 1921.

[148] Died 1 February 1946.

[149] By April 1936 he 'had left Bristol permanently'.

[150] Died 27 February 1945.

[151] A beer and porter taster at George's Brewery.

[152] Philip Hort (1901–1978), was a leading Bristol chartered accountant and freemason, a past-master of The Powell Lodge, Deputy Provincial Grand Master of the Province of Bristol from 1961–1969, and Grand Master of the Mark Degree from 1960 to 1975. Inherited the patronage of the living of Christ Church with St. Ewen from Mrs. Cole, the relict of Canon R. T. Cole.

[153] He died in the twelve months following his resignation.

Ernest Robert Knapp	1977–1980[154]
Hilda Bevan	1978–1979[155]
David Moon	1979–1986[156]
Roger Clive Metcalfe	1981–1984[157]
Dr. Arthur Basil Cottle, F.S.A.	1984–1994[158]
Ena Glide	1987–1991[159]
Louis Anthony Haslett	1991–2000
Dr. Martin John Crossley Evans	1995– present
Stuart Higginbottom	2000– 2004
David Morton Selwyn	2004– present[160]

ACKNOWLEDGEMENTS

The authors wish to thank the officers of Christ Church for their continuing interest and access to the crypt beneath the church, not only in 1958 but again in 2005 and 2007. For the photographic survey conducted in 1958 thanks are due to the late Mr. Frederick Albert Godman (1912–1965) of the University of Bristol's Medical Photographic Department for the loan of cameras and the processing of the film. Mrs. Judy Godman and Mr. Michael Tucker provided invaluable assistance with research and recording.

Thanks are also due to Mrs. Anne Bradley and Ms. Alison Brown, and their colleagues at the Bristol Record Office, who have been tireless in their provision of parish records and vestry minutes as well as the accounts and notes preserved by the Town Clerks of Bristol.

[154] Died 3 October 1987, a member of the council of the Bristol and Gloucestershire Archaeological Society for many years (and later vice-president). He was also honorary secretary for Bristol. Upon his resignation as church warden he was not immediately replaced.

[155] Formerly a member of the congregation of All Saints', Corn Street.

[156] Resigned upon his appointment as one of the church wardens of Christ Church.

[157] Formerly a member of the choir of St. Nicholas, Bristol Bridge. Resigned upon his appointment as one of the church wardens of Christ Church following the death of Vivian George Mildren (1927–1984), who was also the honorary membership secretary of the Bristol and Gloucestershire Archaeological Society. Mr. Mildren served as church warden of Christ Church between 1962 and 1965 and between 1982 and 1984.

[158] Formerly church warden of St. Paul, St. Paul's Road and of St. George, Brandon Hill. Died 13 May 1994, aged 77; president of the Bristol and Gloucestershire Archaeological Society 1987–1988; member of the Diocesan Advisory Committee; 'author, poet, herald and Welshman'; reader in Mediaeval Studies, University of Bristol; author of guides to St. Mary Redcliffe and Christ Church with St. Ewen; author; one of the *Enigma* team at Bletchley Park; head of the Albanian Section of the Foreign Office, 1945–1946; taught himself the language in six weeks and then wrote the Foreign Office Albanian grammar.

[159] Formerly a member of the congregation of St. Thomas, Bristol, and later of All Saints', Corn Street. Miss Glide, a retired school mistress, subsequently became Mrs. McEwen.

[160] Honorary secretary to the Bristol Branch of the Prayer Book Society; editor of the journal of the Jane Austen Society, and former secretary; author.

IX

The Church of St. Thomas the Martyr: Demolition and Re-building 1786–1793

JOSEPH H. BETTEY, F.S.A.

LIKE ITS near neighbour, St. Mary Redcliffe, the church of St. Thomas was founded in the late twelfth century during a prosperous period in Bristol's history when the town expanded rapidly in the area south of the river Avon. The whole district was part of the large parish of Bedminster, and the churches of St. Thomas and St. Mary Redcliffe both remained as chapelries within the parish throughout the Middle Ages. St. Thomas always enjoyed some parochial rights and was effectively regarded as a parish church, although not formally granted independent parochial status until 1852. Having evidently been founded soon after the murder of Archbishop Beckett in 1170, the church was originally dedicated to St. Thomas the Martyr. Henry VIII had a particular dislike of Beckett and in 1538 ordered that he should no longer be regarded as a saint or venerated. The dedication was, therefore, changed to St. Thomas the Apostle, and a new seal made for the church in 1566 bears the legend 'Thomas the Apostle of Christ', but later the church reverted to its original dedication.[1] During the later Middle Ages the district south of the Avon became the industrial quarter of Bristol and was occupied by the crowded workshops of weavers, fullers, dyers, smiths, tanners and carpenters, as well as by shops and alehouses. The busy quays along the banks of the Avon accommodated coastal shipping from South Wales and barges or 'trows' which brought goods down the Severn. Several wealthy and pious merchant families resided in the district, including the Canynges, Stokes and Burtons, and they contributed lavishly both to St. Thomas and St. Mary Redcliffe. St. Thomas's church was on a restricted site, surrounded by streets and houses, so it could not be enlarged or extended like many other Bristol churches, but by the end of the Middle Ages the original twelfth century building had been transformed into an elegant and beautifully-decorated church. No detailed depictions of the mediaeval building have been found, but the illustration in Jacob Millerd's map of 1673 gives a good indication of its external appearance. Millerd was a parishioner and served as church warden

---

[1] Considerable research has been done on the history of the church, especially by the former vicar, the Revd. Charles Samuel Taylor, who was a noted local historian and a Fellow of the Society of Antiquaries. He was editor of the *Transactions of the Bristol & Gloucestershire Archaeological Society* (*T. B. & G. A. S.*), from 1894 to 1896 and from 1900 to 1914. Taylor also published various articles on the records of St. Thomas in the *Proceedings of Clifton Antiquarian Club*. Particularly useful are the following: B.R.O., P/St T/HM/2, Notes on St. Thomas by Charles Samuel Taylor; The Revd. C. S. Taylor, 'The Old Church of St. Thomas the Martyr, Bristol', *T. B. & G. A. S.*, 27, (1904), pp. 340–351; B.R.O., P/St T/HM/32; R.W. Keen, 'The Story of a Bristol Church, St. Thomas the Martyr', (1954). This is an unpublished typescript which provides a wealth of information about the church and its history.

Fig. 1. The interior of St. Thomas, showing the elegant classical design by James Allen and the elaborate altar piece made by William Killigrew in 1716, [from a photograph taken by the author].

between 1676 and 1678. His illustration is evidently drawn with care and accuracy. He shows the church with Thomas Lane and St. Thomas Street on the south and east sides, houses on the north, although with space for a small churchyard on the north side. The elegant fifteenth century tower, which still survives, is depicted surmounted by a large weathercock. (Fig. 2). The weathercock was blown off in 1544 and the church wardens' accounts record the payment of 2d 'to hym that found the weather-cock'. Replacing it cost 9s 11½d. A new one was purchased in 1570, and is described as 'the crowe' in the church wardens' accounts, no doubt referring to the crowing of St. Peter's cock:

> Paid to Richard Myles, tyncker [tinker] for the making of the
> crowe and for metal for the same 10s 0d.
> Painting and gilding 5s 0d
> Ironwork 12d.[2]

There was a small square tower or cupola with large windows, no doubt intended to provide light for the figures over the rood screen. The church wardens' accounts for 1620 record that the three great windows in the cupola were re-glazed with 374 feet

[2] B.R.O., P/St T/ChW/1, (1544); 9, (1570–1).
[3] B.R.O., P/St T/ChW/33, (1620).

of glass costing 4d a foot.[3] Numerous similar entries in the church wardens' accounts indicate the pains they took over the care and maintenance of the fabric. The church consisted of a nave, chancel, two aisles and a tower. The register books of St. Thomas survive from 1552 and the church wardens' accounts begin in 1544. Bequests in wills mention numerous altars, including those dedicated to the Virgin, St. John the Baptist, St. Nicholas and St. Catherine. An altar dedicated to the Holy Cross stood in front of the Rood Screen. There was a guild or fraternity of St. Thomas, and many testators left money for the nearby almshouse which had been founded during the thirteenth century by Simon Burton, and for the maintenance of the water supply for the area which was managed by the church. In 1562 a new 'feather' or subsidiary pipe was laid to bring water from St. Mary Redcliffe to St. Thomas's conduit.[4]

A notable feature of the church is the survival of more than 100 mediaeval deeds, the earliest dating from 1294. They give details of bequests, chantry foundations, offerings to altars within the church and properties given for pious uses, including the maintenance of the lead pipes supplying water to the church and for people living around it. The surviving deeds and wills contain references to chantries in the church, including those founded by the merchants Robert Chepe, Richard Wells, John Stokes and John Burton.[5] Before the Reformation the church was served by six priests and the interior was filled with statues, lights, carved screens and colourful paintings. Further evidence of the opulence of the interior fittings of the church can be seen in the four Limoges candlesticks which are now in the Bristol City Museum, having escaped confiscation under Edward VI. They date from the thirteenth century and are richly inlaid with brightly-coloured enamels.

Two other remarkable survivals are a manuscript Bible of *circa* 1410, beautifully written and decorated, and pages of a fine illuminated missal, which were later used as the covers for church wardens' accounts. The accounts for 1566 contain the entry

> Paid for the newe bynding of the Latten bible, with certain
> quyres of paper too the same viis vid. [6]

The bequests by rich merchants, the support of guilds and fraternities and the income from property possessed by the church meant that St. Thomas was extremely wealthy. The eighteenth century Bristol surgeon and historian, William Barrett, writing shortly before the demolition of the mediaeval church of St. Thomas, commented upon the excellence of its architecture and the splendour of its furnishings, and named it second only to St. Mary Redcliffe among all the Bristol churches. [7] The income of the church wardens of St. Thomas was greatly increased in 1570 when by Letters Patent of Queen Elizabeth they were granted the tolls and custom dues from the Thursday market for cattle and wool which was held in the streets around the church and in the Wool Hall which was on the corner of St. Thomas Street and Thomas Lane. [8] This was an important and well-attended market, and the gratitude of the

---

[4] B.R.O., P/St T/ChW/5–6, (1562).
[5] B.R.O., P/St T/HM/23, Calendar of the Deeds of St. Thomas, compiled by Dr. Elizabeth Ralph, F.S.A., (1954).
[6] B.R.O., P/St T/ChW/7–8, (1566).
[7] W. Barrett, *The History and Antiquities of the City of Bristol*, (Bristol, 1789), p. 557.
[8] B.R.O., P/St T/CH/51–52, Letters Patent of Queen Elizabeth, (1570).

Fig. 2. The Georgian nave of St. Thomas looking west, with its original furnishings. Photograph taken by the Revd. Stanley T. Collins in 1932, [Collection of M. J. Crossley Evans].

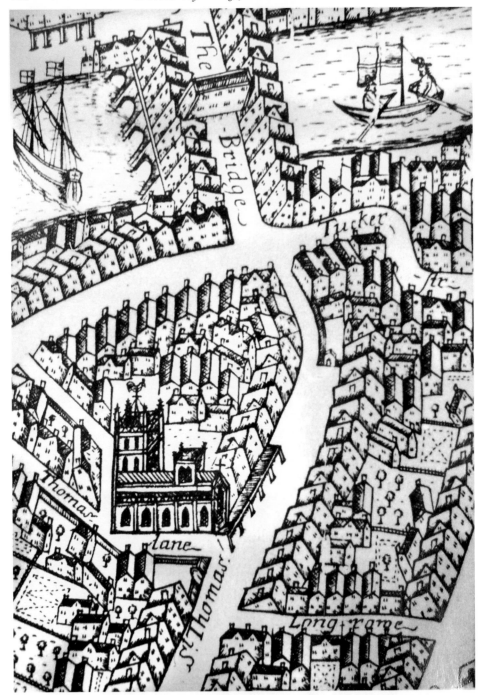

Fig. 3. The church of St. Thomas and its surroundings from Jacob Millerd's plan of Bristol, 1673.

church wardens was recorded in their account book.

> God save Queen Elizabeth and send her grace prosperously to reign over us, for in the fourteenth year of her reign she graciously gave the Market to St. Thomas Parish.[9]

The grant of the market continued to be highly profitable, and writing in 1710 the then vicar of St. Thomas, the Revd. John Gibb,[10] remarked that he could not hold services on Thursdays because of the crowds attending the market:

> There are prayers read at St. Thomas every day of the week except Thursday when the market for cattle hinders the people that they cannot conveniently come to church.[11]

During the seventeenth and eighteenth centuries further wealth came to the church from the growing traffic in shipping on the dockside quays and from newly-established trades such as soap-making, glass production, the wine trade, timber imports and all the commerce connected with the slave trade. Many of the sailors engaged in the slave trade lodged in the numerous inns and taverns around St. Thomas's church, and it was in the *Seven Stars* tavern which still exists beside the church that the Revd. Thomas Clarkson collected much of the evidence about the evils of the trade in 1786 which eventually led to its abolition.

St. Thomas was greatly involved in the fierce religious controversy which raged in Bristol during the early 1530s when radical preachers attacked the established practices and doctrines of the Church, while conservatives strongly upheld the traditional beliefs and ceremonies. This 'battle of the pulpits' which caused so much uproar and division in Bristol started with three Lenten sermons preached during 1533 by Hugh Latimer, who was at the time rector of West Kington in Wiltshire, but was soon to achieve fame as one of the leading reformers. One of his sermons was delivered in the church of St. Thomas where shortly afterwards he was answered by the lively and popular conservative preacher, William Hubberdyne. Another prominent opponent of Latimer's views who preached in St. Thomas's church was Edward Powell, rector of Bedminster and a canon of Salisbury Cathedral. Powell was later to be imprisoned for his refusal to accept the Royal Supremacy over the Church and he was executed at Smithfield in 1540.[12]

The church wardens' accounts continue to illustrate the care and attention which was lavished upon the church throughout the seventeenth century, and contracts from the eighteenth century show the way in which the furnishings of the church were renewed. An elaborate new reredos and altar-piece made of Flemish oak by the Bristol craftsman, William Killigrew, was installed in 1716 at a cost of £170. In 1728 a new organ gallery was erected and the organ-builder, John Harris of London, made a new organ for the church in 1755 costing £360.[13] Two local carpenters, John Llewellin and John Harris were employed in 1755 to make a new floor of English oak

---

[9] B.R.O., P/St T/ChW/9, (1570–1).

[10] The Revd. John Gibb, vicar 1702–1744, prebendary of Salisbury.

[11] Quoted in J. F. Nichols and J. Taylor, *Bristol Past and Present*, II, (Bristol, 1881), p. 230.

[12] B.R.O., P/St T/HM/2, Notes on St. Thomas.

[13] B.R.O., P/St T/ChW/142,/143, (1716 and 1728).

and to provide a complete set of box pews, each six feet high. [14] In 1757 further large sums were spent on repairs to the church. [15]

The regular expenditure and evident care which was bestowed on the church makes it difficult to understand why during the 1780s it was decided that the building was in such a bad state that the only solution was total demolition and re-building. Part of the reason may have been dislike of the gothic architecture and the desire for a modern building in the classical style which had been introduced to Bristol by Redland Chapel which was designed by William Halfpenny for the London merchant grocer, John Cossins of Redland Court in 1741–1743. Later, during Bristol's 'golden age' of wealth and prosperity, the parish churches of St. Nicholas, St. Michael and All Angels on the Mount Without and Christ Church were all re-built. Part of the reason was that the mediaeval interiors were designed for a different style of liturgy and were not well suited to the needs of large congregations listening to the sermons which had become such an important feature of late eighteenth century services. Moreover the church wardens of St. Thomas possessed a regular income and could, therefore, borrow sufficient capital to finance a complete replacement of their church. The structure of the old building may indeed have been in urgent need of repair. None of these possible reasons totally overcomes the lurking suspicion that the surveyors employed to report on the condition of the old building stood to gain greatly by the decision to demolish and rebuild it. It is impossible to know the truth of the matter, but the result was the destruction of the mediaeval church, leaving only the fifteenth century tower. When Joseph Leech, the editor of a Bristol newspaper, attended morning service in St. Thomas's church on Christmas Eve 1845, he sat in one of the high-sided box pews and wondered how the parish could have been persuaded to demolish their beautiful mediaeval church. His conclusion was:

> That the church was originally Gothic, and [...] is now of the classic order of architecture, having undergone a change, about the latter end of the last century, when the declamations of Inigo Jones and Sir Christopher Wren against the Gothic still had some influence, I suppose, on the public mind. [16]

Whatever their reasoning, the church wardens were sufficiently concerned about the fabric of the church in 1786–1787 to employ three surveyors to report on its condition. The men chosen all lived nearby and might be considered unlikely to be completely impartial, since they may have anticipated profitable employment in any building work. They were James Allen, an architect and carver, who lived close to the church in St. Thomas Street, James West, a mason, and Edward Stock, a carpenter. They reported in 1788 that the whole building was in a dangerous condition and that the roof and most of the walls would have to be taken down. Faced with this opinion, the parish vestry decided to proceed with demolition and re-building; the decision was not unanimous but was carried by a majority of the vestrymen. They appointed the local firm of solicitors, Osborne and Seager, to obtain a private Act of Parliament in order that the necessary money could be obtained by loans, parish rates and the

---

[14] B.R.O., St T/ChW/144, (1755).
[15] B.R.O., St T/ChW/145, (1757).
[16] J. Leech, *The Church Goer: Being a Series of Sunday Visits to the Various Churches of Bristol*, (2nd ed., Bristol, 1845), pp. 97–98.

Fig. 4. Prospect of the City of Bristol (1717), by Johannes Kip (1653–1722), showing some of the city's churches, St. Thomas (14); St. Ewen (9); All Saints' (10); St. Nicholas (11); Christ Church (12); St. John the Baptist (13); St. Mary le Port (15); and St. Peter (16), [Bristol City Museum and Art Gallery, K5127].

appropriation of parish and charity funds. The Act was procured early in 1790.[17] The Preface to the Act declared that the church 'is in a ruinous condition, and incapable of being repaired'. It also affirmed that the church possessed properties and the rights to levy tolls at the Thursday market which could be used to pay for a new building, and that the church had £1,500 invested with the Bank of England. The cost of re-building the church and tower was estimated to be £5,000. By the Act, the vicar, churchwardens, vestrymen and other named individuals were appointed as commissioners for overseeing the re-building of the church. The Act of 1790 enabled the parish to raise the necessary money 'by Means the least inconvenient and burdensome to the said Parish'. Money could be collected from ratepayers in the parish, and anyone refusing to pay was to be liable to prosecution and to the seizure of their goods and chattels.

The commissioners moved swiftly to carry out the provisions of the Act. Their minutes show that they met at the *Pope's Head and Pelican* in St. Thomas Street, an hostelry kept by Joseph Pope. The first meeting was held on 12 April 1790, and one of the first actions of the commissioners casts major doubt on the belief that the church was in such a bad condition that complete demolition was inevitable. Thomas Baldwin, the architect of the Bath Guildhall and the city architect of Bath, together with two local architects, William Daniel and Daniel Hague, met to assess the state of the tower. (Figs. 3 and 4). They reported on 29 April 1790 concluding that:

> The Tower is well built and fit to stand, the materials being sound and the Tower perpendicular.[18]

The only faults they noted were that some work was required on the parapet and that the steps needed repair. Faced with this verdict the commissioners agreed that the tower should remain, but that James Allen, the local architect, should still be invited to prepare plans and elevations for the proposed new church. Allen, who had so strongly advised that complete demolition of the old church was urgently necessary, must have had his plans for a new church already drawn. Having been invited on 29 April to present proposals, only four days later, on 3 May 1790, he was able to show the commissioners a complete plan. Little is known about James Allen, except that he was an architect and carver who had become a burgess of Bristol in 1788. He was involved in various minor building projects in Bristol and worked for various churches, including St. Mary Redcliffe. In 1787 his major design for St. Paul's church in Portland Square was turned down in favour of plans drawn up by Daniel Hague, who was later to join with Thomas Baldwin in inspecting the tower of St. Thomas. Like many others, Allen was made bankrupt by the collapse in property prices and building work in Bristol following the outbreak of war against France in 1793. The design for the replacement of St. Thomas's church was Allen's only major project, and its acceptance in 1790 must have been a welcome success for him.[19]

---

[17] B.R.O., P/St T/ChW/147, *Act for Re-building the Parish Church and Tower of St. Thomas within the City of Bristol*, (30 George III 1790).

[18] B.R.O., P/StT/ChW/148, Minutes of the Commissioners; (1790–1825); P/St T/ChW/149, Accounts for Re-building, (1789–1821).

[19] W. Ison, *The Georgian Buildings of Bristol*, (1952), p. 10; A. Gomme, M. Jenner and B. Little, *Bristol: An Architectural History*, (1979), pp. 193–194, 430.

Since the church was closely surrounded by houses, streets and lanes, Allen designed a plain exterior with cement-rendered rubble walls, broken only by a string course, and with simple arched windows. Only at the east end did he provide a dressed ashlar wall with a Venetian-style window and carved garlands, which, no doubt, he carved himself. The interior is impressive, beautifully proportioned, well-lit and spacious. It has a very short chancel, and the emphasis is on creating a space in which congregations could hear the sermons, complete with a three-decker pulpit. There is a nave of five bays and two side aisles supported on rectangular columns. A vaulted ceiling rests on corbels in the form of cherubs' heads on folded wings, doubtless also the work of James Allen. The present church is 32 feet shorter than its mediaeval predecessor and is joined to the tower by a large entrance lobby at the west end. The plaster-covered walls are now painted white, while the whole interior is dignified and impressive. Allen's plan was duly accepted, and at their next meeting on 11 May 1790 the commissioners agreed to advertise for:

> Persons willing to Contract for taking down the walls of the old church and building the new church according to the Plans adopted.

On 8 July 1790 the commissioners accepted the tenders of:

James Wilmot carpenter	£884
John Steele, mason	£1,927
Francis Tozer, tiler and plaisterer	£615 10s od
John Belson, glazier	£38 12s 4d.

The speed and efficiency with which the commissioners pursued their objective, and the rapid progress which was made are extremely impressive. The commissioners met regularly, often at fortnightly intervals, and made speedy arrangements for providing the necessary finance. Collectors were appointed to levy charges on all ratepayers, tickets for £50 each were issued providing interest of 4% to all those willing to support the project, and mortgages were obtained on the security of parish property and the market tolls. Later, further sums were borrowed from individual parishioners. For example, on 28 December 1791 £400 was borrowed from Mrs. Rebecca Bowen at 4%, and a further £300 was borrowed from her on 18 April 1792 'for the purpose of carrying the Act into Execution'. Further sums were borrowed in 1792 from two Bristol gentlemen, Jeremiah Osborne and John Seager.[20] A house built up against the wall of the church was purchased for £300 and demolished, and by the autumn of 1790 the roof of the church had been removed and a shelter erected on scaffolding to safeguard the pews and other furnishings. The work of demolition proceeded rapidly. On 18 May 1791 the mason, John Steele, was paid an additional £70 by the commissioners 'As an encouragement for his going on with Spirit in his Work'. Work was evidently far advanced by 25 July 1792 when Thomas Arundell was appointed to make and paint the iron bars at the windows. The foundation stone of the new church was laid on 16 July 1792. By February 1793 the main structure was completed and John Steele was paid £1,927 for his work and James Wilmot, carpenter, received £1,042. There is no indication of the source of the stone used, presumably much of

---

[20] B.R.O., P/St T/ChW/148;/149 Accounts for Re-building.

the old structure could be re-used, and no doubt additional stone came from local quarries including Dundry.

During the summer of 1793 work on the interior of the church included the installation of the pulpit, the fixing of lights and the finishing of the chancel with Painswick stone. On 7 August 1793 the commissioners met for the first time in the newly-completed vestry and agreed to accept an estimate of £39 from Charles Wilmot, mason, for paving the church. In September 1793 the architect and carver, James Allen, was engaged to make a wooden christening font and to produce carved ornaments for the pulpit. The memory of the change of dedication to St. Thomas the Apostle evidently remained within the parish, since the first service in the newly completed church was held on the feast of St. Thomas on 21 December 1793. Because the new church was largely built on the old foundations, it was not thought to require re-dedication. The re-opening of the church was not marked by a separate wall tablet, but was recorded at the foot of the memorial to John Herman Kater and his family. The inscription reads:

> This Church was Rebuilt and Opened
> For divine worship
> On St. Thomas Day An. Dom. 1793
> The Rev. Benjn Spry, Vicar
> John Herman Kater
> Churchwarden

John Herman Kater had been church warden throughout the whole progress of demolition and re-building. He died in 1803 aged 65, and his monument also commemorates his wife, Mary, and their daughter, Charlotte. He was a sugar refiner and his monument is surmounted by the representation of a sugar loaf and by tools of the trade. The visit of Joseph Leech to St. Thomas's church on Christmas Eve 1845 has already been mentioned. He was greatly impressed by Kater's monument and by the fact that he [Kater] did not attempt to ape the gentry by depicting spurious heraldry but instead 'placed above his mortal remains and mural tablet, a palpable proof of his trade in the shape of a sugar-loaf'.

Joseph Leech commented on the square high-sided pews in the church, which had survived from the earlier furnishings. They had seats on all four sides so that 'people have a sociable and most neighbourly way of looking in one another's faces'. He was impressed by the pre-eminence of the pulpit, and could not see the chancel:

> I believe it has a small chancel, at least I have heard it has,
> but I could not see it, as the pulpit, the reading desk, a row of
> red curtains, and a lofty churchwardens' pew literally shut it out
> from view, and left the stranger to make any mystic conjectures
> he pleased as to what was beyond them.[21]

Minor works on the church continued for some time after 1793 and the commissioners continued to meet, although their meetings were increasingly concerned with finance and the repayment of loans. By 1796 more than £5,855 had been spent on the

---

[21] J. Leech, *op. cit.*, pp. 98–99.

new church. An entry for 17 February 1796 records the bankruptcy of James Allen, the designer of the church, and the commissioners agreed to pay Allen's estate £132 5s 1d 'being his Commission at 2½ per cent on the Extra Work in Building the Church and in full of all other Claims respecting the same'. Finally, on 30 December 1825 the commissioners' work was completed. All the loans were repaid and no debts remained outstanding. They were able to record triumphantly in their Minutes:

> [...] all the Purposes of the said Act of Parliament have been
> Completed and fulfilled and that it will not be necessary to
> Raise any further Rates on the Inhabitants of the Parish. [22]

During the re-building process, scaffolding had been erected and the interior furnishings of the church were protected, so that they could be re-used in the new church. These included the finely-carved altar piece of 1716 by William Killigrew. This spectacular structure includes seven carved candlesticks, the pediment with a pelican in piety, wheat, grapes, flowers and panels originally filled with the Lord's Prayer, the Creed and the Ten Commandments. Also surviving are the gallery, the royal coat of arms of Charles I dated 1637, the carved oak pulpit of 1740 and the Jacobean rest for the ceremonial sword which was carried before the Lord Mayor whenever he attended a service in the church. The eighteenth century box pews with their six-foot high sides and seats on all four sides were also retained.

There was a major restoration of the church in 1878–1880 under the antiquarian vicar, Canon C. S. Taylor, costing £3,887. As part of these changes the high box pews were cut down, the organ was re-built and moved from the gallery, and the chancel was opened up. James Allen's small mahogany font of 1793 was converted into a lectern, and the three-decker pulpit was reduced to its present size. Central heating was installed at this time. In 1907 the panels in the impressive altar reredos were replaced by paintings of Biblical scenes by Fritz von Kamptz of Clifton. They depict the Sermon on the Mount, the Prodigal Son, the Good Samaritan and the Last Supper. Remarkably, St. Thomas survived the bombing during World War II, although neighbouring churches were destroyed or badly damaged. After the war the surrounding population was greatly diminished and the congregation gradually declined. The church was closed in 1979 and was vested in the Churches Conservation Trust in 1988, under whose stewardship the church has been restored to excellent condition. Although we may regret the demolition of what was undoubtedly a fine mediaeval church, the new church designed by Thomas Allen has the finest and most striking Classical interior of any parish church in Bristol, and the retention of so many eighteenth century furnishings from the earlier building adds greatly to its attraction.

[22] B.R.O., P/St T/ChW/148, Minutes of the Commissioners (1790–1825).

X

Blotting out Bristol: Humphry Repton's Royal Fort Red Book

MICHAEL J. H. LIVERSIDGE, F.S.A.

'The perfection of landscape gardening consists in the four following requisites: *First*, it must display the natural beauties, and hide the natural defects, of every situation. *Secondly*, it should give the appearance of extent and freedom, by carefully disguising or hiding the boundary. *Thirdly*, it must studiously conceal every interference of art, however expensive, by which the natural scenery is improved; making the whole appear the production of nature only; and *Fourthly*, all objects of mere convenience or comfort, if incapable of being made ornamental, or of becoming proper parts of the general scenery, must be removed or concealed'.

THIS PASSAGE from Humphry Repton's *Enquiry into the Changes of Taste in Landscape Gardening* published in 1806 reveals the essentially practical approach he applied to the exercise of his art as England's most prolific, and most innovating, landscape 'improver' of the generation after Lancelot ('Capability') Brown.[1] Not only did he create landscapes ranging from intimately scaled country house settings to expansively spreading park scenery encompassing great estates and their wider environs, he also wrote more about the theory and practice of landscape design than any previous author. In his writings he combined drawing together his practitioner's experience as a surveyor and designer with his appreciation of landscape expressed in his capacity as a talented draughtsman and watercolourist. These informed his contributions to the lively debates and controversies surrounding aesthetics that feature so prominently in the landscape literature of the 1790s and 1800s.[2]

As well as the series of books he published, Repton wrote scores of individual essays about specific landscape and garden commissions in the form of illustrated manuscript *Red Books*, each one comprising an account of the conditions and character of the particular site as he encountered it together with his proposals for its improve-

---

[1] For Repton's career and *œuvre*, see : D. Stroud, *Humphry Repton*, (1962); G. Carter, P. Goode and K. Laurie, *Humphry Repton, Landscape Gardener*, (Norwich, University of East Anglia, Sainsbury Centre for the Visual Arts, 1982); S. Daniels, *Humphry Repton: landscape gardening and the geography of Georgian England*, (London and New Haven, 1999).

[2] Repton's principal publications are: *Sketches and Hints on Landscape Gardening*, (1795); *Observations on the Theory and Practice of Landscape Gardening*, (1805); *An Enquiry into the Changes of Taste in Landscape Gardening*, (1806); *Fragments on the Theory and Practice of Landscape Gardening*, (1816). The practical and aesthetic principles which informed his work are more exhaustively documented than any previous landscape designer's: they reveal a mind immersed in the visual vocabulary and controversies of Picturesque theory and taste, but are essentially free from the fanciful extremes in which other writers indulged.

ment.[3] These afford a unique insight into the ways he applied practical solutions to the four fundamental principles summarised in his 1806 *Enquiry*, and they illustrate by example how he used and adapted aesthetic theory to his purposes to compose scenes which reconciled art and nature to 'display the natural beauties, and hide the natural defects of every situation'. With each one Repton supplied his own delicately washed watercolours showing selected views along the principal sightlines of the landscape as he found it and as he proposed to alter it: these 'before' and 'after' pictures he usually contrived by means of hinged inserts which open to reveal the transformation his intervention will accomplish for the landowner. Some of the material from the *Red Books* he incorporated into the volumes he published, but among the thousands of manuscript pages and original drawings they contain there survives a unique record of an artistic vision applied to designing gardens and landscapes. This vividly illustrates how Repton responded to the changing perceptions of nature as eighteenth century sensibilities evolved from artfully composed pictorial constructs into the new landscape sensations that are registered in poetry and painting at the turn of the century and first decades of the nineteenth century. These are reflected in, for example, the poetry of Wordsworth and Coleridge in the *Lyrical Ballads* and in the watercolours of the young Joseph Mallord William Turner and contemporaries such as Thomas Girtin and John Sell Cotman. In this context it is surely no coincidence that Bristol was an important point of intersection between all these writers and artists. Some of Repton's most original schemes were carried out in and around Bristol, notably at Blaise Castle and at Abbots Leigh; the *Lyrical Ballads* was first published by Joseph Cottle from his premises in High Street in 1798; and Turner, Girtin and Cotman, all visitors to Bristol in the 1790s and early-1800s, painted some of their finest early Romantic views recollecting the scenes they experienced in and around the city.[4] Arguably, too, it is no less significant that the new appreciation of nature that defines the Romantic response to landscape which they all reflect occurred in an age that was increasingly urban and industrial—something that Humphry Repton specifically alludes to in his Bristol *Red Book* for The Royal Fort on St. Michael's Hill overlooking the city and port to the south, and looking down towards Park Street and across to Clifton to the west.

Repton's landscaping of the park and gardens adjacent to The Royal Fort in Bristol features in all the accounts of his career, and is generally regarded as a characteristic, if not major, example of his ingenuity in creating an appropriately tasteful setting in the Picturesque idiom for a relatively modest suburban villa. Its treatment in the literature follows Repton's own summary printed in his 1805 *Observations on the Theory*

---

[3] Repton's *Red Books* and his complete works are comprehensively listed in the exhibition catalogue by Kedrun Laurie and the monograph by Stephen Daniels cited above, note 1. See also A. Rogger, *Landscapes of taste, The Art of Humphrey Repton's Red Books*, (2005), for their, and their writer's place in English landscape painting.

[4] Repton's *Red Book* for the Blaise Castle landscape, now inside the City and County of Bristol boundary but at the time in Gloucestershire (Bristol City Museum and Art Gallery), records his first visit there in August 1795 and the completion of his plans in February 1796 ; the Abbot's Leigh (now Leigh Court in Somerset, just across the Avon gorge from Bristol) *Red Book* is dated 1814 (University of Bristol, University Library Special Collections). For Blaise, see J. Dixon Hunt, 'Sense and sensibility in the landscape designs of Humphry Repton', *Studies in Burke and His Time*, 19, (1978), pp. 3–28; the Abbot's Leigh manuscript remains unpublished.

and Practice of Landscape Gardening. Here he presents it as an example of 'what can, and what can not be done by a judicious application of the laws of perspective' to create landscape views that invoke pictorial effect. He shows how to compose optical illusions of scale and distance which operate visually, as in paintings, to convince the eye by means of introducing foreground features that conceal an unsightly middle distance, while opening up views to appropriate what lies farther off but appear to continue and to connect with the pleasure grounds immediately around the house. In other words, a demonstration of the kind of artistic arrangement that a painter makes in selecting and ordering the components of a picture through perspectival manipulation. As he puts it in the *Observations*:

> The Art of Landscape Gardening is in no instance more intimately connected with that of painting than in whatever relates to perspective, or the difference between the real and apparent magnitude of objects, arising from their relative situations; for without some attention to perspective, both the dimensions and the distances of objects will be changed and confounded.[5]

Repton's description of what he accomplished at The Royal Fort continues with a short explanation of his primary intention, to conceal from view the encroaching urban scene of houses advancing up Park Street towards his patron's 'country' villa, as well as those forming Berkeley Square which constituted another disagreeable visual intrusion. As previous writers have pointed out, his landscaping observations (in this instance noting how 'the late prodigious increase of buildings had so injured the prospect from this house, that its original advantages of situation were almost destroyed') often reflect his own negative reaction to the changing nature of the country as a whole in an industrial age.[6] Equally objectionable was the growing urban population, manifested 'by the numerous crowds of people who claimed a right of foot-path through the park' who rendered The Royal Fort 'as public as any house in any square or street of Bristol' and destroyed any pretence of private property or the seclusion and retirement that were intrinsic to a Georgian gentleman's villa retreat as ordained by ancient Roman precedents.[7] Again, Repton is responding with characteristic reactionary spirit to a major social upheaval of the time, one to which as an aspiring gentleman himself he was resolutely opposed ideologically and politically. Blotting out modern Bristol, the place as well as its people, was his priority in recuperating a visually exclusive landscape of (apparent) civility, leisure, culture and cultivated aesthetic pleasure for The Royal Fort.

Repton's motives, as well as his means, are clear enough from the abbreviated account in his 1805 *Observations*. A far fuller version is to be found in the Royal Fort *Red Book*, published here in full together with its complete set of accompanying illustrations (seven watercolours counting each of three 'before' and 'after' pairs separately, plus a diagram in the text: a variant of only one of the pairs and the diagram appear in Repton's published summary version in his *Observations*). The *Red Book*

---

[5] H. Repton, *Observations*, (1805), p. 6.

[6] The most extensive discussion of Repton's social and political views as they are expressed in his writings and communicated through the imagery of his painted and created landscapes is to be found in S. Daniels, *op. cit.*, in which social and economic factors are particularly investigated as integral to the Reptonian visualisation of Englishness.

[7] H. Repton, *Observations*, (1805), p. 7.

now belongs to Yale University (Beinecke Rare Book and Manuscript Library) where it has been since 1916 when The Royal Fort was sold and its contents dispersed. Its whereabouts remained unknown until Repton's surviving manuscripts were comprehensively listed in a gazetteer of his commissions published as part of the catalogue of the major exhibition held at the University of East Anglia in 1983, but until now it has never been separately published.[8]

Repton's Bristol Royal Fort manuscript is in some respects an unusual and unique survival. His *Red Books* were usually produced either when a client had commissioned him to prepare plans and proposals for a landscaping commission, or sometimes one might be conceived by Repton independently as a kind of marketing strategy. By writing and illustrating a detailed project specification setting out the potential of a particular property for improvement, he might persuade a potential patron to undertake the costly business of landscaping an estate. Using the *Red Book* as a means of drumming up business he might hope to convince the recipient that a project would confer the prestige of good taste that improving an estate would bring, not least by demonstrating the possession of wealth and culture that such conspicuous consumption represented. In the case of The Royal Fort, however, the small manuscript volume that Repton presented in 1801 to its owner, the Bristol banker Thomas Tyndall, was a record of what he had done, written *post facto* after the work had been planned and already commenced, as is made clear from the end of the presentation letter that prefaces the text ('I feel doubly flattered in the opportunity you have given me of increasing the peculiar beauties of the Fort […] and for thus allowing me to record the improvements I have had the honor to suggest'), and the dates he gives ('First visit at the Fort Feb 7. 1799. Plans finished at Hare Street near Romford Novr 1801'.).

How, why and when Humphry Repton came to be commissioned to landscape The Royal Fort garden and park has been well-documented. The property around the smart Georgian villa completed in 1760 (attached to earlier Georgian houses remodelled around an inner court) was acquired in 1798 by Colonel Thomas Tyndall whose father, another Thomas Tyndall, had previously inherited it and then sold it to a consortium of property investors in 1792. They planned to develop the whole site on St. Michael's Hill and the surrounding park and fields (some of the area leased from the dean and chapter of the cathedral) as a fine suburb along the lines of similar schemes in Bath. The consortium however failed in the financial crisis, trade recession and property collapse that engulfed the economy after war had broken out with France in 1793. When it reverted to its new owner in 1798 The Royal Fort and its grounds presented a sorry spectacle of abandoned excavations scarring the area, with the Georgian houses and the fine dressed stone villa attached to them still intact but somewhat desolate amid the mounds and trenches of an aborted building site. What Colonel Tyndall took possession of, though, was the former family estate built up from land acquired and leased by successive generations who had prospered from the successful Old Bank founded in 1752 and had become leading members of Bristol's merchant princes. The villa with its celebrated rococo interiors was restored and other minor works were carried out by the architect James Wyatt who had been engaged by the property developers to plan their grand scheme, and he must have been responsible for recommending Humphry Repton as the landscape consultant called in to re-plan the

---

[8] G. Carter, P. Goode, K. Laurie, *op. cit.*

mutilated and disfigured gardens and park in 1799: both he and his brother Samuel Wyatt were professionally associated with the landscape architect.[9]

Repton's 'canvas' consisted of the land bounded on one side by the line of what is now Queen's Road opposite the Triangle and Berkeley Square, the first stretch of Park Row continuing from it towards the old city, and part of Whiteladies Road from its confluence with Queen's Road; behind, the landscaped boundary more or less corresponds to the line now marked out by Woodland Road from Tyndall Avenue to its junction with Tyndall's Park Road. Several of the modern street names record the landscaped area: Park Street climbing up the hill from College Green led to Mr. Tyndall's park, Park Row skirted its edge, Tyndall's Park Road marked a boundary. Woodland Road was another altered later in the nineteenth century development of the area as comfortable Victorian villas for the moderately prosperous middle classes at the upper end and rather less impressive later Victorian terrace houses down to Park Row at the lower end (socially as well as topographically). West Park between Woodland and Whiteladies Roads cut through a farther part of the estate; even the rather mean Victorian brick artisans' houses along St. Michael's Park preserve slightly ludicrously the dignity of their once arboreal situation with its trees and herd of deer.

Victorian residential development was accompanied by sales of land for institutional buildings: Bristol Grammar School, the City Museum, University College, Bristol Baptist College, the Royal West of England Academy. The last remnants of the estate were sold in 1916, and came into the hands of the University of Bristol which has built over much of the land but preserves Royal Fort House with its exceptional original interiors together with its immediate surrounding garden, which still exhibits much of what Repton remodelled from the builders' devastation of the 1790s. The whole extent of the lands on and adjoining St. Michael's Hill that the Tyndall family assembled can be measured in a 1785 surveyor's plan made for Thomas Tyndall (1722–1794) and now in the University of Bristol Library Special Collections (Fig. 1). Comparison with Repton's own plan of the area that he subsequently rescued and landscaped (Fig. 7) shows how he integrated and unified the park, while preserving the separation of the pleasure grounds near to the house (and, as his text makes clear, cleverly affording views out from the gardens over the park and beyond to create extended vistas and pictures eliminating Bristol's polluting population and encroaching streets), which correspond to what survives of his work today, the garden immediately around the house.

[9] The fullest account of the Tyndall family's acquisition of the house and the various parcels of land that eventually formed their Royal Fort property, and of its subsequent development history, is given by J. H. Bettey, *The Royal Fort and Tyndall's Park: the development of a Bristol landscape*, Bristol Historical Association, 92, (1997). For The Royal Fort's architectural history, see: H. Avray Tipping, 'The Royal Fort, Gloucestershire. The Seat of Miss Tyndall', *Country Life*, 1916 (27 May), pp. 646–652; G. Parker, 'Tyndall's Park, Bristol, Fort Royal and the Fort House Therein', *T.B.&G.A.S.*, 51, (1929), pp. 123–141; A. Gomme, M. Jenner, B. Little, *Bristol: An Architectural History*, (Bristol, 1979); T. Mowl, *To Build the Second City: Architects and Craftsmen of Georgian Bristol*, (Bristol, 1991); T. Mowl and B. Earnshaw, *An Insular Rococo: Architecture, Politics and Society in Ireland and England 1710–1770*, (1999). The architect James Wyatt's work for Colonel Thomas Tyndall to restore the villa and re-model parts of the earlier Georgian houses attached to it has not been previously noted, but is recorded by two signed plans dated 1800 preserved with other Royal Fort House documents in the University of Bristol Library in Special Collections.

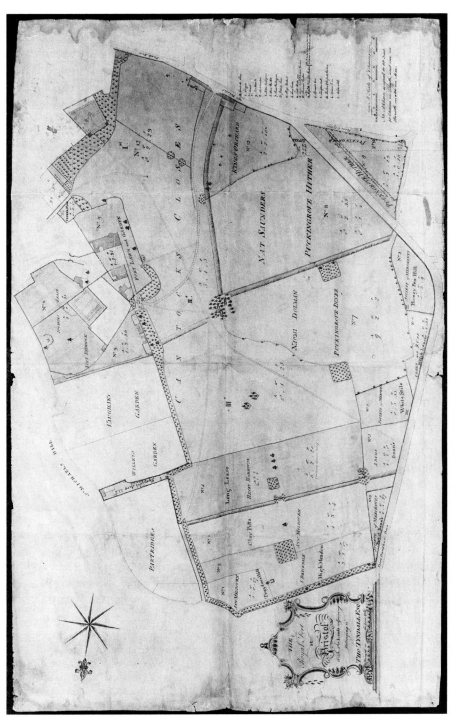

Fig. 1. 'The Royal Fort at Bristol With the Lands adjoining Belonging to Tho Tyndall Esq. Surveyed in the year 1785', estate map showing the parcels of land comprising the Tyndall property. Pen and ink with coloured washes, [University of Bristol Library, Special Collections].

Fig. 2. Samuel Jackson (1794–1869), 'A view from Park Place across Whiteladies Road to the Royal Fort', 1824. The viewpoint is from what is now The Triangle, with Queen's Road (then the continuation of Whiteladies Road) carried over the arch with Tyndall's Park beyond. Watercolour over pencil, [Bristol City Museums and Art Gallery (K2741)].

Repton's Royal Fort *Red Book* is characteristically revealing of his attitude to what might be termed the ideology or the social politics of landscape as something exclusive to the landowning class. The cultured aesthetics that the eighteenth and nineteenth centuries applied to landscape taste reserved it for those who possessed politeness and the education to appreciate it.[10] As an arch conservative in the old Tory tradition he firmly believed in the position that possession conferred: and possession was an entitlement of taste. The urban sprawl that accompanied the early industrialisation and growth of cities threatened the natural order, and like another great landscape artist of the time, John Constable, Repton's politics were expressed in his vision of landscape: continuity and tradition were essential ingredients that would

---

[10] For political interpretations of eighteenth century landscape imagery and landscapes in literature, art and landscaping, see: J. Barrell, *The Dark Side of the Landscape. The Rural Poor in English Painting 1730–1840*, (Cambridge, 1983); N. Everett, *The Tory View of Landscape*, (London and New Haven, 1994); M. Andrews, *Landscape and Western Art*, (Oxford, 1999); T. Williamson, *Polite Landscapes: Gardens and Society in Eighteenth-century England*, (Baltimore, 1995 and Cirencester, 1998). In Everett's words, 'To draw a wood or plant one, to build a folly or cottage, to design in the formal style or the picturesque, to choose to employ one improver over another—these were all interpreted as decisions that expressed a political motivation'.

Fig. 3. Humphry Repton, The Royal Fort, Bristol: 'The view from the principle drawing room', *Royal Fort Red Book*, 1801, No 1. The view before landscaping; The same view after improvement with folding flaps opened left and right. Watercolour over pen and ink, [Beinecke Rare Books and Manuscripts Library, Yale University].

preserve the enduring values of national, patriotic virtues.[11] The Royal Fort set in its wooded landscape at the top of Park Street conveys its owner's status and reinforces by its visible presence, as much as by its physical separation from the public space, a natural social order in which 'nature' itself participates. A vividly radiant watercolour by the Bristol artist Samuel Jackson showing workmen paving the top of Park Street with The Royal Fort behind captures the sentiment that informed Repton's ideal landscape setting: the gleaming house dominates its surroundings, separated from the

[11] Constable's conservative politics were formed in a family whose business and property interests naturally inclined him to adhere to an agrarian capitalist viewpoint: M. Rosenthal, *Constable: The painter and his landscape*, (London and New Haven, 1987).

Fig. 4. Humphry Repton, The Royal Fort, Bristol: 'The view towards the east', *Royal Fort Red Book*, 1801, No 2. The view before landscaping; The same view after improvement with folding flaps opened along lower edge. Watercolour over pen and ink, [Beinecke Rare Books and Manuscripts Library, Yale University].

urbanised and labouring world as a privileged place which represents the authority of a socially ordered, industrious and so politically 'natural' state of affairs (Fig. 2).

In the Royal Fort *Red Book* Repton supplies more than one significant detail to support a politicised interpretation of the landscape he created overlooking Bristol. In re-arranging and framing the scenes viewed from the house he is careful to single out specific elements to emphasise a conservatively traditionalist viewpoint. In one he focuses the revised view on the cathedral and on the animating interest of shipping on the Avon approaching Bristol's quays (Fig. 4:ii). Like John Constable when he painted Salisbury cathedral, the presence in Repton's scene of Bristol's cathedral may be considered symbolic of the continuity of Anglican virtues and Protestant values. Constable's landscapes are also much concerned with the fruitful labour which nurtures prosperity, just as in Repton's scene industrious enterprise is represented by Bristol's merchant shipping (funded, of course, in this case by wise capital investment

Fig. 5. Humphry Repton, The Royal Fort, Bristol: 'The original, & rude state of this ground', *Royal Fort Red Book*, 1801, No 3. The house from the park, showing the excavated foundations for new houses and remnants of seventeenth century fortifications; The same view after improvement, with folding flap opened at left, showing the circuit path inside the pleasure ground surrounding the house. Watercolour over pen and ink, [Beinecke Rare Books and Manuscripts Library, Yale University].

Fig. 6. Humphry Repton, The Royal Fort, Bristol: 'The <u>Fort</u>…restored to its original character of a Castle or Fortress', *Royal Fort Red Book*, 1801, No 4. Repton's imagined transformation
of The Royal Fort into a 'Gothick' mansion, with the wall between the park and the pleasure
ground made into a crenellated feature adding 'extent and magnificence' to the view across the
deer park. Watercolour over pen and ink, [Beinecke Rare Books and Manuscripts Library,
Yale University].

and prudent merchant banking of the kind successive generations of the Tyndall family practiced through their Bristol Old Bank business).[12] Repton's politics often
emerge from what can be inferred from what he insinuates in his commentaries on
landscape improvements and his implicit social views; Constable's are clearly
expressed in some of his letters which indicate how politicised his landscape imagery
can be. In another of the views from the house Repton shows the landscape looking
across to Clifton and the countryside beyond (Fig. 3:ii): Bristol's urban scene and its
unwelcome populace have been rendered invisible so that again the emphasis is on
the élite aspect of an aestheticised appreciation of polite landscape and the presence
of another villa. In other words, Repton carefully chooses what he wants the viewer
to see, and what that comprises is carefully calculated according to class and education. Quite literally, the landscape has been *classified*.

Finally, Repton reveals a synthesis of the Romantic concept of association, in which
a landscape can express sentiments and sensations by the presence in it of features
that provoke or invoke specific meanings, with what is clearly a politically inflected
concluding passage in the Royal Fort text and the illustration he goes out of his way
to include with it.[13] It is a final point which could be mistaken for a *jeu d'esprit* were it
not for the play he makes with the name of the property. What he suggests is a radi-

---

[12] The Tyndalls' role in Bristol's banking businesses in the eighteenth and nineteenth centuries is summarised in S. Cave, *A History of Banking in Bristol*, (Privately printed, London, 1899).
The Old Bank was eventually acquired by the Bank of England.

cal transformation of the whole house, Gothicising it and adding crenellated towers to give it the appearance of what its name suggests—a castle or fortress (Fig. 6).

The Fort, as it was then known, takes its name from a Civil War fortification, one of several on hills originally built around the city to defend it from the Royalists in the 1640s; when Bristol was taken and occupied for a time by Prince Rupert for the King, however, the St. Michael's Hill fort was renamed Fort Royal, and although it and its counterparts were subsequently dismantled the name became the site's primary designation from the Restoration. As the title cartouche for the 1785 estate survey clearly shows, 'The Royal Fort' was how Thomas Tyndall's father and namesake named his house and the surrounding grounds. Extending and re-modelling the house architecturally would give it a Gothic *gravitas* more appropriate both to its name and, in the context of 1799, when Repton first formulated his scheme and 1801 when he wrote the *Red Book* text. Its owner, Colonel Tyndall, was after all one of the commanding officers of a volunteer militia raised in case of need against the French, and what better seat from which to defend British liberty and the legitimate constitutional monarchy against Napoleon's tyranny than The Royal Fort?

Repton expands on the idea of turning The Royal Fort into a Gothic castle in another prominent feature of the last watercolour view in his *Red Book*. As he explains in the text, the view of the house from the park outside the private pleasure ground gardens is interrupted by the necessity of the wall which acts as a barrier to the populace exercising their rights of way across the property. It works in much the same way as a ha-ha from within the private pleasure ground because the inner terrain was modelled to slope up to the top of the wall and planted to conceal its presence.[14] The viewer's eye from inside the garden was thus conducted over the heads of the offending common folk, who were at the same time prevented from seeing into the privileged space of the garden. But, as Repton puts it, 'notwithstanding its great utility, & indeed its absolute necessity' the wall creates a confining impression which can be remedied by turning it into a mock-gothic crenellated feature which 'instead of being objectionable, would contribute to the general extent and magnificence of the whole'. At a stroke it becomes a symbol, a sign of a Romantic historicising association and an ideologically freighted social emblem that makes a political point. Repton's watercolour could not be a clearer demonstration of the order embodied most famously in the lines from the nineteenth century hymn:

---

[13] The suggestive power of features in a landscape to arouse historical and cultural associations was defined by Archibald Alison in his *Essays on the Nature and Principles of Taste*, London, (1790), one of the most influential philosophical and aesthetic works published in the eighteenth century which continued to be reprinted and re-issued almost yearly until the 1850s. For its impact on landscape artists see: L. Hawes, *Presences of Nature. British landscape 1780–1830*, (New Haven, Yale Center for British Art, 1987); M. J. H. Liversidge, 'Rome portrayed: "to excite the sensibility, and awake the admiration of mankind"', in M. J. H. Liversidge and C. Edwards (eds.), *Imagining Rome. British Artists and Rome in the Nineteenth Century*, (London and Bristol, 1996), pp. 38–53; and M. J. H. Liversidge, 'Romantic Redcliffe: Image and Imagination' in A. Heys (ed.), *Thomas Chatterton and Romantic Bristol*, (Bristol, 2005), pp. 53–63; S. A. Jauss, 'Associationism and Taste Theory in Archibald Alison's *Essays*', *Journal of Aesthetics and Art Criticism*, 64, (2006), pp. 415–428.

[14] The wall (in its original form without any 'Gothick' accretions) survives today as the boundary enclosing the Royal Fort garden along what is now University Walk.

> The rich man in his castle,
> The poor man at his gate,
> He made them high, or lowly,
> And ordered their estate.[15]

Repton, one imagines, would have enjoyed the double meaning that can be conjured from the word 'estate' in such a context. Furthermore, the wall brought another benefit to The Royal Fort's polite occupants: the lower orders outside could not only not be seen, they would not be heard either. Although Repton does not expand on the auditory aspect of gardening here, he was certainly aware of it on other occasions: using a wall to keep the socially inferior out of sight also kept them out of earshot, especially with the planting of the sound-absorbing shrubs and trees around the perimeter of the inner garden.

Humphry Repton was a highly successful landscape designer with a sure sense of pictorial composition, Picturesque aesthetics, and practical planting. He was also arrogant. His landscapes and gardens cannot be separated from the social and political ideas (indeed, ideals) to which he subscribed. In understanding what his landscapes aim to achieve his *Red Books* are an invaluable primary source. They are addressed to the proprietors who belonged to the patron class of the educated and politically active establishment, and who represented the natural order in society, just as the landscaper reveals it metaphorically by improving nature. What makes them so especially revealing about how to 'read' a Repton landscape is their conjunction of word and image which renders them for the art and garden historian an extraordinarily rich source for comprehending not just how Repton went about his work, but what was in his mind as he did so. They need to be deciphered visually with a degree of art historical iconological interpretation and contextualisation. Thus, in the Gothicised vision of a remodelled Royal Fort, as indeed on the ground as Repton completed the project, it is important to recognise the deliberate way he gave even more emphasis to the elevated situation of the house so that it so evidently 'lords it' over the meaner Bristolians who are excluded and 'blotted out' from the landscape presented *from* the house *to* its politer occupants. The point is no less clearly conveyed in Samuel Jackson's watercolour from the top of Park Street. Repton, himself a consummate landscape watercolourist, and Jackson both present and represent the house as a signifier of wealth and status in its immaculately ordered 'natural' setting. Both house and landscape are intended to be seen by outsiders to whom they convey the Tyndall family's elevated position and wealth. Contemporary Bristolians would not have missed the point that it was all built on the secure foundation of good banking practice and sound investment. Ironically what Repton created came out the financial collapse of the 1790s which enabled Colonel Tyndall to buy back The Royal Fort after the developers to whom his father had sold it for a fortune in 1792 went

---

[15] Mrs. Cecil Frances Alexander (1818–1895), *'All things bright and beautiful'*, verse 3, from *Hymns for Little Children*, (1848). The verse is now generally omitted when the hymn is sung, (except in a small number of churches such as Christ Church, Broad Street, Bristol) and modern hymnals often exclude it altogether. As a brief internet search entering the first line of the verse shows, it has become one of the most widely used quotations deployed in the titles of articles on contemporary issues appearing in politics, economics and sociology academic journals, as well as in scholarly contributions to the archaeology and history of the middle ages.

bankrupt and their plans imploded in a downward spiral of house prices and negative equity.

Perhaps the art, architectural and garden history which the house, its site and Repton's Royal Fort *Red Book* collectively record have a singular resonance now in an age when popular culture has replaced 'polite taste', and general education has dumbfounded the population. At the higher level the arts and humanities which sustained the civility of 'polite society' in the Tyndalls' day have become an arcane theoretical *cul-de-sac* of scholarly soliloquy, and the civic stability that the family's business, like those of so many other Bristol merchants and benefactors, underpinned has become all too literally discredited. In celebrating Gerard Leighton with this volume, the Bristol and Gloucestershire Archaeological Society happily marks the contribution he personally has made to enabling it over many years to keep alive the best of those values through pursuing and promoting scholarly endeavour, understanding and respecting the cultural inheritance which history and archaeology reveal, conserving and interpreting records and the heritage so that the lessons of the past are passed on, and judiciously managing its business affairs to sustain the intellectual enterprise. In summary, he combines all those qualities that defined the eighteenth century's ideal of the civic humanist as Humphry Repton and Colonel Thomas Tyndall would have known them.

HUMPHRY REPTON, THE ROYAL FORT 'RED BOOK', 1801

Yale University, New Haven, Connecticut;
Beinecke Rare Book and Manuscript Library, Yale University Library

MS Vault, Shelves/Repton

8pp., 29.5 x 22cm.

[Title Page]

THE FORT
near Bristol
a seat of
THOs TYNDALL Esqr

[Presentation Letter]

Sir

 In an extensive exercise of my profession I have constantly digested my ideas of the improvements of every place in writing—& these remarks have generally been accompanied by sketches showing immediately the effect of improvements which were often carried out at leisure—but in the present case it is different—as the effect has been produced on the ground before the plan on paper was completed—and yet in compliance with your request—I submit this small volume to your perusal—and I feel doubly flattered in the opportunity you have given me of increasing the peculiar beauties of the Fort—and for thus allowing me to record the improvements I have had the honor to suggest –

I have the honor to be
Sir, Your most obedient humble Servant
H. Repton

First visit at the Fort Feb 7. 1799
Plans finished at Harestreet near Romford Novr 1801.

Character & Situation

The art of Landscape Gardening is in no instance more connected with that of Painting, than in what relates to the knowledge of perspective, or the difference between the real & apparent magnitude of all objects, arising from their relative situations—for without some attention to the effects of perspective both the dimensions & the distances of objects will be changed & confounded. As few instances have occur'd to me where this can be more forcibly elucidated than in the grounds near the Fort, I shall avail myself of the following sketches to shew what can be done and what cannot be done by the help of perspective.

When I first visited the Fort I found it surrounded by large chasms in the ground & immense heaps of earth & broken rock which had been dug out, to form the cellars & foundations of those additions to the City of Bristol which were afterwards relinquished; the most obvious method of restoring the ground to its original shape—was to return each heap of earth into the hole from whence it was taken—but a little reflection on the character & situation of the place, naturally led me to enquire whether some advantage might not be taken of the mischief that had been done—few situations command so varied, so rich, & so extensive a view as the Fort—on the summit of a hill which looks over the vast City of Bristol, it formerly surveyed the River & the beautiful Country surrounding the City without being incommoded by much view of the City itself—but the prodigious increase of Buildings within the last few years, had so injured the prospect of this House, that the original advantages of situation were almost destroyed, & there was some reason to doubt whether it could ever be made desireable for a villa or a Residence in the Country; because it was not only exposed to the unsightly rows of Houses in Park Street & Barclay Square, but it was liable to be overlooked by the numerous Crouds of People, who claimed a right of foot path thro' the Park immediately before the windows. It was therefore as publick as any House or Square of Bristol, & if the earth had simply been put back to the place from whence it came, the expence of the removal be greater than that which occured to me as more advisable: viz, to fill the holes partly up, by levelling the sides into them, & raising a bank with a wall to exclude the foot path as shown by the annexed Section.

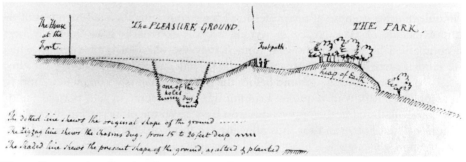

Fig. 7. Cross-section, line drawing.

By this expedient we not only hide the objectionable part of the view by planting the raised heap of earth—but we produce a degree of privacy & seclusion in the valley within the pleasure ground, which was never before known in this exposed situation.

The view from the principle drawing room is so offensively encumber'd by the late increase of the City of Bristol, that it requires very nice management to exclude what ought to be hid, without hiding what ought to be seen. For this purpose I suppose 5 Rods or Poles each ten feet high to be placed at different distances from the eye, & these I have represented in this sketch (No 1; Fig. 3.i) taken from the Windows of the Drawing room—these shew the apparent height of ten feet at the different places, & of course what may be expected of trees planted of any given size at each place, from hence it is evident that a young tree at No 1, will not hide anything for many years except the park wall, a tree of the same size at No 2 will do little more, as appears from the large trees already growing there, but at No 3 where a heap of earth has been thrown to a considerable height, a tree of twice ten feet will hide most of the houses, & in like manner at No 4 & No 5, immediate effects may be produced by judicious planting to see over or under the branches of trees, but since much of this has already been done it is unnecessary further to enlarge on the means previously used to ascertain the effects proposed (Fig. 3.ii).

The view towards the east was improved by the same attention to perspective, and the flat kind of bowling green which I suppose might formerly have been part of the Military esplanade of this fortress & which was partly artificial & supported by a wall, was softened into the gentle hollow described in the drawing No 2 (Figs 4.i, 4.ii) but which I trust the reality far exceeds in beauty. As the original, & rude state of this ground will soon be forgotten I have subjoined the sketch No 3 (Figs 5.i, 5.ii) to shew what is was, rather than to give an adequate idea of what it really now is or soon will be.

The pleasure ground immediately near the house is separated from the Park by a wall, against which the earth is every w(h)ere laid as before described, so as to carry the eye over the heads of persons who may be walking in the adjoining foot path; this wall not only hides the publick passengers from the house, but it prevents the interior ground from being overlooked by them—yet notwithstanding its great utility, & indeed its absolute necessity, the appearance of such a wall from the park gives an air of confinement & the only expedient by which this could be remedied, would be a total change in the character of the place, or rather by altering the house to make it what its name & situation denotes—The <u>Fort</u> might be restored to its original character of a Castle or Fortress—when this wall instead of being objectionable, would contribute to the general extent and magnificence of the whole (No 4; Fig. 6).

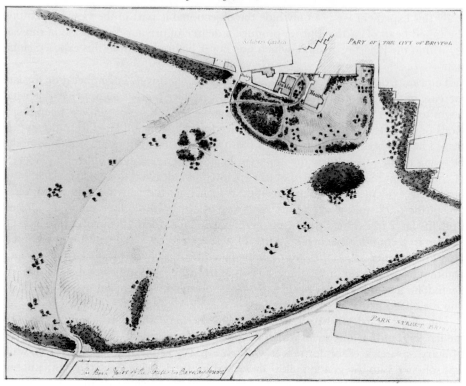

Fig. 8. Humphry Repton, The Royal Fort, Bristol: Plan of The Fort gardens and park as land-scaped and replanted, *Royal Fort Red Book*, 1801, final folio. Pen and ink with watercolour washes, [Beinecke Rare Books and Manuscripts Library, Yale University].

XI

Jane Austen and Bristol

DEIRDRE LE FAYE

IT IS well-known that Jane Austen lived for a time in Bath, and that this city features prominently as setting in both *Northanger Abbey* and *Persuasion*. But little attention has been paid to the question of whether she ever visited Bristol and, if so, when and why and what impressions she acquired of this close neighbour to Bath:—only some 15 miles to the north west—that was yet so very different from it. In her day Bristol was renowned as being a city second in size only to London, a seaport at the heart of transatlantic trade, and a commercial and manufacturing centre sending its goods country-wide; in more modern times Bristol has been described as like the sweaty workman, in leather breeches and shirtsleeves, fairly reeking of the tannery, the soap vats or the docks, while Bath was the holiday resort for the rich, the duchess among cities.[1]

Jane Austen said in one of her letters to her sister Cassandra: 'My preference for Men & Women, always inclines me to attend more to the company than the sight';[2] and this being so, undoubtedly she would have been most interested to observe the inhabitants of Bristol, which was so unlike any other place she knew. Her birthplace of Steventon in Hampshire was no more than a straggling hamlet with a population of less than 200, and Basingstoke, seven miles away, was only a small market town; thanks to staying with her brothers she knew several of the country houses in East Kent, as well as the seaside resorts of Ramsgate and Margate; and she quite often went to London, to visit the theatre and art galleries. Worthing, Dawlish, Sidmouth and Lyme Regis were the other modern seaside resorts visited by Austen family parties; and as her aunt and uncle, Mr. and Mrs. Leigh-Perrot, spent much of their time in Bath and often invited the Austens to visit them there, naturally this inland resort was well-known to Jane by both hearsay and personal experience. Bristol as yet remained unexplored.

At the end of the eighteenth century John Wilkes, a printer, bookseller and stationer in Winchester and proprietor of the *Hampshire Chronicle*, aided by his colleague Peter Barfoot, compiled the massive *Universal British Directory*, and brought it out in five volumes between 1791–1798. Bristol, as might be expected, covers many pages therein, with lengthy descriptions of its public buildings and extensive docks, together with a summary of its various manufactures: it had more than twenty large sugar houses, plus iron foundries, brass works, copper smelting plants, coal mines, soap works, and distilleries, and also produced lead shot, industrial chemicals, china, glass and numerous kinds of fabrics. On its inhabitants Wilkes and Barfoot commented:

---

[1] R. I. James, 'Bristol Society in the Eighteenth Century', in C. M. MacInnes and W. F. Whittard, (eds.), *Bristol and its Adjoining Counties* (Bristol, 1955), p. 231.

[2] D. Le Faye, (ed.), *Jane Austen's Letters* (Oxford, 1995, 1997), p. 179.

Bristol is peopled with an heterogeneous mixture from Wales, Ireland, Scotland, America, Gloucestershire, Somersetshire, and Devonshire, the other neighbouring counties, and almost all parts of England and the world. Here are people of different countries, languages, and religions; so that any general characteristic of its inhabitants cannot be given. Its gentry, merchants, and capital traders, are as polite, and as superb in their town and country houses, *équipages*, servants, and amusements, as any in the kingdom [...] Its shopkeepers are remarkable for their activity, industry, and obliging, upright and punctual, behaviour in their business. Literature and genteel education are much cultivated in Bristol; and it abounds with agreeable women, whose mode of dress, for modest elegance, is universally approved. People of rank and education here, as every where else, pronounce with propriety; but some of the *bourgeois* speak a broad dialect, much worse than the common people in the metropolis, though they are not willing to acknowledge it.[3]

Such a remarkable conglomeration of heavy industry, with the added attraction of literature, genteel education and agreeable women, must have sounded most intriguing to Jane Austen—though one hopes she was able to understand the Bristol accent even if Wilkes and Barfoot found it more incomprehensible than Cockney.

Jane Austen had a number of maternal cousins living in Gloucestershire and Warwickshire, and it is known that she and her elder sister Cassandra visited them at least once in Jane's younger days; travelling from Steventon would in all probability entail passing through either Bath or Bristol—or perhaps both, if they made a round trip. Her first recorded visit to Gloucestershire was in the summer of 1794, when she was aged nearly nineteen; but she may perhaps have made such a journey as early as the spring or summer of 1792, for in 'Lesley Castle', one of the short stories of her *Juvenilia* and probably written that year, a character talks of 'the air of the Bristol-downs, healthy air as it is'; and also comments that February was still 'so unfashionable a season of the year', since the Bristol season, based on attendance at the Hotwells, only started in late March following the end of the Bath season.[4] It cannot however be certain whether Jane had this knowledge from personal experience, or by hearsay from the Leigh-Perrot couple, or from reading contemporary guide-books.

It is however known from her letters that Jane stayed in Bath for three or four weeks with the Leigh-Perrots in their second home in Paragon Buildings, during November/December 1797; and in the summer of 1799 she stayed in Queen Square for six weeks with other members of her family. These visits would have given time for day trips to Bristol, or perhaps even an overnight stay, and Jane could then have acquired the knowledge of Bristol and Clifton that appears in her early novel *Northanger Abbey*, which was composed in 1798–1799, as follows:

> [*It is late February, and the heroine, Catherine Morland, has been in Bath for a few weeks as the guest of Mr. and Mrs. Allen, and has made the acquaintance of the four children of the Thorpe family as well as the Revd. Henry Tilney and his sister Eleanor. The following extracts are taken from chapters 11, 13, 14 and 15.*]

---

[3] P. Barfoot and J. Wilkes, *Universal British Directory*, (London, five vols., 1791–1798); entry for Bristol is vol. II, pp.117–200.

[4] Jane Austen, *Juvenilia*, P. Sabor (ed.), (Cambridge, 2006); Volume the Second, 'Lesley Castle', pp. 153–154, 155–156.

It was too dirty for Mrs. Allen to accompany her husband to the Pump-room; he accordingly set off by himself, and Catherine had barely watched him down the street, when her notice was claimed by the approach of the same two open carriages, containing the same three people that had surprized her so much a few mornings back.

"Isabella, my brother, and Mr. Thorpe, I declare! They are coming for me perhaps—but I shall not go—I cannot go indeed, for you know Miss Tilney may still call." Mrs. Allen agreed to it. John Thorpe was soon with them, and his voice was with them yet sooner, for on the stairs he was calling out to Miss Morland to be quick. "Make haste! make haste!" as he threw open the door—"put on your hat this moment—there is no time to be lost—we are going to Bristol.—How d'ye do, Mrs. Allen?"

"To Bristol! Is not that a great way off?—But, however, I cannot go with you today, because I am engaged; I expect some friends every moment." This was of course vehemently talked down as no reason at all; Mrs. Allen was called on to second him, and the two others walked in, to give their assistance. "My sweetest Catherine, is not this delightful? We shall have a most heavenly drive. You are to thank your brother and me for the scheme; it darted into our heads at breakfast-time, I verily believe at the same instant; and we should have been off two hours ago if it had not been for this detestable rain. But it does not signify, the nights are moonlight, and we shall do delightfully. Oh! I am in such ecstasies at the thoughts of a little country air and quiet!—so much better than going to the Lower Rooms. We shall drive directly to Clifton and dine there; and, as soon as dinner is over, if there is time for it, go on to Kingsweston."

"I doubt our being able to do so much," said Morland.

"You croaking fellow!" cried Thorpe, "we shall be able to do ten times more. Kingsweston! aye, and Blaize Castle too, and any thing else we can hear of; but here is your sister says she will not go."

"Blaize Castle!" cried Catherine; "what is that?"

"The finest place in England—worth going fifty miles at any time to see."

"What, is it really a castle, an old castle?"

"The oldest in the kingdom."

"But is it like what one reads of?"

"Exactly—the very same."

"But now really—are there towers and long galleries?"

"By dozens."

"Then I should like to see it; but I cannot—I cannot go."

"Not go!—my beloved creature, what do you mean?"

"I cannot go, because [...] I expect Miss Tilney and her brother to call on me to take a country walk. They promised to come at twelve, only it rained; but now, as it is so fine, I dare say they will be here soon."

"Not they indeed," cried Thorpe; "for, as we turned into Broad-Street, I saw them—does he not drive a phaeton with bright chestnuts? [...] I saw him at that moment turn up the Lansdown Road,—driving a smart-looking girl [...] I heard Tilney hallooing to a man who was just passing by on horseback, that they were going as far as Wick Rocks."

"Then I will. Shall I go, Mrs. Allen?"

"Just as you please, my dear." [...] And in two minutes they were off. [...]

They were within view of the town of Keynsham, when a halloo from Morland, who was behind them, made his friend pull up [...] and Morland said, "We had better go back, Thorpe; it is too late to go on today; your sister thinks so as well as I. We have been exactly an hour coming from Pulteney-street, very little more than seven miles; and I suppose, we have at least eight more to go. It will never do. We set out a great deal too late. We had much better put it off till another day, and turn round."

"It is all one to me," replied Thorpe rather angrily; and instantly turning his horse, they were on their way back to Bath. [...]

The Clifton scheme had been deferred, not relinquished, and [...] it was brought forward again. [...] Catherine looked grave, was very sorry, but could not go. The engagement which ought to have kept her from joining in the former attempt, would make it impossible for her to accompany them now. [...] Towards the end of the morning however, Catherine [...] walked out into the town, and in Bond-street overtook the second Miss Thorpe, as she was loitering towards Edgar's Buildings between two of the sweetest girls in the world, who had been her dear friends all the morning. From her, she soon learned that the party to Clifton had taken place. "They set off at eight this morning," said Miss Anne, "and I am sure I do not envy them their drive. I think you and I are very well off to be out of the scrape. It must be the dullest thing in the world, for there is not a soul at Clifton at this time of year. Belle went with your brother, and John drove Maria. [...] She was quite wild to go. She thought it would be something very fine. I cannot say I admire her taste; and for my part I was determined from the first not to go, if they pressed me ever so much."

Early the next day [...] the two youngest Miss Thorpes were by themselves in the parlour; and, on Anne's quitting it to call her sister, Catherine took the opportunity of asking the other for some particulars of their yesterday's party. Maria desired no greater pleasure than to speak of it; and Catherine immediately learnt that it had been altogether the most delightful scheme in the world; that nobody could imagine how charming it had been, and that it had been more delightful than any body could conceive. Such was the information of the first five minutes; the second unfolded thus much in detail,—that they had driven directly to the York Hotel, ate some soup, and bespoke an early dinner, walked down to the Pump-room, tasted the water, and laid out some shillings in purses and spars; thence adjourned to eat ice at a pastry-cook's, and hurrying back to the Hotel, swallowed their dinner in haste, to prevent being in the dark; and then had a delightful drive back, only the moon was not up, and it rained a little, and Mr. Morland's horse was so tired he could hardly get it along.

Catherine listened with heartfelt satisfaction. It appeared that Blaize Castle had never been thought of; and, as for all the rest, there was nothing to regret for half an instant.—Maria's intelligence concluded with a tender effusion of pity for her sister Anne, whom she represented as insupportably cross, from being excluded the party.

From these references it can be seen that Jane Austen was thoroughly up to date with the latest social trends and building developments in Bristol and its locality. By the end of the eighteenth century the centre of Bristol had become over-crowded, dark, smoky, noisy and very smelly—all visitors made comments to this effect[5]—and the wealthy merchants were moving into new modern houses outside the old city walls. Kingsdown was the first area to be developed, and other large houses were also built in the surrounding villages of Frenchay, Henbury, Redland and Stapleton. In particular Clifton seems to have been considered the most desirable location, with fresh air, fine views, and the Downs for driving, riding and walking; and development started here about 1785, creating both terraces and individual houses: 'Clifton is universally allowed to be one of the most agreeable, healthy and pleasant villages in the kingdom. The delightful situation of Clifton has long since tempted several persons of large fortune to make it their principal residence, and others continuing to follow their example has occasioned the hill to be almost everywhere covered with respectable mansions, most of them built in freestone in a very elegant style'– a paragraph repeated almost word for word in other guide books for several years to come, with the additional comment in one that: 'This beautiful village [...] furnishes the most charming views over the western part of Bristol, and the Avon, for a considerable way, with its moving scene of ships. It stands on a hill, which rises by a gradual ascent from the river; and is in a great measure covered with elegant buildings.'[6]

The Royal York House Hotel and Tavern had opened in 1790, located on the west corner of Gloucester Place [also called Gloucester Row], in Clifton. It had 'an elegant Ball-room with a good organ: and commands a picturesque view of Leigh woods and the downs. The whole building is a *capital Hotel*, handsomely fitted up; and extremely well calculated for parties who arrive here, or make excursions for a few days to this delightful spot'.[7] By about 1820, the Hotel had been converted into private lodging houses, and the public entertainment rooms were across the road in the Bath Hotel in Sion Place [or Row]—'which is a scarcely less respectable establishment'.[8] The Bath Hotel was rebuilt in 1864 and reopened as the Clifton Down Hotel in 1865; it is now [2009] called Bridge House, and until recently was used as a Visitor Centre for tourists coming to see the Clifton Suspension Bridge.

The Pump-room to which the four young people walked was at the new small spa, the New Hot Wells, which had opened on Sion Hill in the 1780s, and Sion Spring House is its descendant. At this time Clifton did not have its own Assembly Rooms, the building of which only started in late 1806, and the whole area at the top of the hill was referred to loosely as The Mall, consisting of just the east ends of the two terraces which were later expanded into West Mall and Caledonia Place, with an oval lawn or gravelled area in between them.

'Spars' was the generic term for sparkling quartz crystals, in this case those found in St. Vincent's Rocks at the foot of the Avon Gorge; they were known as 'Bristol diamonds' and made into cheap souvenir jewellery. According to the metal salts—manganese and iron—entering into their crystallization, they might be coloured mauve, yellow or red, and so could also be passed off as amethysts, topazes and rubies.

---

[5] D. Lambert, 'The Prospect of Trade: The Merchant Gardeners of Bristol in the Second Half of the Eighteenth Century', in M. Conan, (ed.), *Bourgeois and Aristocratic Cultural Encounters in Garden Art, 1550–1850*, (Dumbarton Oaks, Washington D.C., 2002); p. 124.

[6] P. Barfoot and J. Wilkes, *op. cit.*, II, pp. 127–8; J. Feltham: *A Guide to all the Watering and Sea Bathing Places* (London, n.d., post-1817), p. 298.

[7] *Mathews's Bristol Directory for 1793–4*, p. 104.

[8] J. Feltham, *op. cit.*, entry for Bristol, Hotwells and Clifton is pp. 278–307.

As for the other tourist destinations mentioned by John Thorpe, the contemporary guide books described Kingsweston as the site of 'the delightful residence of Lord de Clifford [...] Few noblemen's seats contain so valuable a collection of original paintings; they are chiefly from the Italian and Flemish schools. The house with the park and gardens laid out in the first style of elegance, may be seen every day in the week [...] the mansion partially shaded by stately trees, presents itself at the extent of a fine lawn, whose sides are deeply fringed by luxuriant elms.'[9] Whether John Thorpe himself really knew what Blaize Castle was—and the naïve Catherine certainly did not—both Jane Austen and her readers would have known that it was only a gothic folly, built on a hilltop by the Bristol sugar merchant Thomas Farr in 1766 to enhance the view from his house at Henbury on the outskirts of the city. The castle has one circular room with three small towers, making it triangular in appearance; Blaize Hamlet, near the Castle, was not built until 1811. Wick Rocks is an outcrop of limestone crags, once used as a quarry, forming a small but picturesque glen on the outskirts of Wick, a Gloucestershire village midway between Bath and Bristol. The Rocks was a well-known local beauty spot of the period, and as late as the end of the nineteenth century all visitors to the area were still being recommended to make an excursion there.[10]

At the end of 1800 the Revd. George Austen suddenly decided to retire from Steventon and move permanently to Bath, leaving his eldest son James to be curate of the village in his place. The Austen sons were now all out in the world and settled in their professions, but Jane and Cassandra were still unmarried, hence their parents may well have thought that living in Bath would enable them to meet more eligible men than was likely to be the case in rural Hampshire. Not many of Jane's letters survive from this time of family upheaval, and although there are some discussions with Cassandra as to where they might choose to settle in Bath, there are only two passing references to Bristol: 'Miss Harwood & her friend have taken a house 15 miles from Bath; she writes very kind letters, but sends no other particulars of the situation— Perhaps it is one of the first houses in Bristol.' And later on, when Jane is talking about buying furniture for the new Bath lodgings once they get there: 'I flatter myself that for little comforts of all kinds, our apartment will be one of the most complete things of the sort all over Bath—Bristol included'.[11]

In the spring of 1801 Mr. Austen, with his wife and daughters, left Hampshire and took a lease of No. 4 Sydney Place in Bath. During the time they lived there they travelled around on summer holidays, mostly in Devon and Dorset; but there is also a reference to a trip to Wales in 1802, in which case they would in all probability have taken the route suggested by the guidebooks, going from Bath to Bristol to cross the Severn at the New Passage, and thence joining the main road leading to Caerwent, Newport, Cardiff, and the rest of the South Wales coast.

Mr. Austen died early in 1805 and, after moving to different lodgings in Bath, Mrs. Austen and her daughters finally left the city in the summer of 1806.[12] On this occasion they definitely did at least pass through Bristol, for they stayed in Clifton for most

  [9] J. Feltham, op. cit., p. 305.
  [10] J. Tunstall, Rambles about Bath and its neighbourhood (Bath, 1847); (7th ed., revised by R. E. Peach, London, 1876), pp. 329–332.
  [11] D. Le Faye, op. cit., pp. 62, 68.
  [12] Ibid., p. 138.

of the month of July, *en route* to their cousins in Gloucestershire. As they were only in holiday lodgings, no address can be found for them there; but on the Sundays during these weeks they would have attended services at St. Andrew's Clifton, and here very probably Jane came across the name of 'Elton' as being one of the important local families, who had a permanent pew in St. Andrews—a name which stayed in her memory.[13] She would also have had time to walk on the Downs and see the 'respectable mansions' which the guidebooks praised; a modern historian mentions a dozen large houses which had been built there during the eighteenth century: Manilla Hall, Clifton Court, Clifton Wood House, Clifton Hill House,[14] also Amherst, Freemantle, Prospect, Beresford, Goldney, Church, Cornwallis, and Grove Houses.[15] It would seem that one at least of these 'elegant buildings' struck her as being particularly ostentatious and hence likely to be attractive to the *nouveaux riches* Bristol merchants; and like the name of Elton, the appearance of this house stayed in her memory.

Later in 1806 Mrs. Austen and her daughters took rented accommodation in Southampton, and eventually moved into their final home, at Chawton in Hampshire, in the summer of 1809. Here Jane revised *Sense and Sensibility*, *Pride and Prejudice* and *Northanger Abbey* for publication, and then wrote three entirely new novels:—*Mansfield Park*, *Emma*, and *Persuasion*. In June 1814 the Austens' friend Martha Lloyd was planning to go on holiday with Captain and Mrs. Deans-Dundas, and Jane wrote to Cassandra: 'Instead of Bath, the Deans Dundases have taken a House at Clifton,—Richmond Terrace—& [Martha] is as glad of the change as even You & I should be—or almost.—She will now be able to go on from Berks & visit them, without any fears from Heat.' However, it seems that this plan had to be changed, for in September 1814 Jane is writing to Martha herself, who was after all staying at Pulteney Street in Bath: 'The weather can hardly have incommoded you by its heat.—We have had many evenings here so cold, that I was sure there must be fires in the Country,— [...] I hope you will see Clifton'.[16]

Jane had started writing *Emma* early in 1814; the action is set in the fictitious village of Highbury, which is said to be not far from Richmond-on-Thames and Box Hill in Surrey, but for the purposes of the plot a female character had to be brought in who was a total stranger to the district—and it was perhaps the thought of Martha Lloyd visiting Clifton which reminded Jane of her own holiday there and the name of Elton, and so paved the way for the creation of Mrs. Elton, late of Bristol and—possibly— Clifton. The personality of Mrs. Elton may have been based on that of a Mrs. Britton, whom Jane had met in Kent in 1813: 'Mrs. Britton called here on Saturday. I never saw her before. She is a large, ungenteel Woman, with self-satisfied & would-be elegant manners'.[17]—but the origins of the character are firmly Bristolian.

[13] M. Elton, *Annals of the Elton Family: Bristol Merchants and Somerset Landowners*, (Stroud, 1994), p. 92.

[14] By 1776 the house was the home of Edward Elton, who was born in 1746, served as warden of the Society of Merchant Venturers in 1770–1771 and died 20 September 1811. His grandfather Jacob Elton (1684–1765) was a younger brother of Sir Abraham Elton 2nd Bart., (1679–1742) of Clevedon Court. Edward's house in Clifton contained three coach houses, three stables and a garden. His wife died in 1780 leaving him with six children under the age of eight and this may have induced him to move to a more manageable house in Clifton at some date prior to 1786.

[15] D. Jones, *A History of Clifton*, (Chichester, 1992), pp. 64–93, 110–133.

[16] D. Le Faye, *op. cit.*, pp. 265, 272.

[17] *Ibid.*, p. 234.

[The Revd. Philip Elton, vicar of Highbury, has gone on holiday to Bath in January, and from there news returns to Highbury that he has very rapidly become engaged to Miss Augusta Hawkins. The following extracts are from Emma, Vol II, *chapters 4, 14 and 15—or chapters 22, 32 and 33 of editions with continuously numbered chapters.]*

A week had not passed since Miss Hawkins's name was first mentioned in Highbury, before she was, by some means or other, discovered to have every recommendation of person and mind; to be handsome, elegant, highly accomplished, and perfectly amiable, [...] [and] in addition to all the usual advantages of perfect beauty and merit, was in possession of an independent fortune, of so many thousands as would always be called ten; a point of some dignity, as well as some convenience; the story told well; he had not thrown himself away—he had gained a woman of 10,000£ or thereabouts; and he had gained her with such delightful rapidity. [...]

Of the lady, individually, Emma thought very little. She was good enough for Mr. Elton, no doubt; accomplished enough for Highbury—handsome enough—[...][but] she brought no name, no blood, no alliance. Miss Hawkins was the youngest of the two daughters of a Bristol—merchant, of course, he must be called; but, as the whole of the profits of his mercantile life appeared so very moderate, it was not unfair to guess the dignity of his line of trade had been very moderate also. Part of every winter she had been used to spend in Bath; but Bristol was her home, the very heart of Bristol; for though the father and mother had died some years ago, an uncle remained—in the law line—nothing more distinctly honourable was hazarded of him, than that he was in the law line; and with him the daughter had lived. Emma guessed him to be the drudge of some attorney, and too stupid to rise. And all the grandeur of the connection seemed dependent on the elder sister, who was *very well married*, to a gentleman in a *great way*, near Bristol, who kept two carriages! That was the wind-up of the history; that was the glory of Miss Hawkins.

Mrs. Elton was first seen at church: but though devotion might be interrupted, curiosity could not be satisfied by a bride in a pew, and it must be left for the visits in form which were then to be paid, to settle whether she were very pretty indeed, or only rather pretty, or not pretty at all [...] [Emma] would not be in a hurry to find fault, but she suspected that there was no elegance;—ease, but not elegance.— She was almost sure that for a young woman, a stranger, a bride, there was too much ease. Her person was rather good; her face not unpretty; but neither feature, nor air, nor voice, nor manner, were elegant. Emma thought at least it would turn out so. [...]

[Emma] had a quarter of an hour of the lady's conversation to herself, and could composedly attend to her; and the quarter of an hour quite convinced her that Mrs. Elton was a vain woman, extremely well satisfied with herself, and thinking much of her own importance; that she meant to shine and be very superior, but with manners which had been formed in a bad school, pert and familiar; that all her notions were drawn from one set of people, and one style of living; that if not foolish she was ignorant, and that her society would certainly do Mr. Elton no good. [...] The rich brother-in-law near Bristol was the pride of the alliance, and his place and his carriages were the pride of him.

The very first subject after being seated was Maple Grove, "My brother Mr. Suckling's seat"—a comparison of Hartfield to Maple Grove. The grounds of Hartfield were small, but neat and pretty; and the house was modern and well-built. Mrs. Elton seemed most favourably impressed by the size of the room, the entrance, and all that she could see or imagine. "Very like Maple Grove indeed!—She was quite struck by the likeness!—That room was the very shape and size of the morning-room at Maple Grove; her sister's favourite room."—Mr. Elton was appealed to.—"Was it not astonishingly like?—She could really almost fancy herself at Maple Grove."

"And the staircase—You know, as I came in, I observed how very like the staircase was; placed exactly in the same part of the house. I really could not help exclaiming! I assure you, Miss Woodhouse, it is very delightful to me, to be reminded of a place I am so extremely partial to as Maple Grove. I have spent so many happy months there! (with a little sigh of sentiment). A charming place, undoubtedly. Every body who sees it is struck by its beauty; but to me, it has been quite a home. Whenever you are transplanted, like me, Miss Woodhouse, you will understand how very delightful it is to meet with any thing at all like what one has left behind. I always say this is quite one of the evils of matrimony."

Emma made as slight a reply as she could; but it was fully sufficient for Mrs. Elton, who only wanted to be talking herself.

"So extremely like Maple Grove! And it is not merely the house—the grounds, I assure you, as far as I could observe, are strikingly like. The laurels at Maple Grove are in the same profusion as here, and stand very much in the same way—just across the lawn; and I had a glimpse of a fine large tree, with a bench round it, which put me so exactly in mind! My brother and sister will be enchanted with this place. People who have extensive grounds themselves are always pleased with any thing in the same style."

Emma doubted the truth of this sentiment. She had a great idea that people who had extensive grounds themselves cared very little for the extensive grounds of any body else; but it was not worth while to attack an error so double-dyed, and therefore only said in reply,

"When you have seen more of this country, I am afraid you will think you have over-rated Hartfield. Surrey is full of beauties."

"Oh! yes, I am quite aware of that. It is the garden of England, you know. Surrey is the garden of England."

"Yes; but we must not rest our claims on that distinction. Many counties, I believe, are called the garden of England, as well as Surrey."

"No, I fancy not," replied Mrs. Elton, with a most satisfied smile. "I never heard any county but Surrey called so."

Emma was silenced.

"My brother and sister have promised us a visit in the spring, or summer at farthest," continued Mrs. Elton; "and that will be our time for exploring. While they are with us, we shall explore a great deal, I dare say. They will have their barouche-landau, of course, which holds four perfectly; and therefore, without saying any thing of *our* carriage, we should be able to explore the different beauties extremely well. They would hardly come in their chaise, I think, at that season of the year. Indeed, when the time draws on, I shall decidedly recommend their bringing the barouche-landau; it will be so very much preferable. When people come into a beautiful country of this sort, you know, Miss Woodhouse, one naturally wishes them to see as much as possible; and Mr. Suckling is extremely fond of exploring. We explored to King's-Weston twice last summer, in that way, most delightfully, just after their first having the barouche-landau. You have many parties of that kind here, I suppose, Miss Woodhouse, every summer?"

"No; not immediately here. We are rather out of distance of the very striking beauties which attract the sort of parties you speak of; and we are a very quiet set of people, I believe; more disposed to stay at home than engage in schemes of plea-sure."

"Ah! there is nothing like staying at home, for real comfort. Nobody can be more devoted to home than I am. I was quite a proverb for it at Maple Grove. Many a time has Selina said, when she has been going to Bristol, 'I really cannot get this girl to move from the house. I absolutely must go in by myself, though I hate being stuck up in the barouche-landau without a companion'; but Augusta, I believe, with her own good will, would never stir beyond the park paling. Many a time has she said so; and yet I am no advocate for entire seclusion. I think, on the contrary, when people shut themselves up entirely from society, it is a very bad thing; and that it is much more advisable to mix in the world in a proper degree, without liv-ing in it either too much or too little. I perfectly understand your situation, how-ever, Miss Woodhouse—Your father's state of health must be a great drawback. Why does he not try Bath?—Indeed he should. Let me recommend Bath to you. I assure you I have no doubt of its doing Mr. Woodhouse good." [...]

Such as Mrs. Elton appeared to her on this second interview, such she appeared whenever they met again,—self-important, presuming, familiar, ignorant, and ill-bred. She had a little beauty and a little accomplishment, but so little judgment that she thought herself coming with superior knowledge of the world, to enliven and improve a country neighbourhood; and conceived Miss Hawkins to have held such a place in society as Mrs. Elton's consequence only could surpass.

From Mrs. Elton's chatter later on in the story, readers learn that Maple Grove is 125 miles from London, which would place it beyond Bristol, to the west or north, and so quite probably in Clifton; but the name of Maple Grove may have been Jane's com-bination of 'Stapleton' to the north-east of Bristol with 'Grove' House in Clifton, thus carefully confusing its location and making it as imaginary as that of Highbury itself. In addition to Maple Grove's park with its paling, Mrs. Elton claims it also has 'an immense plantation all round it! You seem shut out from every thing—in the most complete retirement.' We also learn that, so far from being an ancestral home, the Sucklings only bought the property about twelve years ago, a length of time which makes them feel entitled to despise their nearest neighbours, as Mrs. Elton prides her-self on announcing:

I have quite a horror of upstarts. Maple Grove has given me a thorough disgust to people of that sort; for there is a family in that neighbourhood who are such an annoyance to my brother and sister from the airs they give themselves! [...] People of the name of Tupman, very lately settled there, and encumbered with many low connections, but giving themselves immense airs, and expecting to be on a footing with the old established families. A year and a half is the very utmost that they can have lived at West Hall; and how they got their fortune nobody knows. They came from Birmingham, which is not a place to promise much [...] one has not great hopes from Birmingham. I always say there is something direful in the sound: but nothing more is positively known of the Tupmans, though a good many things I assure you are suspected; and yet by their manners they evidently think themselves equal even to my brother, Mr. Suckling, who happens to be one of their nearest neighbours. It is infinitely too bad. Mr. Suckling, who has been eleven years a resident at Maple Grove, and whose father had it before him—I believe, at least—I am almost sure that old Mr. Suckling had completed the purchase before his death.[18]

A barouche-landau was a new style of four-horse carriage, perhaps the equivalent of some large flashy car, say a BMW, of today's date, and could take up to six people if one was prepared to drive and another to sit on the box beside the driver; a chaise was for two people, or three at a pinch if a fold-out seat was used. Mr. Suckling was certainly well-off, to be able to afford two carriages, with all the stabling, horses and menservants involved in their upkeep, as well as the heavy taxation incurred; though oddly enough, Mrs. Elton never tells us the source of his wealth—which must therefore remain as dubious as that of the Tupmans whom she so roundly condemns.

From Jane Austen's comments in her letters, and from her creation of Mrs. Elton— over-dressed in a white and silver poplin, with lace and pearls—it would seem that although she enjoyed the fresh air of Clifton and thought it much preferable to the steamy heat of Bath, she was not convinced by the *Universal British Directory's* claim that 'Literature and genteel education are much cultivated in Bristol; and it abounds with agreeable women, whose mode of dress, for modest elegance, is universally approved', but viewed the city as a forcing-bed for money-grubbing vulgarians.

As a *coda* to Jane Austen's own knowledge of Bristol, in 1825 Miss Emma Smith, the girl who would three years later marry Jane's favourite nephew, James-Edward Austen-Leigh, was holidaying in Clifton with her siblings Eliza and Charles, staying at 3 Prince's Buildings with their maiden aunt as chaperone. On 28 March 1825 Emma wrote home to her mother in London:

> We have beautiful weather & have made good use of the carriage & horses— Saturday we took Aunt to Henbury—Yesterday we went to the 6 o'clock service at St. Mary Redcliffes wishing to see that magnificent church lighted up. Before the Sermon there must have been 100 lights in it. In the five Chandeliers Eliza counted 60. The Organ is fine & music good but the preacher was dreadful. It was Mr Wish[19] & I heartily <u>wish</u> I may never hear such another again. He preached extempore for an hour his language & composition were worse than I think you can conceive. I longed to get up & go out of church. From the outside the light seen through the Gothic windows had a beautiful effect.

> This morning we have been to see the Sugar baking process—I suppose one of the owners a very intelligent man showed us over and I think it interested Charles

[18] *Emma*, Vol. II, chapters 17 and 18, or 35 and 36 in continuous numeration.

[19] The Revd. Martin Richard Whish (1782–1852), a prebendary of Salisbury cathedral, and vicar of St. Mary Redcliffe; St. John, Bedminster; Abbots Leigh and St. Thomas, City.

much. He makes almost entirely the Patent Sugar which is merely refined by boiling & without Bullocks Blood—The common people he says he believes like the taste of the blood which they can perceive in Treacle. I suppose their profits are very great for he told us they spent <u>twelve thousand £</u> a year. He thinks West India property will improve indeed he says it is now selling at a higher rate than it did. The Jamaica sugar is the best & next that which is brought from the Island of St. Vincent. He told us that excepting the feeling of liberty he thought the Slaves better off than his men, that is to say better fed & clothed. Labour he said is cheaper in Bristol than in London & coals also, they are three pence a Bushel.

The twenty sugar houses mentioned by the *Universal British Directory* in the 1790s had by now dwindled to a mere six: Samuel and James Blackwell; Brice, Stock and Fry; Burge and Chilton; Guppy Bros; Holden and Vining; and John and Francis Savage; but there is no further information as to which one the young Smiths visited.[20] This letter was evidently thought so interesting by Emma's mother that she preserved it, hence its survival in the Austen-Leigh archive.[21]

---

[20] Pigot and Co's *National Commercial Directory*, volume covering Berks, Bucks, Glos, Hants, Oxon (1830; facsimile edn. King's Lynn, 1994).

[21] Austen-Leigh archive, Hampshire Record Office, Winchester, 23M93/72/3.

XII

The Catholic Question in Bristol Public Life, 1820–1829

JOHN R. STEVENS, M.A., (CANTAB)

The terms 'Catholic' and 'Protestant' are used, where occasion demands, in their contemporary sense to denote respectively supporters and opponents of the removal of Roman Catholic civil disabilities ('Catholic Emancipation').[1]

I

ENGLAND UNTIL 1828 was an Anglican Confessional State, eligibility for public office being dependent on communicant membership of the Church of England- the sacramental 'test' which since the reign of King Charles II (1660–1685) had excluded from civil and military office dissenters, Catholic *and* Protestant, from the Established Church. Since 1727, Parliament had passed annual Acts of Indemnity, relieving those who took office in spite of their provisions from the effects of the Corporation and Test Acts (1661 and 1673). This indemnity could, of course, benefit both Protestant and Catholic dissenters.

The position of the Roman Catholics was, however, rather worse than that of Protestant Dissenters. For one thing, aspirants to office were subject to the Oath of (Royal) Supremacy (1562). Although the terms of the Oath had been modified by later Statutes, it was still necessary to abjure the claim to jurisdiction in ecclesiastical *and* civil matters which was still made (theoretically at least) by the Papacy. More practically serious was the requirement of the declaration against transubstantiation, which struck at the heart of Roman doctrine and which excluded Roman Catholics from membership of the House of Commons. It was also clear that any attempt to remove the Catholic disabilities would meet stronger opposition than a similar attempt to aid the Protestant Dissenters. For most Englishmen Protestantism, Englishness and liberty were inextricably linked and Catholicism associated with foreigners and tyranny.

The Catholic question had assumed importance as a result of the Union with Ireland in 1801. (Fig. 1.) The younger Pitt, as Prime Minister, had wished the parliamentary union to be accompanied by the removal of the Catholic disabilities. George III, however, although he had assented to measures allowing Roman Catholics to inherit property (1780), and to build churches (1791), had been implacably opposed to

---

[1] The literature on the question at a national level is voluminous and the writer can do no more than mention here a few secondary authorities, old and new, which he has found particularly helpful, namely: Sir Keith Feiling, *The Second Tory Party 1714–1832*, (1938); Elizabeth, Lady Longford, *Wellington: Pillar of State* (1972); J. C. D. Clark, *English Society 1660–1832*, (2nd. edn., Cambridge, 2000) and R. A. Gaunt (ed.), *Unrepentant Tory: Political Selections from the Diaries of the Fourth Duke of Newcastle 1827–38*, (Woodbridge, 2006).

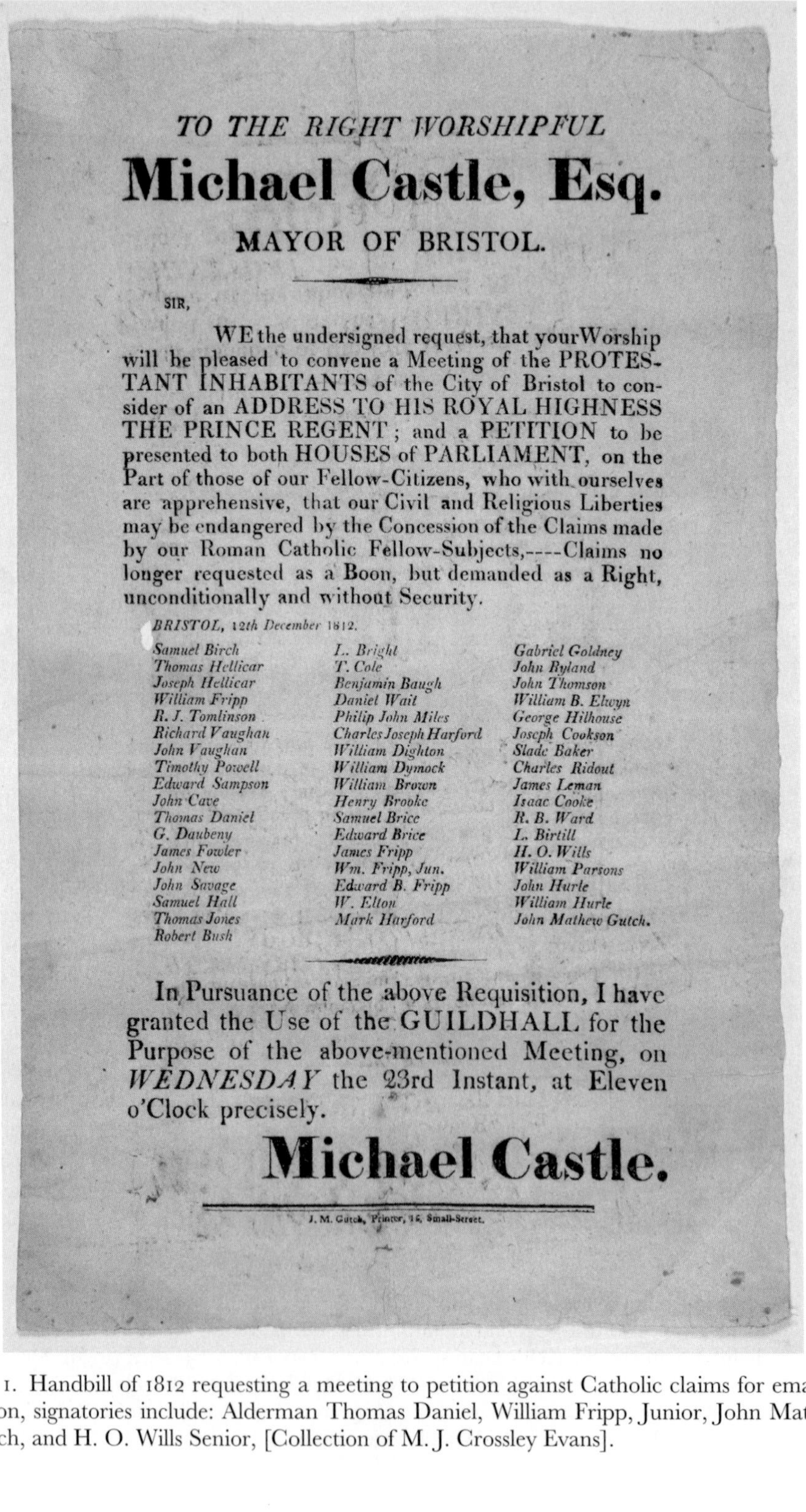

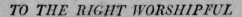

TO THE RIGHT WORSHIPFUL

Michael Castle, Esq.

MAYOR OF BRISTOL.

SIR,

WE the undersigned request, that yourWorship will be pleased to convene a Meeting of the PROTES-TANT INHABITANTS of the City of Bristol to consider of an ADDRESS TO HIS ROYAL HIGHNESS THE PRINCE REGENT ; and a PETITION to be presented to both HOUSES of PARLIAMENT, on the Part of those of our Fellow-Citizens, who with ourselves are apprehensive, that our Civil and Religious Liberties may be endangered by the Concession of the Claims made by our Roman Catholic Fellow-Subjects,----Claims no longer requested as a Boon, but demanded as a Right, unconditionally and without Security.

BRISTOL, 12th December 1812.

Samuel Birch	L. Bright	Gabriel Goldney
Thomas Hellicar	T. Cole	John Ryland
Joseph Hellicar	Benjamin Baugh	John Thomson
William Fripp	Daniel Wait	William B. Elwyn
R. J. Tomlinson	Philip John Miles	George Hilhouse
Richard Vaughan	Charles Joseph Harford	Joseph Cookson
John Vaughan	William Dighton	Slade Baker
Timothy Powell	William Dymock	Charles Ridout
Edward Sampson	William Brown	James Leman
John Cave	Henry Brooke	Isaac Cooke
Thomas Daniel	Samuel Brice	R. B. Ward
G. Daubeny	Edward Brice	L. Birtill
James Fowler	James Fripp	H. O. Wills
John New	Wm. Fripp, Jun.	William Parsons
John Savage	Edward B. Fripp	John Hurle
Samuel Hall	W. Elton	William Hurle
Thomas Jones	Mark Harford	John Mathew Gutch.
Robert Bush		

In Pursuance of the above Requisition, I have granted the Use of the GUILDHALL for the Purpose of the above-mentioned Meeting, on *WEDNESDAY* the 23rd Instant, at Eleven o'Clock precisely.

Michael Castle.

J. M. Gutch, Printer, 16, Small-Street.

Fig. 1. Handbill of 1812 requesting a meeting to petition against Catholic claims for emancipation, signatories include: Alderman Thomas Daniel, William Fripp, Junior, John Mathew Gutch, and H. O. Wills Senior, [Collection of M. J. Crossley Evans].

what he saw as a breach of his Coronation Oath and it became clear Emancipation would not pass in his lifetime. The King was however *non compos mentis* from 1810 until his death in 1820 and the Papal Secretary of State, Ercol Cardinal Consalvi, took the opportunity of a diplomatic visit in 1814 to press the Prince Regent (later George IV) and the Foreign Secretary, Lord Castlereagh, on the question of Catholic Emancipation.[2] The question was given urgency with the founding in 1823 of Daniel O'Connell's Catholic Association, with the purpose of organising and directing the Irish Catholic vote.

The government had been Tory (with insignificant intervals) since 1783. At ministerial level, the Tories were divided. Lord Liverpool (Prime Minister, 1812–1827) was a Protestant moderate whose main concern was cabinet unity: he avoided agitating the question and allowed his cabinet to differ among themselves. Although opposed to Emancipation, Liverpool in 1824 recommended a period of Court mourning on the death of the (Catholic) Jacobite claimant to the British throne, Victor Emmanuel I of Sardinia, whom some thought 'was the lawful King of Great Britain to the day of his death'.[3] Until 1829, most backbench Tory M.P.s and peers were opposed to any concession, taking very seriously their role as defenders of the 'Protestant Constitution'. The Whig opposition in Parliament was largely united in support of the claims both of the Protestant Dissenters and the Catholics. Anti-Emancipation Whigs, such as the Bristol M.P., Henry Bright,[4] were political mavericks.

Like the cabinet, the bishops were divided. During the early 1820s the vast majority of them opposed Catholic Relief Bills in the House of Lords and it was only in the changed circumstances of 1829 that as many as ten voted in favour, although they were still a minority, with the three archbishops and seventeen bishops against. Among the lower clergy, the preponderance of anti-Emancipation opinion was still more marked, with pro-Catholics like the Revd. Sydney Smith,[5] prebendary of Bristol, in a small minority.

As for the Protestant Dissenters, for some Protestantism, and for others liberty of conscience was the decisive factor. The situation was complicated by the fact that until 1828 the Dissenters were, nominally at least, subject to many of the same disabilities as the Catholics and by the rise of heterodox (non-Trinitarian) Dissent, exemplified by the Unitarians and many Presbyterians. At the extreme, heterodox Dissent shaded into Deism and even, it was said, into Atheism and had since the 1790s become associated with the French Revolutionary concept of the 'Rights of Man'. The radical Unitarian minister, the Revd. Joseph Priestley (1733–1804), for example, scientist, supporter of the repeal of the Test Act and of parliamentary reform, had been a prominent advocate of the French Revolution. It can be said that orthodox Dissenters, such as the Congregationalists (or Independents) and the Wesleyans were

---

[2] J. M. Robinson, *Cardinal Consalvi 1757–1824*, (1987), pp. 102–106.

[3] Sir Charles Petrie, *Lord Liverpool and his Times*, (1954), p. 271.

[4] Henry Bright (1785–1869). Bristol West India merchant. Whig; Unitarian. M.P. Bristol 1820–1830. See J. A. Phillips, *The Great Reform Bill in the Boroughs* (Oxford, 1992), pp. 88–92. His brother Richard Bright was the surgeon who discovered Bright's disease.

[5] The Revd. Sydney Smith (1771–1845). Father merchant, mother Huguenot stock. Prebendary of Bristol cathedral 1828–1830 and of St. Paul's cathedral 1830–1845. Preferment came late; hopes of a bishopric were frustrated. See *Oxford Dictionary of National Biography* (hereafter *O. D. N. B.*), (2004), 51, pp. 316–321.

more likely to oppose, and the heterodox more likely to support, the Catholic claims. There were, however, exceptions to the rule: in Bristol the most prominent dissenting clergy on *both* sides of the question were Congregationalists and the city's anti-Catholic Whig M.P. came from a Unitarian background.

Emancipationists grounded their case on political expediency (as far as Ireland was concerned), Christian charity and, in radical circles, 'universal rights'. The opponents of Emancipation appealed to the Protestant Constitution as the bulwark of English liberty. Reference was made to historical episodes from the Reformation onward, in particular to the Glorious Revolution of 1688–1689, when the Roman Catholic King James II, whom, it was said,[6] had aspired to re-impose his Faith in defiance of Parliament and Law, had been deposed in a virtually bloodless coup by his daughter Mary and son-in-law William of Orange. The subsequent constitutional settlement had provided for the regular meeting of Parliament and toleration (but not equal rights) for Protestant Dissenters. The Crown was later settled in the Protestant line (1701), which meant that on the death of James's Anglican daughter, Anne, without issue the throne passed in 1714 to the next Protestant in line, the Lutheran elector of Hanover (George I) rather than James's Roman Catholic son, Mary's and Anne's half-brother, James Francis Edward. It was argued that Roman Catholics, who owed civil as well as religious allegiance to their Church, and were absolved from keeping faith with heretics, would, once admitted to Parliament and to public office, seek to overthrow the Revolution settlement and impose 'Popery and arbitrary power'.

Whig Emancipationists, however, also saw themselves as heirs of the Revolution, taking the view that the Catholic doctrines of allegiance and 'no faith with heresy' had become a dead letter ('old almanacks' in the phrase of the time) and that toleration could now safely be extended to the Catholic community. Whether or not the Roman Church had indeed changed its spots was to be a key question in the debate.

Finally, many Churchmen, *and* orthodox Dissenters, saw themselves confronted by an unholy alliance between Romanism on the one hand and Unitarianism and even Atheism on the other. It was a short step, and a not unrealistic one, to discern a threat to the established order in State as well as Church. Ireland, whose inhabitants were seen as both Catholic and republican, was never far from the surface of the debate.

II

By 1820, the Bristol merchant and banker Richard Hart Davis[7] had sat as the city's Member for eight years. (Fig. 2). A strong Tory and, in Liverpool's words, 'a good Protestant',[8] he had opposed both Parliamentary Reform and Catholic

---

[6] Stuart historians have differed about James's aims, some going so far as to argue he was a ruler ahead of his times, who sought toleration for all rather than hegemony for his co-religionists. For present purposes, we are concerned simply with how James was *perceived* in 1820s England.

[7] Richard Hart Davis (1766–1842). Bristol mercantile family. Merchant trading to West Indies and partner in Harford's Bank. Tory; Anglican. M.P. Colchester 1807–1812 and Bristol 1812–1831. See R. G. Thorne, *History of Parliament 1790–1820: The House of Commons*, (1986), III, pp. 574–576. For another side of his character see: *Harriette Wilson's Memoirs of Herself and Others*, (1929), pp. 54–55, 76; K. Hickman, *Courtesans*, (2003), pp. 154–155.

[8] Lord Liverpool to Lord Bath, 22 February 1820, quoted in R. G. Thorne, *op. cit.*, p. 576.

Fig. 2. Richard Hart Davis M.P., engraved from a painting by Sir Thomas Lawrence, [Special Collections, University of Bristol].

Emancipation. At the General Election which followed the death of George III in 1820, there was little doubt that Hart Davis, as the sole Tory candidate and backed by the Tories' formidable electioneering machine, the White Lion Club,[9] would be re-elected.

The real interest lay in the question of who would accompany him to Westminster as Bristol's other Member. Bristol's Whigs had been divided in recent years. The 'Independent and Constitutional' or 'Union Club' Whigs[10] were disciples of the late

[9] J. A. Phillips, *op. cit.*, pp. 71–83.
[10] *Ibid.*, pp. 75, 83.

Whig chieftain Charles James Fox (1749–1806) and shared his advanced views on Reform, Emancipation and other matters. A more conservative strain of Whiggery was represented by Edward Protheroe Senior,[11] who had obtained a number of Tory votes to be elected with Hart Davis in 1812 and 1818.[12] Protheroe's views on many issues, including Emancipation, were little to be distinguished from those of this Tory colleague.[13]

Protheroe stood down in 1820 and the selection of Henry Bright, son of Richard Bright[14] of Ham Green, as Whig candidate seems to have been intended to heal the rifts in Bristol Whiggery.[15] Like Hart Davis a West India merchant, Bright might be expected to retain the support of the conservatives. But he came of a Unitarian family: his father had campaigned for the repeal of the Test and Corporation Acts and his radical backers included the Revd. John Rowe, colleague of the famous Dr. Lant Carpenter[16] at Lewins Mead Unitarian chapel.

Bright's electioneering suggests a desire to avoid controversy. He expressed general support for Reform and financial retrenchment but avoided specifics, preferring well-tried Whig rhetoric about the 'principles of liberty' and 'the Whig principles of 1688'. There was however one matter on which the electors sought a commitment from the candidate. After Bright's speech at the hustings, the cry rang out: 'The Catholic question! The Catholic question!' Rowe had publicly expressed support for Emancipation.[17] Where did Bright stand himself? He replied:

> I previously avoided [the question] because I felt a strong disinclination to excite religious differences. As I am now circumstanced, however, I cannot refuse to explain my present opinions, although I may differ materially from those with whom I am most closely and dearly connected. After the best consideration I have been able to give to the past events of our history, the moral tendency of the Roman Catholic doctrines[...]the probable political bearing of many of its tenets and even the honest prejudices[...]which assist in keeping alive the rapidly decreasing dread of arbitrary power, I confess I am not a friend to the Catholic cause.[18]

The Tory and Protestant *Felix Farley's Bristol Journal* ('*The Journal*') had earlier expressed the view that 'Mr Bright has [...] little opposition to fear, if he is explicit and open in his opinions on the Catholic question'[19]. So it proved: Bright topped the

---

[11] Edward Protheroe Senior (1774–1856). West India merchant family, also mining interests in the Forest of Dean. M.P. Bristol 1812–1820. R. G. Thorne, *op. cit.*, IV, pp. 898–901.

[12] J. A. Phillips, *op. cit.*, pp. 84–86.

[13] R. G. Thorne, *op. cit.*, p. 899.

[14] Richard Bright (1756–1840). West India merchant. Whig; Unitarian. Bristol common councilman 1783–1835. G. Bush, *Bristol and its Municipal Government 1820–1851*, B.R.S., XXIX, (1976), Appendix 4. M. J. Dresser, 'Protestants, Catholics and Jews: Religious Difference and Political Status in Bristol 1750–1850', in M. J. Dresser and P. Ollerenshaw (eds.), *The Making of Modern Bristol*, (Tiverton, 1996), pp. 92–123, at p. 105.

[15] J. A. Phillips, *op. cit.*, pp. 88–89.

[16] The Revd. Dr. Lant Carpenter (1780–1840). Minister of Lewins Mead Unitarian chapel 1816–1840. Father of pioneering educationalist Mary Carpenter (see note 126 below). *O. D. N. B.*, 10, pp. 233–235 and 237–239.

[17] *Felix Farley's Bristol Journal*, (hereafter *F. F. B. J.*), 4 and 11 March 1820.

[18] *F. F. B. J.*, 11 March 1820.

[19] *F. F. B. J.*, 4 March 1820.

poll with 2,997 votes to Hart Davis's 2,811, the radical Whig, James Evan Baillie, mustering a mere 115 votes.[20]

In the Commons, Bright made good his election pledge, voting against the Catholic Relief Bills of 1821, 1822 and 1825. All three Bills passed the Commons but were defeated in the Lords. In April 1825, he spoke in support of an anti-Emancipation petition from the clergy of Bristol presented by Hart Davis, asking: 'When had Catholics shown themselves favourable to the religious and civil liberties of the people of England?'[21]

The Catholic question was less prominent in the General Election of 1826. For one thing, the positions of Hart Davis and Bright, both of whom stood again, had been made clear. For another, the radical Whigs made slavery the main issue, nominating the former M.P., Edward Protheroe, as an anti-slavery candidate. Protheroe, however, showed a marked reluctance to be nominated and played no part in his campaign.[22] In the event, he polled 1,875 votes, against 3,887 for Hart Davis and 2,315 for Bright.[23] The sitting Members were thus comfortably re-elected and Bright was enthusiastically toasted at Hart Davis's post-election dinner.[24]

The Catholic claims were not altogether ignored. Henry Bush,[25] seconding Hart Davis's nomination, spoke of how his candidate had 'supported our glorious constitution in Church and State', and Bright 'twice took occasion unequivocally to assert that his sentiments in regard to the Catholics remained unaltered, he never had voted for them, and never should'.[26]

Pausing here, Bristol's electorate (unlike many borough electorates before the Reform Act of 1832) was not wholly unrepresentative of public opinion in the city. The franchise was a 'county' franchise, which meant that all owners of freehold property worth 40 shillings were entitled to vote, as were the many freemen of the city- who might become such by residence, marriage or apprenticeship and the payment of a fee- which the political parties were often prepared to fund for their supporters.[27] Pre-1832 *Poll Books* show a fair sprinkling not only of 'gentlemen' but also of 'labourers' among the small tradesmen who made up the bulk of the city's electorate.[28] Thus, insofar as the elections of 1820 and 1826 can be seen as expressive of support for a

---

[20] The Revd. A. B. Beaven, *Bristol Lists: Municipal and Miscellaneous* (Bristol, 1899), p. 171. J. A. Phillips, *op. cit.*, p. 89, note 86. Hart Davis was going through financial difficulties, which may have accounted for his relatively poor showing: J. A. Phillips, *op. cit.*, p. 89, note 87.

[21] *Hansard* (New Series), 4 (1821), p. 1034; 7 (1822), p. 278; 12 (1825), p. 842; 13 (1825), p. 3.

[22] It seems from R. G. Thorne, *op. cit.*, p. 898 that Protheroe had by this time disposed of his own West India interests. For the election campaign, see J. A. Phillips, *op. cit.*, pp. 90–91.

[23] The Revd. A. B. Beaven, *op. cit.*, p. 171.

[24] *F. F. B. J.*, 24 June 1826.

[25] Henry Bush (1795–1857). Father Robert Bush (1761–1829), merchant of Clifton Hill House. Ms. Chronology of James Bush, I, ff. 1, 37, in possession of Dr. M. J. Crossley Evans. Vice-president (jointly with J. M. Gutch– see note 74 below) of the Bristol Chamber of Commerce 1828, president 1834–1837, councillor 1835–1842, master of the Merchant Venturers 1848–1849. The Revd. A. B. Beaven, *op. cit.*, pp. 66, 269. G. Bush, *op. cit.*, Appendix 5.

[26] *F. F. B. J.*, 10 June 1826.

[27] J. A. Phillips, *op. cit.*, p. 75.

[28] See for example, *Bristol Poll Book 1830*. See J. A. Phillips, *op. cit.*, pp. 94–104 for the changes effected by the 1832 Act.

Protestant polity, they would seem to be a fair reflection of Bristolian public opinion, as would indeed be demonstrated in 1829.

III

Protestants felt a keen sense of loss at the death in January 1827 of the King's brother and heir to the throne Frederick duke of York, who had steadfastly opposed the Catholic claims. The Revd. John East, curate to the leading Evangelical the Revd. Thomas Biddulph[29] at St. James, Haymarket, preached a sermon on Sunday 21 January in which he spoke of 'the peculiar nature of our loss as a Protestant people'. East 'improved' the occasion by listing nine crucial doctrinal differences between Protestantism and Catholicism and concluded by emphasising 'the vital consequence of Protestant principles to both our civil and religious liberties, and to our eternal interests'.[30]

In February, the Prime Minister Lord Liverpool suffered a severe stroke. In April, Liverpool was succeeded by his Foreign Secretary, George Canning, a supporter of Emancipation who was also to the Left of his party in his foreign policy. Several Right-wing ministers resigned, among them the seventy-five year old Lord Chancellor Eldon. Eldon was succeeded by Sir John Copley, Master of the Rolls and recorder of Bristol, who became Lord Lyndhurst. The city therefore needed to choose a new recorder.

The corporation of Bristol, like many others at the time, was a self-perpetuating oligarchy. The Tories had wrested control from the Whigs in 1812 and had consolidated their control by filling aldermanic vacancies with their supporters. Municipal Toryism in Bristol was in the words of Graham Bush 'a bastion of the rather old-fashioned Eldonian school'.[31] This is evidenced by the city's choice of recorder in 1827.

The favoured candidate, Sir Charles Wetherell,[32] had been Attorney General but had resigned when Canning took office. A *protégé* of Lord Eldon, he shared his mentor's opposition to the claims of the Protestant Dissenters and the Roman Catholics, and to Parliamentary Reform. Although an able lawyer, his Commons speeches had earned him the reputation of 'a whimsical pedant rather than a formidable debater'.[33] The corporation had initial doubts about his appointment, since votes on 11 and 21 July were tied between Wetherell and the other candidate Sir Nicholas Tindal, but the opposition was withdrawn and on the 28 Sir Charles was unanimously elected.[34]

---

[29] The Revd. Thomas Tregenna Biddulph (1763–1838). Perpetual curate of St James, Haymarket 1799–1838. 'The recognised leader of the Evangelical movement in Bristol (regarded as virtually bishop of Bristol by some)'. *O. D. N. B.*, 5, pp. 678–679.

[30] The Revd. J. East, *The Death of a Protestant Prince Improved by a reconsideration of Protestant principles in contrast with those of the Church of Rome in a discourse delivered in the parish church of St. Philip and St. Jacob on Sunday evening January 21 1827*, (Bristol, 1827).

[31] G. Bush, *op. cit.*, pp. 34–36.

[32] Sir Charles Wetherell (1770–1846). Father dean of Hereford. Chancery barrister: K. C. 1816. M.P. for a succession of pocket boroughs. Solicitor General 1824–1826, Attorney General 1826–1827 and 1828–1829. *O. D. N. B.*, 58, pp. 328–329.

[33] *Gentleman's Magazine*, (2nd Series), 26, (1846), p. 428, quoted in *O. D. N. B.*, p. 328.

[34] J. Latimer, *The Annals of Bristol in the Nineteenth Century*, (Bristol, 1887; Kingsmead Reprints, Bath, 1970), p. 118.

Canning's unexpected death in August led to a period of uncertainty, which only ended with the duke of Wellington succeeding as Prime Minister in early 1828. The government was perceived as having swung back to the Right, and Wetherell again took office as Attorney General, while continuing as recorder of Bristol.

The Election of 1826 is thought to have produced a more Protestant Commons than before. The radical Whig Sir Francis Burdett's motion for Catholic Relief had been narrowly defeated in March 1827 and Canning, although a strong Emancipationist, had not pressed the matter during his short premiership. It is therefore unsurprising that the Whigs began their attack on the Wellington's government in February 1828 with a motion to relieve the Protestant disabilities.

When Lord John Russell's motion to repeal the Test and Corporation Acts came before the Commons on 26 February, the Unitarian Bright voted for the motion, the Anglican Tory Hart Davis against.[35] Neither spoke in the debate. When the motion passed by a majority of 66, including 44 Tories, Wellington and his right-hand man in the Commons, Sir Robert Peel (Home Secretary and Leader of the House) decided to bring Repeal forward as a government Bill, and as such it passed into Law.

Repeal did not arouse great controversy, in Bristol or elsewhere. Dissenters were fellow Protestants, and the orthodox denominations did not differ from the Established Church in fundamentals of belief but rather in points of liturgy and ceremonial, which had probably become less important since the seventeenth century. Furthermore, as has been noted, the annual Indemnity Acts had long rendered nugatory the strict terms of the Test and Corporation Acts. With particular reference to Bristol, Ms. Madge Dresser has written that 'evangelical activity had proved a powerful bonding activity for Church and Chapel'.[36] The Revd. William Thorp,[37] Congregational minister of Castle Green, wrote in 1829 that he was: 'not ashamed to avow myself a conscientious dissenter from the ecclesiastical establishment of my country, which I nevertheless revere, and nothing but scruples of conscience hinder me from entering within her pale',[38] and on his death in 1833, dissenting *and* Anglican clergy were among the pall-bearers.[39]

Nevertheless, a number of Tories and Churchmen opposed Repeal, partly because they opposed *any* weakening of the Church's hegemony and partly because they feared opening the door to the Catholic claims. M.P.s such as Wetherell, and peers like Eldon and the dukes of Newcastle and Cumberland,[40] were becoming known as 'Ultras' (the more extreme of their Whig opponents were starting to be called 'Liberals', both terms being borrowed from contemporary French politics). The *Journal* took an 'Ultra' line on Russell's motion for Repeal, commenting: 'If [the Friends of the Church] make not a stand now, they must soon make one and every

---

[35] *Hansard* (N. S.), 18, (1828), pp. 781, 783.

[36] M. J. Dresser, in M. J. Dresser and P. Ollerenshaw (eds.), *op. cit.*, p. 111.

[37] The Revd. William Thorp (1770–1833). Minister, Castle Green Congregational chapel 1806–1833. Founded Bristol Missionary Society 1812. 'An eloquent man and mighty in the Scriptures' (memorial tablet). The Revd. I. Jones, *Bristol Congregationalism: City and Country*, (Bristol, 1947), pp. 14–15.

[38] The Revd. W. Thorp, *Substance of a Second Speech*, (see note 89 below).

[39] I. Jones, *op. cit.*, p. 15.

[40] G. M. Willis, *Ernest Augustus: Duke of Cumberland, King of Hanover*, (1954), pp. 173–194.

step that they recede [...] is so much vantage-ground occupied for the fresh attack and a further inroad'.[41]

In the House of Lords, the bishop of Bristol, Dr. Robert Gray,[42] (Fig. 3), and the bishop of Bath and Wells (whose diocese then included Bedminster), Dr. George Law,[43] supported Repeal in principle, in common with the bulk of their colleagues, only two of the Bench opposing the Bill on its first reading. Dr. Law found it: 'abhorrent to the principles of genuine religion, that persons should be called upon to take the sacramental test for secular and interested motives', and he regretted differing from his friend Lord Eldon on the point.[44]

Both Dr. Gray and Dr. Law, however, along with six other bishops, supported an amendment moved by Eldon to insert the word 'Protestant' into the declaration to be required of office-holders in place of the test. Dr. Gray considered this necessary to prevent Catholics 'coming into the Corporations' and thus having a say in the administration of money bequeathed for Church purposes. It was 'well known that the Wesleyan Methodists would have no objection to such an amendment'. Other Dissenters, however, might be less amenable. Of the petitions for Repeal before the House, there was 'scarcely one [...] that did not breathe a spirit of ill-feeling towards the Church establishment, nay, that did not express detestation against it'.[45] The Church, in effect, was threatened by an alliance between Catholicism and radical Dissent. Lord Eldon's amendment was nonetheless defeated and the Bill as drawn passed its third reading in the Lords on 28 April.

In June, Dr. Law spoke in the Lords against the Catholic claims. His speech included many of the anti-Emancipation arguments which were to become familiar. He pointed to: 'a manifest difference between political and religious toleration: religious toleration had reference to the intercourse subsisting between man and his Maker, political toleration respected the intercourse between man and man'. He praised the Revolution Settlement, which he hoped 'might prove a rock of ages'. He denied the Roman Church had modified its demand for Catholics' political allegiance, citing recent pronouncements of the Vicars Apostolic. Finally, whilst 'no person could be more anxious [...] to promote the happiness of Ireland', Irish difficulties were in Dr. Law's view more due to lack of employment and absentee landlords than Protestant political hegemony.[46]

July 1828 saw a public disagreement between two Bristol priests (which may have been part of a wider dispute between Franciscans and Jesuits) as to the right of Catholic laymen to interpret the Scripture for themselves. The encounter was marked

[41] *F. F. B. J.*, 1 March 1828.

[42] The Rt. Revd. Robert Gray (1762–1834). Father silversmith, bishop of Bristol 1827–1834. Showed considerable courage in remaining at his post during reform riots of 1831, when his views were not popular. A son became bishop of Cape Town and was active in the doctrinal disputes with Colenso. *O. D. N. B.*, 23, pp. 450–453.

[43] The Rt. Revd. George Henry Law (1761–1845). Father bishop of Carlisle. Eminent brothers included Lord Chief Justice Ellenborough. Bishop of Chester 1812–1824 and of Bath & Wells 1824–1845. 'Distrustful in equal measure of heresy, schism and political agitation'. *O. D. N. B.*, 32, pp. 754–755.

[44] *Hansard* (N. S.), 19, (1828), pp. 184–185.

[45] *Ibid.*, pp. 118–120.

[46] *Ibid.*, pp. 1234–1237.

Fig. 3. The Rt. Revd. Robert Gray, bishop of Bristol, an engraving from a painting by J. W. Wright, [Special Collections, University of Bristol].

by 'personal abuse and scurrilous invective' according to the *Journal*'s correspondent, who went on ironically to congratulate the protagonists on their service to the Protestant cause.[47]

---

[47] *F. F. B. J.*, 19 July 1828. For the divisions within Bristol Catholicism, see P. J. Gilbert, *This Restless Prelate: Bishop Peter Baines*, (Leominster, 2006), pp. 72–73.

The question was now moving towards its crisis. In May, a dispute over the redistribution of parliamentary seats had led to two Canningite ministers, Lord Palmerston and William Huskisson, resigning. Wellington appointed an Ascendancy Irishman, Vesey Fitzgerald, to succeed Huskisson at the Board of Trade. Fitzgerald therefore had to resign his seat of County Clare. His challenger at the ensuing bye-election in June was O'Connell, who, with the support of his Catholic Association, easily triumphed. But he could not take his seat in the Commons.

Wellington and Peel, who had hitherto opposed any concession, now became convinced that Emancipation was a lesser evil than the Irish civil war they thought otherwise inevitable. The government nonetheless delayed announcing their conversion. George IV, who (notwithstanding the affable reception he had given to Consalvi in 1814) shared his father's sensitivities about the Coronation Oath, would require careful handling, as would backbench Tory M.P.s and peers. Political uncertainty led to a rise in the temperature outside Westminster: the autumn of 1828 saw numerous 'monster' meetings and petitions against the Catholic claims from all over England, and similar pro-Catholic manifestations in Ireland.

It was against this background that the Revd. Sydney Smith preached to the mayor and corporation at Bristol cathedral on 5 November. The occasion was the annual 'Gunpowder' Service commemorating the unmasking of Guy Fawkes's Catholic plot to blow up the King and Parliament in 1605. Coincidentally (or providentially), the date later acquired additional significance to Protestants as the anniversary of William of Orange's landing at Torbay in 1688. The corporation expected and usually got a rousingly patriotic and Protestant sermon. This year was to be different.[48]

The Revd. Sydney Smith had earlier in the year been appointed a prebendary of the cathedral. He is remembered today as a wit, but he was also a highly political clergyman, and a strong Whig. With the radical lawyer Henry Brougham he had founded the *Edinburgh Review* and he was associated with the 'Holland House Set' in London, which included the second Earl Grey. Grey and Brougham were in 1830 to become Prime Minister and Lord Chancellor in a Whig government. It is therefore perhaps surprising that the Tory corporation invited Smith to preach, and equally surprisingly nobody seems to have anticipated the Guy Fawkes's Day fireworks which were to ensue: the *Journal* did not even send a reporter to the cathedral.[49]

Smith took as his text St. Paul's *Letter to the Colossians*, 3, vv.12–3: 'Put on therefore, as the elect of God, holy and beloved, bowels of mercies, humbleness of mind, meekness, long-suffering; for-bearing one another, and forgiving one another, if any man have a quarrel against any: even as Christ forgave you, so also do ye'. At one level, therefore, the sermon was simply a plea for 'the sacred principle of charity' to be extended to Catholic fellow-subjects, but Smith went further. Although he began by extolling the superiority of Protestantism, he later appeared to contradict this by asking his hearers to consider that 'in spite of thought and study you may have been mistaken, that other sects may be right'. In any event, he felt: 'God […] will probably save in the latter day [both] the piously right and the piously wrong, seeking Jesus in

[48] For Smith's career in Bristol, his sermon and its results, see the Revd. Canon J. Rogan, 'A Brief Encounter: Sydney Smith in Bristol', in J. H. Bettey (ed.), *Historic Churches and Church Life: Essays in Memory of Elizabeth Ralph*, (Bristol, 2001), pp. 148–167.

[49] *F. F. B. J.*, 8 November 1828.

humbleness of mind'. This was Liberalism with a vengeance! Smith later wrote: 'They stared at me with all their eyes'.[50]

Smith's sermon came as the culmination of a series of disputes between the city and cathedral authorities, and led to the corporation deciding to hold future services at St. Mary Redcliffe.[51] The printed version went through four editions before the end of the year,[52] an indication of the level of interest in the debate, and drew two published responses. The first was a letter to Smith from the Revd. Richard Maunsell, curate of St. James and a colleague of the Revd. Thomas Biddulph. Maunsell began by criticising Smith for lumping the Church of England with 'other sects', when it was not a sect but rather 'that part of the Catholic and Apostolic Church established in our land'. As to Smith's suggestion that both 'the piously right and the piously wrong' might be saved, how could this be reconciled with Our Lord's words, 'No man cometh to the Father but by me'? Smith, in Maunsell's view, was: 'call[ing] upon us to believe that Mahometans and other anti-Trinitarians, and the professed infidel, and the idolatrous Papist were equally as safe as the man who rests his hope in the divinity and atoning blood of the Lord Jesus Christ'. Maunsell's letter contained a wealth of scriptural reference. By contrast, the only piece of Scripture in Smith's sermon was the text, and even this Maunsell considered Smith to have misinterpreted. Smith's 'charity' was really infidelity and as contrary to the love of God 'as east [...] to west'.[53]

The second reply was the anonymous *Strictures*, dedicated to the mayor, sheriffs and common council of Bristol. The author combined religious and political criticisms, bracketing Smith with the radical atheist Tom Paine (1737–1809), a supporter of Revolutionary France. It was a commonplace in Liberal circles that 'the schoolmaster is abroad', meaning the march of intellect would render religious differences unimportant and lead to universal tolerance. The author of the *Strictures* did not accept this: had Protestants 'ceased to be persecuted?' he asked. 'Has Popery changed any of its principles?' Furthermore, with reference to the French Revolution: 'was it worthy of an age of reason, or was it worthy of advanced intellect, to despoil some persons of their property, and deprive others of their lives, under the name of patriotism, perpetrated by the lawless assemblage of the populace, glorying in the title of democrats?'[54]

January 1829 was a month of high tension. Parliament was to meet at the beginning of February and it was rumoured that George IV had been won over and that

[50] The Revd. S. Smith, *A Sermon on those Rules of Christian Charity by which our Opinions of Other Sects should be formed, preached before the Mayor and Corporation in the Cathedral Church of Bristol on Wednesday November 5 1828*, reprinted in *Anti-Catholic Sermons and Tracts* (hereafter *A. C. S. T.*) (Bristol Central Library, Braikenridge Collection, 10821). This volume includes all the sermons and writings quoted hereafter, with the exception of the Revd. John Leifchild's (note 90 below). Smith to E. J. Littleton, quoted in J. Rogan in J. H. Bettey, (ed), *op. cit.*, p. 159.

[51] J. Rogan in J. H. Bettey, (ed.), *op. cit.*, p. 160.

[52] The Revd. R. Maunsell, *A Letter addressed to the Revd. Sydney Smith, Prebendary of Bristol, occasioned by a sermon preached by him in the Cathedral Church of Bristol on the 5 November 1828* (Bristol and London, 1828, reprinted in *A. C. S. T.*).

[53] *Ibid.*

[54] Anon, *Strictures on an Harangue spoken in the year 1825 and on a sermon preached by the Revd. Sidney* (sic) *Smith, a Prebendary of the Cathedral of Bristol, before the Corporation of that City on November the Fifth 1828* (Bristol, 1828, reprinted in *A. C. S. T.*).

the King's Speech would contain a proposal for Catholic Relief. The *Journal* looked ahead with foreboding, Bristol's Whig newspapers the *Gazette* and the more radical *Mercury* with hope (the city's fourth major paper, the *Mirror*, appears to have leaned, both at this time and later, to the Protestant side but tended to avoid editorial comment on the question).[55]

On 29 January, the anniversary of the King's accession, the Revd. Martin Whish[56] (Fig. 4) preached at St. Mary Redcliffe a sermon later published as *Protestantism not Popery the Religion of the Bible*, with a dedication to William Fripp (Junior), alderman of the Redcliffe ward and the sheriffs of Bristol, Charles Walker and Thomas Riddle, all three of whom were prominent in the Protestant cause. Whish's text was *2 Samuel* 23, v. 3: 'he that ruleth over man must be just, ruling in the fear of God'. In contrast to this, 'what [was] Popery but the setting up of man in the place of God?' The following passage well illustrates the politico-theological preoccupations of many opponents of Emancipation.

> When we consider the nature of the new philosophy which overthrew the profession of the Christian religion in France [...] what cause for devout thankfulness to God, that we nationally have escaped hitherto [...] its devastating effects: by having as yet continued to us, under the auspices of the Brunswick Royal House, the blessings of civil and religious freedom; and of a Church, simple in her forms and sound in doctrine; modelled after the primitive ages of Episcopal government; where the best forms of devotion are found, and made venerable by the consecrated talents and worth of its martyred saints; the main colossal pillar on which the ark of our holy religion has hitherto securely rested.[57]

'An Illiberal', writing in the *Journal* a couple of days later, expressed scepticism about the motives of Liberal supporters of Emancipation, who cared for the Catholics: 'not a straw; but as a means of embarrassing the government and promoting their own sinister ends. Had they any real love for rational liberty, they would hesitate to admit to power a sect always opposed to it'.[58]

The meeting of Parliament, and the crisis of the Catholic question, were now at hand.

IV

The measures outlined in the King's Speech on 5 February included Catholic Relief, but also Bills for the suppression of O'Connell's Association and restricting the Irish

---

[55] The *Mercury* appeared on Tuesday, the *Gazette* on Thursday and *F. F. B. J.* and the *Mirror* on Saturday. The gathering crisis may therefore be followed in the *Mercury* for 6, 13, 20 and 27 January; the *Gazette* for 1, 8, 15, 22 and 29; and *F. F. B. J.* and the *Mirror* for 3, 10, 17, 24 and 31 January.

[56] The Revd. Martin Richard Whish (1782–1852). Prebendary of Salisbury cathedral, vicar of St. Mary Redcliffe; St. John, Bedminster; Abbots Leigh and St. Thomas, City. Noted Evangelical.

[57] The Revd. M. R. Whish, *Protestantism not Popery the Religion of the Bible: A Sermon preached on Thursday 29 January 1829, being the Ninth Anniversary of His Present Majesty's Accession to the Throne* (Bristol, 1829, reprinted in *A. C. S. T.*).

[58] *F. F. B. J.*, 31 January 1829.

Fig. 4. The Revd. Martin Whish, vicar of St. Mary Redcliffe, painting by an unknown artist, [reproduced by kind permission of the vicar, church wardens and vestry of St. Mary Redcliffe].

franchise. It was clearly hoped that these Bills, along with the cabinet's resolute stance and the King's apparent consent, would persuade wavering Members to support the main Bill. These tactics would appear to have had some effect, at least to judge by an open letter to his constituents from the formerly Protestant Member for Somerset, Sir Thomas Lethbridge, later published in the *Mirror*.[59] But most anti-Emancipationists,

---

[59] *Mirror*, 21 March 1829.

including the two Bristol Members, remained firm. Peel, whose previous Protestant views had earned him the nickname 'Orange' Peel, now felt honour bound to resign his seat of Oxford University to fight a bye-election.

On 9 February, Hart Davis put before the House of Commons an anti-Emancipation petition from 'a parish in Bristol', declaring that 'an immense majority of his constituents were of the same opinion'; and Dr. Law put before the Lords several petitions from his diocese, expressing the hope that although 'worded in the language of humility and supplication, free from imperious dictation', they would be accorded the same respect as pro-Catholic petitions from Ireland. On the 13th, Hart Davis presented a further petition, this time from St. Augustine's parish, and Dr. Gray presented one from the Bristol clergy.[60]

Back in Bristol, a requisition had been addressed to the mayor to call a public meeting with a view to petitioning Parliament against any concession. The names of the 216 signatories were listed on 7 February in the *Journal* and the *Mirror*. The requisition, like the petitions mentioned above, would seem to have been going the rounds before the announcement of the government's intentions and the *Gazette* suggested some would not have signed had they known the King had apparently now consented to Emancipation. The *Mercury* asserted that a number of signatories had been subjected to 'importunities', although no details were supplied.[61]

The list was headed by the doyen of Bristol Toryism, Alderman Thomas Daniel,[62] (Fig. 5), his fellow aldermen, John Barrow,[63] William Fripp Junior[64] and James George[65] and the city's sheriffs, Riddle[66] and Walker.[67] The other signatories included a number of clergymen, among them the Revds. Thomas Biddulph, perpetual curate of St. James, Haymarket;[68] Fountain Elwin, vicar of Temple; Henry Green, vicar of All Saints'; Robert Watson, rector of Christ Church with St. Ewen, Broad Street[69] (Fig. 6), and Martin Whish, prebendary of Salisbury and vicar of St. Mary Redcliffe,

---

[60] *Hansard* (N. S.), 20, (1829), pp. 134, 153, 297, 329.

[61] *F. F. B. J.* and *Mirror*, 7 February 1829; *Gazette*, 12 February 1829; *Mercury*, 10 February 1829.

[62] Thomas Daniel J.P. (1763–1854). Merchant and West India proprietor. Tory; Anglican. Common councilman 1785–1798, mayor 1798, alderman 1798–1835. G. Bush, *op. cit.*, Appendix 4.

[63] John Barrow (1763–1841). Wool merchant. Tory; Anglican. Common councilman 1816–1828, mayor 1824, alderman 1828–1834. G. Bush, *op. cit.*, Appendix 4.

[64] William Fripp Junior (1785–1871). Father Whig but Anglican. Soap manufacturer. Tory; Anglican. Common councilman 1814–1821, mayor 1820 and 1836, alderman 1821–1845. G. Bush, *op. cit.*, Appendices 4 and 5.

[65] James George (1789–1858). Brewer. Tory; Anglican. Common councilman 1814–1827, mayor 1823, alderman 1827–1835. G. Bush, *op. cit.*, Appendix 4.

[66] Thomas Hooper Riddle J.P. (1794–1848). Lead merchant. Tory; Anglican. Common councilman 1828–1835, sheriff 1829, alderman 1835–1841. G. Bush, *op. cit.*, Appendices 4 and 5.

[67] Charles Ludlow Walker J.P. (1788–1856). Common councilman 1822–1835, councillor (after Municipal Corporations' Act 1835) 1835–1836, sheriff 1825 and 1829, mayor 1835. G. Bush, *op. cit.*, Appendices 4 and 5.

[68] See note 29 above.

[69] The Revd. Robert Watson (c.1758–1842). Rector of Christ Church with St. Ewen, 1816–1842, prior to that vicar of Temple.

Fig. 5. Alderman Thomas Daniel, engraving from a painting by an unknown artist, [in the Special Collections, University of Bristol].

Bedminster, Abbots Leigh and St. Thomas, City[70] as well as the dissenting minister, the Revd. William Thorp.[71]

Lay signatories included John Loudon Macadam[72] the Scottish road maker resident in Bristol, the brothers W. D. Wills and H. O. Wills Junior,[73] tobacco

[70] See note 56 above.

[71] See note 37 above.

[72] John Loudon Macadam (1756–1836) has added his name to the language. Father a minor laird. Lived in Bristol from 1798 to death, although less regularly from 1825. Co-founded Commercial Rooms 1811. Surveyor of roads, Bristol Turnpike Trust 1816–1825. *O. D. N. B.*, 34, pp. 1007–1010. G. Bush, *op. cit.*, p. 9.

[73] H. O. Wills Junior (1800–1871) and W. D. Wills (1797–1865). Tobacco manufacturers. Father H. O. Wills Senior. Family firm adopted their style (W. D. and H. O. Wills). Both brothers sat as Liberals on the post-Municipal Corporations' Act City Council. Generous financial supporters of Congregationalism. *O. D. N. B.*, 59, pp. 426–427; G. Bush, *op. cit.*, Appendix 5; I. Jones, *op. cit.*, p. 81.

Fig. 6. The Revd. Robert Watson, rector of Christ Church with St. Ewen, Broad Street, a painting by Edward Bird R.A., [by kind permission of the church wardens of Christ Church].

merchants and Congregationalists and the *Journal*'s proprietor/editor John Mathew Gutch.[74]

The *Journal* heralded the meeting with a poem, "Up! Protestants, Up!" the last verse running:

> By Wife, Home and Children, by Kindred and King,/ By the one sacred triumph, of which Britons sing,/ By the laws as they are, made to keep Papists down,/ Up! Protestants, Up! And defend Church and Crown![75]

Not all prominent Bristolians supported the requisition. The *Gazette* published a letter from the Revd. Thomas Conolly Cowan, dissenting minister of Bethesda chapel in Great George Street. An Irish Protestant, who claimed to have been active against the

---

[74] John Mathew Gutch (1776–1861). Father antiquary and divine. Friends at school, at Christ's Hospital, included Coleridge and Lamb. Strong but independent Tory: writing as 'Cosmo' attacked dominant merchant influence on corporation 1823. *O. D. N. B.*, 24, pp. 299–301.

[75] *F. F. B. J.*, 7 February 1829.

rebels in 1798, Cowan nonetheless supported Emancipation, which he said would make his native land 'a much safer and pleasanter country in which to reside'. Cowan had been an Anglican clergyman, but his present position was widely regarded as heterodox. He commented that 'we are not without popes of our own', which would seem to be a swipe at the Church of England. Writing to the *Gazette* the next month, the Revd. William Wait, former rector of St. Mary le Port, seems in turn to have taken a swipe at Cowan, referring to former Evangelicals who 'have become Arian and Socinian; for proof of which, alas! We need not go far from home!'[76]

The mayor of Bristol, John Cave,[77] although a Tory, was an Emancipationist. He considered himself bound to call the meeting but declined to attend. The meeting was called for 12 February at the Guildhall, but the venue was later changed to Queen Square. The *Mercury* claimed this was because Cave had indicated he would not let the Protestants pack the meeting, but sheer practicality seems at least as likely: the Guildhall could certainly not have held the number who attended.[78]

Feeling was now at its height and grafitti appeared on walls, much of it 'most irritating and disgusting' according to the *Gazette*, which also mentioned the proliferation of handbills 'alarming the apprehensions of the sober and timid'. The *Mercury* alleged these bills were supplied by Gutch's printing office. On Thursday 12 February, shops were closed and a large crowd, undeterred by rain, converged on Queen Square, where a platform had been erected appropriately enough to the north of King William's statue. J. R. Leifchild, who as a boy accompanied his father the Revd. John Leifchild (Fig. 7) to the meeting later recalled the scene: 'Over that great area [...] a tumultuous mob was gathering [...]. Exclamations most wrathful were heard on all sides, and anon shouts of rivalry and defiance rent the air'.[79]

Church of England clergymen were to the fore, Whish being among the first arrivals. The *Mercury* reported that they and their wardens had spent the last week canvassing for support, and that 'every now and then the suspense of the meeting was relieved by the arrival of some parish procession, headed by their clergy'. From the other side, the *Journal* expressed satisfaction that, as far as they knew, every clergyman was present who was physically able to be.[80]

Estimates of the number present varied. The *Journal*'s was 20,000. The *Mercury* suggested 8,000 but later revised even this figure downwards, and the *Gazette* estimated only about 6,000 were present for the vote. Even the pro-Emancipation London *Times*, however, gave a figure in the region of 13–15,000. This middle figure seems plausible, even if the 20,000 posited by the *Journal* might have been a squeeze, bear-

---

[76] The Revd. Thomas Connolly Cowan (1776–1856). Father a Dublin barrister. Moved to England 1800 and to Clifton 1810. Stipendiary curate (under Whish) St. Thomas, City 1815–1817. Left Church of England 1817. Founded Bethesda chapel 1818, ministered there until 1832. For his colourful career, M. J. Crossley Evans, 'The Life and Times of the Revd. Thomas Connolly Cowan...', in J. H. Bettey (ed.), *Archives and Local History in Bristol and Gloucestershire: Essays in Honour of David Smith* (Bristol., 2007); *Gazette*, 12 February and 12 March 1829.

[77] John Cave (1765–1842). Manufacturer. Tory; Anglican. Common councilman 1822–1835, sheriff 1823, mayor 1829. Bush, *op. cit.*, Appendix 4.

[78] *Mercury*, 10 and 17 February 1829.

[79] *Gazette*, 12 February 1829; *Mercury*, 3 February 1829; J. R. Leifchild, *John Leifchild DD: His Public Ministry, Private Usefulness and Personal Characteristics*, (1865), p. 124.

[80] *Mercury*, 17 February 1829; *F. F. B. J.*, 14 February 1829.

Fig. 7. The Revd. John Leifchild, an engraving taken from a painting by Charles Baugniet in the Braikenridge Collection in the Bristol Central Library, [reproduced by kind permission].

ing in mind the space cleared for the speakers and the presence, in the crowd, of parish and party banners and other *impedimenta*.[81]

According to Leifchild, it was nigh impossible for most of the audience to hear anything: 'Gesticulation [...] was about the only sign that the orators were engaged in addressing the multitude'. The newspapers also referred to this difficulty, although the press was accommodated close to the platform, but, possibly assisted by the speakers

---

[81] *F. F. B. J.*, 14 February 1829; *Mercury*, 17 and 24 February 1829; *Gazette*, 26 February 1829; *The Times*, 14 February 1829.

after the event, and certainly by a degree of cribbing among themselves, they managed to give coherent accounts of the proceedings.[82]

Alderman Daniel, elected to the chair with the assent of both factions, opened the proceedings at 12 noon. The motion for a petition against the Bill was then proposed by the sheriff, Charles Walker, who reminded those present of their ancestors' exertions at the Glorious Revolution and whose speech was punctuated by cries of: 'We will have a Protestant Constitution and nothing but!' Alderman Fripp, seconding, spoke of the situation in European countries living under authoritarian Catholic rule, against which he considered the Protestant Constitution an essential shield.

Two speeches from the Catholic side followed. Charles (later Sir) Charles Elton,[83] a former editor of the *Mercury* and a recent convert from Unitarianism to Anglicanism, was no admirer of O'Connell and stressed that he grounded his case not on 'universal rights' but on 'the opinions of departed statesmen', particularly the 'magnanimous minister' William Pitt. Arthur Palmer,[84] attorney of Park Row, was on the other hand proud to call himself a Liberal, who believed every subject should enjoy the liberties he himself possessed, 'without distinction of creeds or opinions'.

Arthur Chichester now spoke for the Protestant side. A visitor from Exeter, he had clearly acquired a reputation as an orator, for he was greeted with 'most deafening cheers'. He concluded a powerful, populist speech, full of Shakespearean quotation and patriotic allusion, by trusting that 'the British Senate will never surrender the constitution until they are convinced by a declaimer from the Pope that the dispensing power no longer exists'.

The last speaker was Wintour Harris, attorney, who took the Catholic side: 'We feel as Christians that no persons differing from us in religious opinions ought to be incapacitated from filling civil office'.

The Revd. William Thorp, Congregational minister and opponent of Emancipation, now wished to speak but it seems he was surrounded by a hostile group of Irish Catholics and could not make himself heard, eventually retreating after a 'missile' had narrowly missed his head. According to J. R. Leifchild, after the meeting an Irishman tried to beg money from his father to buy shoes, 'for hadn't he flung his best shoe at that ould sinner Thorp to stop his ugly mouth?'[85]

The motion was now put and easily carried. But how substantial was the majority? The *Journal's* estimate of a hundred to one seems exaggerated, Leifchild's account of a substantial Catholic contingent being supported by the *Mercury*, who reported that it was possible for a blue Tory flag to be torn down 'with impunity'. The *Mercury* put the majority at about 2 to 1 and the *Gazette* asserted it did not exceed 3 to 1. The *Times* said 5 in 6 were in favour. Both the Bristol Whig papers and the *Times* said that a third

[82] J. R. Leifchild, *op. cit.*, p. 124; *Gazette*, 19 February 1829, acknowledging assistance of *F. F. B. J.* The following account is based on that in *F. F. B. J.*, the fullest in the Bristol papers.

[83] Sir Charles Abraham Elton 6th Bart., (1778–1853). Published in 1815 *An Appeal to Scripture and Tradition in Defence of the Unitarian Faith* and in 1817, following his conversion, *Second Thoughts on the Person of Christ, on Human Sin and on the Atonement*; *O. D. N. B.*, 18, pp. 342–343. J. A. Phillips, *op. cit.*, p. 87, note 77.

[84] Arthur Palmer (1755–1849). Under-sheriff 1788–1819; president of Anchor Society 1809 and 1826. Prothonotary, Tolzey Court 1789–1838.

[85] J. R. Leifchild, *op. cit.*, p. 125.

to a half of those present did not even raise their hands.[86] This seems surprising, but the problem of audibility may have been a factor when the motion was put to the vote.

The Protestants had however won a clear victory. The *Mercury* took refuge in criticising the quality of the majority. It would, they said, be idle to deny 'that a great majority of the uneducated and unenlightened class of the community' opposed the Catholic claims and they described many of those at the meeting as 'mechanics and labourers of the lowest description' and even as a 'Jack Cade's mob'. The irony of this, coming from a radical newspaper, was not lost on 'A Protestant', writing to the *Journal* of 21 February.[87]

After a letter of support from Hart Davis had been read, three cheers given for the King and court and another for 'staunch Lord Eldon' and the National Anthem sung, the meeting dispersed at around 2 p.m. As the Church bells rang out, the petition of:

> the Magistrates, Clergy, Merchants, Inhabitants and Householders of the City of Bristol, and of its neighbourhood, impressed with a firm conviction, that any repeal of the existing laws [...] would be a violation of our Protestant Constitution as established at the Revolution, dangerous alike to the religious and civil liberties of His Majesty's Protestant subjects of every persuasion, most earnestly and anxiously implore[ing], that no further concessions of political power be granted to Roman Catholics within these Realms

was carried to the Guildhall.[88]

The 'substance' of Thorp's intended speech was now published by John Mathew Gutch as *England's Liberties Defended*. Thorp complained that 'superficial knowledge' of history and Scripture had produced a 'horrid coalition of Atheists, Catholics and Ministers of the Gospel', all advocating Emancipation. The doctrines of Papal Supremacy and 'no faith with heretics' might be 'old Almanacks' but they were 'red-lettered Almanacks and their impress [was] blood'. Nor were they without contemporary relevance: Thorp pointed to the case of a group of English 'liberal' Catholics who had recently questioned these doctrines and had incurred 'the thunder and lightning of the Papal See' for their pains. Once admitted to power, the Catholics, Thorp feared, would work to place on the throne Charles I's descendant Felix, Prince of Sardinia, 'the most bigoted Catholic Prince in Europe' and Jacobite claimant since the deaths of Victor Emmanuel I, King of Sardinia in 1824 and Henry, Cardinal York, in 1807. Thorp considered the Catholics viewed their present Protestant and Liberal allies 'with hatred and contempt'.[89]

The Revd. John Leifchild, Congregational minister of Bridge Street chapel, had told Alderman Daniel that if Thorp spoke at the meeting, he wished to reply. He now replied in writing, under the title *A Christian Antidote to Unreasonable Fears at the Present Crisis*. Leifchild expressed anxiety to contradict opinions of Thorp and his friends 'discreditable to them as Christians and Dissenters'. He praised the 'noble and

---

[86] *F. F. B. J.*, 14 February 1829; *Mercury*, 17 February 1829; *Gazette*, 19 February 1829; *The Times*, 14 February 1829.

[87] *Mercury*, 17 February 1829; *F. F. B. J.*, 21 February 1829.

[88] *F. F. B. J.*, 14 February 1829; *Mirror*, 14 February 1829.

[89] The Revd. W. Thorp, *England's Liberties Defended: The Substance of a Second Speech, after an Interval of 16 years...*, (Bristol, 1829, reprinted in *A. C. S. T.*).

generous' Irish people, who he felt would respond quite as well to conciliation as coërcion.[90]

The stances of Thorp and Leifchild caused further controversy. The *Mercury* urged Thorp to: 'treat the Catholics justly and kindly and you will find they are brethren: you will find that they can fall in with the enlightening and liberalising spirit of the times'. They later accused him of 'violate[ing] the grand principle of Protestantism: the right of private judgment' and even of plagiarism from the Revd. Joseph Fletcher, M.A., whose *Lectures on the Principles and Institutions of the Roman Catholic Religion* had been published in 1817. The *Gazette* reminded Thorp of past persecutions of Dissenters by Anglicans, and wondered whether the 'conscientious scruples' separating him from the Established Church might not be relieved by the offer of 'a snug deanery'.[91]

Leifchild was attacked by the Revd. William Wait in a letter published in the *Gazette* on 26 February. Wait concluded a strong letter by resigning the post of secretary of the Bristol Auxiliary of the London Missionary Society, which he had held jointly with Leifchild. Leifchild responded with some asperity the next week: what proof, for example, did Wait have of his assertion that he (Leifchild) wanted to admit Jews and Infidels to Government? Leifchild added that he was as delighted as Wait himself with the growth of Evangelicalism among Anglican clergy. He nonetheless thought the Law as it stood was 'a species of persecution; and that all persecution for conscience sake is abhorrent to the spirit and letter of Christianity'. Leifchild shared Wait's concern that there should be adequate securities for Protestantism, but was prepared to trust the government to attend to this.[92]

Like the Independents, the Baptists were divided. Their two leading ministers in the city opposed Emancipation. The Revd. Thomas Roberts[93] was one of the signatories of the requisition, and the famous preacher and pastor of Broadmead Baptist chapel the Revd. Robert Hall[94] also firmly opposed Emancipation, viewing Romanism as 'not simply a religion, but a vast politico-religious system, aiming at supremacy [...] that, whilst loudly demanding freedom for itself, would not give it to others'. Whilst having some respect for the heads of the Irish hierarchy Drs. Murray

---

[90] The Revd. J. Leifchild, *A Christian Antidote to Unreasonable Fears at the Present Crisis*, (1829), quoted in J. R. Leifchild, *op. cit.*, pp. 125–126.

[91] *Mercury*, 17 and 24 February and 31 March 1829. *Gazette*, 26 February 1829.

[92] *Gazette*, 26 February and 5 March 1829.

[93] The Revd. Thomas Roberts (1780–1841), minister of Old King Street Baptist chapel 1807–1841; greatly admired by Coleridge and regarded after the death of Robert Hall as the leading Baptist minister in the city; treasurer of the Bristol branch of the Baptist Missionary Society; built new chapel (1815) and encouraged the erection of Buckingham Chapel; Clifton, (1840); actively worked for the emancipation of the slaves; supported the Sunday school movement and missionary work among seamen; M. J. Crossley Evans, *By God's Grace and to God's Glory: An Account of the Life and Times of Buckingham Chapel, Clifton, Bristol 1847–1997*, (Bristol, 1997), pp. 2–3; M. J. Crossley Evans, 'Christian Missionary Work Among the Seamen and Dock Workers of Bristol 1820–1914', in J. H. Bettey (ed.), *Historic Churches & Church Life in Bristol; Essays in memory of Elizabeth Ralph 1911–2000*, (Bristol, 2001), pp. 162–195.

[94] The Revd. Robert Hall (1764–1831). Father Baptist minister. Ministered at Broadmead, Bristol 1783–1790, Cambridge 1790–1806, Leicester 1806–1826, Broadmead again 1826–1831. A youthful admirer of Dr. Priestley, during his first spell at Bristol his views were thought to verge on the unorthodox. Became more orthodox during time in Cambridge. Admirers included Brougham, Sydney Smith and Wilberforce. Rumoured to have been offered high preferment in Church of England. *O. D. N. B.*, 24, pp. 651–653.

and Murphy, Hall said 'there was no guarantee their successors would be men of like character and moderation'. The Revd. Thomas Steffe Crisp, principal of the Baptist college in Stokes Croft, took a different view: when Emancipation passed the Commons, his face 'plainly indicat[ed] the satisfaction he felt'.[95]

The Revd. Fountain Elwin, a friend of and chaplain to the redoubtable Hannah More, preached at the Temple to the mayor and corporation on 1 March and subsequently, at their request, published his sermon under the title *Who is on the Lord's Side?* Elwin concluded by imagining the Protestant martyrs looking down on contemporary England: 'Think of our dying testimony at the stake and of our last words in the flames! It was our glory to kindle the light of a blessed Reformation in England: let it be your glory to prevent that light from being put out'.[96]

An anonymous, scholarly tract addressed to Methodists bore this lengthy title: *Strictures on the Principle, 'Religious Opinions are not a Just Ground of Exclusion from Civil Offices': Including Remarks on the Propriety and Advantages of the National Church Establishment, by A Wesleyan.* The author supported the existence of a 'Protestant National Church' and considered that given the tenets of Roman Catholicism, any Catholic would inevitably oppose such a Church: to do otherwise would be 'in them, wholly inexplicable and unnatural'.[97]

Aimed at a more popular market was *Protestant Constitution and No Popery*, which included graphic accounts of the French massacre of the Huguenots on St. Bartholemew's Day 1572, when every street in the Protestant quarter of Paris 'ran like a rivulet with blood', and of the Irish Rebellion of 1641, when 'even death was the slightest punishment inflicted by these monsters in human form'.[98]

Catholics were portrayed as fanatical, sadistic, possessed of almost supernatural cunning and even, in the satirical poem *Good Morning to your Holiness*, in league with Satan. The Devil comes hot-foot to Rome from Ireland and having slaked his thirst with 'holy water', he recounts to the Pope how 'our cause' is progressing there. He then speaks of his hopes for England, where heretics 'shall soon have fire and steel, Sir'.[99]

Finally, we should mention James Acland's[100] *Bristolian*. Acland was neither a Tory nor a Whig, but an eccentric radical populist, who had already crossed swords with the authorities over his forthright reporting of proceedings in the criminal courts,

---

[95] F. Trestrail, *Reminiscences of College Life in Bristol during the Ministry of the Revd. Robert Hall,* (undated), pp. 97–100. Crisp was assistant minister at Broadmead between 1817 and 1825 and served as principal of the Baptist college between 1825 and his death in 1868, at the age of 80.

[96] The Revd. F. Elwin, *Who is on the Lord's Side? A sermon preached by the Revd. Fountain Elwin, vicar of Temple to the Mayor and Corporation of Bristol on 1 March 1829 and published at their request* (Bristol, 1829, reprinted in *A. C. S. T.*).

[97] Anon. *Strictures, etc. by a Wesleyan,* (Bristol, 1829, reprinted in *A. C. S. T.*).

[98] Anon. *Protestant Constitution and No Popery: with the Infernal Articles of the Creed of the Roman Catholics…with accounts of the bloodthirsty massacre of St. Bartholomew's Day and* […] *the Irish Rebellion of 1641,* (Bristol, 1829, reprinted in *A. C. S. T.*).

[99] Anon. *Good Morning to Your Holiness, or the Devil and the Pope,* (Bristol, 1829, reprinted in *A. C. S. T.*).

[100] James Acland (1799–1876). Clerk and actor before turning to journalism and politics. Later lectured for the Anti-Corn Law League 1838–1846. Pioneering electoral statistician. *O. D. N. B.*, 35, pp. 91–92, (under F. H. McCalmont).

which included personal vendettas against certain of the magistrates, and had led to his incarceration in Gloucester gaol.[101]

Most anti-Emancipationists expressed only veneration for the monarchy, whatever private sorrow they may have felt at George IV's capitulation to his pro-Catholic ministry. Not so Acland. Writing to the heir to the throne, the duke of Clarence, who had spoken in favour of Emancipation in the Lords, Acland bluntly reminded His Royal Highness: 'that the Royal line of Brunswick succeeded to the British throne not by virtue of their superior legitimacy, nor by the right divine of Monarchical descent, but by the free choice of the people of England and by their preference of a foreign Protestant, for a native Catholic, as their Sovereign'. The implication was clear: what the people had given, they could take back again. Wellington was called a 'poltroon', who 'bragged like a coward' and the most foolish Prime Minister 'for a hundred and fifty years at the least', and Peel, 'the unconstitutional leader of an unconstitutional House of Commons', had it was said 'bribed' Members to acquiesce in 'the subversion of the religion of their constituents'.[102]

V

Within a couple of days the petition at the Guildhall reached 24,712 signatures. From the parishes around Bristol, it attracted a further 14,172, making a total of 38,884. This figure attracted the suspicion of the *Mercury*, which pointed to the 1821 census, showing the population of the city and suburbs as 87,779 only.[103] Assuming half this figure were children, and half the remaining half were women, this made the adult male population less than the number of signatories. Even taking into account that the 1831 census was to show a population of 103,386,[104] the figure of 24,712 still seems unusually high.

The *Mercury* alleged widespread double-signing and signing by infants. Both the Whig papers printed the names of 15 boys from the diocesan school, seven of them under the age of 11, who had signed. The *Gazette* challenged the schoolmaster, Samuel Smith, to deny he had frog-marched his pupils to the Guildhall, having exhorted them to sign by telling them that if the Bill passed, they would never be allowed to read their Bibles again; and also amused its readers with nursery rhymes adapted for these juvenile petitioners. One read:

> Sing a song of sixpence, a parchment full of names,/ Eight and thirty thousand, against the Popish claims,/ When the scroll was opened, Old Bags [Eldon] began to sing,/ "Isn't this a famous list to set before the King"?[105]

The *Journal* responded that 'most scrupulous care' had been taken to avoid double-signing and that instructions had been given that no boy under 14 should sign. Whilst it would be difficult to prove such things had not happened 'in a few instances', the

[101] J. Latimer, *op. cit.*, pp. 118–120.
[102] *Bristolian*, 21 March 1829, reprinted in *A. C. S. T.*
[103] *Mercury*, 17 February 1829.
[104] J. Latimer, *op. cit.*, p. 143.
[105] *Mercury*, 17 February 1829; *Gazette*, 19 and 26 February 1829.

Journal asked, in view of the heavy preponderance of anti-Catholic opinion in Bristol, what motive the promoters of the petition would have had for a general resort to such methods?[106]

Across the road at the Exchange, the pro-Emancipation petition of the Friends of Civil and Religious Liberty read:

> That your petitioners have learned with great satisfaction of the benign wishes of our most Gracious Sovereign contained in the Speech from the Throne [...] we earnestly implore your Honourable House to carry into effect His Majesty's benevolent desire to promote the happiness of his people, by considering whether the repeal of these disgraceful Statutes can be carried consistently with the full and permanent security of the Protestant Establishment.[107]

This petition mustered only some 1,700 signatures but gave rise to violence on 13–14 February. A group of men forced their way into the Exchange and overturned the table on which the petition was, and there were similar incidents at other places where copies had been left for signature. Those concerned claimed to have believed the '*pro*' petition to be the '*anti*' one, and thus to have been induced to sign under false pretences. The *Gazette* would have none of this: it was an attempt to force the withdrawal of the pro-Catholic petition, and the attackers were acting at the behest of men who should have known better. The situation deteriorated and arrangements were made to call out the *posse comitatus* (the nearest thing there was to a regular police force) if necessary. The necessity was avoided by the mayor's prudent decision to withdraw both petitions.[108]

Bristol's pro-Emancipation petition was presented to the Commons on 19 February by Sydney Smith's old associate, the Whig M.P. Henry Brougham. Henry Bright said that 'though opposed to the opinions expressed in the petition, [he] felt it his duty to bear witness to the respectability of the signatories'.[109]

A week later, Richard Hart Davis presented the Protestant petition, which gave rise to arguments about double-signing and signing by boys, similar to those already aired in the Bristol press. Double signatures, Hart Davis said, had been struck out, as had those of females, although for himself he regretted 'the most interesting portion of the creation' had been excluded. He felt a female householder had as great a right as a male to express a view on such a vital question. He 'feared he had made out a case of ingratitude, as well as want of gallantry, against his constituents'.[110]

For its time, a remarkable passage! Hart Davis nonetheless drew the line at a suggestion by a Mr. Otway Cave that malefactors at the gaol had been allowed to sign. If this was true, he said, 'it was a most gross abuse of the right of petition'–but this was the first he had heard of it.[111]

---

[106] *F. F. B. J.*, 28 February 1829.
[107] *Gazette*, 12 February 1829.
[108] *Gazette*, 19 February 1829.
[109] *Hansard* (N. S.), 20 (1829), pp. 428–429.
[110] *Ibid.*, pp. 570–581.
[111] *Ibid.* Otway Cave was M.P. for Leicester. As far as the author can ascertain, he was not connected to the Cave family of Bristol. See P. Jupp, *British and Irish Elections 1784–1831*, (Newton Abbot, 1973), pp. 129–135.

Lord John Russell referred to the evidence of signing by boys and wondered 'whether it was not too much to say that we should place greater reliance on the opinions of children under 10 and 11' than on those of 'all the men of genius and talent of the country' who had been considering the question for the last 25 years.[112]

In reply, Bright expressed surprise that the question should be considered one 'for learned statesmen and philosophers' only. He reminded Members they 'were not the representatives of the learned and great only, but also of the common people' and even added that if the petition contained a few double-signings or names of boys, 'he saw no objection to that; it showed a zealous feeling on the subject'.[113]

The Somerset Member, Sir Thomas Lethbridge, although a reluctant convert to Emancipation, made the point that even if 'a few boys' had been allowed to sign, nevertheless 'the incalculably greater number must have been legitimate signatures'. Even Brougham conceded the Bristol petition represented 'the feelings, if not the opinions, of the majority of the people of that City'.[114]

Lord Milton, M.P., asked why this should be: '[he] believed that the strong feeling which prevailed in Bristol and the West of England [...] might be explained by [...] the cruelties practised in that part of the country by the sanguinary instrument of a Catholic tyrant', James II's Judge Jeffreys.[115]

The city's pro-Emancipation petition was presented in the House of Lords, again on 19 February, by the duke of Sussex who, like his brother the duke of Clarence, but unlike his other brothers the late duke of York and the duke of Cumberland, took the Catholic side (Sussex's sympathies were ecumenical and even pan-religious: as Grand Master of the United Grand Masonic Lodge of England, he advocated and encouraged the admission of Jews and Hindus to Freemasonry).[116] It appears the sheriff, Charles Walker, was present in the public gallery.[117] Sussex stated his petition had had to be withdrawn due to threats of violence, and he alleged double, or even triple, signing of the anti-Catholic petitions by Bristol clergymen: of their own parish petitions, the petition of the clergy of the diocese and the main petition. Bishop Gray, in reply, did not deal with this last point directly but emphasised the near unanimity of the various Bristol meetings, of which he had learned from his family, from some of his clergy, who had attended, and from Alderman Daniel.[118]

The subsequent presentation by Dr. Gray of a petition from a Gloucestershire parish led to an intervention by the Whig Lord Lansdowne, which raised an interesting side-issue: non-residence in the Church of England. Lansdowne said the parish was one where Catholicism was increasing because of the lack of a resident Anglican incumbent. He also mentioned a parish in Dorset, which then fell within the Bristol diocese, which he said had been without a clergyman for 30 years and near to which there was a nunnery, the sisters being 'remarkable for their zeal'. Was it surprising that Catholicism was making converts in these circumstances? When

---

[112] *Ibid.*

[113] *Ibid.*

[114] *Ibid.*

[115] *Ibid.*

[116] P. J. A. Jones, 'To what extend did English Freemasonry form itself as a pan-religious society during the period 1813–43?', (University of Bristol undergraduate thesis, 2007).

[117] See note 131 below.

[118] *Hansard* (N. S.), 20, (1829), pp. 376–378.

challenged by Gray to name the parish, Lansdowne said he did not have the name to hand.[119]

There was further discussion in the Lords of the reasons for west-country opinion being so strongly Protestant. The Whig Lord King,[120] like Milton in the Commons, referred to history. In Frome, said Lord King, the names of those condemned to death by Jeffreys had been 'placarded as the victims of the Protestant religion to the cruel tyranny of Rome', and he later fancifully described a petition from a Somerset parish presented by Bishop Law as 'the prayer of the ghosts of the victims of the cruel Judge Jeffreys'.[121]

It is reasonable to assume that folk-memory, fanned by speeches, pamphlets and bills, would have been a factor in producing the large number of signatures to the Bristol petition—although it may be doubted whether it was as strong in the city as in the rural areas instanced by Lord King. Another factor would undoubtedly have been Bristol's large and unassimilated Irish population, which was to reach 4,000 (the largest in the west-country) by mid-century. There had been anti-Irish riots in 1810 and 1825 and as we shall see there was shortly to be another.[122] Then there was Bristol's 'deeply Anglican' civic culture in which, according to Ms. Madge Dresser, 'the vast majority of Bristolians saw themselves as Protestants of a particular type',[123] and which would have provided a fertile soil for the clerical canvassing mentioned above. Finally, we should note the Evangelical activities of bodies like the Bristol Auxiliary of the London Missionary Society in which Anglican and dissenting clergy like the Revds. Martin Whish and William Thorp joined in the leadership of a militant and proselytising Protestantism.[124]

VI

Early in March, news arrived of Peel's defeat in the University bye-election by the strongly Protestant Sir Robert Inglis. Describing the crowds waiting outside the Exchange for the result, the *Mirror* 'could not recollect to have seen such intense interest excited in this City for many years'. The Protestant faction was exultant at the result. The 83 year-old Hannah More wrote to a friend: 'Nothing short of this great event could have induced me to hold a pen'.[125]

In general, however, the tide was flowing strongly in the Catholic direction. In the first week of March, the King, bridling at the government's plan to alter the Oath of Supremacy, dismissed his ministers and attempted to put together a government

---

[119] *Ibid.*, pp. 1302–1303.

[120] Peter, 7th Baron King (1775–1833). Whig family. Presbyterian leanings. A rising political star at the time of his unexpected death. *O. D. N. B.*, 31, pp. 659–660.

[121] *Hansard* (N. S.), 20, (1829), pp. 639–645, 803.

[122] S. Poole, 'To be a Bristolian: Civic Identity and the Social Order', in M. J. Dresser and P. Ollerenshaw (eds.), *op. cit.*, pp. 76–95 at p. 81.

[123] M. J. Dresser in M. J. Dresser and P. Ollerenshaw (eds.), *op. cit.*, at p. 96.

[124] *Ibid.*, p. 109.

[125] *Mirror*, 7 March 1829; W. Roberts, *Memoirs of the Life and Correspondence of Mrs. Hannah More*, IV, (1835), p. 343. She was a close friend of the Revds. Fountain Elwin and Thomas Biddulph and a more cautious one of the Revd. Martin Whish.

under Lord Eldon. The attempt failed and within hours Wellington was back in office. It would now have been clear to any still wavering M.P.s that there was no alternative Protestant administration in sight. Writing to her mother on 5 March, Dr. Carpenter's 21 year-old daughter Mary expressed grudging admiration for the Prime Minister: 'What do you think of the Duke of Wellington? I confess I do not feel much faith in him; but he is a good strong stick that will perhaps cudgel the asses along the road he had chosen to travel'.[126]

A sermon preached on 8 March at St. Thomas, City by the Revd. T. F. Jennings, curate of the parish under Whish, was published later under the title *England's Last Effort*. Jennings concluded: 'and if, Bretheren, after we have used all the means in our power in the exercise of faith and prayer, to avert the threatened calamity, it nevertheless come upon us, it will then be our part to acknowledge a divine hand in the dispensation: "It is the Lord, let Him do what seemeth Him good"'.[127]

On 11 March, the corporation resolved to petition the King to dissolve Parliament, and to offer Lord Eldon the freedom of the city. According to the *Journal*, the vote was unanimous, but the *Mercury* asserted that Cave 'opposed this insult to his Sovereign', as did others they could have named, adding: 'We dare our contemporary to contradict us'.[128]

Sunday 15 March was observed as a fast-day by many Bristol Protestants. Three days later Wetherell spoke in the Commons in the second reading debate. His speech is long and diffuse, and apparently caused some mirth in his Whig hearers, but the central message, his 'contempt' for the 'apostasy' of the government, is clear enough.[129] Wetherell's firmness in the Protestant cause, and his subsequent sacking as Attorney-General by Wellington, made him something of a hero in Bristol, with consequences that will be seen.

That same night (18th), the House divided and the Bill passed its crucial second reading by 353 and 173, Wetherell and the two Bristol M.P.s being among the minority.[130]

On 20 March, a meeting at the White Lion resolved to petition the King, through Eldon, to dissolve Parliament. The *Mercury* called the meeting 'a "hole in corner' affair, although what motive the Protestant faction would have had for secrecy is not clear. Alderman Daniel again took the chair and the motion was proposed by the Revd. Martin Whish and seconded by a Mr. Moore. The Tory common councilman Charles Payne spoke in support, as did Alderman George and Sheriff Walker, who rather imprudently accused the duke of Sussex of 'falsehoods' in his speech in the Lords on 19 February.[131]

A deputation led by Arthur Palmer subsequently waited on Walker and asked him to be specific as to the falsehoods alleged. Walker replied that not having kept a

---

[126] J. Estlin Carpenter, *The Life and Work of Mary Carpenter*, (1879), p. 21.
[127] The Revd. T. F. Jennings, *England's Last Effort: A Sermon on the Roman Catholic Question preached at St. Thomas' Church, Bristol on 8 March 1829* (Bristol, 1829, reprinted in *A. C. S. T.*).
[128] *F. F. B. J.*, 14 March 1829; *Mercury*, 17 March 1829.
[129] *F. F. B. J.*, 21 March 1829; *Hansard*, (N. S.), 20, (1829), pp. 1254–1273.
[130] *Hansard* (N. S.), 20, (1829), pp. 1290–1292.
[131] *Mercury*, 24 March 1829.

memorandum of the speech, he could not satisfy their request, but he refused to withdraw his remark.[132]

Remarks made at the White Lion meeting about the 'unrepresentative' nature of the Commons led the *Mercury* ironically to congratulate 'these gentlemen' on having 'joined the ranks of the Reformers'.[133] It is interesting to note in this context that Ultra dalliance with Parliamentary Reform (although neither unanimous nor consistent) was crucial in bringing about the fall of Wellington's government late in 1830 and securing the passage of the Reform Act of 1832.

The meeting duly resulted in a further address by the corporation 'praying [the King] to dissolve the Parliament, for the purpose of affording his loyal subjects an opportunity of constitutionally expressing their sentiments on the momentous and vital question of Catholic Emancipation'.[134]

The *Journal* of 28 March reported that another loyal address, supportive of the government and the Catholic claims, was lying at Wintour Harris's offices. This had 'been signed by the Mayor, and by a large number of respectable gentlemen'.[135]

Meanwhile, the Bill was going through its committee stage in the Commons. On 24 March, Henry Bright crossed swords with Secretary Peel (who had been re-elected for the pocket borough of Westbury) over Church patronage. Since it was to continue to be a high misdemeanour for a Roman Catholic to advise the monarch on the subject, Peel confirmed one of the Secretaries of State would continue to be a Protestant. Bright was afraid the practicalities of 'discovering the offence' could make the Law nugatory and he wanted the Protestant position secured by specifying that the *Home* Secretary must be a Protestant; else, he feared, there could be nominal compliance with the Law by having a Protestant Foreign Secretary, whilst unbeknown to anyone, the King might be receiving advice on patronage from a Catholic Home Secretary. Peel replied that: 'if he had not entered into detail on the subject it was because he felt perfectly satisfied that the hon. Member was deeply conversant with the principle and practice of constitutional law'.[136] No amendment was made.

Hart Davis made his final contribution on 30 March in the course of the third reading debate in the Commons: 'If he could be persuaded that the Bill would produce permanent conciliation between the conflicting parties in Ireland, he declared before God that it should have had his support; but, believing quite the contrary, it would meet with his decided negative'. He did not consider Emancipation would lead to 'union and concord' in Ireland whilst the Established Church remained Protestant. (There were indeed men in the House that day, Russell among them, who would live to see the disestablishment of the Irish Church in 1869, although, in the event, even this did not lead to 'union and concord'). Hart Davis ended by promising that, on all other issues, the government would have his continued support.[137] He was indeed, unlike many opponents of Emancipation, to remain loyal to Wellington and Peel in the division which brought down the government in November 1830.

---

[132] *Mercury*, 31 March 1829.
[133] *Mercury*, 24 March 1829.
[134] *F. F. B. J.*, 28 March 1829.
[135] *Ibid.*
[136] *Hansard* (N. S.), 20 (1829), pp. 1430–1433.
[137] *Ibid.*, p. 1553.

The Bill now passed its third reading and went up to the Lords, the *Journal* calling for an end to a government whose 'liberalism in religion as well as in commerce' was bringing the country to the 'brink of ruin'.[138]

Recorder Wetherell was to arrive in Bristol on 5 April to carry out the Gaol Delivery. It was anticipated he would be met by possibly disorderly demonstrations of support. Sir Charles appealed for calm, as did the magistrates, these appeals being echoed by the press, both Whig and Tory. It is, however, to be doubted that the *Mercury*'s satirical tone was best calculated to allay strife:

> Let him enter the City as a Judge with proper decorum, let him deliver the Gaol impartially, and they may afterwards stick him on the charger in Queen Square with his back to the glorious immortal [William III] and fall down and worship him if they wish.[139]

The appeals for calm were in any event disregarded, the recorder's carriage being accompanied into the city by shouts of 'No Popery! Wetherell for ever!' The *Mercury* said this was the work of 'fifty or a hundred boys' only, but according to the *Journal* a large crowd was present to welcome the recorder. He was greeted similarly on his arrival at the Guildhall on subsequent days.[140]

Violence erupted on the night of Monday 6 April when, the *Journal* was sorry to report, the mob 'committed great excesses', smashing the windows of the Catholic Chapel in Trenchard Street and those of several houses in Marsh Street, 'occupied by the lower orders of the Irish'. These Irish, according to the *Mercury*, did not retaliate, 'their good sense being greater than that of the faction that insulted them'. The *Mercury* also mentioned attacks on the houses of a Mr. Fenning, described as 'Agent for Catholic Publications', who lived next to the Chapel in Trenchard Street, and of a Mr. Cossen, straw-hat maker of Castle Street.[141]

One of the ring-leaders of the mob, Richard Johnson, a chimney-sweep known as 'one-eyed Dick', was convicted by the magistrates on 9 April and committed to pay a 20 shillings fine and five shillings costs, which sums were, to the dismay of the *Mercury*, soon paid by well-wishers, Johnson thus being set at liberty once more.[142]

At the mayor's dinner for Wetherell, a number of those present deliberately emptied their glasses before the toast to Wellington was drunk, and at the sheriffs' dinner the healths were drunk not only of the recorder but also of Lord Eldon and Alderman Daniel, 'the father of the City'.[143]

The Bill quickly went through all stages in the Lords, passing the third reading on 10 April. Dr. Law was among the last to speak, his speech being interrupted by shouts of 'Divide!' Dr. Law maintained to the last his opposition to any concession to adherents of a religion 'totally and diametrically opposed to our own, and opposed, in such a hostile manner, as to render the grant of political power to them, highly dangerous'. He added that, 'another thing weigh[ed] heavily on his mind [...] I do not mean to

---

[138] *F. F. B. J.*, 4 April 1829, quoted by M. J. Dresser in M. J. Dresser and P. Ollerenshaw (eds.), *op. cit.*, p. 112.

[139] *F. F. B. J.*, 4 April 1829; *Mercury*, 31 March 1829.

[140] *Mercury*, 7 April 1829; *F. F. B. J.*, 11 April 1829.

[141] *F. F. B. J.*, 11 April 1829; *Mercury*, 7 April 1829; *Mathews's Bristol Directory 1829*.

[142] *Mercury*, 14 April 1829.

[143] *Ibid.*

contend that *vox populi* is at all times *vox Dei* but I do contend that Government was ever intended, not for the benefit of the governors, but of the governed'. Dr. Law concluded by trusting that he had 'discharge[d] my duty, as a Protestant Bishop, faithfully and honourably'.[144]

The *Journal* of 11 April published 'A Prophesy':

> In eighteen hundred and twenty-nine,/ Atheists, Papists and Whigs combine-/ In eighteen hundred and thirty-two,/ The people will find out who are who![145]

1832 was expected to be the year of the next General Election, parliaments then expiring after six years. In fact, 1832 was to mark an era in English history for quite different reasons, which neither the *Journal*, nor anyone else, foresaw.

VII

Reviewing the Catholic question, in Bristol as elsewhere, the historian is struck above all by the topsy-turvy nature of the responses evoked. We have seen in these pages a conservative bishop coming close to equating *vox populi* with *vox Dei*, and we have seen radical Whigs dismissing a popular mass-meeting as a 'Jack Cade's mob'. It would be easy to multiply instances. The paradox arises essentially from the realisation, on both sides, that, to quote the late Maurice Cowling in another context, 'the conclusions of a pessimistic sub-section of the intelligentsia were in many ways the opinions of the people'.[146]

Many of the arguments, on both sides, may strike the modern reader as quaint. The claims of the Roman Catholics would probably now be urged mainly as a matter of 'human rights': then, more often than not, it was a question of political expediency and/or Christian charity, with advocates of the 'Rights of Man' attracting the suspicion of Protestants and Catholic moderates alike. It is perhaps still more difficult to enter into the minds of those opposed to Emancipation. The effort must be made, however, since the arguments they raised, about civil allegiance and the place of religion in society, are of permanent interest and importance.

Protestant doubts about Catholic loyalty to the Crown proved (in England at any rate) happily unfounded. In their fears for the place of the Church of England, indeed of Christianity itself, in a secular liberal state, they were, however, prescient. Only superficially is it a paradox that the passing of the Catholic Relief Act was crucial in setting one young Tory Anglican clergyman, the Revd. John Henry Newman, on a road which led eventually to a cardinal's hat. This and other developments of the Victorian age, and their influence on Bristol life, are however beyond the scope of the present paper.

---

[144] *Hansard* (N. S.), 20, (1829), pp. 677–678.
[145] *F. F. B. J.*, 11 April 1829.
[146] M. Cowling, *Religion and Public Doctrine in Modern England*, (Cambridge, 1980), p. 432.

ACKNOWLEDGMENTS

For the provision of information, advice and assistance, thanks are due to the staffs of the Bristol Central Library, Bristol City Record Office and Bristol Museum and Art Gallery, to Mr. David Fogden and Mrs. Marianne Pitman of Clevedon Court, to Mr. Michael Richardson special collections' librarian of the University of Bristol, to Mrs. Joyce Morris and above all to Dr. M. J. Crossley Evans, who has given freely of his time and knowledge of the period. Any errors which remain are the author's own. Thanks are also due to Dr. Wilson and Mrs. Winnie Wong who typed the manuscript, to the Bristol & Gloucestershire Archaeological Society for a grant from its research fund (in the name of Miss Irene Bridgeman) which made the illustrations possible, to Miss Ann Pethers for photography and to the following bodies and individual who gave permission for the use of the illustrations: the church wardens of Christ Church with St. Ewen, Bristol, the vicar and church wardens of St. Mary Redcliffe, Bristol, the University of Bristol, and Dr. M. J. Crossley Evans.

XIII

Parochial burials in Bristol in the eighteenth and nineteenth centuries, exemplified by Christ Church, City

M. J. CROSSLEY EVANS, F.S.A.

Should your sickness prove incurable
(For here below there is nothing durable)
Before you finish your affairs
Pray give direction to your heirs,
That James shall serve your funeral
And o'er you spread the sable pall:
He truly mourns when he attends
The last sad offices to friends.

Advertising jingle of Mr. Isaac James, book seller, tea dealer, glover, seller of patent medicines, stationer, bookbinder, undertaker, and proprietor of a circulating library at 10 Wine Street, *c.* 1799, parishioner of Christ Church and later deacon of Broadmead Baptist Chapel.[1]

IN SPITE OF the huge increase in the population of the city of Bristol between the Middle Ages and the mid-eighteenth century, the provision for burials in the city had hardly increased. Between then and first half of the nineteenth century provision was expanded by the addition of burial grounds including St. Paul, Portland Square;[2] St. George, Brandon Hill,[3] and Holy Trinity, St. Philip; Portland and St. Philip's Wesleyan chapels; the Moravian chapel in Upper Maudlin Street; Zion Independent chapel, Bedminster; the Jews' burial grounds at St. Philip's Marsh and Temple; the Unitarian burial ground at Brunswick Square; St. Joseph's Roman Catholic chapel, Trenchard Street, and the field in Clifton where the pro-cathedral was erected; Bristol Infirmary burial ground off Johnny Ball Lane, and by five small grave yards commercially run by undertakers where, in at least two of them during the 1840s, two or three dozen bodies were said to be interred each Sunday.[4]

In May 1836 the chronic shortage of space was addressed by the formation of the Bristol Cemetery Company, which obtained a 28–acre site on the Bath Road, part of

---

[1] Bristol City Library, Reference Section, Braikenridge Collection, XV, pp. 372, 373.

[2] *27 Geo. III, cap. 49,* (1787), *An Act for Dividing the parish of Saint James [...] and for building a church, and providing a cemetery or church yard, and parsonage house within the new parish.* This was a local Act.

[3] Burials also took place in the crypt of the church until 1854.

[4] The Quaker burial grounds situated at Redcliffe pit and near the Quaker workhouse in St. Philip's probably dated from the second half of the seventeenth century.

which was laid out as a cemetery and consecrated in October 1840.[5] One of the 140 proprietors behind the company was Isaac Niblett (1792–1868), a resident of the parish of Christ Church, whose wife died before the cemetery was opened and was consequently buried in the crypt of the parish church.[6] The cost of the new cemetery was almost £17,000.[7] The move was not universally welcomed, particularly by the clergymen, who received significant additions to their income from surplice fees which they received for conducting burials in their churchyards. The bishop of Gloucester and Bristol, Dr. Monk, championed their cause. He successfully insisted that a clause was added to the Act of Parliament ensuring that the parochial clergy would continue to obtain their ten shilling fee and that the parish clerk would receive his shilling for the funeral of any parishioners interred in Arno's Vale.[8] These fees, when added to the cemetery's charges, made burial there prohibitively expensive. Consequently in 1842 there were only 25 burials in the cemetery and during the first seven years following its opening, the annual average number of internments was under a hundred.[9]

Following the outbreak of cholera in 1849 Mr. G. T. Clark of the Board of Health collected statistics on the state of public health in the borough in a series of hearings held between 13 February and 2 March 1850. In his report he stated that there were 61 places of burial in the city,[10] including church crypts, and churchyards and independently and commercially run burial grounds, which between all of them were estimated to cover no more than 14 acres. The report stated that 'the great majority, being full to repletion, were unfit for further interments; and burials in the vaults under parish churches were also strongly condemned'. On 18 January 1854 all the church wardens in the city were notified by the Home Secretary's Office that Lord Palmerston intended to use the clauses of the *Second Burials' Act* (1853)[11] to recommend the Privy Council to forbid burials in church crypts and parochial and commercial burial grounds. The crisis caused in Bristol by Lord Palmeston and the *Second Burials'*

---

[5] Established by an *An Act for establishing a general Cemetery for the Interment of the Dead in or near the City of Bristol, 7 Gul. & 1 Vict. cap. 131*, (1837). This was a local Act passed on 15 July 1837.

[6] Susanna Niblett died 7 February 1838, aged 61, Isaac died 11 December 1860 and was buried in Arno's Vale. There is a tablet to them both in Christ Church. See: Anon, *Arnos Vale Bristol: A Victorian Cemetery*, (Bristol, 2007), p. 55.

[7] J. Latimer, *The Annals of Bristol in the Nineteenth Century*, (Bristol, 1887), p. 226.

[8] S. Rutherford, *The Victorian Cemetery*, (Oxford, 2008), p. 19. See B. Drummond, *The New Eden: An Introduction to Arno's Vale Cemetery*, Bristol, (Bristol, 2005), pp. 6–7.

[9] J. Latimer, *op. cit.*, p. 226.

[10] J. Latimer, *op. cit.*, pp. 313–315. Of the 61, 37 belonged to the Church of England, and the following to undertakers; Francis's, West Street; Thomas's, Clarence Place, Castle Street; Dolman's, Pennywell Street; and Howland's, Newfoundland Street. The Infirmary graveyard in Johnny Ball Lane was also closed. It was sold by the Infirmary and cleared for the purposes of housing in 2005. The burial grounds connected with St. Andrew's and St. John the Evangelist, Clifton and Dowry Square Chapel, Hotwells, were not closed until July 1871, following a government order, J. Latimer, *op. cit.*, p. 458.

[11] This widened the scope of the Metropolitan, or First, Burial Act, *15 &16 Vict. cap. 85*, passed on 1 July 1852, which superseded *13 & 14 Vict. cap. 52, The Metropolitan Interments' Act*, (1850).

Act (16 and 17 Vict. cap. 134)[12] resulted in three parish burial grounds receiving a temporary lease of life, before the provision to discontinue burials in the churches and burial grounds of the city became effective towards the end of the year, thus ending a practice which had been universally practised in the city since time immemorial.[13] Within a short period the old cemeteries were re-utilised: the Rackhay burial ground, Back Street, which was attached to the parish of St. Nicholas, was turned into the playground of the parish school as early as 1858,[14] and many others in the last years of the nineteenth century, such as that at Temple, were laid out as gardens.

This study looks in detail at burials in the parish of Christ Church, Broad Street during the eighteenth and nineteenth centuries and seeks to place the problems faced by the parochial authorities into their historical context.

INTRODUCTION

In Bristol, as in the country as a whole, all parishioners, irrespective of their religious allegiance, had the common law right to be buried in the churchyard of the parish in which they resided. In the case of those who died in St. Peter's Hospital, which acted as the workhouse for the diseased and infirm poor of the city, in 1720 the Corporation of the Poor authorised that the guardians could contribute up to eight shillings for the 'coffin and all other charges for burying one poor person in their respective parishes'.[15] The burial of non parishioners who either died in the parish, or whose families lived in the parish, could be granted as a favour, but not as a right, by the parson and the church wardens together, the latter acting as the guardians of the rights of the parishioners. The parishioners had no right to determine where either they or their family members were buried, this was at the sole discretion of the parson.

In populous parishes the burial rights of parishioners were of considerable concern, and jealously guarded. The judgement of Lord Stowell in 1820 made a number of important observations on the custom of burial.

> For persons of abject poverty [...] What is called a shell is used, and which I understand to be an imperfect coffin, and in very populous parishes it is used successively for different individuals.

---

[12] This was passed 20 August 1853, and extended the scope of the first Act beyond London. Its terms did not affect either Jewish or Quaker burial grounds. There was an amending Act (*17 and 18 Vict. cap. 87*, 1854), by part 1 of which the city council were given the power to provide a municipal cemetery. Part 12 enacted that no burial should take place within a hundred yards of a dwelling house. *18 &19 Vict. cap. 128* (1855), established Burial Boards; and *18 & 19 Vict. cap. 79, (1855)*, dealt with the burial of poor persons by the guardians and the overseers of the poor.

[13] D. Large, *The Municipal Government of Bristol 1851–1901*, B.R.S., 50, (1999), pp. 120–121; see The Revd. O. Chadwick, *The Victorian Church, Part One: 1829–1859*, (1987), pp. 326–327.

[14] J. Latimer, *op. cit.*, p. 356.

[15] E. E. Butcher, *Bristol Corporation of the Poor, Selected Records 1696–1834*, B.R.S., III, (1932), p. 94, 11 August 1720.

He noted that at one time unconfined funerals were not infrequent, although by the eighteenth century a coffin was an essential element of a decent funeral, even for the poor.[16] This is confirmed by the previous quotation from the Bristol records of the Corporation of the Poor. Lord Stowell goes on to state that the body 'is to be returned to his parent earth for dissolution'. Consequently he upheld the existing legal doctrine that the grave was only the *domus ultima* and not the *domus aeterna*. The common church cemetery was not:

> The excusive property of one generation now departed; but is likewise the common property of the living, and of generations yet unborn, and subject only to temporary appropriation.

Only in rare cases should a parson give:

> Exclusive title in a part of the public cemetery [churchyard] to the succession of a single family, or to an individual who has a claim to such a distinction [...] Even a brick grave, without such authority, is an aggression upon the common freehold interest, and carries the pretensions of the dead to an extent that violates the just rights of the living [....] In populous parishes, in large and crowded cities, the exclusive possession is unavoidably limited; for, unless limited, evils of formidable magnitude would take place. Churchyards cannot be made commensurate to a large and increasing population: the period of decay and dissolution does not arrive fast enough in the accustomed mode of depositing bodies in the earth, to evacuate the ground for the use of succeeding claimants.

A case of 1615 indicated that a body had only the right to remain in the ground 'for such time as is necessary for the complete dissolution of the remains' and this time varied from place to place due to differences in soils and climate.[17]

Under the terms of the 85th Canon of the 1604 Canons, the church wardens were responsible for the care and maintenance of the churchyard, and the parishioners were bound to pay for the repair of its fences, walls, and railings at their own charge, together with the churchyard, paths and its gates or stiles. The parson owned the freehold of the church and churchyard during his period in office and had the ownership of any hay or grass cut in the churchyard.[18]

CHURCHYARDS IN BRISTOL

The mediaeval city churches north of the river Avon with attached churchyards were: St. Stephen, All Saints' (the churchyard was built upon in the early nineteenth century), St. Werburgh, Corn Street, (cleared and built upon in the late nineteenth century), St. Peter, Castle Green; St. Philip and St. Jacob; St. John the Baptist; St. James, Horsefair (partly cleared in the 1950s by the corporation for road widening and

---

[16] The Revd. P. C. Jupp and C. Gittings, *Death in England: an illustrated history*, (Manchester, 1999), p. 193; C. Gittings, *Death, Burial and the Individual in Early Modern England*, (1984), chapter 3.

[17] H. W. Cripps, *A Practical Treatise on The Law Relating to the Church and Clergy*, (8th ed., 1937), pp. 564–589.

[18] J. N. Spellen, *The Churchwardens' Assistant*, (5th ed., 1859), pp. 38–39.

improvements); St. Michael and All Angels on the Mount Without, which was rebuilt in the eighteenth century, and has a crypt beneath; St. Mary le Port (cleared in the 1960s) and St. Augustine the Less (cleared in the 1960s and 1970s).

Some information about burials in the church and churchyard of St. Mary le Port was recorded during the excavations conducted in 1962–1963, but the study was not detailed or systematic. The record of the burials and the graves, although sparse, noted that the brick-lined burial vaults beneath the church floor were generally painted white or purple, and capped with a pennant sandstone ledger slab at floor level. The excavators believed that at one time many thousands of people were buried in the church and churchyard, and that the detritus from the remains disinterred when creating new burial places was disposed of in stone-lined vaults, building construction trenches and the west cellar, which was to the north of the chancel. The coffins were of wood and lead, with one of nineteenth century date, made of zinc. The excavations revealed some fine copper alloy coffin fittings, breast plates delicately engraved with the name and age of the deceased, grip plates and their handles (usually six in number), and additional decorative coffin furniture and brass studs, of eighteenth and nineteenth century date. Some of the more recent human remains retained hair, now 'ginger' and 'organic residues'. These were unceremoniously removed to cemeteries elsewhere in the city. The cellar of what is believed to have been the priests' house, north of the chancel, and known at one time as the east cellar, may have been used as a charnel. Subsequently, and certainly by the late 1870s, it had became the boiler house for the church heating apparatus, and by the 1840s, the room above it had become the vestry. Between the seventeenth and nineteenth centuries the small north churchyard which lay between the church wall and St. Mary le Port Street was 'sacrificed to commerce', and built upon. The main churchyard was situated to the south of the church and was bounded by Butter Market Passage. During this period the ground beneath the church floor was honeycombed by many brick-lined tombs. The faculty granted in 1875 for extensive improvement work in the church undertaken in 1877 stated: 'that in consequence of the interments which have taken place in former times in the church it is advisable for the health of the congregation that the vaults throughout the church should be properly sealed with a layer of concrete and the church newly paved'.[19]

The church of St. Augustine the Less, College Green was damaged during the air raids in 1940, and following closure it was demolished in 1962. In 1881 Nicholls and Taylor stated that 'in vaults beneath the floor of the church are about 800 leaden coffins containing the remains of as many parishioners'.[20] Eric Boore noted that the church contained 70 vaults with numerous memorials, wall tablets and ledger slabs. Road improvements in 1892 and 1894 saw a reduction in the area of the graveyard from 2,445 square yards to 1,423 square yards: a loss of 42%, and 2,524 burials were removed in the process.[21] The burials were removed from the vaults following the

[19] L. Watts & P. Rahtz, *Mary le Port, Bristol: Excavations 1962/3*, (Bristol, 1985), pp. 33, 86, 105, 112, 115, 116, 123–125, 128–129, 168–175, 192–194.

[20] J. F. Nicholls and J. Taylor, *Bristol Past and Present*, II, (Bristol, 1881), p. 238.

[21] E. J. Boore, 'Excavations at St. Augustine the Less, Bristol, 1983–84', *Bristol and Avon Archaeology*, 4, (1985), pp. 21–24.

demolition of the church and buried in Canford. In 1971 the remaining part of the churchyard was cleared, and the bodies removed and reburied, some of them in South Bristol Cemetery. In 1983 the site of both the church and the churchyard was excavated prior to the erection of an extension to the Swallow Royal Hotel.[22] At St. Augustine's three basic types of vault were identified; the rectangular family vault which often took several coffins side by side and sometimes was approached by steps; the rectangular vault the width of only one coffin; and the coffin-shaped vault with its head to the west which was also the width of one coffin. Many of these were of eighteenth century date and cut into vaults of earlier date. Some had brick floors, and many were painted internally with lime.[23] In 1819 the churchyard was described as overcrowded.[24] Vaults of all three types were also found in the churchyard, together with extensive disarticulated human remains, coffin fragments and coffin furniture left during the earlier clearances.

The problems caused by the shortage of space to bury the dead within the city were not confined to the parishes of Christ Church, Broad Street, or St. Augustine the Less. An Act of Parliament, *14 Geo III cap. 55, (1774)*, 'for making commodious ways and passages within the parish of Saint Stephen' noted that the 'churchyard or burying place next to the said church is too small for the necessary interment of the dead', and authorised the purchase of three old ruinous buildings for the purpose of extending the burying ground:

> Provided always [...] that the said burying-place shall not extend into any part of the said street or way called Pile End, so as to narrow the same street or way; nor shall the said Burying-place extend within eight feet of the Back Part of the houses and Buildings [...] on the north side of Clare Street.

A witness stated before the House of Commons in 1774 that due to the inadequacy of the size of the churchyard and the large number of burials 'the ground had become raised five feet above the natural level'.[25] In 1794 the parochial cemetery of St. Stephen, situated at the south end of Prince's Street and conveyed to the parish by the corporation in 1676 at a fee farm rent of 3s 4d p.a., was conveyed back to them on the request of the common council for a sum of £1,000; the parishioners noting that that 'the said churchyard, owing to the numerous interments there will, in a short time, be rendered of no use to the parish, and has long been considered and indicated as a nuisance'. It was subsequently used for commercial uses and warehouses were erected on the site.[26]

'The Bristol Churchgoer' towards the end of his life published a description of St. Werburgh's church in Corn Street. He describes a visit made in the 1840s 'through the churchyard on the north side, entering from Small Street. It is quite another place from this little-frequented passage'. He describes the small burial-ground 'packed with the remains of many centuries of parishioners, and of the existence of which is a

---

[22] E. J. Boore, *Excavations at St. Augustine the Less*, (Bristol, 1983).

[23] E. J. Boore, 'Excavations at St. Augustine the Less, Bristol, 1983–84', *Bristol and Avon Archaeology*, 4, (1985), pp. 21–33.

[24] E. J. Boore, *op. cit.*, (1985), pp. 23, 29.

[25] J. Latimer, *The Annals of Bristol in the Eighteenth Century*, (Bristol, 1893), p. 399.

[26] *Ibid.*, p. 497.

mere accident'.[27] Towards the end of the nineteenth century St. Werburgh fell a victim to its declining resident population, the demands for street improvements, and the
clamours of the leaders of commerce. When St. Werburgh was taken down in the
Spring of 1878, we are told that: 'forty large chests of human remains, and about a
hundred leaden coffins were removed to Greenbank Cemetery at a capital outlay of
about £700'. These were removed both from the crypts underneath the church and
from the churchyard, which was completely cleared. It was estimated that the cemetery level of the churchyard was originally twelve feet below the level of the fifteenth
century building.[28]

The scant respect accorded to the dead by the living was commonplace in the eighteenth and early nineteenth centuries, and in a world dominated by the deities of
pragmatism and commerce everywhere the dead made way for the living. Whatever
men might say each week in church at the recital of the Creed about their bodily resurrection in the last days, these former 'temples of the Holy Spirit' were viewed and
treated in a curiously detached manner by those who came after them. During the re-
building of the church of St. Thomas the Apostle between 1789 and 1793 no thought
was given to the fate of the bodies disturbed or exhumed as a result of the demolition
of the old church. Consequently we find that on 28 March 1791 it was decided that
'the corpses now lying in the Churchyard above ground, which had been taken from
the inside of the Church, should be again buried in the Church against the walls next
to Saint Thomas Lane'.[29]

THE PARISHES OF CHRIST CHURCH AND ST. EWEN IN THE EIGHTEENTH CENTURY

At the time that the first plans of Bristol were drawn to scale in 1671 and 1673 the city
of Bristol is believed to have had about 20,000 inhabitants within the mediaeval city.
The 1696 assessments upon births, marriages, burials, bachelors of 25 years and
upwards and childless widowers give a detailed picture of the population of the city at
this time.[30] From the same assessments we learn that St. Ewen's parish, at 0.7 acres,
and Christ Church parish with a total acreage of 4.8 (out of a total of 737.7 in the
parishes and Castle precincts) were the smallest and the fifth smallest parishes respectively in the city, but they were amongst the most densely populated and prosperous
with no poor listed as living in either.[31] A detailed description of both parishes is to be
found in Bishop Secker's Diocese Book, compiled by Dr. Thomas Secker in 1735–1737
whilst he was bishop of Bristol. The Book was continued by Dr. Thomas Newton, the
bishop between 1761 and 1781. The number of houses in the city increased from 4,311

[27] J. Leech, *Supplemental Papers by the Church Goer*, (Bristol, 1888), p. 25.

[28] J. Latimer, *The Annals of Bristol in the Nineteenth Century*, (Bristol, 1887), p. 461.

[29] The Revd. M. Paterson, 'Saint Thomas the Martyr, Bristol', typescript booklet in the possession of the author, (1950), p. 33.

[30] This was made under the Act of *6 & 7 Gul. & M., cap. 6* , which enabled Bristol to raise money for the war against France, and was commonly known as the Marriage Act. It was in force between 1695 and 1706.

[31] E. Ralph, and M. E. Williams, *The Inhabitants of Bristol in 1696*, B.R.S., XXV, (1968), pp. xx, xxii, xxiv, 21–30, 49–51.

in 1712 to 5,701 in 1745 and continued to rise. In these years, St. Ewen's parish had between 25 and 27 houses, which may have corresponded to the number of resident families in the parish. The number of families resident during the later part of the century declined from 22 in 1766 to 19 in 1784. In contrast Christ Church parish, although small, saw an increase in the number of houses in the parish from 100 in 1712 to 164 in 1735. By 1766 there were 210 families resident. By 1784 this had declined to 126. In contrast St. James had about 2,500 families in 1784, St. Mary Redcliffe almost 600, St. Philip and St. Jacob 2,600, and St. Nicholas 350 families.[32] James Sketchley in his *Bristol Directory 1775* estimated that the population of the city was then 35,440, although the late Bryan Little in his introduction to the reprint of the original believed that this estimate was probably too low.[33]

THE EXISTENCE OF A CRYPT AT CHRIST CHURCH, BROAD STREET.

In considering burials in Christ Church, Broad Street, in the eighteenth century we need to know if the church possessed a crypt, which was often known as a crowd.[34] There is no mention of Christ Church possessing a crypt in William Worcestre's *Topography* of 1480, but the absence of a mention of one is not conclusive.[35]

A number of the ancient city parish churches were provided with crypts of considerable architectural importance, such as that of St. John the Baptist, with its guild of the Holy Cross founded in 1465.[36] It was much desired as a place of burial, and masses were held here every day. St. Giles's church, which was formerly over the gate in Small Street, also had a crypt which once served as the mediaeval synagogue, and was later used to store merchandise. It became redundant, possibly in the early fourteenth century. St. Leonard's church also contained a small crypt on the north side[37] and other crypts which remained long after the church was demolished in 1766.[38] The records of the mediaeval crypt of St. Nicholas, destroyed in 1940, have been most recently described by Dr. Joseph Bettey, in his excellent essay 'The Pre-Reformation Records of St. Nicholas, Bristol'.[39] The crypt at St. Nicholas was used for services. Masses were said for the souls of the fraternity of the Holy Cross, which met there, and the wealthier citizens of the parish were buried in the crypt. Like St. John the Baptist, St. Nicholas had a number of chantries which owned houses in the city, the

[32] P. McGrath, (ed.), '*A Bristol Miscellany*', B.R.S., XXXVII,(1985), pp. 21–70.

[33] *Sketchley's Bristol Directory 1775*, (Kingsmead Reprints, Bath, 1971).

[34] *The Shorter Oxford English Dictionary*, (1933), I, p. 429, the origin of the word is unknown.

[35] F. Neale, 'William Worcestre: Bristol Churches in 1480', in J. H. Bettey (ed.), *Historic Churches and Church Life in Bristol*, (Bristol, 2001), p. 33.

[36] H. C. M. Hirst, *History of the Church of St. John the Baptist, Bristol*, (Bristol, 1921), pp. 26–29, 32–37.

[37] C. Burgess (ed.), *The Pre-Reformation Records of All Saints' Church, Bristol*, Part 3, B.R.S., 56, (2004), p. 19, Constance Hatter in her will (1460) asks to be buried in 'the crowde of St. Leonard'.

[38] J. Bindon, 'On the Desecrated and Destroyed Churches of Bristol', *Memoirs Illustrative of The History and Antiquities of Bristol*, (1853), pp. 118–141.

[39] J. H. Bettey (ed.), *op. cit.*, pp. 55–72.

rents of which were used to finance the masses for the dead. The fraternity had its own altar, pews and church wardens. St. Nicholas's parochial cemetery was on Welsh Back (with a small chapel dedicated to St. John the Evangelist, which was acquired by the church in 1383) and measured 156 feet long by 38 feet wide.[40]

A number of other churches, such as St. Leonard, and St. John the Baptist, owned detached churchyards. The latter was given to the church in 1390 and measured 94 feet in length and 59 feet in width.[41] The other churches within the heart of the ancient city: St. Stephen, St. Werburgh, All Saints', Christ Church, St. Ewen. St. Mary le Port, and St. Peter, all had churchyards attached to the parish church. Of these churches we know that All Saints' had a small crypt entered close to the entrance to the church,[42] and that St. Ewen possessed a crypt. This is discussed in greater detail elsewhere in the volume. No crypt appears to have existed at St. Lawrence, which was situated on the city wall adjacent to St. John the Baptist.[43] This was the only one of the walled churches to have been without a crypt.

Although we have no plan of a crypt or crypts at Christ Church prior to the demolition of the old building, we know that Canon M. A. R. T. Cole, the rector between 1903 and 1938, believed that the nineteen tenements and a garden given by Richard Erle in 1491 for a chaplain to say mass daily in the chapel of St Michael within the church for himself and his wife, related to a chapel within the crypt of the church.[44] The chantries of the church were well endowed and contrary to the usual despoliations of the chantries under Edward VI's commissioners in 1549, much of their property remained attached to the church. By letters patent in 1599, Queen Elizabeth I granted them to the church wardens and parishioners.[45] The church wardens' vouchers for the period of the demolition and re-building of the church at the end of the eighteenth century also clearly prove the existence of one or more crypts under the main body of the church.[46]

[40] R. H. Leech, *The Topography of Medieval and Early Modern Bristol*, B.R.S., XLVIII, (1997), p. xxviii. This was extant as late as the 1950s.

[41] R. H. Leech, *op.cit.*, (1997), p. xx for St Leonard, and p. 162 for St John; H. C. M. Hirst, *History of the Church of St. John the Baptist, Bristol*. (Bristol, 1921), pp. 61–62.

[42] Information from Messrs. David Moon and Roger C. Metcalfe, church wardens of Christ Church with St. Ewen, City. In 2005 it was overrun by swarms of large rats which both fed on the shrivelled human cadavers which were entombed there, and nested and bred among the coffins and human remains, emerging at night time, bloated from their charnel feasting, a parody of the aldermen and citizens who once inhabited the streets above.

[43] J. Bindon; *op.cit.*, (1853), p. 133.

[44] Conversations with the late Revd. C. M. J. Turner (1913–1997); W. Barrett, *The History and Antiquities of the City of Bristol* (Bristol, 1789), pp. 466–467.

[45] These endowments are still managed by the trustees of the Christ Church Lands Trust; T. J. Manchee, *The Bristol Charities, Being the Report of the Commissioners For Inquiring Concerning Charities in England and Wales so far as Relates to the Charitable Institutions in Bristol*, I, (Bristol 1831), pp. 342–348.

[46] B.R.O., P/XCh/ChW/4, church wardens' vouchers 1772–1800.

CHRIST CHURCH, BROAD STREET, AND ITS
CHURCHYARDS *c.* 1737–1783

Prior to 1745/6 the only burial place for the small but populous parish of Christ Church was a small enclosed graveyard on the north side of the church approximately 25 yards long by 12 yards broad and one and a half yards deep.[47] It was not surprising that by 1745/6 the churchyard was 'so very small and full of corpses that there was not room for the inhabitants to bury their dead'.[48]

There were occasionally references to clearances in the church yard prior to 1746 and we find in August 1737 a payment to four labourers for a day's work to remove tombstones from the congested churchyard to enable further burials.[49] Burials provided a regular source of revenue for the church, which in 1738 amounted to £3.13.4.[50] The cost to the parish of paupers who died in the Poor House and who were formerly resident in the parish was not inconsiderable, and it was customary for the Corporation of the Poor 'to allow two shill[ing]s for ye burying any poor person out of ye Mint'.[51]

The small churchyard to the north of the church was provided with its own skull house in which the disinterred bones from the churchyard were placed until, with decreasing space, it was necessary to place them elsewhere[52] Due to the considerable overcrowding in the churchyard it was necessary to use a measuring rod, rather similar to a gimlet in shape with a 'nose' on the end, which could be thrust into the earth to search for the outline of coffins and human remains in order to determine where new graves were to be dug in the churchyard.[53]

To meet the problem of the overcrowded churchyard on 28 February 1745/6 the vestry instructed the church wardens and others to 'treat with the parish of St. John the Baptist, City of Bristol, also with the corporation of the said city of Bristol, or any other person or persons whosoever whom it doth or may concern in order to obtain a new church yard or buryall place' and they were given power to do whatever 'as in their discretion shall be fitt and convenient'.[54] Their work involved employing a lawyer to draw up the surrender of leases between the vestry and William Fisher and William Okey to enable them to make a new church yard in Duck Lane, and to grant them the remainder of their old lands in the form of a new lease.[55] Thereafter work progressed rapidly and in June Thomas Paty producing a pair of freestone piers probably for the entrance to the new graveyard. At some stage between the end of June and September 1746 the churchyard was consecrated with some pomp by the bishop, Dr. Joseph Butler. The stage erected in the new ground for the use of the bishop and

---

[47] B.R.O., P/XCh/ChW/4 (vi), church wardens' vouchers 1762–1772.
[48] B.R.O., P/XCh/ChW/7.
[49] B.R.O., P/XCh/ChW/4 (ix); p. 31.
[50] *Ibid.*, p. 32.
[51] *Ibid.*, p. 37.
[52] *Ibid.*, p. 40.
[53] B.R.O., P/XCh/HM/1(c), p. 96, 22 September 1763. When I was assistant to the sexton at St. Bartholomew's, Thurstaston, Wirral, in the 1970s something similar was still in use.
[54] B.R.O., P/XCh/HM/5, pp. 61–63.
[55] B.R.O., P/XCh/ChW/4 (ix), extracts of the church wardens' accounts 1714–1799, No 45, 1 May 1746, 11 June 1746.

attendant officials was covered by 39 yards of scarlet Colchester baize. By the time that the bishop's butler was paid ten shillings and sixpence as a gift and all the legal business was attended to and the ecclesiastical fees paid, the work represented a considerable financial investment by the parish.[56]

Following the consecration of the new graveyard, the vestry met on 8 October 1746 and noted that:

> Whereas the church yard adjoining to this parish church of Christ Church by the frequent interment of deceased persons is so filled that without the utmost inconvenience it will not bear any additional corpses therefore at a meeting of the vestry it is this day agreed that all avenues whatsoever leading to the said church yard shall be wholly shut up and the church yard cleaned and sown with grass seeds. And that no burial shall be made in the same during the space of fourteen years to commence from this day, and whereas as a new yard has been opened for the very purposes and ends for which the old has been used and has and with the approbation of the Lord Bishop of this diocese who upon representation of the premises has been pleased to consecrate the same It is further ordered and resolved that the said new yard be henceforth made use of as the sole burying yard And for the prevention of indecencys which often happen by opening graves before a reasonable time is expired It is also resolved that the graves shall be at the least six feet in depth, and that the west end be appropriated for the interment of parishioners, and the east end for strangers, that the corpses on each side be placed in a straight line side by side as near as conveniently maybe, and that the liberty of placing tombs or flat grave stones over any grave be allowed to none but only head and feet stones.[57]

The church wardens' accounts record various work undertaken in the old churchyard in the years that follow, including tidying up and sowing hay seed in March 1747/8, and taking down one of the brick walls of the old churchyard.[58]

By 1762 the new churchyard in Duck Lane was full and on the 21 July John Daniel, a stone mason, was asked by the vestry if it was possible to lower the old churchyard. A month later he confirmed that the Duck Lane churchyard was 'full and unfit for the reception of any more corps'. He advised that the old churchyard should be re-opened for burials but that 'it ought to be lowered to the level or even with the pavement of the church and the mould thereof carryed to the other church yard'. It was decided that the vestry should apply for a faculty from the bishop's court to remove the gravestones and earth.[59] John Masters, one of the church wardens, placed an advertisement in the weekly *Sarah Farley's Bristol Journal*, to ask for tenders to undertake the work. These appeared in three successive issues between 25 September and 9 October 1762.[60] An estimate for the work at the churchyard has survived:

---

[56] B.R.O., P/XCh/ChW/4 (iii), vouchers marked No 42, No 43, No 44, No 45, No 47, The freestone piers cost £6. 3. 10½.

[57] B.R.O., P/XCh/HM/5, pp. 67–71.

[58] B.R.O., P/XCh/ChW/4, (iii), voucher marked No 48.

[59] B.R.O., P/XCh/ChW/7; P/XCh/ChW/4(v), church wardens' vouchers 1757–1772.

[60] B.R.O., P/XCh/HM/5, pp. 125, 127, 129, 21 July, 17 August, 20 September 1762, pp. 143, 145, 147, 13 June, 13 July 1763; P/XCh/HM/1(c), p. 23; P/XCh/ChW/4(v), church wardens' vouchers 1757–1772.

Digging and screening 450 lds of earth at 6d.p.ld.	£11.05.0
Wheeling thorough the church at 2d. p.ld.	£3.15.0
Filling into the cart at 1d. p.ld	£1.17.6
Halling at 6d.p.ld.	£11.05.0
Laying and speding the same at 1d p.ld	£1.17.6
Extraordinary work in mooving toombs and sinking holes	
under to berury bones & others if any	£5.00.0
	£35.00.0[61]

In the estimate given by Luke Spencer Senior, of Frogg Lane, he noted that 'no tombe stones to be moved but left in the said churchyd and all the vaults to be cleard to the said and beforementioned leavel of the [...] paving floor stones and all the sculls and bones of the dead boddies to be psvd [*sic*] and reserved on one side'.[62] A place was to be cut in the newly levelled churchyard in Duck Lane, six feet square to receive all the human remains and the tombstones were to be set aside in the churchyard,[63] as required by the bishop's faculty 'so as to preserve the inscriptions thereon from being defaced, in the best manner they can'.[64]

Richard Rogers was given the contract to lower the churchyard to the level of the pavement leading to the tower of the church. Besides burying all the bones and corpses found in the old churchyard, Rogers was required to level the churchyard in Duck Lane and we find that Dean Bayley, the senior church warden paid Rogers, who had employed two men for two days to take down a wall in the Duck Lane churchyard removing the grave stones, and cleaning the bones out of the skull house and putting them in a vault.[65] This may have been similar to the one designed under the tower of the new church (1786) (see Fig. 4, p. 117). At the same time the church-yard gate in Duck Lane was repaired.[66]

From an early date the sexton appears to have paid the set fees for interments to the parish clerk, who accounted for them to the church wardens. For example, between April and December 1760, Henry Mattock accounted for five burials each at mark [13/4d]. In 1762 William Redwood, the clerk, noted two payments of a mark and one of a noble [6/8d] 'for the ground of Mr Smith's child'. All of these are likely to have been in Duck Lane as the upper churchyard was not then reopened for buri-als and there is no mention of burial in the church crypt.

By the fact that the vestry decided in October 1746 that no further burials should take place in the upper churchyard for fourteen years we can be fairly certain that the church officers were content that by the end of 1760, the flesh would have fallen from even the most recently interred bones. In the end the small five-sided churchyard in Duck Lane, measured by the Revd. Canon M. A. R. T. Cole in the 1900s as being 50

---

[61] B.R.O., P/XCh/ChW/4 (vi), church wardens' vouchers 1762–1772; P/XCh/HM/5, pp. 143, 145, 147, 13 June and 13 July 1763; for estimates by Luke Spencer and Abraham Browning for lowering the churchyard P/XCh/ChW/21.

[62] B.R.O., P/XCh/ChW/21 (c), 30 September 1762.

[63] B.R.O., P/XCh/ChW/21 (a, b).

[64] B.R.O., P/XCh/ChW/7.

[65] B.R.O., P/XCh/ChW/4 (vi), the receipt is dated 25 October 1763 and the work cost 12 shillings.

[66] B.R.O., P/XCh/ChW/4 (v), 30 September 1762.

Table 1. Burials in the churchyards of Christ Church, Broad Street, 1750 -1763[67]

March 1750–February 1751	31
March 1751–November 1751	16
January 1752–December 1752	20
January 1753–December 1753	26
January 1754–December 1754	22
January 1755–December 1755	26
January 1756–December 1756	22
January 1757–December 1757	26
January 1758–December 1758	25
January 1759–December 1759	28
January 1760–December 1760	27
January 1761–December 1761	31
January 1762–December 1762	36
January 1763–December 1763	28
Total	364

feet long by 42 feet six inches, 12 feet six inches, by 50 feet and 29 feet 2 inches, was not full until almost seventeen years had elapsed and almost 500 corpses had been crammed into the site of two tenements.

Unfortunately, we do not know when the church officers thought that the Duck Lane burial ground would be fit to be re-opened after its closure in 1763, but the preceding two years had seen an unprecedented increase in the number of burials from an average of 25 in the 1750s to 31 in 1761 and 36 in 1762. At the earliest they cannot have planned to re-open the Duck Lane (or the lower burial ground as it was also then called), before the end of 1777, if not long afterwards. Given that the upper churchyard was then approximately 75 feet long by 36 feet broad it is possible that this area could have held the majority of the 535 burials recorded in the church register between 1764 and 1785.[68] What we do not know is the number of wealthier people who chose to be buried in neither the upper or lower churchyards, but opted to be buried in the church crowd or crypt. This had a number of attractions, not least of all being its general inaccessibility to the city's trainee surgeons and their teachers, whose need for fresh subjects upon whom to practise their skills was insatiable, and the subject of considerable local contemporary interest and anger.[69]

---

[67] Based on figures from P/XCh/R/1(d), which includes burials 1721 to 1812.

[68] Canon Cole in his memorandum book on the churchyard, now in possession of the author, states that a terrier of the church glebe land, dated 9 August 1804, records that on the north side the upper churchyard was then 55 feet six inches long and on the south side 54 feet and in breadth 33 feet, and on the other side 46 feet and six inches. It was made smaller during the re-building of the church between 1784 and 1790. See p. 239 for its measurements pre-1786.

[69] There are a number of accounts of grave robbery in Bristol during this period, the most recent and comprehensive being, M. E. Fissell, *Patients, Power and the Poor in Eighteenth-Century Bristol*, (Cambridge, 1991), pp. 14, 140–143, 165–167, 199–200.

Table 2. Burials in the churchyards of Christ Church, Broad Street, 1764–1785

1764	27		1775	21	
1765	32		1776	24	
1766	32		1777	20	
1767	20		1778	25	
1768	31		1779	31	
1769	11		1780	21	
1770	22		1781	28	
1771	27		1782	27	
1772	26		1783	28	
1773	16		1784	23	
1774	21		1785	22	
	265			270	= 535

The church wardens' vouchers for the period 1762 to 1772 give evidence of the differing costs of burial in the church and churchyard:

Mr Willmots fun[era]l		Mrs Coxs fun[era]l	
Ground	13.4	Ground	6.8
Minister	10.0	Minister	10.0
	£1.3.4		16.8
Received this money of ye clark____		Recd this of ye clerk	_____
23 March 1764	_____	23 March 1764[70]	_____

Work was continually required to keep the floor of the church in order and in June and July 1769 we find the church wardens making payments for raising tombstones in the church and for taking up and relaying sections of the church pavement.[71]

THE SEXTON *c.* 1720–1854

The sexton was the key figure in the organization of burials in the parish. By custom and practice the sexton of Christ Church appears to have been appointed by the vestry, rather than by the parson and churchwardens. Together with the parson, the sexton was entitled to receive fees for every burial which took place in the church or the churchyard, which were usually set throughout the diocese by the bishop. As long ago as 1725 it had been decided by the ecclesiastical courts that the office of sexton could be held by a woman. Christ Church employed its first sextoness between 1732 and 1735 and widows, wives and daughters of those who held the post occupied the position of parish sexton for much of the second half of the eighteenth and the first half of the nineteenth century. In a judgement in 1789, Lord Kenyon stated that the office of sacrist had been rarely held, except in cathedrals, since the days of the

[70] B.R.O., P/XCh/Ch W/4 (vi).
[71] B.R.O., P/XCh/ChW/4 (ix), p. 118.

reformation, but in practice many sextons, like those at Christ Church, undertook this role and were responsible for such things as the washing and the care of the surplice. At Christ Church the sexton was paid a small salary, £4 per annum, independent of burial and other fees, and may well have received a gratuity from the executors of the deceased when undertaking such offices as tolling the passing bell on the death of a parishioner.[72] The vestry minutes clearly show that the sexton of Christ Church performed a variety of tasks; pew opener, sacristan, cleaner and parochial beadle. For instance we find in the vestry minutes in October 1753, that he filled the role of pew opener: 'every person is to be acquainted that the sexton will have orders to fill [the pews] if not filled by the respective family to whom it is allotted at the reading of the psalms'. The sexton was paid ten shillings in June 1759 for cleaning and looking after the church's branches or candelabra. These payments appear regularly in the church wardens' vouchers.

Thomas Brown's bill for work during one half year in 1760 survives and includes expenditure on scouring paper, sweeping the chimney (of the vestry), pens (for the vestry), brushes, a besom, mops, coal and candles. His widow, Avis, succeeded him in office and in 1761 made charges for carrying water, washing the surplice, sand (for the floor, or for scouring pewter), soap, a watering pot and '7 days work for my maid's cleaning ye church 10.6d'. The following year she charged for making a dozen towels and washing them, turpentine, a coal box, a spade and pail and greens for dressing the church (probably with holly and ivy at Christmas).[73]

In September 1766 the sexton and his wife were paid an additional £4 per annum for providing fire and candles in the vestry and for cleaning. These responsibilities included care of both the churchyards. On the 7 October 1766 the vestry:

> ordered that the sexton do put the ch.yd. adjoyning to the ch. in good order and keep it so for the future and not to permit the same to be made use of by any person for any purpose whatsoever. That no door ways be opened into said ch.y.d., and that the sexton do keep the keys thereof and of the Bone House.

We find Mrs. Barnett performing the role of beadle, collecting the key to the parochial chest and running errands for the vestry. Following a meeting of the vestry in February 1773, when one of the members was not present, 'a message was sent to him by the sexton woman today that the vestry is met'.[74] One of the questions which cannot be answered from the records is whether the sextons cut the ground (or raised the existing ledger slabs), and dug the graves themselves, or employed others to do it for them, paying the grave diggers from the burial fees they received from the executors or the family of the deceased. One of the sextons, Robert Barnett, also augmented his income by acting as the sexton of the Mayor's Chapel in 1784.[75]

The wealth of records which have survived for the parish of Christ Church tell us a little about those who held the office of sexton in the eighteenth and nineteenth centuries. William Cole, the sexton who died in June 1732[76] was succeeded by his

[72] H. W. Cripps, op. cit., pp. 177, 588.
[73] B.R.O., P/XCh/ChW/4 (v).
[74] B.R.O., P/X Ch/HM/5, pp. 8, 113, 138, 174, 183–184.
[75] B.R.O., P/XCh/ChW/4 (ix), p. 136.
[76] B.R.O., P/XCh/R/1 (d), which includes burials 1721–1812.

Table 3. Sextons of Christ Church, Broad Street *c.* 1720–1885/6

Name	Date Appointed	Date Resigned/ Dismissed/ Died	
William Cole		1732	a
Widow Cole	1732	1735	b
Francis Searchfield, cordwainer	1735		
Joyce Searchfield, widow		1753	
Thomas Brown, staymaker	1735	1761	c
Avis Brown, widow	1761	*c.* 1766	
Robert Barnett	1766	1800	d
Mrs. Mary Barnett	1766	1809	e
Miss Mary Frances Barnett, Assistant	*c.* 1800	1809	f
George Jones	1809	1821	g
Charlotte Jones	1821	1847	h
Miss E. Jones	1848	1854	
Mrs. Taylor	1854	1856	
John Olliver [*sic*]	1857	before 1862	i
Miss E. Olliver, or Oliver	before 1862	*c.* 1874	
Mrs. Fitzgerald	*c.* 1874	1885/6	

a Buried 23 June 1732.
b P/XCh/HM5, p. 45. 12 December 1735 discharged, paid to Lady Day.
c Buried 4 February 1761.
d Appointed 5 September 1766, buried Lower Churchyard 16 December 1800.
e Buried Duck Lane, 18 April 1809, sexton 43 years.
f Buried 6 March 1809.
g Parish clerk and sexton, lived in All Saints' Street, buried 26 November 1821, aged 55.
h Succeeded Mrs. Hannah Smith as sexton of St. Ewen in 1829. She may have been assistant to George Jones as sexton of Christ Church as early as 1817. Of Narrow Wine Street, buried 17 August 1852, aged 74.
i Sexton and Beadle. He appears to have been the last parish clerk of Christ Church.

widow, who held the post for three years, but was discharged by the vestry in December 1735.[77] Her successor, Francis Searchfield or Satchfield, was a cordwainer. He was also succeeded by his widow, Joyce, who was discharged from office by the vestry, probably on the grounds of infirmity on 12 November 1753, but paid until St. Thomas's Day, and granted the benefit of the Easter collection.[78] The custom appears to have been established to appoint a poor tradesman to the post of sexton. Thomas Brown, who was in office between 1753 and his death in January 1761 was a staymaker.[79] He was succeeded in turn by his widow. In September 1766 the vestry appointed Robert Barnett (otherwise Burnett or Barnatt) and Mary, his wife, jointly as sextons. Robert died in 1800. Mary remained in post for almost 43 years until

[77] B.R.O., P/XCh/HM/5, p. 45, 12 December 1735, she was paid until Lady Day.
[78] *Ibid.*, p. 87.
[79] B.R.O., P/XCh/R/1 (d); P/XCh/HM/5, p. 87, 12 November 1753.

August 1809, although in her later years she appears to have exercised her office through her daughter, Mary Frances Barnett.[80] Mary Barnett's monument which could be seen in the churchyard in Duck Lane as late as 1920 stated that she 'filled the situation of sexton [...] with the highest integrity' and noted that she was 'universally esteemed and beloved'. This is borne out by events following the death of her daughter. On 30 March 1809 the vestry resolved that George Jones, who had been appointed parish clerk by the rector, Dr. Ireland, should be appointed sexton on the understanding that he made an allowance to Mrs. Barnett during her life time. George Jones received other payments from the church including four guineas *per annum* for singing in the church choir.[81] He was subsequently succeeded as sexton by his widow, daughter, or daughter-in-law, at some time before his death in November 1821, and this person may have acted as his deputy as early as 1817.

Although the post of sexton was usually a lowly one, it was respected. It is perhaps worth recording that the poet Thomas Chatterton (1752–1770)'s, uncle, or great uncle, John Chatterton, was the sexton of St. Mary Redcliffe for twenty years between 1732 and 1752.[82] The Chatterton family had held the post of sexton at Redcliffe, 'time out of mind'. Occasionally sextons were financially and socially men of position and Thomas Bolt (died 1766), sexton of the parish of St. Augustine, kept at least one servant, lived in a substantial well-furnished house which contained pictures, a small library, a well-equipped kitchen full of brass, pewter and copper, and left an estate valued at £327.[83]

The vestry minutes for 21 April 1791 show that the sexton's tasks at Christ Church after the re-opening of the church continued to include the filling of all unoccupied seats after the psalms had been read.[84] The sexton also continued to undertake the responsibilities occasionally undertaken elsewhere by respectable, elderly widows who were called 'pew openers'. No doubt these services occasionally elicited gratuities from visitors to the church at service times.

The income derived from burials was a useful source of funding for the church. In the nineteenth century the usual annual receipts ranged from £5.13.4 (1833/4) to £1.3.4 in 1848/9 and 1849/50. The cost of the ground for the use of burials generally ranged from

---

[80] B.R.O., P/XCh/HM/5, p. 184, 7 October 1766. Mary Barnett was buried in the Lower Churchyard in Duck Lane on 18 August 1809. Mary Frances Barnett, her daughter predeceased her and was buried on the 6 March 1809. B.R.O., P/XCh/HM/6, unfoliated, indicates that Mrs. Barnett resigned as sexton in 1800 in favour of her daughter. In fact the latter acted as her deputy. See also Canon Cole's MS. notebook on the tombstones p. 37, in possession of the author.

[81] B.R.O., P/StE/V/3, f. 7.

[82] J. H. Ingram, *The True Chatterton; A New Study From Original Documents*, (1910), pp. 20, 25. His epitaph ran: 'Near this place in a cold bed of another's making lies John Chatterton, who was Death's chamberlain Here for twenty years And after having provided lodgings for Various Passing Travellers, Lay down himself, A. D. 1752 of his sojourning 48. When living, John, Pursuant to his trade, Many Good Beds for weary Pilgrims made; May the same kindness now for their Host receive, Dead John will be among them by their Leave'.

[83] E. and S. George, (ed.), *Bristol Probate Inventories*, Part III, B. R. S., 60, (2008), pp. 189–195; E. and S. George, *Guide to the Probate Inventories of The Bristol Deanery of The Diocese of Bristol (1542–1804)*, (Bristol, 1988), p. 24. It is possible that he was the cathedral sexton rather than the sexton of the church of St. Augustine the Less.

[84] B.R.O., P/XCh/HM/6.

a noble (6/8), to a half a noble (3/4). In 1847 we find the parish paying amongst its incidentals the costs of coffins for Mrs. Ditchett (8/-) and Mrs. Hollister (5/6). The last receipt for burial fees (16/8) is listed in the church wardens' account for 1853 and there is no record of a payment for the only funeral taken in 1854.[85] The burial register covering the years 1813 to 1854 shows a gradual decline in the number of respectable tradespeople being buried in the parish church, many of whom moved their residences out of the city into the wealthier suburbs from the 1820s onwards (see the biographical details of the church wardens of St. Ewen found elsewhere in this volume see pp. 152–154). This is coupled with a proportional increase in the number of burials of people resident in the slums of the Pithay and its adjoining courts and purlieus, such as Cider House Passage, Tower Lane, and Bedlam Court. There was a steady decline in the number of burials in 1851, 1852 and 1853, and the last burial took place on 8 January 1854.

By 1822 Charlotte Jones, the sexton, was receiving £13.16.10 from the church wardens for her wages, whilst the parish clerk's income amounted to £10.7.8 for serving as parish clerk and as a result of the monies bequeathed to him at an endowed annual sermon, together with £2.13.0 for serving as the parish constable. These sums remained constant for many years, the clerk and the sexton each receiving £10 p.a. with the addition of various sundries.

THE RE-BUILDING OF CHRIST CHURCH AND THE CLEARANCE OF THE HUMAN REMAINS 1786 TO 1790

The perilous state of the fabric of the old church necessitated the demolition of the building and its re-erection.[86] The timescale of the work was short and the clearance of the site undertaken with great haste. The new church was designed by Thomas Paty and possibly also by his son William, with whom he was in partnership. We know that the new crypt was part of this design and also that an integral feature was a cemetery under the tower, which was initially designed to contain the remains of the leading families in the parish rescued from the old church. This is discussed in detail by Mr. Colin Godman elsewhere in this volume. Charles Viner of Bath organized the taking down and the re-building of the cemetery and the moving of the dead.[87]

The work commenced in the autumn of 1786 and Viner received the first instalment of payment for the work on 12 January 1787. The work on the clearance of the churchyard and crypt began in mid-October, once the heat of the summer and the dangers posed by meat flies, bluebottles and maggots had passed. The work was macabre with many of the recently interred bodies in an advanced state of putrefaction. The horrors of the work, largely undertaken in the dark by the light of tallow candles, and the distressing sights and smells, called for a constant supply of ale and the semi-inebriation which will have followed must have led to the behaviour later recorded by Robert Southey, and to the corpses being treated with scant respect. An

[85] B.R.O., P/XCh/Ch W/19, pp. 39, 778, 90, 93, 105.

[86] *25 Geo. III, cap. 95* , (1785). The structure of the church may have been damaged by the vaults cut into the crypt(s) and floor of the church.

[87] B.R.O., P/XCh/ChW/4 (vi), church wardens' vouchers 1772–1800. The cost of the work was £125.2.6½; B.R.O., P/XCh/ChW/1, his bill for building the church, tower, and cemetery [crowd] was £1, 930. 0. 0.

account of the daily ration of ale allowed to the workmen from 16 to 25 October survives, and generally amounts to 18 quarts a day.[88] The ledger slabs over the graves and the floor of the crypt were lifted between the 10 and 18 October and 88 loads were transported away from the site. In conjunction with this work between the 14 and 18 October some 49 loads of rubble, probably largely from the vaults, were also removed from the church.[89] A detailed account of the wages paid week on week, from 21 October 1786 and ending in the week commencing 2 January 1787 by the foreman Edward Lacey, to the day labourers, has survived. Each week a gang of men ranging in number from six to 17, were employed for generally two and a half or three days, receiving between one shilling and ten pence and two shillings a day.[90] The invoices reveal the scale of the operation:[91]

To Diging a Hole in St. Phillips Church Yard to Bury the Bones and Leveling the Dirt

1786, Novr 5	£. s. d.
Joseph Bateman 5 Days	9. 2
Richard Francomb 5 D[itt]o	9. 2
John Smith 5 D[itt]o	9. 2
To 12 Men 2 Nights takeing the bones and buring them	1. 2. 2
Novr 8	
To 7 Load of Bones Hald away	7. 0
Novr 9	
To 6 Load of Bones Halld away	6. 0
Novr 11	
To 6 Load of Old Coffin Boards	6. 0
To 4 New Baskets to Carry the Bones in	2. 8
Novr 18	
To Joseph Bateman 4 Days	7. 4
Novr 25	
To Joseph Bateman 3 Days	5. 6
To 12 Men takeing the bones and burying them	11. 0
To 5 load of Bones Halld away	5. 0
Decr 9	
To Joseph Lovell 3 days	5. 6
Decr 16	
To Joseph Lovell 2 Days	3. 8
To 3 Load of Bones Halld a way	3. 0
To 9 Men taking the bones and burying them	8. 3

[88] B.R.O., P/XCh/ChW/4 (viii), marked 'No 2 E. Lacey. The bill for 154 quarts of ale amounted to £4. 6. 9.

[89] Ibid., marked 'No 3 Edw. Lacey.

[90] Ibid., marked 'No 1, Day Work £31.10.8½'. P/XCh/ChW/4 (ix), p. 137, notes that the church wardens paid Edward Lacey ten guineas as part of his charge for 'removing the dead bodies'.

[91] B.R.O., P/XCh/ChW/4 (viii), marked 'No 4 The Exor of Mr Edward Lacey'. Lacey never lived to be paid for his work. Edward Arnold, his wife's second husband received £15.2.9 in cash on account on 21 October 1791, and a further account of Jones and Lacey was received on 13 November 1792.

These accounts allow us to see in considerable detail the remnants of centuries of human remains in the crypt and some of the more recently deposited human remains from the upper churchyard being removed from the shell of the church at night time through the south door into Wine Street, perhaps shielded by the wooden scaffolding from the eyes of the curious. The workmen would have been illuminated either by horn lanterns or by flambeaux and the jumbled and disarticulated human remains carried on the back of numerous covered carts to be deposited in an unmarked, and according to the records of SS. Philip and Jacob, an unrecorded, pit in their church-yard. Robert Southey, the poet, then a youth of 12, living in Wine Street, either wit-nessed or was informed of what happened during the clearance of the vaults and the upper churchyard. Almost twenty years later, writing in March 1806, he recalled: 'sad things were said of the indecencies that occurred in removing the coffins for the new foundations to be laid'.[92] The memory of what happened at this time, the indignities, and the rude handling of the dead of previous centuries, who were consigned to a common pit in the churchyard of SS. Philip and Jacob, passed away, and was not transmitted by word of mouth from one generation to another.[93] The Revd. Henry Rogers (1810–1849),[94] who was curate at Christ Church in the 1830s to the Revd. Robert Watson and founded the first parish school,[95] was a popular and zealous min-ister. No vestigial echo of these macabre events could have reached him when he wrote of the church: 'that two of her sister churches, S. Ewen and S. Andrew have been […] levelled with the ground, and their holy earth by impious hands desecrated to worldly purposes, she still[…]remains […]the shrine of honoured dust[…]she even yet guards the remains of those who lived and died'.[96]

The re-building of the crypt required rough ashlar, or partly dressed stone, stone rubble, and bricks. Following the rapid erection, there was a partial collapse of the arches and vaulting.[97] Messrs. Richard Hill & Son, whose main trade was painting, billed for daywork under the date 3 November 1787: 'To Labour in removeing Cornish Tiles after the cemetery fell in [&] alterations in the ceiling after it was Lathed & Roughed in per Order Mr Paty 19.1'.[98] Messrs. Jenkins and Lovell, the

---

[92] The Revd. C. C. Southey, (ed.), *The Life and Correspondence of Robert Southey*, III, (Bristol, 1850), p. 35. Letter to Grosvenor C. Bedford, dated Keswick, 6 March 1806, quoted in J. F. Nicholls and J. Taylor, *Bristol: Past and Present*, II, (Bristol, 1881), pp. 171–173.

[93] It is interesting to note that by the 1830s all the space under the floor of Bath abbey had been used for interments. *The Bath Weekly Chronicle* for 2 June 1836 records a meeting in the Guildhall in which a Dr. Wilkinson stated that 'in the Abbey it has been found necessary to periodically remove the surplusage of the remains and it might be said that of the persons buried there antecedent to twenty years ago, not a particle now remained'.

[94] J. Foster, *Alumni Oxonienses, 1715–1886*, III, (Oxford, 1888), p. 1219, he was third son of George Rogers of Clifton, mat. University College, Oxford, 21 October 1830, scholar 1830–1833, B.A. 1834, M.A. 1837, vicar of All Saints', Corn Street, 1841, died 7 November 1849.

[95] B.R.O., P/XCh/HM/6, the vestry presented him with a gratuity of 20 guineas in 1840 as a mark of its appreciation.

[96] The Revd. H. Rogers, *The Calendars of Al-Hallowen, Bristowe: An attempt to Elucidate Some Portions of The History of the Priory or Ffraternitie of Calendars*, (Bristol, 1846), pp. 48–49.

[97] B.R.O., P/XCh/ChW/4 (ix), p. 147; extra work included: 'Penant steps to church yard as per 2nd drawing £6. o. o. ; 40 perch of stone to springing of cemetary £6. o. o; 525 perch of mortar in arches pillars & backing in cemetary £17.10.0'. Bill of Charles Viner dated 10 November 1789, marked No. 2.

[98] B.R.O., P/XCh/ChW/4 (viii).

contractors, were paid £35 for 'making, halling & fixing the Centerns [*sic*], Boards &c for ye Crowd a second time as per Agreement'.[99] There was also a charge for removing all the rubble from the arches of the crowd which could not be re-used. This setback must have caused a noticeable delay to the completion of the work on the church.

The clearing of the upper churchyard and the completion of the cemetery under the tower appears to have taken place between January and April 1789:

1789 17 Jan(uary)[100]

Placing stone in cemetery 5 days a mason	£ 0.15. 0[101]
5 days a mason 2.6 d(itt)o a mason 2.	£ 1.02. 6[101]
5 days a labourer [2 lb] candles 1.04, Beer 1.0	9. 10[101]

[January] 31

Moving dead on the north side of the church	11. 0[101]
2 days a mason at 3.0 [ ] 1.6 d[itt]o a Boy 1.0	
I lb of candles 8d a pint of Rum 1.0	1. 8[101]

Feb[ruary] 7

Altering steps and making drains	
5 days a mason 3.0	15. 0[101]
5 days each 2 Labr and a Boy	£ 1.00. 0[101]

Mar[ch] 21

Moving deabl [?] for Sanders at back door	
1 day a mason 3.0 d[itt]o a Mason 2.4 & 4 days each 2 Labourers 1.6	17. 4[101]

{March} 28

To d[itt]o & relaying Tombs & Walling up the opening between the Tower & Mr Brownes	
2 days a mason 3.0 & 5 days a mason 2.4	17. 8[101]
5 days each 2 Labourers	15. 0[101]
Paid the Grave digging of St James's for Removing 5 Corpse's	6. 6[101]

Ap[ri]l 4

Moving dead relaying Tombs &c	
2 days a mason 3.0 & 3 days a mason 2.4	13. 0[101]
3 days each 2 Labourers	9. 0[101]
130 Bushels of Lime 2 ½ & 61 Bushells of Coarse Lime 1d	£ 1.12. 2[101]
Repairing Wall that was broke by drawing Holes for Girders of the Building in Wine Street 1 day a man 2.4 6 boardes of mortar 3d	3. 10[101]
To overcharge in Mr. Wests valuation of old Stones	£ 12. 7. 0[101]

---

[99] B.R.O., P/XCh/ChW/4 (viii), the bill is dated March 1788.

[100] B.R.O., P/XCh/ChW/1.

[101] There is no record in the relevant parish registers of the re-burial of these five bodies in the churchyard of St. James.

What happened to the remains of those people buried in the crypt and upper church-yard whose husbands and wives, children and parents were still alive and expected their mortal remains to be united in death with their loved ones? The wealthy banker, Thomas Tyndall of the Royal Fort, rescued the remains of his wife, and of his cousin and namesake, and we presume that he also secured the remains of those of the numerous other members of his family who had been buried in the old church.

Canon M.A.R.T. Cole compiled a volume of plans of the new church and church-yards and transcribed all the gravestone and memorial inscriptions visible between 1915 and 1922. Many of these stones have now perished or become illegible. By using his papers and the burial registers it is possible to reconstruct a number of cases where corpses from the old church were rescued from the vaults, stored (we know not how or where) and restored to the new church. These include James Banister (1772),[102] whose widow Ann was buried in the new crypt in 1796;[103] Robert Bolster, gentleman (1767);[104] Christopher Raymond (1754) with four of his children, whose widow Dorothy (*née* Tyndal) was buried in the crypt in 1802;[105] and most interestingly of all, Thomas Holmes, merchant of the parish of St. Nicholas, and sometime deputy governor of the Incorporation of the Poor[106] and his daughter Elizabeth, who died unmarried, aged 29, on 19 January 1772. Like the others whose names are recorded on this list, their memorial which adorned one of the walls of the old church, was taken down and re-erected in the new structure. Carved by James Paty, it is of a particularly high standard of workmanship. Mary Holmes (1704–1789), widow of Thomas, recovered the bodies of her husband and her beloved daughter. She was subsequently buried in the crypt, probably with her husband, but noted on the family's memorial monument in the church, that their daughter was buried in the 'cemetery under the tower,' a fact which is discussed elsewhere in this book in an essay by Mr. Colin Godman. We do not know the fate of the body of the Revd. Daniel Debat, which was only placed in the vault under the chancel a little before the demolition of the church. It is, however, believed that the remains of a former rector, the Revd. Charles Brent, remained in the church, although his funerary monument was moved to Wraxall in Somerset.

BURIALS 1790–1854

The rate of burials in the churchyards in the period 1785 to 1790 remained constant with 22 including the rector in the chancel in 1785; 16 in 1786; 22 in 1787; 19 in 1788; 25 in 1789 and 1790.[107] The first mention of the situation within the church where a

---

[102] He died 25 October 1772, aged 66.

[103] She died 26 December 1796, aged 80 and was living in 5 Queen Square in 1775.

[104] He died 4 March 1767 aged 80. His wife and two children were buried in the old church and he is termed on his memorial tablet, which was still extant in 1922 'a sincere friend and a Christian'.

[105] He died 28 February 1754, aged 52, she died 7 March 1802, aged about 103, her father was Athelstone Tyndal [*sic*]. One of their daughters Ann, (1723–1810), was an undertaker. Ann Raymond and Co. upholders is listed at 48 Wine Street in 1775.

[106] The Revd A. B. Beaven, *Bristol Lists; Municipal and Miscellaneous*, (Bristol, 1899), p. 362. He was deputy governor between 1740 and 1741 and died 24 July 1761, in his 73rd year.

[107] B.R.O., P/XCh/R/1(d).

particular person was buried occurs in 1785, but it is only occasionally used in the years immediately following. During the period 1786 to 1790 there were 92 burials including 23 people from St. Peter's Hospital, who were probably all buried in the Duck Lane cemetery, together with people from other parishes (Clifton, St. James, St. Stephen, St. John the Baptist and St. Nicholas) who were buried in the crypt or parish churchyards. William Baylis (1788), a linen draper and haberdasher of 55 Wine Street,[108] a parishioner, was one of the first to be buried in the new crypt followed by Peter Goodwin from St. Stephen's parish, a retired linen draper and haberdasher, formerly of 49 Wine Street, who was allowed to be buried in a crypt under the chancel in 1790.[109]

During the clearance of the crowd and upper churchyard between 1786 and 1789 most burials must have taken place in the lower churchyard in Duck Lane. The other two places of burial were brought into use immediately after the church was rebuilt. Excluding the fragments of three stones recorded by Canon Cole, which must have come from the old church,[110] the earliest date of death recorded on a stone in the crypt records the last resting place of Sarah, wife of George Salway, who died 25 May 1786, aged 26 and was buried in her own church, St. Ewen, prior to being moved to the crypt of Christ Church in 1793.[111]

The upper churchyard also contained the remains of people whose families were determined to secure their remains following the decision to demolish the church and take down the upper cemetery. The majority of stones which remain are now illegible but Canon Cole's rough plan and transcriptions survive. His father made no such record of the stones which were moved when the choir and clergy vestries and the baptistery were built in the 1880s and 1890s. Canon Cole noted that a gravestone dated 1765 formed part of the ceiling over the safe in the choir vestry, but gave no transcription and it cannot now be seen. Among those buried in the upper churchyard was Catherine White, who died on 19 January 1785, daughter of William White, the keeper of the White Hart Inn in Broad Street, who hired chaises and from whose premises one of the London coaches departed; [112] Mrs. Ann Jackson (1781), hosier of 57 Broad Street; the wife, mother in law and son of John Crocker (1719–1803), peruke maker of 60 Wine Street;[113] the Combes family;[114] and Allis Williams (1723–1775), 'of

---

[108] William Baylis died aged 49, his family monument, carved in marble is situated in the porch.

[109] Buried 4 February 1790; he must have been friendly with the rector as burial here was in his particular gift.

[110] One records the death of Sarah, daughter of John and Elizabeth Clark, died 16 May 1737, aged 3 years; another the death of an unnamed wife of Walter Townshend who died 8 September 1740 and Elizabeth his second wife, died 9 October 1767; and a Mr. or Mrs. Whittock who died November 1731 aged 69 together with one Hooper. All the stones were difficult to decipher when Canon Cole made his transcriptions.

[111] She was one of two former residents of St. Ewen to be buried in Christ Church in 1793.

[112] The Lodge of Jehosaphat of Free and Accepted Masons met here between 1775 and 1785, and as it was customary for inn keepers to be masons it was possible that White was one, A. C. Powell and J. Littleton, *A History of Freemasonry in Bristol*, (Bristol, 1910), pp. 74 and ff.

[113] His wife was Sarah, his mother-in-law, Martha Marchant and his son John Crocker Junior, fellow of Wadham College, Oxford.

[114] Mr. Combes died 11 July 1762, aged 62, Hannah, his daughter, 13 May 1765, aged 22; Elizabeth Combes died 9 March 1770, aged 37 and Mary Combes died 16 March 1772, aged

the parish of Hyreffield [*sic*][115] in the county of Gloucester'.[116] By the entrance to the crypt there is a stone which formerly bore an inscription to the memory of John Palmer of the parish who died in 1765 and James, who died in 1792.[117] By the time that Canon Cole had made his plan the stones in the upper churchyard had all been moved from their original positions.

In 1785 the burial records of the church begin, occasionally, to list the burial places of the dead.[118] This was strictly observed in the registers between 1798 and 1812. In the latter year the type of register changed and precluded the capture of this kind of information.

Table 4. Place of burial in Christ Church with St. Ewen 1798–1812

Year	Crowd	Chancel	Lower Churchyard	Upper Churchyard	Total
1798	1	0	11	4	16
1799	5	0	10	2	17
1800	4	1	10	9	24
1801	3	0	8	9	20
1802	3	0	7	4	14
1803	0	0	6	8	14
1804	1	0	7	0	8
1805	4	1	10	3	18
1806	2	1	8	3	14
1807	3	0	7	2	12
1808	9	0	1	3	13
1809	4	0	10	4	18
1810	1	0	6	5	12
1811	3	0	5	4	12
1812	2	0	10	2	14
Total	45	3	116	62	226

The tendency for the poor to end up in the Duck Lane Cemetery at this time is reinforced by the fact that a number of those buried in the lower churchyard in 1801 are marked as being 'poor'.

During the period 1813 to 1852 there were 684 burials in the parish, excluding those in 1814 for which we do not have figures, and there were a further six burials in 1853 and one in 1854. The gentle decline in the number of burials in the parish over time between 1813 and 1854 has not been explained. The ground plan of the crypt drawn by Canon Cole in 1920 would indicate that there was room for further vaults and intramural burials.

---

72. They may have been related to William Combes, who in 1775 was living 73 Castle Street and is called 'tin plate worker and coffin plate chaser'.

[115] Probably Haresfield. I am grateful to Mr. David J. H. Smith for this information.

[116] She died 21 November 1775.

[117] In 1775 there was a Palmer and Son woollen drapers and slop sellers at 35 Corn Street.

[118] B.R.O., P/XCh/R/1(d), the Revd. Daniel Debat in the chancel on 10 April and Susannah Lewis in the church on 25 April.

Table 5. The number of burials by year in the parish of Christ Church with St. Ewen 1813 to 1852[119]

1813	18	1823	14	1833	26	1843	14
1814	?	1824	24	1834	13	1844	18
1815	22	1825	15	1835	15	1845	15
1816	23	1826	17	1836	15	1846	11
1817	15	1827	22	1837	20	1847	24
1818	21	1828	14	1838	17	1848	24
1819	16	1829	16	1839	21	1849	15
1820	20	1830	9	1840	21	1850	11
1821	21	1831	20	1841	19	1851	9
1822	20	1832	33	1842	10	1852	6
Total	176		184		177		147

Routine maintenance was carried on to both churchyards. In July 1836 the vestry gave instructions for the churchyard to be levelled and the tombstones regulated.[120] We have a description of the upper churchyard as it appeared to an occasional visitor in the early 1840s:[121]

> It was a cold and dreary afternoon in November when I entered the churchyard, a narrow strip of ground, lying between the north side of the Church and the back of the White Hart Inn. The hue and aspect of mortality around me were in unison with the melancholy progress of decay, the harbinger of the falling year; nor shrubs nor flowers bloomed upon the graves, but the tall sickly, meagre grass, heavy with damp, bent over the mouldering stones. Chill, comfortless, and depressing are the thoughts of death, in a spot so desolate, so penned in by houses that the sunlight of Heaven rarely shines upon the narrow beds where sleep the countless dead, while the many voices of human life resounding in the air sicken the ear with their jarring contrast to the deep silence of the congregated dust below.

The Bristol Times for 17 August 1850, in part of an occasional series entitled 'Parochial Pencillings', talks of: 'looking out on the little secluded graveyard, with its grey weather-worn tombstones, beneath which so many a Christ Church patriarch lies mouldering'.[122]

The lower burial ground in Duck Lane was kept in order in the 1830s and 1840s and we find the vestry ordering work to be undertaken there in February 1843.[123] Following the cessation of burials in 1854 the place was allowed to fall into decay. When the Revd. Edward Pattinson Cole became rector of the parish in 1880 he found

[119] B.R.O., P/XCh/R/4(a) Burial Register 1813–1854.
[120] B.R.O., P/XCh/HM/6, 4 July 1836. The church wardens asked for planks for use in burials in the two churchyards on 2 May 1837, which was agreed by the vestry.
[121] S. G. Tovey, *Cursory Observations on the Churches of Bristol By An Occasional Visitor*, (2nd ed., Bristol, 1843), pp. 106–107.
[122] Bristol City Library, Reference Section, Braikenridge Collection, XV, p. 59.
[123] B.R.O., P/XCh/HM/6, 19 February 1843.

the Duck Lane churchyard neglected and containing only ten gravestones, the oldest ones dating from 1769 and 1799.[124]

His son, writing in 1942 following the demolition of one of Messrs. Frys' factories adjoining the cemetery, stated that the graveyard had been put in order following the construction of the factory in the late 1890s. His father had the stones re-laid in the form of a cross. The workers often used the grounds as a place of recreation in their lunch hour. Canon Cole related:

> The graveyard was so packed with human remains that the greatest care had to be taken to prevent the bones from spreading while the foundations of the adjacent factory were being put in. When my father first came to Christ Church there were still living those who could remember burials taking place in this graveyard, and told of the careless manner of conducting funerals in it- namely, how quantities of bones were unearthed when a grave was opened and hidden behind boards during the funeral service, and when this was over they were shovelled in again, the skulls being pitched in, "dap, dap, dap, like so many coconuts".[125]

Mr. John Edward Heal, the former parish secretary, and patron of the living of Christ Church with St. Ewen, remembers the forlorn and dilapidated graveyard in the late 1940s and early 1950s. The Duck Lane cemetery was finally swept away in the post-war development of the city.

The crypt of Christ Church is now used as a solicitor's archive and its ledger slabs are no longer visible. All that remains above ground to remind us of the practice of burial in Christ Church is the presence of a few broken and largely illegible pennant slabs in the upper churchyard, worn by use and the inexorable hand of time, which cover the remains of some of the former residents of the parish. Hemmed in by the Grand Hotel, the vestries of Christ Church and the rear of the properties belonging to the Christ Church Lands Trust situated in Broad Street, the spot is even more melancholy and neglected than it was when it was described in the early 1840s. It serves as a place to contemplate futurity, the vanity of human desire and the apophthegm:

> In the grave all looks alike, Lazarus' sores will make as good dust as Jezebel's paint.[126]

ACKNOWLEDGEMENTS

I wish to record my gratitude to Mr. and Mrs. Colin Godman; to the Revd. Dr. Peter Jupp, one of the leading authorities on the subject of the burial of the dead, for discussions on this subject made during his visits to Bristol, and to the law librarian of the University of Bristol; Mr. Vivian George Mildren (1927–1984), church warden of

---

[124] One of the stones was to the memory of James Langford who died 10 February 1769, aged 45 and his family, and the other was to Mary Weaver who died October 1799 and her family. The latter was one of two of the ten stones to have disappeared by the time that Canon Cole made his transcriptions between 1915 and 1922.

[125] *The Bristol Evening Post*, 8 July 1942, from the papers in the B.R.O., P/XCh/HM/8.

[126] H. Montagu, 'Death Common to all', *Contemplatio Mortis et Immortalitatis*, (1639).

Christ Church and Dr. Arthur Basil Cottle, F.S.A., (1917–1994), church warden of St. Ewen; to the Revd. Charles Maurice Joseph Turner (1913–1997), *quondam* joint-patron of the living; Mrs. Edith Stephanie Ryder (1918–2009), daughter of the Revd. Hugh Carlo Bellasis Roden (1886–1970), rector of Christ Church with St. Ewen between 1941 and 1952; Dr. Elizabeth Ralph F.S.A., (1911–2000); Mr. John Edward Heal, patron of the living, and Mr. Roger Clive Metcalfe, church warden of Christ Church, for their extensive and detailed knowledge of this well-loved church and parish, which they have generously shared with me over a period of thirty years.

XIV

The Restoration of the Funerary Hatchments and the Royal Coat of Arms in Christ Church with St. Ewen, Bristol

K. WOODGATE-JONES, F.I.I.C.

INTRODUCTION[1]

ONE OF the many city churches damaged during the air raids of 1940–1941 was Christ Church with St. Ewen, Broad Street, which narrowly escaped destruction during the 'Great Air Raid' which took place on Sunday 24 November 1940.[2]

The heat from the fires outside the church was so intense that the windows on the south and east sides of the church were damaged and the stained glass they contained destroyed, either shattered by the blasts, or melted in the heat generated from the burning shops in Wine Street which adjoined the south wall. The organ gallery remained intact although a number of lead pipes in the organ were damaged and one was melted in the heat.[3] The organ case and gallery were blistered and smoke damaged, and subsequently repaired between August and December 1953. Two of the mullions on the south wall nearest to the east end were destroyed and the ceilings of the south aisle and part of the central aisle were scorched. The cinders from the burning shops in Wine Street entered the church through the melted and shattered windows and landed on the pews, the cushions, the hassocks, and inside the organ pipes. It was only by chance that the interior of the church did not become engulfed in flame and the following morning the verger found the hassocks and cushions smouldering and on the point of combustion.[4]

Two of the additional casualties were the funeral hatchments which hung on the west wall between the windows and the gallery. These were severely damaged by the smoke and heat. The hatchment of Thomas Tyndall (1722–1794) of the Royal Fort House, which was hung higher than the other was particularly badly damaged and the paint was blackened by the smoke and bubbled, blistered and crazed in the heat.

In 2007 the parochial church council of Christ Church with St. Ewen decided to have all four hatchments within the church and the Royal coat of arms in the vestry cleaned and stabilized. Generous grants were pledged to enable the work to be

---

[1] The introduction on pp. 257–269 is written by Dr. M. J. Crossley Evans.
[2] The Revd. C. M. J. Turner, *Christ Church or Holy Trinity, Bristol*, (Bristol, 1955), pp. 33–37.
[3] H. Byard, 'The Historic Organs of Bristol and Gloucestershire', *T. B. & G. A. S.*, XCIII, (1974), p. 164, states that the damage to the organ was only rectified in 1969.
[4] This is partly based on an account written by Canon Cole following a visit to the church made on 29 August 1941, which is in possession of Dr. M. J. Crossley Evans, and partly taken from conversations with the late Revd. C. Maurice J. Turner.

undertaken, and they were examined *in situ* by Miss Kate Woodgate-Jones on 10 June 2007. Grants were received from the Vice-Chancellor of the University of Bristol, Professor Eric Thomas D.L.; the St. Ewen's Lands' Trust; the St. Andrew's Conservation Trust; and the Cottle Trust, which transferred its residential funds to the church for this purpose in memory of Dr. Arthur Basil Cottle F.S.A. (1917–1994), church warden of St. Ewen between 1984 and 1994; past-president of the Bristol and Gloucestershire Archaeological Society and reader in Mediaeval Studies at the University of Bristol.

FUNERARY HATCHMENTS

Until the mid-nineteenth century it was customary after death for the coat of arms of an armigerous person to be painted in oils upon canvas or on wooden board in the form of a funeral escutcheon. Following the funeral the hatchment was placed over the front door of their house as a sign of mourning, where it remained for the period of a year.[5] The arms were placed in a black, lozenge-shaped wooden frame, usually between five and six feet in height. The escutcheon informed the passer-by of the rank and marital status of the deceased. After the period of mourning the hatchment was hung in the parish church where the funeral had taken place.[6]

Bachelors had their arms displayed complete with helmet, crest, mantling and motto on a black ground. Husbands had their arms complete, impaled with those of their wives. In all cases the ground was: *per pale* black and white, with black on the dexter side and white on the sinister, showing that the wife had survived her husband. Where the wife predeceased her husband the ground was painted *per pale* white and black, the sinister part was black and the dexter half white.[7] The escutcheons of widowers and widows differed from those of husbands only in that the background was wholly black. The achievements of arms for wives were the same as their husband's minus the helmet crest, mantle and motto. Sometimes the motto of the deceased was not used on the hatchment but was replaced by the single word: '*Resurgam*'.[8] The arms of both spinsters and married women were painted on a lozenge shaped shield.

[5] Sometimes this was not possible and the hatchment was hung on the outside of the first floor façade. An advertisement in the 1841 *Mathews's Bristol Directory* for Edward A. Bird, a linen draper, silk mercer and undertaker of 29 Corn Street, who specialised in 'family mourning', illustrates this line of his business by including a small engraving in the advertisement which shows a hatchment affixed over the upper part of a window. The hatchment was removed the day following the expiry of the year of mourning.

[6] J. Litten, *The English Way of Death: The Common Funeral Since 1450*, (1991), p. 189.

[7] Anon., *A Glossary of Terms used in British Heraldry*, (Oxford, 1847), pp. 3–7; G Cadogan-Rothery, *Concise Encyclopaedia of Heraldry*, (1915), p. 333; T. Woodcock and J. M. Robinson, *The Oxford Guide to Heraldry*, (Oxford 1990), p. 179; A. C. Fox Davies, *The Art of Heraldry: An Encyclopaedia of Armory*, (1986), pp. 476–477; *Chamber's Encyclopaedia*, (New edition), V, (1890), p. 583; H. Clark, *An Introduction to Heraldry*, (1859), pp. 67–68; S. T. Aveling (ed.) *Heraldry: Ancient and Modern, including Boutell's Heraldry*, (1898), p. 158; F. E. Hulme, *The Principles and Practice of Heraldry*, (1892), p. 196; H. Clark, (revised by J. R. Planché), *An Introduction to Heraldry*, (1906), pp. 69–70; C. Lynch-Robinson and A. Lynch-Robinson, *Intelligible Heraldry: The Application of a Mediaeval System of Record and Identification to Modern Needs*, (1948), pp. 125–127.

[8] J. P. Brooke-Little, *Boutell's Heraldry*, (Revised edition, 1978), pp. 148–150.

THE TYNDALL HATCHMENTS AND MOURNING

The Tyndall hatchments would each have been used in the traditional 'lying in state'. Although we cannot be certain what the arrangements were when Thomas Tyndall I died in Berkeley Square in 1794, the other members of the family are likely to have been placed encoffined on a heraldic pall surrounded by candles in the small drawing room in the Royal Fort House looking over the gardens. The room would have been shuttered, hung from floor to ceiling in black and dominated by the funerary hatchment. At least three areas of the house would have been hung with mourning: the entrance hallway, the drawing room, where the family would have received visits of condolence during the year of mourning, and the small drawing room where the corpse would have rested prior to the funeral. The hatchment would then have appeared in a prominent position in the funeral procession[9] on its way from The Royal Fort to Christ Church, where it would have been attended by mutes and either borne in procession together with the customary tray bearing black ostrich feather plumes, or attached to the catafalque.

HATCHMENTS IN BRISTOL CITY CHURCHES

By the time that the Phillimore volume covering Bristol in *the Hatchments in Britain* series was published in 1988, only a small number of hatchments could be located in the city of Bristol, and this number included the four in Christ Church with St. Ewen. The four hatchments in Christ Church can be confidently dated to the period 1794 to 1841. The other locations of hatchments in Bristol are: St. George (one, 1818); SS. Philip and Jacob (five, 1790, 1818, 1837, 1854, and one of unknown date); The Lord Mayor's Chapel (six, two unidentified and four for former mayors, 1737, 1743, 1818, and 1855) and three from the Blaise Castle Museum, (provenance unknown)[10]. These are probably only a fraction of the number which would have been found in the city churches prior to the late Victorian restorations of the 1870s and 1880s. Further losses were experienced in the widespread destruction of the churches in the old city during the air raids of 1940–1941.[11]

A study of watercolours in the Braikenridge Collection reveal that the walls of a number of the city churches were once adorned with hatchments which are not now extant. A watercolour of 1828 painted by James Johnson showing the interior of St. James Haymarket, reveals a hatchment on the north wall of the central aisle, and his

---

[9] J. Litten, *op. cit.*, (1991), pp. 190–191.

[10] P. Summers and J. E. Titterton, *Hatchments in Britain*, VII, [Cornwall, Devon, Dorset, Gloucestershire, Hampshire, Isle of Wight and Somerset], (1988), pp. 68–73. The Kingscote/Beaufort hatchment was given to the city of Bristol in 1934 by the Torquay Motor Company. It is signed by William Edkins and has been held by the Bristol City Museum and Art Gallery since 1990 under the number T8390.

[11] St. Werburgh's, Corn Street, was demolished in the road widening scheme in the 1870s. The air raids destroyed St. Peter, St. Mary le Port, St. Nicholas, and Temple, and St. Augustine the Less was demolished after the war. No hatchments are recorded in: St. Stephen, All Saints', St. John the Baptist on the Wall, St. Mary Redcliffe, St. Thomas the Apostle, St. Michael and All Angels on the Mount Without, or St. Paul, Portland Square.

painting of the interior of St. Peter, executed at the same time, shows hatchments on the east wall of the north aisle and on the south wall of the central aisle.[12] These had gone from St. Peter before 1909 when Charles Boucher, writing in our *Transactions* deplored the loss of the Royal coat of arms and the destruction of 'the interesting hatchments'.[13] In the same year Dr. Alfred Harvey noted that the only two churches without Royal coats of arms in Bristol were Christ Church and St. James, 'the latter being a church which has been swept absolutely clean of all old furniture whatever'.[14]

William Henry Goldwyer (1762–1820), a noted Bristol surgeon and oculist and the Provincial Grand Master of the Freemasons' in the Province of Bristol, was buried in the crypt of St. Nicholas. After his funeral a hatchment with his arms impaled with those of the order was hung over the entrance to Freemasons' Hall in Bridge Street. Subsequently it was hung in the crypt of St. Nicholas. When the crypt was restored in 1893 it was acquired by Freemasons' Hall, Park Street, where it was hung in the lodge of instruction. It perished in the destruction of the hall on the night of 24 November 1940.[15] When Richard Smith the Younger (1772/3–1843), the noted surgeon and freemason died, a hatchment was also placed on Freemasons' Hall in Bridge Street where it remained for a year. It would then have been transferred to Smith's parish church, Temple,[16] in accordance with the prevailing custom. This is not known to have survived the blitz.[17]

THE TYNDALL FAMILY

The Tyndall family were originally Gloucestershire yeomen. In 1674 Onesiphorus Tyndall I (1657–1748) settled in Bristol and having obtained the freedom of the city in 1680 established himself as a drysalter and grocer. In 1696 a number of members of the Tyndall family were resident in the parish of Christ Church including Athelstone Tyndale [*sic*] and Hester his wife, Onesiphorus and Elizabeth Tyndale, and Onesiphorus, Thomas, William and Joseph Tyndale.[18] The older Onesiphorus Tyndall established a considerable fortune, which was partly based on his trade with the West Indies. A Unitarian, he served as the treasurer of Lewin's Mead chapel in 1704 and subsequently was a common councilman between 1703 and 1712 and sheriff in 1707–1708.[19] He was the father of at least three sons. John, who died unmarried in

[12] Bristol City Museum and Art Gallery, Braikenridge M 2808, P. Brown, 'Centuries of Change: Bristol Churches since the Reformation', J. H. Bettey, (ed.) *Historic Churches and Church Life in Bristol*, (Bristol, 2001), pp. 113, 121–122.

[13] C. E. Boucher, 'St. Peter's Church, Bristol', *T. B. & G. A. S.*, XXXII, Part II, (1909), p. 300.

[14] A. Harvey, 'Church Furniture and Decoration of the Renaissance Period in Bristol', *T. B. & G. A. S.*, XXXII, Part I, (1909), p. 162.

[15] A. C. Powell and J. Littleton, *Freemasonry in Bristol*, (Bristol, 1910), p. 179.

[16] He was buried under a flat tombstone in the churchyard of Temple, G. Pryce, *A Popular History of Bristol: Antiquarian, Topographical, and Descriptive*, (Bristol, 1861), p. 306.

[17] A. C. Powell and J. Littleton, *op. cit.*, p. 203.

[18] E. Ralph and M. E. Williams, (eds.), *'The Inhabitants of Bristol in 1696'*, B.R.S., XXV, (1968), p. 23.

[19] He died 27 August 1748, aged 91. The Revd. A. B. Beaven, *Bristol Lists: Municipal and Miscellaneous*, (Bristol, 1899), p. 311.

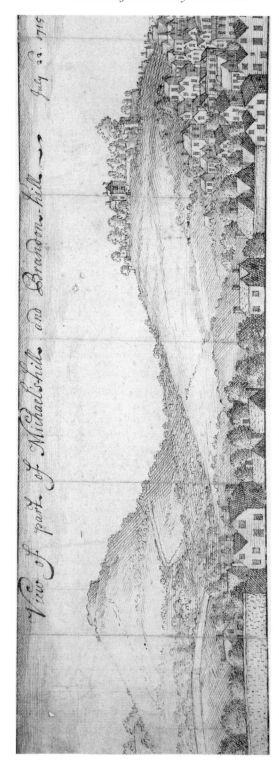

Fig. 1. Engraving of part of St. Michael's Hill and Brandon Hill, dated 22 July 1715. Artist and Engraver unknown. This shows St. Michael's Hill before Thomas Tyndall erected the Royal Fort House *c.* 1758–1760, [Bristol City Museum and Art Gallery, Ma 4381, part of the Heber Mardon bequest].

1743/4, served on the common council between 1740 and 1741 and left his house in the Royal Fort (Fig. 1) to his brother, Onesiphorus Tyndall II (1689–1757), who was a drysalter, a West India merchant,[20] and one of the founders of the Old Bank, otherwise Tyndall, Lloyd and Co., which opened its offices in Broad Street on 1 August 1750.[21] Onesiphorus Tyndall II was a freeman of the city and the last verderer of Kingswood Forest, an honour he purchased whilst speculating in coal. The second Onesiphorus married Elizabeth Cowles of Bristol in 1717.[22] His younger brother, Thomas Tyndall (1690–1735), was a merchant living in the parish of St. James. All three brothers were buried in Christ Church, Broad Street. It is also the last resting place of Elizabeth, the wife of Onesiphorus Tyndall II.[23] Although the family chose to be entombed in the church there is no record of any member of the family being baptised there from at least 1730 onwards, nor is there evidence that they played any part in the life of the church and the parish, although their other business, Tyndall, Power and Townsend, drysalters, was situated at 51 Wine Street, known as the 'Dutch House', (opposite to Christ Church).[24]

THE TYNDALL HATCHMENTS IN CHRIST CHURCH WITH ST. EWEN

The history of the hatchments on the west wall of the church and the identification of the people they commemorated had largely become a matter of speculation by the

---

[20] It is not known if he was associated with the firm of slave factors Tyndall and Assheton, based in Jamaica, but it has been suggested that he may have been an owner of the *Cato*, a slave ship active between 1729 and 1730, which imported ivory and redwood into Bristol, D. Richardson, (ed.), *Bristol, Africa and The Eighteenth-Century Slave Trade to America, Vol. 1, The Years of Expansion 1698–1729*, Bristol Record Society, XXXVIII, (1986), pp. 178, 184.

[21] He was senior partner between 1750 and 1757.

[22] G. Parker, 'Tyndall Park, Bristol, Fort Royal and the Fort House Therein', *T. B. & G. A. S.*, LI, (1929), pp. 134–138; C. H. Cave, *A History of Banking in Bristol from 1750 to 1899*, (privately printed, Bristol, 1899), p. 43.

[23] B.R.O., P/XCh/R/1(d), Christ Church, baptisms 1721–1812, marriages 1721–1754 and burials 1721–1812, unfoliated; Elizabeth, wife of Onesiphorus Tyndall (or Tindal) buried 17 December 1730; Thomas Tyndall from St. James, 11 December 1735; John Tyndall, buried 12 March 1743/4; Onesiphorus Tyndall buried 3 June 1757. Other members of the family whose exact relationships have not been positively identified were also buried there: Elizabeth, 6 September 1747; Onesiphorus, 7 July 1752, (*The Gentleman's Magazine*, XXIII, (1753), p. 200 called 'Esq: merchant at Bristol'); and Athelstone 14 February 1754. His daughter, Dorothy (*c.* 1699–1802) married Christopher Raymond (*c.* 1700–1754) of the parish, and they, together with a number of their children were buried in the crypt and commemorated by a marble funerary monument. Thomas Tyndall's son and namesake, Thomas Tyndall F.R.S. (*c.* 1717–1766), the King's proctor, died in London and was brought back to Christ Church to be buried on 16 September. Other members of the family buried in the church were Alicia, daughter of Thomas and Marianne Tyndall, on 28 December 1793, who died on the 24th aged 5 years, and her sister, Alicia Tyndall who was buried on 17 March 1806.

[24] *Sketchley's Bristol Directory 1775*, (Kingsmead Reprints, Bath, 1971), p. 99; R. H. Leech, *The Topography of Medieval and Early Modern Bristol: Part 1: Property Holdings in the early Walled Town and Marsh Suburb North of the Avon*, Bristol Record Society, XLVIII, (1997), p. 197; this property was leased to Onesiphorus Tyndall I in 1698, and considerably added to by him.

Fig. 2. Thomas Tyndall II, Marianne his wife and their family (*c.* 1798), from a painting by Sir William Beechey, R.A., in the drawing room of the Royal Fort House, [reproduced by the kind permission of the University of Bristol].

time that the Revd. Maurice Turner wrote his history of the church in February 1955.[25] He postulated that looking from the east end to the west they commemorated:

Onesiphorous Tyndall died 1757[26]   Marianne Tyndall died 1805
Thomas Tyndall died 1804   Thomas Tyndall died 1794[27]

When Catherine Constant undertook her study of funeral hatchments in Bristol she identified two of the hatchments correctly.

The first was the one which commemorates Thomas Tyndall II who died 23 July 1804 aged 40,[28] and was a partner in the Old Bank between 1795 and 1804. He was appointed lieutenant colonel of the Royal Bristol Volunteers in 1803[29] and served as a deputy lieutenant for Bristol and Gloucestershire. In 1786 he married Marianne, daughter of Lambert Schimmelpenning.[30] His arms are shown on a 'Dexter background sable', 'Argent a fess gules between three garbs sable (Tyndall), impaling, azure two keys in saltire or (Schimmelpenning). Crest: a demi-lion rampant gules holding a garb or; mantling: gules and argent'. His obituary notice in the *Gentleman's Magazine* states: he 'died in the prime of life' and was 'buried at Christ church, not with military honours, that being declined by the family, but as a private gentleman'.[31] *Felix Farley's Bristol Journal* stated that: 'as an officer and a private gentleman he had gained the universal esteem of his comrades and fellow citizens'.[32] Thomas Tyndall II and Marianne had a large family, eleven children, most of whom are depicted with their parents in the painting by Sir William Beechey R.A. (1753–1839), which hangs in the drawing room of Royal Fort House.[33] (Fig. 2).

The second hatchment correctly identified by Constant commemorates Marianne, widow of Thomas Tyndall II, who died 'after a short but severe illness'[34] on 15

[25] Thomas Tyndall I, II and III and their respective wives are all commemorated by armorial marble tablets within the church.

[26] This supposition was also incorrectly made by Canon Cole, B.R.O., P/XCh/1/16.

[27] The Revd. C. M. J. Turner, *op. cit.*, p. 38.

[28] B.R.O., P/XCh/R/1(d), Christ Church, baptisms 1721–1812, marriages 1721–1754 and burials 1721–1812, unfoliated. He was buried on 30 July 1804 in the crowd or crypt.

[29] R. Winstone, *Bristol: As It Was 1866–1860*, (Bristol, 1967), plate 74 shows Mr. William Horwood (1772–1864), who served in the volunteers between 1797 and 1814. It is stated here that his captain [*sic*] 'Thomas Tyndall Esq., died in his arms', which would indicate that Thomas Tyndall II died whilst on exercise with the volunteers.

[30] C. H. Cave, *op. cit.*, p. 51. *Mathews's Bristol Directory*, (1793–4), p. 72. He was an insurance broker, and is called here, 'gentleman' of 'Orchard Street'.

[31] *The Gentleman's Magazine*, LXXIV, Part II, (1804), p. 786. The date of his death is given as the 16th.

[32] *Felix Farley's Bristol Journal*, 28 July 1804, p. 3.

[33] The children were: Thomas III (1787–1841); Alicia (1788–1793); Onesiphorus III (1790–1869), keeper of Falkland Palace, changed his surname to Bruce 1829; Marianne (1792–1864), later Mrs. Marcus McCausland; William, (1793–1863); Henrietta, born 1794, later Mrs. Conolly Gage; Caroline, (1796–1843), later Mrs. Robert Bright; Charles, born 1797; The Revd. George Tyndall (1798–1848), fellow and later sub warden of Merton College, Oxford, rector of Lapworth, Co. Warwick; Edward Tyndall, (1800–1849) and Alicia, (*c.* 1801–1806). I am grateful to Dr. Brian R. Pollard, *quondam* lecturer in Physics at the University of Bristol, for this information.

[34] *Felix Farley's Bristol Journal*, 16 November 1805, p. 3.

November 1805 aged 41.[35] It is painted on a lozenge, to show that the person commemorated was a woman, and is surmounted by a cherub's head. The hatchment displays the same coat of arms as her husband, recorded above. Both Thomas and Marianne Tyndall are also commemorated within the church by a marble tablet with their armorial achievements painted above the inscription.[36] Her obituary notice says that 'a numerous and young family are thus left to deplore the loss of their parents within a few months'.[37] As their eldest son, Thomas, was only 17 at the time of the death of his father and unable to take his seat as a partner in the Old Bank, his mother looked after his interests until her death.

The third hatchment was not identified by Constant. It shows the same crest and the mantling as the first hatchment with the arms of Tyndall, impaling: 'Ermine on a cross sable, a castle triple-towered argent' for the Hill family. As the background is all black we can be certain that the arms are those of Thomas Tyndall III, who died 21 March 1841 aged 53.[38] He was a partner of the Old Bank between 1809 and 1841.[39] Tyndall was married in 1812 to Mary Sybella (*née* Hill), eldest daughter of Jeremiah Hill (1752/3–1831), of Down House, Gloucestershire.[40] She died at Weymouth on 13 August 1822 aged 31 and was brought back to Christ Church to be buried in the family vault.[41] It is probable that her death would have been also commemorated by a hatchment, which disappeared either at or prior to the restoration of the church in 1881–1883.[42] Both husband and wife are commemorated in an armorial funerary monument inside the porchway, or vestibule, of Christ Church.

The fourth hatchment was also not identified by Constant. It bears the Tyndall coat of arms alone, but with the crest and mantling as described on the first hatchment. This belonged to Thomas Tyndall I, who died at his residence in Berkeley

---

[35] B.R.O., P/XCh/R/1(d), Christ Church, baptisms 1721–1812, marriages 1721–1754 and burials 1721–1812, unfoliated. She was buried on 23 November 1805 in the crowd or crypt.

[36] She was the daughter of Lambert Schimmelpenning of 28 Orchard Street. Schimmelpenning and Co. were insurance brokers at 4 Exchange; *Sketchley's Bristol Directory 1775*, (Bath, 1971), p. 86.

[37] *The Gentleman's Magazine*, LXXV, Part II, (1805), p. 1173.

[38] B.R.O., P/XCh/R/4 (a), p. 66, burials 1813–1854, buried 29 March 1841, aged 52 [*sic*]; *The Gentleman's Magazine*, XV, (New Series), Part I, (1841), p. 555. The date of death that is given is 24 March, and his age 52.

[39] Elsewhere his bank directorship is said to have ended in 1837, C. H. Cave, *op. cit.*, pp. 52, 248–249.

[40] The Revd. A. B. Beaven, *op. cit.*, p. 295. Jeremiah Hill was master of the Merchant Venturers' between 1791 and 1792. *Mathews's Bristol Directory*, (1793–4), p. 43, Jeremiah Hill and Sons, merchants, St. Stephen Street; *The Universal British Directory 1793–1798*, II, part I, p. 153, the firm are stated to have been Spanish wool merchants.

[41] B.R.O., P/XCh/R/4 (a), p. 23, burials 1813–1854, buried 21 August 1822; *The Gentleman's Magazine*, XCII, Part II, (1822), p. 285, the date is given as 14 August.

[42] Their son, Thomas Onesiphorus Tyndall (1814–1869) of Royal Fort House, was the last male member of the family in the direct line. In 1842 he married Caroline Lucy (1809–1882), a twin, and one of the eight daughters of Sir Charles Abraham Elton Bart., (1778–1853), of Clevedon Court, Somerset. He died leaving six daughters (two predeceased him); M. Elton, *The Annals of the Elton Family: Bristol Merchants and Somerset Landowners*, (Stroud, 1994), p. 164. He was buried in Arno's Vale Cemetery, *Arrowsmith's Dictionary of Bristol*, (1st edition, 1884), p. 173.

Square on 17 April 1794, aged 72.[43] He built Royal Fort House, which was completed in 1760, for his young wife, Alicia (*née* Smith), a West Indian heiress from Barbados, whom he married in 1756. She died tragically young from the effects of childbirth, on 2 February 1764 aged 31,[44] leaving him with the care of a son only a few days old.[45] Fine marble busts once believed to represent each of them, Mrs. Tyndall wearing an elegant hat, were recorded by the late Professor Basil Fletcher as forming part of the drawing room fireplace.[46] Mrs Tyndall was buried in Christ Church.

The actual order of the hatchments in 2007, looking from the east end was:

Thomas Tyndall, died 1794	Thomas Tyndall II died 1804
Marianne Tyndall, died 1805	Thomas Tyndall III died 1841

THE TYNDALL CREST AND ACHIEVEMENT OF ARMS

The Tyndall Crest is described by Fairburn as 'a demi-lion rampant, [supporting] a garb',[47] but no colours are specified for either part of the crest. Sir Bernard Burke describes the family's arms as 'Ar. a fess gu. between three garbs sa.'.[48] In other words a red bar between three black wheat sheaves on a silver background. The crest and the coat of arms appear on the three Tyndall funerary monuments in Christ Church with St. Ewen's, City, and the crest and coat of arms also appears on the decorative stonework of their family home, Royal Fort House, in the tympanum of the pediment.[49] The crest again appears in the tympanums above the two garden doors, one from the small drawing room and the other from the hallway under the main staircase, both situated on the south front, and all carved splendidly by Thomas Paty.[50]

---

[43] He was born in Christ Church parish and baptised at Lewins Mead Unitarian Chapel on 26 March 1723, B.R.O., 39461, I am grateful to Dr. B. R. Pollard for this reference. C. H. Cave, *op. cit.*, pp. 47, 248–249. Cave gives two dates for the marriage of Thomas Tyndall to Alicia Smith, 1754 and 1756. B.R.O., P/XCh/R/1(d), Christ Church, baptisms 1721–1812, marriages 1721–1754 and burials 1721–1812, unfoliated. He was buried on 24 April 1794; *The Gentleman's Magazine*, LXIV, Part I, (1794), p. 388, notes the death 'At his house in Berkeley Square, Bristol, Thomas Tyndall, Esq., banker'. *Felix Farley's Bristol Journal*, 19 April 1794, p. 3. His death is said to have taken place on Thursday evening. His son lived on Clifton Hill before repurchasing the Royal Fort.

[44] B.R.O., P/XCh/R/1(d), Christ Church, baptisms 1721–1812, marriages 1721–1754 and burials 1721–1812, unfoliated. She was buried on 6 February 1764.

[45] In North Cerney, Gloucestershire there is a funeral hatchment for Thomas Tyndale [*sic*] who died 29 July 1783, aged 52 [*sic*], showing his arms, as those of the family of the Royal Fort House, impaled with those of his wife, Elizabeth, *née* Cox, of Avening. P. Summers and J. E. Titterton, *op. cit.*, p. 73. This Thomas Tyndale matriculated at Magdalen Hall, Oxford on 10 May 1746, aged 17, J. Foster, *Alumni Oxonienses 1715–1886*, Part II, IV, (Oxford, 1888), p. 1456. *The Gentleman's Magazine*, XXX, (1764), p. 349, where the date of his marriage is given as 17 July 1764.

[46] B. A. Fletcher, *The Royal Fort Bristol: The Story of an Ancient House*, (no place of publication or date, but probably Bristol, *c.* 1956), pp. 24–25. Mr M. J. H. Liversidge believes that these representations were derived from a contemporary design book, (private communication).

[47] J. Fairbairn, (Revised by L. Butters), *Fairbairn's Crests of the Families of Great Britain and Ireland*, (Poole, 1986), p. 472 as Tindall, Plate 84, cr. 7.

[48] B. Burke, *The General Armory of England, Scotland, Ireland and Wales*, (1884), p. 1041.

[49] W. Ison, *The Georgian Buildings of Bristol*, (1952), pp. 192–193.

[50] A. Gomme, M. Jenner and B. Little, *Bristol: an architectural history*, (1979), pp. 155–159.

THE ROYAL ARMS IN CHRIST CHURCH

The Royal coat of arms was set up in churches following Henry VIII's Act of Supremacy. In 1933 Professor Edward Fawcett published an article in our *Transactions*[51] on 'the Royal Arms of Gloucestershire Churches' and attempted to catalogue those to be found both in Bristol and Gloucestershire. Our current honorary general secretary, John Loosely, is in the process of coordinating a further survey to update Professor Fawcett's work.

In the 1933 survey Professor Fawcett noted that: 'in many cases the condition of the arms, more especially if painted on canvas, is deplorable'.[52] In the 19 places of worship in Bristol recorded as having Royal coats of arms, three are listed as having representations of the Brunswick coat of arms used by George III between 1801 and 1816. Two are believed to have been destroyed during the war; namely those on the front of the west gallery of Clifton parish church and the one over the north door of St. Augustine the Less, College Green. The other survives in Christ Church with St. Ewen, which in 1933 was housed on the south wall of the vestry. Professor Fawcett described it as being: 'wood panelled framed, upper edge convex, lower concave, has fitted an arch; 5′ x 5′. Since 1933 the Lord Mayor's Chapel has acquired a Brunswick coat of arms in a wooden frame, now situated in the south wall of the nave. In the 1980s it hung on the wall between the north transept and the vestry. Its origins are unknown.

The history of the Christ Church version of the Brunswick arms is revealed in a manuscript notebook kept by the Revd. Canon Edward Pattinson Cole and his son, the Revd. Canon Marwood Anselm Rauceby Thorold Cole, who held the living successively between 1880 and 1938.[53] The Royal coat of arms seen by Professor Fawcett in the early 1930s originally came from the church of St. Leonard, Stanton Fitzwarren, in the deanery of Cricklade, Wiltshire, and was presented to Canon Rauceby Cole by Canon William Masters.[54] It is possible that it was hung in the church before being moved to the choir vestry in the late 1920s. In 1936 Professor Fawcett gave this Presidential Address to our Society and developed and expanded the work which he had published three years before on Royal coats of arms. In it he states that Canon Cole saved the specimen in Christ Church from destruction and offered it a home. Professor Fawcett believed that it had originally been placed between a chancel arch and a barrel vault and commented upon the heraldry: 'the general details seem to be correct, save Scotland's fleur de-lis and the chain of the unicorn which does not descend between the fore legs'.[55]

It is curious that Professor Fawcett makes no mention of a small unfinished Victorian Royal coat of arms painted in oil, which was presented to the church by Canon Rauceby Cole and hung over the west door, inside the church, to commemorate the coronation of George V in 1911.[56] It was in place in the late 1920s, and had

[51] *T. B. & G. A. S.*, LV, (1933), pp. 105–134.

[52] *Ibid.*, p.106.

[53] In possession of the author, p. 133.

[54] J. Foster, *Alumni Oxonienses 1715–1886*, III, (1888), p. 927, the Revd. William Caldwell Masters, born 1844, B.A. Magdalen College, Oxford, 1865; M.A. 1869; vicar of Long Marston, Hertfordshire 1871–1885, and rector of Stanton Fitzwarren from 1885.

[55] *T. B. & G. A. S.*, LVIII, (1936), p. 60.

[56] *Ibid.*, pp.131, 159.

been removed before Fawcett's visit *c.* 1933. It had certainly disappeared from the church before 1970.[57]

MICHAEL AND WILLIAM EDKINS

Canon Cole claims that the small unfinished Victorian Royal coat of arms painted in oil in Christ Church with St. Ewen was executed by Michael Edkins. A Michael Edkins was a painter of coaches, scenery, porcelain and glassware. He painted the Theatre Royal in the 1760s and the Merchants' Hall in 1775, more than sixty years before this coat of arms was executed.[58] In *Mathews's Bristol Directory*, (1793–4), a Michael Edkins, painter, is listed at 37 Bridge Street.[59]

This Michael Edkins was the father of William Edkins who is described in 1817 as living in Bridge Street and having painted the banner of the Deputy Provincial Grand Master of the Freemasons' of Bristol.[60] In 1820 he painted, at a cost of £5, the Royal arms, crest, supporters and mottos on a hatchment in St. Werburgh's in memory of the recently deceased George III.[61] He worked on the Council House between 1823 and 1825[62] and his firm is called in the directories of the 1830s and 1840s 'William Edkins and Son, city painters, tillers, plasterers &c.' and listed with an address in Charlotte Street, Queen Square. The business was still operating in the 1880s.[63] A file held in the Bristol City Museum and Art Gallery viewed by kind permission of Mrs. Sheena Stoddard, the keeper of Fine Art, notes that the Fry collection of trade cards in the Blaise Castle Museum contains a business card for William Edkins in which he is called: 'successor to his late father, Michael Edkins, coach, sign and house painter,

---

[57] Information from Mr. R. C. Metcalfe, church warden of Christ Church with St. Ewen.

[58] W. Ison, *op. cit.*, pp. 125, 127, 136. This Michael Edkins was thought to be the artist of the small landscape in the dining room of Royal Fort House.

[59] *Mathews's Bristol Directory*, (1793–4), p. 31. B.R.O., Will of Michael Edkins, painter, died July 1811, dated 24 June 1811, proved 19 November 1811, left under £100. He lived with his son William, to whom he left his whole estate. His sons William and Michael were baptised at St. Mary Redcliffe on 25 May 1764 and 10 August 1768 respectively. Michael Edkins senior married Elizabeth James at St. Augustine the Less on 28 April 1755.

[60] A. C. Powell and Littleton, *op. cit.*, p. 174. He was a negligent and unsatisfactory master of The Moira Lodge of Honour in 1830, *ibid.*, p. 565; S. S. Herron, *An Essay on the History of the Moira Lodge of Honour No. 326 (Province of Bristol) 1809 to 2009*, (Bristol, 2009), pp. 19, 67.

[61] B.R.O., P/StW/ChW/3 (d). He was then listed as a painter at 37 Bridge Street, his father's address in 1793–1794.

[62] A banner painted by William Edkins was hung from the balloon used by James Sadler (1753–1828), the first English aeronaut, in his ascent from Bristol in 1810, M. D. Crane, 'Sadler's Balloon Ascent from Bristol in 1810', *Avon Past*, No. 3, Autumn 1980, pp. 28–32; J. Penny, *'Up, up and Away! An account of ballooning in and around Bristol and Bath 1784 to 1999'*, Bristol Historical Association, 97, (Bristol, 1999), p. 11. As a child I remember a fragment of this balloon, which I believe was made of silk, and was then in the possession of Mrs. Lilian Mary Sadler (1896–1979), the widow of Roy Lowton Sadler of Willaston, Wirral.

[63] J. Winstone, *Bristol Trade Cards: Remnants of Prolific Commerce*, (Bristol, 1993), p. 63, carries a trade card for the firm from the 1880s and states that Edkins and Sons, builders and house decorators, were specialists in paper hanging.

glass enameller, hatchments, escutcheons, pictures cleaned and lined'.[64] In 1841 he was responsible for the execution of the coat of arms of Thomas Tyndall III displayed on his funerary hatchment within Christ Church with St. Ewen. The 1837 edition of *Mathews's Bristol Directory* lists a Michael Edkins, painter, at 10, Charles Street, who may well have been William's brother.[65]

The frame for the coat of arms of George III which was erected in St. Werburgh in May 1820 was made by Joseph Panting, carpenter, builder and undertaker of Charles Street, who charged £2. 3s .od for the frame and 'staining' (query, varnishing?) the hatchment painted by William Edkins and it is probable that he was employed conjointly with the Edkins family in this line of work.[66]

THE BRUNSWICK ARMS

As a result of one of the articles of the Treaty of Paris, and in anticipation of the union of Great Britain with Ireland, on 1 January 1801 George III officially ceased to be styled King of France and formally renounced the title borne by all of his predecessors since it was adopted by Edward III (1327–1377).[67] The French *fleurs-de-lis* were removed from the arms of England by Royal proclamation. From 1801 until 1837 the Royal arms was re-marshalled thus: quarterly, 1 and 4 England; 2 Scotland and 3 Ireland, and overall an 'inescutcheon of pretence' with the arms of Hanover: 'Per pale and per chevron: 1, gules, two lions passant guardant, in pale or, for Brunswick; 2, or, semee of hearts, a lion rampant azure, for Lunenburgh; 3, gules a horse courant argent, for Westphalia; and overall and inescutcheon gules, charged with the golden crown of Charlemagne'. Between 1801 and 1816 George III's arms were ensigned with the electoral bonnet of Hanover, as depicted on the arms in Christ Church with St. Ewen, which in the latter year was replaced by a royal crown, upon Hanover being raised to the status of a kingdom.[68] These arms were borne by George III between 1816 and 1820, George IV from 1820 to 1830 and William IV from 1830 to 1837.

[64] Information kindly supplied by Mrs. Sheena Stoddard, keeper of Fine Art at Bristol City Museum and Art Gallery.

[65] *Mathews's Bristol Directory*, (1837), p. 85. In the 1839 edition, p. 88 he is listed at 10 Charles Street and 12 Dighton Street and in the 1840 edition, p. 94 he is listed at 10 Charles Street and 8 Duke Street. An M. A. Edkins is listed at the Duke Street address from 1841 until the 1847 edition, but does not appear in 1848. William Edkins had two sons called Michael, one who died in 1817 as an infant, the other who was baptized at St. Mary le Port on 19 March 1820. I am indebted to Mr. Matthew Cole for this information,

[66] B.R.O., P/StW/ChW/3 (d). Information kindly supplied by Mrs. Sheena Stoddard, keeper of Fine Art at Bristol City Museum and Art Gallery.

[67] Louis XIV had such an exalted view of kingship that he allowed his cousin James II , who lived in exile in France between 1688 and his death in 1701, to touch for the king's evil in his capacity as *de jure* King of France, based on the claims of Edward III.

[68] S. T. Aveling, *op. cit.*, pp.24, 28; F. J. Grant (ed.), *The Manual of Heraldry*, (Edinburgh, 1924), pp. 135–136; J. P. Brooke-Little (ed.), *op. cit.*, pp. 215–216; T. Woodcock and J. M. Robinson, *op. cit.*, pp. 189–191.

THE RESTORATION OF THE FUNERARY HATCHMENTS AND THE ROYAL COAT OF ARMS IN CHRIST CHURCH WITH ST. EWEN, BRISTOL

Thomas Tyndall I, 1794
Size: 1525mm x 1525mm

Description:
Oil on coarse canvas, pine strainer with mortise and tenon corner joints. The frame is a flat wood section, 190mm wide and 45mm deep. The section is painted matt black and has a gold moulded inner rebate 15mm wide.

Condition:
The canvas is impregnated both front and back with red lead oil paint. This was a standard procedure to limit the free absorption of moisture into the fabric support.

The location of this Hatchment on the west wall of the church meant it suffered the full force of the adjacent fire (cf. introduction). The surface is totally scorched and blistered. The intensity of the heat has severely damaged and denatured the original oil paint and what remains of the surface is friable and vulnerable.

There are areas of loss distributed throughout the surface which vary in severity. Most of these are seen where the surface has blistered, contracted and fallen away.

The larger blisters are noted in the upper section of the Hatchment where the heat

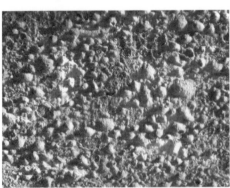

was the most intense; however, in the lower part, where the application of paint was thinner, the surface has been reduced to loose powder.

The Hatchment is so blackened that it is almost impossible to ascertain the existing condition of the original paint layer and what percentage of it remains intact. The actual losses are obvious but the paint layer could well have been affected by the extreme heat and in consequence, its appearance diminished.

Treatment:
The fire damaged paint layer is to be softened and re-affixed to the ground and canvas.

Once the surface has been fully secured, the hatchment is to be cleaned of all material foreign to the original.

The deficiencies in the paint and ground layers are to be made good with the use of a gesso compound stopping.

The damages will be re-touched initially in watercolour followed by dry pigment in a medium of Acryloid B 72.

On completion of treatment, a layer of varnish is to be finally applied.

Thomas Tyndall II 1804
Size: 1575mm x 1575mm

Description:
The hatchment is oil on coarse canvas stretched over a pine strainer with centre cross bars, the width of the strainer bars is 83mm and the depth 15mm. The frame is a flat wood section 90mm wide, 30mm deep and has a gold moulded inner rebate 20mm in width

Condition:
It would seem that this Hatchment has been inexpertly cleaned and roughly repaired at some time in the past. The lower section has several old areas of damage as noted:

(i) a hole, 50mm x 45mm, at the lower tip of the shield and further smaller holes in this area with total loss of support, ground and paint layers. These areas of damage have been roughly patched with a cotton fabric adhered with white lead and subsequently the losses have been filled with a compound of this paint. The damages and surrounding area have been crudely re-painted

(ii) in the Shield the upper left sheaf of wheat and the background is re-painted

(iii) in the Shield details of the shadows in the gilded keys are worn

The original paint layer appears abraded. Many of the finer details of this work have been removed in over-cleaning and have then been inexpertly re-painted. This is particularly noticeable in the gilded areas where thin stains have been used to produce the more decorative details.

The surface film is heavily oxidised with accumulations of dirt and discoloured varnish trapped in the interstices of the canvas weave.

Treatment:
The Hatchment is to be cleaned of the oxidised surface film, together with the most disturbing of the over-paint.

The crude patches and the adhesive is to be removed from the back of the canvas and new canvas inserts are to be fitted.

A gesso filler is to be used to replace the ground, and the stoppings are to be toned with watercolour to match the priming.

The painting is to be re-touched using a dry pigment in an acryloid medium.

On completion of the above treatment a suitable varnish will be finally applied.

Marianne Tyndall 1805
Size: 1525mm x 1525mm

Description:
Oil on coarse canvas stretched over a pine strainer with a centre cross bar; width of strainer bars 83mm x 15mm in depth. The frame is a flat wood section painted matt black measuring 90mm wide and 30mm deep with gold moulded inner rebate 20mm wide.

Condition:
Verso: The back of the canvas has been painted with a black paint. There are two old patches in the right corner.

Recto: The painting has a red lead priming. Water damage has weakened the lower right edge and this has rotted and completely broken away from the auxiliary support. The extent of the missing paint and ground layers in this area is measured as an average depth of 50mm from the outer edge. Nothing remains of the original in this area.

The surface of the work is blackened and desiccated. It would seem that the severity of the heat of the fire has caused the surface film to move and contract, forming a hardened compacted crust.

Two punctures are seen through the canvas in the left corner with loss of both ground and paint layers; these correspond to the patches seen on the back of the canvas. Several other small areas of damage are noted, these are distributed throughout the painting.

Movement of the canvas against the inner edges of the strainer bars has left linear impressions on the front of the work around all four sides.

Treatment:
The rotted edge is to be 'strip lined' in order to re-attach the weakened original canvas to the auxiliary support. A length of linen fabric is to be attached to the original canvas using Parafilm 'M' as an adhesive. The reinforced edge is to be re-tensioned over the strainer.

The total loss of the ground and paint layer in this area are to be replaced with a gesso layer followed by a rabbit skin and calcium carbonate compound. This filling is to be toned with watercolour to match the red lead priming.

The paint layer is to be cleaned.

The puncture holes in the left corner are to be treated locally and the losses are to be filled.

The damages will be re-touched with watercolour followed by dry pigment in an acryloid B 72 medium.

A suitable varnish of Ketone N resin with a percentage of bleached beeswax is to be finally applied.

Thomas Tyndall III 1841
Size: 1650mm x 1650mm
This Hatchment is signed lower left edge W Edkins & Son. Pinxt[69]

Description:
Oil on coarse canvas tensioned over a pine stretcher. The stretcher has staggered, each corner contains one wedge.

The width of stretcher bar is 90mm, the depth of the stretcher bar is 25mm. The frame is of a flat wooden section painted matt black 200mm wide x 50mm deep with a gold moulded inner rebate 25mm wide.

Condition:
Unlike the previous three hatchments this later one, dated 1841, shows no sign of having a red lead priming.

Verso: Two old patches are seen on the back of the canvas adhered with white lead. The lower left edge is water stained.

Recto: The lower right edge, which corresponds to the water stained *verso*, is damaged. The canvas has weakened and become friable and there is loss of both ground and paint layers along the full length of this edge.

---

[69] William Edkins and Son are listed as 'city painters, tillers and plasterers' in *Mathews's Bristol Directory & Almanac* for 1829, 1835 and 1845.

There is damage in the lower left quarter of the shield which measures 60mm x 25mm. There are several small puncture holes. These are distributed throughout the painted surface.

The surface film is heavily oxidised orange/brown with dirt and discoloured varnish seen lodged in the interstices of the canvas weave and along the strokes of the impasto brushwork.

Treatment:
The Hatchment will be cleaned of all material foreign to the original.

The losses will be made good with the use of a gesso filler.

Initial re-touching will be executed in watercolour.

Final re-touchings are to be carried out with dry pigment in an acryloid B 72 medium.

A suitable varnish is to be finally applied.

Treatment general to all the Hatchments:
The Hatchments were originally held in their frames with hand cut screws through the frame, strainer and canvas. The extraction of these screws in order to remove the canvas and support from the frame has left 10mm diameter holes both front and back of the work.

- the screw holes will be filled in the back of the wooden auxiliary supports, (the holes through the canvas will be hidden by the frame rebate)
- the localised treatment of boring insects is to guard against further infestation
- the frames are to be cleaned and then minor repairs are to be carried out

Royal Coat of Arms
Size: sight edge 1195mm x 1400mm, framed 1350mm x 1600mm

The shape of the Royal Arms is noted with a convex upper edge and a concave lower edge *

* Mention is made in the introduction that these Royal Arms were made to fit above a 5´ x 5´ arch

Description:

Verso: Six horizontal pine planks of varying widths, the top and bottom segments cut to form; the upper segment convex and the lower concave. There are two vertical struts which have been dovetailed into the horizontal planks, these are noted from the inner edge of the frame left and right o/c 335mm. The struts are dovetailed into the horizontal planks which make up the support. The back of the painting and frame have been treated with a matt black paint which has decayed.

Frame: The frame section is 80mm in width and 70mm in depth. It is an intricate cut moulding of the period, the gold inner rebate is an integral part of the moulding. The frame has a black gloss painted finish with the inner rebate painted gold. The corners of the frame are strengthened with metal straps varying slightly in length but these are, on average, 300 mm in length. The straps are fastened with hand cut screws.

Condition:

Recto: Apart from small indentations, scratches and abrasions the Coat of Arms is generally in relatively good condition. However, there are two visually disturbing areas of damage:

(i) in the left side, an area of the upper curve of the lion's tail, a deep vertical gouge measuring 150mm x 25mm This damage is seen 75mm from the left side

(ii) an area of wear extending 140mm x 100mm in the lower edge of the belt surrounding the shield through the lettering of 'PENSE'. The letter 'N' and the letter 'S' have been completely worn away

There is evidence of active borer infestation along the upper edge of the panel.

Treatment:

The insect borer is to be treated in order to prevent continuing infestation

The painting will be cleaned of all material foreign to the original

The most disturbing of the losses will be filled

Re-touchings will be carried out in watercolour followed by dry pigment in a medium of Acryloid B 72

A varnish of Ketone N with a percentage of bleached beeswax is will be finally applied

Frame: The fixing holes and damages marking the outer edges of the frame will be filled and re-touched before the frame is polished with a wax polish

XV

Bristol and the Foundation of its Madrigal Society

JAMES HOBSON, B.A., P.G.DIP., (LAW)

THE BRISTOL Madrigal Society is often to be found proudly cited in articles from the mid-nineteenth century onwards when discussing music-making in the city, and rightly so: its foundation in 1837 marks it as one of the earliest societies established outside London with the specific aim of madrigal singing.

The inspiration for a madrigal society was born not only of a series of lectures that were delivered in the city in 1837, and which sparked excitement and enthusiasm for renaissance madrigals, but also because of a paucity of music-making there, where in the thirty years prior to the B.M.S.'s foundation there was a musical *lacuna* which was waiting to be filled.

Bristol had been in a sort of musical recession in the early years of the nineteenth century. A critic of the city, who chose wisely to remain anonymous, complained in the *Monthly Magazine* of 1799:

> Perhaps there is no place in England where public and social amusements are so little attended to as here. From this circumstance, the inhabitants have been stigmatized with a want of taste, and described as the sordid devotees of Pluto's. [1]

London critics have traditionally been harsh in their judgement of the provinces, but even Bristol newspapers of the early 1800s supported the view that there was very little concert life in the city. Fashionable society no longer appeared content to attend the recitals and concerts of chamber music which had been the mainstay of both domestic and public life in the eighteenth century.

The Hotwells Pleasure Gardens, a popular venue for musical entertainments in the eighteenth century, had fallen into decline, partly due to the awkward access to Hotwells from the city and from the newly-desirable Clifton, and as a result, the Gardens had closed by the beginning of the nineteenth century. However, the Clifton Assembly Room and Hotel in the Mall opened in 1811, and it replaced a somewhat less popular assembly room that had been attached to the Gloucester Hotel near Dowry Square, in Hotwells, and which was *below* Clifton, in every sense of the word. The new Assembly Room and Hotel was spacious and elegant. It offered its patrons 'a noble reception saloon and tea room, with convenient lobbies, a billiard room, etc.' and 'every accommodation for both families and individuals, even to sets of apartments/drawing rooms, a coffee room, a shop for pastry and confectionery, with an adjoining room for soups, fruits and ices; hot, cold and vapour baths'. [2]

---

[1] *The Monthly Magazine; or, British Register;* (1799), Part I.
[2] *Clifton at Play* (November, 2003). Accessed 10 September 2008 http://www. cliftononline.net/f_people_preview2.asp

If dancing was to overtake the waning popularity of music-making and concert attendance, then Bristol society showed its preference with its feet. Towards the end of 1811, the old Assembly Rooms in Prince Street—originally built in 1754—underwent considerable internal alteration and were re-opened the following year under the name of the Regency Theatre. However, the first season of concerts was a failure with poor attendance and by 1813, 'it was noticed in the newspapers that the theatre had sunk to giving entertainments on the musical glasses'.[3]

Others tried and failed: subscription concerts had once attracted keen audiences, but by the early nineteenth century their popularity had all-but gone. Andrew Ashe, a celebrated Irish flute player, had become director of the Bath Subscription Concerts in 1810. With successes in Bath behind him, he organized a series of concerts at the Assembly Rooms in Prince Street in the winter of 1820–1821. However, he faced competition from another series organised by Mr. Greethead in Bath that same season. As a result, Ashe's own concert series suffered. Early the next year, Ashe announced another series of subscription concerts, but there were complaints about the choice of programme, and the series was cancelled due to insufficient patronage. Disappointed, Ashe decided to depart for Dublin, but not before he gave one final concert at the Theatre Royal on the 7 February 1822. The concert received a very generous notice in *Felix Farley's Bristol Journal*, but the correspondent also wrote:

> Mr. Ashe, having bid us adieu we must heartily wish him every success in his future progress through life, and sincerely hope Thursday's profits may prove some slight remuneration for his losses in this city. But are we never again to be delighted with sweet sounds? Is Bristol really to be without her entertainments? We trust not; if not for the pleasure, for the honour of our city.[4]

The correspondent went on to consider how Bristol might best create a regular series of successful subscription concerts by means of a group of financiers rather than an individual. However, it wasn't for another ten years, in 1832, until the great London impresario and musical director, Sir George Smart, came to Bristol and organized at the Theatre Royal, the longed-for subscription concerts.

Undoubtedly, in the 1820s and early 1830s, Bristol was a less attractive place to live than it had been before. The city's population was rapidly increasing, but its means of accommodating it was not. Between 1801 and 1830, Bristol's population doubled. This increase of population was slightly below the national average—from 61,000 in 1801, to 104,000 by 1832—but it still reflected a staggering rise of 42%.[5]

Questions arose as to how Bristol would cope with this explosion; how and where the city would house its new inhabitants; what provision would be made for the poor. Unfortunately, Bristol didn't really have any answers. Little new building took place in the first few decades of the nineteenth century, except in Clifton, where the new merchants' houses were built away from the city centre; thus the increased population of the city was squashed into and around the old mediaeval city.

The increasing population was caused, in part, by the fact that by 1817, two years after the end of the Napoleonic wars, Britain had demobilized 300,000 soldiers and

---

[3] J. Latimer, *The Annals of Bristol in the Nineteenth Century* (Bristol, 1887), p. 48.

[4] *Felix Farley's Bristol Journal*, 10 February 1822.

[5] Figures sourced from national censuses. I am very grateful to Dr. Alan Jocelyn at U.W.E. for this information.

sailors, all without any pension or gratuity for their services, whilst the post-war government struggled with an enormous national debt of £861,000,000. By 1830, the result of this and a succession of poor harvests, led to a national state of economic distress, resulting in the worst depression of the nineteenth century.

The depression was particularly widespread in the South and West of England and Bristol had a dense and pauperized population who lived in and around the city centre. To make matters worse, the city centre's floating harbour, created in 1809, had become one huge cesspool. Despite being a great feat of engineering, it had caused the natural removal of sewerage by the river flow virtually to cease, and at the height of a cholera epidemic in 1832, 600 people died.

There can be little doubt that such squalor and poverty did not enhance Bristol's reputation as a place of entertainment, and nor was there any great musical progress. It seems likely to imagine that as their city began to burst at the seams all around them, the comfortable classes initially shut their eyes to the problems in the hope that they might not be affected, and chose to carry on as before.

However, the mid-1830s saw both a cultural and financial revival. Concerts began to be advertised more regularly in the newspapers: churches in Clifton held benefit concerts; balls were held weekly at the Assembly Rooms; the Theatre Royal had a constant stream of visiting acts and travelling theatre troupes; and in 1835 the first season of the Bristol and Clifton Philharmonic Society was announced.[6]

It must be remembered that during the same period when professional musicians had been suffering, organised amateur music-making reflected similar difficulties, and none more so than in the exclusive male bastion of the Bristol Catch Club.

Glee and catch clubs had played a small but significant role in the amateur musical life of towns and cities across Britain from the second half of the eighteenth century onwards, and membership of nearly all of them was exclusively male. The often-vulgar catch (whose vulgarity was deemed, by eighteenth century taste, as unsuitable for the ears of ladies) had its roots firmly in the seventeenth century,[7] but from it developed the more poetic glee. The two forms had certainly found a happy union by the late eighteenth century when many publications included both catches and glees in a single volume, the 'indelicate' catches being dropped, or sometimes simply modified, in order not to offend genteel sensibilities.[8]

Most of what is known about the Bristol Catch Club comes from notes penned into the opening pages of the first volume of a set of five that contain the first twenty 'collections' of *Warren's Catches*.[9] Four of the volumes (one having been unaccountably

---

[6] *F.F.B.J.*, 23 December 1835.

[7] For an excellent account of the origins of catching in England, read the first chapter of B. Robins, *Catch and Glee Culture in Eighteenth-Century England*, (Woodbridge, 2006).

[8] There are many editions, printed from *c.* 1770 onwards, of collected works, and volumes by single composers such as Samuel Webbe the elder's, *The Ladies Catch-Book, being a collection of Catches, Canons and Glees, the words of which will not offend the nicest delicacy*, (*c.* 1775).

[9] *Warren's Catches* were published from 1765 onwards by Thomas Warren (*c.* 1730–1794), a member of, and scribe to, the Catch Club, founded in London in 1761. The various supplements or 'collections', published from 1765 onwards were bound together in single volumes and they were eventually published under the title of *A Collection of Vocal Harmony consisting of Catches, Canons and Glees, to which are added several Motetts and Madrigals composed by the Best Masters. Selected by Thomas Warren*, (*c.* 1775).

lost) are now in Bristol Central Library.[10] They belonged first to the Bristol Catch Club, from its institution in 1774, and then afterwards to a member of the Club, the eminent Bristol surgeon and freemason, Richard Smith, junior (1772–1843).[11] The volumes each contain many partsongs, glees, catches, and a number of English madrigals from the late-sixteenth to the early-seventeenth centuries.

In his notes, Smith tells us that his father—also Richard Smith, and who was also a surgeon at the Bristol Infirmary—joined the Bristol Catch Club in 1785. Further, he writes that other members included four clerics; two attorneys-at-law; a merchant; a silk mercer; Colonel Andrewes of the Somerset Militia; the organist, director, composer and publisher Robert Broderip[12]; and the cathedral organist, Rice Wasbrough.

When Richard Smith junior joined the club in 1796, several of his father's contemporaries were still members, and they were joined by other members of the Wasbrough family and also a customs officer; James Hillhouse, Esq., a shipbuilder; a doctor; an attorney-at-law; Dunbar—'a private gentleman' and Applewaite—'a West Indian'.[13] These men, who demonstrate a diversity of professions, were all joined together in one harmony, which embodies a chief point that the social, and potential business opportunities afforded by these clubs and societies were as important as their musical purpose. The historian of the catch and its clubs, Brian Robins, quotes from the preface to John Arnold's collection of part songs, catches, canons and glees, *The Essex Harmony*, of 1769, making the point that the cultivation of singing in the provinces would serve a social purpose:

> It would not only prevent the many Accidents, Mischiefs, and other bad consequences, generally attending those Diversions of Heroism, Cudgeling, Football Playin[g] &c. but would be a means of encouraging the practice of one of the greatest of Sciences. What can be more agreeable or commendable for Country Choirs, than to meet […] and thereby entertain themselves and Friends, with such harmonious and inoffensive Mirth; which may not only introduce Peace and Tranquility in a Neighbourhood, but the Practiceing of Part-Songs and Catches,

[10] Bristol Central Library, shelfmark bl 21952.

[11] Two rather macabre anecdotes about Richard Smith junior appear in a nineteenth century publication: 'In 1802, two women were executed at St Michael's Hill gallows for infanticide. The bodies, according to the judge's sentence, were taken for dissection to the Infirmary […] the brain of one of the two women was dissected and lectured upon by Mr. Richard Smith'. The authority for this story is a manuscript note by Mr. Smith himself, who appears to have revelled in operations upon malefactors'. And even more shocking: 'In April, 1821, a man named John Horwood was hanged at the usual place, for the murder of a girl, and his body also fell into Mr. Smith's hands'. The following tradesman's account is the first manuscript contained in the book in the Infirmary library: 'Bristol, June, 1828. Richard Smith, Esq. Dr, to H. H. Essex. To binding, in the skin of John Horwood, a variety of papers, etc., relating to him, the same being lettered on each side of the book, 'Cutis vera Johannis Horwood' £1.10s,' J. Latimer, *op. cit.*, pp. 17–18. This volume is now in the B.R.O., 35893/36/v.

[12] Robert Broderip (*c.* 1758–1808) was probably a brother of Francis Fane Broderip of the London publishing houses, Longman & Broderip and Broderip & Wilkinson. He was appointed organist of the Mayor's Chapel in Bristol in 1780. In 1795, Robert Broderip published and dedicated a collection of duets, glees and catches to 'Members of the Bristol Catch Club and Cecilian Society'.

[13] G. Hooper, 'A Survey of Music in Bristol with Special Reference to the Eighteenth Century', (M.A. thesis, University of Bristol, 1963), pp. 200–205.

which will be a means of greatly improving several Country Choirs in their Knowledge of Musick. [14]

The Bristol Catch Club survived into the early nineteenth century.[15] In 1804 Robert Broderip issued a second *Collection of Duets, Rotas, Canons, Catches and Glees*, dedicated to 'Members of the Catch Club and the Cecilian and Amphion Societies'. Little is known about these latter two societies. In fact, the identity of the Amphion Society remains unknown, but Hooper notes that 'on Friday 7 December 1798 the Gentlemen members of the Cecilian Society gave a Grand Concert in aid of the Public Subscription for the benefit of the Widows and Orphans of those Brave Men who had fallen in the Glorious Battle of the Nile'.[16] It might be reasonable to suppose, therefore, that if the *gentlemen* members of the Cecilian Society were singled out, then there might also have been *lady* members. Many of the compositions in Broderip's *Collection of Duets, etc.* have a distinct soprano line, which also points in the direction of possible intended female participation, especially if Broderip hoped to make good the sales of his music in Bristol.[17] How, or when, the Bristol Catch Club came to an end is not recorded, but no newspaper references to it appear after 1810.

According to Smith's account, there was a subsequent twenty-two year break, consistent with the decrease in other musical activity in Bristol. He then goes on to describe the founding of the St. Austin's Glee Society, which met at his home, and he records the first and subsequent members of the Society:

> The St. Austin's Glee Society began at my house, 38 Park Street on the 22nd of Sept. 1832. Present, Austin Phillips played the piano, Robert Nokes Williams, Joseph Wilcox of the Cathedral, Edward Gee, surgeon. In October, George Edwards at the Music Warehouse, Upper Arcade. William Lye Seagram joined, now a surgeon at Warminster. William Turner, a visitor. 10th November, Alfred Bleeck, whom God preserve, joined. December, William Goldyer, Hotwells, joined. May 1833, Charles Turner was engaged. Stephen Pratton, a visitor. James England joined in January 1833. George Turner, visitor. Thomas Browne, Schoolmaster at Brislington. Thomas Muller Evans, attorney, joined. Charles J. Fripp, Architect, joined. The last meeting was 13th of March 1834, the 50th time, when to be rid of a troublesome member the Society was dissolved—but it soon rose again from its ashes and the new Club was therefore called

---

[14] B. Robins, *op. cit.*, p. 89.

[15] The Bristol Catch Club also seems to have been 'available' for other events. Reference to them appears in *Bonner and Middleton's Bristol Journal* of 3 June 1786 for an evening of entertainment advertised at the Old Trout Tavern in Cherry Lane, off Stokes Croft when 'Comus' Court' would be held on 6 June. It stated that 'the Gentlemen of the original Catch-Club, Castle Ditch, have generously offered their kind Assistance for that Night only'. In 1795, they appeared at the Theatre Royal in King Street, giving a programme of music between a performance of *King Lear* and a farce called *The Positive Man*. A Ladies' Night concert was given on 29 March 1810. G. Hooper, *op. cit.*, p. 206.

[16] Infuriatingly, Hooper doesn't disclose his sources for these quotations. G. Hooper, *op. cit.*, p. 206.

[17] David Johnson points out, however, in his article 'The 18th-Century Glee', *The Musical Times*, 120, (March 1979), that composers very often deliberately left vocal lines in scores without specifying if they were intended for a soprano or tenor voice, for example, in an attempt to increase sales.

The Phoenix Glee Society.

The first meeting was at my house the 20 March 1834—it was formed by Richard Smith, Alfred Bleeck, J. Wilcox, G. Edwards, James England, W. L. Seagram. Master William Pratten was made honorary member, also C. J. Fripp. P. H. S. Marsh joined—a teacher of music, William Strong, Book Seller. 1835 Stephen Pratten—teacher of music joined. The last meeting was the 19th of July 1838— when will the next be?

R.S. 25th December 1842.

It is evident that the Glee Society continued to sing from *Warren's Catches*, as the note of presentation of the volumes from Richard Smith to 'fellow-surgeon' Alfred Bleeck—on Bleeck's birthday, 25 December 1842—charges Bleeck that he may have them on condition that he sing certain of the catches nominated in the volumes, and to drink to the memory of his old friend, Richard Smith. Smith went on to stipulate 'that the said worthy camarado, Alfred Bleeck, Esqr, shall not part with them, so long as he is able to bear a bob in a catch, glee or madrigal'.

Several of the men in Smith's Phoenix Glee Society were among either the founding twenty-two members, or soon joined, the Bristol Madrigal Society after Edward Taylor, the journalist-musicologist, came to Bristol in January 1837.

Felix Farley's Bristol Journal of Saturday 31 December 1836, announced Taylor's imminent arrival:

Bristol Institution. On Thursday, January 5th, 1837, at Two o'clock, Mr EDWARD TAYLOR, of London, will commence at the Bristol Institution, Park-street, a course of four Lectures on ENGLISH VOCAL HARMONY, with numerous Illustrations.

The Bristol Institution for the Advancement of Science, Literature and the Arts was founded in 1822, and simultaneously, under its wing, so was the Bristol Literary and Philosophical Society, by a group of men, many of them clergymen. We know that the Institution and Society were very broad in their combined interests, hosting an annual art exhibition, encouraging scientific research, and founding a museum—in whose collection of fossils Charles Darwin took an interest in the 1850s[18]—and providing historical artefacts for researchers of antiquity.[19] Taking into consideration the advertisements for forthcoming lectures and talks, to be found most particularly in the *Bristol Mercury* and *Felix Farley's Bristol Journal*, the Bristol Institution was the most likely, if not the only, place in Bristol where Taylor's lectures would be given.[20]

[18] Charles Darwin corresponded with the curator of the museum of the Bristol Institution, Samuel Stutchbury (1798–1859). The *O.D.N.B.* says 'In 1831 Stutchbury became curator at the Bristol Institution, where he published significant papers on conchology and palaeontology and made the museum one of the best in Europe' D. F. Branagan, 'Stutchbury, Samuel (1798–1859)', *Oxford Dictionary of National Biography*, (Oxford, 2004).

[19] 'Many sculptures extant in public and private collections, especially those splendid casts from the island of Egina, now in the Bristol Philosophical and Literary Institution, represent several archers drawing the bowstring'. George Agar Hansard, *The Book of Archery*, (1841) p. 428.

[20] Advertisements for public lectures in Bristol to be found in either of these newspapers clearly signal the Bristol Institution as the prime venue.

Felix Farley's Bristol Journal went on to clarify just what the attendees might expect:

In the approaching course, (to commence next Thursday) Mr. Edward Taylor will give a history of madrigal and glee singing. The subject has never been treated connectedly by any of our musical historians, and there is no work from which the matter of the lectures can be derived. The illustrations extend, in an almost unbroken series, from the middle of the sixteenth century to the present time; and the performance of these enables the lecturer to point out the varied graces, or it may be the defects, of the respective compositions. Besides several of our chief provincial towns, the course has been given in five of the metropolitan Institutions, and always to crowded audiences. The subject, in Mr. Taylor's manner of treating it, has uniformly proved attractive and entertaining, and when the nature of the course is fully known among us, there is no room to doubt but that it will be highly popular here as it has been on all other places, through its novelty and its sources of interest & information.[21]

Taylor's lectures had enjoyed particular success in London because they reflected a growing interest in the study and revival of old music.[22] By the 1830s, interest had also been revived in the music of the Tudor composer, Thomas Tallis.[23] The Devonian baronet and president of the Madrigal Society, Sir John Leman Rogers (1780–1847), had succeeded in organising an annual service, devoted to the music of Tallis at Westminster Abbey and on 21 January 1836, Rogers delivered a lecture, followed by a performance of Tallis's forty-part motet, *Spem in alium*,[24] and so undoubtedly, Taylor's lectures were warmly received in this field of growing interest.

Taylor had become music critic of the *Spectator* magazine in 1829, only a year after its re-revival in 1828. Although he was a late-comer to music as a profession,[25] Taylor soon established himself as a musician worthy of note. He was appointed Gresham

---

[21] *F.F.B.J.*, 31 December 1836.

[22] For example, Vincent Novello's *Fitzwilliam Music* had first appeared early in 1826. It was a collection of pieces largely by renaissance Italian composers, taken from the Fitzwilliam collection of manuscripts at the University of Cambridge, and it had been very well received. In the same year, Samuel Wesley attempted to publish a collection of pieces by William Byrd, drawn also from the same collection. The project was only thwarted by the difficulty of collaboration with the University Council, whose apparent unwillingness to grant a licence to Wesley had all-but stalled the proceedings, and yet there had been strong support for the publication amongst potential subscribers. See Phillip Olleson and Fiona M. Palmer's article: 'Publishing Music from the Fitzwilliam Museum, Cambridge; the work of Vincent Novello and Samuel Wesley in the 1820s', *Journal of the Royal Musical Association*, 130.1, (2005), pp. 38–73.

[23] For further reading, see S. Cole's excellent *Thomas Tallis and his Music in Victorian England*, (Woodbridge, 2008).

[24] Husk, William H, 'Sir John Leman Rogers, Bart.', *Grove's Dictionary of Music and Musicians*, (1879–1890). In 1836 the motet was sung to the words 'Sing and Glorify'.

[25] Taylor was born in Norwich and was an ironmonger and then a civil engineer until 1825 when the business which he ran with his brothers failed and he turned to singing and lecturing in 1827. Successes as a performer and as a conductor at that time cemented his career. Leanne Langley. 'Taylor, Edward'. *Grove Music Online* (Accessed 10 October, 2008).

professor of music in 1837.[26] His lecture tour of English Vocal Harmony had begun in 1832 at the London Institute, and it was then received with great popularity as he went about the country delivering it to learned societies of the land.[27] Writing about Taylor's later lectures after his appointment as Gresham professor of music, William Henry Husk, in the first edition of Grove's *Dictionary of Music and Musicians* wrote:

> They were admirably adapted to the understanding of a general audience; they were historical and critical, excellently written, eloquently read, and illustrated by well-chosen extracts from the works described, efficiently performed.[28]

It does not seem unreasonable to believe that this description would also serve for the lectures delivered at Bristol on the 5, 9, 12 and 16 January 1837. According to Herbert Byard in his history of the Bristol Madrigal Society,[29] each lecture was given in the afternoon of the appointed date and repeated in the evening of the following day (See Fig. 1).

In his biography of Robert Lucas Pearsall,[30] Edgar Hunt wrote of Taylor's lectures and the foundation of the B.M.S.:

> Of the audience [at Taylor's lectures] some twenty-two [...] were so attracted by the beauty and superiority of the old madrigals which had been performed as illustrations, that they resolved to combine for the study and practice of this special branch of musical composition, hitherto unexplored as far as Bristol was concerned.[31]

That some sort of 'magical' effect had enchanted the listeners is without doubt, but that they were 'hitherto unexplored as far as Bristol was concerned' is probably an exaggeration. The madrigals included in *Warren's Catches*, were certainly known to some of the men who had sung with Richard Smith, and who attended Taylor's lectures. It is perhaps more accurate to consider that inspired by Taylor's lectures, and more specifically by the music contained therein, these men saw an opportunity to form a society, run along similar lines to the Madrigal Society in London, and which would also provide a social forum with a desirable artistic cause—that is to say, the revival of English and Italian renaissance madrigals.

---

[26] The appointment of Gresham professor of music dates to 1596, when the terms of the will of the City liveryman, Sir Thomas Gresham, established seven professorships in various academic disciplines, including music. The holder of the office is expected to deliver a specified number of public lectures per year for an annual stipend.

[27] According to an itinerary penciled into his notes, which are kept at the R.C.M. (shelfmark MS2153), Taylor's tour took him to Halifax in 1832; Birmingham and the Royal Institute in 1833; Oxford 1834; Norwich and Brighton 1835; Liverpool, Manchester and Hull 1836; and Leeds and Bristol in 1837. He continued lecturing from the same notes until 1848.

[28] W. Husk, 'Taylor, Edward', Grove's *Dictionary of Music and Musicians*, (1879–1889).

[29] H. Byard, *The Bristol Madrigal Society*, Bristol Historical Association 15, (Bristol, 1966).

[30] E. Hunt, *Robert Lucas Pearsall, the 'compleat gentleman' and his music (1795–1856)*, (Chesham Bois, 1977).

[31] *Ibid.*, p. 180.

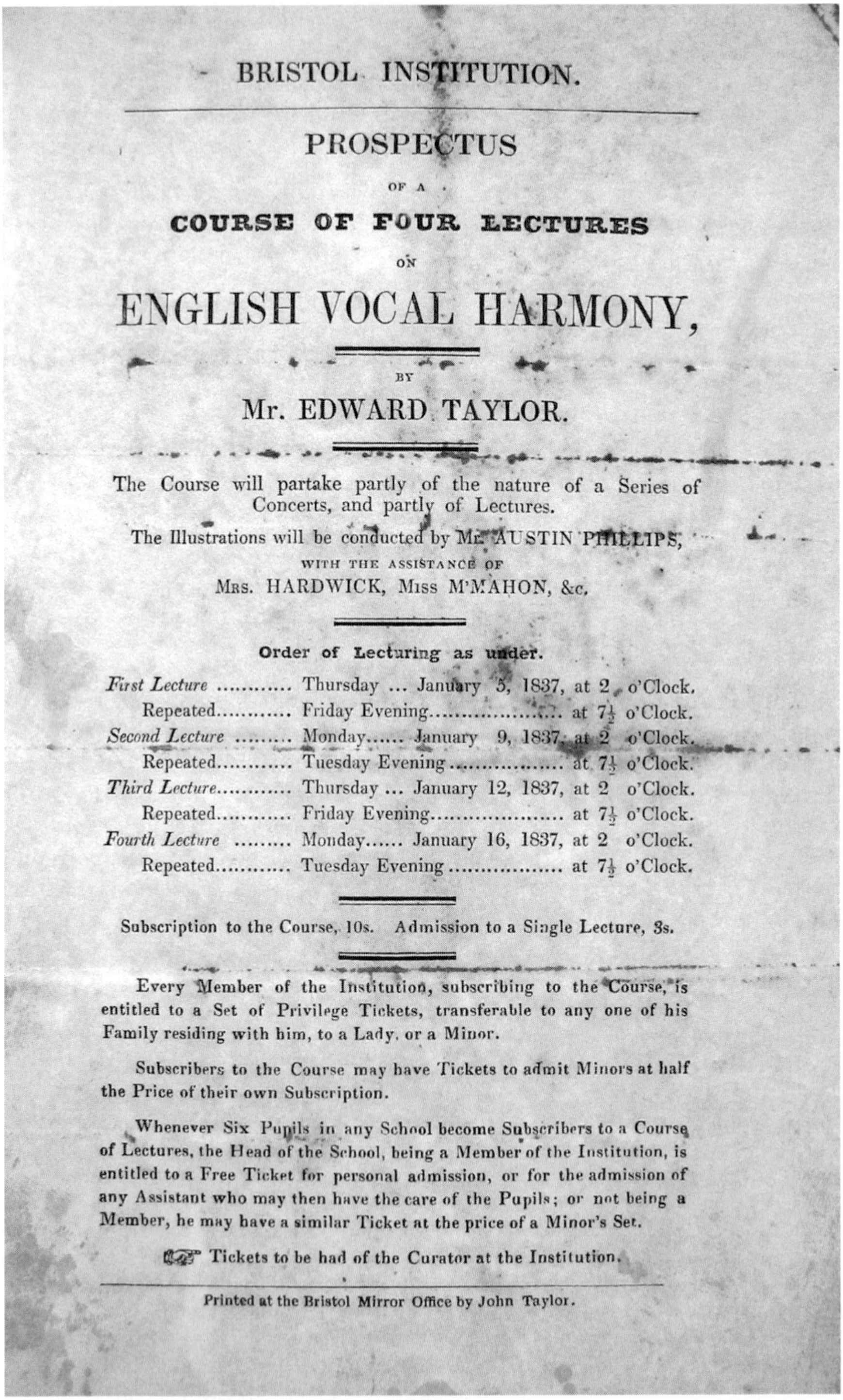

BRISTOL INSTITUTION.

PROSPECTUS

OF A

COURSE OF FOUR LECTURES

ON

ENGLISH VOCAL HARMONY,

BY

Mr. EDWARD TAYLOR.

The Course will partake partly of the nature of a Series of Concerts, and partly of Lectures.

The Illustrations will be conducted by Mr. AUSTIN PHILLIPS,

WITH THE ASSISTANCE OF

Mrs. HARDWICK, Miss M'MAHON, &c.

Order of Lecturing as under.

First Lecture .... Thursday ... January 5, 1837, at 2 o'Clock.
Repeated............ Friday Evening.................... at 7½ o'Clock.
Second Lecture .... Monday...... January 9, 1837, at 2 o'Clock.
Repeated............ Tuesday Evening .... at 7½ o'Clock.
Third Lecture............ Thursday ... January 12, 1837, at 2 o'Clock.
Repeated............ Friday Evening.................... at 7½ o'Clock.
Fourth Lecture .... Monday...... January 16, 1837, at 2 o'Clock.
Repeated............ Tuesday Evening .... at 7½ o'Clock.

Subscription to the Course, 10s.   Admission to a Single Lecture, 3s.

Every Member of the Institution, subscribing to the Course, is entitled to a Set of Privilege Tickets, transferable to any one of his Family residing with him, to a Lady, or a Minor.

Subscribers to the Course may have Tickets to admit Minors at half the Price of their own Subscription.

Whenever Six Pupils in any School become Subscribers to a Course of Lectures, the Head of the School, being a Member of the Institution, is entitled to a Free Ticket for personal admission, or for the admission of any Assistant who may then have the care of the Pupils; or not being a Member, he may have a similar Ticket at the price of a Minor's Set.

☞ Tickets to be had of the Curator at the Institution.

Printed at the Bristol Mirror Office by John Taylor.

Fig. 1. Prospectus for Mr. Edward Taylor's Lectures (1837), [The Bristol Chamber Choir archive, Special Collections, University of Bristol].

Alfred Bleeck
Surgeon at the Bristol Infirmary and First President of the B.M.S. 1837–1867.

Robert Lucas Pearsall
Composer and First Honorary Member of the B.M.S. 1845.

John Davies Corfe
Organist of Bristol cathedral and First Director of the B.M.S. 1837–1865.

Fig. 2. Three Founding Members of the Bristol Madrigal Society, [The Bristol Chamber Choir archive, Special Collections, University of Bristol].

In the Bristol Madrigal Society archive there is a scrapbook, compiled by Daniel Rootham, musical director of the Society from 1865 until 1915. It contains some extraordinary letters and extracts that shed a great deal of light on the events of January 1837. Rootham had obviously taken an interest in the earliest days of the Society, and George Powell, sometime manager of the *Bristol Mercury and Post*, wrote to Rootham with his recollections of Taylor and the Bristol Madrigal Society:

Jan 13th, 1885

My Dear Mr. Rootham,

So far as memory serves me touching the matter I named to you when speaking of the origin of the Madrigal Society, the facts were as follows. Near the close of 1836, I received a letter from a friend in London informing me that Mr. Edward Taylor, a musical gentleman of eminence (I do not think that he was at that time Gresham Professor), was endeavouring to awake an interest in English Chamber Harmony & that he purposed lecturing in Bristol on the subject.

The letter asked me if I would send the names of a few citizens who would be likely to lend a helping hand to such an object; this I did. Shortly afterwards Mr. Taylor came to Bristol and brought a letter from Mr. Henry Phillips stating that the Lectures were of much interest and social value and asking me if I would give good notices of them in the Mercury and endeavour to induce the other Bristol papers to do the same. At that time, I had not the pleasure of any personal acquaintance with Mr. Phillips but he said he wrote to me as being known to some Bristol families. I readily complied with his request.

I attended and reported the Lectures.[32] They were illustrated musically and a selection of Madrigals sung by Miss McMahan, Mrs. Hardwick, Mr. Wilcox, Mr. George Turner, Mr. James England, Mr. Austin Phillips & the Lecturer himself. I well remember the solemn dignity with which Mr. Taylor pleaded the cause of the Madrigal, the only description, he contended, of genuine English Music. About that time, Mr. Bleeck, the father of the respected proprietor of the Bath Chronicle […] was in the habit of having glee parties at his residence. I had not the privilege of a personal acquaintance with Mr. Bleeck till some considerable time afterwards but I heard of these parties from Mr. Wilcox and other friends, and I believe that the formation of the Madrigal Society grew out of Mr. Edward Taylor's lectures and Mr. Bleeck's Glee parties. I do not recall any positive personal evidence of that fact, but it has always been a belief with me and I fancy that I have said so much to Mr. Bleeck himself.

I pen you this poor narrative at your own request, and if its length bores you, you must blame yourself.

I am, My Dear Mr. Rootham,

Very Truly Yours,

George Frk. Powell

---

[32] These were duly reported in the *Bristol Mercury* on Saturday, 21 January 1837.

Henry Phillips (1801–1876), referred to in the letter, was a well-established opera and oratorio singer in London. Bristolian by birth, he had been the *protégé* of the conductor, Sir George Smart, who himself had some connection with Bristol's music since the 1820s.[33] We do not know what Henry Phillips's association was with Taylor, but it would indicate that he had both knowledge of the content of Taylor's lecture, and of Taylor himself. Furthermore, there may have been a family link between Henry and Austin Phillips.

Even if Henry Phillips were not of Austin's family, nepotism still had its part to play: Mrs. Hardwick was Austin Phillips's sister, and beside their appearance at Taylor's lectures, they were often to be found participating in Clifton concerts. Likewise Miss McMahon, appears in several announcements in *Felix Farley's Bristol Journal* for her Bristol concerts. Amongst the gentlemen, George Turner, Mr. (Joseph) Wilcox and Austin Phillips were lay clerks in the cathedral choir.[34] James England *may* have been a lay clerk, although whether he was employed between 1829 and 1836, can only be conjecture.[35]

What we know about the foundation of the Society is due largely to well-recorded minutes in the archives of the Bristol Madrigal Society, now deposited with Special Collections' at the University of Bristol's Arts and Social Sciences Library.[36] The first two pages of the first minute book read as follows:

> On the 14th January 1837 some Gentlemen who were very desirous to promote Madrigal singing in this City, met at Mr. Austin Phillips', to consider of the practicability of forming a Society for that purpose.
>
> Mr. Edward Taylor of London was present, who imparted much information on the subject.
>
> It was admitted that a Madrigal Society could be established in Bristol, and for this purpose, an adjournment to 28th January was determined upon, on which occasion Mr Salter was called to the chair, and
>
> It was Resolved

---

[33] Sir George Smart (1776–1867) conducted concerts in aid of the Bristol Infirmary in 1814 and 1821, and, as mentioned earlier, in 1832 he organized a series of subscription concerts at the Theatre Royal in King Street.

[34] Corroborated with a list of lay clerks of Bristol cathedral held in the Bristol Record Office. The list itself is written by another lay clerk, E. T. Morgan, compiled in 1912 from existing cathedral records. The lay clerks are listed by date of employment by the cathedral. However, there is a noticeable gap in the records between 1829 and 1836, possibly due to loss of some records in the riots of 1831, and fires later in the nineteenth century. B.R.O., DC/A/7/14/1.

[35] His name does appear in the cathedral records of 1825 on a certificate of apprenticeship: 'I hereby certify that Ed Turner [a chorister] was bound apprentice to James England to learn his business of piano forte tuner and repairer for 6 years by indenture. 1st June 1825. Chas. Hodges'. B.R.O., DC/A/11/1/1.

[36] The collection came to the university in 2008 with the consent of Bristol Chamber Choir, the successor to the B.M.S. Previously it was in the care of the Bristol Central Library, where it had been deposited *c.* 1994 by Miss Enid Hunt for safe keeping, however it had never been incorporated into the library or separately catalogued.

That the following named gentlemen be appointed to wait upon Mr. Corfe, to request he will allow his name to put upon the provisional Committee.

Mr. Phillips, Mr. Turner, Mr. Salter

It was Resolved

That the following gentlemen be a provisional Committee for the purpose of obtaining information, and the formation of Rules be submitted to a general Meeting of the Society at the earliest opportunity.

Mr. Bleeck, Mr. Corfe, Mr. Phillips, Mr. W Rankin, Mr. Salter.

It was Resolved

That the following gentlemen who have signified their intention of joining the Society be considered Members, from this day:

Mr. Bleeck, Mr. Corfe, Mr. Coles, Mr. Geo. Barrett, Mr. John Barrett, Mr. Geo. Edwards, Mr. T. Edwards, Mr. Harwood, Mr. Hardwick, Mr. F. Jones, Mr. Kingdon, Mr. ~~Machin~~, Mr. T. B. Miller, Mr. T. Miller, Mr. A. Phillips, Mr. R. L. Pearsall, Mr. C. M. Powell, Mr. E. Rankin, Mr. T. W. Rankin, Mr. Trimnell, Mr. Geo. Turner, Mr. Salter, Mr. Willcox, Mr. ~~Cowley~~'

And on the following page:

February 24 1837

A General Meeting was held this day, at Mr. Bleeck's, for the purpose of having submitted to it the Rules which had been prepared by the provisional Committee, and which, as eventually adopted will be found on page 4. Mr. Bleeck was in the Chair, and

It was Resolved

That Mr. Bleeck be appointed President of the Bristol Madrigal Society

That Messrs. Salter and Phillips be appointed Vice Presidents.

That Mr. Corfe be appointed Director

That Mr. T. Wright Rankin be appointed Secretary.

That the Bristol Madrigal Society hold its first Meeting on Wednesday the 1st March next.

There remain five gaps in Table 1 where, to date, there is no traceable identity— and some of these might never be solved, as there are, for example, seven 'F. Jones' in *Mathews's Directory* alone. However, those others, whose identity is known, provide an interesting cross-section of trades and backgrounds amongst the seventeen of them. As Bristol was a port, it seems only natural to find a wine and spirit importer in their number, and there are tradesmen who might be found in any town—a saddler, a saddle-tree maker,[37] a bookseller and lawyer. The extraordinary man in their midst

---

[37] A saddle-tree is the wooden frame around which the leather of a saddle is placed and stitched, thus forming the foundation of the saddle.

Table 1. The First Twenty-Two Members of The Bristol Madrigal Society and their Professions (where known) [38]

Alfred Bleeck	Surgeon
John Davies Corfe	Organist, Bristol cathedral
Mr. Coles	
George Barrett	Piano Teacher, Seller and Tuner
John Barrett	Piano Teacher, Seller, Tuner and Lay Clerk
George Edwards	Organist and Piano Teacher
Thomas Edwards	Piano Teacher
Mr. Harwood	
Mr. (J.) Hardwick	Bookseller
Mr. F. Jones	
Mr. Kingdon	Saddler
Mr. T. B. Miller	Gentleman
Mr. T. Miller	
Austin Phillips	Music & Singing Teacher and Lay Clerk
Robert Lucas Pearsall	Composer
Mr. C. M. Powell	Gentleman
Mr. E. Rankin	Solicitor
Thomas W. Rankin	Wine and Spirit Importer
Thomas Trimnell	Saddle-Tree Maker and Lay Clerk
George Turner	Piano Teacher and Lay Clerk
Mr. R. Salter	
Joseph Wilcox	Lay Clerk

was Robert Lucas Pearsall (1795–1856), a Bristolian and a barrister who had left the city for Germany in 1825, in pursuit of a new life of musical study, composition and research. The death of his mother in 1836 had caused Pearsall to return to Bristol to tie up the affairs of her estate, and his extended stay coincided with Taylor's lectures. Although Pearsall returned to Germany and later moved to Switzerland, he maintained a close interest in the affairs of the Bristol Madrigal Society from afar. He went on to write some of his finest compositions, chiefly madrigals and part songs, for the Society, amongst which are two magical eight-part works, *Lay a Garland*, and *Great God of Love*, the latter dedicated to John Davies Corfe. He was elected the first Honorary Member of the Bristol Madrigal Society in 1845.

There are two possible identifications for John Barrett. A John Barrett who is recorded as having entered the cathedral choir as a lay clerk in 1796 and he remained there until his death in 1842. The second possibility is that the John Barrett listed in the minute book of the B.M.S. was the son of the lay clerk, John Barrett, senior. John Barrett, junior, sang as a chorister in the cathedral between 1815 and 1823.[39] Thus,

---

[38] Information derived from *Mathews's Bristol Directory*, (Bristol, 1837).

[39] Receipts from the cathedral archive, now held at Bristol Record Office, show that John Barrett, junior, received £27.10.0 from the cathedral as his 'augmentation'—or salary—for services as a chorister between 21 December 1815 and 3 April 1823. It is signed by him and witnessed by his father, John Barrett, senior. B.R.O., DC/A/11/1/1.

George Barrett is probably either the son or the brother of the B.M.S. member. He is not listed with a profession in *Mathews's Directory* for 1837.[40] George Edwards's name had already appeared twice before, once as a member of St. Austin's Glee Society, which he joined in October 1832, and then as a founding member of the new Phoenix Glee Society in 1834. His address is given in *Mathews's Directory* for 1837, as the Music Warehouse, 31 Upper Arcade—and this is confirmed by Richard Smith in his account (although Smith appears to have compiled his history in 1842 for the presentation of the volumes to Alfred Bleeck). Whether Thomas and George Edwards are related is not clear. The fact that they are both piano teachers and founding members of the B.M.S. may be sheer coincidence—Edwards, like Jones, is a common name in Bristol. Mr. J. Hardwick is also listed in *Mathews's*: his premises were at 7 Corn St, where he is cited as an 'English and Foreign Bookseller, Printseller, Stationer and Binder'. He was also the brother-in-law of Austin Phillips, and married to Mrs. Hardwick (perhaps not so surprisingly!), one of the singers employed by Taylor for his lectures.

Mrs. Hardwick and Miss McMahon are not referred to again after the lectures, and it had obviously been determined by the time that the group met at Austin Phillips's house on 14 January—two days before Taylor gave his final lecture—that there was to be no place for women in the B.M.S.

Both Joseph Wilcox and Austin Phillips had made previous appearances in Richard Smith's St. Austin's Glee Society when it was formed in 1832, although of the two of them, only Joseph Wilcox is listed as a member of its subsequent re-invention, the Phoenix Glee Society. Richard Smith's note concerning the transition from St. Austin's to The Phoenix Glee Society tantalizingly refers to the need 'to be rid of a troublesome member.' Could it possibly have been Austin Phillips? In the copy of *Mathews's Directory*, 1836, in Bristol Central Library, p. 139, the entry for Phillips describes him as 'Organist of St. Michael's', but a previous owner of the *Directory* has written, indelibly, 'dismissed' beside it.[41] Perhaps Phillips was the sort of man whom trouble followed.

It appears to have been perfectly commonplace—and logical, really—that in many, if not all, provincial cathedral cities, members of the cathedral choir, and often

[40] George Barrett was paid £19.10.0 for his services to the cathedral as a chorister between 1823 and 1830. B.R.O., DC/A/11/1/1.

[41] Austin Phillips may well prove to be one of the most interesting of all the founding members of the B.M.S. Piecing together what little information there is about him to date, it would appear that he emigrated to New York, on the maiden voyage of the *S.S. Great Western* from Bristol on 8 April 1838. A song, entitled '*Farewell Awhile My Native Shore,*' by Austin Phillips, a song written for Mr. Wilson, 'first sung aboard the Great Western Steam Ship on her voyage from Bristol to New York.' It was dedicated to the directors of the Great Western Steam-Ship Company and published in Bristol by J. Cockram. John Wilson was a popular opera singer who made a two-year tour of the United States, leaving Bristol in 1838. It transpires that he had sung in the London première of *The Siege of Rochelle*, which had also starred the same Henry Phillips who had first written to George Powell, introducing Edward Taylor. Austin Phillips appears again from 1841 onwards, as a composer of songs published by Atwill of New York. His last hitherto recorded work, was published in 1847, a ballad concerning the US-Mexico war (information from the William R. and Louise Fielder Sheet Music Collection, Stanford University, U.S.A.). Phillips died in New York in April 1851. See J. Hobson, 'Austin Phillips', *CHOMBEC News*, 5, (Summer 2008), pp. 11–13.

the organist, were of huge importance to their local musical societies and concerts. Robins points clearly to instances of this, particularly in connection with catch clubs, in several British cities in the late eighteenth century. Norwich cathedral lay clerks founded Norwich's Harmonic Society, while at Salisbury, the four main singers in the catch club were all cathedral songmen, and the clubs at Lichfield and Chichester were equally well supported by cathedral musicians. [42]

Taylor must have made his audiences aware that the Madrigal Society (of London) had always relied on two rather special elements: a handful of boys hired out from the choirs of St. Paul's cathedral, Westminster Abbey, and the Chapel Royal, to sing the soprano line, and some of the vicars choral from the same foundations who were paid to sing and lead the other parts. It is not yet known whom Taylor enlisted for help in the other cities where he delivered his lectures, but as we have already seen in Bristol, three, if not four, of his singing men were members of the cathedral choir, and it is likely that he sourced his musical illustrators from similar foundations in the other towns he visited.[43]

As long as the participation of some of the choristers from Bristol cathedral could be assured, and with the implicit assistance of the organist and master of the choristers, John Davies Corfe,[44] then there was little to bar the way of the establishment of a madrigal society in Bristol. From the support of the twenty-two men assembled at Alfred Bleeck's house on 28 January, there seems to have been no lack of enthusiasm to do so.

The first entry in the B.M.S. minute book is from 28 January 1837, and therefore records the meeting at Austin Phillips's retrospectively. Regrettably, it fails to tell us who was at that very first meeting on 14 January,[45] but it would appear, judging by the election of a representation to attend upon him, that Corfe was not there, and that the vital issue of recruiting the choristers, on which the future of the B.M.S. hung, was yet to be tackled.

An approach must have been made to Corfe by 28 January, at least to co-opt him onto the provisional committee of the B.M.S., as his name appears amongst the twenty-two men who showed their intention to join the Society on the same date.

Taylor had obviously left Bristol by this stage, and the provisional committee members of the new B.M.S. were tackling the issues of the formalisation of rules and regulations without his help. However, the committee had written to Sir John Leman

[42] B. Robins, *op. cit.*, pp. 202–203. This may also have been true at Ely, where Highmore Skeats the Younger was the cathedral organist. He succeeded his father and namesake in 1804, who subsequently became the organist of Canterbury cathedral.

[43] See note 27.

[44] Corfe, appointed organist at Bristol cathedral in 1825, was the son of the organist of Salisbury cathedral, Joseph Corfe, sometime conductor of the Salisbury catch club.

[45] To enforce this, a letter from Henry Oldham in Dan Rootham's scrap-book writing about his reminiscences of the founding of the B.M.S., relates how he regretted not being able to accept an invitation from Austin Phillips to meet Taylor at Phillips's home on 14 January 1837. Unfortunately, there are no letters in Rootham's book where anyone recalls being at Phillips's house.

Rogers, president of the Madrigal Society since 1828.[46] Exactly what they asked of him, and what he replied to those questions, is now lost. The answer from Rogers was originally pasted to p. 4 of the first minute book and, on the opposite page, a copy of the first set of rules of the Society, but both had been removed without permission at some point within the subsequent forty-three years.[47] A note, scribbled into the margin of p. 5 by the Secretary, dated 1880, deplored this fact. It might be imagined that the committee were seeking Rogers's counsel, or possibly patronage, for the Society.

The Society next met on 24 February 1837, for a general meeting to consider the rules which the provisional committee had drawn up. At the same meeting, the officers of the B.M.S. were nominated. Whether they were elected by ballot or simply established by merit is not recorded, but the five of them, Alfred Bleeck as president, Austin Phillips and Richard Salter, as vice-presidents, J. D. Corfe as director and T. W. Rankin as secretary were confirmed on that day.

Presumably, in the intervening four weeks between 28 January and 24 February, Corfe had been persuaded to provide the choristers for the Society, and also to undertake the paid post of director.

As was the case with the Madrigal Society in London, the president was to choose the music to be sung, and the director executed the president's wishes accordingly. The last entry in the minutes for 24 February stated that the Bristol Madrigal Society would convene for its first meeting, five days later, on Wednesday 1 March 1837.

Having looked more closely at the background of the Society's establishment, it is evident that it was not such a simple case of a number of men clubbing together to promote madrigals. There was, no doubt, an element of snobbery played out in the apparent emulation of the well-to-do Madrigal Society in London, but there is also evidence that the foundation of the B.M.S. owes a certain amount to a very real desire to revive and to learn from old music that appealed to the ears and to the sensibilities of the founding members, and to place firmly behind them the musically-impoverished preceding decades.

These men could not have known that one hundred and seventy two years later, their Society would still exist, albeit in the newer guise of the Bristol Chamber Choir, and that their names would be venerated for their foresight in providing Bristol with a musical foundation in which the city would take such great pride. Perhaps their greatest legacy, however, was in acting as the creative catalyst for one of their founding members, Robert Lucas Pearsall, whose compositions for the Bristol Madrigal Society set him apart as one of the most important English madrigalists of the nineteenth century.

---

[46] Rogers was also responsible for the foundation of the Devon Madrigal Society in 1830. It met in Exeter on a monthly basis and was run along identical lines to its London counterpart— that is to say, with an appointed director of music, trebles drawn from the cathedral and paid singers from amongst the lay clerks. Rogers was president. He must have been constantly traveling, as he rarely missed a meeting of the Devon Madrigal Society, or any of the Madrigal Society in London.

[47] The B.M.S. did not issue a new full set of rules until 1858. However, it would appear that many of the first rules were found unsatisfactory within a relatively short time. Some of the fines imposed for lateness or absence were deemed unfair and were revised within the first few weeks.

ACKNOWLEDGEMENTS

The author would like to thank Ms. Elena Antoniou and the committee of the Bristol Chamber Choir (formerly, the Bristol Madrigal Society) for permission to reproduce the photographs and prospectus which are held in the Special Collections of the University of Bristol.

XVI

Dr. Pusey: Visitor to Bristol

LORNA F. HUGHES, B.A. (OXON)

PART ONE: 'THY HOUSEHOLD THE CHURCH':
BEGINNINGS

THE NAME of Edward Bouverie Pusey is often linked with those of John Henry Newman and John Keble, as a founder member and leader of the Oxford Movement. This is not quite in accordance with historical exactitude, for Dr. Pusey was not associated with the Movement at its inception; his leadership of it came later still. The name of Richard Hurrell Froude was better known in the earliest days.

The Oxford Movement: Twelve Years 1833–1845 was the first full historical account, published posthumously in 1891, its author having died the previous year. This was the Revd. Richard William Church, who in 1871 became dean of St. Paul's. He wrote this history at the request of Dr. Pusey; by then he was in his seventies and had deeply reflected upon the events of that intensely-experienced period in his younger life. His book is still regarded as one of the classic works on the Oxford Movement; the biography of Dean Church in the *Oxford Dictionary of National Biography* recognizes it as a fine literary work as well as a history: 'evocative and influential' with 'some of the elements of a tragedy, hingeing on the fall of a protagonist and concentrated within the classical unities of time and place'. The portrait of Newman is of 'a lost leader driven out of Oxford by lesser men'.[1]

Born in 1815, the Revd. William Church was some years younger than the other Oxford men so far mentioned, but he knew them well as he pursued an academic career within the University until 1847. The Revd. John Keble lived from 1792 to 1866. He was a fellow and tutor of Oriel College, as Newman also was, and he was highly regarded as a poet, his best known work being *The Christian Year* (1827). It was hugely popular in the nineteenth century, but is not much read today. Even so, it has given us some well-loved hymns, one being *New every morning is the love*, another *Blest are the pure in heart*; both hymns seem to express something of the essence of Keble's spirituality. He was professor of poetry at the University from 1831 until 1841. Church describes him as having 'a temper of singular sweetness and modesty, capable at the same time, when necessary, of austere strength and strictness of principle'.[2]

Keble was generous in inviting some of the undergraduates to his Gloucestershire home to read with him during the long summer vacation, and it was through this that

---

[1] *Oxford Dictionary of National Biography* (hereafter *O.D.N.B.*), (Oxford, 2004), 11, p. 585.
[2] The Revd. R. W. Church, *The Oxford Movement: Twelve Years 1833–1845*, (New York, 1932), p. 24.

he and Richard Hurrell Froude became intimately acquainted. Two other friends who stayed during the summer of 1823, whose names came to be associated with the Oxford Movement, were Isaac Williams, and Robert Wilberforce, one of the four sons of the great William Wilberforce.

Froude, born in 1803, died young (1836) from consumption, but was known as a fearless, dynamic personality, one given to strong utterance. He and Robert Wilberforce were both appointed fellows and tutors of Oriel College in 1826. The ability and fiery energies of Froude did much to drive forward the Movement in its early days.

Pusey lived from 1800 to 1882 and Newman from 1801 to 1890. Sensitivity is the quality of character most emphasised by Church in his descriptions of Newman:

> In spite of his enthusiasm and energy [and] his unceasing work [...] there was always present this keen sensitiveness, the source of so much joy and so much pain. He would not have been himself without it. But he would have been a much more powerful and much more formidable combatant if he had cared less for what his friends felt, and followed more unhesitatingly his own line of judgement [...] The experience of later years shows that he had despaired too soon.[3]

Newman was ordained priest in 1825 and became vicar of the University Church of St. Mary the Virgin. Here began his preaching of the famous Sunday afternoon sermons (later published as *Parochial and Plain Sermons*, in eight volumes, between 1834 and 1842). These sermons had a profound effect upon those who heard them: there were many who never forgot them. Richard William Church was one of those who were entranced and inspired by them; the following extract shows how influential these sermons were, and also suggests a certain personal magnetism in Newman himself:

> The profound influence they exerted at the time lay in their call to holiness, a call which could not be dissociated from the charisma of the preacher himself, who avoided all the usual oratorical devices of the pulpit, but whose rapt intensity and low, soft, but strangely thrilling voice left unforgettable memories with many of his listeners.[4]

The Revd. Dr. Owen Chadwick, in his scholarly two-volume work *The Victorian Church*, is another who recognizes the impact of Newman's sermons upon those who heard them, and the uniqueness of the experience:

> From the pulpit of St. Mary's they learnt obedience, holiness, devotion, sacrament, fasting, mortification, in language of a beauty rarely heard in English oratory.[5]

Clearly, then, the Oxford Movement started amongst men of inspirational character, high academic standing and dedication. Its context was entirely Anglican, since Dissenters, Protestant and Roman Catholic alike, were at that time excluded from the University. Newman's 'call to holiness' was soon to become one of the great features

---

[3] *Ibid.*, pp. 187, 188.
[4] *O. D. N. B.*, 40, p. 645.
[5] The Revd. O. Chadwick, *The Victorian Church Part I*, (3rd ed., 1971), p. 169.

of the Movement, coming at a time when apathy towards religion was fairly general, and an increasingly materialistic outlook was becoming ingrained in society.

In his *Apologia Pro Vitâ Suâ* Newman defines the start of the Movement as Keble's preaching of the Assize Sermon on 14 July 1833: for Newman, it was a seminal event:

> I have ever considered and kept the day as the start of the religious movement of 1833.[6]

By this date Keble had taken on the curacy of his elderly father's parish of Coln St. Aldwyn, Gloucestershire,[7] later serving as vicar of Hursley in Hampshire, from 1836 until his own death in 1866. He devoted himself to the cure of souls there, to the instruction and pastoral care of the parishioners. As professor of poetry he continued to be involved with the academic life of Oxford, but was inevitably somewhat distanced from it; his modesty, shyness and lack of worldly ambition were qualities of character which fitted him for the role of a country parson, towards which he was deeply attracted.

In view of this, the controversialist tone of the Assize Sermon, which it was his duty to preach at St. Mary's, on the invitation of the Vice-Chancellor, was all the more notable. Its title alone, *On National Apostasy*, has a challenging ring. The sermon reflects the political dimension of the Oxford Movement. Under the reforming Whig administration of Lord Grey, ten Irish dioceses, including two archbishoprics, were amalgamated with other dioceses nearby. Keble spoke out forcefully against erastianism, or state control over the Church. He warned that the Church was the holy Church of God, God-appointed, God-directed, and not an appendage of the state. If men stood by and let the state interfere with the Church they would be guilty of apostasy. He emphasised the spiritual authority of the Church and of the episcopate, this at a time when the bishops were generally unpopular, partly because of their opposition to the 1832 Reform Bill. Some bishops had suffered attacks in the streets; in the 1831 Bristol Riots the bishop's palace (then next to the cathedral) had been burnt down. The wider context of the sermon was a perception of an increasing materialism and secularisation throughout society. Keble voiced some pressing concerns, and what he said was felt to have particular contemporary relevance. The topic and style of the sermon certainly bear out Church's perception of Keble's 'austere strength and strictness of principle'.[8]

If the start of the Movement can be dated from Keble's sermon, its end was the secession, in October 1845, of John Henry Newman to the Roman Catholic Church. This is the twelve-year span of Dean Church's history. The dates are convenient for reference, though in reality neither a beginning, and still less an end can be so neatly pin-pointed. Significantly, Church saw Newman's secession as a beginning, quite as

---

[6] The Revd. J. H. Newman, *Apologia Pro Vitâ Suâ*, (1908), p. 35.

[7] Keble was born in Fairford, Gloucestershire, where his family resided until his father, the Revd. John Keble Senior's death in 1835. Following ordination, Keble served the cure of the two small Gloucestershire parishes of Eastleach and Burthorpe. On his departure from Oxford in 1823 Keble added a third, Southrop, where he resided and took occasional students. The combined income from all three parishes was modest. He remained a resident in Gloucestershire between 1823 and 1835, with a short break between 1825 and 1826, and refused all preferment in order to be able to assist his father in his parochial duties.

[8] See note 2.

much as it was, in one sense, an end. The title of the chapter on Newman's secession is *The Catastrophe*, and it shows the author's keen awareness of paradox. More secessions followed Newman's and these were cataclysmic events: however, they marked the start of the phase which took the influence of the Movement outside Oxford. From then on it began to touch the lives and everyday religious experience of ordinary people in parishes up and down the land, and has continued to do so.

In 1833 the Assize Sermon raised awareness of the challenging situation facing the Church and it was then that Newman, Keble and Hurrell Froude agreed that some action was needed. They were not the only ones who thought so. It was a Cambridge man, Hugh James Rose, priest, teacher and outstanding divine, who called a meeting for discussion at his Hadleigh rectory. Hurrell Froude was present at this meeting, the principal outcome of which was the launching of the Tracts, whereby the Oxford Movement came to be known also as the Tractarian Movement. The first *Tracts for the Times* were issued in the form of short pamphlets on religious doctrine. They were terse in style and strongly worded: as Church puts it: 'They were clear, brief, stern appeals to conscience and reason [...] like the short, sharp, rapid utterances of men in pain and danger and pressing emergency'.[9] They were penned by Newman, Keble, his brother Thomas Keble, Froude, and Isaac Williams, together with a few other contributors.

From the Tracts, from the sermons of Newman and others, and from articles in periodicals such as *The British Critic*, the aspirations of the Oxford Movement came to be promulgated. Crucial to its ethos were: recognition of the links of the Anglican Church to the Ancient Church and the continuing Catholic heritage of the Anglican Church; scholarship, centred on the teaching of the Early Fathers and Caroline Divines; the primacy of the sacraments of the Church; the primacy of the apostolic succession; personal holiness of life; renewed dedication and reverence in church worship.

The Tracts were speedily produced; eventually there were to be ninety. It was in 1834 that Edward Bouverie Pusey came to be publicly associated with the Movement, for it was in that year that he was persuaded by Newman to contribute a Tract. (Fig. 1.) He produced *Thoughts on the Benefits of the System of Fasting enjoined by our Church*. In 1835 he composed a long Tract on the sacrament of baptism. The academic reputation of Dr. Pusey was already well established. Since 1828 he had been the regius professor of Hebrew and a canon of Christ Church, and was revered as a man of almost formidable scholarship. Church says that he was: 'without question the most venerated person in Oxford'.[10] It was no wonder then that the Tract on fasting was longer and weightier than any of those that preceded it, its format and style resembling those of a learned treatise rather than a pamphlet. In *An Introduction to the Oxford Movement* Michael Chandler sums up the influence of Dr. Pusey: 'there was a sense of gravitas about Pusey which all recognized'.[11] It is interesting that Newman recognized and appreciated 'gravity' in Pusey, along with other rather similar qualities of character: 'Dr. Pusey's influence was felt at once. He saw that there ought to be more sobriety,

---

[9] The Revd. R. W. Church, *op. cit.*, p. 110. Also cited in M. Chandler, *An Introduction to the Oxford Movement*, (2003), p. 27.

[10] The Revd. R. W. Church, *op. cit.*, p. 327.

[11] M. Chandler, *op. cit.*, p. 27.

Fig. 1. Dr. Pusey in old age in his study, [taken from the frontispiece of the 1900 edition of Maria Trench's *The Story of Dr. Pusey's Life*].

more gravity, more careful pains, more sense of responsibility in the Tracts and in the whole Movement, […] He at once gave us a position and a name […] He was a man of large designs; he had a hopeful, sanguine mind'.[12]

The Tracts were controversial and open to the charge of 'popery'. Dr. Pusey's Tract on fasting caused some stir, as the practice of fasting was considered by many to be outmoded and extreme, and therefore 'Roman'. This reaction might be a predictable one, but opponents of the Movement were liable to consider all the Tracts as 'trying to establish Roman Catholic doctrines within the Church of England'.[13] It is worth noting Pusey's surprise at the public reaction to his Tract. Chandler cites the following extract from a letter found in H. P. Liddon's *The Life of E. B. Pusey D. D.* (four volumes, 1893–1897):

> I was not prepared for people questioning, even in the abstract, the duty of fasting […] I assumed the duty to be acknowledged and thought it only undervalued.[14]

Dr. Pusey seems to have had little awareness of public opinion; Newman by contrast was an acute judge of prevailing public moods.

Newman's secession came after a long and difficult period of soul-searching, when he became convinced that he had finally lost faith in the Church of England as the authentic Catholic Church. He was received into the Roman Catholic Church on 9 October 1845. The belief of Pusey and Keble in the catholicity of the Anglican Church did not waver, and Dr. Pusey then became, reluctantly, the recognized leader of the Oxford Movement.

In June 1828 Pusey married Maria Raymond Barker, and in November he was appointed regius professor of Hebrew. The post was attached to a canonry of Christ Church and his priestly ordination followed on 23 November. A house on the corner of the great quadrangle of Christ Church College went with the appointment. Here they settled into married life; theirs was a hospitable household with many visitors. Overall, however, it was not an easy life, for Dr. Pusey had to face much public controversy because of his key role in the Oxford Movement. On at least one occasion he was the victim of outright injustice. In their private lives, too, he and his wife knew tragedy. One of their daughters died in infancy and their two eldest children both suffered serious illness. Only the youngest, Mary, had good health. Maria Pusey as a girl was tall, strong and athletic; Liddon describes her as 'a handsome woman and handsomely dressed'.[15] Even so, she became consumptive and died after only eleven years of marriage, in 1839. Their daughter Lucy died of the same disease in 1844. It was when Maria was gravely ill that Lucy and her sister Mary started school in Clifton, Bristol.

---

[12] The Revd. J. H. Newman, *op. cit.*, pp. 61, 62.

[13] M. Chandler, *op. cit.*, p. 29.

[14] *Ibid.*, p. 28. Source given as the Revd. H. P. Liddon, *The Life of E. B. Pusey D. D.*, I, (1893), p. 280.

[15] The Revd. H. P. Liddon, *op. cit.*, I, p. 194.

PART TWO: 'SEE, I HAVE REFINED YOU; I HAVE TESTED YOU IN THE FURNACE OF ADVERSITY'. BRISTOL, CLIFTON AND HORFIELD

'Came to Clifton'[16] is Maria's diary entry for 18 April 1838. She had been staying at the London home of Lady Lucy Pusey,[17] mother of Edward, and had there consulted a physician as her deteriorating health was giving concern. So too was the condition of their young son, Philip Edward, who, at six years old, had been struck down with a severe disabling illness, the effects of which were to be life-long. A letter written from Clifton to John Henry Newman conveys the anxious concern of the parents, confiding their despair at 'the hopelessness of the restoration of our dear boy'.[18] Philip did, however, live to be almost fifty, and took delight in aiding his father's academic researches, in pursuit of which 'he shrank from no journey, however toilsome'.[19]

The family already had a link with Clifton, since a close friend, Mrs. Rogers[20] (often referred to as Miss Rogers), ran a school in Royal York Crescent, assisted by several of her daughters. Mrs. Rogers had formerly been governess to Maria at Fairford in Gloucestershire. (Maria was well educated: she worked for her husband on the translation from Latin of St. Augustine's *Confessions*, and also on St. Cyprian. She was one of many translators for Pusey's *Library of the Fathers*). The Clifton school appears each year in *Mathews's Bristol Directory* from 1822 through to its closure in 1855. It was a ladies' boarding school situated in numbers 2 and 3 Royal York Crescent. These houses were much later converted into apartments and are now known as Eugenie House, in honour of a former pupil of the school. Eugenie, who, together with her sister Paca, daughters of a Spanish nobleman, attended the school for a brief period in 1837.[21]

---

[16] M. Trench, *The Story of Dr. Pusey's Life*, (2nd ed., 1900), p. 125. Maria Trench originally wrote anonymously. Her book is the source of most of the more personal information on Dr. Pusey and his family included in this paper. In her preface she emphasises that Dr. Liddon's *Life of E. B. Pusey D. D.* 'must ever remain the great and abiding monument to Dr. Pusey' (Preface p. xiv). Her book was written at the wish of his daughter Mary, and was intended as a more personal memoir. Many personal letters of Dr. Pusey were made available to the author.

[17] Daughter of the earl of Harborough.

[18] M. Trench, *op. cit.*, p.126.

[19] *Ibid.*, p. 525.

[20] Ann Rogers died 9 November 1855, aged 92. Her husband was Richard Rogers, late of Hackney, Middlesex, died at Royal York Crescent on 9 February 1823, aged 59. They were buried in Clifton parish church with two of their daughters. At least five of their daughters taught at the school: Ann, who died 15 June 1846, aged 53; Sarah, born London, alive 1851; Hannah, the third daughter, born London died 8 December 1854, aged 61; Mary I. Rogers, born Cussop, Herefordshire, 1804, alive 1851; Lucy B. Rogers, alive 1851. Mrs. Rogers employed three further resident school mistresses, including a granddaughter, at the time of the 1851 census, and had six domestic servants and 15 resident pupils. This information was kindly supplied by Mrs. M. V. Campbell of Bickley, Cleeve, Somerset.

[21] Eugenie is remembered for her subsequent marriage to Napoleon III whereby she became empress of France. The Pusey sisters were not quite contemporary with her as they did not enter the school until the autumn of 1838. They might have heard stories of her, for at least once she attempted to abscond from the school, being found on board a ship by one of the ever-vigilant daughters of Mrs. Rogers!

After their visit to Clifton in April 1838 the family went to Weymouth, which was known for its healthful climate. 'Miss' Rogers visited them there in August, when Maria's diary notes illness confining her to bed from the 8th to the 15th, when 'Miss Rogers and Mary left for Clifton'.[22] Mary was only five years old. On the day following her departure her father writes forlornly to Newman: 'We parted yesterday with our little Mary who was too much for her strength; happily her former governess, a friend, now keeps a school; so she is gone under her special care, not as to school'.[23]

Mary must have settled well at the school, for in 1840 Perceval Ward, a family friend, wrote this charming note to Dr. Pusey: 'I saw your little Mary again before I left Clifton; she is very well. She has quite won the hearts of my mother and sisters by her gentle and lively manners. It is quite delightful to see her attachment to Miss Rogers, who appears a most sensible and good person.'[24]

Lucy, their eldest child, nine at the time of Maria's death, joined the school a little after Mary, 'Maria being no longer equal to the charge'.[25] Philip went to school in Brighton. As a result of the children's schooling their father became a regular visitor to Clifton and Brighton, preaching in both places. From the memoir that she wrote later on, we can see that Mary had some happy recollections of the Clifton days when her father used to stay 'in the house next to Miss Rogers'.[26] (Mary married the Revd. J. G. Brine in 1854 and was the only child to survive both parents). She recalls: 'the delightful walks we had with him over some downland to Bristol Cathedral, and there I learnt first, for the rest of my life, never to look about me in church'.[27] This downland must have been Brandon Hill, which would make a pleasant walk from Clifton to Bristol cathedral. It is amusing to contrast Mary's lively enthusiasm with the disconsolate attitude of poor Eugénie towards Clifton life: she complained: 'Do not think there are any public amusements here. Everyone stays at home, and one never sees a fashionable man in the street'.[28]

Following Maria's death, the family friendship with Mrs. Rogers continued; indeed Dr. Pusey wrote to her on the day after Maria died, 27 May 1839. 'My dear friend, I have little to add about the last hours of your dear child's earthly life; it was closed in mercy sooner than we expected. I administered the communion to her between twelve and one that day.'[29] The letter continues in a most confiding tone. It is one of many which reflect the close friendships of Dr. Pusey's life. It is interesting too that Maria is seen as a 'dear child' of Mrs. Rogers: relations between pupil and governess were not always of that character! The gift of an east window to St. Andrew's, the parish church of Clifton, in memory of Maria, was made by her husband and Mrs. Rogers. The church was bombed in the Blitz of December 1940 and mostly destroyed; the tower alone survived, but was demolished in 1954.

Dr. Pusey continued to correspond with Mrs. Rogers during the controversies of 1843 which culminated in the condemnation of his sermon preached before the

---

[22] *Ibid.*, p. 134.

[23] *Ibid.*

[24] *Ibid.*, pp. 161–162.

[25] *Ibid.*, p. 135.

[26] *Ibid.*, p. 234.

[27] *Ibid.*, p. 195.

[28] Quoted in P. Turnbull, *Eugénie of the French*, (1974), p. 24.

[29] M. Trench, *op. cit.*, p. 145.

University at Christ Church. This was *The Holy Eucharist, a Comfort to the Penitent.* The condemnation resulted in his being suspended for two years from preaching within the University (neither did he preach anywhere else during that time). A letter to Mrs. Rogers written just after his suspension in June 1843 shows that even at this very critical time in his public life, his thoughts were for his children and for her, and any possible adverse effects on the school:

> One thing I have thought of for some time, whether, if this event did happen, it ought not to occasion a suspension of my visits to Clifton, for, hitherto, however people spoke against me, no authority had decided upon me; now a body which, however constituted, is the representative of the University has declared that I have taught doctrines at variance with those of the Church of England; and parents might well have misgivings about me. There is no reason to decide at once; your kind visit to the sea with us cannot prejudice your school more than hitherto; so to this, please God, I shall look forward. My love and blessing to the dear children.[30]

Much has been written, from Church and Liddon onwards, on the injustice of the University authorities in their proceedings. A very brief outline will show not only what Dr. Pusey went through, but the general attitude of the University towards Tractarian doctrine. The sermon drew extensively upon the Early Fathers and attested the doctrine of the Real Presence, that is, the real though spiritual presence of Christ in the Eucharist. The Vice-Chancellor received a complaint about the sermon from Dr. Faussett, the Lady Margaret professor of Divinity; six doctors of divinity were appointed to investigate the sermon. One of these was Faussett himself; four of the five others were known to be hostile to the Tractarians. Dr. Pusey was not allowed to be present at any of their meetings or to defend the sermon. All the proceedings were carried on in secret, finally concluding that 'he had preached certain things which were either dissonant from or contrary to the doctrine of the Church of England'.[31] It seems that they could not agree amongst themselves exactly what these 'certain things' were. Dr. Pusey himself was magnanimously concerned that, since the sermon was based so extensively on the Early Fathers his judges might end up condemning one of them 'when they thought they were only condemning me'.[32]

When his suspension became known there were protests. Two of the signatories to a memorial from London were Mr. Justice Coleridge and W. E. Gladstone. Trench says bluntly that 'his judges found themselves in a hole'.[33] She also cites the interesting case of one of the Revd. John Keble's curates, a deacon, being refused priestly ordination (in 1841) for his belief in the Real Presence. Keble was deeply distressed for the curate, of whom he thought very highly, and because he felt that the refusal was really directed at his teaching.

At the same time as the anxieties about the sermon were paramount there were also very serious worries over the health of Lucy. She had never been strong and her father was keenly aware of the frailty of both the older children: close upon the first anniversary of Maria's death he alluded in a letter to Newman to 'the season of the

---

[30] *Ibid.*, p. 210.
[31] M. Chandler, *op. cit.*, p. 74.
[32] The Revd. H. P. Liddon, *op. cit.*, II, p. 312.
[33] M. Trench, *op. cit.*, p. 211.

year and my children's frail lives'.[34] In May 1843 there had been fears for Lucy of the possible onset of consumption, although these had then been dispelled by a decided improvement. However, during the Lent of 1844 rapid consumption set in and Lucy died in Clifton soon after Easter, in her fifteenth year. She was buried with her mother in Christ Church cathedral.

Lucy had always been very dear to her father; even when very young she had shared many of his aspirations. Her confirmation at the age of twelve had been a great joy and he wrote to John Keble: 'dear Lucy whom you contributed to prepare for confirmation is going on very lovelily'.[35] She became her father's 'dearest friend and companion, entering warmly into all his hopes and plans for the restoration of religious communities in England'.[36] This was a most significant aspect of Dr. Pusey's work, and Lucy hoped to become a *Soeur de la Charité* in a sisterhood ministering to the sick or to the poor. When she made her first Communion on Trinity Sunday 1841 she knelt by the side of Miss Marian Hughes who, under the spiritual direction of Dr. Pusey, took religious vows of poverty, chastity and obedience. She is believed to be the first person to have taken such vows within the Church of England. She later went on to become superior of the convent of the Holy Trinity in Oxford. Chandler tells us that she and Lucy were both attracted to the concept of holiness of life through Newman's sermons. Lucy's death at such an early age was a sad end to bright hopes. Long afterwards, her sister Mary came to feel that the confirmation had dedicated Lucy to the higher service of God in heaven, and that the same thing had happened to Mary's own daughter:

> My own eldest child made (her first Communion) in St. Barnabas Church at Oxford [...] in three short months to be called, as my eldest sister was, by rapid consumption, to the accepted dedication of their lives to God's service.[37]

Lucy's great hopes of entering Religious Life had inspired Helena Richards, a close friend at school, with similar high ideals; sadly Helena too died before her hopes could be realized, but her cousin joined the Devonport sisters in 1849, under the direction of Miss Lydia Sellon. Helena's father was the Revd. Henry Richards, incumbent of Holy Trinity, Horfield from 1828 until 1864, and so Dr. Pusey preached at Horfield as well as at St. Andrew's Clifton. It seems that a friendship between the Pusey and Richards families had originated from Maria's marriage. Her family were the Raymond Barkers of Fairford Park in Gloucestershire. A gift to Holy Trinity Horfield of a small one-manual organ was made, during the incumbency of the Revd. Henry Richards, by the Revd. Raymond Barker of Fairford Park. In his *Horfield Miscellanea*, the Revd. Fanshawe Bingham, a later incumbent (1878–1899) refers to this small organ as being in Holy Trinity until 1885, when it was replaced. (It was sold to Elberton Church). The school friendship of Lucy and Helena must have continued a well-established family friendship.

[34] *Ibid.*, p. 167.
[35] *Ibid.*, p. 195.
[36] *Ibid.*, p. 182.
[37] *Ibid.*

The text of one of the sermons preached by Dr. Pusey at St. Andrew's Clifton is held in the Bristol Room at the Central Library, College Green. Its title is *A Sermon Preached at the Parochial Church of Saint Andrew, Clifton, in behalf of the Society for the Propagation of the Gospel*. Dr. Pusey preached several sermons in aid of good causes. It was preached in Advent 1840 and published the following year. It is illuminating to consider the sermon within the context of what we know of St. Andrew's Church. Consecrated in 1822, it was the original parish church of Clifton, with, finally, ten daughter churches. It stood at the end of the avenue now known as the Birdcage Walk, called in the 1850s the Pleached Walk, where the lime boughs were being trained round the railings. The walk leads through the main graveyard of the church (there is a second graveyard on Lower Clifton Hill, the 'Strangers' Burial Ground').

It was a church frequented by the rich and fashionable, and it features at length in an article by Joseph Leech, a journalist who wrote a series of articles under the soubriquet of *The Church Goer*. He paints an astutely observed portrait of the typical Sunday at St. Andrew's, together with some sharply satirical comment, aimed to draw attention to the unjust neglect of the needs of the poor of the parish, and the scandal of pew rents and reserved seats left unoccupied:

> Young and old, all finely clad, nodding plumes and flowing dresses swept on, and still the expectants stood by the porch, seeming more uncomfortable and more painfully embarrassed as others were accommodated; and the well trained sextoness flitted by from time to time, affecting, of course, to understand nothing of the significant, though almost imploring glances, meant to make interest, as it were, for the humblest portion of the humblest pew in the church [...] It is not the church of the poor man; he has no business there in that atmosphere of *eau de Cologne* and *bouquet de la reine*, where the glitter of gilt-edged prayer books and the rustle of brocades present sounds and sights extraordinary to humble comprehensions.[38]

Abandoning description for forthright denunciation, he then declaims: 'You that thirst, come not near the sacred, soft-cushioned preserve—the privilege which one man pays for, under the invidious pew system, of shutting another out of the house of God'.[39]

Such, then, was the context of the 1840 sermon. Reading the text we immediately see that it is an erudite sermon, with many Biblical quotations, its themes clearly argued, with an earnest, even impassioned fluency. The text is Matthew 24:14: 'And this gospel of the Kingdom shall be preached in all the world for a witness unto all nations; and then shall the end come'. This 'end' Dr. Pusey sees not as an end in time 'for time has no relation to God but to us only who are now subject to it'.[40] Rather, it is an end which is being ever and presently worked out in the ongoing struggle between goodness and the very real power of Satan, 'his wrath the hottest when his Kingdom is most threatened'.[41] The present time is seen as one of particularly intense

---

[38] J. Leech, *The Church Goer Being a Series of Sunday Visits to the Various Churches of Bristol*, (3rd ed., Bristol, 1850), pp. 17, 18, 19.

[39] *Ibid.*, p. 18.

[40] The Revd. E. B. Pusey, *A Sermon Preached at the Parochial Church of St. Andrew, Clifton, in behalf of the Society for the Propagation of the Gospel*, (Bristol, 1841), p. 9.

[41] *Ibid.*, p. 4.

struggle, where 'everything seems to be hurrying on upon a gigantic scale'.[42] With a sombre and yet homely touch, the preacher declares: 'Evil is so mixed with good in this sad world'.[43]

The argument moves on to the profound responsibilities of the nation towards the empire, of which he is by no means uncritical, since 'our Indian empire [was] gained by ambition and cupidity and long held by denial of Our Lord'.[44] As the acquisition cannot be undone, however, missionaries are needed to extend the work by now already begun, since 'God has awakened us from that sin which he most hates—luke-warmness—and has put into our mind some thoughts of self-denial and charity'.[45] Here the sermon challenges all complacent notions of charity, appealing to the wealthy congregation to give in a spirit of self-denial and humility, in recognition that 'nothing we have is ours';[46] that charity and almsgiving should not be an occasional act, less still a matter of self-congratulation, but simply 'the continued habit of our lives'.[47]

This was indeed true of Edward and Maria Pusey, for they gave anonymously, over a period, £5,000 to the Bishop of London's Fund to provide new churches to meet the spiritual needs of a rapidly expanding population, mainly of poor, working people. They agreed between themselves to live more simply: they gave up their carriage and horses; Maria sold her jewellery. After Maria's death her husband was the anonymous donor who founded St. Saviour's Church to minister to those working in the manufacturing industries of Leeds. In his personal life Dr. Pusey followed a way of austere simplicity, as he grew older inclining more and more towards asceticism.

Another Bristol sermon of 1840 was preached at St. Paul's Portland Square. This was *Christ the Source and Rule of Christian Love*, and was preached on the Feast of Saint John the Evangelist, in aid of a new church to be erected in an outlying district of that parish. This 'outlying district' was Horfield, a rapidly developing suburb by the 1840s, though it had been for hundreds of years no more than a small village—the 'Horefelle' of the Domesday Book.[48] The records of the diocese of Bristol say that Horfield was an ancient parish, and it is known that there was formerly a church there dedicated to St. Andrew. According to a brief history obtainable from the present day church, it was re-dedicated to the Holy Trinity at an unknown date before the nineteenth-century. A chapel within the church, now known as the Lady Chapel, continued for some time under the dedication to St. Andrew. According to the Revd. Fanshawe Bingham, the church was enlarged in 1831 and then again in 1847 when the whole of the nave and chancel were rebuilt. The church was re-opened on Thursday 11 February 1847 when the Venerable Archdeacon Thorpe preached; the evening sermon was preached by the Revd. Sir George Prevost, a friend of Dr. Pusey. Dr. Pusey himself preached the following Sunday. The largely rebuilt church was re-consecrated by Dr. James Henry Monk, bishop of Gloucester and Bristol on 22 December

---

[42] *Ibid.*, p. 10.
[43] *Ibid.*, p. 14.
[44] *Ibid.*
[45] *Ibid.*, p. 21.
[46] *Ibid.*, p. 23.
[47] *Ibid.*
[48] This was a manor held by the bishop of Bristol.

1847. The 1840 sermon at St. Paul's Portland Square was therefore preached in aid of some very extensive building work, all of which took place during the long incumbency of the Revd. Henry Richards.

In his booklet on the impact of the Oxford Movement in Bristol, Canon Peter Cobb describes the re-opening ceremonies, with reference to the *Bristol Journal* and *Bristol Mirror* of 13 February 1847. The rebuilt church was filled with beauty and colour, with 'the raised chancel glowing with colour from the stained glass' and 'The Communion table, which was in fact a moveable stone altar, covered with a "gorgeous carpet [...] of rich green silk with gold fleur-de-lis and stars", designed by the architect William Butterfield'.[49] Canon Cobb also emphasises the great significance of the occasion, quoting from the *Bristol Mirror*: 'We did feel that the English Church was neither a mere institution of three hundred years' growth, nor formed by man's device, but is founded upon the Holy Apostles, Jesus Christ himself being the chief corner stone.'[50] Holy Trinity Church was 'the first clear manifestation of the Oxford Movement in the area' and 'all the key figures [...] were present'.[51] Besides those already mentioned, Canon Cobb says that the Epistle was read by the Revd. James Woodford, and the Gospel by the Revd. Henry Eland. The former became vicar of St. Mark's, Easton, and later bishop of Ely, the latter of St. John's, Bedminster, where he remained all his life. From Bingham we learn that the moveable stone altar was in fact an innovation of Dr. Pusey himself. 'It was owing to Dr. Pusey's influence, so I am informed'.[52]

In the second volume of Robinson's *West Country Churches* we read of 'a wooden pulpit, quite a disfigurement to the church, but interesting historically as the one in which Dr. Pusey preached when he was refused a hearing at Clifton'.[53] This pulpit was later removed to St. Edmund, Horfield, where the original building had been a school room before it became the Mission Church of St. Edmund. This church was on the Gloucester Road and was closed in 1978. In 2007 it was demolished to make way for new housing. The pulpit is believed to have perished.

Of Dr. Pusey's being 'refused at Clifton', despite his having regularly preached there, and his preaching instead at Horfield, we learn much of interest from the *Church Goer*. He was to have preached at St. Andrew's on the Christmas Day of 1846, but there were threats from 'two or three red-hot gentlemen' of their walking out of church 'with marked and significant stampings' if he mounted the pulpit.[54] The reverend doctor consented, for the peace of the church, to forgo his permission to preach at Clifton. According to Leech it was not unknown at this period of intense controversy for whole congregations to arise and walk out, hence the difficulty encountered by anyone desirous of hearing 'one of the great Oxford dons and especially the Hebrew professor'.[55] The secession of John Henry Newman to the Roman Catholic

---

[49] The Revd. P. G. Cobb, *The Oxford Movement in Nineteenth Century Bristol*, Bristol Historical Association, 68, (Bristol, 1988), p. 7.

[50] *Ibid.*

[51] *Ibid.*

[52] The Revd. F. Bingham, *Horfield Miscellanea*, (Portsmouth, 1906), p. 79.

[53] W. J. Robinson, *West Country Churches*, (Bristol, 1914), II, p. 156.

[54] J. Leech, *The Church-Goer's Rural Rides; or Calls at Country Churches*, (3rd ed., Bristol, 1851), pp. 221, 222. Bingham refers to the same incident (*Horfield Miscellanea*, p. 79). He gives the source as Liddon's *Life of E. B. Pusey*, III, p. 138.

[55] J. Leech, *Rural Rides, op. cit.*, p. 221.

Church in 1845 had in many minds engendered suspicion against his close friends, and had fostered a feeling then current that the Tractarians were under-cover Papists, and that there existed 'an Anglo-Catholic plot to subvert the Church of England'.[56] Many of the opponents of the Tractarians were at this time watching and waiting for Pusey to follow Newman, and, says Leech, 'impatiently and petulantly demanding the reason for his stay'.[57] Leech comments further: 'If he abides with us he will have established his character for fixed and founded principle under an ordeal severe and trying'.[58] Such long continuing controversies and further secessions after Newman's must have tested his steadfastness severely, but he had, according to Dean Church, great reserves of strength: 'An inflexible patience, a serene composure, a meek, resolute self-possession was the habit of his mind and never deserted him in the most trying days'.[59]

On Christmas Day 1846, then, he preached at Horfield instead of at Clifton, and he preached again at Holy Trinity two days later on the Feast of St. John the Evangelist. Leech writes of Horfield as a little country church, a 'rural ride' outside the city, into Gloucestershire. He implies that a fashionable church such as St. Andrew's would be much more likely to encounter trouble from the presence of a controversial preacher than would a little-regarded rural church in an 'outlying district'. Even so, he refers to the 'daring' of the Revd. Henry Richards in opening his doors 'to a man who wanders about like an ecclesiastical Cain'.[60] Bingham, too, remarks: 'It seems evident that the visits of Dr. Pusey to his personal friends at Horfield Rectory excited the fears of some in Horfield as well as at Clifton and Bristol.'[61]

The Church Goer was present on that December afternoon and wrote one of his best pieces, a wonderfully evocative description of the occasion. The shadowy interior of the church, dimly lit by four candles in the fading winter twilight; the frail and humble figure of Dr. Pusey; the melancholy sense of the year drawing to its close; the solemnity of the text and the delivery of the sermon itself—all are beautifully suggested in the following passage from Leech's article. He had obviously been deeply impressed by the earnest, quiet conviction in the preaching and by 'a beauty of holiness, a Christian spirit so broad and Catholic, so deep and devotional'.[62]

> The little church was filled—a flock of more than ordinary numbers having collected together to be devoured by the "ravening wolf from the banks of Isis" as a Birmingham platform man called the Professor some time ago. The people were mostly parishioners, though there were some who, like myself, took a crisp cold walk from Bristol through curiosity, and others, admirers of the Doctor, who came from Clifton in flys, and followed his footsteps with all the affection and fidelity of devoted disciples for a world-driven but patiently enduring master. The heavy shadows of a winter evening were beginning to fill the church, and cast an

[56] The Revd. P. G. Cobb, *op. cit.*, p. 22.
[57] J. Leech, *Rural Rides, op. cit.*, p. 225.
[58] *Ibid.*
[59] The Revd. R. W. Church, *op. cit.*, p. 134.
[60] J. Leech, *Rural Rides, op. cit.*, p. 222.
[61] The Revd. F. Bingham, *op, cit.*, p. 75.
[62] J. Leech, *Rural Rides, op. cit.*, p. 229.

additional gloom on the Christmas evergreens; and this, with the fact of our being near the close of another year, and the apparently proscribed character of the man who was about to preach, imparted something very sombre and peculiarly subdued to the scene [...]

The incumbent and curate were officiating: and in a pew under the pulpit, in a plain black gown, sat the man whose name is known throughout the Kingdom— arraigned on the platforms of our great cities, and pronounced with something like a supernatural sense of dread by the smallest coteries of the remotest village—one of no high and haughty bearing, however, with authority in his eye or command- ing intellect enthroned on his brow; but drooping his head meekly on his breast he seemed rather to shrink from than challenge observation. Of all the simple people that crowded that simple church not one looked more humble or more unconscious of self, or of the stealthy or fixed glances which were directed to him from time to time by the stray comers, some of whom, I have little doubt, expected to see the celebrated Pusey (an heresiarch in the eyes at least of half the Church), of some fearful outline, differing from other men in his form and visage. No horn or cloven hoof, however, protruded to reward their curiosity [...]

Thus it was that I was enabled, without prejudice or horror at the name of Pusey, to sit down and judge for myself, while I watched, with the interest of an observer merely, the manner, person, and preaching of a remarkable man.

While the last Psalm was being sung, the Professor left his pew (no officious sexton leading the way) and ascended to the pulpit on the floor of which he knelt down in private prayer until the singing had concluded, when he rose and prayed in a con- trite and almost thrilling tone. Yet there was nothing affected in all this; on the con- trary, whatever Doctor Pusey's opinions and doctrines may be, so far as man can judge of man, you would have said his character was that of pious humility and self- abasement.

His text was taken from the 21st chapter of Revelations. "And he said unto me it is done. I am Alpha and Omega, the beginning and the end". Never before did I hear so beautifully *evangelical* a sermon as this from the man who has given a name to a party which is supposed to represent a different principle in the church. It had but one fault, it was fifteen minutes too long. Nevertheless, it was listened to through- out, by that little crowded church-full, with fixed and rapt attention, though it was neither declamatory, noisy nor eccentric; but plaintive, solemn and subdued, breathing all through, I may say, a beauty of holiness and a Christian spirit so broad and Catholic, so deep and devotional, that while the most jealous Protestant could find nothing in it he might not approve, the most bigoted Roman Catholic could not enter an exception to a single expression that it contained. I never recol- lect so feelingly apposite a sermon for the close of the year [...] We seemed, as it were, to look back with him from an eminence in serious review upon the trans- actions of the year, ere it had yet passed from our sight, while ever and anon in touching recurrence and solemn fall, came the words "It is done", which were every time, with some beautiful feature of novelty, illustrated and enlarged upon [...] at moments you could almost fancy you were hearing an office for the departing year [...] The very gloom of the little church seemed in keeping: yet this plain and apparently unpretending man, of mild manners and of middle years and stature, who now preached a sermon more perfectly free from controversy than ever I before heard, had himself been foremost in the greatest controversy of the age.

"Who be he that preached", said one young rustic maiden to another as we left the church: "a monstrous nice man, but dreadful long".

"Don't you know", replied the other; "it is that Mr. Pewdsey, who is such a friend to the Pope; but come along, or we'll be late for tea", and away they trotted.

Now, whether Dr. Pusey be a friend to the Pope or not, the reader has his portrait as faithfully and impartially as I can paint it.[63]

He also preached on two occasions at St. James's, Horsefair. This was at the morning and evening services on Wednesday 6 November 1850, and the *Bristol Mercury* of 9 November carried a detailed report:

The notorious connection of the rev. doctor with the recent movement in the church caused an unusual degree of interest to be felt on the occasion. The sacred edifice was crowded in every part with most miscellaneous congregations, for in the morning we noticed among the multitude which attended, the pastors of some of our dissenting congregations, the Rabbi of the Jewish synagogue, some Roman Catholics and one or two members of the Society of Friends [...] Those who attended from motives of mere curiosity were doomed to disappointment, for he made no reference in the course of his very beautiful, scriptural and eloquent sermon to any controversial matter: on the contrary he inferentially rebuked those who had come to hear him in that expectation by the few words in which he in any way alluded to himself:

"With unwillingness would I, in this house of God, say one word of myself; yet for fear of being misunderstood in these days of doubt, misgiving and disquiet I will state that I have come here among you [...] for one single end, that of asking you who are able to supply the heavy expenses attending the daily worship of God in this parish church".[64]

The appeal for funds is then made in a vein broadly similar to that at St. Andrew's already described. The evening discourse was 'of a most eloquent and practical character',[65] and the hearers were urged to seek above all things the Kingdom of God, for then 'the windows of heaven were most freely and immediately opened to such as sought';[66] this was shown in the recent activity discernible in the church; 'subject of congratulation when contrasted with the dreary sleep of [the] last century'.[67]

The daily services for which money was to be raised were choral celebrations of the morning and evening Office. Commitment to the holding of more regular and frequent services, both of daily prayer and of the celebration of the Eucharist was a

---

[63] *Ibid.*, 222–230 *passim.*
[64] *Bristol Mercury*, 9 November 1850, p. 8, column c.
[65] *Ibid.*
[66] *Ibid.*
[67] *Ibid.*

pronounced feature of the way worship was changing under the Tractarian influence; Bingham notes that after the enlargement of Holy Trinity, Horfield, Matins and Evensong were said daily, and early morning celebrations of the Eucharist were instituted on feast days, one example being a 6:30 am celebration on Ascension Day. Chadwick notes that the Evangelicals too, always known for their zeal and sense of commitment, increased the frequency of services and encouraged a greater sense of reverence.

The fact was, however, that in November 1850 it was no straightforward matter for the Revd. J. H. Woodward, incumbent of St. James, to invite Dr. Pusey to preach. Chadwick makes brief mention of this visit of Dr. Pusey to St. James, as occurring, significantly, on the day after Guy Fawkes's Day. 1850 was the year in which a Roman Catholic hierarchy was set up in England and Wales, with twelve episcopal sees and the archbishopric of Westminster. Pope Pius IX established the new sees on 29 September. Dr. Wiseman, rector of the English College at Rome from 1828 to 1840, was made a cardinal and archbishop of Westminster (remaining so until his death in 1865). Rome had attempted to forestall outrage in England, and any threat of resurgence of the old 'No Popery' riots. As the following passage will show, they had planned a strategy but had failed to appreciate the intensity of feeling generated by national history; they had acted as if it were entirely a matter of timing:

> The government was Whig and partly dependent on the Catholic votes of the Irish. As Parliament was not sitting, no questions could be asked in the House of Commons. The titles of [the new] sees kept the law of England. The Pope and his advisers believed that they had done all that was necessary to secure favourable circumstances. They overlooked considerations of moment. They wanted speed while the Anglican soul was in turmoil, and therefore failed to realize that the brief would look like a spoon to stir the boiling pot. They were not sufficiently aware how hallowed to England was the name of Westminster. And above all they reckoned without the exuberance of Wiseman. He found himself a cardinal and an archbishop, the first in England since the reign of Bloody Mary, and his heart was moved to exult.[68]

Dr. Wiseman compounded feelings of resentment by his almost immediate issue of a pastoral letter to be read out in the churches, the language of which was construed as triumphalist, even if he had not intended it to be such. The implication seemed to be that the establishment of the hierarchy was a crushing blow to the Church of England. The Roman Catholic sees were intended to minister to a greatly increased Catholic population, with many Irish immigrants, but in the fervid climate of the times the whole process was termed Papal Aggression. One of the new sees was designated for Bristol, and in December 1850 Dr. J. W. Hendren was enthroned as Roman Catholic bishop of Clifton. This took place at the Church of the Apostles, which then became known as a pro-cathedral.

A short time before the bishoprics were established, Dr. Wiseman had persuaded Newman, who 'since 1845 had spoken nothing outside his communion'[69] to give a series of lectures in London. Newman prepared these with reluctance, too hastily and against his better judgement. The result was *Lectures on Certain Difficulties Felt by*

---

[68] The Revd. O. Chadwick, *The Victorian Church, Part I*, (3rd ed., 1971), pp. 290, 291.
[69] *Ibid.*, p. 288.

Anglicans in Submitting to the Catholic Church. According to Chadwick, 'it was the only book by Newman which many Anglicans found it impossible to forgive'.[70] In it he argued that the Church of England was spiritually dead, and 'a mere collection of officials depending for a living on the supreme civil power'.[71] Newman, like Dr. Wiseman, now saw the Oxford Movement as never at home in the Church of England, and the natural goal of its adherents, Rome. Thus pressure greatly increased upon Dr. Pusey and other Tractarians remaining within the Church of England.

In the days leading up to 5 November 1850 there were processions in which effigies of Wiseman and some of the Pope were paraded in the streets, as guys, and then burnt. The 'No Popery' placards were sometimes accompanied by others with 'No Puseyites' or 'No Tractarians'. It may be of interest to recollect here that such occurrences were not new: as early as Easter Day 1837 Dr. Pusey had recorded:

> The walls of Oxford have been placarded for the last week with Popery of Oxford and its citizens have been edified with the exhibition of Newman's and my name as papists.[72]

A few days after the demonstrations of 5 November, an address to the bishop of Gloucester and Bristol, Dr. James Henry Monk, from the rural dean and clergy appeared in the *Bristol Mercury*. The text of this address is a striking proof of the strength of feeling that was aroused when it became known that a Roman Catholic bishop of Clifton was to be enthroned. The loyalty of the rural dean and clergy to Bishop Monk is expressed as follows:

> We are anxious to offer the most efficient opposition to this schismatical intrusion upon your lordship's rightful authority in the church of Christ, and to resist, as God shall grant us grace, this presumptuous attempt to give increased influence to the unscriptural doctrines and practices of the Church of Rome, which appear to us to be daily assuming a more offensive and dangerous form.[73]

On the same day there also appeared, from the bishop of London, (Bishop Blomfield) a condemnation of 'Puseyite practices' as 'tending to lead weak and imaginative minds to Rome'.[74] The above extracts are to be found in the *Bristol Mercury* of 9 November, the same date as the report of Dr. Pusey's sermons at St. James. Just before this, at the end of October, Bishop Blomfield had delivered a charge in which the aggression of the papists had been denounced, together with 'insidious imitations of Rome lately introduced into Anglican worship'.[75] This was reported in the press with strong approbation. It is therefore abundantly clear that Dr. Pusey preached at St. James at a time of national tumult, and when there was an upsurge of feeling against the Oxford Movement.

---

[70] *Ibid.*, p. 289.
[71] *Ibid.*
[72] M. Trench, *op. cit.*, p. 109.
[73] *Bristol Mercury*, 9 November 1850, p. 2, column d.
[74] *Ibid.*, p. 8, col. c.
[75] Quoted by the Revd. O. Chadwick, *op. cit.*, p. 295.

In addition to all this, the *Bristol Mercury* of 9 November revealed what had been going on locally, behind the scenes. Dr. Pusey was originally to have preached on 9 October at St. James, but this was postponed. An article of 9 November shows that Bishop Monk, on hearing that the reverend doctor had been invited to preach, approached Woodward, requiring 'that he might not be permitted to do so'.[76] When Woodward asked if there would be proceedings against him if the doctor preached, the bishop replied in the negative, but said he 'should be better pleased if his request were complied with'.[77] It was therefore a decision of some moment on the part of Woodward to invite Pusey to preach, in defiance of the request (albeit moderately urged) of his bishop.

Reading the papers of the following year, 1851, we learn of the secession to the Roman Catholic Church of the Revd. J. H. Woodward, reported in the *Bristol Mercury* of 17 May. The following extracts are again a clear testimony of the intensity of feeling which was incited by secessions, and by the practices which were supposed to influence people towards Rome. The press of the day was of course not subject to the standards that apply now, and the vehemence of some of its language must at times have inflamed passions and prejudices to fever pitch. Conversion to the Roman Catholic faith was reported not as 'conversion' but as 'perversion', hence a *Bristol Mercury* editorial of 24 May 1851 headlined 'Perversion at Our Doors', from which the following extracts are taken:

> The spirit of priestcraft should be exorcised in every quarter. Puseyism lies snugly folded up for the moment in the bosom of the Church of England. It should be forthwith voided. High Churchism should be taught […] that a church appointed by the State […] must be amenable to the power which gave it being.[78]

One might reflect, on the last sentence particularly, with reference to Keble's 1833 Assize Sermon! In the previous week's paper, church congregations were reminded of their duty:

> To cease attendance at the first sign of Romish practices, and not to appear to condone them by enduring them […] until the minister is pleased to announce his own perversion.[79]

The actual announcement of Woodward's secession (he was followed two months later by his wife and eight children) also appears in the *Bristol Mercury* of 17 May. Here the tone is, in part, one of genuine regret for the loss of one who was for long 'an ornament' in an evangelical ministry.[80] There is a measure of rather contemptuous 'compassion for intellect overthrown and mind prostrated', but also respect for 'purity of motives evinced by the vastness of the sacrifice'[81] made by the married man with eight children who could never join a celebate priesthood.

Woodward's secession (and those of two of his former curates) may indeed have cast suspicion in some minds upon Dr. Pusey, but in fact in the early 1850s his regu-

---

[76] The Revd. P. G. Cobb, *op. cit.*, p. 15.
[77] *Ibid.*
[78] *Bristol Mercury*, 24 May 1851, p. 8, column b.
[79] *Bristol Mercury*, 17 May 1851, p. 5, column f.
[80] *Ibid.*
[81] *Ibid.*

lar visits to Bristol were drawing to a close. By then Mary had left school and in 1854 she was married. Even so, his involvement in ecclesiastical life in Bristol was significant on at least two further occasions.

In 1850 he was elected a member of the Bristol Church Union, to which Keble already belonged. (It had been founded in 1844 for the defence of Church Schools against State interference.) In this period of Papal Aggression, when public opinion had swung quite violently against the Oxford Movement, the then dean of Bristol, the Very Revd. Gilbert Elliott, was one more strident voice of opposition to the Tractarians, declaiming 'We have not only to contend against Romish papacy but we have to contend against Anglo papacy',[82] and demanding 'Is it not high time that the Tractarian treason should no longer be permitted to train converts to Rome?'[83] At this point many members of the Church Union thought it imperative, given the gravity of the situation, 'to make some kind of anti-Roman declaration to prove their loyalty to the Church of England'.[84] Even Keble thought a 'very moderate but quite real disavowal of Rome'[85] was needed. The Revd. W. Palmer, vice-president of the Union, brought forward a strongly worded resolution. Dr. Pusey was adamant in his opposition to the motion and argued against it on the grounds that bitterness and aggression were themselves unchristian, and he insisted on 'the impropriety of making antagonism to the Church of Rome the basis of religious union'.[86] He saw this issue as one whose effects would be on-going: 'I fear that it will be a hard struggle; but it is of very great moment. It is one to determine the whole course of the movement'.[87] His arguments won Keble round, and after intense debate in the crowded assembly the motion for the anti-Roman declaration was defeated. Pusey's uncompromising stance greatly assisted in the longer term towards an ecumenical movement. Ecumenism was an ideal to which he had all his life aspired: his three-part *Eirenikon* was written as a plea for union between the Church of England and Rome—though he never expected to see it in his lifetime. The entry in the *Oxford Dictionary of National Biography* says: 'Pusey must be regarded as one of the leading ecumenists of the nineteenth century',[88] drawing attention to his role as one who tried to 'reconcile' and 'explain' which he did 'with singular reasonableness and charity'.[89]

He was also involved in the question of the development of ritual practices. Broadly speaking, it was this debate that became, from the 1860s onwards, the arena for the next era of ecclesiastical controversy. The very words Puseyite and Puseyism are significant here, since, in common parlance, they were understood to refer to ritualistic practice. The coinage of these words (which were normally used pejoratively) from his name must have been distasteful to him, for his was a sensitive nature; more importantly, the words were profoundly ironic, as Dr. Pusey had little or no personal inclination towards

---

[82] A. S. Graeme, *Observations upon a Speech, recently delivered by the Dean of Bristol*, (Bristol, 1851), p. 10.

[83] The Revd. P. G. Cobb, *op. cit.*, p. 14.

[84] *Ibid.*, p. 15.

[85] *Ibid.*, also M. Trench, *op. cit.*, p. 354.

[86] M. Trench, *op. cit.*, p. 354.

[87] Quoted in the Revd. P. G. Cobb, *op. cit.*, p. 15. Source given as P. Butler (ed.), *Pusey Rediscovered*, (1983), p. 351.

[88] *O.D.N.B.*, 45, p. 595.

[89] *Ibid.*, p. 598.

ritual. That he did not endorse it is clearly shown in a pleasant letter to Revd. G. R. Prynne, who was for a time one of the curates at St. Andrew, Clifton, and who was influenced by Dr. Pusey's upholding of the practice of confession within the Church of England. Dr. Pusey was of the opinion that ritual must never become an end in itself, and that it should feature, if at all, only within a context of sound church teaching and dedicated pastoral care. As he expresses it in the letter:

> I have long felt that we must win the hearts of the people and then the fruits of reverence will show themselves. To begin with outward things seems like gathering flowers and putting them in the earth to grow. If we win their hearts all the rest will follow.[90]

It is of interest that he himself actually defined Puseyism, in reply to a lady who had enquired its meaning when it came into common usage about 1840. Liddon cites a reply to the enquiry, which was a long and thorough letter of explanation, typical of the doctor's conscientiousness and courtesy. The following is a brief summary of six points which he took to be comprehended in the term:

> High thoughts of the sacraments, particularly Baptism and the Eucharist;
> High estimate of Episcopacy;
> High estimate of the visible Church, the body of Christ;
> Regard for ordinances such as daily public prayers, fasts and feasts;
> Regard for the visible part of devotion;
> Reverence for and deference to the Ancient Church.

To this he added: 'What people mean to blame is what to them appears an excess' (of any of these).[91] The clear implication is that a pejorative usage of the word was usual.

Controversies over ritualism raged fiercely, as we see from Canon Cobb's short study of the Oxford Movement in Bristol, or Forster Alleyne's *All Saints', Clifton*. It was, after all, contention over ritual that caused the closure, for fifteen years, of the beautiful church of St. Raphael, Cumberland Road. The Revd. R. W. Randall was the first vicar of All Saints', Clifton, consecrated in 1868. (Fig. 2.) He was a conscientious, dedicated man, who instituted the daily Office, daily Eucharist, children's services with instruction in the catechism, and who encouraged church missions and parish retreats. He had held always that the law was his 'guiding principle'[92] and that he had scrupulously followed the Prayer Book rubric, and yet, in 1877, proceedings were started against him under the *Public Worship Regulation Act* of 1874. He felt driven to the very point of making his resignation. Canon Liddon (whose father lived for many years in Clifton) and Dr. Pusey begged him to stay on. The latter, by then aged seventy-seven, wrote to him: 'I would gladly go to prison for you'.[93] This would have been said in all sincerity; it would have been consistent with his action in going to Bethnal Green to assist the rector there in visiting the sick and dying in the cholera outbreak of 1866.

Five priests in all served prison sentences under the 1874 Act. The situation only improved when the Act came to be seen as unworkable, and Bishop Ellicott (Fig. 3)

---

[90] M. Chandler, *op. cit.*, p. 107.
[91] The Revd. H. P. Liddon, *op. cit.*, II, p. 140.
[92] F. M. Alleyne, *All Saints', Clifton*, (Bristol, 1893), p. 12.
[93] The Revd. P. G. Cobb, *op. cit.*, p. 23.

Fig. 2. The Revd. Richard William Randall, D.D., (1824–1906), dean of Chichester 1892–1902, photographed in London by Samuel A. Walker, *c.* 1870, [Collection of M. J. Crossley Evans].

declared that to settle 'the ritual question by any definite enactments is hopeless and mischievous';[94] but this was not until 1890. Dr. Pusey died in 1882. In his long association with Bristol, and in his life outside Bristol, he saw many vicissitudes. As he grew older he became more withdrawn and the progress of the Oxford Movement no longer depended so much on him. His steady character, however, meant that he was always 'the stabilizing force of the Catholic revival, steadfast in his loyalty to the Church of England, quietly persistent in his teaching about the meaning of the sacraments and their value'.[95]

[94] *Ibid.*, p. 26.
[95] *O.D.N.B.*, 45, p. 594.

BISHOP OF GLOUCESTER

Fig. 3. Dr. Charles John Ellicott (1819–1905), bishop of Bristol and Gloucester 1863–1897, and of Gloucester 1897–1905, *c.* 1900, [Collection of M. J. Crossley Evans].

PART THREE: 'THAT THY CHURCH MAY JOYFULLY SERVE THEE IN ALL GODLY QUIETNESS': TOWARDS A CLOSE

It is intriguing to try to imagine how Edward Bouverie Pusey was regarded in Bristol in his day. He was necessarily a controversial figure because he was at the head of a controversial religious movement: yet controversy was markedly absent from the sermons he preached: at Horfield 'he preached a sermon more free from controversy than ever I before heard',[96] says Leech, while at St. James his beautiful and scriptural sermon made no reference 'to any controversial matter'.[97]

---

[96] J. Leech, *Rural Rides, op. cit.*, pp. 222–230 *passim.*
[97] *Bristol Mercury*, 9 November 1850, p. 8, column c.

That so quiet and humble a man should ever have attained notoriety was due in part to misrepresentations of him and of Tractarian teaching in the press: even the fact of his staying within the Church of England was often treated with suspicion or contempt. As Leech said: '[They] taunt him with duplicity in remaining—they impatiently and petulantly demand the reason for his stay'.[98] Some of the popular ideas that got about concerning him were quite wild; rumour had it that he slaughtered a lamb every Friday! Leech might indeed question whether at Horfield they expected to catch sight of a cloven hoof.

But the activity of the press was only one factor in a very turbulent period. It would be hard to overestimate the effects upon the public perception of Pusey of such events as the condemned sermon of 1843 (when he feared that parents might withdraw their children from Mrs. Rogers's school); or the secessions of Newman and others;[99] or the period of Papal Aggression. There was a heady current to these times, in which almost anyone might have got caught and swept along.

Some genuine perplexity about Tractarian teaching might have played a part in the misconceptions that beset him in Bristol and elsewhere. To present doctrine to the public is seldom simple. One of Pusey's sermons on the Eucharist had seven hundred pages of notes appended to it! Practices such as confession and fasting, together with his work in directing the first Anglican religious community (founded in Park Village, London, in 1845) must all have added to the belief that he was 'such a friend to the Pope'[100]—an impression firmly fixed in minds more subtle and more learned by far than that of the bucolic lass of Horfield.

His limited awareness of public opinion probably saved him from pain on some occasions. Lack of awareness, in his case, was more of a strength than a weakness, because it proceeded from his unworldliness, his humility, and above all from his freedom from consciousness of self. This was something Leech experienced with striking clarity as the doctor knelt to pray in the Horfield pulpit. The same impression was one which greatly struck the young Richard Meux Benson (founder of the first male religious community, the Cowley Fathers, in 1865). It is illuminating to read of the comparison he made as an undergraduate at Oxford between Newman and Pusey: of Newman he felt: 'That this man was preaching from his heart [...] "And intellect moreover vibrated in every syllable of his sermon"', he was to write years after. Yet he realized with curious insight the weakness of the preacher—his too great self consciousness and occupation with himself. In after years he would compare him with Pusey, 'who had no magic, no silver voice, who spoke in ponderous sentences, and who yet was so self-emptied that he was actually the greater of the two'.[101] And so it was that Dr. Pusey let the bandwagon of public opinion pass him by, while he quietly got on with doing what he believed to be right.

---

[98] J. Leech, *Rural Rides, op. cit.*, p. 225.

[99] These events provided an important impetus for the erection of Buckingham Baptist Chapel in Clifton, see M. J. Crossley Evans, *By God's Grace and To God's Glory: An Account of the Life and Times of Buckingham Chapel, Clifton, Bristol, 1847–1997*, (Bristol, 1997), pp. 1–4.

[100] See extract from his sermon at Horfield. J. Leech, *Rural Rides, op. cit.*, pp. 222–230 *passim*.

[101] M. V. Woodgate, *Father Benson of Cowley*, (1953), pp. 15, 16.

Something that fascinated Leech was the sense of incongruity between the unremarkable looks and frail appearance of this 'poor, plain, pensive man'[102] and his prominence in the Church and public life. Observing him officiating at Holy Communion at St. Andrew in the early 1840s Leech thought:

> He seems to have the capacity neither physical nor moral for battling in the vanguard of a great movement. There is none of that vigour or strength or activity of character required for one taking the part and position he does in the Church of England of the nineteenth century.[103]

Here he made an error of judgement, in equating lack of physical vigour with lack of moral strength. Leech, and no doubt others too, came in time to recognize the exceptional moral stamina so fundamental to his character, which brought him through that 'ordeal severe and trying'.[104] It is doubtless true that physical vigour was lacking, for the private sorrows of his life and his habitual ascetic disciplines took a heavy toll.

The Bristol sermons drew the crowds. The sensation-seekers got nothing, but the big congregations listened with almost spell-bound attention. Liddon and others insist that he was no orator, but as the able and observant J. B. Mozley said: 'Pusey seemed to inhabit his sentences'.[105] This sense of a strong spiritual presence and the passionate, though quiet conviction in his preaching, must have carried his hearers with him. A profound sense of the present reality of God must have enlightened all, so that many were drawn, as Leech was, to 'a beauty of holiness'[106] in this man.

His personality, therefore, found its truest expression not in public life, but in the spiritual and the personal. It is very evident from his letters that he had a real capacity for friendship and this was a feature of his time in Bristol. He also acted as a spiritual friend or guide ('confessor' would have been the more usual term in the nineteenth century) to many, including the founding sisters of the Park Village community, one of whom was Jane Ellacombe, daughter of the vicar of Bitton. This important aspect of his work did not feature largely in Bristol and can receive brief mention only, but it speaks of his complete dedication to the things of the kingdom of heaven, and of his gift of realizing the deep spiritual longings of people, and his nurturing of those seekers. When St. Saviour's in Leeds was consecrated, a week of mission celebrated its opening. He met there a twelve-year-old child, to whom he afterwards wrote:

> Seek that your first waking thought should be of God. It is a very blessed practice that the first word pronounced by the lips should be, very reverently, JESUS. May he keep you for ever in his holy keeping.[107]

His greatest gift to Bristol was that which he strove to impart to all: his inspired vision of a purer, holier church, and of lives of personal sanctity spent in the service of God.

---

[102] J. Leech, *The Church Goer*, *op. cit.*, p. 20.
[103] *Ibid.*
[104] J. Leech, *Rural Rides*, *op. cit.*, p. 225.
[105] Quoted in M. Trench, *op. cit.*, p. 308. Source given as Liddon, *op. cit.*, III, pp. 59, 60.
[106] J. Leech, *Rural Rides*, *op. cit.*, pp. 222, 229.
[107] M. Trench, *op. cit.*, p. 305.

ACKNOWLEDGEMENTS
Sincere appreciation is due to the staff of the Reference and Lending departments of the Bristol Central Library, for their courteous assistance in accessing books and news items, as well as for their technical dexterity in operating machinery. My very sincere gratitude goes to Dr. M. J. Crossley Evans for his unfailing encouragement and patience, and very generous loan of books from the rich resources of his library. His enthusiasm for research has been a constant inspiration.

XVII

'A Grand City': Kilvert and Bristol

JOHN TOMAN B.A., B.PHIL.

'LIFE, MOVEMENT AND WORK'

THE VALUES and experiences linking Kilvert to Bristol were both deep and varied. His *Diary* entry for 23 October 1872 contains some of the factors that made the city important to him. He was attending a conference of clergy and laity at the Victoria Rooms, Clifton, but, being Kilvert, ever responsive to beautiful autumn weather, he stayed only long enough to hear the bishop's address:

> At luncheon I was tempted to cut the afternoon Conference. The weather was so glorious that it seemed a pity to sit in a stuffy room any longer. So I mouched and stealing down Park St. unobserved I breathed freely again in College Green. I made a pilgrimage to the Cathedral where I was ordained Deacon and Priest. The Church was very quiet and once more I knelt in the old place upon the same marble altar steps.[1]

With its frank, personal tone and picture of himself as a naughty schoolboy, assuaging his guilt at playing truant from a religious conference by revisiting the cathedral where he was ordained in 1864, the entry is characteristic of *Kilvert's Diary* and helps to explain its appeal. A year later almost to the day (24 October 1873), he visited Bristol again this time for a cultural event—the Bristol Music Festival—in company with several ladies, two of whom were his sisters, Fanny and Dora. They had come specially to hear the *Messiah*. Kilvert hated crowds and was not pleased at having to struggle with the mass of other people who, like him, were eager to obtain the unreserved seats. 'People were wedged in the doorway and were shot in like cannonballs by the terrible pressure from behind,' he wrote.[2]

On 1 October 1874, Kilvert was pursuing his courtship of Katharine Heanley whom he had met seven weeks before at the wedding of his cousin, Adelaide Cholmeley, to Charles Heanley. Adelaide was living at 1 Carlton Place, Clifton, and Kilvert took the opportunity of visiting her there when Katharine was also visiting from Lincolnshire. When he visited Adelaide again at Carlton Place on 10 December 1874, his courtship of Katharine was running into difficulties and he walked with his friends Jessie and Ella Russell 'over the Suspension Bridge along the edge of Nightingale Valley and through the Leigh Woods beautiful even in winter.' His mind

---

[1] W. Plomer (ed.), *Kilvert's Diary. Selections from the Diary of the Revd. Francis Kilvert*, 2, (1971), p. 282.

[2] *Ibid.*, 2, p. 386.

Fig. 1. The antiquary John Britton, F.S.A., (1850), taken from part 1 of his *Autobiography*, [Collection of M. J. Crossley Evans].

would have turned to 21 August 1874 when he had sat with Adelaide on a seat over-looking the Suspension Bridge while they talked of Katharine and he wrote:

I shall never now see the Suspension Bridge from the Cliff without thinking of Kathleen[*sic*]. The Bridge, the river at low tide, the steep lofty Cliffs, and the green-foliaged dingle and slopes of Nightingale Valley are now inextricably bound up with thoughts of her.[3]

---

[3] *Ibid.*, 3, p. 72.

The *Diary* entry for 4 March 1876 concerns another romantic liaison. The affair with Katharine had faded and the new girl was Ettie Meredith Brown, who lived near Kilvert's Langley Burrell (Wilts.) home. On his way to Carlton Place, he went to Williams, the Bristol book-binder, to have Ettie's name stamped on the leather cover of a manuscript book of his poems, an Easter present for her. Another family connection that took him to Clifton concerned his sister Emily. She was married to an Indian Army officer and she had returned from India in late April 1875, leaving him there. She wanted to set up home in Clifton in the meantime and Kilvert accompanied her there on 21 May to search for a suitable house to rent. They finally chose 'a whole comfortable house at 16 Sion Place' (near the Suspension Bridge but since demolished).

The most significant element in Kilvert's 23 October 1872 *Diary* entry recording his visit to Bristol, in terms of the image he held of the city, is his statement: 'It is a grand city. How much grander than Bath. I breathe freely here. Here is life, movement and work instead of the foolish drawl and idle lounge'. The statement is highly revealing. He knew that Bristol would have difficulty surpassing Bath's elegant terraces and beautiful setting. However, when he said that Bristol was 'a grand city', he was not thinking of physical charms. 'Grand' is almost invariably used in the *Diary* to mean morally wholesome, morally admirable. He recognised that Bristol's appearance could leave something to be desired, referring to it on one visit as 'the vast smoky town'.[4] However, in that phrase lies a clue to the basis of his admiration. His family, originally from Shropshire, had migrated to Bath in the last quarter of the eighteenth century and lived there for over 50 years, before moving to Wiltshire. In this period, the Kilvert family embraced Evangelicalism, which does much to explain Kilvert's endorsement of the virtues of energy and work. He was brought up to value work as appears in his poem 'Honest Work', which begins: 'Honest work is always holy, / Howsoever hard and lowly'. His diary is filled with portraits of small farmers and labourers who provided for their families and remained independent of parish relief by dint of hard work. The virtue of raising oneself through effort and perseverance was also instilled into the diarist, represented by such figures as John Britton (1771–1857), (Fig. 1), the Wiltshire antiquary and topographer,[5] who achieved national eminence from humble beginnings and was commemorated in a poem by Kilvert's uncle Francis, and Richard Hurd (1720–1808), bishop of Worcester,[6] the subject of a biography by uncle Francis. In addition, Kilvert's sister Emily wrote that *Old England: A Pictorial Museum of Regal, Ecclesiastical, Municipal, Baronial and Popular Antiquities* (1844) by Charles Knight (1791–1873) was a formative influence on all the Kilvert children.[7] The volume is permeated by a vision of social progress achieved through work, invention and philanthropy. The Evangelicalism of Kilvert's father, his uncle Francis, and

---

[4] *Ibid.,* 3, p. 32. In another entry (3, p. 89) he referred to 'the murky smoky city'.

[5] Britton wrote (with Edward Brayley) *The Beauties of England and Wales: or Delineations Topographical, Historical and Descriptive of Each County* (various publishers, 1801–1818). Kilvert's father recalled reading its earliest volumes as a child. See 'Memoirs of the Revd. Robert Kilvert' in *More Chapters from the Kilvert Saga,* (Kilvert Society, Leamington Spa, no date), p. 18. Kilvert showed extensive knowledge of Britton's volumes in his diary.

[6] In *Memoirs of the Life and Writings of the Right Rev. Richard Hurd,* (1860), he emphasised 'his gradual ascent ... from an inferior to an exalted station', (p. vi).

[7] E. Wyndowe, 'Rambling Recollections', in *More Chapters from the Kilvert Saga,* p. 89.

(probably) his grandfather, of whom more will be said later, was committed to this idea of work and progress.

The same can be said of the Quakerism that provided a key dimension of Kilvert's sensibility. The family of his mother, the Colemans of Kington Langley near Chippenham, were Quakers for several generations (and originally merchants), and she attended the Moravian school at East Tytherton (its motto was 'Busyness') founded by the Quaker and (later) Evangelical preacher, John Cennick (1718–1755). Kilvert came under additional Quaker influence in the Claverton (Bath) school run by his uncle Francis, whose wife Sophia had been raised in the London home of the Quaker merchant, Thomas Woodruffe. She wrote an educational treatise, *Home Discipline*, which is filled with Evangelical and Quaker ideas. In the following extract from it, she highlighted the Quaker virtues of work, usefulness and philanthropy:

> The riches which have flowed in upon this society, consequent on its habits of patient industry and acknowledged integrity, have tended to bring it conspicuously in contact with many of the most useful institutions in the kingdom for ameliorating the sufferings of mankind.[8]

It can be assumed that she inculcated Quaker virtues into the boys of her husband's school, where Kilvert boarded from 1851 to 1858.[9]

William Penn, the Bristol Quaker leader, was evidently important to Sophia Kilvert's husband from the fact that among his literary papers was found a bookplate of Penn negotiating with the American Indians. It was a scenario emblematic of Quaker wisdom and tolerance. The bookplate is from *A Portraiture of Quakerism* by the Revd. Thomas Clarkson (1760–1846), the anti-slavery campaigner.[10] There is evidence to show that uncle Francis Kilvert passed on to Kilvert, as Kilvert's mother did, a Quaker view of Nature that derived in part from Wordsworth, who was influenced by Quakers in his youth.[11] The Penn family had its roots in Gloucestershire and Wiltshire, facts that would have helped to make it significant for the Kilverts.[12] The latter may have felt a special affinity with the Penn family because the history of one of Mrs. Kilvert's Coleman ancestors paralleled that of William Penn. An American descendant of the Colemans referred to a Thomas Coleman (1602–1685), 'the founder of our family in this country', who emigrated in 1635 to Boston, Massachusetts. He was 'one of the associate proprietors of the Island of Nantucket about 30 miles south of the Massachusetts coast'.[13]

---

[8] *Home Discipline, or, Thoughts on the Origin and Exercise of Domestic Authority*, (1847), p. 156.

[9] Kilvert made a number of favourable references to Quakers in his diary.

[10] Much of Clarkson's evidence about the slave trade was gathered in Bristol. *A Portraiture of Quakerism* (3 vols.) was published in London in 1806.

[11] Wordsworth was a close friend and neighbour of Clarkson in Grasmere. See J. Toman, *Kilvert's Diary and Landscape*, (Cambridge, 2009), chapter two.

[12] John Penne was born in Minety (Wilts.) in 1500 and his grandson, William (born 1548), lived in Bristol and died in Malmesbury (Wilts.) in 1610.

[13] Letter dated 26 December 1895 from Walter Tomlinson Coleman of Brooklyn, New York (collection of genealogical notes about the Coleman family, Wiltshire Record Office, 873/161).

BRISTOL AND QUAKERS

In a city of 'life, movement and work', one would expect to find Quakers because it would provide opportunities for their particular attitudes and skills. In the eighteenth century, 'The city's population included the highest percentage of Quakers anywhere in England'.[14] Such prominent Bristol Quaker families as the Frys, Champions, Harfords and Goldneys are synonymous with the city's industrial and commercial heritage. Long-standing links between Kilvert's family and the Goldneys would no doubt have coloured Kilvert's attitude towards Bristol. 'The Goldneys were merchants of wealth and importance at Bristol for many generations [...] A branch of the family settled in Chippenham, Wiltshire, in the 15th-century, and has been instrumental in the development of the important cloth manufactories in the West of England'.[15] The Coleman antecedents of Kilvert's mother (born 1808) rubbed shoulders with Goldneys at the Chippenham Monthly Meetings of Quakers in the late seventeenth and early eighteenth centuries. The notes to the Chippenham Minute Books describe the Chippenham Meeting as:

> A better educated and wealthier one than the Wilts. East Meeting, containing eleven yeomen—substantial farmers owning their own land—and a number of manufacturers, shopkeepers, and craftsmen connected with the clothing trade.[16]

The trade of Adam Goldney II is given in Appendix II as 'linen-draper'.

Kilvert was always drawn to landed families, especially ones who had exerted beneficent influence over a community for many generations, as, for example, the Clutterbucks of Widcombe (near Bath)—'the old family, the beloved and honoured family'.[17] The Goldneys were another such and reverence for them as Quakers and for their long service as Chippenham's bailiffs, mayors and M.P.s lay at the bottom of Kilvert's alarm when it appeared that Gabriel Goldney (1813–1900, 1st Baronet 1880) might lose the 1874 Chippenham election. A 'Radical' (i.e. Liberal) candidate had presented himself. 'We thought Goldney was going to walk over the course without opposition', Kilvert wrote nervously. Nevertheless, Goldney won and, while enjoying a lift into Chippenham in Goldney's brougham, Kilvert 'congratulated him heartily on his success'.[18]

The Goldney family's relationship with Bristol began when Gabriel Goldney (1589–1670) sent his second son Thomas there as an apprentice to a grocer. Having acquired his own grocery business, Thomas I became an important figure in Bristol's newly formed Society of Friends, and his son (also a grocer), Thomas II (1664–1731), bought what became Goldney House. He began to show the interest in metal trades that allied him with the Champion family. Thomas II was an early investor in the

---

[14] M. E. Fissell, *Patients, Power and the Poor in Eighteenth Century Bristol*, (Cambridge, 1991), pp. 6–7.

[15] *Burke's Peerage and Baronetage*. The Quaker influence on Kilvert is explored in J. Toman, 'The Kilvert Quaker Background: A story that could not be told', *Kilvert Society Journal*, No. 24, September 2007.

[16] Wiltshire Record Office 1699–79, Chippenham Monthly Meeting Minute Books 1669–1709, transcribed by N. Saxon Snell with notes by B. Saxon Snell..

[17] *Kilvert's Diary*, 3, p. 241.

[18] *Ibid.*, 2, p. 408 and p. 410.

Coalbrookdale iron works of the Quaker Abraham Darby. Coalbrookdale goods—pig iron, hollow ware (such as pots and furnaces), cylinders and other parts of Newcomen steam engines—were being sent by trow down the Severn to Bristol. In 1752 came the move into banking that was characteristic of so many, particularly Quaker, trading families: Thomas III and five partners opened a bank (Goldney, Smith and Co.) in Corn Street. The partners—one was Richard Champion of the metal dealing family, another was Morgan Smith, a sugar refiner—were all Quakers.[19] The Goldney wealth helped William Penn in 1708 to secure Pennsylvania when his right to it was challenged: Henry Goldney, cousin of Thomas Goldney III (1696–1768), lent Penn £3,300.[20]

THE POPE FAMILY AND THE SUGAR TRADE

In many respects the family of Kilvert's close friend, Andrew Pope epitomised Bristol's 'life, movement and work'. Their friendship dated from 1867 when they found themselves fellow curates in parishes either side of Hay-on-Wye:– Kilvert in Clyro (from 1865), Pope in Cusop (from 1867). The two men often dined, lunched, and walked the countryside together. Kilvert was best man at Pope's wedding on 9 September 1874 when he married Harriet Mary Money Kyrle of Much Marcle, Herefordshire. (Fig. 2).

During the twelve-year friendship of the two clergymen, Kilvert must have learnt the story of the rise to eminence of the Pope family. It was notably successful in the sugar trade, which 'was the greatest success story in Bristol's eighteenth century Atlantic trade, [...] the most remunerative' of all Bristol's trades.[21] The Pope sugar business owed its origin to the merchant (and Baptist) Thomas Ellis, who bought Whitson Court in 1665 and developed it as a sugar house, in which sugar, imported from the West Indies, went through a refining process culminating in the baking of 'loaves' of sugar by charcoal fires. The Pope family too had Baptist and Congregationalist affiliations; a significant number of businessmen in the sugar trade were Quakers. The sugar trade developed at a time of fierce competition in Bristol's industrial history, when 'every man was out for himself', and Michael Pope and his partners, John Whiting and Nehemiah Webb, who were typical of the sons of clothiers, yeomen and of other men of humble occupation drawn from surrounding country districts into the city's grocery and sugar refining businesses,[22] began life there as grocers. Michael Pope, 'bold, energetic' and with a sharp sense of business, continued in that field until 1682 when he and his partners bought Whitson Court, named after the Whitson manor estate, on part of which Bristol Royal Infirmary now stands. Whitson Court was an extensive property comprising warehouse, mill house, cooper-

[19] P.K. Stembridge, 'The Goldney Family. A Bristol Merchant Dynasty', B.R.S., Bristol, XLIX, (1998), pp. 3, 24, 30, 34, 62.

[20] See W. Dixon, William Penn: An Historical Biography, (1851), p. 416.

[21] K. Morgan, Bristol and the Atlantic Trade in the Eighteenth Century, (Cambridge, 1993), pp. 221–222.

[22] I. V. Hall, 'Whitson Court Sugar House, Bristol, 1665–1824', T.B.&G.A.S., 65, (1944), pp. 9–10. The Pope family came from Brislington in Somerset in the seventeenth century; Whiting was the son of an Upton (Gloucs.) mason.

Fig. 2. The wedding of the Revd. Andrew Pope, 9 September 1874, taken at Homme House, Much Marcle, Herefordshire. The Revd. Francis Kilvert, the best man, is to be seen bearded and seated, to the far right, [By kind permission of the Kilvert Society].

age, drying rooms, workshops, counting house and stables.[23] Because water was extensively used in the refining process of sugar, sugar bakers sought sites on the banks of rivers and, for transport purposes, near main roads.[24] There was great competition to acquire good sites and ambitious men could see that furtherance of their interests depended on having political influence in Bristol so they aspired to become city councillors, or mayor, or to attain high position in religious associations. 'Thus a ring of interest developed in the local sugar trade and Bristol was ruled by its sugar lords'.[25]

The influence of the sugar trade was felt beyond Bristol in surrounding counties as is evident from the number of estates in Somerset, Gloucestershire and Herefordshire founded on sugar interests. One of these estates—that of the Cornewall family of Moccas Court, Herefordshire—features in *Kilvert's Diary*. When Kilvert became vicar of Bredwardine, Sir George Cornewall was his local squire and Kilvert may have known the source of the wealth of the family because, on the basis of his fanciful claim to have kinship with it, he investigated its history.[26] An eighteenth century Sir George

---

[23] D. Jones, *'The Bristol Sugar Trade and Refining Industry'*, Bristol Historical Association, 89, (1996), p. 10.

[24] K. Morgan, *op.cit.*, p. 216.

[25] I. V. Hall, *op. cit.*, p. 11.

[26] *Kilvert's Diary*, 3, pp. 165, 346, 357–358.

Fig. 3. The Revd. Andrew Pope (1844–1924), c. 1905, [By kind permission of the Kilvert Society].

Cornewall was heavily involved in a West Indian sugar plantation.[27] It was the sugar trade that drove Bristol's economy in the eighteenth century and was its greatest source of wealth.[28] It boomed most spectacularly in the period when Michael Pope was establishing his sugar house: 1700 to the late-1720s saw a 54% increase in imports.[29] Bristol had twenty sugar refineries by 1750 and sugar imports doubled between 1748 and 1775, making it second only to London as a sugar port.[30] Its reputation as a centre of trade and as one of the five largest English cities would have been a formative element in Kilvert's consciousness as he grew up.

When he made his contrast between Bristol and Bath in terms of the one being a place of work, the other of idleness, it was Bristol's reputation as an industrial centre he was highlighting: 'Bristol was a leading centre of growth industries between 1660 and 1800: sugar refining, soap-making, glass and pottery manufacture, and the metal industries all flourished in the city during that period'.[31] There was some industrial

---

[27] See S. Seymour, S. Daniels and C. Watkins, *Estate and Empire: Sir George Cornewall's Management of 'Moccas', Herefordshire and 'La Taste', Grenada, 1771–1819*, University of Nottingham, Department of Geography, Working Paper 28, (1994).

[28] K. Morgan, *op. cit.*, p. 185.

[29] *Ibid.*, pp. 13, 15.

[30] *Ibid.*, pp. 186, 188.

[31] *Ibid.*, p. 219.

activity in Bath but it was small and dated largely from the start of the nineteenth century.[32] Neale summed up the nature of Bath in the eighteenth century: 'for men and women of property and wealth it offered brief moments of social communion wrapped in a cocoon of pleasure in pleasant surroundings remote from the competitive reality of the economic life of property and wealth,' adding 'It was a pre-industrial city'.[33] This ethos was the basis of Kilvert's characterisation of Bath in terms of 'the foolish drawl and the idle lounge', a critical viewpoint fully expressive of his Quaker and Evangelical background that valued energy, enterprise and usefulness. Bath did not experience, as Bristol did, direct experience of the eighteenth century West Indian sugar trade but its beneficiaries gave the former much of its character, as is evident from the oft-quoted passage in Smollett's *Humphrey Clinker* (1771):

> Every upstart of fortune [...] presents himself at Bath. Clerks and factors from the East Indies loaded with the spoil of plundered provinces; planters, Negro drivers [...] from our American plantations [...]; contractors who have fattened in two successive wars on the blood of the nations; insurers, brokers and jobbers of every kind; men of low birth, and no breeding, have found themselves suddenly translated into a state of affluence.[34]

It was in order to service Bath's rich, fashionable and idle that Kilvert's grandfather set up there a coach-building business (in which sugar actually played some small part: the spirits distilled from molasses, the lowest grade of sugar, were basic to the varnishes used by coach-builders). It should be remembered that in the Kilvert family's history in Bath trades of various kinds played a significant role. Kilvert's grandfather had moved there in company with other, largely Shropshire, businessmen in the late 1770s to early 1780s. These men were involved in ironmongery, wine shops, corn and coal businesses, and several of them were Quakers or Nonconformists. The Clutterbuck family, the Bath patrons of the Kilverts, also had Quaker and Unitarian links and became bankers in the city.

The family of one of the Shropshire businessmen, Frederick Falkner, a cousin of Kilvert's father, progressed from being wine merchants to bankers in a pattern that closely resembled the Pope family's progress. After Michael Pope's death in 1723, 'the Popes, during the next two generations elevated their social position; they prided themselves as Merchant Venturers, entered the City Council, served as sheriffs and mayors, [...] became local bankers'.[35] They also became lawyers and clergymen. Andrew Pope I, great-grandfather of the Andrew of *Kilvert's Diary*, (Fig. 3), was Bristol's mayor in 1775. At the start of the nineteenth century, the family moved to an estate adjacent to Hampton Road and Cotham Road, part of which is now the site of Cotham Comprehensive School.[36] Andrew Pope II sold all his interests in the Whitson Court business in 1808, the year he became a partner in the Tolzey Bank.

---

[32] R. S. Neale referred to a number of small factories in the 1820s and 1830s in *Bath 1680–1850: A Social History*, (1981), p. 270. The Revd. R. Warner spoke of 'useful manufactories' outside the city at Twerton; see *The History of Bath*, (Bath, 1801), p. 215.

[33] R. S. Neale, *op. cit.*, p. 38.

[34] Quoted in H. Torrens, *The Evolution of a Family Firm: Stothert and Pitt of Bath*, (Bath, 1978), p. 1.

[35] I. V. Hall, *op. cit.*, p. 63.

[36] E. West, 'Rev. Andrew Pope', *Kilvert Society Newsletter*, Aug. 1983.

The Pope family's rise from grocers and sugar bakers to bankers and public figures typified not only Bristol as a city, but also the model of enterprise and self-help that had been held up to Kilvert from childhood. At that time, and at the time of his visits to Bristol, the city would still have appeared as a flourishing place, even though from long before his birth in 1840 it was in decline commercially.[37] During his lifetime, its shipbuilding, sugar refining, cocoa, chocolate and tobacco manufacture continued to prosper.[38]

ST. MARY REDCLIFFE AND CHATTERTON

Kilvert's 'pilgrimage' to Bristol cathedral where he was ordained is indicative of an important trait in his character, one that his background greatly encouraged: a veneration for the past, represented often by ancient buildings. The Kilvert children were brought up with antiquarianism, chiefly because their uncle Francis was an antiquary.[39] This partly explains Kilvert's intense interest in Bristol's church of St. Mary Redcliffe. It seems that whenever he visited the city, he would squeeze in a 'pilgrimage' to the church if he possibly could, as, for example, on 23 October 1872, when he recorded paying 'a flying visit to the glorious church of St. Mary Redcliffe at last completed by a noble spire', the last words suggesting a steady concern with the history. He also went to St. Mary Redcliffe (S.M.R. henceforth) before going on to hear *The Messiah* during his 24 October 1873 visit. It has been noted already that *The Beauties of England and Wales* by the antiquary/topographer John Britton figured in Kilvert's background. In the Somerset volume, S.M.R. is described as 'the finest parochial church in the kingdom',[40] a phrase repeated in another work known to the diarist by William Howitt, who observed that 'Mr. Britton has been almost as enamoured of it as was Chatterton himself'.[41] Britton wrote his own study (1813) of S.M.R., the dedication of which (to the Bristol Quaker, Charles Joseph Harford) stated: 'As a whole it is grand and imposing, and its details are beautiful, curious and elegant'. Central to Britton's account of it was 'an essay on the Life and Character of Thomas Chatterton [who] had enrolled its name in the annals of poetry'. Chatterton's writings, Britton said, 'gave the church and the surrounding scenery a powerful, but adventitious, interest'.[42] For Howitt too the church's association with the poet was vital to its appeal: it had, he wrote, 'awoken the soul of one of its lovers' (i.e. Chatterton). Britton's links with S.M.R. continued long after his 1813 study, for he was involved in its restoration. An 1842 appeal for funds for this work, including reconstruction of its spire, referred to reports by him on the structure.[43] (Fig. 4). Kilvert's 1 October 1874

---

[37] B. W. E. Alford, 'Economic Development of Bristol in the nineteenth century: an enigma?' in P. McGrath (ed.), *Essays in Bristol and Gloucestershire History*, (Bristol, 1976), pp. 252–254.

[38] K. Morgan, *op. cit.*, p. 223.

[39] In the early nineteenth century, when he was growing up in Bath, the city boasted a circle of antiquarians.

[40] Vol. 13, part II, p. 670. This volume was written by the Revd. J. Nightingale.

[41] W. Howitt, *Homes and Haunts of the Most Eminent British Poets*, 2, (1849), p. 234.

[42] J. Britton, *An Historical and Archaeological Essay relating to Redcliffe Church Bristol*, (1813), p. 2.

[43] M. Q. Smith, *St. Mary Redcliffe: An architectural history*, (Bristol, 1995), p. 142. See also entry on Britton in the *Oxford Dictionary of National Biography*.

Fig. 4. The Renovation of the spire of St. Mary Redcliffe: the spire completed (1872), [The Reece Winstone Collection].

Diary entry shows again his concern with the repair: 'The Church is still under repair, the roof of the nave being now nearly restored'.

A shared interest in antiquarianism was one of the things that attracted Kilvert to Chatterton (1752–1770). Peter Ackroyd said of the latter: 'He pursued that antiquarian passion [...] which seems inseparable from the native genius' and the moment when the old chests in the muniment room of S.M.R. were opened and Chatterton gained possession of old manuscripts, 'must stand as one of the most important scenes in English literary history'.[44] On the basis of those manuscripts and other sources, Chatterton, while still an adolescent, wrote a series of poems and prose works which he claimed had been written by Thomas Rowley, an imaginary monk of the fifteenth century. They were initially accepted as genuine but later rejected as forgeries.[45]

Chatterton's family was a poor one. His father, who died some months before his son's birth, was the school master of the Free School in Pile Street in Redcliffe. (Fig. 5). Later, the family moved to 'a dark old house on Redcliffe Hill'.[46] A sub-chanter in Bristol Cathedral, he was also a man with antiquarian interests. The Chatterton men had been for several generations sextons of S.M.R. and from childhood Thomas had developed 'a passion for this lovely structure'.[47] Charles Knight, in the *Old England* volume that Kilvert's sister said was a 'never failing source of pleasure' to her and her siblings,[48] repeated the famous story of how Chatterton, 'on some sudden impulse, [would] throw himself on the green sward and, fixing his eyes upon the venerable structure, was lost in a species of ecstasy'. Knight's characterisation of Chatterton as 'one of the proudest, because one of the poorest and most sensitive, of poets that ever trod the earth' was probably a key element in Kilvert's conception of him. Knight stated that the youthful poet (he was only 17 years 9 months old when he died) had a name 'suggestive of melancholy considerations', and to contemplate his poetry inevitably meant contemplating 'the awful shadow of the boy-suicide'.[49] One must assume that this 'shadow' possessed Kilvert on his 23 October 1872 visit to S.M.R. when he wrote 'Poor Chatterton. Poor Chatterton' (the phrase appears in Knight's account). The shadow also falls across Kilvert's 1 October 1874 *Diary* entry when he, in company with Katharine Heanley and Jessie Russell, 'ascended the spiral staircase to the Muniments Room and saw the old worm-eaten remnants of the chests in which Chatterton "the marvellous boy, the sleepless soul that perished in his pride" averred that he had discovered the poems of Rowley the monk'. Kilvert added, partly (one assumes) because he had Katharine Heanley with him, 'it was a very happy day'.

The quoted lines ('the marvellous boy' etc.) in Kilvert's entry are from Wordsworth's poem *Resolution and Independence*, which is about his encounter with an old man whose existence depends on the meagre income he derives from gathering and selling leeches. In essence, he represents 'Honest Work' that was central to

---

[44] N. Groom (ed.), *Thomas Chatterton and Romantic Culture*, (Basingstoke, 1999), p. 1, preface.
[45] They are currently being reassessed and considered as a new form of fiction.
[46] J. C. Nevill, *Thomas Chatterton*, (New York, 1970), p. 11.
[47] W. Howitt, *Homes and Haunts of the Most Eminent British Poets*, 2, (1849), p. 235.
[48] E. Wyndowe, 'Rambling Recollections', *op. cit.*, p. 89.
[49] C. Knight, *Old England: A Pictorial Museum of Regal, Ecclesiastical, Municipal, Baronial and Popular Antiquities*, 1, (New York [1847], 1987), p. 303. This huge book (800 double-column pages) was in itself an education in antiquarianism.

Fig. 5. Chatterton's birthplace, [copyright *Wikipedia*].

Kilvert's moral outlook (Wordsworth referred to the leech gatherer's 'honest maintenance'). The old man's independence reminded the poet of others who were 'deified'
by their determination to help themselves and he cited Robert Burns, who 'followed
his plough', and Chatterton, 'the marvellous boy'. However, the recollection (particularly of the latter) led him to the reflection that 'We Poets in our youth begin in
gladness; / But thereof come in the end to despondency and madness'. A number of
other poets had written similar poems on Chatterton's fate and they helped to fashion a Romantic cult. Groom observed that the Chatterton myth is one 'built literally
on madness', adding that what captivated writers and painters about it is the 'nostal-
gic and elegiac figment of Chatterton'. Henry Wallis's famous painting *The Death of
Chatterton*, (1856), which must have been known to Kilvert, is 'the most enduring image
of Romanticism […] this angelic poet has suffered for his genius—starving and destitute, mad and suicidal and now dead'.[50] Groom has challenged the story of
Chatterton's suicide, seeing it as the result of an overdose of opium and arsenic.[51]

[50] N. Groom (ed.), *op. cit.*, pp. 3, 8.
[51] N. Groom, 'The Death of Chatterton' in A. Heys (ed.), *From Gothic to Romance: Thomas
Chatterton's Bristol*, (Bristol, 2005), pp. 116–125.

It is probable that Kilvert knew the series of watercolours painted around 1800 by Turner, Girtin, Cotman and Varley, which reinforced S.M.R.'s Romantic image. They are watercolours which represent 'the church and its setting transfigured by powerfully imaginative and intensely poetic responses', emphasising its historical and picturesque associations, antiquarian interest, and with strong 'romantic overtones'.[52] Kilvert's taste in painting shows an attraction towards exactly the kind of content and tone found in these watercolours. Billingham noted that 'he required elevating subject matter and dramatic interpretation' and that he favoured the 'tenebrosi' (sombre, melancholic) style of Baroque painting—all of which elements are present in the watercolours.[53] The engraving of S.M.R. (no. 1043) that Kilvert had seen in *Old England* is notable for the way the shadow of the tower (minus spire) falls ominously across figures in the foreground. Kilvert was also drawn to paintings that told stories, particularly dramatic and touching ones, and the antiquarian books by Knight and Britton that he knew from childhood are replete with such material. Kilvert was attracted to Chatterton's Rowley poems because they linked together S.M.R.'s story with that of the merchant, William Canynge, and Bristol at the time of the Wars of the Roses. Heys argued that 'Bristol is as much part of Chatterton as Chatterton is part of Bristol; the two are inextricably linked'.[54] Similarly, Nevill noted that Chatterton, 'a romanticist at heart', found satisfaction in creating a 'half real, half imagined [Bristol] of medieval days'.[55] Kilvert's 'pilgrimages' to other historic buildings are marked by the love of the picturesque, the historic, the poetic, the antiquarian that characterises his *Diary* entries on S.M.R. His background bred this response but it was also an element of his personality and his literary taste.[56] In one *Diary* entry, he wrote: 'I like wandering about these lonely, waste and ruined places'.[57] And his accounts of visits to old buildings often have a melancholy, elegiac quality[58] and the awareness of change that is also a feature of his taste in painting.

It is unsurprising therefore that he warmed to both the personality and the image of Chatterton, epitomised by S.M.R. He and Chatterton come together most clearly in their disposition towards melancholy, their love of ancient buildings, of the romance and mystery of the past. S.M.R. was the 'metaphorical gateway' through which Chatterton's imagination 'worked itself back into the great field of the past'.[59] The same might be said of Kilvert, who had been brought up by his uncle Francis to

[52] M. J. H. Liversidge, 'Romantic Redcliffe: Image and Imagination', in A. Heys, (ed.)., *op. cit.*, p. 53. The watercolours—*South Porch of S.M.R.* (1792) by Turner, *S.M.R.* (1800–01) by Girtin, *S.M.R.. Dawn* (1801–02) by Cotman, and *S.M.R.* (1806) by F. C. Lewis after John Varley—are reproduced in Liversidge's essay. Varley's *S.M.R. from the north* (1802) had appeared in Britton's, *The Beauties of England and Wales*, 13, part II, (1813).

[53] R. Billingham, *The Rev. R. F. Kilvert and the Visual Arts*, (Kilvert Society, Hay-on-Wye, no date), p. 6.

[54] A. Heys, *op. cit.*, p. 9.

[55] J. C. Nevill, *op. cit.*, p. 30.

[56] For the cult of mourning in which he was raised, and his love of graveyards, see J. Toman, *Kilvert's Diary and Landscape* (Cambridge, 2009), chapter one.

[57] *Kilvert's Diary*, 1, p. 307.

[58] For example, Wadham College (Oxford), Old Sarum, Stonehenge, Restormel Castle, the ruined church of Llanlionfel, and the ruined farmhouse of Whitehall.

[59] D. Masson, *Chatterton: A Story of the Year 1770*, (1874), p. 42.

admire eighteenth century writers and by his father to love Scott's novels, which reanimate a past of feudal values and ancient buildings.

THE CLERGY DAUGHTERS' SCHOOL

One of Kilvert's visits (4 June 1874) to Bristol took him to the Clergy Daughters' School (C.D.S.) in Great George Street (off Park Street), to see Janet Vaughan, daughter of his very close friend, the Revd. David Vaughan (1819–1903), rector of Newchurch, Radnorshire. Vaughan was of Radnorshire peasant farming stock. Educated at an elementary school, he worked on his father's farm before entering Lampeter College on 1 October 1845, aged 26, in order to train for the ministry. The majority of the students were sons of Welsh farmers and most were ordained, usually to serve parishes in their native counties. Students at Lampeter College did not receive degrees but only certificates.[60] Vaughan typified the individual from a humble background whom Kilvert had been brought up to admire. Kilvert admired Vaughan, not only for his hard work and self-improvement, but also for his Evangelical piety.

The original C.D.S. was founded for poor Evangelical clergymen like Vaughan, who had several daughters to educate. The Revd. William Carus Wilson (1791–1859) had set up the first C.D.S. at Cowan Bridge, Yorkshire, in 1824. It had gained notoriety from its portrayal as 'Lowood' in Charlotte Brontë's *Jane Eyre* (1847) as a place of harshness and cruelty. The school was seen to meet a need and similar institutions were established in Brighton, Warrington, Dublin and Bristol. The Bristol C.D.S. began in Gloucester in 1831. Teaching covered 'the Christian religion according to the Church of England, the 3Rs, English grammar, geography and 'the use of the globes, and plain needlework'. Pupils were to leave at fourteen to be employed in 'useful domestic offices'.[61] Persistent illness of pupils throughout much of 1832, caused by faulty drains, led to the school's removal to Bristol in 1833 where it was located in the Old School House at the Royal Fort, St. Michael's Hill. Illness, including diphtheria, kept breaking out in the 1850s and the school's honorary physician recommended a move to new premises. The Revd. Alfred Peache, a governor, offered to buy the house, known as the Old Mansion House, at the top of Great George Street, for which he paid £2,750. (Fig. 6). The house stood in grounds occupying the whole of the top of the hill. The formal re-opening of the school took place on 10 February 1862, at which time there were 36 pupils. Its extreme Protestant bias may be glimpsed from the Committee's declaration of its fierce adherence to 'Principles [...] consistent with Evangelical and Protestant truth'.[62]

Janet Vaughan became a pupil in January 1874. She was then just fourteen and Kilvert had known her since she was five. He had become particularly fond of her and showed it in physically demonstrative ways surprising to twenty-first century readers of *Kilvert's Diary*. However, Victorians went in for a good deal of touching, hand-holding and kissing among friends. Kilvert is regularly found kissing young girls, often in

---

[60] The College was later granted the right to confer degrees– the B.D. in 1852 and the B.A. in 1865.

[61] *St. Brandon's School: 150 Years 1831–1981*, (Bristol, 1981), p. 12; B.R.O., 40398/SG/7/8.

[62] B.R.O., 40398/M/1/6, Committee Minutes, 30 May 1873.

Fig. 6. Detail from the façade of the Clergy Daughters' School, Brandon Hill, [copyright John Toman].

their parents' presence. When he walked into the C.D.S. on 4 June 1874 she unself-consciously greeted him with 'a long loving kiss'. He attached great value to such displays of affection partly because Evangelicalism did, partly because he was a man of strong passions, and partly because he craved spontaneity and naturalness in (especially women's) behaviour. His attitude emerges clearly in his observation on entering the school that though Janet was 'much grown', she was 'as sweet and simple and affectionate as ever'. Of course, he was sexually attracted to her but most commentators on *Kilvert's Diary* agree that his behaviour towards young girls was innocent and involved no misconduct. The natural warmth between him and Janet was, however, to incur the disapproval of the C.D.S. They went out of the School into the garden at the rear into 'a secluded walk, dark and shady […] called in the school traditions the "Poet's Retreat"'. They carved their names on a beech tree 'whose bark was grimy black with Bristol smuts' and generally behaved like lovers. He had called into the market earlier to buy Janet 'a nosegay of roses'.

Their behaviour in the garden was observed, as is recorded in the committee minutes of 12 February 1875, which relate how 'a note from the Revd. Kilvert addressed to Jeanetta Vaughan'[63] had been laid before the committee. 'It appeared that Mr. Kilvert was a friend of the family, but had called at the school last half year, and had conducted himself in a trifling way in the garden in the presence of the school, which conduct he followed this half year by the letter produced, in which he alluded to the circumstances in language calculated to lower the tone of the school'. The minutes' language had been carefully selected to register the moral outrage felt by the committee. Miss Winter, the school principal, had intercepted Kilvert's letter and brought it to the governors' attention. On 10 December 1874 he was aware that his visit to Janet on 4 June had occasioned comment. He had gone to Bristol in December to see Adelaide Cholmeley, and she and her friends were, he wrote, 'in fits of laughter at the story of my visit to the young ladies' school in Great George Street when the Lady Principal was horrified to discover that I was not as she had thought "quite an old gentleman"'.[64] Amusement later gave way to anger on 19 March 1875 when a *Diary* entry noted that he was 'very annoyed' to learn from one of Janet's sisters of Miss Winter's actions. Janet's father was told by the school's honorary secretary that if Janet continued to receive letters from Kilvert the Revd. Mr. Vaughan must withdraw her. A 'very satisfactory letter' (the words of the 4 June 1875 committee meeting) was received from Vaughan and the outcome of the affair was a change in the school rule which stated that no unmarried male relation of a pupil was allowed to come to the school. Kilvert had thus left his mark on the school, in addition to his initials on a tree in its garden. (The tree exists no longer because the garden is a car park.) The mark Janet left consisted in her academic achievements. She was in the sixth form for the whole of 1879 and was one of two pupils awarded prizes for painting and drawing. School records show that she achieved distinctions in French, Latin, Arithmetic and Mathematics in the Higher Oxford Local Examinations, although this was in 1885, after she had left. She was offered a scholarship at Newnham College, Cambridge, but there is no record of her being a student there.

BRISLINGTON HOUSE

Masson, in his 1856 book on Chatterton, observed: 'A medical friend of ours avers that he never knew a man of genius who had not some aunt or other in a lunatic asylum'.[65] Kilvert was not a man of genius but he met the medical friend's criterion. Perhaps because he knew something of the anguish attending the decision to place someone dear in an asylum, he was careful to record instances of it in his diary. In one of them, he was personally involved: 'Ellen Clifford told me that my poor old

[63] Committee minutes of 30 May 1873 record approval of the admission of 'Jeanne Jane Vaughan'. The school register lists her as 'Janetta'.

[64] *Kilvert's Diary*, 3, p. 120.

[65] D. Masson, *op. cit.*, p. 40.

nurse Mary Strange was taken to the lunatic asylum at Devizes last Thursday'. She went 'resignedly', he recorded, 'but she said sorrowfully that she thought it very sad that she should be obliged to spend the rest of her life in such a place'.[66] That Kilvert was preoccupied with such cases is clear from their frequency in the *Diary*.[67] His aunt Emma, wife of the Revd. Edward Kilvert, younger brother of Kilvert's father, was a patient in Brislington House and visiting her there was another of Kilvert's links with Bristol. He wrote on 2 November 1874: 'By the 12.40 train [...] to Keynsham with my Father on our way to pay a visit to Aunt Emma at Dr. Fox's private lunatic asylum at Brislington'.

Brislington House had been founded by Dr. Edward Long Fox (1761–1835) of the Quaker Fox family, which had several strands in the west. Trade was a dominant element in the family's history: several family members were merchants and businessmen. Medicine was another significant element. Edward's father, of the Falmouth strand, was a doctor as were many of his descendants. Edward Fox helped in his father's Falmouth general practice and in a Plymouth practice until 1786 when he became physician to Bristol Royal Infirmary, living first at 16 Castle Green, later at 45 Queen Square. Always keen to explore new treatments, he studied mesmerism and tried it on his Infirmary patients.[68] He pioneered the treatment for the insane known as 'Moral Therapy' or 'Moral Treatment' in 1790 at his small Quaker asylum at Cleeve Hill, Downend, Bristol. The treatment has been described thus: 'a mild regimen centred on the placement of the patient in a carefully designed environment and one that tried to minimise the use of physical forms of restraint'.[69]

A desire to expand his treatment and his income led Edward Long Fox to begin building Brislington House in 1804 on former common land near the village. Costing an enormous £35,000, it opened in 1806. Hickman stated that 'it was aimed predominantly at an élite private clientèle',[70] as its buildings and setting confirm. Kilvert found it very impressive: 'Brislington Asylum is a fine palatial-looking building very beautifully situated on the high ground between Keynsham and Bristol, and the grounds are large and well kept'.[71] (Figs. 7a, 7b). There were several detached houses in the grounds for nobility and their servants and a number of large 'cottages', one for Fox's own family. The year after he died (1835), two of his sons, Francis and Charles (both doctors), published *History and Present State of Brislington House*, which described the place and its rationale. It noted that 'intimidation' was once seen as 'the only means by which lunatics could be governed', with much use of 'corporal punishment and personal restraint'. Patients were usually accommodated in buildings not designed for them, whereas Edward Fox's asylum was purpose-built in a setting 'to which his taste gave an imposing appearance, having laid it out in diversified walks and extensive plantations [...] in a well-wooded estate'.[72] The landscape Fox designed

[66] *Kilvert's Diary*, 3, pp. 301–302.

[67] *Ibid.*, 1, pp. 88, 275; 2, p. 272; 3, p. 221.

[68] G. Munro Smith, *A History of the Bristol Royal Infirmary*, (Bristol, 1917), pp. 474–475.

[69] C. Hickman, 'Moral therapy, asylums and gardens', *Journal of Medical Biography*, 15, (2007), p. 187.

[70] *Ibid.*, p. 187.

[71] *Kilvert's Diary*, 3, pp. 103–104.

[72] Anon., *History and Present State of Brislington House, near Bristol*, [...], (Bristol, 1836), pp. 3–4.

Figs. 7a, and 7b. Two illustrations of Dr. Fox's Asylum, taken from Anon, *History and Present State of Brislington House, near Bristol, an Asylum for the cure and reception of Insane Persons, established by Edward Long Fox M.D., A.D. 1804*, (Bristol, 1836), [Special Collections, University of Bristol].

complemented its beautiful setting.[73] John Perceval, a patient there from January 1831 to May 1832, wrote: 'Dr. Fox's madhouse stood in a very fine and picturesque country and near a steep and wooded bank that bordered the river. At one elevated spot commanding a view down the valley, there was a natural or artificial precipice', to which patients were often and bizarrely (for some were suicidal) led. Perceval himself recorded: 'My voices commanded me to throw myself over'.[74] One wonders whether

[73] Hickman examines the landscape's role in Brislington's therapy in 'The "Picturesque" at Brislington House: the role of landscape in relation to the treatment of mental illness in the early nineteenth-century asylum', *Garden History*, (2005), 33, pp. 47–60.

[74] G. Bateson (ed.), *Perceval's Narrative: A patient's account of his psychosis 1830–1832*, (1962), p. 116. Originally published as *A Narrative of the Treatment Experienced by a Gentleman during a State of Mental Derangement* by John Perceval, (1840).

Perceval's case was known to the Kilvert family because he was the fifth son of Spencer Perceval, Britain's first Evangelical Prime Minister, whose assassination in 1812 was, Kilvert's father recorded, 'marked in my memory as with the point of a diamond'.[75] John Perceval's relatives had chosen Brislington House partly because of its picturesque setting;[76] the Kilvert family, fond of the countryside, probably did the same for the sake of Kilvert's aunt Emma. Its country-house appearance would also have recommended it for people of their station. Its main virtue would have been that it was the brain-child of an enlightened Quaker.

Inevitably, the questions must be asked: was Fox's treatment of patients effective or notably humane? Bateson, in his introduction to Perceval's narrative, stated that it was impossible to answer these questions on the basis of one patient's testimony. He believed that the effect of Fox's methods was reduction of the patient's sense of his own worth and responsibility, which was the effect of methods used in the early 1960s, when Bateson was writing. Perceval complained of being treated as a child, of being humoured, of the way staff took his deranged behaviour to be his real self. He resented the way he, a gentleman, was placed in 'the common sitting-room of madmen'. He also objected that an Evangelical Anglican like himself should be entrusted to the care of what he called a 'sectarian' (i.e. a Quaker).[77] It seems that the Brislington House staff was preoccupied with keeping wards quiet, something which communicated itself to Kilvert visitors to aunt Emma. On 22 December 1873, Kilvert recorded his father's visit to her: 'He brought back a very good account of her. She was quiet and natural'. When Kilvert himself went to see her, the matron told him that aunt Emma was having 'a bad day', as she termed it; she was 'more violent and excitable than usual. She asked us to go out into the garden to see her where she was sitting quietly, rather than bring her into the house where she might make a great noise'. In his account of this visit, Kilvert included remarks indicating some unease about the institution. His aunt was, he said, 'dingily dressed in black' and was 'full of grievances': that she was 'in daily danger of her life and was cursed and swore at for a "damned bitch"'.[78] Some resentment of her treatment comes through in another *Diary* entry about the visit of Kilvert's father when she 'did not use quite so many oaths and curses as usual. But Dr. Charles Fox sat by all the time, and she did not scruple to say in his presence that his house was a hell upon earth'.[79] On 29 December 1878 she died, her torments over, and Kilvert wrote: 'The poor darkened restless brain is at rest now'.

CONCLUSION

Kilvert is an enigmatic figure, a man full of contradictions, and this emerges in his stance towards Bristol. The city was important to him because it symbolised modernity and progress yet was indissolubly linked with S.M.R. and Chatterton, which together signified the romance and mystery of the past. Kilvert lived and worked in

[75] R. Kilvert, *Memoirs*, p. 37.
[76] *Perceval's Narrative*, p. 117.
[77] *Ibid.*, pp. 122–123.
[78] *Kilvert's Diary*, 3, p. 104 (2 November 1874).
[79] *Ibid.* 2, p. 54, (5 October 1871).

the countryside but was drawn to scientific and technological things because he believed in social amelioration, which Bristol, as the capital of the west, represented. For him, Bristol meant commerce and industry, but it also meant passion, intimacy and beauty. He valued it both for its culture and for its religious traditions, especially its Quakerism. His forebears were people like the Goldneys—yeomen and business-men—and they exemplified the same rise from humble beginnings. He felt attached to Bristol because the Goldneys were Quakers, with roots not only in Wiltshire, his home county, but in the Quaker community around Chippenham to which his mother's family belonged. In addition to the many meanings—cultural, moral and religious—that Bristol possessed for Kilvert, there was an overriding personal one: it had provided a home for members of his family and for his lovers.

XVIII

Captain Francis George Irwin: his private press and his Rosicrucian rivals

ROBERT A. GILBERT, B.A., Ph.D.

FRANCIS GEORGE Irwin (1828–1893) was a soldier by profession, an occultist by inclination and a Bristolian by adoption. He was born in Armagh on 20 June 1828[1] but the details of his family and education are unknown, and the first official record of Irwin is of his enlistment, at the age of 14, as a bugler in the Corps of Royal Sappers and Miners (the forerunner of the Royal Engineers) in 1842. His military career lasted for 25 years and included service in England, in the Baltic theatre during the Crimean War, and in Gibraltar, from where he returned to England in 1863, having attained the rank of colour-sergeant. He was finally discharged from the army in 1867.

Following his discharge Irwin made Bristol his adopted home and in August 1867 he took up a second military career as adjutant, with the rank of captain, to the Administrative Battalion of the Gloucestershire Royal Engineer Volunteer Corps.[2] The unit was based in Avon Street and Captain Irwin set up home nearby at No. 1 Brislington Crescent (later to be re-numbered as 52 Bath Road), with his wife Catherine, and ten year old son, Herbert.[3] He was an efficient and active adjutant, to the extent that in 1882 he established *The Sapper*, a journal for the Corps that he also edited. It may be noted, however, that Irwin neither printed nor published *The Sapper*.[4]

On retirement from his post in 1884 Irwin was awarded the rank of major, and promptly set out with Sir Charles Warren, who had known him in Gibraltar, as an unofficial aide-de-camp in the Bechuanaland Field Force, remaining in South Africa

---

[1] This is known from a horoscope, undated but *c.* 1875, drawn up by Irwin himself, now in the High Council Library of the *Societas Rosicruciana in Anglia* (S.R.I.A.). For an account of Irwin's life, see C. W. Wallis-Newport, 'From County Armagh to the Green Hills of Somerset: the career of Major Francis George Irwin; (1828–1893)', in *Ars Quatuor Coronatorum, Transactions of Quatuor Coronati Lodge No. 2076*, (hereafter *A.Q.C.*), 114, (2001), pp. 112–181.

[2] In 1880 the administrative battalions were formed into a consolidated body; the Bristol Engineer Corps, as it became, was the only case in which a separate battalion was formed from an existing administrative corps.

[3] As with much of Irwin's private life, details of his marriage are sketchy. He was presumably married at Gibraltar in 1856, as his son, Herbert Thomas F. Irwin, was born on 3 June 1857. Herbert Irwin became a medical student but died from an overdose of laudanum on 8 January 1879.

[4] *The Sapper*, which was printed by A. Heath, 38 Park Street, Bristol and published 'by authority of the Lt. Col. Commanding the First Gloucestershire Engineer Volunteer Corps', ran for ten issues from September 1882 to January 1884.

until the end of 1885. The remainder of his civil life was uneventful, but Major Irwin had another, more private life that was, to him, of equal or perhaps greater significance than his public persona. And because of its perceived significance Irwin preserved the records of that private life in the form of unpublished manuscripts, notebooks, scrapbooks and an extensive correspondence with his colleagues and fellow enthusiasts.[5] Nor do these records stand alone; they can be dovetailed neatly into other archives and printed sources so that a curious byway of esoteric activity, with its own local printing and publishing history, can be fully mapped out.

When he was not engaged in his work with the Volunteers, Irwin devoted his time to the twin pursuits of occultism and the obscure fringes of Freemasonry.[6] For Irwin the two were inextricably intertwined, but he took no known part in any of the masonic activities within the masonic Province of Bristol—perhaps because his personal viewpoint was (as it still is) almost universally rejected by what might be termed 'orthodox' freemasons.[7] One consequence of this distance between Irwin and his fellow masons in the city was that, in this context, he can be said to have been *in* Bristol but not *of* it. But if Irwin, as an occultist, can be seen as an odd man out, the fruits of his metaphysical alienation were far stranger.

Occultism may be defined as a collective term for the various doctrines, theories, ideas and principles believed to underlie and hold together the practices of magical, divinatory and related arts and sciences, such as alchemy, astrology, tarot and all forms of contact with the spirit world.[8] In academic circles it is now fashionable to use the terms 'esotericism' or 'rejected knowledge' rather than 'occultism', which is seen as both pejorative and too narrow,[9] but in the Victorian era it was recognised as a

---

[5] The bulk of Irwin's archives are contained in the Library and Museum of Freemasonry, Great Queen Street, London (L.M.F.M.), which is accessible to the public, and in the High Council Library of the S.R.I.A., which is private. A further part of his 'esoteric' correspondence is held in the library of the Yarker Trust, but this is not open to the public.

[6] Although Freemasonry is the most well-known of the various fraternal associations, its institutional structure is perhaps less familiar to the general reader. In England the basic unit is the private Lodge, and these lodges are grouped under a series of Provincial Grand Lodges—the different Provinces being based on the historic English counties—with overall control exercised by the United Grand Lodge of England. Freemasonry had been established in Bristol by 1724, and by the middle of the nineteenth century there were estimated to have been some 200 freemasons in the city. The various individual lodges have met since 1818 at Freemasons' Hall, which was, until 1871, situated in Bridge Street, and from 1872 to the present day in Park Street.

[7] In addition to the three basic 'Craft' degrees, there are many other forms of masonic ceremonial activity within Freemasonry that constitute what are termed the 'Additional Degrees'. All of these are concerned with instilling moral precepts into their members and they do not, in any sense, constitute a part of occultism.

[8] This is my modification of the definition given in J. Gordon Melton (ed.), *Encyclopedia of Occultism & Parapsychology*, (4th ed., Detroit, 1996). See Vol. 2, p. 948.

[9] Antoine Faivre uses the term 'Western esotericism' to encompass both the illumination and saving knowledge (*Gnosis*) that characterise 'speculative mysticism' (*i.e.* the type of Theosophy espoused by Jacob Boëhme and his followers) *and* the more morally acceptable of the occult sciences (*Access to Western Esotericism*, (Albany, 1994), p. 36). The expression 'rejected knowledge' was introduced in 1972 by the printing historian Ellic Howe, who applied it to 'an important reservoir of 'hidden knowledge' based upon an ingenious construction of arbitrary relationships between different symbolical systems, *e.g.* the Cabbalistic Tree of Life, astrology,

wholly appropriate label for the activities of Irwin and his fellow enthusiasts. Such activities were not, however, widely followed. Occultists in general comprised a very small minority of the adult, literate population of the United Kingdom,[10] and Irwin's circle was very much a minority within that minority.

Irwin was concerned with both the theory and the practice of occultism, and it is clear from the contents of his library and from his writings and correspondence— almost entirely unpublished—that his principal concerns were alchemy, astrology, crystal gazing, Mesmerism, Spiritualism and Rosicrucianism. The last of these pursuits was, as we shall see, introduced to Bristol by Irwin, but others already had followers in the city.

Both alchemy and, to a much greater degree, astrology were practised and promoted in the late eighteenth century by Ebenezer Sibly (1751–1799), a physician, astrologer and prolific author on the occult sciences who was also much involved with the odder fringes of Freemasonry.[11] Sibly was born and raised in Bristol but spent much of his later life in London, although most of his immense survey of occultism, *A New and Complete Illustration of the Occult Sciences*, published in sixty parts between 1784 and 1791, was produced during a later stay in Bristol. A later, and more successful *émigré* Bristolian astrologer was Robert Cross Smith (1795–1832), who practised his art in London and wrote under the pseudonym of 'Raphael'. In 1824 Smith became editor of *The Straggling Astrologer*, a recently established weekly 'popular' journal devoted to astrology, but the journal failed before the year was out and Smith turned to producing almanacs, at which he was highly successful.[12]

Other astrologers did ply their trade in the Bristol area, not always with happy results. In January 1852 a Bath astrologer, Francis Copestick, was gaoled, under the Vagrancy Act of 1824, for 'Fortune-telling'.[13] This was not an uncommon fate for professional astrologers at that period, but there was a demand for their services and the risk was presumably outweighed by the potential rewards. These are exemplified by the charges made by a 'Professor Cattell' of 15 Upper Perry Hill, who in 1893 advertised that 'he drew up brief charts for 1s 1d, Seven Years' Events for 2s 6d, and a

---

alchemy, the Tarot trumps and so on.' (*The Magicians of the Golden Dawn*, (1972), p. *xxii*). It must be emphasised, however, that the Victorian occultists who made the connections between different systems of symbolism did not see the relationships they constructed as being in any sense arbitrary.

[10] An analysis of the available evidence indicates that the maximum number of those committed to active engagement in any organised form of occultism varied from *c.* 4,000 in 1870 to *c.* 6,000 in 1900. As a percentage of the total population of the country—slightly in excess of 21,000,000 in 1870, and of 30,000,000 in 1900—and reducing these figures by 75%, in order to remove those excluded from active involvement by reason of age, sex, illness, poverty, lack of education, or the pressures of employment or of social disapproval, these figures represent 0.076% and 0.08%, respectively of that total.

[11] For Sibly see Eric Ward, 'Ebenezer Sibly: a man of parts', *A.Q.C.*, 71, (1958), pp. 48–52 , and Patrick Curry, 'Ebenezer Sibly', *Oxford D.N.B.*, online edition.

[12] Smith compiled *Raphael's Prophetic Messenger* from 1827 until his death in 1832, but his pseudonym was retained: there were five other 'Raphaels', the last being Robert Cross (1850–1923).

[13] For the furore over Copestick's case, see Christopher Cooke, *Curiosities of Occult Literature*, (1863), pp. 20–35.

nativity for 5s.'[14] Irwin, who died in that year, would not have been a customer, for he was a competent amateur astrologer, well skilled in this 'art' and had drawn up his own horoscope long before.[15] But was Irwin also competent in other areas of occultism? On this there are mixed opinions.

Walter Spencer, a masonic publisher and a well-informed if disillusioned Rosicrucian—he openly derided the *Societas Rosicruciana in Anglia*—described Irwin, who had introduced him to the Society, as being a 'real enthusiast, probably the only one within its ranks'.[16] Against this view must be set the comments, with due allowance for their intellectual snobbery, of A. E. Waite, one of the few objective historians of occultism: '[Irwin] was a believer in occult arts within the measure of a thinking and reading person of his particular mental class [...] [who] was satisfied apparently with the pursuits of spiritualism'.[17]

Spiritualism had been imported to England from the United States of America in 1852, and spiritualist *séances* in Bristol predated Irwin's arrival in the city. A Signor G. Damiani,[18] then living in Clifton, gave evidence to the Committee of the London Dialectical Society for their *Report on Spiritualism* of 1869. His testimony included accounts of spiritualist activity in Clifton, beginning with a *séance* in 1865, which,

> took place at No. 13, Victoria Place, Clifton,[19] the medium being Mrs. Marshall[20] [...] I found assembled at this *séance* some forty gentlemen, lawyers, physicians, clergymen and journalists, besides a fair sprinkling of ladies.[21]

In addition to this Sgr. Damiani had encountered 'a boy medium, between ten and eleven years of age', and 'another medium, aged fifteen, also resident at Clifton', and he listed as *habitués* of *séances*, 'Messrs. Watson, Blackwell,[22] and John Beattie,[23] all of

---

[14] Owen Davies, *Witchcraft, Magic and Culture 1736—1951*, (Manchester, 1999), p. 245.

[15] See note 1.

[16] Walter Spencer, *Freemasonry: its outward and visible Signs. A description of the Jewels, Clothing, & Furniture, for all Degrees, with convenient Index*, (Revised edition, 1880), p. 96. In addition to praising Irwin and decrying the S.R.I.A., Spencer refers to his own collection of Rosicrucian books and manuscripts, to which Irwin presumably had access. And see below, p. 348, note 46.

[17] A. E. Waite, *The Brotherhood of the Rosy Cross*, (1924), p. 570.

[18] *Mathews's Bristol Directory*, (1868), p. 132, professor of Italian language and literature, of 2 Pembroke Villas, Pembroke Road.

[19] *Ibid.*, pp. 174, 378, 13 Victoria Place South was the home of Benjamin Hall, no profession or occupation is listed. In 1883 and 1891 he was resident at Brooklyn Villa, 66 Oakfield Road, Clifton. *Mathews's Bristol Directory*, (1883), p. 12; (1891), p. 255.

[20] Possibly Mrs. Mary C. Marshall, 8 Arlington Villas, Clifton; *Mathews's Bristol Directory*, (1868), p. 233.

[21] *Report on Spiritualism of the Committee of the London Dialectical Society*, (2nd ed., 1873), p. 194.

[22] Possibly William Blackwell, of Polygon Cottage, Clifton; *Mathews's Bristol Directory*, (1868), p. 91, no occupation is given.

[23] *Ibid.*, pp. 86, 378, Beattie and Bark, photographic artists, Strathern House, next to Victoria Rooms, 1 (note not 2), Westbourne Place, Clifton. By 1874 he appears to have retired and was resident at 2 Richmond Hill, (*ibid.*, p. 147); he was there in 1883 (*ibid.*, p. 125), and was dead by 1886 when Mrs. Beattie was living at this address, (*ibid*, p. 125).

Bristol or Clifton'.[24] One of these gentlemen, John Beattie, who lived at 2 Westbourne Place, Clifton, identified himself as a 'Christian spiritualist'.[25] Spiritualism in Bristol at this period was thus, it would seem, thoroughly middle-class and respectable.

It is not known when Irwin first took up Spiritualism, but his first recorded involvement with Bristol spiritualists took place in 1870, when he was 'mesmerised', in order to relieve insomnia, by George Tommy[26], a medium with an office in Unity Street.[27] Irwin continued to visit Mr. Tommy, socially as well as spiritually, and obtained from him various periodicals issued by James Burns, a London publisher of spiritualist works. By 1874 Irwin was evidently well-known in local spiritualist circles and was invited by Tommy to meet 'Mr. Beattie and a few friends [...] for the purpose of organising a Psychological Society'[28] (the title usually given to provincial spiritualist institutions), although nothing seems to have come of this venture. It is probable that Irwin was not enthusiastic, for, unlike Signor Damiani, he was not initially concerned to converse with the dead through professional mediums. Irwin preferred to receive private 'Spiritual communications' from both departed occultists and angels by way of questions and answers obtained through table-tipping,[29] and he recorded many of these in private journals, two of which, from 1872 and 1873, survive.[30]

He also made use of crystal-gazing as a means of spirit communication, and borrowed from his friend and frequent correspondent, Frederick Hockley, manuscripts which he transcribed and occasionally purchased. And it was through Hockley that he learned of Lieutenant Morrison's experiments with the crystal, and of the activities of a Hampshire crystal-gazer, Robert Fryar.[31] Morrison was an astrologer, whom Irwin believed, wrongly, to be a fellow freemason, and it was probably wishful thinking on Irwin's part that led him to take seriously Morrison's spoof quasi-masonic degree of 'Astrological Master Shewing the Death of Hiram according to Astronomy'. That he carefully transcribed its ritual gives force to another comment by Waite that

---

[24] *Report on Spiritualism of the Committee of the London Dialectical Society*, (2nd ed., 1873), pp. 197–198 and 202.

[25] See his letter in *The Spiritualist*, Vol. 1, 15 May 1870, p. 7.

[26] *Mathews's Bristol Directory*, (1868), p. 322, of Brandon House, Brandon Hill; (*ibid.*, 1874), p. 244; 7 Unity Street, College Green; (*ibid.*, 1883); 13 Melrose Place, Clifton. He does not appear in the Directory for 1886.

[27] George Tommy to F. G. Irwin, 31 March 1870, (L.M.F.M.). Tommy then lived at 12 Clare Street, Bristol, but worked from Unity Street.

[28] Tommy to Irwin, 10 October 1874. The meeting was to be held on 14 October.

[29] Table-tipping, or Table-turning, is the practice of obtaining answers to questions by the movements of a small table on the basis of an agreed letter code. Such movement was assumed by the sitters to be due to spirit activity but to a sceptic it was the result of unconscious—or perhaps, conscious—pressure on the part of the sitters.

[30] *Spiritual Journal*, No. I and No. II, (1872–73), Small 8vo, 67 pp. (L.M.F.M.).

[31] Lieutenant Richard James Morrison (1795–1874) was a retired naval officer who embarked on a successful career as a professional astrologer, under the pseudonym of Zadkiel. He produced an annual almanac designed for astrologers, as opposed to the 'man in the street'. For Fryar, see below pp. 351–353. See also J. Hamill (ed.), *The Rosicrucian Seer: Magical Writings of Frederick Hockley*, (New edition, York Beach, 2009), *passim*.

Irwin 'was a zealous and amiable Mason, with a passion for Rites and an ambition to add to their number'.[32]

Irwin was initiated into Freemasonry at Gibraltar in 1857 and took to it with vigour. He had not lost his enthusiasm when he settled in Bristol, but with few exceptions his masonic activities were confined to Somerset.[33] Much as he enjoyed these, his real love was for a curious offshoot of English Freemasonry, the *Societas Rosicruciana in Anglia*.[34] This society was founded in London in 1867, by and for freemasons who were concerned with studying the precepts of the Rosicrucians: the mythical fraternity of mystics and alchemists, allegedly established in the early seventeenth century. Irwin was one of the earliest members, joining the society in October 1867, but he rarely attended the quarterly meetings, presumably because he lacked the opportunity of travelling to London. To overcome this difficulty, Irwin drew together a number of fellow enthusiasts with the aim of founding a local branch of the society, which came into being in December 1869 after it had been agreed that,

> Captain Irwin, of Bristol, be permitted to form a College at Bristol, restricted to the number of 12 members, including himself as Chief Adept.[35]

As events turned out, the Bristol College would be, in a reversal of Irwin's situation, *of* Bristol but not *in* it.

A week before the chosen date—29 December 1869—of its first meeting, a printed summons for the 'Rosicrucian Society of England [...] Provincial College of Bristol and Neighbouring Counties', was sent by the two nominated officers of the new college (Irwin as 'Chief Adept' and Benjamin Cox, the town accountant of Weston-super-Mare, as 'Provincial Secretary-General') to the twelve candidates for admission. Nine of these were residents of Weston-super-Mare, so it was most appropriate that the meeting was held in the town's Masonic Hall. Among them was Thomas Clarke, a newspaper proprietor, who lived at Victoria Quadrant, and who would print both the future summonses of the College and its *Rules and Ordinances*.[36] Of the remaining candidates, only one came from Bristol. Lieutenant Henry Wiltshire, of Hillside Villa, Totterdown, was Irwin's fellow officer in the Volunteer Engineers, but on the day he did not attend, and he made no further attempt to join Irwin's Rosicrucians.

---

[32] Waite, *loc. cit.* Irwin's transcription is in L.M.F.M. (Accession No. 15,570). He noted that candidates for the degree must be 'Master Masons of good standing, [who] have a taste for astrology and be able to erect a Horoscope the figure of which must be sent in with his application to join the Order,' and that the room in which the ceremony takes place 'is hung with astrological figures emblems & instruments'.

[33] Irwin was initiated on 3 June 1857 (the day of his son's birth), in Lodge No. 325 under the Grand Lodge of Ireland. For his masonic career, see Wallis-Newport, *op. cit.*, pp. 122–127 and 139–150.

[34] For a general history of the society, see T. M. Greensill, *A History of Rosicrucian Thought and of the Societas Rosicruciana in Anglia*, (2nd revised ed., London, privately printed, 2003).

[35] *The Rosicrucian, a Quarterly Record of the Society's Transactions*, edited by R. W. Little and W. R. Woodman, Vol. 1, No. 5, July 1869, p. 54.

[36] *Rosicrucian Society of England [...] Rules and Ordinances of the Provincial College of Bristol and Neighbouring Counties, A.L. 5869 A.D. 1869*. 'Frater Clarke, "Gazette Office", Weston-super-Mare', [1869], 8 pp, plus printed wrappers. Copies are held by L.M.F.M. and the High Council Library, S.R.I.A.

The Bristol College was not a success. Details survive for only five further meetings between February 1871 and April 1873: manuscript minutes of four of them, and a printed summons for the fifth.[37] There were occasional meetings at later dates, but the precise details remain unknown because of the laxity in filing reports by the society's officers in London.[38] Over the entire period of its existence, the Bristol College acquired only 24 members, most of whom took no part in its activities after their admission. Of these, eight were Bristolians, six of them joining at the last recorded meeting, which took place at 'The Masonic Hall, 23 Brislington Crescent, Bristol' on 14 April 1873.[39] They included a local clergyman, the Revd. J. B. Spring of Fishponds,[40] but none of the members were prominent in local society, in civic affairs, or in masonic circles.

Some of them, however, were eager to be instructed in Rosicrucianism. Shortly after the first meeting of the Bristol College, Benjamin Cox, the secretary, wrote to Dr. Woodman, who was Secretary-General and *de facto* editor of the society's journal, *The Rosicrucian*, requesting him to:

> Please send to Frater Townsend [*i.e.* Capt. J. Townsend, R.N., of Iona Villa, Weston-super-Mare] the 7 Nos. of the Rosicrucian and continue the same for future quarters. I will send you up the money for the same when I forward you the fees for the new members of our College. [41]

Captain Townsend presumably received the journal, and attended all of the meetings held in Weston-super-Mare, but his enthusiasm for the society did not extend to travelling to Bristol for the last recorded meeting of the College.

The Rosicrucian played an important part in the affairs of the S.R.I.A., being a regular source of information on the society's meetings, current officers and of articles on various esoteric and masonic topics. In the journal's early years its printing and distribution were overseen solely by Dr. Woodman, variously at Stoke Newington and at Exeter after he briefly moved home in 1873,[42] but it is far from certain that his personal enthusiasm for Rosicrucianism was shared by more than a small minority of the members, Irwin prominent among them.

Irwin felt that 'no meeting of R.C. shd. take place without a paper being read & the subject discussed by the Fraters. These papers in my opinion shd be confined to the occult mysteries.'[43] In this respect he fully did his duty. At the one known meeting in Bristol Irwin delivered two papers, one on 'the Cabbala, and some of the mystic signification of numbers', and another on 'the Religious aspect and utility of

---

[37] The Minutes, and copies of the printed summonses, are in L.M.F.M..

[38] At least two meetings certainly took place, as the papers delivered were subsequently printed, but the dates are not known.

[39] This was not an official Masonic Hall but a private house, and I assume that Irwin hired a suitable room from the occupier, one Alfred Sayce, who does not seem to have been a freemason, or to have had any other connection with Irwin.

[40] There is no mention of him in the 1874 edition of *The Gloucester and Bristol Diocesan Kalendar*.

[41] Letter, 11 January 1870, H.C. Library, S.R.I.A.

[42] Nos. 1 to 20, July 1868 to May 1873, were printed at Stoke Newington, while Nos. 21 to 26 (November 1874) were printed at the *Gazette* office in Exeter. Later issues were printed in central London.

[43] Irwin to T. Blair, 12 August 1879. L.M.F.M.

Astrology'.[44] Later in 1873, possibly in August, Irwin read a paper by Frederick Hockley on crystal-gazing, 'Evenings with the Indwellers of the World of Spirits', and it was presumably at this meeting—whenever it *did* take place—that another Bristol freemason, a Brother Ansaldo, was admitted.[45] One further paper, a 'Speech' on Rosicrucianism in general, by Walter Spencer, was delivered, but it is not known when.[46] Nor were lectures the only means by which Irwin sought to instil Rosicrucian precepts into the members of his college.

They were encouraged to study the symbolism of the intricate and rather pleasing lithographic certificate that Benjamin Cox had designed for them in 1871,[47] and in October 1876 Irwin began to print 'Rosicrucian' leaflets on a small private press that he set up at his home in Brislington Crescent. He had previously experimented with printing between 1859 and 1861, when he produced ephemeral material for use in his masonic lodge at Gibraltar,[48] but 'The Rosicrucian Press' was a ramshackle affair and in most respects it must be judged a failure.

Irwin made use of a primitive hand press of unknown make, and although his type-setting was adequate, his presswork was not. The press was in operation for three years, but its output was small. Eight leaflets were printed; all of them except the final piece, a memorial to his son Herbert, are on hermetic and Rosicrucian topics, and all of these are crudely printed in blue ink on blue paper.[49] Irwin did not advertise his

---

[44] See *The Rosicrucian*, Vol. 2, No. 20, May 1873, p. 26. The text of these papers was not printed.

[45] Ansaldo appears as a member on a return made to the High Council in January 1874.

[46] The speech was printed in *The Rosicrucian*, Vol. 1, No. 4, October 1875, pp. 86–92, but the date of delivery is not given.

[47] The certificate has no imprint, but was almost certainly lithographed by J. Lavars & Co. of 51 Broad Street, Bristol. In a letter to Irwin of 25 April 1877, Cox writes 'Yesterday I received the certificates from "Lavers" [*sic*] I will now fill them up and forward them for your signature'. This can refer only to a later batch of certificates for the Bristol College. It is illustrated in H. C. Bruce Wilson, *Early History of the S.R.I.A., Chapter III*, [the Bristol College], (London, 1944), p. 13.

[48] Examples of these are bound into a notebook of Irwin's, labelled *Bibliotheca Masonica*, in the High Council Library of the S.R.I.A.

[49] The eight titles are as follows. All save the last are printed in blue ink on blue paper. The number of copies printed is not known, but copies of the eight pieces are known gathered together and stuck into plain wrappers, presumably to be given to friends after Herbert Irwin's death.

Hours with the Brotherhood of Light. 4pp No imprint. 8, 10, 1876.

[Supplementary leaf] 2pp, 15, 10, 1877.

[Swastika] *Hours with the Brotherhood of Light.* Single leaf, undated, and with no imprint.

Extracts from my Rosicrucian Note Book. [I] The Rosicrucian's Prayer. Printed at the Rosicrucian Press, Bristol, By, Frater F. G. Irwin. IX. [Three variants, one without imprint]. Single leaf.

Extracts from my Rosicrucian Note Book, II. Oracle I [II, III], Printed at the Rosicrucian Press. By Frater. F. G. Irwin. IX. Single leaf, undated.

Extracts from my Rosicrucian Note Book, III. Brotherhood of the Brilliant Cross. Printed at the Rosicrucian Press. Bristol. 7.4.1877. By Frater F. G Irwin. IX. Single leaf.

Extracts from my Rosicrucian Note Book, IV. The Smaragdine Table. Printed at the Rosicrucian Press. Bristol. 9.4.1877. By Frater F. G. Irwin. IX. Single leaf.

In Loving Remembrance of Herbert F. Irwin, Born 3 June, 1857, Passed to the higher life 8 January, 1879. 4 pp., printed in black on white paper. No imprint.

press and there is no reference to it in any of the publications of the S.R.I.A.; it is thus probable that the only persons who were aware of its existence were the members of the Bristol College and his closest Rosicrucian correspondents. Its purpose was evidently the instruction of members of the Bristol College in the principles of Rosicrucianism, but the leaflets that issued from the press do not appear to have had the desired effect—very few copies have survived, and none at all that can be linked to any of the members, who do not seem to have kept them even as curiosities.

The Rosicrucian Press might yet have continued, but the tragic loss of his son in January 1879 caused Irwin to reduce greatly his masonic and quasi-masonic activities. The Bristol College was already moribund and the society's journal, *The Rosicrucian*, ceased publication in October of that year. Irwin felt that this was the final blow to the college, a view he expressed later in a letter to Cuthbert Peek, Woodman's successor as Secretary-General: 'I fear that without a recognised organ such as "The Rosicrucian" we have little chance of reviving the Order in the west of England.'[50] In this Irwin was proven right, and a subsequent attempt in 1906 to resuscitate the Bristol College came to nothing despite the enthusiasm of two local members of the S.R.I.A.: Tudor Trevor, who was the local secretary of the Church of England Temperance Society, and Sholto Henry Hare, J.P.,[51] notable only for his membership of an obscure masonic body which Irwin had been instrumental in establishing in Bristol. At least in name.

'The Primitive & Original Rite of Freemasonry', or 'Swedenborgian Rite', was imported to England from Canada in 1876 by John Yarker, a Manchester businessman and pre-eminent promoter of dubious masonic degrees.[52] He promptly appointed Irwin as his deputy to oversee the 'Western District' and to establish 'Emmanuel Lodge and Temple No. 1' at Bristol. This was warranted on 13 January 1877 but followed the example of the Bristol College and moved immediately to Weston-super-Mare, where its first meeting in the real world took place on 30 May. Exactly what had preceded this meeting is unclear. Benjamin Cox, who was to be the first master of Emmanuel Lodge and Temple wrote to Irwin in February to advise him that, 'I have copied the minutes of E.L. & T. No. 3 [*sic*] ... [but] ... I do not see any date when the meeting was supposed to have been held. This omission might be of importance at some future time'.[53] He was also concerned that the members would have no idea how to work the ceremony at the first meeting while ignorant of its purpose, content and text.

No minutes survive for any of the lodges of the Swedenborgian Rite, but the printed summons for the May meeting at Weston-super-Mare includes a surprising item that reads,

[50] Letter, 1 May 1881. L.M.F.M. Sir Cuthbert Peek was also a noted amateur meteorologist and astronomer. He had an observatory at Rousdon in Dorset, where he lived.

[51] *Mathews's Bristol Directory*, (1874), p. 186, of Knole Park, Almondsbury; *ibid.*, (1883), p. 174; (1886), p. 199; (1891), p. 258 , of Alva House, Clifton Down.

[52] For an account of the Swedenborgian Rite, which had no connection with either the doctrines of Emanuel Swedenborg or the New Church that propagated those doctrines, see R. A. Gilbert, 'Chaos out of Order: The Rise and Fall of the Swedenborgian Rite', *A.Q.C.*, 108, (1995), pp. 122–149.

[53] Letter, Cox to Irwin, 12 February 1877, in L.M.F.M.

   Also, W. Bro. George F. Tuckey, P.M., together with a number of other distinguished Brethren of Bristol and Gloucestershire, for the purpose of forming a
Lodge and Temple in the Province of Bristol.

That a second body for Swedenborgian freemasons in the district should have been
needed at all, let alone so soon after the first, seems inconceivable, but 'Cagliostro
Lodge & Temple No. 7' was duly formed at Keynsham on 16 June 1877. Whether or
not ceremonies were worked at Keynsham is unknown, but although George Tuckey
resigned in 1878, Cagliostro Lodge and Temple survived in name, under the direction
of one of its founders, J. T. Hallam[54] of Stokes Croft, Bristol, until 1908 when the
Swedenborgian Rite finally faded away.
   Irwin also retained membership and nominal authority in this most insubstantial of
Rites until his death, but his enthusiasm for Freemasonry was waning, as he noted in
a letter to Dr. Westcott:

   I am becoming year by year more lukewarm in Masonry—I find the majority of
   masons content themselves with talk—and never dream of carrying out practically
   what they pretend to admire so much.[55]

Spiritualism and other aspects of occultism, however, continued to draw him,
although he was not active in any local bodies,[56] except in the Brotherhood of the
Cross of Light (*Fratres Lucis*), an esoteric Order that he had created in November 1873
after receiving its supposed history and rituals from the long dead Count Cagliostro,
by way of crystal-gazing with Herbert Irwin as the seer. The purpose of this Order
was the study and practice of:

   Natural magic, Mesmerism, the science of life and death, immortality, Cabala,
   alchemy, necromancy, astrology and magic in all its branches.[57]

It is not known if the three certain members of the Order—Irwin, Cox and Frederick
Hockley[58]—ever met to work its ceremonies, but it seems highly improbable that any
of these alarming magical arts were put into practice at Brislington or anywhere
else—even though Irwin had both earlier and later encounters with magicians.
   During a visit to Paris in 1874 Irwin apparently met Éliphas Lévi—otherwise
the Abbé Constant—who had made magic respectable with his two books on the

---

   [54] *Mathews's Bristol Directory*, (1874), pp. 185, 341, John Thomas Hallam, clerk of the church
of St. Thomas the Apostle, City, of 22 Webb Street, Pennywell Road. He was still clerk in 1891;
(1880), p. 221, carver and guilder of 63 Stokes Croft; (1886), p. 197 as before; (1891), pp. 256,
585.
   [55] Letter, Irwin to W. Wynn Westcott, 4 September 1886. In L.M.F.M.
   [56] Irwin read the works of Mme. Blavatsky and had become a Fellow, as members were
then described, of the Theosophical Society, but its Bristol Lodge was not founded until June
1893, one month before Irwin's death, and there is no record of his being involved with any
other branch of the society.
   [57] J. Hamill, *op. cit.*, p. xxi–xxii, quoting a letter of 1874 from Irwin to Cox.
   [58] It is possible, but not certain, that Herbert Irwin and K. R. H. Mackenzie, another
prominent creator of quasi-masonic degrees, were also members.

subject,[59] but he declined to have anything to do with the most famous of magical societies, the Hermetic Order of the Golden Dawn, when it was founded in 1888, even though its Osiris Temple was established at Weston-super-Mare under the leadership of Benjamin Cox. Instead, in 1890, he joined a rather more ill-disciplined magical body, the Celestial Brotherhood of the astrologer John Thomas, better known as Charubel. But this Order worked by post, and finding its chief to be wanting in esoteric knowledge he left before the end of the year.[60] It would seem that Irwin preferred magical texts to magical ceremonies.

And there were many such texts, as both printed books and manuscripts, in his impressive library, which had been built up over many years. Irwin received regular catalogues from both English and German booksellers who specialised in the occult, and he was quite prepared to pay high prices when necessary. Thus, in 1874 he spent £2.10.0 on two books by the English Rosicrucian, John Heydon.[61] After his death Irwin's masonic books and manuscripts were given by his widow to the library of the United Grand Lodge of England, while most of his esoteric books were sold at auction. Some of these, including the unpublished manuscript of Irwin's long and rambling Rosicrucian work, *The Star Rising in the East* (1874), appeared in a catalogue issued by the Bristol booksellers, William George's Sons, but most of his books cannot now be traced.[62]

Bristol was not, however, fertile ground for booksellers and publishers specialising in the occult. There were few local enthusiasts for the subject matter and, apart from Irwin and Cox, there are no known local collectors of such books at that time. It was almost inevitable that the one specialist publishing house in the area would fail dismally, and a matter of great surprise that it was ever established.

It was the creation of Robert H. Fryar (1845–1909), who between 1884 and 1898 published, or co-published, from his home in Bath thirteen titles of the 'Bath Occult Reprints'—a series of English alchemical, hermetic and theosophical texts and translations.[63] In addition, he issued four titles on what was politely termed 'esoteric physiology', distributed packs of Tarot cards, and carried on his various trades of clerk, Mesmerist and accountant. He was no more successful at any of these than he had

---

[59] *Dogme et Rituel de la Haute Magie*, (Paris, 1854) and *Histoire de la Magie*, (Paris, 1860). Substantial extracts from both works were issued in English translation, by A. E. Waite, in 1886 as *Mysteries of Magic*.

[60] For Irwin's career in the Celestial Brotherhood, see R. A. Gilbert, 'The Disappointed Magus: John Thomas and his "Celestial Brotherhood"', *Theosophical History*, Vol. 8, No. 3, July 2000, Fullerton, CA., pp. 103–107. Irwin's name in this Order was Arokiel.

[61] An invoice from a London specialist, George Bumstead, recording this purchase is bound up in Irwin's *Bibliotheca Masonica*, in the High Council Library, S.R.I.A. Many catalogues formerly belonging to Irwin are in the L.M.F.M., and a bound volume of them is in the possession of the author.

[62] The auction in question cannot be identified, but it is referred to in a letter of the Revd. W. A. Ayton, an early member of the Golden Dawn, and took place in 1895. William George's Sons Catalogue 214, *Bibliotheca Antiqua et Curiosa. Old Books of Past Centuries, including Occultism in its various forms* (n.d. but *c.* 1895) includes forty-four items from Irwin's library. The ms of *The Star Rising in the East* is now in the High Council Library, S.R.I.A..

[63] From 1878 to 1893 Fryar and his family lived at 8 Northumberland Place, and thereafter, until 1909, at 2 Prospect Terrace, Highmere Grove, Tyning Lane, Bath.

been as a Crystal-gazer and copyist of magical manuscripts at Southsea in the early 1870s,[64] but it was the last of these activities that had brought him to the attention of Captain Irwin.

There is no record of Irwin buying manuscripts from Fryar, which had been recommended to him by Frederick Hockley as 'worth the money he charges',[65] nor is there any evidence that he met Fryar in person. He did, however, receive prospectuses for the 'occult reprints', six of which were the work of his Rosicrucian friends, John Yarker and William Wynn Westcott—neither of whom held a high opinion of Mr. Fryar, although they appreciated his attempts to promote occultism. Yarker wrote of him that 'he is a man whom I should scarcely like to make an intimate of, yet I have always willingly helped him for the sake of the Occult Sciences.'[66] Yarker also noted that Fryar was not a freemason, but he had been involved, briefly, with the supposedly Rosicrucian, 'Hermetic Brotherhood of Luxor', a body that made use of the 'Taro' and of 'Magic Mirrors', both of which were sold by Fryar. After a bout of mutual recrimination Fryar severed his connection with this Brotherhood in 1886 and confined his Rosicrucianism to the works he published.[67]

Fryar's venture, however, needed more than the lukewarm support of occultists to guarantee it success. He was further hampered by insufficient working capital, ignorance of the publishing trade, and over-confidence in his own abilities; he also had no established customer base. As a consequence he issued his titles in strictly limited editions, of 100 or 200 copies, to subscribers whom he had difficulty in finding in sufficient quantity (the most elegant of his books, *The Isiac Tablet*, which Westcott had subsidised, includes a 'Remainder List of the "Bath Occult Reprints."'). It is possible that Irwin was among the purchasers of *The Isiac Tablet* and the *Exposition of the Hieroglyphical Figures*, as prospectuses for both titles are bound into his *Bibliotheca Masonica*, but if he did have copies they have not survived.

Fryar also suffered from what he later described as 'The Bath Book Scandal of 1889', when his works on 'esoteric physiology' (*i.e.* sexual practices) 'were withdrawn from circulation, 1889, in deference to the National Vigilance Association'.[68] This setback was compounded in 1893 when rival, and rather better editions of two of his

---

[64] In 1870 Fryar published, at Portsea, a pamphlet on *The History and Mystery of the Magic Crystal*, and both he and his wife were active as spiritualist mediums and crystal-seers.

[65] Letter, Hockley to Irwin, 18 June 1874 (L.M.F.M.). Fryar's charges were 15s, 25s and 30s.

[66] Letter, Yarker to Westcott, 20 January 1887, in the High Council Library, S.R.I.A. John Yarker was the editor of *"Aureus:" The Golden Tractate of Hermes Trismegistus*, (1886), and of two *Continuations* of the Rosicrucian text, the *Comte de Gabalis*, (1897); while Westcott had written *The Isiac Tablet of Cardinal Bembo*, (1887), translated the *Sepher Yetzirah, The Book of Formation*, (1887), and supplied a Preface to Nicholas Flammel's *Exposition of the Hieroglyphical Figures*, (1889).

[67] *Lucifer*, Vol. 1, No. 2, 15 October 1887. p. 159. See also J. Godwin, C. Chanel & J. P. Deveney, *The Hermetic Brotherhood of Luxor. Initiatic and Historical Documents of an Order of Practical Occultism*, (York Beach, 1995).

[68] Invictus [R. H. Fryar] (ed.), *The Letters of Hargrave Jennings Forming the Unabridged Correspondence with the Editor of the Bath Occult Reprints between 1879 and 1887*, (Bath, 1895), p. 57. The National Vigilance Association was formed in August 1885 'for the enforcement and improvement of the laws for the repression of criminal vice and public immorality'. Fryar's activities would have been investigated by the Association's Bristol and South Western Counties branch, but I have been unable to trace any relevant reports or public complaints of the time.

titles, *The Divine Pymander* and the *Sepher Yetzirah*, were issued by the Theosophical Publishing Society. Fryar's later publications were no more successful than the earlier ones, and after 1898 he re-invented himself as an accountant, and the House of Fryar came to an end. He did, however, retain some of his occult interests, in Spiritualism if not in Hermetic or Theosophical societies.

In this he followed Irwin, but for more material reasons: towards the end of his life Fryar appealed for help from spiritualists by way of letters to the journal *Light*.[69] These failed to produce material results, whereas Irwin succeeded on a more ethereal plane when, on behalf of George Tommy, he attended a *séance* in London, with the medium William Eglinton. According to Irwin, he took a box containing two slates, that been locked previously by Tommy in Bristol, to London for the *séance*, during which 'writing was distinctly heard, and upon opening the box and taking out the slates the words "Will this do, Mr. Tommy?" were discovered on the inside of one of the slates.'[70]

The incident is risible in terms of validating spirit communication, but it *is* evidence of Irwin's continuing involvement with Spiritualism, which long predated Herbert Irwin's death. He held a firm belief in human survival of bodily death, and his enthusiasm for *séances* was not something generated by grief. It was, however, unusual, as support for Spiritualism was not fashionable locally at that time and no organised spiritualist society existed in Bristol during the nineteenth or early twentieth centuries. A similar situation prevailed in many other parts of the country also, and the development of Spiritualism as a popular movement did not take place until after World War One.[71]

Indeed, local enthusiasm for *any* branch of occultism, as distinct from folk beliefs and practices, had never been substantial: a state of affairs reflected in the meagre support for Irwin's Rosicrucian and other esoteric endeavours, and in Fryar's failure to generate demand for his publications. A lack of active participants also precluded the success of any institutional form of occultism: the Bristol Rosicrucian College, the Golden Dawn Temple at Weston-super-Mare, and the embryo Bristol Lodge of the Theosophical Society all foundered and orthodox Freemasonry resolutely set its face against anything remotely related to occultism.[72]

There would be little change in the situation until the second half of the twentieth century. Both the Theosophical Society and the Golden Dawn were revived in Bristol, but on a small scale, and the Hermes Temple of the latter—membership of which was supposedly secret—rarely had more than twenty members, despite the energetic promotion of the Order during the 1920s by Catherine Hughes, and the

---

[69] See, *e.g.*, his letter in *Light*, Vol. 28, No. 1416, 29 February 1908, p. 108.

[70] *Light*, Vol. 4, No. 199, 25 October 1884, p. 440.

[71] In her survey of Spiritualism, *Nineteenth Century Miracles*, (Manchester, 1884), Emma Hardinge Britten, one of its more popular protagonists, noted that support was weak in the 'west and south of England' (p. 218). See also G. K. Nelson, *Spiritualism and Society*, (1969).

[72] The Osiris Temple was defunct by 1895; the attempt to revive the Bristol College of the S.R.I.A. in 1906 had failed; and the Theosophical Society was riven by internal dissent, culminating in the then president of the Bristol Lodge, F. H. Palmer, returning its charter—torn into fragments to prevent its re-use (personal communication from Mr. Palmer's daughter).

more discreet support of her brother and fellow-member, the poet Donald Hughes.[73]

Irwin had played no part in creating or promoting the Golden Dawn, but after his death he was promoted into its pantheon of notional adepts[74]—a fate he would not have appreciated, as the furrow that he ploughed was a lonely one, albeit deeply satisfying to himself, and it is perhaps appropriate, if surprising, that the location of his last resting place, and even the details of his funeral, remain unknown.

---

[73] Catherine Hughes joined the *Stella Matutina*, the new name for one branch of the Golden Dawn, in 1909 and was working the Hermes Temple by 1916. During the 1930s and 1940s it was located at No. 6 Hillside, Cotham. A somewhat inaccurate list of the members is given in Ithell Colquhoun, *Sword of Wisdom. MacGregor Mathers and the Golden Dawn*, (1975), p. 196.

[74] R. A. Gilbert, *The Golden Dawn, Twilight of the Magicians*, (Wellingborough, 1983). See p. 102. Irwin died on 26 July 1893.

XIX

They came, they stayed and they went: musicians and Bristol in the nineteenth century

STEPHEN BANFIELD, M.A., D.Phil., F.R.C.O.

EVERY YEAR in late September a cohort of fresh young men and women arrives in Bristol, unpacking its belongings somewhere in Clifton and saying gruff farewells to wilting parents who recognise that their offspring are passing out of their control into that of this bustling provincial city. Some have come from the residential suburbs and towns nearby; more from distant parts of the south and all too occasionally from the north of England; some, already alone as they boarded the plane, from overseas. Bristol will take them in and spin them around as students for three, four, five or six years. Then they will move back, move on, or settle locally.

This is our contemporary version of a youth demographic that has been playing itself out with varying formulae for centuries. For centuries Bristol has been the biggest town west of London and, long before the suspension bridge and the M5 set their spectacular seals on the spanning of distance, the gateway to or from the south west peninsula. They have come, they have stayed, or they have gone—including musicians.

Two musicians in widely differing periods arrived in Bristol from the far west of Cornwall, just as workers still arrive today seeking better economic and personal prospects than the Lizard or Penwith can offer. One was a singer, the other an organist and composer. In spite of their disparity they represent part of a pattern.

Charles Incledon was born in St. Keverne, which if only it had had a market in its spacious but sleepy main square would have been the southernmost town in mainland Britain. Its residents certainly had enterprise in the eighteenth century, for in 1762, the year before Incledon's birth, five local smugglers brought home 218 barrels of brandy.[1] His father was a doctor, but Incledon must have been fascinated by the nearby sea with its dreadful rocks, the Manacles, for after serving under William Jackson as a chorister in Exeter Cathedral, he joined the navy.[2]

Incledon made his name as a singer in Bath and Bristol. He became the leading English tenor of his day, retained his strong west country accent, and held audiences entranced with his nautical scenas, acted on the stage with dramatic backdrops. One such, the cantata *Black Ey'd Susan* with words by John Gay, was composed by Bristol's Robert Broderip, his family name best known for publishing and piano manufacture. The cantata was printed by the firm in 1785. According to the title page, Incledon

---

[1] A. K. Hamilton Jenkin, *Cornish Seafarers*, (1932), reprinted in *Cornwall and its People*, (Newton Abbot, 1970), p. 12.

[2] O. Baldwin and T. Wilson, 'Incledon, Charles', S. Sadie and J. Tyrrell, (eds.), *The New Grove Dictionary of Music and Musicians*, (London, 2/2001), xii, p. 146.

sang it 'at the Subscription Concerts in Bristol and Bath', and it was evidently popular, for a second edition appeared four years later.[3] Incledon had only just joined the Bristol and Bath players in 1785 (the two cities for many years ran their theatres as a single company), but he was not much valued for his acting.[4] After five years his singing took him to Covent Garden, where Haydn heard him in William Shield's *The Woodman* in 1791, and he eventually sang as tenor soloist in the first London performance of *The Creation*. Grove refers to his 'somewhat flashy personality'.[5] Bristol did not forget Incledon, and when he returned to the Theatre Royal in March 1805 to play Don Carlos in Sheridan's *The Duenna*, 'nearly fifty pounds was turned away from the box office'.[6]

Born almost a hundred years later, William Coulson Tregarthen was another Cornish musician whose career was nurtured in Bristol before he passed on to broader horizons. He came from seafaring stock. Two sea captains, James and F. B. Tregarthen, lived in St. Mary's, Isles of Scilly, during the nineteenth century, and ships mastered by one or other of the Tregarthens arrived at and departed from Bristol repeatedly during the same period, as did young Tregarthens who were taking and passing their Marine Board examinations.[7] A Mr. Tregarthen of Cardiff took part in the Weston-super-Mare regatta of 1888.[8] William's father, however, was a clothier from St. Mary's who had set up as a tailor in Penzance, where William was born.[9] One of William's elder brothers, James Coulson Tregarthen (there were five children altogether), would distinguish himself as a naturalist and the author of books such as *Cornwall and Its Wildlife* (1924). He wrote a whole series on what was clearly a winning formula, beginning with *The Life Story of the Otter* (1909) and continuing with biographies of the hare, the badger and the fox. Once again smuggling hovers in the margin of our narrative with the subject of his later book *The Smuggler's Daughter: a romance of Mount's Bay* (1932).

William Tregarthen attended Penzance Grammar School from 1867 to 1873, and then followed a common route for boys with broken voice who wished to pursue music as a 'trade' by becoming the articled pupil of a church or cathedral organist, in this case George Riseley of Bristol. This was an apprenticeship available, with luck, to families of modest means (another tailor's son, Ivor Gurney, would later undertake it in Gloucester) in the days when Oxford or Cambridge would have presupposed more preparatory support, generally a public school education, and the Royal College of Music with its scholarship provision was not yet open. Tregarthen studied with Riseley from 1873 to 1878. Until 1876 Riseley was organist of All Saints', Clifton, where Tregarthen became his assistant in May 1873. Riseley must have thought highly enough of him to arrange for cathedral experience, not in Bristol where the

---

[3] There is a copy in the Special Collections of the Bristol University Library, Restricted M1619, vocal score [*c.* 1790]

[4] K. Barker, *The Theatre Royal Bristol, 1766–1966: two centuries of stage history*, (1974), p. 54.

[5] O. Baldwin and T. Wilson, *loc. cit.*

[6] K. Barker, *op. cit.*, p. 75.

[7] *Bristol Mercury*, 21 September 1867, p. 6; 10 June 1871, extra sheet; 18 October 1873, p. 7; 17 August 1878, p. 7.

[8] *Bristol Mercury*, 15 August 1888, p. 6.

[9] This and many of the following details are taken from the family website, www.tregarthen.com, accessed 27 August 2008.

aged John Davis Corfe, his own master, had been in post for half a century,[10] but at Gloucester under Samuel Sebastian Wesley. Perhaps a meeting occurred in April 1874 when Wesley, in one of his very last public engagements, opened the new organ in the Victoria Rooms, Clifton.[11] Tregarthen studied with Wesley from January to October 1875; Wesley was then at the end of his career and can have been hardly any more sprightly than Corfe. Whether he studied organ playing or composition is not known.

Corfe died early in 1876 and Riseley succeeded him as cathedral organist, taking his young pupil with him as sub-organist. Tregarthen also held posts at St. John the Evangelist, Clifton, (April 1873 to October 1875)[12] and St. Paul's, Clifton (from October 1875)[13]. At St. Paul's he helped a student, who can have been only a year or two younger than himself, Edmund Mackie,[14] to win a choral scholarship to Magdalen College, Oxford.[15] He was not helping himself by attempting, without qualifications, to develop a musical career in an English provincial city, even in those high Victorian times when new churches were springing up like mushrooms in fashionable suburbs, each wanting a mighty organ with someone to play it and train a surpliced choir.[16] In February 1877 he was living at 15 Victoria Place, hardly the address for an ambitious young gentleman, if this was the cramped *cul de sac* of tiny workmen's houses in the back end of Bedminster.[17] In the following year he did what many Penwithians of his generation were doing and emigrated to South Africa, leaving behind a modest trail of hymn tunes attesting to local affection: 'St. Buryan', 'Cornwall', 'St. Paul' and 'Coulson', published in *The Monthly Hymnal* (Glasgow, 1877). He took with him an honorary membership of the newly founded Trinity College, London, no doubt a useful paper credential for uncertain conditions ahead.[18]

Exit Tregarthen from the musical annals of Bristol. How strange this coming and going would have seemed to Corfe, had he lived to witness it, or even to Riseley, born in Bristol and himself an articled pupil of Corfe, following a choristership at the

[10] John Davis Corfe was born in Salisbury, where his father was cathedral organist in succession to his grandfather.

[11] P. Horton, *Samuel Sebastian Wesley: a life*, (Oxford, 2004), pp. 302–304.

[12] We do not know the strength of his choir, but the services at the church were both choral and semi-choral, the chants were Anglican, the psalms were chanted, *Monk and Ouseley's Psalter* was used and the hymnal was *Ancient and Modern*, (new edition). S. Colborn, *The Bristol, Clifton, and Suburban Guide*, (Bristol, 1878–9), p. 42. [Ed.]

[13] His choir consisted of 16 trebles, 4 altos, 8 tenors, and 11 basses [S. Colborn, *op. cit.*, p. 45]; the choir used Anglican chants, the *Cathedral Psalter*, it chanted the psalms and used *Hymns Ancient and Modern*, (new edition). Sunday services were fully choral and week day services semi-choral. [Ed.]

[14] Son of the chaplain of the Bristol Infirmary.

[15] *Bristol Mercury*, 19 February 1876, p. 6.

[16] This was an emotive issue. Bristol was traditionally Evangelical in its churchmanship and its churchmen were against Tractarian innovations. In 1878 there were only 14 surpliced choirs in the 42 Bristol churches and in five out of the 13 in Clifton, including All Saints', St. John the Evangelist, and St. Paul. S. Colborn, *op. cit.*, appendix following p. 80, see also *The Gloucester and Bristol Diocesan Kalendar*, (Gloucester, 1874). [Ed.]

[17] In 1878–1879 he is stated to have lived at Prospect House, Oakfield Road; S. Colborn, *op. cit.*, p. 45. [Ed.]

[18] *Bristol Mercury*, 26 January 1878, p. 8.

cathedral. Yet Tregarthen was by no means a lone musical emigrant from Bristol and its hinterland. Two instances from earlier in the century concern men, probably casual acquaintances, who headed for North America within a couple of months of each other in 1838 due to unpropitious career prospects in Bristol.[19]

The singer and composer Austin Phillips left Bristol for New York because of bankruptcy the previous year. William Hodges was organist of two Bristol city churches, St. James Haymarket and St. Nicholas. Widowed three years earlier and failing to gain a cathedral post, he emigrated to Toronto, moving swiftly on to New York where he was organist of the important Trinity Church for nearly a quarter of a century.

Hodges returned twice to Bristol and died there, with Corfe still doggedly at his post at the cathedral all the time Hodges was educating the musical tastes of a fashionable Manhattan congregation. Indeed Corfe assisted at his funeral. But a return was not the rule, and in general when you said farewell to someone on the quayside in the nineteenth century it was for good.

As three of the four cases described so far may suggest, emigration was a larger fact of musical life in the nineteenth century than has been previously noticed; but it was one of a number of demographic career patterns into which Bristol's musicians fitted. As this article's title indicates, there were others. Working with a collection of around 75 genteel (as opposed to proletarian) musicians born between *c.* 1760 and 1880 for whom biographical facts have been easily retrieved, initially from Brown and Stratton's *British Musical Biography*, patterns emerge which whilst not rigid are certainly striking.[20] The list of these musicians is given in Figure 1.

In the nineteenth and early twentieth centuries Bristol was a regional centre as well as a portal for the British Empire, and thereby also for a British cultural formation, now sometimes termed 'the British World' (of which Hodges never doubted the U.S.A. was a part). By reference to these factors it is possible to detect some trends among the apparently diverse lives of musicians whose careers included time spent in Bristol.

Those musicians who came to Bristol having already established a musical identity in some other region include Beachcroft, Greenwood, Hudson, Hunt, Milani, both Peppins, Rainforth, Roeckel and Daniel Rootham. Beachcroft, a pianist and composer, was assistant music master at Clifton College and a pupil of Sir Walter Parratt. Greenwood was born in Lancashire but came to Bristol aged 19 and gained a lay clerkship at the cathedral, also becoming organist of various suburban churches: Bedminster, Westbury-on-Trym, Kingsdown. He was music master at Colston School and Bristol Grammar School and died in Clifton. Hudson, a violinist and composer, had been born in Hull and pursued a career there before coming to Clifton. Milani was a violinist from Frankfurt and came to Bristol as a violin teacher *via* a post at Blundell's School, Tiverton. Of the Peppins, Arthur joined the music staff of Clifton College; he had been Sir George Grove's secretary at the Royal College of Music. His brother was a singer and the precentor at Bristol cathedral. Both Hunt and Rainforth are rare examples of musicians leaving London for the provinces.

[19] S. Banfield, 'Bristol's music and musicians in region, nation and empire', *British Music*, xxviii, (2006), pp. 30–55; J. Hobson: 'Austin Phillips', *CHOMBEC News* 5, (Summer 2008), pp. 11–13.

[20] J. D. Brown and S. S. Stratton, *British Musical Biography*, (Birmingham, 1897).

George A. Ames (1827–1893)

John Carlowitz Ames (1860–?)

Joseph Humfrey Anger (1862–1913)

George Barrett (1814–1891)

John Barrett (1812–1886)

John Barrett (1837–?)

Richard Owen Beachcroft

Cornelius Bryan (c.1775–1840)

Percy Buck (1871–1947)

Cedric Bucknall (1849–1921)

Henry Elliott Button (1861–1925)

John Cockram

William Edward Cockram (1836–1870)

Sydney Coles (1852–?)

John Davis Corfe (1804–1876)

Charles Cummins (1785–?)

William Fear Dyer

George Edwards

John Emdin (1784–1827)

Charles Eulenstein (1802–1890)

James Foster (1807–1885)

W. E. Fowler

Edward Bowles Fripp (1787–1870)

Charles Joseph Frost (1848–?)

James Greenwood (1837–1894)

The Revd. Frederick Kill Harford (1832–?)

Basil Harwood (1859–1949)

The Very Revd. Stephen Georgeson

Hatherly (1827–?)

Edward Hodges (1796–1867)

Thomas Howell the elder

Thomas Howell the younger (1783–?)

Arthur Hudson

Hubert Hunt (1865–1945)

Charles Incledon (1763–1826)

Jane Jackson (c.1834–1907)

Charles Warwick Jordan (1840–?)

Joseph Kemp (1778–1824)

Joseph Philip Knight (1812–1887)

Frederick Charles Maker (1844–1927)

Bertram von der Mark

Clara Meller (1856–?)

Otto Milani (1866–1923)

Philip Napier Miles (1865–1935)

Robert Lucas Pearsall (1795–1856

Arthur Hamilton Peppin (?-1929)

G. F. E. Peppin

Austin Phillips (?-1851)

William Lovell Phillips (1816–60)

Henry Pope

Robert Sidney Pratten (1834–1868)

Elizabeth Rainforth (1814–1877)

Thomas German Reed (1817–1888)

George Riseley (1845–1932)

Joseph Leopold Roeckel (1838–1923)*

Cyril Rootham (1875–1938)

Daniel Wilberforce Rootham
   (1838–1922)

Fred W. Rootham

Mabel Margaret Rootham

Samuel Rootham

George Sampson (1861–?)

George Frederick Stansbury
   (1800–1845)

Joseph Stansbury

Miss Stansbury

Alfred Stone (1841–1878)

William Frederick Taylor (1835–1887)

William Coulson Tregarthen
   (1856–1942)

Thomas Trimnell (?-1865)

Thomas Tallis Trimnell (1827–1897)

William Frederick Trimnell

Austin T. Turner (1823–?)

John Wasbrough (?-1829)

Charles Wesley (1757–1834)

Samuel Wesley (1766–1837)

Fig. 1. Some Bristolian musicians in the nineteenth century.

* Also called Röckel, L. J. de Bekker, *Stokes' Cyclopaedia of Music and Musicians*, (1911), pp. 554–555, [Ed.].

Rainforth was a London soprano (the first Arline in Balfe's *The Bohemian Girl*) who retired from the metropolis to Bristol, dying in Redland. Hunt, like Riseley a major force in Bristol music, was organist of Bristol cathedral from 1901 to 1945 and conductor of the Bristol Madrigal Society and the New Philharmonic Society. Father of the recorder player and musicologist Edgar Hunt, he arrived in Bristol after 15 years in London as an organist and professional violinist in the Blagrove Quartet. As he came from cathedral stock and had been a chorister and an articled pupil at St. George's, Windsor under Elvey and Parratt, his decision to accept a provincial cathedral appointment was not surprising.[21] Roeckel was a pianist, composer and teacher of distinguished German pedigree (his father was a famous opera singer, his uncle the composer Hummel). He was born in London and settled as a young man in Bath together with his brother Eduard some time in or before 1861. He moved on to Clifton while Eduard stayed there. A third brother, August, languished in a German prison for 13 years after the Dresden uprising of 1849, a fine mess he got Wagner into. Rootham's family came from Cambridge; Dan himself was a chorister at St. John's College (whither his son would return) and a pupil of Walmisley. He moved to Bristol and became a cathedral lay clerk when his father died in 1852. (Clara Butt was one of his pupils.) In these instances Bristol was a career magnet with a drawing power superior to that of places such as Tiverton and Hull and in two cases London, but only in the fields of public education, cathedral music (consolidated by church organist posts and choral conductorships), and in the private teaching opportunities that Clifton could offer.

By those who stayed is meant individuals whose entire musical career was in Bristol and who in most cases were either born or nurtured there. They would appear to include the Barretts, Bryan, Bucknall, John Cockram, Corfe, Dyer, Emdin, Foster, Jackson, Maker, Napier Miles, Riseley, Fred and Samuel Rootham, Stone, Taylor, Thomas Trimnell, W. F. Trimnell, and Wasbrough. It makes for a long list, longer than the nineteenth century revolution in transport might have presupposed. Most of the names in this category represent organists, teachers and cathedral singers; some were also minor composers, with one or two interesting variants such as Bucknall, who was a micologist of national distinction and founded the university orchestra. Bucknall was organist of the Victoria Rooms and of All Saints', Clifton.[22] The latter was an important Victorian church designed by G. E. Street R.A. and the prestigious post of organist and choirmaster recurs in musical annals.

Almost a hundred years earlier Wasbrough was Bristol cathedral organist (1807–1825) while Bryan was organist of the mayor's chapel and St. Mary Redcliffe.[23] Bryan published a number of compositions, including two sets of *Effusions for the Organ*. Cockram was a music-seller in Bristol, Dyer organist of St. Nicholas and conductor of the Bristol Church Choral Union festivals, Taylor a pianist and composer. William Frederick Trimnell was an organist and director of music at Clifton College, and Fred

[21] J. A. Bennett: 'Hubert Hunt: Musician and Mason (1865–1945): his contribution to the musical scene of Bristol and beyond', Bristol Masonic Society lecture, 30 May 2002.

[22] He used Gregorian chants regularly in worship. [Ed.]

[23] For Bryan see, A. C. Powell and J. Littleton, *Freemasonry in Bristol*, (Bristol, 1910), p. 200. He died at a rehearsal of his opera *Lundy* as a result of falling down a trap door used for hauling scenery up and down. The opera was never performed. [Ed.]

Rootham was a piano teacher. Stone was a music teacher in various schools, an organist (St. Paul's, Clifton; Arley chapel; Highbury chapel), conductor of the Orpheus Glee Society, chorus master of the Bristol Festival, and editor of the revised *Bristol Tune Book* (1876). Jackson, a prolific salon composer, was one of the daughters of Bristol's leading painter, Samuel Jackson. She married Joseph Roeckel.

At the earlier end of the nineteenth century, there are some remarkably long musical careers in Bristol. Corfe has already been mentioned. Thomas Trimnell (father of William Frederick) was a cathedral lay clerk of such long standing that the dean and chapter eventually retired him on a pension. George Barrett was the organist at Holy Trinity, Hotwells, for 52 years, his father Slater Barrett having been in the Bristol cathedral choir for nearly 60 years. Dan Rootham conducted the Bristol Madrigal Society for 50 years in succession to Corfe. Riseley also stayed a long time, as organist of the Colston Hall as well as of the cathedral, and as conductor of the Bristol Orpheus Society, the Bristol Monday Popular Concerts and the Bristol Festival. However, his influence spread to the metropolis and he began to commute, making an impact on the national scene by teaching the organ at the Royal Academy of Music, giving a Royal Albert Hall series of organ recitals and taking his choir to London and to the Queen at Windsor. Samuel Rootham sought the opposite of Riseley's glamour from his Bristol base: 'In a quite unobtrusive way he has done much good work', Brown and Stratton commented, mentioning his teaching at the Blind Asylum and conducting the Redland Park Hall Band.[24] Emdin and Foster were musical amateurs (Foster was a builder) and as composers probably wrote little beyond songs and hymn tunes. Napier Miles was also an amateur but as a rich, philanthropic one (his father developed the Avonmouth docks), he was able to accomplish far more, composing symphonic works plus operas, some of which were produced and so have a place in the story of British opera.[25]

Five of the above (Beachcroft, Arthur Peppin, Hunt, Riseley and Fred Rootham) were founders of the Bristol Music Club in 1903, its tiny concert hall easily overlooked even by pedestrians on St. Paul's Road, Clifton, yet rare in possessing its own premises and justifiably proud in having Joseph Joachim, the great Hungarian violinist, as its first president. While Riseley made a national impact, Hunt did not need to, for he flourished in the best years of the cathedral organist's profession. Maker might seem to epitomise the inconsequential musical jobber. His *British Musical Biography* entry reads: 'Organist and composer, born at Bristol. Chorister in Bristol Cathedral, and pupil of Alfred Stone. Organist of Milk Street Methodist Free Church; Clifton Down Congregational Church; and from 1882 of Redland Park Congregational Church. Has composed a cantata "Moses in the bullrushes" [*sic*]; contributed tunes to the Bristol Tune Book; Issued a collection of original tunes; Anthems, etc'.[26] True, nobody sings *Moses in the Bulrushes* these days. Yet 65 works composed by him and published in London appear in the British Library catalogue, and he wrote the hymn tune for 'Dear Lord and Father of mankind' preferred today in the U.S.A to that of Parry. The extraordinary thing about these people, domestic and foreign-bound, is that nearly all of them composed music, however modest in scale, managed to get it

[24] J. D. Brown and S. S. Stratton, *op. cit.*, p. 354.
[25] See E. W. White, *A History of English Opera*, (London, 1983), pp. 397, 400.
[26] J. D. Brown and S. S. Stratton, *op. cit.*, pp. 268–269.

published, and kept on doing so. It was clearly a viable part of their freelance portfolio, and it is impossible to overestimate the scope of what we might now call three commercial 'rackets' for musicians in the nineteenth century: the church, the school and home study.

So much for those who came or stayed. Of those who went, London claimed many born or brought up in Bristol: William Edward Cockram (son of John), Frost, Harwood, Incledon, Jordan, Kemp, William Lovell Phillips, Pope, Pratten, German Reed, Sampson, G. F. Stansbury, the two young Wesleys, and probably John Carlowitz Ames. This was almost inevitable for singers and instrumental *virtuosi*, as it still is; less so for church-based musicians. In addition to Incledon, Cockram, Pope and Stansbury were singers, and Pratten a flautist. The Wesleys were child prodigy keyboard players. Most of them stayed in London, although Sampson appears to have moved on to Brighton.

What is striking is how few went to other provincial regions: Coles, Fripp, Knight (the first two organists, the third a song-writer), Cyril Rootham, Thomas Tallis Trimnell, and Turner. Even then, the majority migrated to places where they had strong ties, geographical or familial. Rootham returned to his grandfather's city, Cambridge, and Fripp and Knight remained within the west country. Fripp ended his days in Teignmouth, and Knight became vicar of St. Agnes in the Isles of Scilly, although he was to die in Great Yarmouth. Apart from Coles, who left Bristol aged 20 or 21 for an articled pupilship in London and whose subsequent career was spent in Eastbourne, only Trimnell and Turner ventured into unconnected regional territory. Both were born in Bristol, within four years of each other, and were choristers (Trimnell was also an articled pupil). Trimnell went to Chesterfield and Sheffield, Turner to a post as vicar choral at Lincoln cathedral, and for both of them there was probably an element of *Wanderlust*, for both subsequently moved abroad, Trimnell to New Zealand in 1886 at the age of 58 or 59, taking up organist's posts in Auckland and at St. Peter's, Wellington, Turner to Australia in 1854, where he settled in the gold-rush town of Ballarat and presided over an increasingly lively musical scene.[27]

For whatever reasons, those who went abroad form a longer and more interesting list than those who left for other regions within Britain, especially if one extends the catchment area from Bristol to the whole of Somerset. They comprise Anger, Harford, Hatherly, Hodges, Meller, Austin Phillips, Tregarthen, Thomas Tallis Trimnell and Turner, plus Ernest Slater (1860–1936), born in Taunton, and Joseph Summers (1839–1917), from Charlton Mackrell near Yeovil. All but one of them remained within the British world, however far afield that might take them. That includes Leipzig with its anglophone colony of residents (not just in music) as part of the British world. Meller, a pianist born in Clifton and educated first in Bristol and then in London, went to Leipzig for further study in 1871 and stayed there because she married a famous German musicologist, Hermann Kretzschmar. ('Give my regards to Clara', Grieg writes in his letters to Kretzschmar.)[28] The exception was Hatherly, a priest, organist, musicologist and composer, who joined the Greek Orthodox church 'and in 1875 became proto-presbyter of the Patriarchal

[27] See Anne Doggett: 'And for Harmony Most Ardently We Long': musical life in Ballarat, 1851–1871, (Ph.D. dissertation, University of Ballarat, 2006).
[28] Personal communication from Daniel Grimley.

Œcumenical Throne of Constantinople' before returning to Bristol.[29] The others colonised, in addition to Leipzig, all the Dominions—Australia, Canada, South Africa, New Zealand—plus Gibraltar, India and the U.S.A.

Hodges, Phillips, Tregarthen, Trimnell and Turner have already been mentioned. Anger, from the Swindon district, came to Bristol as a young organist in 1889. Although he stayed only two years, he made his mark with a splendid madrigal, 'All on a summer's morning', dedicated to one of the pillars of the Bristol Madrigal Society, John Barrett, another member of that markedly entrenched family, before moving on first to Ludlow and after a further two years to Canada. Harford, an amateur composer born in Clifton, educated at Rugby and Oxford and then ordained, spent only a short period as chaplain to the bishop of Gibraltar before retreating to Westminster Abbey as a canon, but his imperial experience possibly rubbed off on him, since he was 'active in the attempt to popularize the National Anthem in India'.[30] Slater took jobs in London before becoming organist and choirmaster at St. John's, Calcutta, in 1885. Summers, the son of a stonemason, was clearly restless, holding posts at Bradfield College, and in Weston-super-Mare and Notting Hill prior to emigrating to Australia in 1865, where he joined his brother who was already working there as a sculptor.

How did the emigrants fare abroad, and how would they have fared had they stayed at home? Opinion is divided as to whether the British musical profession was declining in the nineteenth century, but it was certainly becoming more crowded and competitive.[31] Population and educational growth contributed towards this, as did ease of travel and communication, which made people more mobile, even if this study has demonstrated that they were not as indiscriminately mobile as might have been expected. Whether or not demand was actually matching supply at home, there was a perception that it was not. Overseas it was everywhere outstripping it, and if this did not necessarily lead to satisfied customers it was undoubtedly a seller's market. Thus Trimnell and Turner, 'two little boys' (to quote the imperial song revived by Rolf Harris) who must have known each other as choristers, achieved acclaim as musical pioneers in the Antipodes, at least in their own day and in one case in a doctoral dissertation in ours. Anger and Tregarthen established dignified careers in their chosen colonies, Anger in the theory department of the Toronto Conservatoire, as director of music at the Church of the Ascension in that city, and with the Toronto Philharmonic, Tregarthen eventually as organist of St. George's, Johannesburg, following posts in Port Elizabeth, Queenstown, and elsewhere. Beyond this, both made unsuccessful bids for transnational apotheosis by composing patriotic songs that they hoped would become national anthems, Anger 'Hail Canada!' in 1911, Tregarthen 'Behold the night' in 1927, published 'in English, Dutch and Kafir', as the title page announces.[32] Slater certainly made a go of Calcutta, where he remained at least until

---

[29] J. D. Brown and S. S. Stratton, *op. cit.*, p. 188.

[30] *Ibid.*, p. 183.

[31] See A. V. Beedell, *The Decline of the English Musician: a family of English musicians in England, Mauritius, and Australia*, (Oxford, 1992). Nicholas Temperley takes issue with the thesis implicit in Beedell's title in his 'Foreword', T. Ellsworth and S. Wollenberg, (ed.), *The Piano in Nineteenth-Century British Culture*, (Aldershot, 2007), pp. xv-xix.

[32] Copies of all three versions, signed by Tregarthen, are in the British Library, shelfmark B.512, p. (17).

early 1912, when the *Musical Times* reported that at St. Paul's Cathedral, Calcutta he had been 'personally complimented by the Queen-Empress upon the excellence of the service music provided on December 31', though he disappears from the record after that until *The Times* notes his death in England in 1936.[33] Summers enjoyed a somewhat chequered and litigious career in Australia. He rose to hold a number of important posts in Melbourne, and eventually wrote a published autobiography. He became insolvent, sued the local paper for caricaturing one of his 'musical productions', and eventually moved on to Perth. Here the object of his litigation was a priest who owed him a libretto. Still, he remained in good enough official odour to found the Philharmonic Society and the Liedertafel in Perth, and to compose and publish an effective male-voice motet, 'O where shall wisdom be found?', performed at the first Commencement of what is now the University of Western Australia,[34] founded in 1911.

More Bristol musicians of the nineteenth century will come to light. It is difficult to tell whether or not Brown and Stratton, on whom so much of the material for this article has relied, found all the best ones (however obscure they now seem) through their research, undertaken more than a century ago. The newly digitised Bristol daily press has not yet been scoured for further professionals, or indeed for further details of those musicians mentioned in this article, and the amateur scene should be certainly researched too. The parents of Alfred Hill (1870–1960), the first native-born Australian composer of eminence,[35] emigrated from Bristol in 1852. His father was a hat maker and talented amateur violinist.[36]

Naturally the emigrants with their intrinsically adventurous lives have interested me the most. Did Bristol have more than its fair share of them? To answer the question it would be necessary to compare numbers and proportions with those of other cities over the same period—Birmingham, say, or Leicester—and even then the sample would probably be too small to mean much. But my guess is that it did. Bristol's economic growth slowed markedly in the nineteenth century, and its musical importance declined as Manchester, Birmingham and the seaside resorts gained orchestras, bands, patrons and more affluent publics. True, it gained from Bath's decline (very few of the musicians mentioned in this essay were active there, in contrast with the previous century), and Clifton was a unique hothouse of musical gentility. An overriding factor, however, may have been Bristol's traditions of exchange and venture as a port, counteracting the effects of economic stagnation. Perhaps it was salt in the blood and the gulls on the quay that led not just Incledon to sing his cantata about black-eyed Susan and her sailor, and the Tregarthens to cross the oceans, but many another budding organist, teacher, singer or amateur *aficionado* to take their music overseas.

---

[33] *Musical Times*, liii, (1912), p. 124; *The Times*, 1 September 1936, p. 1. It would be good to know whether Gordon Slater, O.B.E. (1896–1979), a well-known composer for the organ who became organist of Lincoln cathedral, was Ernest Slater's son.

[34] See J. Summers, *Music and Musicians: personal reminiscences, 1865–1910*, (Perth, 1910); R. S. Stevens: 'Summers, Joseph (1839–1917)', *Australian Dictionary of National Biography* online, (www.adb.online.anu.edu.au).

[35] He grew up and began his career in New Zealand.

[36] J. M. Thomson, 'Hill, Alfred (Francis)', *Grove*, xi, p. 503.

XX

Lovers of Dickens: The formative years of the Bristol and Clifton Dickens Society[1]

LIONEL R. REEVES, B.ED.

THE BRISTOL and Clifton Dickens Society, founded in April 1902, is the oldest such organisation in Great Britain. Charles Dickens was born on 7 February 1812 at Portsmouth, but is thought of as a man of Kent, or of London, so why was it that Dickens enthusiasts in Bristol came to lead the way where others were to follow?

The Society was the brainchild of a twenty-two year old journalist, James William Thomas Ley.[2] Educated at Bristol Grammar School, he was articled to the *Bristol Daily Mercury* and was, not unlike Dickens himself, a reporter 'of exceptional energy and activity'. He also had a passion for the works of Charles Dickens, and it was said of him, 'that if the text of *Pickwick Papers* should ever be lost, he was the man who might restore it from memory'.[3] Ley was also impressed by the author's active involvement in enterprising philanthropy and his influence in effecting social change.[4] The Dickens Society that Ley envisaged would continue this work in the name of Dickens and be decidedly different from other literary organisations.

Although the popularity of Dickens had not diminished during the thirty years since his death in 1870, Ley saw the demise of many of the author's friends and associates as 'the snapping of another link in the chain which connects this generation with that of Charles Dickens'.[5] This also applied to local devotees of the author. Some had already died, including James Verry Staples of Clifton,[6] who had read *A Christmas Carol* to the poor at the Bristol Domestic Mission Institution in 1843 and afterwards corresponded with Dickens; Miss Mary Carpenter, whose *Reformatory Schools* [...] (1851) was favourably reviewed by James Hannay in Dickens's journal, *Household*

References. *B. D. M.* = *Bristol Daily Mercury*; *B. E. P.* = *Bristol Evening Post*; *B. E. W.* = *Bristol Evening World*; *B. G.* = *Bristol Gazette*; *B. T.* = *Bristol* Times; *B. T. & M.* = *Bristol Times & Mirror*; *B. T. & F. F. J.* = *Bristol Times & Felix Farley's Journal*; *C. C.* = *Clifton Chronicle & Directory* (weekly, published on Wednesdays); *D.* = *The Dickensian*; *T.* = *The Times*; *W. D. P.* = *Western Daily Press*.

[1] There are few early documents. The first minute book in the Bristol and Clifton Dickens Society archive is from 1929.
[2] Honorary general secretary of the Dickens Fellowship 1904–1909, a founder of *The Dickensian*, died 21 August 1943. His annotation of Forster's *Life of Dickens* is still a standard work.
[3] *T.*, Monday, 23 August 1943 p. 6, col. e.
[4] *B. D. M.*, Thursday, 13 February 1902 p. 3, col. c. Kindly supplied by Dr. M. J. Crossley Evans.
[5] *B. D. M.*, Wednesday, 6 February 1907, p. 4, col. g.
[6] See G. Storey, (ed.), *The Letters of Charles Dickens*, IV, p. 95; VII, p. 1, and XII, p. 674.

Words;[7] and Dean Gilbert Elliot, whom Dickens had applauded for his anti-Tractarianism, wishing him to be made bishop of Exeter! In a private capacity Dickens had also acted as an intermediary between the dean and his second wife when their marriage ran into difficulties.[8]

Ley would not have known of the latter circumstance and was probably unaware that a current residentiary canon at the cathedral, who spent three months of each year in Bristol to carry out his duties, had received part of his education at a London boarding school where two of Dickens's seven sons were pupils. The Revd. Alfred Ainger[9] had been introduced into the Dickens household in his youth and taken part in a number of their family theatricals and later lectured on his experiences.

Ley was conscious that fewer and fewer Bristolians now recalled the excitement of seeing the 39 year old Dickens perform with his company of amateur players at the Victoria Rooms in November 1851.[10] A specially-written play by Sir Edward Bulwer Lytton,[11] *Not So Bad As We Seem*, had been the main attraction and Mark Lemon[12] had collaborated with Dickens to write the accompanying farce, *Mr. Nightingale's Diary*, in which Dickens assumed seven characters.[13] So successful was the scheduled performance that another was hastily convened and staged two nights later.[14]

Of those who crowded into the Bristol Athenaeum on 19 January 1858, to hear Dickens read from *A Christmas Carol* for the benefit of the institution, how many now remained?[15] Who now recalled, a few months later, reading the bewildering press reports that Dickens had legally separated from his wife on grounds of their incompatibility[16] or were present when Dickens was enthusiastically received at the Victoria Rooms at the opening of his first provincial public reading tour on 2 August 1858?[17] Dickens returned to Bristol five times, the last being on 20 January 1869, during his farewell reading tour.[18] All were memorable occasions.

After the death of Charles Dickens on 9 June 1870, his weekly journal, *All the Year Round*, continued to be conducted by Charles Dickens—his eldest son! John Forster

[7] Dickens was unable to show Mary Carpenter (1807–1877) around the rehabilitation home for young prostitutes he managed, but sent her a letter of introduction. See *ibid.*, VII, p. 907.

[8] See M. Slater, (ed.), *Dickens' Journalism*, II, (1996), pp. 310–315.

[9] The Revd. Alfred Ainger (1837–1904) author, essayist and biographer of Charles Lamb, see E. Sichel, *The Life and Letters of Alfred Ainger*, (1906), chapter 1, kindly made available by Mr. Andrew Phillips, chapter clerk of Bristol cathedral.

[10] *B. T.*, Saturday, 15 November 1851, p. 6, cols. a-c. See J. Latimer, *The Annals of Bristol in the Nineteenth Century*, (Bristol, 1887), p. 329.

[11] Sir Edward Bulwer Lytton Bart. (1803–1873), English novelist and man of letters. Dickens named his last child, born 1842, Edward Bulwer Lytton Dickens. See P. Schlicke, (ed.), *The Oxford Reader's Companion to Dickens*, (Oxford, 1999), p. 63.

[12] Mark Lemon (1809–1870), co-founder and editor of *Punch* from 1841 until his death. See P. Schlicke, (ed.), *op. cit.*, p. 326.

[13] L. R. Reeves, 'Charles Dickens: The Bristol Connection', *The Temple Local History Group Newsletter* No. 1/88, pp. 34–43.

[14] John Forster was the only player to be replaced at the second performance.

[15] *B. G.*, Thursday, 21 January 1858, p. 5, col. d.

[16] *B. G.*, Thursday, 19 June 1858, p. 6, col. b.

[17] *B. T. & F. F. J.*, Saturday, 7 August 1858, p. 6, col. d.

[18] *B. T. & M.*, Tuesday, 26 January 1869, p. 3, col. b.

issued the official biography of his close friend, and Dickens's daughter Mary, with her aunt Georgina Hogarth, edited a collection of his letters to compliment it.[19] Many of Dickens's family and friends wrote their reminiscences of him. New editions of the novels appeared and 'Collected Editions' included his journalism and other material. Theatrical versions of his novels continued to be popular. Henry Irving,[20] whose relatives lived in the city, played 'Mr Jingle' at London's Lyceum theatre and Martin Harvey[21] the part of Sydney Carton in *The Only Way*, a re-working of *A Tale of Two Cities*. Elocutionists, in imitation of Dickens, also gave recitals and readings from his works.

Foremost among the latter was the Revd. Charles Clark, who in January 1867, at the age of twenty-nine, began his pastorate of Broadmead Baptist Chapel, Bristol. His dramatic style of preaching and magnetic charm secured his appointment, and soon the 650–seat chapel was regularly filled to overflowing. One can only speculate whether he attended Dickens's reading at the Victoria Rooms on 12 April 1867. Two years later Clark took up an appointment at Albert Street Baptist Chapel, Melbourne. Whilst there he gave his first lecture on Dickens and subsequently made several reading tours of the colonies: Australia, New Zealand, South Africa; and also America. These readings built up an enviable reputation for him, both as a preacher and as an exponent of the works of Dickens. The Revd. Charles Clark and his wife retired to Bristol in 1887, 'as he liked Clifton better than any other place he had seen on his travels'.[22] His talents undiminished, he continued to give recitals from the works of Dickens to popular acclaim. (Figs. 1 and 2).

Such was the climate in which the Bristol and Clifton Dickens Society was born. Having formulated his ideas, J. W. T. Ley consulted others about his plans. The biographer of Dickens and critic, George Gissing,[23] sent an encouraging reply:

> I heartily sympathize with the objects you have in view; the idea of a subscription on behalf of suffering children in Charles Dickens's name seems to me particularly happy. You will remember, of course, that one of the best of his admirable speeches was that he delivered for the children's hospital in London. There is no danger that

---

[19] Their editing removed references to Dickens's intention of visiting the Very Revd. Gilbert Elliot, dean of Bristol, and also of his first meeting with Robert Gay Barrow, his great uncle John's eldest son. See G. Storey, (ed.), *op. cit.*, VI, (1988), pp. 537–553.

[20] Sir Henry [John Henry Brodribb] Irving (1838–1905), the first actor to be knighted (1895) for his services to the theatre.

[21] (Sir John) Martin Harvey (1863–1944), Overshadowed by *The Bells*, Irving's portrayal did not receive critical acclaim. See L. Irving, *Henry Irving*, (1951), pp. 109, 207, 301. Bristol had to wait to see Martin Harvey in his greatest role as Sydney Carton. The part was first played here by William Haviland. D. Carleton, *The Prince's of Park Row*, Bristol Historical Association, 55, (Bristol, 1983), note 22, p. 15.

[22] *C. C.*, 1 April 1903, p. 5, col. h; Dr. M. J. Crossley Evans, 'The Revd. Charles Clark', unpublished lecture delivered to the Bristol and Clifton Dickens Society, 2005.

[23] George Robert Gissing (1857–1903), prepared an abridged and revised edition of Forster's life of the novelist for Messrs. Chapman and Hall in 1902. Gissing was a novelist and one of the foremost early critics of Dickens. His works included: *Charles Dickens: A Critical Study*, (1898). See: P. Schlicke, (ed.), *op. cit.*, p. 249.

Fig. 1. The Revd. Charles Clark, [Collection of M. J. Crossley Evans].

Dickens will be forgotten, but it is good to come together then at stated times and remind one another of the great work he did in English literature and English life.[24]

A letter to the editor of the *Bristol Daily Mercury* dated 11 February 1902 and signed, 'A Lover of Dickens', offered an opportunity to the 'great many lovers of Dickens in Bristol' to form a society 'to consist entirely of avowed lovers of the master—ladies included' and suggested that monthly meetings 'of a social character' were held and that 'on the anniversary of Dickens's birth the members might meet together and drink to his immortal memory. Of course, the object of the society would be the furtherance of those grand principles of humanity which "Boz" tried to implant'. The letter concluded by saying that a favourable response might result in a planning meeting being convened to further these objectives.[25]

A positive response came from 'K. A. N.' who recommended that the Revd.

24   P. Constillas, *Gissing's Writing on Dickens,* (1969), p. 10.
25   *B. D. M.,* Thursday, 13 February 1902, p. 3, col. c.

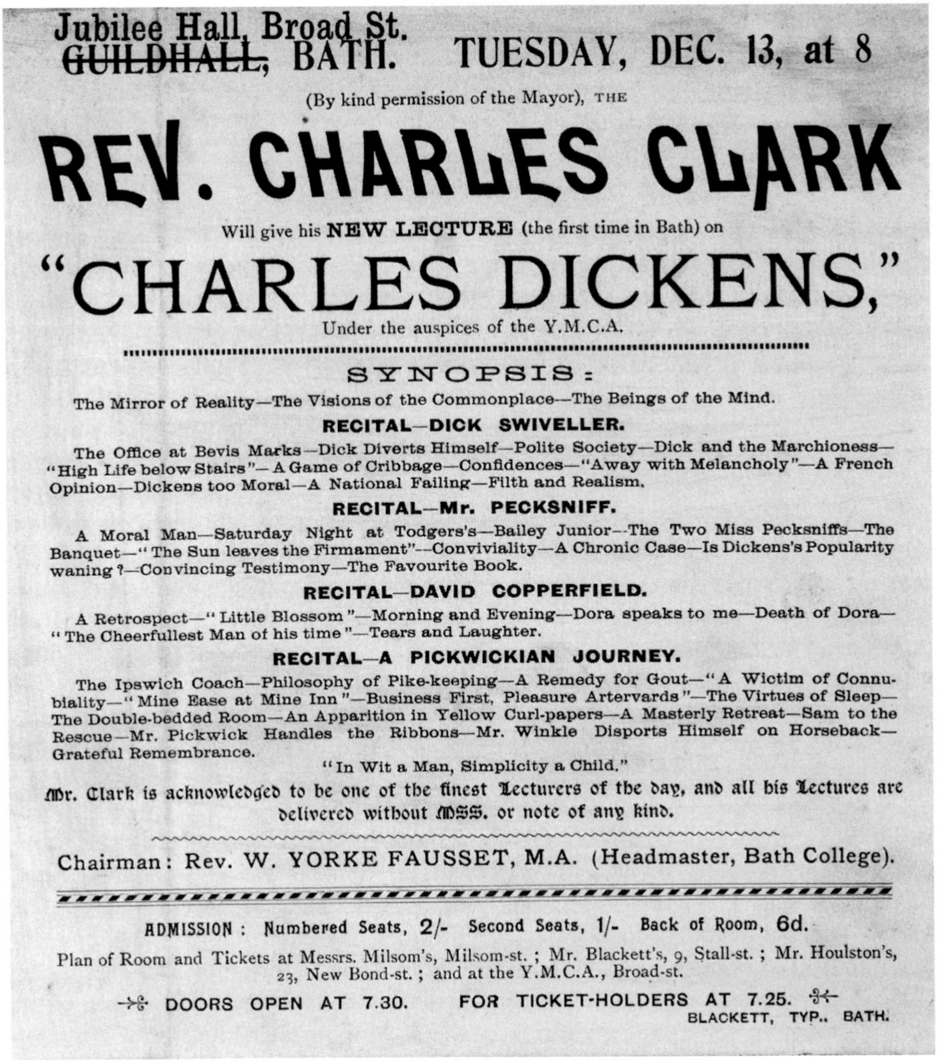

Jubilee Hall, Broad St.
~~GUILDHALL,~~ ~~BATH.~~   TUESDAY, DEC. 13, at 8

(By kind permission of the Mayor), THE

REV. CHARLES CLARK

Will give his **NEW LECTURE** (the first time in Bath) on

"CHARLES DICKENS,"

Under the auspices of the Y.M.C.A.

SYNOPSIS:

The Mirror of Reality—The Visions of the Commonplace—The Beings of the Mind.

RECITAL—DICK SWIVELLER.

The Office at Bevis Marks—Dick Diverts Himself—Polite Society—Dick and the Marchioness— "High Life below Stairs"—A Game of Cribbage—Confidences—"Away with Melancholy"—A French Opinion—Dickens too Moral—A National Failing—Filth and Realism.

RECITAL—Mr. PECKSNIFF.

A Moral Man—Saturday Night at Todgers's—Bailey Junior—The Two Miss Pecksniffs—The Banquet—"The Sun leaves the Firmament"—Conviviality—A Chronic Case—Is Dickens's Popularity waning?—Convincing Testimony—The Favourite Book.

RECITAL—DAVID COPPERFIELD.

A Retrospect—"Little Blossom"—Morning and Evening—Dora speaks to me—Death of Dora— "The Cheerfullest Man of his time"—Tears and Laughter.

RECITAL—A PICKWICKIAN JOURNEY.

The Ipswich Coach—Philosophy of Pike-keeping—A Remedy for Gout—"A Wictim of Connu- biality"—"Mine Ease at Mine Inn"—Business First, Pleasure Artervards"—The Virtues of Sleep— The Double-bedded Room—An Apparition in Yellow Curl-papers—A Masterly Retreat—Sam to the Rescue—Mr. Pickwick Handles the Ribbons—Mr. Winkle Disports Himself on Horseback— Grateful Remembrance.

"In Wit a Man, Simplicity a Child."

Mr. Clark is acknowledged to be one of the finest Lecturers of the day, and all his Lectures are delivered without MSS. or note of any kind.

Chairman: Rev. W. YORKE FAUSSET, M.A. (Headmaster, Bath College).

ADMISSION : Numbered Seats, 2/-   Second Seats, 1/-   Back of Room, 6d.

Plan of Room and Tickets at Messrs. Milsom's, Milsom-st. ; Mr. Blackett's, 9, Stall-st. ; Mr. Houlston's, 23, New Bond-st. ; and at the Y.M.C.A., Broad-st.

DOORS OPEN AT 7.30.   FOR TICKET-HOLDERS AT 7.25.

BLACKETT, TYP., BATH.

Fig. 2 One of the Revd. Charles Clark's popular lectures, advertised to take place in Bath in 1898, [Collection of M. J. Crossley Evans].

Charles Clark should be approached.[26] This was endorsed by 'A. J. T.' who pointed out that a society such as that proposed already existed in London and that the sec- retary, Mr. Edwin Drew,[27] might be able to help. 'A. J. T.' had been invited on the anniversary of the birth of Dickens when flowers were placed on his grave. He noted that the society also gave occasional concerts for charitable purposes. The correspon- dent advised that a Bristol Dickens Society should:

Let its chief concern be to aid and sympathise with the Tiny Tims and poor Joes,

[26] *B. D. M.*, Tuesday, 18 February 1902, p. 3, col. d. (correspondent unidentified).
[27] Edwin Drew claimed his name was used by Dickens as the inspiration for the main char- acter in the novel, *The Mystery of Edwin Drood*.

to help the Bob Cratchits and to convert the Scrooges! Whatever is done, don't let the pledging of the Immortal Memory—probably a dinner at which this sentiment will be submitted—be the chief idea. The memory is secure as regards immortality or oblivion, as the work of the great artist will keep it alive. If the proposed society comes into being, it will prosper, succeed, and flourish in just the degree that it deserves to according to the good it does, the charity it dispenses, and the help it lends to those in need.[28]

Another supporter, Mr. Edward George Follwell,[29] looked forward to a 'Bristol School of Dickens Students', with the Revd. Charles Clark as tutor and instructor'.[30] Within a week 'A Lover of Dickens' revealed himself as J. W. T. Ley. Supporting 'A. J. T.' he wrote that he 'never meant to suggest that the annual toasting of the immortal memory of "Boz" should be the chief object of the society'. Ley had written to both Edwin Drew and the Revd. Charles Clark, and had not received answers. Again Ley invited supporters to write to him. The reply from Edwin Drew, pledging support and practical help, was printed in the same issue.[31] The Revd. Charles Clark's response came two days later. He acknowledged that lovers of Dickens 'would appreciate an occasional gathering', but he doubted the practicality of maintaining 'a society for the systematic study of his works, and the furtherance of the grand principles of humanity which "Boz" tried to impart'. Although reluctant to discourage so laudable an idea, he advised, 'I feel that it should be well considered before anything is attempted'. He concluded by saying 'It is clear to me that much responsibility and labour would have to be undertaken by some person in order to keep such a society in vigorous life and I must frankly say—that I am not in a position to accept such responsibility'.[32]

'A. J. T.' was Alfred James Tonkin, a clerical tailor and designer of university academic robes, the senior partner of George Tonkin and Sons, tailors and church furnishers of 9 Park Street, Bristol and 156 Strand, London. He was a leading freemason; member of the Phonetic Society and the R.S.A., and an ardent collector of Dickensiana.[33] Ley and Tonkin now joined forces; the latter offering his home for planning and committee meetings and contributing half a guinea towards expenses.[34] They elicited several encouraging letters. Henry Fielding Dickens K.C.,[35] son of the author, would be 'interested to hear how the scheme prospers' and drew attention to the All Around Dickens Club in Boston U.S.A., and the Boz Club[36] in London, of which he was a member. 'The only difficulty we experience is in keeping the

---

[28] *B. D. M.*, Thursday, 20 February 1902, p. 8, col. f.

[29] Edward George Follwell, 1901 census, of 84 Claremont Street, Stapleton Road, aged 23. Provision merchant's clerk, born London, gave Dickens talks and recitations, *B. D. M.*, Thursday, 10 March, 1904, p. 5, col. e.

[30] *B. D. M.*, Monday, 24 February 1902, p. 9, col. c. See also Thursday, 10 March 1904, p. 5, col. e.

[31] *B. D. M.*, Tuesday, 25 February 1902, p. 3, col. c-d.

[32] *B. D. M.*, Wednesday, 26 February 1902, p. 3, col. e.

[33] *Who's Who in Freemasonry 1913–1914*, (1913), pp. 367–368, kindly supplied by Dr. M. J. Crossley Evans.

[34] *B. E. W.*, Monday, 16 January 1956, p. 2, col. c.

[35] Later Sir Henry Fielding Dickens, (1849–1933).

[36] Founded in 1900, its last meeting was held in 1914.

membership down'. Supportive messages also came from, among others, the popular comedian, John Laurence Toole,[37] whose career Dickens had helped to launch; Dickensian writers, Percy Fitzgerald,[38] (Fig. 3), and Frank Marziels;[39] and F. C. Burnand,[40] the editor of *Punch*.[41]

The foundation meeting of the Society was held at the Hannah More Hall, Park Street, on Thursday, 3 April 1902 with A. J. Tonkin in the chair. Among the letters of apologies received was one from Mr. William Rennison Maby,[42] a brass player of the Theatre Royal orchestra, who had been among the musicians when Dickens performed at the Victoria Rooms in November 1851.[43] The Revd. Charles Clark may have thought it inappropriate to send a message and the promoters had to be content with a reported conversation printed in the *Clifton Chronicle* the previous day, in which the minister, 'looked forward hopefully to being more free to join later on'.[44] The objectives of the proposed society were set out before the enthusiastic gathering prior to the motion from the chair that a 'Bristol and Clifton Dickens Society' be formed. The seconder was a Mr. Harvey. Among those participating in the ensuing debate were: Mr. George Rennie Powell,[45] the Stapleton registrar and a notable journalist

[37] Lessee and manager of Toole's Theatre, London, born 1830, died 30 July 1906. He was a popular performer at the Prince's Theatre in Park Row, and a member of the Bristol Arts Club. D. Carleton, *op. cit.*, p. 7, and note 12. See G. Storey, (ed.), *op. cit.* VI, (1999), p. 607, XI, (1999), pp. 470–471, and his obituary by J. W. T. Ley, *The Dickensian*, II, (1906), pp. 234–236.

[38] Percy Hetherington Fitzgerald M.A., F.S.A. (1834–1925), became first president of the Dickens Fellowship. See *Cassell's Saturday Journal*, 1 May 1901. Fitzgerald wrote an estimated 200 books, created 60 sculptures and wrote 20 books on Dickens. He often wrote 'carelessly and never [...] produced a book entirely free from foolishness and complacency'; S. Monod, '1900–1920: The Age of Chesterton', *D.*, 66, no. 361 (1970), pp. 109–110. P. Schlicke (ed.) *op. cit.*, (Oxford, 1999), p. 236.

[39] Sir Frank T. Marziels, author of *Life of Charles Dickens*, (1887), and co-author of a life of Thackeray in the same year.

[40] Sir Francis Cowley Burnand (1836–1917), provided the libretto for some of Sir Arthur Sullivan's early comic operettas such as *Cox and Box*. He was editor of *Punch* between 1862 and 1906.

[41] *C. C.*, 2 April 1902, p. 5, col. c.

[42] William Rennison Maby (1814–1903), was 88, and one of the oldest freemasons in the city. He was a member of The Royal Clarence Lodge No. 68, trumpeter to the Provincial Grand Lodge, and Provincial Grand Steward (1900). In 1829 he was a member of the band which played for Princess Victoria when she visited Clifton and was presented to the Queen during her visit to Bristol on 15 November 1899. Trumpet major in the Gloucestershire Yeomanry, he played the cornet and was a fine actor, performing with James Henry Chute. At the funeral A. J. Tonkin (and G. Webb) travelled with the family to Arno's Vale Cemetery. A wreath from Mr. and Mrs. A. J. Tonkin is mentioned in the report. *B. D. M.*, Tuesday, 24 March 1903, p. 7, col. c. (Obituary); A. C. Powell and J. Littleton, *Freemasonry in Bristol*, (Bristol, 1910), pp. 338–339, 602.

[43] *C. C.*, 28 May 1902, p. 5 col. e. See also *C. C.*, 9 April 1902, p. 2.

[44] *C. C.*, 2 April 1902, p. 5, col. c.

[45] Mr. George Rennie Powell in the 1901 census was aged 56 and his occupation is given as author, journalist; *Wright's Bristol Directory* for 1902 gives him as registrar of births and deaths, Ballivor, 36 Nevil Road, Bishopston. *The Clifton Chronicle and Directory*, 8 July 1914, p. 2, col. e., reports that on 30 June he retired after 37 years as registrar of births and deaths for the

Fig. 3. Percy Fitzgerald, [Collection of M. J. Crossley Evans].

and performer;[46] Mr. W. J. Kidner, the conductor of the Bristol Glee Club; Mr. John Jones Sheasby,[47] a professional swimming instructor; and Mr. A. Burnett. A committee was appointed to draft rules etc., and to report at the next meeting.[48]

An immediate challenge to the title chosen for the Society came from Mr. Richard Drewett Robjent[49], who, as a member of the Bristol Athenaeum, may have heard

---

sub-district of Stapleton. He was then aged 70 and had been appointed one of the Guardians of the Clifton Union on 25 March 1877. G. R. Powell and his father, George F. Powell, former editor of *the Bristol Daily Mercury*, were both theatre critics. With his brother F. Clover Powell, he wrote quite successful plays, *The Faithful Heart* played over a hundred performances in London. He was a member of the Bristol Arts Club and author of *The Bristol Stage*, (1919). D. Carleton, *op. cit.*, p. 4, notes 6 and 7, and p. 9.

[46] *C. C.*, 8 July 1914, p. 2, col. e.

[47] John Jones Sheasby, 1901 census, aged 54, professional swimming master, 1 Sunningdale, Alma Road. Later of 14 Aberdeen Road.

[48] *C. C.*, 9 April 1902, p. 2, col. a.

[49] 'A worthy upright citizen, whose one aim was to do good'. Since his retirement from the probate office he had devoted his energies to writing to the press on numerous subjects.

Dickens read from *A Christmas Carol* in 1858.[50] His letter published in the *Western Daily Press* on 5 April opined: 'There is no such place as Clifton, separate and apart from Bristol' and expressed the view that the new Society should be simply called 'The Bristol Dickens' Society',[51] a suggestion not taken up.

A fortnight earlier, the Revd. Charles Clark had delivered his popular No. 1 Dickens lecture at the Bristol Y. M. C. A. Hall, 'his last lecture of the session'.[52] It was the last lecture he gave. Towards the end of April he took to his bed suffering from bronchitis with complications. The *Bristol Daily Mercury* kept its readers informed of his steady recovery and at the beginning of July it reported that Mr. Clark was able to take some exercise on the Downs.[53] Mr. Ley, on behalf of the Bristol and Clifton Dickens Society, wrote expressing sympathy and wishing him a 'speedy and complete restoration to health.' Mr. Clark, in his reply, stated that he was schooling himself to patience.[54]

At the foundation meeting, the membership of the fledging Society was six. It had, however, increased by the time the first committee was formed. It comprised of four maiden ladies, the Misses Bruford,[55] Dugdale,[56] Peacock, and Thatcher,[57] and Mrs. Tonkin, and four gentlemen, Messrs. A. J. Tonkin (acting vice-president), J. W. T. Ley (honorary secretary and treasurer), Frederick Drew Tonkin and George Rennie Powell, under the presidency of the city librarian, Edward Robert Norris Mathews, F.R.Hist.Soc.[58] (Fig. 4).

Promotional circulars from J. W. T. Ley were sent out to prospective members setting out the objects of the Society:

1. To form a bond of union among lovers of Dickens, of both sexes, and to encourage the general study of his works.
2. To hold Meetings of a Literary and Social character periodically.
3. To arrange from time to time Excursions to places immortalised in the works of Charles Dickens.

[50] *B. G.*, Thursday, 6 May 1858, p. 6, cols, d—e. Dickens had become a life-member of the Bristol Athenaeum.

[51] *W. D. P.*, Saturday, 5 April 1902, p. 6, col. f.

[52] *B. D. M.*, Thursday, 20 March 1902, p. 6, col. c.

[53] *B. D. M.*, Monday, 7 July 1902, p. 3, col. a.

[54] *B. D. M.*, Friday, 26 September 1902, p. 5 col. a.

[55] Miss Nancy Bruford was a colleague of Mr. Ley's on the *Bristol Mercury*, *B. E. P.*, Wednesday, 2 April 1952, p. 2, cols. b-f.

[56] Miss Ethel M. Dugdale, daughter of Mr. Robert Dugdale, J.P., and member of the National Federation of Church School Teachers. In the 1901 census, she was living at home at 38 Bushy Park, aged 22, a teacher. She died at Ilfracombe in 1910. The Society sent 'a large wreath of their emblem flower (scarlet geraniums)', *W. D. P.*, Friday, 18 February 1910, p. 7, col. d. *W. D. P.*, Saturday, 19 February 1910, p. 7, col. e.

[57] Miss M. Thatcher. In 1902 she was living at 12 Tamworth Place. A music teacher, she later resided at 134 Cotham Brow.

[58] *B. T. & M.*, Monday, 9 October 1911, p. 9, col. a. Born 1851, died January 1919. Educated Queen Elizabeth's Hospital School, librarian of the Bristol Museum and Library 1883; chief librarian of Bristol Public Libraries 1893–1919; W. T. Pike (ed.) *Bristol in 1898: Contemporary Biographies*, I, (Brighton, 1898), p. 82; J. Lyes, *Bristol 1914–1919*, (Bristol, 2003), p. 31. Resided at 11 Henleaze Gardens. See *Arrowsmith's Dictionary of Bristol*, (2nd ed., Bristol, 1906), pp. 237–238; a freemason and a member of The Royal Sussex Lodge of Hospitality, No. 187.

Fig. 4. Mr. Norris Mathews, the first president, [from W. T. Pike, (ed.), *Bristol in 1898: Contemporary Biographies*].

The proposed annual subscription was five shillings for 'Active Members' and ten shillings and six pence for 'Honorary Members'. There was no commitment to charitable work, but Ley said of Dickens that: 'No writer has so moved the souls of men to sympathy with the poor and unfortunate, and particularly with unhappy children', adding, 'He taught us our duty to our fellow-men better than we knew it before'.[59]

The circular drew support from Lord Rosebury, and C. E. Hobhouse M.P. for east Bristol. The leading actor of his generation, Sir Henry Irving, 'agreed most heartily with the objects of the society'. There were detractors, however. Sir Michael Hicks-Beach, the Chancellor of the Exchequer and Member for west Bristol expressed 'no special interest in the subject.' The duke of Beaufort and the Right Hon. Lewis Fry of Goldney House were the Society's first honorary members.[60]

To stimulate interest J. W. T. Ley contributed occasional articles to the weekly *Clifton Chronicle*. The first of these, 'Why I Love Dickens' gave eight reasons for appreciating Dickens: his humour; his pathos; his unequalled ability to blend them; the

[59] Bristol Central Library, Circular, May 1902, B. 4287.
[60] *B. D. M.*, Monday, 2 June 1902, p. 3, col. a; *C. C.*, 28 May 1902, p. 4, col. a; *C. C.* 4 June 1902, p. 4, col. f.

realism of his characters; their individuality; his descriptive powers; his status as the apostle of Christmas, and his humanity. 'I only wish that more of our young people would try to read him instead of the cheap light trash that they devour nowadays in such quantities'. Continuing to call himself 'A Lover of Dickens', he signed the column and subsequent articles, 'J. Dubu Teley', derived, of course, from his name. Later articles during the year were: 'The Pathos of Dickens'; 'Dickens's Women Characters'; 'Charles Dickens: reform by satire'; and 'Dickens and Christmas'.[61]

In fulfilment of the Society's third object, the first meeting was an excursion to Bath, on Saturday, 5 July 1902, to explore the places of Dickensian interest, with particular reference to incidents in *The Pickwick Papers*. Of the four Bath guides who escorted them around the city that afternoon, Councillor T. Sturge Cotterell,[62] and Mr. Lewis Vigis[63] were to play their part in furthering the Bristol Society.[64]

The formation of a Dickens Society in Bristol received nationwide support and presumably alerted the existing *ad hoc* groups in London to the potential of an international federation of Dickens societies. As a result, on 6 October 1902 a foundation meeting was held in the capital. The objects of the proposed organisation reflected those crystallised in Bristol but the title 'Society' was rejected in favour of 'Fellowship', reflecting 'companionship among admirers of the author' and so The Dickens Fellowship was born. Honorary posts of vice-president were established and offered to those who had kept Dickens's memory green. Among the first vice-presidents (complimentary appointments) were the Revd. Charles Clark, Sir Henry Irving, and J. L. Toole.[65] The good wishes of the Bristol and Clifton Dickens Society, were sent by J. W. T. Ley. A warm reply was received from Bertram Waldrom Matz, the first general secretary of The Dickens Fellowship,[66] and a lasting friendship developed between the two men ahead of their first meeting at Bath four months later.[67]

In Bristol, advertisements announced that 'The President, Norris Mathews, Esq., F.R.Hist.S.,' would give the inaugural lecture of the Bristol and Clifton Dickens Society at the Museum Lecture Theatre on Monday 13 October 1902.[68] Mr. Mathews was a well-established speaker and the press reports record how skilfully he engaged with a large audience of members, friends and the general public. Unsupported by notes, he concluded the evening with a recital to illustrate Dickens's pathos, humour and dramatic power; Scrooge's encounter with the final phantom and his changed

---

[61] *C. C.*, 28 May 1902, p. 3, col. a; *B. D. M.* Saturday, 28 June 1902, p. 10, cols, a–b; *B. D. M.*, Saturday, 26 July 1902, p. 3, col. e; *B. D. M.*, Saturday, 30 August 1902, p. 8, col. c.

[62] Later Alderman Thomas Sturge Cotterell, a director of Cotterell Brothers Ltd., wallpaper manufacturers, M.B.E., J.P., mayor of Bath 1930–1931. Born 1865, died 1950, councillor 1895–1911 and from 1921; Anon., *A History of the Mayors of Bath*, (Bath, 2006), p. 11.

[63] Lewis Vigis died 1904 aged 56. Chemist and druggist of 12 Chapel Row, Bath. Founder member of the Dickens Fellowship, collector of Dickensiana.

[64] *B. D. M.*, Monday, 7 July 1902, p. 3, cols, b–c; A clipping from the *The Bath Chronicle*, 10 July 1902.

[65] Photocopy of Dickens Fellowship enrolment certificate, 1903. Kindly supplied by Dr. M. J. Crossley Evans.

[66] B. W. Matz (1865–1925). Publisher, later first editor of *The Dickensian*. Author of numerous works on Dickens. S. Monod, '1900–1920: The Age of Chesterton', *D.*, 66, no. 361 (1970), p. 110.

[67] *D.*, vol. xxii, no. 1 Jan 1926 p. 12 kindly supplied by Dr. M. J. Crossley Evans.

[68] *C. C.*, Friday, 10 October 1902, p. 4, col. d.

relationship with his clerk from *A Christmas Carol*; the altercation between Sairey Gamp and Betsy Prig from *Martin Chuzzlewit*; the sacrifice of Sydney Carton from *A Tale of Two Cities*.[69]

Syllabuses for the Society's first session were issued to members and copies sent out to interested parties. One of the latter was Miss A. E. Bayly,[70] a popular novelist writing under the pseudonym 'Edna Lyall', who responded by sending her best wishes for the Dickens Society, remarking how much her family were enjoying reading *Martin Chuzzlewit* aloud in the evenings.

The first meetings were held at Stuckey's Restaurant in Wine Street. In November five readings were shared between the president, the vice-president, A. J. Tonkin, other members of the committee and H. Theo. Jones, who would soon establish himself as a notable performer of the works of Dickens.[71] The following month it was announced that J. W. T. Ley had been elected a 'Corresponding Member of the "All Round Dickens Club", Boston U.S.A.'. Mrs. Adelaide Gardener, the club's founder, became a corresponding member of the Bristol and Clifton Dickens Society, and would help to shape its development by supplying 'useful budgets and suggestions'.[72]

'J. DuBu Teley's 'Dickens and Christmas' in the *Bristol Daily Mercury*, noted above, may have been the catalyst for a proposal in the leader column of its rival *Western Daily Press* on Christmas Eve 1902:

> The great novelist and analyst of the popular emotions flung off the galling fetters of the age of severe utilitarianism, and led the way in freeing the pent-up tide of human sympathy and geniality. By means of his writing he cast a fresh halo round the great Christmas anniversary. He opened up hearts that had long been impenetrable to the influences of kindly feeling and generosity [...] In various cities of England Dickens societies have quite recently been formed. Bristol has been in the forefront of this movement, and we may, with all deference, suggest to those so identified that they might take up in earnest a proposal to perpetuate the memory of Dickens by some fitting monument.[73]

In reply, two supportive letters, both dated 25 December, appeared in the Boxing Day issue. E. R. Norris Mathews addressed a letter from the Central Library endorsing 'the timely and sensible words you have uttered' and J. W. T. Ley wrote: 'That suggestion has my fullest sympathy, and the sympathy of every lover of the great novelist'. Both correspondents however, drew attention to a clause in Dickens's will, 'I conjure my friends on no account to make me the subject of any monument, memorial or testimonial of any kind whatever.' And there the matter rested—for the time being.[74] For this reason when the bronze statue of Dickens commissioned by the Chicago World Fair from the New York sculptor, Frank Elwell, and exhibited in 1894, was sent to England as a gift from the American people, Sir Henry Dickens

---

[69] *B. T. & M.* Reprint, Tuesday, 14 October 1902, held in Bristol Central Library, B. 3512.

[70] *B. D. M.*, Friday, 5 December 1902, p. 3, col. c. Ada Ellen Bayly, died 8 February 1903, author of such works as *To Right the Wrong*, (1892), and *In Spite of All*, (1901).

[71] *B. D. M.*, Wednesday, 19 November 1902, p. 6, col. f.

[72] *B. D. M.*, Thursday, 13 June 1907, p. 5, col. b.

[73] *W. D. P.*, Wednesday, 24 December 1902, p. 5, col. f.

[74] *W. D. P.*, Friday, 26 December 1902, p. 6, col. b.

insisted that it was not unpacked and asked for it to be returned to America. Today it stands in a park in Philadelphia.

In January 1903 the *Clifton Chronicle* noted that, in a departure from the usual readings and debates, a programme of non-Dickensian pianoforte duets, songs, sketches and recitations had been arranged for the first part of the evening. Afterwards Mr. Lewis Vigis[75] presented his 'Dickens and Bath' perhaps in preparation for celebrations ten days later. Mr. Vigis returned to address the March meeting on 'Dickens's Lore and Characters' and the *Clifton Chronicle* published the full text of both lectures.[76]

On Saturday 7 February 1903, the ninety-first anniversary of Dickens's birth, the corporation of Bath marked the day 'in a way that it has not been celebrated in England before', by arranging the unveiling a tablet to Dickens on 33 St. James's Square, which had been the home of Walter Savage Landor.[77] Here Dickens had stayed and here the character of 'Little Nell' had been conceived.[78] Henry Fielding Dickens K.C., the only surviving son of the author, was to have unveiled the plaque to his father, and the 'astonishingly popular' novelist, Hall Caine[79], was to have unveiled a plaque to Landor on his later home in River Street. Both gentlemen were unable to attend, so Percy Fitzgerald, an associate of Dickens, founder of the Boz Club and president of The Dickens Fellowship, performed both ceremonies. The president, vice-president, honorary secretary, and other members of the Bristol and Clifton Dickens Society were present. An exhibition of Dickensiana 'in the temporary Dickens museum' was considered to be 'unique, and has been gathered from all parts of the country'. Items loaned by members of the Bristol Society, (mainly pictures) came from the collections of A. J. Tonkin, J. W. T. Ley and Lewis Vigis.

Percy Fitzgerald's most controversial suggestion, at the unveiling did not escape the attention of the reporter from the *Western Daily Press*. The editorial on the following Monday returned to the question of whether or not Dickens's expressed wish that his friends should not make him the subject of any statue or monument should be binding on their descendents? 'Mr. Fitzgerald clearly thinks not' and the editorial challenged the 'numerous Dickens societies throughout the country [...] to discuss the ethics of the whole question'. Indeed they could have called upon Dickensians further afield to talk the matter over as The Dickens Fellowship already had branches in Austria, Sweden, Norway, Italy, South Africa, the United States and Canada. Whether or not the Bristol and Clifton Dickens Society rose to the challenge is not known and no response appeared in the correspondence columns.[80]

[75] *B. D. M.*, Friday, 16 September 1904, p. 6, col. e.
[76] *C. C.*, 28 January 1903, p. 2, cols, a–b; 8 April 1903, p. 2, col. a; 15 April 1903, p. 2, cols a–b; 22 April 1903, p. 3, cols e–g.
[77] Walter Savage Landor (1775–1864), poet and man of letters. Dickens named his fourth child in 1841, Walter Landor Dickens. See P. Schlicke, (ed.), *op. cit.*, pp. 315–316.
[78] Newspaper clipping from *The Bath Herald*, 7 February 1903.
[79] Sir Thomas Henry Hall Caine (1853–1931). Romantic novelist, perhaps most famous for *The Christian*, (1897).
[80] *B. D. M.*, Monday, 9 February 1903, p. 3, cols a–c.

A Dickens dinner was held that evening in the long card room at the Assembly Rooms, which since the publication of *The Pickwick Papers*, was associated with Mr. Pickwick's game of whist with 'three thorough-paced female card-sharpers'. Councillor Thomas Sturge Cotterell took charge of the arrangements and produced a specially designed menu with appropriate culinary quotations from Dickens printed above each course—on this occasion, all but one from *The Pickwick Papers*. It was the start of a tradition that was adopted by The Dickens Fellowship for their annual conference banquets. Musical items included songs written by Dickens, such as *The Ivy Green*.[81] The mayor of Bath, Alderman J. E. Henshaw J.P., presided. Apologies were received from the Lords Roberts and Rosebery and the Very Revd. Samuel Reynolds Hole, dean of Rochester.[82] Henry Dickens followed up his apologies with a telegram, in which he remarked that: 'The love which the people still bear for my father's memory is extraordinary in its extent and depth'. The Revd. Charles Clark also heartily wished he could have been there, but regretted that it would be months before he was well enough even to take such an easy journey as to Bath.

Percy Fitzgerald proposed the toast to 'The Immortal Memory of Charles Dickens'. His ebullient praise of Dickens was liberally peppered with anecdotes and personal recollections. The toast was drunk in silence, 'in the genuine Dickens gin punch, hot—a delightful drink,' ran one report 'after tasting which we can forgive Mr. Pickwick and his friends their occasional indiscretions in the way of taking a little too much.'[83]

Among the toasts was one 'To all lovers of Dickens'. Many writers had their admirers, some their adorers, but few—and Dickens was the greatest of them—had their lovers. Mr. Lewis Vigis had the pleasure of toasting the 'The Dickens Fellowship' and gave his paper on 'Dickens and Bath'. E. R. Norris Mathews was amongst the responders to 'The Visitors' informing the company present that the Bristol and Clifton Dickens Society would be holding a dinner in April, although there is no record of one being held or cancelled.[84]

It was during these proceedings at Bath that J. W. T. Ley was first introduced to B. W. Matz, in the company of E. P. Haslam. Through them Ley would be appointed assistant editor of a new periodical, *The Easy Chair*, and subsequently its editor.[85]

The March meeting, at the Hannah More Hall, included the Society's first staging in full costume—a dramatisation of the 'Trial Scene from the Pickwick Papers'.[86] It would become a great favourite with the public and a vehicle for raising money for good causes.

March 1903, however, would be remembered, not for costumed performances, but for the death of the Revd. Charles Clark on 29 March.[87] Messages of condolence were

---

[81] From *The Pickwick Papers*, chapter vi. Set to music by Henry Burnett, Dickens's brother-in-law.

[82] The Very Revd. Samuel Reynolds Hole D.D. (1819–1904), close friend of John Leech, the artist, and of W. M. Thackeray, dean of Rochester, 1887–1904, a famous grower of roses. See: B. Massingham, *Turn on the Fountains: A Life of Dean Hole*, (1974).

[83] *B. D. M.*, Tuesday, 10 February 1903, p. 3, col. b.

[84] *B. D. M.*, Tuesday, 10 February 1903, p. 3, col. b.

[85] *D.*, vol. xxii, no. 1, January 1926, p. 12. Kindly supplied by Dr. M. J. Crossley Evans.

[86] *B. D. M.*, Wednesday, 4 March 1903, p. 6, col. e.

[87] *B. D. M.*, Monday, 30 March 1903, p. 5, col. g.

received from many parts of the world and the funeral on 2 April 1903 at Christ Church, Sneyd Park, (where the Clarks worshipped), attracted a large congregation: Norris Mathews and A. J. Tonkin represented the Bristol and Clifton Dickens Society; and J. W. T. Ley, The Dickens Fellowship. There was also a large gathering at Redland Green for the interment just inside the cemetery gates and among the floral tributes was one from the Bristol and Clifton Dickens Society.[88]

Although the Revd. Charles Clark was almost certainly never a member of the Bristol and Clifton Dickens Society, honorary or otherwise, he was universally acknowledged as one of the most eminent exponents of Dickens and as already noted helped to create a climate in Bristol in which the Bristol and Clifton Dickens Society could flourish. It was therefore appropriate that at the end of April the Society should determine 'to raise a fund for the erection of a memorial to the late Revd. Charles Clark'.[89]

A committee was formed of representatives of the city and three members of the Bristol and Clifton Dickens Society: A. J. Tonkin (vice-president), J. W. T. Ley and Mr. Ebenezer H. Julian.[90] A circular, and collecting cards with 'a capital portrait' of the deceased were issued. In London, members of The Dickens Fellowship supported the venture in honour of one of their vice-presidents and donated one guinea from their funds.[91] Other donations ranged from 6d to six guineas. On Christmas Eve, 1903, without ceremony, an obelisk of Aberdeen Peterhead granite, designed by G. Tuckfield and Co. of Arno's Vale, was placed over the grave of the Revd. Charles Clark. Beneath the deceased's name and dates was inscribed -

'Lord keep my memory green'
This memorial was erected by the Dickens
Fellowship and many loving friends in
Great Britain and Australia.

The report in the *Bristol Daily Mercury* reminded its readers that 'the subscriptions were raised by the Bristol and Clifton Dickens Society'.[92]

At the end of the Society's first session Norris Mathews regretfully resigned the presidency, due to pressure of work associated with the construction of the Central Library, College Green, and the proposed extension of the city's boundaries in 1904.[93] Thus it was when the second session opened in October 1903, the Society was without a president, and A. J. Tonkin, the vice-president, stepped into the breach. It was at this juncture that an application for affiliation to The Dickens Fellowship was successfully concluded and a month later it was announced that the Revd. Ambrose

[88] *B. D. M.*, Friday, 3 April 1903, p. 3, col. d.
[89] *B. D. M.*, Tuesday, 28 April 1903, p. 4, col. h.
[90] Mr. Ebenezer H. Julian of Sneyd Lodge, Sneyd Park. 1901 census, aged 43, living on his own means.
[91] *B. D. M.*, Monday, 18 May 1903, p. 5. col. d.
[92] *B. D. M.*, Saturday, 23 January 1904, p. 7, col. d.
[93] G. F. Stone: *Bristol: As It Was—And As It Is*, (Bristol, 1909), pp. 251–252; for Mathews's involvement in the design of the building, see A. Beeson: *Bristol Central Library and Charles Holden*, (Bristol, 2006).

Fig. 5. The Revd. Ambrose Nichols Blatchford, [from *Greater Bristol by Lesser Columbus*, (1893)].

Nichols Blatchford B.A., (Fig. 5), minister of Lewin's Mead Unitarian Church, had accepted the presidency. Well-known throughout Bristol as a great raconteur, under his leadership the continuing success of the Society was assured.[94]

The session closed on Primrose Day, (19 April) 1904 with an announcement that 'since its affiliation to The Dickens Fellowship' the membership had greatly increased. The main attraction was a repeat performance of 'Bardell *versus* Pickwick'. The large Hannah More Hall was packed and following a programme of musical items and Dickens recitations, the Revd. Ambrose Blatchford gave a short speech bearing testimony to the good that Dickens had done for English literature and our national life and accreting that:

[94] *B. D. M.*, Monday, 30 November 1903, p. 5, col. d. Ambrose Nichols Blatchford, (1842–1924). He died on 24 April 1924. Assistant minister Lewin's Mead 1866–1876, minister from 1876–1915. W. T. Pike, (ed.) *op. cit.*, p. 109; Anon, *Greater Bristol by Lesser Columbus*, (1893), pp. 131–133. He gained his name as 'The Press Chaplain' through his connection with most of the West of England journalists, *B.E.P.*, 24 April 1989, an article entitled 'Concise history of long running ministry'.

Fig. 6. Charles Andrews, Collection of M. J. Crossley Evans].

> If there were a Dickens Society in any city or township in the kingdom, that city should be the city of Bristol, which was so long the home and field of usefulness of their always-to-be-regretted friend, Charles Clark.

He noted how appropriate it was that the proceeds of the evening were devoted to the Guild of the Brave Poor Things in memory of the writer who created 'Tiny Tim'. The Guild, founded by Miss Ada Vachel, provided activities for children and others with a variety of disabilities, seeking to offer them companionship and to raise their self-esteem.[95] The Bristol and Clifton Dickens Society adopted the organisation as its 'special charity' and introduced an annual collection for its benefit at the Society's December meetings. 'Bardell v. Pickwick' was reported in glowing terms in the *Clifton Chronicle*. George Rennie Powell 'representing his original character of Sergeant Buzfuz, a part in which he gained a reputation nearly thirty years ago at the Prince's Theatre' received particular praise. Frederick Bowles Down was applauded for his portrayal of Sam Weller, and Charles Andrews (Fig. 6), was said to have given a

---

[95] F. M. Unwin, *Ada Vachel of Bristol*, (Bristol, 1928), p. 45.

'never to be forgotten performance' as Nathaniel Winkle as well as managing the production. All three were to become leading members of the Society.[96]

The Society's first outing to Bath was repeated on 2 July 1904, to cater for the rising number of new members. Mr. Lewis Vigis led the party on this occasion. The press announcement also informed its readers that, 'Mr. J. W. T. Ley had resigned the office of hon. secretary and treasurer prior to his moving to London'.[97]

An outing to Portishead was organised for the Saturday preceeding the August Bank Holiday Monday to say farewell to Mr. Ley. The president was away on holiday sailing in Devonshire, and so the task of making the presentations fell to A. J. Tonkin. 'The present status of the Society—indeed, its very existence—was due' he said, 'to Mr. Ley's untiring efforts in regard to its foundation and his hard work since.' Further plaudits followed and Mr. Ley was left in no doubt that they sincerely hoped that he 'may rise to the top of the literary ladder [...] he was so skilfully ascending.' Amid a cheering company he was presented with three-volume editions of *Chambers' Cyclopaedea of English Literature* and *Chambers' Book of Days*, together with a *Concordance to Shakespeare*, a gold scarf pin, 'the badge of The Dickens Fellowship' and a silver-mounted pipe. In thanking them, Mr. Ley expressed the hope of seeing them all on his future visits to Bristol.[98] Within two months of his arrival in London, Ley was elected to the council of The Dickens Fellowship. At the first meeting Ley attended, he was elected the honorary general secretary, to enable B. W. Matz to be the first editor of the organisation's monthly journal, *The Dickensian*, first issued in January 1905.[99]

The new honorary secretary and treasurer of the Bristol and Clifton Dickens Society was Charles Andrews, a popular Dickens recitalist. Following a business meeting in September 1904, at which it was agreed to support The Dickens Fellowship by donating one guinea to their Charity Fund, a new promotional circular was printed. A. J. Tonkin was re-elected vice-president and five women and seven men served on the committee. As previously noted, the duke of Beaufort and the Right Hon. Lewis Fry were the Society's first honorary members, having each contributed half a guinea. Their number was augmented by the addition of Mrs. Charles Clark, who may have joined their ranks in appreciation of the Society's efforts in raising funds for her late husband's memorial. The other honorary member was Mr. Thomas Thatcher, a well-known College Green bookseller and stationer.[100] The circular gave a revised statement of the Society's aims and organisation. 'Whilst affording its members opportunities for entertainment, enlightenment, the exchange of views and personal intercourse centring in their favourite author, it seeks to be of some real use to our local and other charities'. The Society, now standing on a sure financial footing, held its monthly meetings on the third Tuesday of the month at the Church Missionary Society's Hall in Park Street. The honorary membership payment scheme was discontinued and the annual subscription halved to two shillings and six-pence.[101]

---

[96] *C. C.*, 27 April 1904, p. 2, col. e.
[97] *B. D. M.*, Friday, 24 June 1904, p. 5, col. a.
[98] *B. D. M.*, Monday, 1 August 1904, p. 6, col. c.
[99] *D.*, vol. xxii, no. 1, Jan 1926; information kindly supplied by Dr. M. J. Crossley Evans.
[100] Aged 61 in 1901, based at 44–45 College Green.
[101] Bristol Central Library, Second Circular, B. 4288.

The 1904–1905 session opened in October with an advertised reading of one of Dickens's lesser-known stories 'The Tale of Private Richard Doubledick' given by the Revd. A. N. Blatchford. The performance was 'delightfully touching' but presumably rather shorter than required and Charles Andrews, 'at very short notice', contributed 'Bob Sawyer's Supper Party'. Between the recitals A. J. Tonkin reminded members that their object 'was to spread the love of humanity which Dickens ever taught and practised, and thus give practical effect to his teachings by following his example.'[102]

Edmund Tolson Wedmore,[103] a gifted musician with a keen interest in poetry and art, lectured at the November meeting on 'Dickens in Kent', 'illustrated by a series of coloured views of the objects of interest'.[104] It was the first of a number of lectures he gave ranging from 'Pictures of Animal Life in Dickens' to 'Scenes of Clerical Life in Edwin Drood'. Mr. Wedmore was a devout and active member of the Society of Friends at the Hampton Road Meeting House, Redland. He served on the committee of the Dickens Society for many years and was subsequently elected a vice-president in recognition of his services.[105]

At the December meeting, Mrs. Louie A. Field-Tonkin, the vice-president's wife, became the Society's first female lecturer. 'The Humanity of Dickens' was published in the *Clifton Chronicle* a few days before Christmas and served as a fitting prelude to Mr. H. Theo. Jones's part-read, part-performed declamation of *A Christmas Carol* that 'reminded his audience of the late Revd. Charles Clark, and the older members [...] of Charles Dickens himself.' The meeting closed with a collection for a 'deserving cause' which had been brought to the Society's attention.[106]

The opening months of 1905 were marked by two innovations: a high-spirited conversazione and the first annual dinner, on the anniversary of Dickens's birth. Many of the hundred or so people at the conversazione attended in costume as characters from the novels, and a ballot for the most idealistic characterisations was taken. Miss Bruford received a hand-painted plaque for her representation of 'The Vengeance'[107] *(A Tale of Two Cities);* Mr. John Jones Sheaseby, a silver-framed portrait of Dickens, for his 'Daniel Peggotty' *(David Copperfield)* and a consolation prize was given to Miss Rose Peacock for her 'Kate Nickleby'. All the recipients were members of the committee.[108]

The dinner was held at Chivers' Restaurant, Queen's Road on the 93rd anniversary of Dickens's birth. Mr. A. J. Tonkin, in the chair, read a telegram of greetings from Henry Dickens in which he reminded them of his father's motto, 'Courage, perseverance'. In proposing the toast to the 'Immortal Memory of Charles Dickens', the

---

[102] *C. C.*, 26 October 1904, p. 8, col. d.

[103] Mr. Wedmore was aged 53 at the time of the 1901 census. Sugar and fruit merchant later of 14 Cambridge Park, Redland. He played Mr. Pickwick's lawyer in the trial scene. Died 26 August 1920. A keen musician and a member of the University and Literary Club, he gave a lecture under their *aegis* to an audience of 400 members of the club and guests at the Victoria Rooms on the subject of 'The Harp, Ancient and Modern', on 16 October 1893, Anon., *The University and Literary Club 1890–2008*, (Bristol, 2009), p. 23.

[104] *B. D. M.*, Thursday, 17 November 1904, p. 6, col. g.

[105] *C. C.*, Thursday, 2 September 1920, p. 11, col. b.

[106] *C. C.*, 21 December 1904, p. 9, cols, e.

[107] *A Tale of Two Cities*, book II, chapter 22.

[108] *W. D. P.*, Thursday, 19 January 1905, p. 9, col. c.

chairman said that the popularity of the author knew no bounds and stated as proof of this fact, the membership of The Dickens Fellowship now stood at 7,000 world-wide. In replying to a toast to the Society, the honorary secretary said that in three years their membership had risen from 20 to 100.[109]

Another annual event, 'A Musical and Dramatic Evening' took place in the Lesser Colston Hall on 4 April 1905 in aid of the 'Guild of Poor Things'.[110] The evening was patronised by a number of distinguished gentlemen including Sir Michael Hicks-Beach, who had evidently acquired an interest in Charles Dickens after all! The hall was crowded for the entertainment that included a recitation by H. Theo. Jones of 'Mr. Bumble's Courtship' and another performance of the trial scene from *The Pickwick Papers*, which was well received.[111] Sixteen guineas were raised for the Guild,[112] an amount not exceeded until 1920.

The committee were well aware of the asset the Society possessed in their president, who enjoyed a well-deserved popularity in Bristol. 'He is a come-at-able man and is ever ready with a cheery word of encouragement and counsel for the lowliest' enthused one local journal.[113] As the long-established pastor of Lewin's Mead Unitarian Church, he was a talented orator who could draw large audiences. So what better way was there to open the fourth session than the Revd. A. N. Blatchford giving a public reading of *Somebody's Luggage*, the 1862 Christmas story published in Dickens's weekly journal, *All the Year Round*. For this meeting the Hamilton Rooms, 40 Park Street, was hired, presumably because of its larger capacity than the C. M. S. Hall. As anticipated, there was a good response and the reader was praised for his 'excellent interpretation'.[114]

A programme of meetings and social events had now been established. A popular recital to open the season; papers; readings; discussions; Christmas celebrations; a Dickens birthday dinner on 7 February; a conversazione; a charity musical and dramatic evening at the Lesser Colston Hall; a summer outing; and a whist drive.

There was only 'a fair attendance' in November for a paper on *Bleak House* but a lively discussion was recorded. Charles Andrews introduced 'Christmas Books and Stories' in December and members read short excerpts they had chosen.[115] The next day, Mr. H. Theo. Jones, now generally recognised as a first-class elocutionist, gave a recital of *A Christmas Carol* under the patronage of the Bristol and Clifton Dickens Society at the Y. M. C. A. Hall, St. James's Square. Many of the audience remembered the last time the '*Carol*' had been performed there, by the late Charles Clark. Mr. Jones was competing that night with a recital of the same work, at the Victoria

[109] *C. C.*, 15 February 1905, p. 2, col. f.

[110] For 80 years the Society's 'special charity' was 'The Guild of the Poor Things', re-named 'The Guild of the Handicapped' in 1918. In the re-organisation of the Bristol Municipal Charities in the mid-1980s it was felt that the guild had lost its identity and it was decided by the members of the Society at the A. G. M. to adopt a different charity during the coming year.

[111] *B. T. & M.*, Wednesday, 5 April 1905, p. 5, col. f.

[112] *B. D. M.*, Tuesday, 5 September 1905, p. 5, col. 6.

[113] Photocopy of 'Clifton Society' cartoon, 29 January 1903, held at Bristol Central Library, RL 2D2, B6562, kindly supplied by Dr. M. J. Crossley Evans.

[114] *B. D. M.*, Wednesday, 20 September 1905, p. 6, col. e.

[115] *D.*, vol. II., no. 1, January 1906, p. 21.

Rooms, by the popular young school master, Gustav Adolf Widmann[116], and the Cambrian Glee Singers. The critic of the *Bristol Daily Mercury* wrote that Mr. Jones, performing without note or book, had excelled himself and called upon him to keep up the 'praiseworthy custom set by his distinguished predecessor'.[117] Responding, again under the patronage of the Dickens Society, Mr. Jones returned in December, 1906 with the Revd. A. N. Blatchford in the chair.[118] This time there was no direct competition, although fellow Dickensians, Charles Andrews and Sam Tucker[119] also gave public performances of the 'Carol' that month elsewhere in the city.[120]

The third 'object of the Society', as already noted, was 'To arrange from time to time Excursions to places immortalised in the works of Charles Dickens'. Bath was popular and on 9 June 1906, The Dickens Fellowship arranged another visit to the city. Councillor T. Sturge Cotterell welcomed and took charge of the party, which consisted of 51 people. Charles Andrews, and possibly others from Bristol joined the company. A 'realistic' recital of 'Bob Sawyer's Party' from *The Pickwick Papers* was the after tea entertainment given by the Revd. Professor Baynham 'of Bristol',[121] (Fig. 7).

The Dickens Society's own outing, on the following Saturday, was to Limpley Stoke and although there were the usual components of tea with strawberries and cream followed by sports, the main attraction was a conducted tour of Winsley Sanatorium for the treatment of the poor suffering from tuberculosis. The institution was supported by the Bristol health authorities, who paid for twenty beds to be reserved for its citizens.[122] It seems likely, that in the apparent absence of local places associated with Dickens the next best course was to emulate their hero and visit institutions as he had done. Their guide, Councillor Dyer, addressing them at Boule's Tea Gardens, regretted the expenditure of £2,500 per patient at a similar institution in Sussex, which had silver-plated sinks and other luxury fittings, while Winsley served the four counties of Gloucestershire, Somerset, Wiltshire and Bristol, and needed more beds to meet their requirements.[123]

A guided tour of the nautical school at Portishead formed part of the summer excursion in 1908[124] and a ramble to Shirehampton was arranged for September. Miss Thatcher was convinced that the identification of a lane in Westbury-on-Trym, was the one described by Dickens in chapter 38 of *The Pickwick Papers*. So it was reported in the *Bristol Daily Mercury* that a 'pilgrimage was first made to the lane where

---

[116] Gustav Adolf Widmann, born Bristol, June 1881. 1901 census, aged 19, assistant school teacher.

[117] *B. D. M.*, Thursday, 14 December 1905, p. 7, col. g.

[118] *B. D. M.*, Thursday, 13 December 1906, p. 6, col. e.

[119] Sam Tucker, 1901 census, aged 40, Vivian Villa, 25 Nottingham Road. Civil Service Post Office.

[120] Thursday, 6 December 1906, p. 5, col. d (Andrews); *W. D. P.* Wednesday 19 December 1906, p. 3, col. d. (Tucker).

[121] *D.*, II, July 1906, p. 190. The Revd. Professor Baynham F.E.I.S., formerly professor of English Literature and Elocution at the University of Glasgow and member of the Boz Club. Professor Baynham was obviously well-known in Bristol as an exponent of the works of Dickens. We find him giving a recital of *A Christmas Carol* to the members of the University and Literary Club in 1894, Anon., *The University and Literary Club 1890–2008*, (Bristol, 2009), p. 23.

[122] G. F. Stone, *op. cit.*, p. 106.

[123] *B. D. M.*, Monday, 18 June 1906, p. 6, col. d.

[124] *B. D. M.*, Monday, 29 June 1908, p. 6, col. f.

Fig. 7. The Revd. Professor Baynham, a popular lecturer on the works of Dickens, [Collection of M. J. Crossley Evans].

Sam Weller met the "pretty housemaid Mary"'.[125] The lane was already dubbed 'Sam Weller's Lane' and the tradition persists, despite the fact that Dickens is supposed to have discovered the location during a visit to Bristol as a newspaper reporter in 1835, some months before he was approached to write *The Pickwick Papers*.[126]

[125] *B. D. M.*, Monday, 7 September 1908, p. 6, col. e.
[126] *Bristol & Clifton Dickens Society Newsletter*; Sylvia Kelly, September 2008; Lionel Reeves, April 2009.

A. J. Tonkin, the hard-working vice-president, wrote occasional articles on Dickens for *The Clifton Chronicle*. Many were transcripts of his lectures. The first, in August 1903, posed the question, 'Was Dickens Unjust to Women?' Opening with, 'I submit that the great author has not been unjust in the creation of his women characters,' Mr. Tonkin examined, in detail, a number of female characters and drew the conclusion that we must base our judgments of the accuracy of their portraits on our study of the times in which they were placed by their author. Other articles discussed 'David Copperfield', 'Tom Pinch' and 'Edwin Drood'.[127]

The Society was sufficiently well-established by 1906 for it to appear in the second edition of *Arrowsmith's Dictionary of Bristol*, where readers were given a synopsis of the activities and achievements of the Society to date.[128]

At the opening of the 1906–1907 session the number of people present to hear the Revd. A. N. Blatchford's reading of *A Tale of Two Cities*, is described as 'satisfactory', a reflection, perhaps, of the membership levelling out at about a 100.[129] Among the speakers at the annual dinner were the Revd. Professor Baynham and Mr. James Baker F.R.G.S., F.R.Hist.S.[130] A conversazione brought a 'most successful' session to a close in April.[131]

Change, however, was in the air. From October 1907 the Society met at the Literary and Philosophical Club[132] in Berkeley Square, with A. J. Tonkin in the chair as the Society was again without a president. Mr. H. Theo. Jones, now honorary secretary and treasurer, gave a recital taken from *Dombey and Son* to a crowded room that 'left nothing to be desired'. Many new members were enrolled.[133] With Mr. and Mrs. Tonkin at the helm, the Society would not flounder. The November meeting was arranged by the gentlemen of the committee and the ladies took over in December.

---

[127] *C. C.*, 5 August 1903, kindly supplied by Mr. Andrew Palmer; 18 August 1909, p. 3, col. b—c; 13 April 1910, p. 7, col. b-d; 5 August 1911, p. 7, col. a-d.

[128] *Arrowsmith's Dictionary of Bristol*, (2nd ed., Bristol, 1906), p. 133.

[129] *B. D. M.*, Thursday, 8 November 1906, p. 6, col. d.; Friday, 9 November 1906, p. 4, col. f.

[130] *B. D. M.*, Thursday, 7 February 1907, p. 5, col. f. James Baker (1847–1921) was the founder of a well-known publishing house in Clifton and a founder member of the Bristol and Gloucestershire Archaeological Society in 1876. He served on our council for many years representing the city of Bristol, and died in June 1921. A journalist, he travelled extensively and published numerous travel works and novels, making a particular study of the Austro-Hungarian empire and was made a knight of the Imperial Order of Franz Josef. He lived at Sewelle Villa, 1 Goldney Road, Clifton. It was said that he had done much 'to promote the position of the [archaeological] society'. It was largely due to his efforts that Stokeleigh camp was presented to the National Trust in *c.* 1909. The B. & G. A. S. is currently represented on the National Trust's management committee for Leigh Woods by Mr. H. G. M. Leighton. The Society's representation came about as a result of the work of James Baker. *T. B. & G. A. S.*, XLI, Part 2, (1919), p. 131; XLIII, (1921), p. 2; *W. D. P.*, 25 June 1921.

[131] *C. C.*, 24 April 1907, p. 5, col. f.

[132] This club was founded for persons of literary and scientific tastes in September 1890 and met in two houses originally purchased to provide an episcopal palace for the bishop of Bristol. *Arrowsmith's Dictionary of Bristol*, (2nd ed., Bristol, 1906), p. 108. The club was subsequently renamed The University and Literary Club in 1908, Anon. *The University and Literary Club 1890–2008*, (Bristol, 2009), p. 5. The Revd A. N. Blatchford was proposed as a member of its committee in 1890, *ibid.*, p. 13, a position that he did not take up.

[133] *B. D. M.*, Friday, 25 October 1907, p. 6, col. e.

Thus a tradition was established of holding a 'Gentlemen's Night' and a 'Ladies' Night' each session, generating a spirit of genteel rivalry and resulting in a wider participation by the membership at large. There was further development in 1910, when the gentlemen met for an informal 'Friendly swarry, consisting of a boiled leg of mutton, with the usual trimmings, Pickwick pudding, pipes, wine and music' at St. Stephen's Restaurant, Baldwin Street.[134]

In November 1907 it was announced that Richard Pape Cowl M.A., professor of English at University College, Bristol, and secretary of the committee formed with the object of obtaining a charter for the University College, had accepted the presidency.[135] (Fig. 8). Professor Cowl chaired his first meeting in December in a room festively decorated with ivy and geraniums (the Dickens emblem). The annual Christmas collection was donated to the Bristol Children's Hospital.[136]

In January 1908 James Baker lectured to the Society on 'The Bohemia of Today', dispelling his audience's pre-conceptions with limelight views of the scenery and social conditions of the country. Old castles, almost hidden by forests, were grim reminders of past battles between the Hussites and the Romanists and he spoke of the hatred that still existed between the Germans and the Czechs, with whom his sympathies lay.[137]

The anniversary birthday dinner was held at the Bristol Restaurant, Wine Street. The president, in proposing 'The Immortal Memory of Charles Dickens' drew a heading in the *Bristol Daily Mercury*, 'Professor R. P. Cowle [*sic*] criticises the writings of Dickens'. He is reported to have said:

> There were societies in memory of Villon, the French poet, and Omar Khayyam. These societies had fortunately, he thought, few members, and they were generally those who had lost something of the best of life. Then there was the Shakespeare Society, and again, they had a class of literary society such as the Burns Society and the Dickens Society. The last two societies were something of the same type. As far as the Dickens Society was concerned, their interest in Dickens was not purely a literary one. If they were literary critics they might discover and discuss the flaws that existed in the works of Dickens. They would recognise the confined range within which Dickens conceived and created character, that many of his characters were somewhat unreal or histrionic [...] exaggerated, and some almost past the borderline of caricature, or that his plots were ill-constructed, incoherently involved, and form a tangled web that the utmost patience and ingenuity on the part of the readers could hardly unravel [...] it might be said that his humour tended to the

[134] *W. D. P.*, Wednesday, 19 January 1910, p. 5, col. f.

[135] Professor Cowl, a scholar of Trinity College, Dublin, was a lecturer in English Language and Literature and special lecturer in Middle English, at the University of Birmingham from 1899 until 1905. He was appointed to Bristol in 1905 and was the only holder of a 'chair' at University College not to be re-appointed when the College was granted its charter in 1909. His honorary research professorship, granted in 1909, came to an end in 1912. The controversy about the end of his research professorship resulted in extensive press coverage, which was condensed and reprinted for circulation to the University Court, the Bristol corporation and others as *Bristol University: What the London Press Says* (1913) and R. P. Cowl, *A Brief Statement*, (1913). His future career is unknown.

[136] *B. D. M.*, Friday, 20 December 1907, p. 6, col. d.

[137] *W. D. P.*, Friday, 17 January 1908, p. 5, col. f.

Fig. 8. Professor Richard Pape Cowl, [from Special Collections, University of Bristol].

grotesque, sometimes to the farcical, and that his pathos was often forced or that it bordered [...] upon the ludicrous.

He went on to extol Thackeray's range of vision but concluded that 'Dickens commanded the admiration and affection of his countrymen in a sense that Thackeray never did', an opinion which was greeted with applause. Professor Cowl then outlined Dickens's strengths asserting that he was a great benefactor of his race. It was also announced that the Society's membership had risen to 120.[138]

---

[138] *B. D. M.*, Saturday, 8 February 1908, p. 8, col. a.

The February meeting was devoted to 'Lesser known characters in Dickens's books'. These included Mr. Bagnett in *Bleak House* selected by Miss Lilian Hughes,[139] who commented that 'Mr. Bagnett's admiration for his wife, who helped him so much was a splendid argument for women's suffrage'.[140] The conversazione held in Whatley Hall, which had recently been refurbished, brought the session to a close in April. The proceedings were as varied as usual, but Charles Andrews probably stole the show, performing sketches from *Barnaby Rudge*, in full costume complete with a substitute raven—a jackdaw loaned for the occasion by Captain G. B. Villiers, superintendent of the Zoological Gardens. The highlight of the evening, however, was when the president, Professor Cowl, presented the Society's first certificate of life-membership to the Revd. A. N. Blatchford.[141]

The superior facilities at Whatley Hall probably influenced the decision to make it the Society's headquarters from the 1908–1909 session. At the same time, the scope of the away engagements, entertainments given at various venues in aid of good causes, was extended to take Dickens readings and recitals into the poorer parts of the city,[142] indicating that they were not viewed solely as money-raising operations. The Revd. A. N. Blatchford opened the new session with his 'Inspector Bucket the Detective', a narrative collated from *Bleak House*. Taking a strand from one of the novels was a logical development from the usually short character sketches. At the conclusion of the reading, it was announced that Miss Mary Angela Dickens,[143] granddaughter of the novelist, was in the audience. Acknowledging the warmth with which she, 'a stranger in this city' had been received, Miss Dickens expressed the hope that, 'it may be your good pleasure to wish me success in my undertaking'.

Bearing in mind Miss Hughes's opinions expressed a few months earlier, one can only speculate on whether or not the audience anticipated what was to follow:

> I am in Bristol connected with the League that has for its object the opposition to the vote for women, and I would like you to study both sides of the question before giving your voices to either. Of course Charles Dickens's granddaughter is not Charles Dickens by a long way, but she is proud of the honour of her relationship, and loves the thought that she is following a line of action that would have had his sympathy, to believe in the humanity of womankind at its best, and for this reason she asks you not to be hard upon her, to pledge yourself to no line of action unless you honestly believe such a line will be best for woman herself [...] I ask you to do this in memory of and for the sake of him in whose name we meet tonight.[144]

It is unlikely that members of the Society, had ever been challenged in such a way before!

Professor Cowl was in the chair for the anniversary birthday dinner at Whatley Hall, but breaking with custom, E. R. Norris Mathews, the first president, was invited to pro-

---

[139] Miss Lilian Hughes, 1901 census, aged 25, of 7 The Avenue, Clifton, daughter of James Silcott Hughes, Accountant/Insurance.
[140] *C. C.*, 19 February 1908, p. 2, col. a.
[141] *B. D. M.*, Friday, 17 April 1908, p. 6, col. d.
[142] *B. D. M.*, Monday, 7 September 1908, p. 6, col. e.
[143] Daughter of Charles Dickens Junior. Novelist. Died 7 February 1948.
[144] *B. D. M.*, Friday, 16 October 1908, p. 5, col. g.

pose the toast 'To the Immortal Memory of Charles Dickens'.[145] He recalled the preliminary meetings of the Society; the work of A. J. Tonkin and J. W. T. Ley in preparing the initial programme. The Society had emerged from its infancy and given evidence of its growth and healthy existence; 'The genius of Charles Dickens' he declared, 'would ever shine brilliantly', optimistically adding, 'The ideals and reforms which he originated would no more be forgotten in our national history than would be the life work record of Carlyle, of Ruskin or Addison. Never was Dickens more appreciated and read than he is today'. The honorary secretary, H. Theo. Jones in responding, said their members came from all over the city and suburbs as well as the country parts of Somerset and Gloucester. 'The visitors', were toasted by Sam Tucker and Mr. H. E. Chattock in responding referred to the 'proposed permanent memorial' to Dickens and he opined that his works would continue to be read after buildings had crumbled away. At a late hour, the celebrated actor Bransby Williams,[146] (Fig. 9), who was appearing as Abanazar in *Aladdin* at the Prince's Theatre, joined the company and entertained them with three short Dickens sketches and expressed a wish that he might do something more for the Society while he was in Bristol, 'perhaps in aid of a charity which was his favourite way of showing his love for Dickens's memory'.[147]

The session of 1909–1910 saw a great increase in membership, 60 joining at the preliminary whist drive at the Imperial Hotel on Whiteladies Road. The Revd. A. N. Blatchford again gave the opening lecture, 'An appreciation of Charles Dickens'. Eulogising, with obvious scriptural overtones, he stated that Dickens: 'was the kindly physician to humanity, who, seeing its weak points and neglected sores, bound up the wounded in that true charity which covered a multitude of sins, and pouring in the oil and wine of his encouragement and sympathy, he tried to heal and to send men back to the ranks once more, strengthened for the struggle of life'.[148]

Several new members were enrolled in January when Professor Cowl gave an exposition of the genius of Dickens in relation to the age in which he lived. It was the professor's opinion that Dickens could not reach his ambition of artistic perfection and that if he had succeeded in so doing, his novels would have been of less value. 'There was something invaluable in the realism of Dickens, reality made his characters live [...] The realism describes inanimate life, and this, as done by Dickens, was very great, showing very clear knowledge and closeness and an extraordinary fineness

---

[145] *The Calendar of University College, Bristol, 1908–1909*, p. 41, shows that Norris Mathews was one of the two assessors of the College's Library Committee. Cowl was also a member of the Library committee.

[146] Bransby William Pharez, stage name Bransby Williams, (1870–1961), music hall artiste, famous for his monologues and character sketches. Began presentations of character studies from the works of Charles Dickens in the 1890s and continued until the 1950s, successfully transferring his art to the medium of television and appeared in film. He was inspirational and numbered amongst his *protégés* Eric Jones-Evans, a noted Dickensian performer, for whom he wrote forewards to: *In the Footsteps of Barnaby Rudge: A Selection of the Character Sketches from Charles Dickens' Famous Novel of the Gordon Riots on 1780*, (1947); and *Character Sketches from Charles Dickens*, (1947). Bransby Williams was the author of two books of character sketches from Charles Dickens and of works such as *The Old Time Actor and Penny Showman*, (1913).

[147] *B. D. M.*, Monday, 8 February 1909, p. 6, cols. a-b.

[148] *C. C.*, 3 November 1909, p. 2, col. 5.

Fig. 9. Bransby Williams one of the greatest Dickensian interpretators *c.* 1910, [Collection of M. J. Crossley Evans].

in the perception of detail'. By way of illustrating his point, the president concluded the evening with a recital of the Eatanswill election, from *The Pickwick Papers.*[149]

At the anniversary dinner in 1910 a bust of Dickens on a pedestal was prominently displayed in front of the central table[150] and the toast list 'was a model of brevity'.

---

[149] *C. C.*, 26 January 1910, p. 3, cols, a-b.
[150] The bust made of parian ware is in the safe keeping of the president of the Society and is still used on special evenings.

Toasting 'The Immortal Memory of Charles Dickens', Professor Cowl sympathised with those who thought praising Dickens was superfluous but concentrated on the ways in which he had expressed his humanity by interesting his fellow men in the lives of the poor and ridiculing the shams and corruptions employed to advance social change. James Baker toasted 'Our Guests' and in response Mr. William Edward Hicks[151] speculated:

> Supposing Dickens, instead of being brought up as he was, had been a fortunate youth, sent to Eton and then gone on to Balliol. No doubt his original genius would have been there, but it would have taken other forms. His essays would have been gone through by professors and tutors, who would have marked out a great deal, pruned his style, corrected him in many respects, and produced probably a cultured, accomplished, clever man, but not the Dickens they knew, not the Dickens they loved.

The membership of the Society had now risen to 200.[152]

The earliest copy of a programme in the Society's archive is for the annual Dramatic Evening in aid of 'The Guild of the Brave Poor Things' at the Lesser Colston Hall in April 1910. From it we learn that the musical element of the occasion had been curtailed; that 'Mr. Bumble and Mrs. Corney' (played by Mr. and Mrs. Tonkin) was still a favourite and the main attraction remained 'Bardell v. Pickwick'. The presentation was accurately costumed, 'props' introduced, and the players were skilfully 'made-up' by Harry Webb.[153] The tradition of Mrs. Cluppins being played by a man[154] that had been maintained in the early years of the Society had now been abandoned. One reviewer remarked that the familiar themes added to the enjoyment. There, was a full house, some 'latecomers' being turned away.[155] The capacity of the hall was 700.[156] Messrs. James Baker and E. T. Wedmore are serving on the committee and the dedicated Mr. and Mrs. Tonkin are now life members. (Figs. 10a and 10b)

H. Theo. Jones did not take part. With his wife, he had attended the annual dinner in February 1909; stepped down as secretary later that year; and given readings of the *Carol* in December.[157] It is possible that he was nursing a sick wife, for her death is recorded at the A. G. M. in September 1911. Mr. Jones remained in Bristol but is apparently no longer an active member of the Society.

The Society's affiliation to the Dickens Fellowship was seen as contributing to its success and members were encouraged to visit the headquarters in London,[158] where

---

[151] W. T. Pike, *op. cit.*, II, (Brighton, 1899), p. 280. Born 1852. Assistant editor, *Western Daily Press*, 1883–1891. Night editor of the *Western Daily Press* from 1891 onwards.

[152] *W. D. P.*, Tuesday, 8 February 1910, p. 10, col. c.

[153] *B. E. P.*, Wednesday, 2 April 1952, p. 2, col. d.

[154] A popular local actor, William Fosbrooke (Funny Fosbrooke) had played Mrs. Cluppins at the Prince's Theatre, when George Rennie Powell impersonated Buzfuz, *Ibid.*, col. e. See also K. Barker, *The Theatre Royal, Bristol, 1766–1966: Two Centuries of Stage History*, (1974), pp. 145, 170.

[155] *W. D. P.*, Thursday, 21 April 1910, p. 5, col. e.

[156] *Wright's Bristol Directory*, (1910), p. 946.

[157] *W. D. P.*, Saturday, 4 December 1909, p. 4, col. f; Thursday, 21 December 1909, p. 3, col. f. He was one of those to whom C. F. W. Dening dedicated his *Old Inns of Bristol*, (Bristol, 1943).

[158] *C. C.*, 16 November 1910, p. 5, col. f.

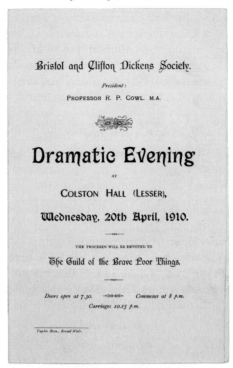

Figs. 10a and 10b. Programme for the Dramatic Evening 1910, [Collection of M. J. Crossley Evans].

preparations were underway for celebrating the centenary of Dickens's birth in 1912. With this in mind, the Bristol Society offered to host the Fellowship's 6th annual conference in 1911, an invitation warmly accepted.[159] It was held at Whatley Hall, Clifton, on Saturday 7 October with the president, John Cuming Walters[160] in the chair. Welcoming delegates to Bristol, Professor Cowl outlined the progress that the Bristol Society had made. The membership had increased to almost 200 and on the charitable side, constant requests were received for entertainments to raise funds to assist deserving causes; nearly £50 had been raised during the previous year. Speaking of the Fellowship, Mr. Walters was able to report that their surplus funds had doubled in a year, and although they had not reached their target of 10,000 members, the membership had increased to 6,075. Plans for the Dickens Centenary included a series of dinners for poor children; performances of the plays of Dickens in London theatres; a series of lectures in London and a sermon in Westminster Abbey. Commemorative badges would be awarded for long and active service to the Fellowship. Sir Luke Fildes, R.A., 'fellow worker and friend of Charles Dickens' was elected President of the Fellowship for the coming year.[161] Professor Dowden (Dublin) and Mr. G. W. Davis (London) were elected vice-presidents and the serving vice-presidents were re-elected for the year 1911–1912. In the afternoon delegates were taken for a drive to view the sights of Bristol and were entertained to tea at Goldney House by the Right Hon. Lewis Fry.

Although there was a good attendance at the dinner, there were many notable absences, including the Lord Mayor of Bristol, the duke of Beaufort, Sir Herbert Ashman, Bart., Sir Luke Fildes, the Revd. A. N. Blatchford, Walter Dexter, and J. W. T. Ley. Despite the inclusion of ladies, only Mrs. Newcombe of Bethlehem U.S.A. was invited to speak, responding to the toast, 'Other Branches'. In the press reports of those attending, no other ladies are listed.

Following the loyal toast, E. R. Norris Mathews, proposing 'The Dickens Fellowship', said: 'They had a real fellowship not only with the good-hearted Dickens, but with the immense family of men, women, and children whom he had created in his books, and who were to them more or less intimate acquaintances'. Responding, Percy Fitzgerald said that the Fellowship had gathered up the traditions of Dickens that would otherwise have been dispelled and scattered. Of Dickens's wide circle of friends, only Marcus Stone[162] and himself now remained [*sic*]. Mr. Fitzgerald stated that he had set up five bronze busts of Dickens, all of his own workmanship, and he thought that the public would insist on a national memorial being set up during his centennial year. J. Cuming Walters proposed the toast to the 'Immortal Memory of Charles Dickens'.[163]

The opening meeting in the centennial year in January 1912 took the form of the Society's first social. It was deemed a great success. The honorary secretary read out

[159] *C. C.*, 4 October 1911, p. 6, col. c.

[160] Died 16 July 1933. President of The Dickens Fellowship 1910–1911, the editor of the *Manchester Evening Chronicle* 1902–1906, and for 25 years the editor of *The Manchester City News*. He wrote extensively on Dickens.

[161] Born 1843, died 27 February 1927. Illustrator of books and painted portraits. Knighted in 1906, K.C.V.O., 1918.

[162] Born 1840, R.A., 1887. Illustrated the works of Dickens in his youth. Died 24 March 1921.

[163] *B. T. & M.*, Monday, 9 October 1911, p. 9, cols, a-b.

several letters of thanks from various charities for whom Dickens evenings had been arranged. The Y. M. C. A. Cricket Club had benefited by over £10; the Zion Chapel, Bedminster restoration fund received £12; the Knowle Sunday Schools received £6, and as a result of the Christmas collection, the Guild of the Brave Poor Things were presented with £1. 17s. 4d.[164] The Society's talented performers were very popular. Previously, in November 1910, the Christ Church Men's Club decided to stage a concert with 'an unusually good programme' to relieve their financial deficit. It was agreed that 'If only the services of the Bristol and Clifton Dickens Society could be enlisted [...] there would be no doubt as to the result'.[165] The evening at the Grand Spa Hotel raised £25. 12s. 9d.[166] At that time, the amount raised by the Society for charity averaged £30 a month.[167]

Returning to 1912, notices of events for the 7 February celebrations began to appear in the press. Gustav Adolf Widmann, 'a Bristolian born and bred' and 'a worthy successor of Charles Clark' returned to perform a centenary Dickens recital, this time at the Y. M. C. A. Hall.[168]

On 6 February 1912, the *Western Daily Press* declared:

> The whole of this week is a Dickens week. [...] The interest that is being taken in the centenary differs altogether from that which is usually given to the celebration of literary anniversaries. These, as a rule, are of interest only to persons who are proficient in literature, who are either authors themselves or are critical students of more contemporary writers. But Dickens appeals to the general public.[169]

In the same issue there was a letter from Edward G. Follwell who went further and wished to be the spokesman for 'that great community of "little people" [...] of no fame, no notoriety, no standing' who felt that they knew Charles Dickens. 'There are many [...] in Bristol who love and cherish his memory [...] I will think of these as I reverently place my modest flower upon Dickens's tomb in the Abbey on Wednesday'.[170]

The next day, Edgar W. Down[171] in a lengthy reply as honorary secretary of the Bristol and Clifton Dickens Society, expressed his great pleasure in reading Mr. Follwell's tribute, and adding his own praises he said that Dickens 'was a man with a message, whose religion and philosophy embraced mankind; he taught men to believe in the good that was in them, and that they could "rise on the stepping stones of their dead selves to higher things"'.

Edward James Thomas[172] of Redland claimed that Dickens had 'provoked more laughter, induced more smiles with his dry humour than any other soul on the planet

---

[164] *C. C.*, 10 January 1912, p. 6, col. d.
[165] *C. C.*, 16 November 1910, p. 7, col. c.
[166] *C. C.*, 7 December 1910, p. 2, col. d.
[167] *C. C.*, 21 December 1910, p. 8, col. h.
[168] *C. C.*, 24 January 1912, p. 3, col. f: *B. T. & M.*, Thursday, 8 February 1912, p. 7, col. c.
[169] *W. D. P.*, Tuesday, 6 February 1912, p. 4, col. g.
[170] *Ibid.*, p. 3, cols. f-g.
[171] *Mathews's Bristol Directory*, (1905), p. 362, hatter and hosier of 19, 20, 21, and 22 Lower Arcade, Broadmead. Born Cardiff 1872/3, aged 28 at the time of the 1901 census.
[172] Edward James Thomas, 1901 census, aged 36, 28 Collingwood Road, Redland. Assistant with the Ordinance Survey.

for a hundred years'.[173] The following day, Willie Ernest Cannings wrote of the *Western Daily Press* leading article, 'It especially appealed to me because of its critical, as well as laudatory character'. His own appreciation of Dickens had been tempered by reading the works of Galsworthy, Shaw and Wells, but he took issue with the expressed opinion that reading Dickens was only for enjoyment rather than reform, although he thought it likely that Dickens's influence would wane over time with the spread of real education.[174]

There was extensive newspaper coverage of the Dickens celebrations in London with wreath-laying on his grave in Westminster Abbey, but there is no mention of a tribute from Bristol. There were also reports from Rochester and Gloucester in England and New York, Bethlehem and San Francisco in the U.S.A. The only event in Bristol seems to have been Gustav Widmann's Dickens recital at the Y. M. C. A.[175] 'Since the death of the Rev. Charles Clark', wrote one critic, 'Mr. Widmann has been the most prominent local reciter of selections from Dickens'. There is no mention of the Bristol and Clifton Dickens Society even holding their annual dinner, possibly because two dinners had been arranged in the previous year, although Edgar Down's letter quoted from above includes the following:

> And as I lift my glass tonight, together with those who are united with common feeling of gratitude and affection, I shall pay tribute to the immortal memory of a man whose [...] life was gentle, and the elements so mixed in him, that Nature might stand up and say to all the world, "This was a man!"

The following day, (8 February), Bransby Williams paid a flying visit to the Bedminster Hippodrome to give an afternoon performance of a dozen or so Dickens character studies, to a full house.[176] In the evening he accepted an invitation from the Bristol Playgoers' Club to hear the Revd. A. N. Blatchford present his 'Sydney Carton' reading at Fortt's Assembly Rooms in the Royal Parade. Not to disappoint the members, Mr. Williams took to the stage at 10.35 pm and brought the evening to a close with his impersonations of Sergeant Buzfuz, Uriah Heep and Dan'l Peggotty.[177]

The absence of any activity by the Bristol and Clifton Dickens Society passed without press comment, but the leader column in the *Bristol Times and Mirror* on 9 February singled out the Society for criticism:

> Yesterday Sir Luke Fildes, president of the Dickens Fellowship, appealed to our readers to become members. We trust that the appeal will meet with a large response. The Fellowship aims at doing some of the things that Dickens did— helping good and resisting evil. It cares for the Tiny Tims, who are still to be found, and often with less fortunate surroundings than the original had. Bristol has a Dickens Society, which claims to be doing something of the same kind, but we are disappointed to find that its most recently reported efforts are not quite on the lines Dickens would have approved. [The details quoted above follow]. To call the chief

[173] *W. D. P.*, Wednesday, 7 February 1912, p. 5, col. d.
[174] *W. D. P.*, Thursday, 8 February 1912, p. 3, col. e.
[175] *B. T. & M.*, Thursday, 8 February 1912, p. 7, col. c.
[176] *C. C.*, 14 February 1912, p. 2, col. c.
[177] *B. T. & M.*, Friday, 9 February 1912, p. 6, col. f.

of these efforts charitable is to stretch the meaning of the word "charity" beyond anything that Dickens would have permitted. What amount was sent to provide pocket-handkerchiefs for the natives of Africa is not disclosed,[178] but we can well understand a society which calls cricket clubs and chapel painting charities, and aids them in the proportion of pounds to shillings for the Tiny Tims, making strenuous efforts to send out the pocket-handkerchiefs. We wonder what Dickens himself would have said about such "charities", as are here set down to the credit of the Bristol Dickens Society.[179]

No officer or member of the Society chose to defend their fundraising record by replying to this editorial, but a tragic incident at Soundwell provided the Dickensians with an opportunity to demonstrate care and make a practical response. At 7.15 pm on 13 July 1912, William Nichols, a blacksmith, whose sight had been seriously impaired in an industrial accident and was unable to work, shot at his wife outside their home. Missing his wife Louisa, his 70 shots blinded Worthy Brown, a passing postman making his evening deliveries.[180] The *Evening Times & Echo* opened a fund in aid of Mr. Brown,[181] and on 6 November the Dickens Society performed their own five-act dramatisation of *A Tale of Two Cities,* at the Lesser Colston Hall. It proved a 'great success',[182] and raised £14 for the support fund.[183] The annual collection for the Guild of the Brave Poor Things in December netted £2. 18s. 6d, the highest collection the Society had ever taken at a December meeting, and a committee decision increased it to £5.[184] The total donation to the Guild that year was £10.[185] The person responsible for this re-assessment of charitable giving may have been A. J. Tonkin who was now president, having succeeded Professor Richard Cowl at the A.G.M. in October.[186] At the last meeting of the centennial year, Wednesday, 18 December, Mr. Frank Giddings[187] was presented with a framed life-membership certificate in recognition of his seven years service as honorary treasurer, during which period the membership had risen from 90 to over 300.[188] Mr. Tonkin would hold office until his sudden death in 1922,[189] giving the Society stability in what were to prove turbulent years. In 1913 the Bristol Society withdrew its affiliation to The Dickens Fellowship[190] and the Society's brass plate on All Saints' Hall, Clifton, (its new headquarters), led to

[178] A reference to the missionary work of Mrs. Jellyby in *Bleak House,* see chapters iv, v, &c.

[179] *B. T. & M.,* Friday, 9 February 1912, p. 5, col. g.

[180] *B. T. & M.,* Friday, 16 August 1912, p. 6, col. e.

[181] *B. T. & M.,* Monday, 2 September 1912, p. 3, col. d.

[182] *C. C.,* 13 November 1912, p. 6, col. c.

[183] *C. C.,* 27 November 1912, p.3, col. f.

[184] *C. C.,* 25 December 1912, p. 8, col. b.

[185] Guild accounts, B. R. O. 39842.

[186] *B. T. & M.,* Friday, 16 August 1912, p. 6, col. e. *C. C.* 9 October 1912, p. 2, col. c; 'compelled him to reside in London'; D. Carleton, *A University for Bristol,* (Bristol, 1984), p. 28.

[187] Francis John (Frank) Giddings, 1901 census, aged 24 living at 18 Elmgrove Ave., Easton. Insurance clerk.

[188] *C. C.,* 25 December 1912, p. 8, col. b.

[189] *B. T. & M.,* Thursday, 30 November 1922, p. 6, col. a.

[190] *C. C.,* 29 October 1913, p. 6, col. b.

protest letters in the press against Charles Dickens being associated with the church.[191] The privations placed upon the Society during the 'Great War' tested its resourcefulness and ability to survive, but it kept going. Mrs. Louie Tonkin was appointed the Society's first lady president on the death of her husband.

The Bristol and Clifton Dickens Society today owes much to the pioneers in its formative years. Fund-raising in the name of Dickens continues, and takes the form of prepared readings and talks to other groups, with an annual collection still taken at the December meeting. The proceeds are currently sent to the Julian Trust, which is dedicated to assisting the homeless in Bristol. A 'book of the year' is recommended for study by the book group. In 1934 the Society 'joined hands' again with The Dickens Fellowship as branch no. 124. Bristol is recognised as one of the Fellowship's most active branches and international Dickens conferences were held here in 1993 and 2003.

Presidents of the Bristol and Clifton Dickens Society

Mr. Edward Robert Norris Mathews, F.R.Hist.S., F.R.S.L.	1902–1903
The Revd. Ambrose Nichols Blatchford, B.A.	1903–1907
Professor Richard Pape Cowl, M.A.	1907–1912
Mr. Alfred James Tonkin	1912–1922

Honorary Secretaries of the Bristol and Clifton Dickens Society

Mr. James William Thomas Ley	1902–1904
Mr. Charles Andrews	1904–1906
Mr. H. Theophilus Jones[192]	1906–1909
Mr. Charles Andrews[193]	1909–1910
Mr. Edgar W. Down[194]	1910–1912
Mr. Sam Tucker	1912–1912

Honorary Treasurers of the Bristol and Clifton Dickens Society

Mr. Francis John 'Frank' Giddings	1905–*post* 1912

[191] *C. C.*, 12 November 1913, forward.

[192] Jones is shown as secretary in *D.*, vol. II, no. 11, November 1906, p. 322.

[193] *B. D. M.*, Friday, 26 November 1909, p. 6, col. d., 'Mr. C. Andrews, who Dickensians were pleased to welcome back in the position of honorary secretary'. Mr. Andrews is still honorary secretary at the A. G. M. in September 1910 reported in *C. C.*, Wednesday, 28 September 1910, p. 3, col. c. At the meeting he gave a report and was 'presented with a certificate of Honorary Membership'. At the same meeting 'Mr. Edgar W. Down was re-elected honorary secretary and Mr. F. J. Giddings again chosen treasurer'. From this it seems likely that Jones stood down before the end of the 1908–1909 season, Down took over and Andrews was elected at the A. G. M. at the beginning of the 1909–1910 session, or maybe 're-elected' was a reporter's error.

[194] *C. C.*, Wednesday, 9 October 1912, p. 2, col. c. 'Mr. Down [...] regretted that through business pressure and ill health he was forced to resign the post of secretary'. Sam Tucker was elected honorary secretary and Francis John Giddings re-elected honorary treasurer and made a life member.

ACKNOWLEDGEMENTS
I am indebted to Dr. M. J. Crossley Evans for invaluable help providing all the illustrations and augmenting the references, and for his inexaustable patience; Mr. Anthony Beeson, Art Librarian, and the staff of Bristol Central Library reference department for generous professionalism; the staff of Bristol Records Office; Ms. Anne Murch; Mr. Andrew Palmer, LL.B., D.M.A.; Mr. Andrew Phillips, chapter clerk of Bristol cathedral; and Mr. Michael Williams, B.A., Adv. Cert. Ed.

XXI

The Society's Archives: Gloucestershire Archives D7996

DAVID J. H. SMITH, M.A., F.S.A.

IN THE long tenure of office of Gerard Leighton our Society has been twice blessed. Firstly, he has meticulously cherished the Society's assets both financial and real, and kept careful records of how he has done so. Secondly, he has placed in the Society's archives not only his own papers but also the records he inherited from his father's long and distinguished membership. As a result we have information about the Society's activities in the interwar period, especially in the Bristol area, which is not available elsewhere.

Over many years the Society's minute books and other records were deposited by various officers in both the Bristol and Gloucestershire record offices. In 1996 by mutual agreement the records at Bristol were all transferred to Gloucester. They were allocated the reference D7996. Since then further deposits have been made, amounting in all to some 16 disparate groups of papers, some quite large. In 2006 and 2007 these were amalgamated, sorted and listed by the present writer. A summary of the resulting catalogue follows. For further details and itemized references consult the full catalogue in Gloucestershire Archives. Following existing practice these documents are all available for immediate consultation save for some membership records to which a 30–year rule applies. Significant groups of related documents are also held in two other places: the Society's Library and the Special Collections held in the University of Bristol's Arts and Social Sciences Library.

The material in the Society's Library comprises four distinct groups, shelved next to the *Transactions*. The first is a single green volume of meetings programmes covering the period August 1876 to September 1896. Included are other items relevant to the venues such as maps including a map of ancient Bristol; a map of Cheltenham made for the Social Science Conference, 1878; as well as an appeal to fund a new drawing of the Woodchester pavement, 1881; a prospectus for the proposed publication of Smyth's *Lives of the Berkeleys*; and a prospectus for an edition of the Winchcombe cartulary, 1887. There is a list of contents at the front of the volume.

The second group comprises five red volumes of meetings notices. The first four cover the period 1897 to 1920 (meetings were suspended between August 1914 and July 1919). The third volume (1906–1910) also contains a catalogue of old Bristol plans, coins, and antiquities displayed at the Bristol meeting held on 17 July 1906. The fifth volume relates to the joint meeting with the Royal Archaeological Institute, 11–16 July 1921, and contains (loosely inserted) some letters of Roland Austin. It is possible that this series was compiled by him.

The third set is of two green volumes containing only meetings programmes, 1897–1911. The last set is of three green volumes of meetings programmes compiled by Canon Bazeley and given to the Library by Colonel Arthur Lloyd-Baker in 1953.

The set covers the period 1897–1909. Each volume has a table of contents in the front and all include many photographs of places visited, mostly general views but some containing architectural detail.

The material in the University of Bristol's Special Collections, of which details have been kindly furnished by Dr. M. J. Crossley Evans, comprises two main groups being DM 1605 and 2080. DM 1605 comprises the papers of H. C. "Len" Prior, relating to the Bristol section and his period as secretary, 1986–1989, and a Bristol section minute book 1922–1983 with related papers from the 1960s onwards. DM 2080 comprises the papers of Dr. Crossley Evans accumulated during his long and distinguished service to the Society. These both duplicate and amplify the official papers catalogued below and comprise A.G.M. notices, rules, and council papers for the 1980s, and 1990s; committee papers for the 1990s and 2000s; *Newsletters* numbers 2–49 (Editors: Miss Elizabeth Ralph, No. 1, March 1977 (missing)-No. 4 February 1979; Mr. G. T. St. John Sanders, No. 5, September 1979–No. 12, February 1983; Mr. D. J. H. Smith, No. 13, September 1983–No. 20, February 1987; Dr. M. J. Crossley Evans, No. 21, August 1987–No. 42, February 1998; Dr. Suzanne Clarke No. 43, August 1998—), programme cards; Bristol section papers for the 1980s and 1990s; correspondence 1980s-2000s, including with Miss P. C. Bath, G. C. Boon, Mrs. M. V. Campbell, Dr. E. Christmas, Dr A. B. Cottle (papers when meetings' secretary), Canon J. E. Gethyn-Jones, L. V. Grinsell, Dr. N. M. Herbert, H. G. M. Leighton, M. J. H. Liversidge, Dr. E. Ralph, Canon J. Rogan, D. J. H. Smith, J. Somerville, the Very Revd. A. G. G. Thurlow, and Canon D. Walker.

Papers concerning the Society may also be found in the files of individual correspondents amongst the papers of Dr. Arthur Basil Cottle (1917–1994), a past-president and meetings' secretary of the society, in DM 1582. The University's Library store contains a bound leather volume with the armorial book plate of Frederick St. John Bullen (113540), which contains the general arrangements, the programmes and the archaeological notes for the annual Spring and Autumn meetings of the Society beginning with the meeting held in London between 11 and 16 July 1898 and ending with that held in Cirencester between 16 and 18 July 1907.

THE CATALOGUE

1. Rules, 1948–1999. 11 items.

The Society was established on 1 April 1876. Its object 'whilst not excluding matters of general antiquarian interest, shall specially be the cultivation of the Archaeology of Bristol and Gloucestershire'. By 1894 the object had been rephrased as 'to promote an interest in the antiquities of Bristol and Gloucestershire, and to encourage the study of archaeology' and has thus remained.

The Society established its rules at its first Annual General Meeting on 22 April 1876. These were published in the first volume of *Transactions*. Revisions have usually been printed, but with exceptions: for example, the major alterations approved at the Annual General Meeting for 1964 never appeared in the *Transactions*. The rules have also been printed separately from time to time. These examples are not a complete set and the versions published in the *Transactions* should also be consulted.

2. General Meetings, 1918–2003. Notices of meetings, annual reports and accounts, meeting papers and notices and reports of Special General Meetings. 21 files and 9 documents.

Annual General Meetings were originally held at the summer field meeting. In 1953 the Annual General Meeting was moved to March or, occasionally, April. Lists of officers elected for the year, the annual report of Council, the annual accounts and the report of the meeting are all published in the *Transactions*. The report of the meeting takes the place of minutes, so the only records of an Annual General Meeting not published are the notices of the meeting and the lists of candidates for election to Council and, latterly, to its committees. In earlier periods these were sometimes included in the Council minute books.

3. Council minutes, agendas and meeting papers, 1876–2004. 18 volumes, 7 files and 1 bundle.

Additional matter may be found in some minute books such as copies of the rules, minutes of committees, meeting notices and agendas, and draft notices and lists of nominations for Annual General Meetings. Summaries of the main business of the committees are included in the minutes of Council.

4. Finance and General Purposes Committee minutes and agenda papers, 1946–2004. 8 files.

The earliest minutes were included with the minutes of Council. The Society's financial year originally ran from 22 to 21 April. This was altered to the calendar year with effect from 1 January 1895. Council appointed a Finance Committee during the year ending 4 August 1908. It was established as a standing committee in new rules approved on 22 July 1918. In 1930 the name was expanded to its present form.

5. Membership records: registers, circulars, prospectuses, lists circulated to officers, 1881–2006. 18 volumes, 2 binders, 1 file and 19 documents.

Lists of members' names and addresses were published in the *Transactions* every year until 1948 since when they have appeared at irregular intervals. Because of the personal information in these records, documents containing entries less than 30 years old are not available for consultation.

6. Financial records: ledgers, cash books, accounts, balance sheets and correspondence, 1876–1996. 26 volumes and 2 files.

The annual accounts are published in the *Transactions*.

7. Excavations and Buildings Committee minutes and agenda papers, 1985–2005. 6 files.

8. Excavations and Buildings correspondence and case files, 1948–1995. 26 bundles and 11 files.

During the Society's year 1919–1920 an excavations fund was established and a committee was appointed to manage this. Minutes of the Committee were recorded in the Council minute books from 1927. It had become a standing committee by July 1935.

The Committee was re-named 'Excavations and Buildings' in 1946. From about 1970 until the early 1990s its main business was the monitoring of listed building consent applications in liaison with the Council for British Archaeology. Changes in the way these applications were dealt with and the increasing professionalism of archaeology in general reduced the business of the Committee and in July 2005 its meetings were adjourned *sine die*.

9. Publications Committee minutes, meetings and correspondence including files relating to some volumes published in the Gloucestershire Record Series, 1950–2005. 23 files and 1 binder.

From its inception publication has been a central part of the Society's activities. The *Transactions* have been published without interruption since 1876 (save in wartime) and within a decade the first monograph was produced in the shape of Smyth's *Lives of the Berkeleys*. So it is surprising that no separate committee was created to supervise publication until much later. Occasionally *ad hoc* committees were set up for specific purposes, such as, for example, to create a general index to the *Transactions*, but until 1948 no committee for publications existed. In 1954 and 1958 the editor, Miss (later Dame) Joan Evans, gave some shares anonymously to the Society with the intention that the income from dividends should ensure the regular publication of the *Transactions*. On 12 January 1990 H. G. M. Leighton and Miss Ralph made a statutory declaration as to the circumstances of this gift which was published in *Transactions* 108, pp. 216–217.

In 1943 Alfred Bruce Robinson bequeathed a reversionary interest in £6,000 to the Society on the death of his wife, to enable the Society to publish parish registers and other records of genealogical and ecclesiastical importance. Mrs. Robinson died in 1948 and the bequest was then paid in eight instalments of £375. In 1950 the Robinson Bequest Committee was established and was re-titled the Records Section Committee in April 1951. It was not regarded as a standing committee though members were elected annually. The Records Section published volumes at irregular intervals for sale to members and to the public. In 1960 an unsuccessful attempt was made to establish an independent record series and in 1970 there was a move to broaden the scope of Records Section publications which also failed. On 28 March 1979 the committee was reconstituted as the Publications Advisory Committee. In about 1985 the committee took over responsibility for the Society's stock of publications from the Library Committee. In January 1988 the committee was renamed the Publications Committee.

In 1987 a Special General Meeting was held as a result of which the Gloucestershire Record Series was established. It publishes a volume each autumn which is supplied to members paying a supplementary subscription and is also available for sale.

10. Library Committee: minutes, 1961–1990, 3 volumes; loans registers, 1933–1987, 4 volumes; and correspondence, 1951–1999, 7 files.

From its inception the Society has collected books by purchase, gift or bequest. In 1881 the establishment of a library and museum in Bristol and Gloucester was formally announced and a catalogue of books already acquired was published. In the following year an *ad hoc* committee was established to allocate books and objects between Bristol and Gloucester. However in 1887 it was decided to bring all the books to Gloucester. A further catalogue was published in 1892. In 1896 Bellows, the Society's printers, set aside a room for the library in their premises in Eastgate. This room also housed the library of the Cotteswold Naturalists' Field Club, jointly stored in specially built cupboards, some of which remained in use in the Society's publications store until 2008.

In 1904 a renewed attempt was made to establish a library in Bristol. Despite this, only two years later the room in Eastgate had become too small and in 1913–1914 the library in Gloucester was moved into the City Library and the Library Committee was constituted with Roland Austin as its first secretary. In the revised rules approved on 22 July 1918 both the Finance and Library committees were established as standing committees. In 1933 the books at Bristol were moved from Red Lodge to the City Museum and Art Gallery.

By 1957 the library at Gloucester contained 5,701 volumes and in the following year it was moved to St. Michael's Rectory, by then in use by the city library. Two years later an *ad hoc* committee was set up to review the library. In 1977 it was moved back into the main building of the former city library in Brunswick Road. In 1983 the last few books still in Bristol were added to the main and now only library in Gloucester. Responsibility for the storage and management of the Society's stock of publications was vested in the Library Committee until about 1985 when it was transferred to the Publications Committee.

In 1996 the Society was given notice by the County Librarian that the Brunswick Road library could no longer house the Society's books. After considerable discussion, including a special general meeting, the Society was able to negotiate an agreement with the Cheltenham and Gloucester College of Higher Education, now the University of Gloucestershire, which houses its books with the University's archives at Francis Close Campus at Cheltenham.

11. Committee for Archaeology in Gloucestershire: minutes, agendas, correspondence and papers, 1974–1999. 27 packets.

Following discussions which began in December 1974 the Committee held its first meeting on 3 May 1976. Its aims are to bring together in a single forum the archaeological organisations in Gloucestershire so as to co-ordinate representations to government and local authorities and to stimulate interest in archaeology. Its annual report is published in the *Transactions*.

12. Field Meetings and lectures: circulars, programmes, accounts, correspondence, guides to places visited and related papers, 1888–2003. 8 packets, 7 bundles, 4 files, 1 volume and 36 items.

From its inception field meetings were at the heart of the Society's activities. Until 1953 the Annual General Meeting was held during the summer residential meeting. Until 1978 these were reported in the *Transactions* and since then short notes have appeared in some *Newsletters*. In 1952 a committee was set up to help plan meetings but this seems not to have remained in being for very long.

In 1903–1904 programmes of lectures were held during the winter in Bristol and Gloucester, organised by the Secretaries for the respective districts. These were not held every year. Since 1979 regular programmes of lectures have been arranged at Gloucester and Bristol, though in Gloucester there was a hiatus during 1988 and 1989.

In addition to the records listed here there are several bound volumes in the Society's library, housed (2009) beside the *Transactions* (see pp. 401–402 above). These mainly comprise prospectuses for meetings which often contain similar information to the published reports. However some include fliers circulated with the *Transactions* relating to other Society activities, photographs taken during field meetings, plans of places where meetings were held, occasional letters, exhibition catalogues, programmes for joint meetings with other organisations, and miscellaneous related ephemera.

13. Bristol and Gloucestershire Archaeological Trust, 1929–1952: minutes, accounts and correspondence. 3 volumes, 1 bundle and 1 file.

The Trust was established on 5 November 1928 and its governance and objects were set out in a Memorandum published in the *Transactions* 50, p. 380. Its main purpose was to accept custody of buildings and monuments for preservation and protection. It was abolished during the financial reconstruction of the Society after 1948.

14. Correspondence with officers, 1922–1987. 16 files and 3 documents.

For the preservation of many of the records (other than minutes) prior to 1948 the Society is indebted to Wilfrid Leighton. Miss Ralph became secretary for Bristol in 1943 and her correspondence sheds light on the rift between her predecessor as Honorary General Secretary, the Revd. F. W. Potto Hicks, and Roland Austin. This was only resolved when Miss Ralph accepted the suggestion of Mr. Hicks to act as his assistant for a year prior to standing for election as his successor at the Annual General Meeting of 1948. Other topics include Miss Evans's agreement to edit the *Transactions* on the resignation of Roland Austin in 1950, attempts to establish a records society, the re-starting of the *Victoria County History* in Gloucestershire and discussions between officers on matters of policy.

15. Miscellaneous items, *c.* 1890–2000. 2 files, 1 packet, 1 bundle and 44 documents.

Amongst the items which cannot be classified are circulars and appeals relating to the preservation of antiquities and some printed ephemera which may not survive elsewhere (for a list see the full catalogue in Gloucestershire Archives).

Appendix: D7996: Acc 8042. Photographs purchased for Record Series volume 11 *Early* acta *of Gloucester Abbey*.

As part of the agreement with Professor Robert Patterson, editor of this volume, a substantial budget was made available for the purchase of copies of documents to enable him to do most of his preparation in the United States. More than 250 such copies were acquired. After publication these were deposited in the Gloucestershire Record Office. An itemized list has been prepared so that researchers may readily identify copies of original documents held in other repositories which they wish to consult.

Index

Illustrations are denoted by page numbers in *italics* or by (*illus.*) where figures are scattered throughout the text. The letter n following a page number indicates that the reference will be found in a note.

The following abbreviations have been used in this index: b. – born; B. & N.E.S. – Bath & North East Somerset; C – century; d. – died; *fl.* – *floruit*; Glam. – Glamorgan; Hants. – Hampshire; Herefs. – Herefordshire; J.P. – Justice of the Peace; Lancs. – Lancashire; m. – married; M.P. – Member of Parliament; N. Som. – North Somerset; N. Yorks. – North Yorkshire; Northants. – Northamptonshire; Notts. – Nottinghamshire; Oxon. – Oxfordshire; S. Glos. – South Gloucestershire; Shrops. – Shropshire; Som. – Somerset; U.S.A. – United States of America; Wilts. – Wiltshire